THE
THEOLOGY OF
MARTIN LUTHER

THE
THEOLOGY
OF
MARTIN
LUTHER

PAUL
ALTHAUS

Translated by
Robert C. Schultz

FORTRESS PRESS PHILADELPHIA

This book is a translation of *Die Theologie Martin Luthers,* second edition, published in 1963 by the Gütersloher Verlagshaus Gerd Mohn in Gütersloh, Germany.

Library of Congress Catalog Card Number 66-17345

ISBN 0-8006-1855-6

Printed in the United States of America

1-1855

15   16   17   18   19   20

FROM THE PREFACE TO
THE GERMAN EDITION

THIS BOOK has grown out of the lectures and seminars on Luther's theology which I have held regularly at the Universities of Rostock and Erlangen since the early 1920's. Many of the studies made in preparation for these lectures and many of my essays on Luther, particularly those which were presented to conferences of the *Luther-Gesellschaft* during the past decades, have—with considerable alteration—become part of this book.

My purpose in this book is the same as in my lectures, to present a comprehensive overview of the basic elements of Luther's theological work. I have not undertaken to summarize the results of "Luther research" or even to contribute to it through presenting the results of my own special investigations. And I have only occasionally entered into an explicit discussion of the results of this research. It has not been possible for me to follow and evaluate completely the vast number of studies on Luther's theology now being produced by Evangelical scholars as well as increasing numbers of Roman Catholic scholars—although I think that I am familiar with the most important of these studies. As a result the bibliographical references in the individual chapters are quite modest and incomplete.

I have tried to present a living picture of Luther's theology on the basis of my own ongoing study of the sources, and so to present this picture that it will be fruitful for theological study—and thereby also fruitful for the proclamation of the gospel in our time. This book was not written for specialists, but is directed to the broad range of theologians and pastors and, beyond them, to all who are in any way engaged in the ministry of the word and desire to use what they learn from Luther in their ministry.

I thus did not undertake a historical description of the development of Luther's thought. The formative period of Luther's theology, together with all the important questions connected with it, has not been considered. The development of his thought from his earlier to his later years is discussed only at some very important points. Apart from this, his theology is understood as unified and consistent at all important and decisive points throughout all stages of his development. Luther's polemical opposition to scholastic theology and the Roman Catholic Church are, for the most part, expressed only implicitly, that is, in the presentation of the antitheses necessary to an understanding of the substance of his position.

It is my intention that this book systematically present and interpret Luther's teaching. I hope that this will enable the reader to see that Luther's understanding of the gospel remains a vital reality in spite of everything in his theology which reflects the conditions of his times and which we cannot use. If we seek to deepen and renew our understanding of the gospel and prepare for the unity of the church, Luther's theology will be extremely significant for the present and future not only of the Lutheran Church but of all Christianity.

Since this book attempts to facilitate the kind of study of Luther's theology that will be helpful in the present situation, I have as much as possible permitted Luther to speak for himself. The notes not only indicate the source, but very frequently contain the text of the passage under discussion.[1] They are intended not only to support the presentation but to permit the reader to hear Luther's own voice. Any presentation of Luther's theology must, in comparison with the inexhaustible riches of his writing and preaching, always be more abstract and less concrete than Luther's own presentation. The frequent quotation of his own words is offered as a counterbalance to this.

Even a comprehensive presentation such as this can be only an incomplete selection, in terms of both the total scope of Luther's theology and of the range of individual topics. Luther's theology is a way of thinking. Completeness could therefore neither be sought nor achieved. This is true not only of the number of writings that are referred to but also of the variety of topics discussed. It was necessary to emphasize central points and to exercise limitations. Luther's later disputations have been used fully and often.

---

[1] See the Translator's Note.

That is only proper. In these disputations, and in the theses written for them, Luther not only expresses himself very briefly and forcefully, but also discusses the most important theological topics in a remarkably direct and vital manner.[*]

In presenting Luther's position, I have emphasized particularly its biblical foundation by making repeated references to it. Only in this way can we do justice to the distinctive character of his theology; Luther constantly developed his theological position by interpreting and referring to passages of Scripture. And this presentation tries to reflect that fact adequately. I have especially and repeatedly emphasized Luther's relationship to the Apostle Paul and considered not only the agreement but also the differences between their respective theologies.

Just as this comparison is intended to help the reader to think for himself about the subject under discussion, so the entire presentation—even where this is not stated explicitly—has been determined by the question concerning the truth of the gospel. Occasionally this leads us to ask critical questions of Luther the theologian. That is also part of the "systematic" intention of this book.

The various chapters of this book correspond only in part to a systematic presentation of the Christian faith. Some of them focus on a specific topic. Others, for example, chapters 5 and 19, view larger areas of theology from a specific dimension. Under these circumstances the repetition of some material and of some references to Luther's writings is not inappropriate.

The references to Luther's writings are not intended as isolated proof passages. In most instances, the significance of a particular statement requires an awareness of the material that comes before and after it. In a series of references, the first reference(s) applies to the quotation(s) in the text; any further references refer the reader to parallel passages.

I need not use many words to express how much I have learned from the great Luther interpreters of the past and from my own contemporaries.[*] In studying their work, one of course notices the

---

[*] I have discussed Luther's ethics in my book, *Die Ethik Martin Luthers* (Gütersloh: Mohn, 1965), of which an English translation is now being prepared.

[*] For my evaluation of their work, see "Die Bedeutung der Theologie Luthers für die theologische Arbeit," *Luther-Jahrbuch* (1961), pp. 13 ff.

danger which threatens every attempt to present material from the past in a way that will be of vital significance for the present situation, that is, to present Luther the theologian as the supporter of the author's own theology. If one is aware of this difficulty, however, one can consciously guard against it. The selection of topics as well as the balance and emphasis both in the totality and in the individual details of this book reflect the present situation and the author's own theological viewpoint. I confess, however, that I have strenuously tried to resist the temptation to capture Luther in my own dogmatical frame of reference—to say nothing of presenting his thought in the language of some contemporary school of theology. Should someone, however, notice that this presentation of Luther is, in many important points, very close to my dogmatics and find this suspicious, he should also consider that the reason may be that I have learned very much from Luther for my own work.

Erlangen,
Advent, 1961.

PREFACE TO THE
AMERICAN EDITION

I AM VERY HAPPY that this book has been translated and made available to my fellow Christians in the English-speaking countries. I am especially grateful to the translator, who is particularly well qualified for this task, for his competent and accurate translation.

May this book lead many into a more intensive study of Luther's own writings. The intensive study of Luther's theology has been and will continue to be a dynamic process leading to theological renewal.

Erlangen,
April, 1966.

TRANSLATOR'S NOTE

IN THE PROCESS of translation, some changes have been made in the notes. Insofar as I was able, I have attempted to provide cross references between Althaus' references to the critical edition of Luther's Works (*WA*) and the available modern translations. Such references to English translations are indicated by a semi-colon after the *WA* reference. When the English translation is based on a different version of the text than that specifically referred to, the translation is preceded by "cf."

Althaus frequently paraphrases the quotations from Luther's Latin works and gives the Latin text in a footnote. In this case, I have ordinarily omitted the text from the note and given only the *WA* reference. This change explains the variation in the structure of the notes; in sections largely based on Luther's Latin works, there are relatively fewer quotations in the notes than in other sections.

In translating the quotations from Luther's works, I have gratefully used the available modern translations. This, hopefully, will make it easier for the reader in referring to these translations. It will, I hope, also avoid some of the distortions that occur in translating brief passages out of context. I silently made whatever changes were necessary to preserve Althaus' emphasis, to make the text of the quotation fit into the flow of thought, and to conform to the basic editorial policy adopted for this volume. I am grateful to Concordia Publishing House and Fortress Press, the joint publishers of *Luther's Works* (*LW*), for permission to use longer quotations. In the process of searching out the corresponding passages in the translations, I have learned a new respect for all who have labored to make Luther's works available in translation. They cannot all be mentioned by name; but it is my hope that the cross references to their translations will make it easier for the interested reader of this volume to use and benefit from their work.

It was my privilege as a student to hear the lectures on which much of this book is based. I am happy to have had the opportunity to participate in making them available in translation, not only because of my own desire to present the author with a tangible token of gratitude for the courtesy and kindness which he has shown to me personally, but also because I have in my own ministry experienced the stimulation and insight which this book can give. The congregations which I have served while preparing this translation have profited from these labors. And I have tried to carry out the author's intention of presenting an introduction to Luther's theology that could be used by the layman as well as by the pastor.

CONTENTS

APPENDIXES

INDEXES

ABBREVIATIONS

BC — *The Book of Concord,* translated and edited by Theodore G. Tappert, *et. al.* (Philadelphia, 1959).

BOW — Martin Luther, *The Bondage of the Will,* translated by J. I. Packer and O. R. Johnston (Westwood, N. J.: Fleming H. Revell, 1957).

CW — Paul Althaus, *Die Christliche Wahrheit,* 3rd edition (Gütersloh: Bertelsmann, 1952).

GA — Karl Holl, *Gesammelte Aufsätze zur Kirchengeschichte* (3 vols.; Tübingen: Mohr, 1932), vol. 1, 6th ed., vol. 3, 2nd ed., vol. 3, ed. Hans Lietzmann.

LCC — *Library of Christian Classics,* John T. McNeill and Henry P. van Dusen, General Editors (Philadelphia: Westminster, 1953-   ).

LCC 15 — Martin Luther, *Lectures on Romans,* translated and edited by Wilhelm Pauck. *LCC,* vol. 15 (1961).

LCC 18 — *Luther: Letters of Spiritual Counsel,* translated and edited by Theodore G. Tappert. *LCC,* vol. 18 (1955).

LT — Theodosius Harnack, *Luthers Theologie,* 2 vols. 1st edition (Erlangen: Blaesing, 1862-1886). 2nd edition (Munich: Kaiser, 1927). Page numbers are ordinarily those of the 1st edition. Vol. 2 of the 2nd edition gives the page numbers of the 1st edition in the margin.

LW — American Edition of Luther's Works (Philadelphia and St. Louis, 1955-   ).

PE — *Works of Martin Luther,* 6 vols., (Philadelphia, 1915-1943).

MPL — *Patrologia, Series Latina,* 221 vols. in 222, edited by J. P. Migne (Paris, 1844-1904).

RW — *Reformation Writings,* translated by Bertram Lee Woolf (New York: Philosophical Library, 1953-   ).

S-J — *Luther's Correspondence,* 2 vols., edited by Preserved Smith and Charles M. Jacobs (Philadelphia: United Lutheran Publication House, 1913-1918).

WA — *D. Martin Luthers Werke.* Kritische Gesamtausgabe (Weimar, 1883-   ).

WA, Br — *D. Martin Luthers Werke.* Briefwechsel (Weimar, 1930-1948).

WA, DB— *D. Martin Luthers Werke.* Deutsche Bibel (Weimar, 1906-   ).

WA, TR— *D. Martin Luthers Werke.* Tischreden (Weimar, 1912-1921).

INTRODUCTION

1

THE AUTHORITY OF SCRIPTURE
AND OF THE CREEDS

INTENSIVE study of Luther's theology is particularly rewarding because of his originality. The voice with which Luther speaks to us is unmistakably his own. Luther however did not intend to say anything particularly original. He felt he was commissioned only to explicate rightly the truth contained in the Holy Scriptures and the dogma of the orthodox church. All of his theological work presupposes the authority of Scripture and the derived authority of the genuine tradition of the church.

We shall begin at this point: All Luther's theological thinking presupposes the authority of Scripture. His theology is nothing more than an attempt to interpret the Scripture. Its form is basically exegesis. He is no "systematician" in the scholastic sense, and he is no dogmatician—either in the sense of the great medieval systems or in the sense of modern theology. He wrote neither a dogmatics, nor an ethics, nor a *Summa:* he never produced anything like Melanchthon's analyses of individual doctrines (*loci theologici*) or Calvin's *Institutes of the Christian Religion.*

Luther was professor of biblical exegesis at the University of Wittenberg. The major part of his literary work consists accordingly of exegetical lectures on the Old and New Testaments. Some he edited himself; some were edited by others. Together with these lectures stand the sermons. Again, some were prepared for publication by Luther himself; others were taken down and published by his students. In these sermons we again hear Luther explicating biblical material. His larger and smaller topical writings too are saturated with quotations from Scripture and are largely exegetical in character. Luther also prepared theses for his students to defend in the open disputations that were part of the examinations for the theological degrees; and although he tried to cast these in the sharpest and briefest theological form possible, he constantly makes explicit as well as implicit references to biblical texts, using the language of his Latin Bible, the Vulgate.

A comparison of this aspect of Luther's work with the great theological works of scholasticism reveals the new and characteristic thrust which dominates Luther's theological method. There is no precedent for the way in which Luther, as an exegete and as a preacher, thinks in constant conversation with Scripture. Almost every single step in his theology receives its basis and direction from Scripture. To be sure, he also cites the church fathers and can occasionally—as in *The Bondage of the Will*—even call on philosophy or natural reason to provide secondary proof for theological theses. So far as his theology as a whole is concerned, however, that remains a secondary and peripheral addition to his method.[1]

It is instructive to compare Thomas Aquinas and Luther on this point. Of course, Thomas also quotes Scripture; but in addition, we find references to the philosophical and ontological reflections of Aristotle and of Thomas himself. In contrast to this, Luther is always primarily oriented to Scripture, and often only to Scripture. In saying this, I do not mean to deny the influence which Occamistic philosophy actually had on Luther; what we are concerned with here however is the conscious intention of Luther's theological method. He distinguishes what he can say on the basis of Scripture from his own theological opinion. Since the latter cannot be proved from Scripture, Luther feels that no one is bound to accept it.[2] For this reason he claims only that he has himself understood—and taught others to understand—the Holy Scripture some-

---

[1] See *WA* 8, 120; *LW* 32, 248 f. Luther is, as a matter of principle, distrustful of and doubtful about the use of philosophical concepts and arguments in discussing theological questions. "I would prefer not to use them at all in theology." *WA* 39[1], 228; cf. *ibid.*, p. 227. Philosophy has had and still has "harmful and disadvantageous results in theology." *WA* 39[1], 228. "Philosophy by nature flatters reason; theology, however, lies far beyond all human comprehension." *WA* 39[1], 229 This is why Luther advises his pupils to avoid using philosophical concepts in theology whenever possible. If they still wish to use them, then they must first "purify" them for theological use: "Give them a bath first!" *WA* 39[1], 229; cf. *ibid.* p. 231. Cf. *WA*, TR 5, 5245.
[2] This is how Luther treats purgatory. *WA* 7, 450, *LW* 32, 95. "But if you wish to discuss this question then you must leave room for surmise and differences of opinion, as I do. Do not make your own ideas into articles of faith." *WA* 7, 455; *LW* 32, 98.

what better than the scholastic theologians had and sometimes better than the early fathers.[•]

At this point, it is not a question of how far Luther may have gone in one-sided or forced interpretations of the Scripture. Neither would we speak about his criticism of the canon. These matters do not alter the fact that Luther—even when he criticized Scripture—never wanted to be anything else than an obedient hearer and student of the Scripture.

In this Luther was a perfect example of his own teachings concerning the authority of Holy Scripture in the church. The Scripture is the record of the apostolic witness to Christ and is as such the decisive authority in the church. Since the apostles are the foundation of the church, their authority is basic. No other authority can be equal to theirs.[4] Every other authority in the church is derived from following the teaching of the apostles and is validated by its conformity to their teaching.[5] This means that only the Scripture can establish and substantiate articles of faith. The Scripture offers all that is necessary to salvation. Christians need no other truth for their salvation beyond that proclaimed in Scripture. This applies to articles of faith as well as to ethical instruction. As the later dogmaticians put it, Scripture is "sufficient."[•] No dogma or rule of the church not already contained in Scripture is necessary for salvation.

[•] "I know and am assured, by the grace of God, that I am more learned in the Scriptures than all the sophists and papists." *WA* 15, 216; *LW* 40, 55. "Although we do not want to boast that we are superior to the early fathers, . . . we still must confess and cannot deny that we, by the grace of God, have clearer insight into many passages of Scripture than they had." *WA* 19, 50. "I understand the Holy Scriptures much better (although still only a little)." *WA* 53, 256.

[4] "No authority after Christ is to be equated with the apostles and the prophets. . . . Only these who ought to hand down the articles of faith are to be called the foundation of the church." *WA* 39ɪ, 184. "The apostles who are sent to us by a sure decree of God are infallible teachers." *WA* 39ɪ, 48.

[5] "Whatever they wish to teach or legislate, they ought to follow and accept the authority of the apostles." *WA* 39ɪ, 185.

[•] "All articles are sufficiently established in the Holy Scriptures, so that it is not necessary to establish any beyond these. All commandments of good works are sufficiently stated in the sacred Scripture so that it is not necessary to formulate any beyond these." *WA* 30ɪɪ, 420. Cf. *WA* 39ɪ, 47; *LW* 34, 111. "Nothing in respect of either faith or morals can be established as necessary to salvation beyond what is taught in Scripture." *WA* 39ɪɪ, 43. "No one is bound to believe more than what is based in Scripture." *WA* 7, 453; *LW* 32, 96.

Neither the church therefore nor any of her representatives, not even the councils, have the authority to establish new articles of faith or new commandments.[7] This does not mean that the teachers of the church and their theological work and teachings are to be despised and rejected. Their validity however depends on their conformity to Scripture.[8] They must substantiate their statements from Scripture and may be judged and criticized on the basis of Scripture. For it "alone is the true lord and master of all writings and doctrine on earth."[9] Scripture alone is the authority capable of deciding in cases of doctrinal controversy.[10] Furthermore, the statements of the teachers and fathers of the church are never placed on a level with articles of faith.[11] For they do not provide the unconditional certainty which the conscience needs and which Scripture, the word of God, gives. We may trust unconditionally only in the word of God and not in the teaching of the fathers; for the teachers of the church can err and have erred. Scripture never errs.[12] Therefore it alone has unconditional authority. The au-

---

[7] "The church of God has no power to establish any article of faith and it neither has established nor ever will establish one. The church of God does not have the power to command any good works and it never has commanded nor ever will command one." *WA* 30[II], 420. "This means that the Word of God shall establish articles of faith and no one else, not even an angel." *WA* 50, 206; *BC*, 295. "A council has no authority to establish new articles of faith, despite the fact that the Holy Spirit is present with it." *WA* 50, 607; *PE* 5, 243. "In the realm of the church, the rule is: 'God's word abides forever,' and we must judge by it and not seek to make new or different words of God and to establish new or different articles of faith." *WA* 50, 617; *PE* 5, 254 f. "Nothing should be asserted in questions of faith without scriptural precedent." *WA* 8, 108; *LW* 32, 230.

[8] "Accordingly their [the fathers'] authority is worth most when it has clear scriptural support." *WA* 8, 79; *LW* 32, 189. Cf. *WA* 18, 656; *BOW*, 130.

[9] "Therefore, necessity forces us to run to the Bible with the writings of all teachers, and to obtain its verdict and judgment upon them." [Here follows the footnoted quotation in the text.] *WA* 7, 317; *LW* 32, 11. Cf. *WA* 8, 99; *LW* 32, 217.

[10] *WA* 7, 97.

[11] "For what is asserted without the Scriptures or proven revelation may be held as an opinion, but need not be believed." *WA* 6, 508; *LW* 36, 29. "Whatever is taught in the church of God without the word is ungodly blasphemy. And it is blasphemy and heresy for anyone to assert that it is an article of faith." *WA* 54, 425. "It will not do to make articles of faith out of the holy fathers' words or works." *WA* 50, 206; *BC*, 295. Cf. *WA* 8, 108; *LW* 32, 231.

[12] "But everyone, indeed, knows that at times they [the fathers] have erred as men will; therefore, I am ready to trust them only when they prove their opinions from Scripture, which has never erred." *WA* 7, 315; *LW* 32, 11. Cf. *WA* 18, 656; *BOW*, 130. "No one shall attempt to create or find any comfort except in the word of God. . . . Therefore you should not accept the teachings of the holy fathers as though your conscience could trust and find

thority of the theologians of the church is relative and conditional. Without the authority of words of Scripture, no one can establish hard and fast statements of dogma in the church.[12]

Those parts of the tradition of the church however which prove to be based on Scripture also have authority, even though it is only a derived authority. This was Luther's attitude toward the three so-called ecumenical creeds of the ancient church. Luther accepted them, not because they had been adopted by councils (that does not guarantee their orthodoxy), but because he was convinced that they conform to Scripture.[13] He therefore explicitly accepted them for himself and emphasized them, especially against the anti-Trinitarians. Beginning in 1533, the oath required of students receiving the doctor's degree at Wittenberg included the subscription to these three creeds. Luther published them with his own commentary in 1538. In 1528, he had expressly confessed his agreement with their content.[14] Now, ten years later, he wishes "once again to bear witness that I hold to the true Christian church, which up until now has preserved these creeds or confessions."[15] He praises the Apostles' Creed as "the finest of all, a brief and true summary of the articles of faith." He values the Athanasian Creed as "a creed that protects" the Apostles' Creed.

With these creeds, Luther accepted the basic dogmas of the early church on the Trinity and the person of Christ. He also agreed with the church in its rejection of the heretics.[17] On individual

---

comfort in them." *WA* 12, 413. "Hold to Scripture and the word of God. There you will find truth and security—assurance and a faith that is complete, pure, sufficient, and enduring." *WA* 7, 455; *LW* 32, 98.

[12] *WA* 8, 97; *LW* 32, 215.

[13] Cf. *WA* 50, 283; *LW* 34, 229 for Luther's acceptance of the trinitarian formula.

[14] Speaking of the "sublime article of the divine majesty," that is, the Trinity, Luther says: "All this has been maintained up to this time both in the Roman Church and among Christian churches throughout the whole world." *WA* 26, 499; *LW* 37, 361. (Cf. pp. 362 ff.) With reference to the entire creed, he says: "This is my faith, for so all true Christians believe and so the Holy Scriptures teach us." *WA* 26, 509; *LW* 37, 372. Luther advises a Christian who is attacked for accepting the article of the Virgin Birth to make this reply: "I have here a little pamphlet called the creed; and it contains this article. This is my Bible; it has stood for a long time and still stands without being disproved. I stand by this creed: I was baptized into this faith and I shall live and die by it." *WA* 37, 55.

[16] *WA* 50, 262; *LW* 34, 201.

[17] *WA* 26, 500; *LW* 37, 361. *WA* 50, 267 f.; *LW* 34, 207 ff. Cf. *WA* 10I.1, 191.

points, however, Luther frequently criticized the terminology of the
dogmas; he maintained for himself and granted to others freedom
not to use the terminology, provided that the substance of the
dogmas was preserved.[18]
The authority of the word of God which confronts us in Scripture and in the creeds establishes itself in our spirit and heart
through experience. Of course, Luther also knows that there are
elements of Christian truth which are beyond experience and must
simply be "believed." But when it comes to the heart and center
of the gospel, the message of sin and grace, Luther appeals not
only to Scripture and the consensus of the church, but also to his
own experience in spiritual matters.[19] There can be no doubt that
experience is one of the principles of his theology. It is, of course,
not a source of knowledge in and by itself, but it definitely is a
medium through which knowledge is received. Theological knowledge is won by experiencing it.

This is the ground on which Luther's theology stands. He intends to bring the old truth of Scripture and of dogma out of
obscurity into the light, and to let its real meaning shine forth.
His theology is intended as a commentary, an exposition of the received texts of Scripture and of the creeds. In this process of exposition, the old truth admittedly becomes new truth because it is
received in a new situation by men whose theological concerns and
frame of reference are determined by medieval theology. And Luther knew that situation at first hand. He knew from experience
the agony of asking its deepest questions—and also the freedom of
the man who has found the answer. His new interpretation in turn
brings with it its own tensions and contradictions, as we shall see,
particularly with reference to his attitude toward Holy Scripture.
Luther however never casts any doubt on the basic validity of the
authorities.

[18] "We must preserve the substance but are quite willing to use whatever
terms you please." *WA* 39[II], 305. "Even if my soul hated this word, *homo-
ousios,* and I refused to use it, still I would not be a heretic. For who compels
me to use the word, providing I hold to the fact defined by the council on the
basis of Scripture?" *WA* 8, 117; *LW* 32, 244.
[19] *WA* 8, 110; *LW* 32, 234. "I am at least partly informed concerning Holy
Writ and besides I have to some extent tested these spiritual matters in experience." *WA* 8, 127; *LW* 32, 258.
   Cf. the discussion of the relationship between Scripture and experience in
the knowledge of sin on pp. 141 f.

2

THE SUBJECT MATTER
OF THEOLOGY

LUTHER very carefully considered the subject matter of theology. Theology is concerned with the knowledge of God and of man. It is therefore both theology in the narrower sense—the doctrine of God—and anthropology. These two are inseparably joined together. God can be properly known only in terms of his relationship to man; and man can be properly known only in terms of his relationship to God. Theology is thus concerned neither with an objective doctrine of God nor with an anthropology that asks questions about man other than those involving his relationship to God. Both sides of this relationship are determined by the fact that man is a guilty and lost sinner and that God is the justifier and the redeemer of precisely this kind of man. This highly existential twofold theme of man's guilt and redemption—this and nothing else—is the subject matter of theology. "Whatever one seeks apart from this is error and idle gossip in theology."[1] This means that theological knowledge of God and of man is "relative" knowledge in the sense that each is known only in relationship to the other, a relationship that is ontological as well as personal. This is what Luther means when he says, "Christ is the subject matter of theology."[2]

What is the significance of this for the relationship of theology to philosophy?[3] Philosophy is also concerned with man, with man as a rational being and as the bearer of reason, which is the source of all culture. Philosophy however is not concerned with man as "theological" man, with man in his relationship to God. Philosophy thinks of man in immanent categories. Compared with the-

---

[1] WA 40ⅠⅠ, 327; cf. LW 12, 310 f. Cf. WA, TR 5, 5757.
[2] WA, TR 2, 1868 and frequently; cf. the index in WA, TR 6.
[3] See The Disputation Concerning Man, WA 39Ⅰ, 175 ff.; LW 34, 137-144. Cf. also WA 40ⅠⅠ, 327; LW 12, 310 f.

ology therefore it knows almost nothing about man.' It knows
neither where he comes from, nor what he is here for, nor where
he is going. It can describe the purpose of his existence only in
terms of an ordered society—Luther was thinking of Aristotelian
philosophy. At the decisive point therefore philosophy knows
nothing about the essential nature of man. That is quite natural.
For we men can know our essential nature only when we view
ourselves "in our source, that is, in God."⁵ Then we see the individual man and all of mankind in its primal perfection as God
created it, in its fall into sin, under the power of death and the
devil, and as freed through Christ, that is, as guilty and pardoned
man. At the same time, theology shows man eschatologically, in
terms of the life for which God originally created him and which
God intends to give him in the future through restoring and per-
fecting the image of God.' Philosophy however does not view man
eschatologically. Only theology therefore is able fully and completely to describe the essence of man; and it can do this on the
basis of Scripture.'

Obviously, philosophy also speaks about God.' He appears in
metaphysics as the object of speculative thought. Here one can
gain some knowledge of God, of his providence, and of his control
of the world. All this, however, remains "objective." The decisive
question about God's attitude and approach to *me*, the individual
man, remains unanswered. On this basis, one may have a religious
view of life but cannot be certain about God as a person and about
God's personal relationship to man. "Plato can assert neither that
God cares about us nor that he hears and helps the needy. He
stays within the limits of metaphysical thought."⁹ That is, however, not yet the true knowledge of God.

This is true not only of philosophy; Luther asserts that scholastic
theology and non-Christian religions such as Islam are limited in

---

⁴ *WA* 39ᴵ, 175; *LW* 34, 137 f.
⁵ *WA* 39ᴵ, 175; *LW* 34, 138.
⁶ *WA* 39ᴵ, 177; *LW* 34, 139 f.
⁷ "Theology . . . from the fulness of its wisdom defines man as whole and
perfect." *WA* 39ᴵ, 176; *LW* 34, 138. "Philosophers and Aristotle are not able
to understand or define what the theological man is, but by the grace of God
we are able to do it, because we have the Bible." *WA* 39ᴵ, 179; *LW* 34, 142.
⁸ *WA* 40ᴵᴵᴵ, 78 f. Cf. *WA* 44, 591.
⁹ The quotation in the text continues: ". . . like a cow staring at a new gate."
WA 44, 591.

the same way. These can say very many things about the essence of the deity and even about its personal being. But the most important matter of all is God's attitude toward us and what he wills to do with us; and that remains unknown to them. Such knowledge lies outside reason's area of competence; in these matters only the word of God gives certainty.[10] Philosophy can express nothing but the limited content of human reason.

---

[10] *WA* 40ᴵᴵᴵ. 78.

Part One

THE KNOWLEDGE OF GOD
The Word of God and Faith

3

THE GENERAL AND THE
PROPER KNOWLEDGE OF GOD

G OD CAN be known to a certain extent even where the biblical revelation, the word, and faith are not known. For Luther, the witness of the Holy Scripture established this beyond all doubt. And his observation of the religions confirmed it. Luther also cited the religious views of classical authors, especially Cicero, in support of this view.

Luther reaffirms and elaborates Paul's assertion (Rom. 1:20)— that God has always been known through his works of creation— with the comment: The veneration of various gods in the idolatrous pagan religions presupposes that men carry within themselves a conceptual notion of God and of the divine being. Without that, it would have been impossible for them to call their idols "gods," to ascribe divine attributes to them, to worship them, and to pray to them. Men have this idea of God, however, as Paul says, from God himself.[1] God has thus given men knowledge of himself. And this knowledge cannot be eradicated from the human heart. "This light and understanding is in the hearts of all men and can be neither suppressed nor put out."[2] The Epicureans and other atheists have tried to deny it, but they can do so only by doing violence to themselves. Atheism is opposed by the secret voice of conscience.[3]

All men have been given a general knowledge not only of God's

---

[1] WA 56, 179; LCC 15, 23. WA 40¹, 607; LW 26, 399. WA 40¹, 608; LW 26, 400. WA 19, 205.

[2] WA 19, 205.

[3] "There are people like the Epicureans, Pliny, and others who deny it with their mouths [that there is a God]. But they must force themselves to do so; and by trying to extinguish the light in their hearts they act like men who plug their ears and close their eyes so that they may neither see nor hear. This does not solve their problem, however, for their conscience tells them something else." WA 19, 206. "This basic theological 'insight of the conscience' is in every mind and cannot be obscured." WA 56, 177; LCC 15, 24.

metaphysical attributes, such as his omnipotence and omniscience,[4] but also of his ethical attributes. This knowledge includes the awareness that God is the giver of all good, that he is kind and gracious, and that he is willing to help a man who calls on him in time of need.[5] "Natural reason must confess that all good comes from God." "The natural light of reason is strong enough to regard God as good, gracious, merciful, and generous; that is a strong light." But this knowledge of God has a twofold limit. First, although reason knows all this about God, it cannot produce the certainty that God really wants to help *me*. The experiences of life repeatedly speak against this possibility; and since the mere thought of God cannot assert itself against this experience, a man's actual situation is always one of doubt. A man may really believe that God is ready to help others—but the same man does not dare to believe that God will help him.[6] Second, although reason has the idea of God, it lacks practical experience of him. It knows *that* God is; but it does not know *who* God is. On the contrary, it always applies the idea of God to something that isn't God at all. It "plays blindman's buff with God," reaches out to grab him but misses him, and grasps not the true God but idols, either the devil, or a wish-fulfilment dream of the human soul—and such a dream also comes from the devil. Human reason does not know who the real God is. That knowledge is taught only by the Holy Spirit.[7]

---

[4] Luther can therefore also appeal to this knowledge to support his assertion that God works all in all and knows everything that will happen. *WA* 18, 709, 718, 719; *BOW*, 203, 216, 218.

[5] Luther lists God's mercy ("gracious to those who call on him") as one of the attributes which every man knows. *WA* 56, 177; *LCC* 15, 23. This is particularly clear in *WA* 19, 207 ff., where Luther refers to the fact that even though the sailors described in the story of Jonah were heathen, they "each cried to his own god" [Jonah 1:5].

[6] "It [reason] does indeed believe that God is able to do this and knows what to do, how to help, and how to give. It cannot, however, believe that God really wants to do this for me. Its attitude is inconsistent. It believes that God has the power to help, but doubts that God wants to help—because in the time of trouble it feels that the opposite is true. [Even the sailors in the story of Jonah] believe that God wants to help others; but this is as far as they can go and they cannot rise above this." *WA* 19, 296.

[7] "Reason knows that there is a God. However, it knows neither who the true God is nor what he is like. . . . Reason plays blindman's buff with God; it makes all kinds of attempts to grasp him but always without success. It invariably misses him. For this reason, it always identifies as God something that is not God and denies that the real God is God at all. It would do none of these things if it did not know that there is a God—or if it knew who God is and what he is like. Therefore it simply jumps in and gives divine titles

The foregoing is based on Luther's commentary on Jonah, but Luther's lecture on Romans 1:23 ff. expresses the same thought. Pagan religion has the concept of God and to this extent it knows about God. It began to err however because it did not let the God it originally knew remain in his "nakedness" and worship him as such. On the contrary, it arbitrarily concretized him according to its own wishes and thus equated him with an idol of the kind that men seemed to need and want. "Everyone wanted to find God in that which pleased himself." Therewith the primal knowledge of God was corrupted and, as Paul puts it, the truth of God changed into a lie (Rom. 1:25). Such an idolization of God occurs not only in gross idolatry but also in the "spiritual and subtle" forms of idolatry: for example, when the true God is made over to fit the pattern of one's own moralistic work righteousness. Luther thus places Christian moralism in the same category as pagan worship of idols. The essence of both is idolatry.

Elsewhere, Luther expressly distinguishes between the general (*generalis*) and the proper (*propria*) knowledge of God. The former knows that God is, that he has created the world, is righteous and judges; but it lacks the certainty about what God thinks of us and about his intention to save us sinners—and it is this which constitutes the true and proper knowledge of God.[10] Luther also describes this difference between the knowledge which is given to all men and that knowledge which is first disclosed through the word of God and the Holy Spirit as the difference between "superficial" [*von aussen*] and "inside" [*von innen*] knowledge of God.[11]

---

and honor to what it thinks is God, while actually never hitting upon the true God but always upon the devil or its own thoughts which are controlled by the devil. So there is a great difference between knowing *that* there is a God and knowing *who* he is and what he is like. Nature knows the first and it is written in all hearts. The second is taught only by the Holy Spirit." *WA* 19, 206 f.

[8] *WA* 56, 177; *LCC* 15, 23. Cf. Luther's explanation of the First Commandment in his *Large Catechism*. *WA* 30¹, 135; *BC*, 367.

[9] *WA* 56, 179; *LCC* 15, 26.

[10] *WA* 40¹, 607; *LW* 26, 399.

[11] "Men see that the heavens and the earth are so wisely governed and then, on the basis of this external government and the nature of creation, they draw the weak conclusion that there is one God. . . . Such a knowledge of God, which is based merely on the fact that the earth remains and the heaven does not fall down, is weak and superficial." *WA* 45, 90 (Rörer's notes). "What a profound and generous idea God had, to so pour out his mercy that we may know what he thinks and what he intends and through his revelation, see his heart."

"Superficial" knowledge is gained when reason—on the basis of what it observes of the reality of the world, its continued existence, and the apparently wise way in which it is governed—deduces the existence of one God who rules the world with retributive righteousness. Luther, of course, recognizes that such cosmological and teleological syllogizing is "sickly" and "weak."[12] Through deduction of this kind however one still does not know what God intends with men. Reason cannot have this "inside" knowledge; reason cannot have it because it is beyond reason. This knowledge is given to us only through the incarnation of the Son, when God "pours out his mercy" and thus opens his heart to us; only Scripture imparts to us that knowledge. This is what Luther means when he says that the superficial knowledge of God leads to monotheism but not to a knowledge of the Trinity.[13] The Trinity is the "inside" of God. At first glance, one might think that Luther uses the term, "inside knowledge" ("what takes place within the Deity"),[14] in different senses: at one time with reference to the attitude of God's heart toward sinful man and at another time with reference to the trinitarian nature of God. For Luther however each of these is contained in the other; knowledge of the Trinity includes knowledge of the incarnation of the Second Person, and it is this knowledge of the incarnation which teaches us how God feels about us in his heart.

This means then that the general or natural knowledge of God so remains within the limits of the law that the gospel is hidden from it and unknown to it. Even a legalistic piety can speak of God's goodness, but that is not the same as knowing that God is merciful and accepts sinners. "The heathen can only reach the point of saying: God will hear the good, but not the godless—

WA 45, 93; cf. *Ibid.*, pp. 90, 92. Cf. the same sermon, in the edition based on Rörer's notes, in Cruciger's *Sommerpostille. WA* 21, 509 f.

[12] *WA* 39[II], 346. In this connection, Luther also says that the heathen, e.g., Cicero, have seen God's governing activity and recognized that he rules the world; but they have not known that God creates out of nothing and thus have not known the most important thing about God's creative activity.

[13] For the relationship of this "inside" knowledge of God to the Trinity, see *WA* 45, 90 f.; *WA* 21, 509. Cf. Luther's use of the phrase, "what God is in himself," *WA* 49, 238 f.

[14] *WA* 45, 92 f. The discussion shows that for Luther there is no other answer to the question as to what God thinks than that given us through the knowledge of the Trinity and the incarnation and work of the Son.

they cannot go beyond this."[15] There are two types of knowledge about God, legalistic and evangelical—the one comes from the law and the other from the gospel. Reason—and this is also true of philosophy—can attain to the legalistic but is limited to it and cannot of itself reach the evangelical. Legal knowledge knows God's "left hand," evangelical knowledge knows God's "right hand."[16] In order really to know God, one must "hold to His right hand." Only then do we know what God thinks of us and what his intentions are toward us. The God whom we learn to know through the law shows us his back [Exod. 33:18-20]; it is through the gospel, through Christ, that "we learn to look straight into the face of God."[17]

---

[15] *WA* 39II, 278.

[16] *WA* 46, 667 ff., 672; *LW* 22, 147, 150, 153, 156 f.

Cf. "Reason is confined to the first type of knowledge of God which proceeds from the law; and it speaks a vague language. . . . Reason can arrive at a 'legal knowledge' of God. It is conversant with God's commandments and can distinguish between right and wrong. The philosophers, too, had this knowledge of God." *WA* 46, 667 f.; *LW* 22, 150 f.

[17] *WA* 46, 669, 672; *LW* 22, 153, 157.

4

GOD IN HIMSELF AND GOD AS
HE REVEALS HIMSELF

FOR LUTHER, there is a contrast between man's attempt to find
and know God on his own and the knowledge and encounter
which God gives through His word, and this contrast is of decisive
importance. This theme runs through Luther's entire theology, in
all phases of its development, and Luther repeatedly discusses it.[1]

---

[1] The following discussion in this chapter is based on the passages here
quoted, which are illustrative of the several points made.
"Some through their speculations ascend into heaven and speculate about
God the creator, etc. Do not get mixed up with this God. Whoever wishes to
be saved should leave the majestic God alone—for He and the human creature
are enemies. Rather grasp that God whom David [Psalm 51] also grasps. He
is the God who is clothed in his promises—God as he is present in Christ. . . .
This is the God you need. May you as you are yourself never be confronted by
the unclothed God. . . . We know no other God than the God clothed with his
promises. If he should speak to me in his majesty, I would run away—just as
the Jews did. However, when he is clothed in the voice of a man and accom-
modates himself to our capacity to understand, I can approach him." WA 40ᴵᴵ,
329 f.; cf. LW 12, 312 f.
"Every word of Scripture comes from the revealed God. We are able to
grasp him in a specific place to which he is bound by his words. Thus the God
of the children of Israel was in the temple in Jerusalem, in the promises, and
in specific signs. In the same way, we do not now discuss a vagabond [vanum =
vagum (?)], naked God but rather one who [has clothed himself] with definite
signs in [some specific] place." WA 40ᴵᴵ, 386. Cf. the same passage in its
more extensive version, WA 40ᴵᴵ, 386; LW 12, 352.
"God also does not manifest himself except through his works and word,
because the meaning of these is understood in some measure. Whatever else
belongs essentially to the Divinity cannot be grasped and understood." WA 42,
9; LW 1, 11.
"It is folly to argue much about God outside and before time, because this
is an effort to understand the Godhead without a covering, or the uncovered
divine nature. Because this is impossible, God envelops himself in his works
and in certain forms, as today he wraps himself up in baptism, in absolution,
etc." WA 42, 10; LW 1, 11.
"It is therefore insane to argue about God and the divine nature without
the word or any covering. . . . Whoever desires to be saved and to be safe
when he deals with such great matters, let him simply hold to the form, the
signs, and the coverings of the Godhead, such as his word and his works. For
in his word and in his works God shows himself to us." WA 42, 11; LW 1,
13. [Luther is referring to God's historical "works" in redeeming his people.]
"But those who want to reach God apart from these coverings exert themselves to ascend to heaven without ladders (that is, without the word). Over-

Philosophical and scholastic theological speculation about God also belongs to the category of man's autonomous search for God. Such speculation seeks to know God in himself, in his majesty—as he is in heaven. The corrupted nature of sinful man cannot, however, achieve this. For if man does achieve it, what he confronts is absolute majesty, naked and unveiled. Sinful man however is not capable of dealing with this divinity. Whoever thus tries to fly directly to heaven with his own thoughts "falls, overpowered by that majesty which he sought to grasp in its nakedness." God cannot meet us when he is clothed in his majesty. If he came thus, we could not grasp him and we would find the brilliance of his glory too terrible to bear. Man and God in his majesty are enemies. Prior to eternity, we shall not see God face to

---

whelmed by his majesty, which they seek to comprehend without a covering, they fall to their destruction." *WA* 42, 11; *LW* 1, 14.

"Since our corrupted nature is completely unable to grasp the Divinity, we are not able to bear the sight of God as he is, God has therefore chosen to take hold of our nature which is corrupted and infected with satanic poison and to involve it in these external manifestations and sacraments so that we may be able to grasp him." *WA* 39^I, 217.

Concerning the work of the Holy Spirit, Luther says: "His ministry is thoroughly external and completely available to our senses; then we shall see him face to face [I Cor. 13:12] as he is. Now however we see and we hear the Holy Spirit in the dove, in tongues of fire, in baptism, and in a human voice." *WA* 39^I, 217. "The Holy Spirit is now truly present among us and works in us through the word and sacraments. He has covered himself with veils and clothing so that our weak, sick, and leprous nature might grasp him and know him. If he came to us in his majesty, we would not be able to comprehend him and to bear so bright a light. So it is that he comes to us in his prophets; and he is in truth bodily and substantially present and works in us through the word and sacraments." *WA* 39^I, 244.

In addition, cf. *WA* 39^I, 246; *WA* 50, 647 (*PE* 5, 292 f.), and *WA* 40^{III}, 52 ff. In interpreting Psalm 121, Luther says, "God wills that we should worship him at the place which he has chosen; he does this so that he may forbid all autonomous religion and worship." *WA* 40^{III}, 52. "He has freed us from the danger implicit in external places. . . . Our place [of worship] is Jesus Christ, because God has decided that he will not be heard anywhere except through this Man. Outside of Christ there is no basis on which we can pray, hope, be religious, or live." *WA* 40^{III}, 53. "Thus you may find God in Christ, but you cannot find God outside of Christ even in heaven." *WA* 40^{III}, 56; cf. *ibid.*, p. 54.

Cf. Luther's interpretation of Ps. 130, *WA* 40^{III}, 335 ff.: "The Jews had their God contained, as I have said, in his place of mercy, the temple. . . . Thus today we are able to speak neither about nor with God except in our place of mercy, that is, in Christ who is our mercy seat." *WA* 40^{III}, 336. "Seeking God outside of Jesus is [the work of] the devil; if the anxieties of conscience come, despair will result; and if meaningless religion grows, pride will follow." *WA* 40^{III}, 337. "God . . . does not allow us to find him in our thoughts. If we could do this, we would not need God; but because we need him, he has designated a place and a person—showing us where and in what way he ought to be found." *WA* 40^{III}, 338. Cf. *WA* 37, 43.

face as he is in his deity, majesty, and glory. In this life God neither wants to meet us in that way nor does he want us to try to approach him thus. Rather, he adjusts himself to our human ability to comprehend him. Therefore he does not present himself to us uncovered, but covers and clothes himself with a mask so that we may bear him and grasp him. God thus comes to us hidden by "fog and shadows" that he has made for our benefit.[*] This also means that he concretizes, humanizes, and incarnates himself for us. He does not permit us to find him wherever we may happen to want to seek him. He is not a vagabond and wandering God but has definitely limited and bound himself to a specific place; for Israel, it was the tabernacle, the mercy seat of the ark of the covenant, the temple, and Jerusalem. And he directs men to seek and find him not in heaven but in this place. The infinite creator and Lord of heaven and earth accepts limitations. He confronts Israel in a specific history of real acts and signs, in his prophets, and in promises so specific that one may experience their fulfilment. All these are the clothes which he has put on, his masks and disguises.

We Christians, unlike the men of the Old Testament, are no longer directed to a geographical location. What Jerusalem and the temple once were for them, Christ now is for us. His humanity is the place to which God summons us. Christ alone is the sanctuary and the mercy seat of the New Testament. Only here is God now present with men; and it is here that we must speak with him, for he will hear us only here. If we seek God outside of Christ, we will not find him even if we look for him in heaven.

Christ himself is present to us in a very earthly way. Everywhere in the history of revelation God embodies himself for us. His Spirit came in the form of a dove and of the fiery tongues of Pentecost. And God still embodies himself for us. The Holy Spirit comes to us and brings Christ to us through the external, physical, sensible means of the word, of the human voice, and of the sacraments. All these words and sacraments are his veils and clothing, his masks and disguises with which he covers himself so that we may bear and comprehend him.[*] Only in eternity will this minis-

---

[*] *WA* 39¹, 245.
[*] *WA* 17ᴵᴵ, 262 f.

try of the Spirit, these coverings and external means become un-necessary.

Luther asserts this in opposition not only to man's speculation about God but also to all of man's attempts to take the initiative in finding God. It is thus directed also against the other religions and, beyond that, against every attempt by Christians autonomously to construct a picture of God on the basis of their own thoughts. In this connection, he often places the Jews, the Moslems, and the papists in the same category. In all of them, he finds only that human self-reliance and arbitrariness which insists on dealing with God on the basis of man's own ideas rather than obediently meeting him at the place which he has appointed.[4] It is not enough to say that we can find God only in some specific place; we must also remember that he can be found in only one specific place and not in others. Luther was very serious about this. He could say that whoever seeks God outside of Jesus finds the devil. This means that such autonomous attempts can, in every case, result only in something completely contrary to God and produced by the devil. Thus if a man experiences anxiety of conscience and does not seek God in Christ, he ends in despair; and if the same man commits himself to a religion that is meaningless because it is Christless, he may find peace in it but he becomes proud—and both pride and despair are the work of the devil. "Anyone who has a god, but does not have his word, has no god at all."[5]

Luther uses a variety of expressions to convey the antithesis between:

God in himself	God as he reveals himself
The absolute God	God of the fathers
God in his (absolute) majesty	God of the children of Israel
The naked God	God clothed (in his promises)
	God covered (by a mask or as a person who is tempered or attuned to us)
	God veiled
God apart from the word and the promise	God bound to the word
	God revealed by his word

---

[4] *WA* 40^{III}, 335.
[5] *WA* 30^{III}, 213.

God in heaven	God in the man Christ
God speculatively conceived	God made manifest
The vagabond [*vagus*] God	The identifiable [*sigillatus*] God who confines himself to a definite place by means of his word and specific signs

5

THE THEOLOGY OF
THE CROSS

IN THE *Heidelberg Disputation* of 1518, Luther describes the essence of true theology as theology of the cross [*theologia crucis*]. The opposite of this is the theology of glory [*theologia gloriae*][1].

Luther's basic statements on the theology of the cross also indicate the contrast between these two types of theology: "That person does not deserve to be called a theologian who looks upon the invisible things of God as if it were clearly perceptible in those things which have actually happened. He deserves to be called a theologian, however, who comprehends the visible and manifest things of God seen through suffering and the cross."[2]

In order to understand these theses, one must keep Exodus 33:18 ff. and Romans 1:20 ff. in mind; for Luther's concepts are taken from these two passages. In Exodus 33, Moses asks, "Show me thy glory." God answers, "You cannot see my face; for man shall not see me and live." Instead of this, God places Moses in a cleft of the rock and holds His hand before him until His glory has passed by. Then God takes away his hand and Moses sees God's back, but not his face full of glory.

Luther's characterization of false theology is taken from Romans 1:20.[3] He urges men to turn away from the kind of theology there described. In doing so he uses Paul's words in I Corinthians 1:21 ff.: "For since in the wisdom of God, the world did not know God through wisdom, it pleased God through the folly of what we preach to save those who believe." The theology described in Ro-

---

[1] Cf. Walther von Löwenich, *Luthers Theologia Crucis* (4th ed.; Munich: Kaiser, 1954).
[2] *WA* 1, 361 f.; *LW* 31, 52. Theses 19 and 20 of the *Heidelberg Disputation*.
[3] The Vulgate text of Rom. 1:20, "*Invisibilia enim ipsius . . . per ea quae facta sunt; intellecta conspiciuntur,*" is echoed in Luther's theses.

mans 1:20 was possible when man was first created. But men have misused it. Now it no longer makes them pious, but rather fools. God therefore now follows another method. What is now important is not the knowledge of God's invisible nature in his works but the knowledge of his back side visible through sufferings. God's invisible nature is opposed to the visible; his back side is in opposition to the glory of his face. His invisible nature is described in terms of his majestic attributes (cf. Rom. 1:20) and his visible back side in terms of his humanity, weakness, foolishness (cf. I Cor. 1:25). Furthermore, knowledge of God from his works and knowledge of God from his sufferings are also opposed to each other. "Because men misused the knowledge of God through works, God wished again to be recognized in suffering, and to condemn wisdom concerning invisible things by means of wisdom concerning visible things, so that those who did not honor God as manifested in his works should honor him as he is hidden in his suffering. . . . Now it is not sufficient for anyone, and it does him no good to recognize God in his glory and majesty, unless he recognizes him in the humility and shame of the cross."[4] Thus God's revelation and his hiddenness in suffering (Luther refers to Isaiah 45:15) are also opposed to each other. That is, whether direct or indirect, the knowledge of God is paradoxical. The theology of glory corresponds to Philip's request in John 14:8, "Show us the Father." Jesus' answer, however, calls this man who is looking for God elsewhere, back to Himself, "He who has seen me has seen the Father." For this reason true theology and knowledge of God are to be found in the crucified Christ.[5]

The theology of glory knows God from his works; the theology of the cross knows him from his sufferings. The context of these statements in Luther's disputation and Luther's references to Romans 1:20 and I Corinthians 1:21 ff. make it clear that Luther uses "works" to describe God's works in creation and "sufferings" to describe the cross of Christ. In the same breath, however, he deepens the meaning of these expressions: Luther uses "works" not only in the sense of God's works but also in the sense of man's

---

[4] *WA* 1, 362, *LW* 31, 52 f.
[5] "He who does not know Christ does not know God hidden in suffering." *WA* 1, 362; *LW* 31, 53.

works; and "sufferings" refers not only to Christ's suffering but also to man's suffering. Luther makes the transition from the one to the other as though it were self-evident. This is not an unclarity or a logical confusion in his thought but a legitimate assertion, the validity of which is deeply rooted in the material under discussion. For Luther, concern for the true knowledge of God and concern for the right ethical attitude are not separate and distinct but ultimately one and the same. The theology of glory and the theology of the cross each have implications for both. Natural theology and speculative metaphysics which seek to learn to know God from the works of creation are in the same category as the work righteousness of the moralist. Both are ways in which man exalts himself to the level of God. Thus both either lead men to pride or are already expressions of such pride. Both serve to "inflate" man's ego.* Both use the same standard for God and for man's relationship to God: glory and power. In this connection, Luther speaks not only of the glory of God but also of man's love for the glory and glamor of his own works.

God, however, wishes to be known and honored according to a different standard. The cross is opposed to both elements of the theology of glory, and that in two senses, as the cross of Christ and as the cross of the Christian. The theology of the cross works with a standard exactly contrary to that of the theology of glory and applies it both to man's knowledge of God and to man's understanding of himself and of his relationship to God. This standard is the cross. This means: The theology of glory seeks to know God directly in his obviously divine power, wisdom, and glory; whereas the theology of the cross paradoxically recognizes him precisely where he has hidden himself, in his sufferings and in all that which the theology of glory considers to be weakness and foolishness. The theology of glory leads man to stand before God and strike a bargain on the basis of his ethical achievement in fulfilling the law, whereas the theology of the cross views man as one who has been called to suffer. Man's cross "destroys man's self-

---

* Luther says that a man's pride is inflated by his knowledge of God's invisible nature as well as by a knowledge of man's own works. "It is impossible for a person not to be puffed up by his good works. . . . That wisdom which sees the invisible nature of God in works as perceived by man is completely puffed up, blinded, and hardened." *WA* 1, 362; *LW* 31, 53.

confidence" so that now, instead of wanting to do something himself, he allows God to do everything in him. Such a man has been led from moralistic activism to pure receptivity.[7]

Luther recognizes the inner relationship and even the identity of religious intellectualism and moralism. He shows that both are in opposition to the cross. These are two of the deepest insights of his theology. The cross simultaneously destroys both natural theology and the self-consciousness of man's natural ethos. Luther's statement "God is known only in suffering" is an ambiguous statement or—more correctly—it points to the deep correlation between the suffering Christ, in whom God makes himself known, and the suffering man, who is the only man able to enter into community with God.

Luther's transition from the cross of Christ to the suffering of the Christian and from the weakness of God in Christ to the demolition of man's moralistic self-confidence is significant in yet another way. It means that the knowledge of God is not theoretical knowledge but rather a matter of man's entire existence. We cannot view the cross as an objective reality in Christ without at once knowing ourselves as crucified with Christ. The cross means: God meets us in death, in the death of Christ, but only when we experience Christ's death as our own death. The death of Christ leads us to an encounter with God only when it becomes our death. Contemplating the death of Christ necessarily becomes a dying together with him.

In summary, Luther's theology of the cross means that the cross conceals God and thus marks the end of all speculation about God on the part of self-confident reason. The cross is the symbol of judgment over man and thus marks the end of all achieving of fellowship with God on the part of the self-confident moralistic man. The cross makes itself available only to experience; more accurately: only to the suffering of God prepared by him for us through and with Christ.

---

[7] "He, however, who has emptied himself through suffering no longer does works but knows that God works and does all things in him. For this reason, whether God does works or not, it is all the same to him. He neither boasts if he does good works, nor is he disturbed if God does not do good works through him. He knows that it is sufficient if he suffers and is brought low by the cross in order to be annihilated all the more." *WA* 1, 362 f.; *LW* 31, 55.

In his commentary on Thesis 20 of the *Heidelberg Disputation* Luther is obviously treating "works" as God's works of creation; he even refers explicitly to Romans 1:20.[8] Beginning with the discussion of Thesis 21, however, the matter is not so certain. There Luther says that the theology of glory "prefers works to suffering and glory to the cross."[9] On the basis of what precedes this statement one might again think of God's works. But the sentence is ambiguous, and there is no doubt that the next sentences refer to the works of men. Luther refers to the "theologians of glory" as "'enemies of the cross of Christ' for they hate the cross and suffering but love works and the glory of works." They consider the cross to be an evil. The "friends of the cross," however, consider it a good because "through the cross works are dethroned and the old Adam, who is especially edified by works, is crucified." Luther is no longer speaking about the works of God but about the works of men by which they "edify" and assert themselves. Luther continues, "It is impossible for a person not to be puffed up by his good works unless he has first been deflated and destroyed by suffering and evil until he knows that he is worthless and that his works are not his but God's."

In like manner, Luther moves from the idea of Christ's sufferings, in which God is hidden, though wanting to be known, to the idea of man's sufferings. Man's sufferings, as indicated by the passage just quoted from the close of Luther's discussion of Thesis 21, are contrasted to man's works and to the claims which man makes on the basis of his ethical activity. The enemies of Christ's cross are also enemies of their own cross. They do not want to go the way of suffering. The ambiguity of the concepts "suffering" and "works" and the change in their usage—after speaking of man's works throughout Thesis 21, Luther once again speaks of God's works in Thesis 22—makes the entire section very difficult to understand. It is understandable that some have attempted to avoid the difficulty by interpreting each of the two concepts in only one sense. This is what Carl Stange intended when he interpreted "works" as referring only to man's good works and not to God's works.[10] But this understanding of the section cannot be maintained in view of the clear text, and it robs Luther's thoughts of their real depth and boldness.

---

[8] *WA* 1, 362; *LW* 31, 52 f.

[9] *Ibid.*

[10] *Die ältesten ethischen Disputationen Luthers* (Leipzig: A. Deichert, 1904), p. 67.

The theology of the cross permeates all of Luther's theological thinking. All true theology is "wisdom of the cross."[11] This means that the cross of Christ is the standard by which all genuine theological knowledge is measured, whether of the reality of God, of his grace, of his salvation, of the Christian life, or of the church of Christ. The cross means that all these realities are hidden. The cross hides God himself. For it reveals not the might but the helplessness of God. God's power appears not directly but paradoxically under helplessness and lowliness. Thus it is that God's grace is hidden under his wrath and that his gifts and benefits are "hidden under the cross," in other words, under "trouble and disaster."[12] The world sees only the wrath and the trouble. Since we and our hearts are part of that world, we too feel only wrath and trouble. God's reality thus completely contradicts the world's standards. In the eyes of the world—and they are also our eyes—God's truth

---

[11] *WA* 5, 42, 45; *LW* 14, 305, 309.

[12] "God's gifts and benefits are so hidden under the cross that the godless can neither see nor recognize them but rather consider them to be only trouble and disaster." *WA* 31¹, 51; cf. *LW* 14, 58.

"Thus the favor bestowed by God on this little group is completely hidden from the world and appears to be nothing but eternal wrath, punishment, and torment from God himself." *WA* 31¹, 91; *LW* 14, 58.

"Outwardly His grace seems to be nothing but wrath, so deeply is it buried under two thick hides or pelts. Our opponents and the world condemn and avoid it like the plague or God's wrath, and we too do not feel much differently about it.

"Peter says truthfully (2 Peter 1:19) that the word is like a lamp shining in a dark place. Most certainly it is a dark place! God's faithfulness and truth always must first become a great lie before it becomes truth. The world calls this truth heresy. And we, too, are constantly tempted to believe that God would abandon us and not keep his word; and in our hearts we begin thinking he is a liar. In short, God cannot be God unless he first becomes a devil. We cannot go to heaven unless we first go to hell. We cannot become God's children until we first become children of the devil. All that God speaks and does the devil has to speak and do first. And our flesh agrees. Therefore it is actually the Spirit who enlightens and teaches us in the Word to believe differently. By the same token the lies of this world cannot become lies without first having become truth. The godless do not go to hell without first having gone to heaven. They do not become the devil's children until they have first been the children of God. . . .

"To summarize, the devil does not become and is not a devil without first having been God. He does not become an angel of darkness unless he has first been an angel of light (2 Cor. 11:14). . . . 'I know well that God's word must first become a great lie, even in myself, before it can become truth. I also know that the devil's word must first become the delicate truth of God before it can become a lie. I must grant the devil his hour of godliness and ascribe devilhood to our God. But this is not the whole story. The last word is: "His faithfulness and truth endure forever." ' " *WA* 31¹, 249; *LW* 14, 31 f.

seems to be a lie and the world's lies seem to be the truth. The world—and Christians also belong to this world—judges God on the basis of what he does with his own and concludes that he is a devil.[13] The devil, however, appears to be God, the Lord of the world. That is the terrible impression the reality of the world gives. All men, including the Christian, must endure before the miracle of faith can occur. The man·who believes must repeatedly pass from this experience to that faith which recognizes the reality of the grace, truth, and faithfulness of God hidden under its opposite.

Luther makes the same point when he discusses the hiddenness of Christ's kingdom. Both pagans and Jews are scandalized by the assertion that the Crucified One is king. That contradicts both their reason and their experience.[14] The salvation which this king brings to his people is exactly the opposite of what every man hopes to get from God's king—the cross and death, the world's hatred, and the like.[15] Thus God's children are hidden from the world and even from themselves.[16] Neither they nor the world recognizes them for what they are before God. Psalm 1 calls the righteous "blessed." However "the blessedness of this name is hidden in the Spirit, i.e., in God, so that it cannot be known except through faith or experience. . . . The man whom the prophet here calls blessed is unanimously declared by the world to be the most

---

[13] "He [God] makes himself look like a devil." *WA* 41, 675.

[14] "It is most difficult of all to recognize as king, one who died such a desperate and shameful death. The senses are strongly repelled by such a notion, reason abhors it, experience denies it, and a precedent is lacking. Plainly this will be folly to the Gentiles and a stumbling block to the Jews (I Cor. 1:23) unless you raise your thoughts above this." *WA* 5, 68; *LW* 14, 342.

[15] "Under this King's reign all the things you hoped for in the law are condemned and all the things you feared are to be loved. He offers the cross and death. . . . You must die if you would live under this King. You must bear the cross and the hatred of the whole world." *WA* 5, 69; *LW* 14, 342.

[16] "But because this is the wisdom of the cross, God alone knows the way of the righteous. It is hidden even to the righteous; for His right hand leads them in such a wonderful way that it is not the way of the senses or of reason but of faith alone, which is able to see even in darkness and behold the invisible." *WA* 5, 45; *LW* 14, 309.

For another description of Christians as hidden from even themselves, cf. *WA* 31¹, 249; *LW* 14, 31 f. (quoted above in n. 12).

"All his people are concealed [*inwendig*] and hidden even from themselves." *WA* 9, 196.

"A Christian is even hidden from himself; he does not see his holiness and virtue, but sees in himself nothing but unholiness and vice." *WA*, DB 7, 420; *LW* 35, 411.

wretched of all, as Isaiah looked upon Christ, the Head and Model of the blessed, whom he calls the lowest of all [Isa. 53:3]."[17]

This theology of the cross also determines Luther's view of the church. The true church of Christ cannot be identified with the historical institution which calls itself the church and with its errors, sins, divisions, and heresies. Rather the true church is hidden under this empirical reality. We shall return to this point when we discuss Luther's doctrine of the church. The earthly appearance of the church is an offense: "The devil can cover it over with offenses and divisions, so that you have to take offense at it. God too can conceal it behind faults and shortcomings of all kinds, so that you necessarily become a fool and pass false judgment on it. Christendom will not be known by sight, but by faith. And faith has to do with things not seen."[18]

The theology of the cross also determines Luther's understanding of justification. The man with whom God deals is a sinner, a man who experiences and feels nothing except the wrath of God. It is precisely this man, however, who is supposed to dare to believe the word of the gospel and think of himself as righteous and well pleasing to God. God's "yes" to him is hidden in a severe "no." But faith is the art of comprehending God in his opposite and "of holding fast to the deep and hidden 'yes' under and above the 'no' by firmly trusting in God's word."[19]

All this makes it clear that the theology of the cross results in a new understanding of what we call "reality." True reality is not what the world and reason think it is. The true reality of God and of his salvation is "paradoxical" and hidden under its opposite. Reason is able neither to understand nor to experience it. Judged by the standards of reason and experience, that is, by the standards of the world, true reality is unreal and its exact opposite is real. Only faith can comprehend that true and paradoxical reality. As a

---

[17] *WA* 5, 36; *LW* 14, 298. In the same context Luther alludes as follows to one of his favorite passages (Ps. 4:3). "Thus God exalts his saints [*mirificavit Dominus sanctum suum* . . .] , that the height of misfortune becomes the height of prosperity." *WA* 5, 41; *LW* 14, 304. Luther translates this passage *"dass der Herr seine Heiligen wunderlich führet."* Luther also quotes the same verse in connection with his doctrine of justification. This too is evidence of the fact that the justification of the sinner is a special part of God's activity described in general terms under the theology of the cross. Cf. p. 227.
[18] *WA*, DB 7, 418; *LW* 35, 410.
[19] *WA* 17ᴵᴵ, 203.

result, throughout Luther's theology of the cross the viewpoint of reason, the senses, experience, and the "world" appears in opposition to the viewpoint of faith (and the experience granted to it).[20]

This means that faith by its very nature always conflicts with that reality which the world and our own reason and experience of the world is able to see. The Christian is constantly attacked by temptation. Luther's understanding of *Anfechtung*[21] as an essential characteristic of Christian existence is part of his theology of the cross. The Christian's existence is in danger because he stands in the midst of reality under that impression of it which reason and rational experience have given him. To believe means to live in constant contradiction of empirical reality and to trust one's self to that which is hidden. Faith must endure being contradicted by reason and experience; and it must break through the reality of this world by fixing its sights on the word of promise.

This presupposes that faith is not a position on which one takes a stand but a constantly new movement. The empirical reality of human existence and of the world, the experience of trouble, of wrath, and of death, does not cease and cannot be avoided. The Christian can only overcome it constantly by holding fast to the word in faith. The Christian is always tempted to allow his impression of reality to make him doubt the truth of God and view it as a lie. He cannot possess the heaven of community with God without repeatedly making that descent into hell which takes place when he doubts and even despairs of God's grace.[22] Faith thus stands in constant conflict; and it comes to life only when it breaks through the reality accessible to reason. This fact finds theological expression in the need to present many Christian truths in paradoxical statements. Luther's thoughts on the wrath of God will give us more specific examples of this. A systematic presentation must express not only the viewpoint of faith but also the temptations and doubt in which faith is born and to which it is always related. Only so can it describe faith's break with the frame of reference available to reason. The theology of the cross is the the-

---

[20] Cf. the discussion of faith and experience on p. 55.
[21] [This word has been translated in various ways, e.g., trials, temptations, assault, perplexity, doubt.—Trans.]
[22] Cf. *WA* 31¹, 249; *LW* 14, 31 f. (see n. 15 of this chapter).

ology of faith: the theology of faith is and remains, however, the
theology of temptation [*Theologie der Anfechtung*]. The theological
thinking and speaking does not occur apart from doubt and temptation, and faith's overcoming of temptation; rather it is and remains
a thinking within this process, that is, thinking within the framework of *Anfechtung*.

Luther feels that since man's fall into sin true theology is possible only as theology of the cross. For Luther, as for Paul (I Cor.
1:21), the theology of the cross was originally not the only possibility. Luther can say that the wisdom with which a man learns to
know God in his works is, in itself, just as good as God's law. Like
all good gifts, however, this one is used by the sinner to exalt himself. Therefore only the theology of the cross now leads to a true
knowledge of God.[*] The close connection which Luther establishes
between the theology of the cross and man's sinfulness does not
nullify the fact that this theology is also intimately connected with
and expresses Luther's understanding of God's being God. The
theology of the cross means that God hides himself in his work
of salvation and that he acts and creates paradoxically while camou-
flaging his work to make it look as though he were doing the opposite. In this Luther feels that God glorifies himself as God. God
has power to create out of nothing; he can even create something
out of its opposite. This is demonstrated by the reversal of all
earthly standards and relationships. God shows that he is God
precisely in the fact that he is mighty in weakness, glorious in lowliness, living and life-giving in death. Thus in Luther's thinking,
the theology of the cross and God's being God are most intimately
connected.

It is hardly necessary to add that in his theology of the cross
Luther follows Paul's lead. He gives new force and power to the
statements of Paul in I Corinthians 1:18 ff. and in II Corinthians
about the way in which God's life works in death and his strength
in helplessness. Paul was Luther's predecessor in understanding the
cross as the valid standard for the knowledge of God and for man's
understanding of himself.

---

[*] Thesis 24 of the *Heidelberg Disputation*. "Yet that wisdom is not of itself
evil, nor is the law to be evaded; but without the theology of the cross man
misuses the best in the worst manner." *WA* 1, 363; *LW* 31, 55.

6

THE WORD OF GOD AND THE
SPIRIT OF GOD

GOD ENTERS into a saving encounter with man only by "clothing" himself and causing himself to be found at a place he
himself has designated.[1] This particular place is Christ. Where,
however, can we find Christ? How is he present with us and
known to us? "No one will find him any place except in God's
word."[2] He comes to us only through the gospel which testifies to
Christ. This testimony is given in the Holy Scripture insofar as
both Old and New Testaments "preach Christ" [*Christum treiben*]
—to use Luther's expression.[3] This gospel constantly comes to us in
the proclamation of the church. It comes also in that word of
promise which Christians speak to one another and which ministers
of the word in particular are authorized to speak to the people
committed to their care. The word proclaimed by the church cannot be thought of as Christian apart from the biblical word from
which it obtains its life. One may, however, not think of the biblical word without the contemporary living proclamation, that "shout-
ed word" which Luther felt is the original as well as the essential
form of the gospel.[4] Both Scripture and the spoken word however
are external words; that is, they are not primarily a direct mystical
communication from God's spirit to man's spirit but a word which

---

[1] See pp. 21 ff.
[2] "How, then, do we have Christ? After all, he is sitting at the right hand of
the Father; he will not come down to us in our house. No, this he will not do.
But how do I gain and have him? Ah, you cannot have him except in the
gospel. . . . And since Christ comes into our heart through the gospel, he
must also be accepted by the heart. As I now believe that he is in the gospel,
so I receive him and have him already." *WA* 10ᴵᴵᴵ, 349; *LW* 51, 114. "Christ
cannot be known except through his word; without this word Christ's flesh is
of no help to me even though it were to come today." *WA* 10ᴵᴵᴵ, 210. Cf. *WA*
12, 414.
[3] [A more literal but perhaps too colloquial translation of *Christum treiben*
would be "to push Christ." The parallel to the salesman's jargon gives some
connotations that "to teach Christ" does not.—Trans.]
[4] *WA* 40ᴵᴵ, 410 f.; *LW* 12, 369. *WA* 50, 240; *BC*, 310.

comes to men from the outside and is brought and mediated to
them by other men. This is closely connected to the fact that
Christ in his humanity, that is, in his historicity, is God present
with us. Just as he became man bodily, so he also comes to men
through the human and historical means of the "external word."
Through this human witness to him, Christ himself comes to men
with his salvation; it is here that he is present with us and for us,
and we are with him.[5] Human preaching is therefore "God's word."

God's word, however, is never merely an external word, spoken
by human lips and heard with human ears. On the contrary, at
the same time that this word is spoken, God speaks his truth in
our hearts so that men receive it not only externally but also in-
ternally and believe it. This is the work of the Spirit of God. "In
my sore distress He came to me through His eternal word and
Spirit."[6] We must now ask about the relationship between the external word and the inner word which God speaks to the heart.
For Luther they are most intimately connected. His expressions on
this can be summarized in two sentences: (1) The Spirit does not
speak without the word. (2) The Spirit speaks through and in the
word.

First, God does not give his Spirit until the external word has
preceded. Thus he does not give his Spirit directly, "without
means," but rather through means.[7] Luther continually asserted
this against the spiritualists and enthusiasts of his time.[8] "Faith

---

[5] "When you open the book containing the gospels and read or hear how
Christ comes here or there, or how someone is brought to him, you should
therein perceive the sermon or the gospel through which he is coming to you,
or you are being brought to him. For the preaching of the gospel is nothing
else than Christ coming to us, or we being brought to him." *WA* 10I,1, 13;
LW 35, 121. "Christ rules in us and yet we can neither feel him nor grasp him
but can comprehend only the word. So it is that he comes and kindles faith."
WA 9, 632.
[6] *WA* 31I, 99; *LW* 14, 62. "When the word shines into a man's heart . . ."
WA 32, 343; *LW* 21, 55.
[7] In explaining why God does not carry out his work in men without the
word, Luther says that although he could do it without the word, he does not
wish to do so. "It has pleased God not to give the Spirit without the Word,
but through the Word; that he might have us as workers together with him,
we sounding forth without what he alone breathes within wheresoever he will."
WA 18, 695; *BOW*, 184.
[8] Cf. the well-known statement on Enthusiasm in the *Smalcald Articles*. "In
these matters, which concern the external, spoken word, we must hold to the
conviction that God gives no one his Spirit or grace except through or with the
external Word which comes before. Thus we shall be protected from the en-

comes only through the work of the Holy Spirit and that is done only through the external word. Therefore, contrary to what some think, one must first hear this external word and not despise it. For God will not come to you in your private room and speak to you. He has therefore arranged that the external word should be preached and go before—so that after a man has heard the word with his ears and grasped it with his heart, the Holy Spirit, the real teacher, comes and gives power to the word so that it takes hold."[*] "We must not, as the sectarians do, imagine that God comforts us immediately, without His word."[10] The activity of the Holy Spirit in the heart is therefore always dependent on the previous hearing of the "external word." This also means that the Spirit speaks nothing else except the external word. There are no new revelations. He makes the external word powerful within us. He gives the external word power to strike man's heart. The content of the Spirit's speaking is therefore also completely bound to the word. If God would speak without means, as the spiritualists thought he should, and if the Spirit were free from the word, he could inspire anything that one might think of. That would mean, however, that some way of salvation other than the gospel of Jesus Christ would have been opened and that God would encounter sinful humanity in some way other than through the humanity and historicity of Jesus, to which the word witnesses. The fact that the Spirit is bound to the word means that our salvation is bound to the human life of Jesus Christ. The fact that the Spirit works only through the word preserves the unequivocal meaning of God's speaking in law and gospel. Spiritual speaking "without means" can mean many things; the word, however, is unequivocal.

Secondly, all this applied to the word means that the word itself is spiritually powerful. It does not remain outside of the hearer but enters into him. The external word itself becomes the inner word; it works in the heart and thereby proves that it is God's word. The Spirit does not work alone without the word but rather in and through the word.[11] It has the power to bring Christ

---

thusiasts—that is, from the spiritualists who boast that they possess the Spirit without and before the Word." *WA* 50, 245; *BC*, 312.
[*] *WA* 17ᴵᴵ, 459 f.
[10] *WA* 31ᴵ, 99; *LW* 14, 62.
[11] *WA* 9, 632 f.

into our hearts. It is able "to satisfy the heart" and to "so gain control over a man that he feels caught by it and is compelled to admit that it is true and right."[11]

The word has the divine power to convince our spirit of its truth, that is, that it is God's word. Therefore the gospel does not need to be authorized or guaranteed by some other authority such as the church. No one needs to tell me where the word of God, the gospel, is. We simply feel it; the word takes us captive and proves to us directly that it is God's word. This is the "testimony of the Holy Spirit" in the heart.[12] Luther can describe that inward event in which man is made certain of the gospel as both the self-testimony of the word and the testimony of the Holy Spirit. For these two are the same.

Word and Spirit therefore not only belong together but constitute an indissoluble unity. Luther illustrates this from nature and from human speech. The word and the Spirit are related to each other like the heat and the light which the sun always produces together, or like the voice and breath in speaking. "One cannot separate the voice from the breath. Whoever refuses to hear the voice gets nothing out of the breath either."[13]

The first point that Luther makes with these examples is that we cannot have the Spirit without the word. But do they also mean that the Spirit is always present where the word is? As we have seen, Luther emphasizes that the word is master of the heart. Yet at the same time, he distinguishes the working of the Spirit from the hearing of the word. The fact that the external word enters and overwhelms the heart is therefore not the result of an inherent dynamic which the word possesses in itself. On the contrary, the activity of the Spirit which always occurs through the word, must first be added to the preaching and hearing of the external word; and it is not always added at once. It exists as a second factor together with the preaching and hearing of the word.[14]

---

[11] *WA* 10I,1, 130.
[12] "We should, therefore, not believe the gospel because the church has approved it, but rather because we feel that it is the word of God. . . . Everyone may be certain of the gospel when he has the testimony of the Holy Spirit in his own person that this is the gospel." *WA* 30II, 687 f.
[13] *WA* 9, 633. Cf. *ibid.*, p. 632.
[14] Compare Luther's usage of "afterwards" (*darnach*) in *WA* 9, 632. and *WA* 17II, 460. It is clearly evident that this "afterwards" does not refer to a

"It is easy enough for someone to preach the word to me, but only God can put it into my heart. He must speak it in my heart, or nothing at all will come of it. If God remains silent, the final effect is as though nothing had been said."[16] There is no doubt of the fact that God does work with his Spirit through the word. He has, however, not delegated the power of his Spirit to the word but rather works freely through the word in the manner appropriate to the specific situation. He does not give the preacher control over his Spirit. Sometimes the preaching and the hearing must wait for him. We have to pray for the gift of the Spirit to accompany the word. The preachers can preach the law and the gospel. But they have no control over the way in which they strike and convert people. God himself controls that. So God's Spirit must work together with the preaching. It is God who converts men. Through his activity the Spirit makes the word effective on whomever he chooses, and whenever he chooses.[17] Both the "on whomever" and the "whenever" are important. The "whenever" means that we must wait for the Spirit; and God sometimes waits awhile before allowing the word to be effective in the heart. The Holy Spirit knows very well how to remind the heart and give new power to the word which may have been heard ten years before. This means that the word can often remain in the heart many years without having any effect; and then God's Spirit comes and makes the previously heard word effective.[18] God is, however,

---

temporal sequence but rather only to the fact that the activity of the Spirit is essentially bound to the word. Luther can also emphasize that the Spirit comes just as soon as the word is proclaimed. "Thus Peter in Acts [2:14] teaches nothing else than the word; and yet as soon as he speaks it the Holy Spirit comes and enlightens them [his hearers] and kindles faith in them; all that they have done is to sit still." *WA* 9, 633. But the Spirit does not always come at once.

[16] *WA* 10^{III}, 260. *WA* 17^{II}, 174.

[17] See n. 5. "God wills that we should teach the law. When we have done this he himself shall see who will be converted by it. He will certainly turn anyone whom he wishes to repentance whenever God wills. . . . The gospel is for all but not all believe. The law is for all but not everyone feels the power and significance of the law. I thus repent whenever God strikes me with the law and with the gospel. We are not able to say anything about the time and the hour. God himself knows when he wills to convert me." *WA* 39^{I}, 369. After preaching "leave the matter in God's hands; he will move whatever hearts he will." *WA* 39^{I}, 370. Cf. *ibid.*, pp. 404, 406.

[18] "Comfort does not come to us without the word, which the Holy Spirit effectively calls to mind and enkindles in our hearts, even though it has not been heard for ten years." *WA* 31^{I}, 100; *LW* 14, 62. Cf. "And according to the time and the need you will receive help and salvation from heaven above;

free not only to determine the "when" but the "on whom."[19] The law and the gospel are preached to many who do not receive the Spirit and thus do not receive the word to their salvation. Why God does this sort of thing is his secret. He has not revealed it to us and we must leave it to his judgment.[20] This is all the more necessary in cases where God uses his commandment and external word to move a man to resistance—as he did, for example, with Pharaoh.[21]

All this emphasis on God's freedom to add his Spirit to the external word when and as he wills in no way changes the fact that the Spirit is bound to the word. In receiving God's Spirit man always remains completely dependent on the external word. He should stay with it and wait with patience—in the certainty that God will deal with him in any case only through the word and will give his Spirit sooner or later. This promise of God is valid for everyone who preaches and hears the word. It is not negated by the ultimate possibility that God might also refuse to give his Spirit. He who speaks in the name of God and he who hears should both hold fast to this promise; that is, they should remain faithful in preaching and in hearing. Precisely because no one knows exactly when God will speak to the heart through his Spirit, it is necessary to keep on hearing the word. "Since the preachers have the office, the name, and the honor of being God's co-workers, no one should think that he is so learned or so holy that he may despise or miss the most insignificant sermon. This is especially true because he does not know at what time the hour will come in which God will do His work in him through the preachers."[22]

Luther never tired of emphasizing all of this in opposition to the spiritualistic enthusiasts. He knew very well that God's speaking is always a spiritual and inner moving of the heart, always a matter of God reaching in and touching the heart at just that mo-

---

either a brother will come to you and speak the external word or the Holy Ghost himself will work in your heart and cause you to remember such an external word." *WA* 38, 205. Cf. *WA* 40[II], 410; *LW* 12, 369.

[19] "[God] uses this same [gospel] for giving faith and his Holy Spirit wherever he wills." *WA* 30[III], 180.

[20] "But the Holy Spirit is not given to all who are contrite. Why is he given to some and not to others? I would answer that this has not been revealed to us but rather is to be left to the judgment of God." *WA* 39[I], 578.

[21] *WA* 18, 711; *BOW*, 207.

[22] *WA* 17[II], 179.

ment. It is by God's will, however, that this inner spirituality is completely bound to the external word preached and heard by human beings. God speaks directly to the heart only through the external word; and in this direct communication he says nothing else than what the external word says. This direct communication gives the power to the word by which the word impresses its content on the heart. The Spirit works only by gaining power over men in this way through the word.

Luther knows too that the Spirit can work directly and "without means," and the enthusiasts assert that he works through means. Each, however, thinks of this as taking place at a different point and in a different way. The enthusiasts teach and practice methods of preparing oneself to receive the Spirit. Luther rejects such a technique of treating souls. "God's word comes to me without any preparation or help on my part."[23] There is only one true preparation; and that is to preach, to hear, and to read the word. In doing that, however, I do not depend on my own power and activity—as the enthusiasts do with their methodology—but expose myself alone to the spiritual power of God in his word.[24] And there is no direct working of God which makes such hearing of the word unnecessary. The enthusiasts teach a working of God through means, that is, human preparation, precisely at the point at which it dare not be asserted because it limits the freedom of God. And these enthusiasts teach that God works without means precisely at the point where God has made the Christian dependent on the means of grace. Luther rejects the spiritualists' position on both points because of his understanding of justification. Luther preserves both the fact that God has bound himself to the word and the fact that he remains free.

God's word in the hand of his Spirit is simply indispensable for man's soul and spirit. The soul is created for the word, and it cannot live without the word of God. It can get along without everything else but not without the word. And when it has the word, it needs nothing else; for in the word it finds the essence of all

---

[23] *WA* 12, 497.
[24] "I am able to do this much: I can go and hear or read or preach the word so that it enters into my heart. That is the true preparation, which does not lie in human power and capability but rather in God's power." *Ibid.*

good and therefore full satisfaction.* The word is thus the one and only unconditional authority over the soul and the spirit. The soul can be determined and ruled only by God's word and not by some earthly power—for like the word itself—it is "eternal." It transcends everything within this world. That is its dignity and its freedom.*

---

* "The soul can do without anything but the word of God; and apart from the word it has no means of help. When it has the word, however, it has no need of anything else. In short, it possesses food, joy, peace, light, ability, righteousness, truth, wisdom, freedom, and sufficient to overflowing of everything good." *WA* 7, 22; *RW* 1, 358; cf. *LW* 31, 345.

* "The human soul is eternal and transcends all temporal categories. It can, therefore, be approached and ruled only through the eternal word." *WA* 11, 409; *PE* 4, 76. "For God cannot and will not permit anyone but himself to rule over the soul." *WA* 11, 262; *LW* 45, 105.

7

FAITH

A T THIS point in our study of Luther's theology we shall not consider all aspects of faith. Before we can discuss the content of faith and the extent to which salvation depends on it, we must first consider God's word and its two forms of law and gospel. The meaning of faith in Jesus Christ can become clear only within the context of the doctrines of justification and of the person and work of Christ. At this point we are concerned with the essential structure of faith, that is, with its relationship to the word of God, with its personal character, and with its relationship to experience and to reason.

FAITH AND THE WORD OF GOD

The Object of Faith Is God in His Word

We cannot discuss Luther's understanding of faith without referring to God's word. Each is closely connected with the other. We cannot therefore discuss Luther's understanding of the word of God without referring to faith. For it is the nature of God's word both to call us to faith and to work faith in us. Faith however is characterized by its orientation to the word. God's word and faith are interrelated because of their very nature.

Luther's concept of faith has nothing in common with any attempt to create strength and courage within ourselves by our own efforts, such as "positive thinking," nor is it related to a psychological condition of confidence which can exist without an object of trust and apart from a personal relationship. Faith exists only as a response to God's word. The word alone gives it its basis and content. This word is the word of "promise," that is, of the gospel. God's law is written in the hearts of all men. Everyone knows at least something about it before it is proclaimed to him. The law is therefore not the object of faith, at least not in the same sense

that the gospel is. "Faith is nourished only by the word of God. . . .
Where there is no promise of God there is no faith."[1] (Luther accepts Paul's assertion in Romans 4:13 ff. that faith and the promise
of God belong together.) For this reason the hearing of the word
precedes faith, as both Luther and Paul repeatedly emphasize,
(Rom. 10:14; Gal. 3:2) "Faith comes only through hearing," that
is, through hearing the preaching of the gospel.[2] For Luther then
faith means accepting God's promise from the heart and taking a
chance on it. Faith is an act of the will with which a man "holds
to" the word of promise.[3] "In faith you must put everything except
the word of God out of your mind. . . . Faith depends only and
simply on the word, never loses sight of it, and sees nothing else."[4]
    The word is the object of faith; this means that faith trusts God
himself or Christ. For God and Christ present themselves to us
in the word.[5] "Believing the word," therefore means the same as
believing "in God through the word."[6] Faith thus trusts directly in
God. The word of the promise which I believe does not have
authority in itself, as though it were a universally valid truth that
demonstrates its own validity; rather it possesses the personal authority of my God and Lord who speaks to me in this word. It
thus does not convey a purely objective truth but rather is a word
of acceptance and summons, of promise and command, which God
personally addresses to me. Faith therefore is always a direct relationship to God himself and to Christ. To believe means to accept
God in his word as truthful and thus to recognize and honor him
as God. Faith is unconditional trust of God in his word. Nothing
else that a man does gives God as much honor as faith does, for
faith takes God seriously as God. Unfaith denies that God is God.
The insight that faith honors God and fulfills the First Commandment is extremely characteristic of Luther's understanding of faith.

---

[1] *WA* 6, 363 f.; *LW* 35, 92. "The promise is received in faith." *WA* 39^{II},
207.
[2] *WA* 17^{II}, 73, 176 f.
[3] "It is the nature of faith that the will holds to the word which provides
invisible joys, help, and defense." *WA* 40^{III}, 50.
[4] *WA* 10^{III}, 423.
[5] "Be grateful that you have my word and myself in my word." *WA* 31^{I},
456; *LW* 14, 134. Other expressions: "The word . . . is God himself." *WA* 8,
49; *LW* 32, 146. "When the word of God is taught, . . . God himself is then
present." *WA* 8, 50; *LW* 32, 147.
[6] *WA* 10$^{\mathrm{I,1}}$, 129.

Luther sees faith not only anthropocentrically, as the only way in which man is saved and wins eternal life, but also theocentrically. God's honor is at stake in faith. When "the soul firmly believes God's word, it considers him to be truthful, good, and righteous. Thereby it pays him the highest honor it can: It admits that he is true and does not dispute the fact. Thus it honors his name. This also means that we can do no greater dishonor to God than not to believe him."[7] To use Luther's well-known phrase from the *Large Catechism*, "Faith and God belong together."[8] They are correlated in two ways. First, true faith can never have any other object than God, for only God can be unconditionally trusted.[9] Secondly, only that faith which unconditionally trusts God really treats him as God. Faith is this relationship to God; and God is the One in whom we can and must believe. If we want to express what faith is, we must speak about God. And if we want to say who God is, we must speak of faith.

Man's faith gives God the honor due his deity. Luther summarizes this with the bold assertion that "faith creates the deity." Feuerbach referred to such statements to illustrate his thesis that the idea of God is anthropologically derived through man's objectivication of his own being (man created God in his own image). Karl Barth feels that Feuerbach's appeal to Luther is not wholly unjustified, and he asks whether the occurrence of such statements in Luther does not indicate that Luther failed adequately to protect the irreversibility of the relationship between God and man and assert the unconditional priority and initiative of God in that relationship.[10] The truth of the matter is, however, that Feuerbach errs in quoting Luther to prove his position; and Barth's concern is unfounded. No line of development connects Luther with Feuerbach. For when Luther says that "faith creates the deity," he immediately adds "not in [God's] person but in us."[11] It goes with-

---

[7] *WA* 7, 25; *RW* 1, 362 f.; cf. *LW* 31, 350 f.
[8] *WA* 30¹, 133; *BC*, 365.
[9] "Reason itself teaches and Scripture confirms the fact that no man should be made the object of the heart's confidence and trust; this belongs only to the true God, since he alone is eternal and immortal and in addition is also all-powerful so that he also can do what he wills." *WA* 37, 42.
[10] *Protestant Thought: from Rousseau to Ritschl*, trans. Brian Cozens (New York: Harper, 1959), p. 359.
[11] *WA* 40¹, 360; cf. *LW* 26, 227.

out saying that God really exists as God without us and before we believe. However, he also wants to be God "in us." He is God "in us" only when we let him be our God in faith. So it is for the sake of his deity that God thus waits for us to believe and commands us to believe. And it is in this sense that another of Luther's bold statements is to be understood: "Outside of faith God loses his righteousness, glory, riches, etc. and has no majesty or deity where there is no faith."[12] This means neither more nor less than the explanation of the first petition in the *Small Catechism* means when it says: "To be sure, God's name is holy in itself, but we pray in this petition that it may also be holy for us."[13]

The priority of God and the irreversibility of the relationship between God and man are asserted in the fact that faith does not create the word but rather hears and receives it. And the grace offered to us in the word must be grasped in faith. Until then, it is not real to us. And it is in only this sense that our own thinking and attitude, our faith or unfaith, creates reality for us. Our thinking about God, our believing or not believing, is not merely a subjective factor without meaning and significance for reality; it rather determines God's transcendent relationship to us.[14] "As you think, so it happens." "If you believe that He is your father, your judge, your God, then this is what He is." "If you think of God as wrathful, He is. Thus His activity orients itself to our thoughts."[15] Such statements are not Luther's autonomous theological self-expression but only an explanation of the word of Jesus, "Be it done for you as you believe."[16]

In grasping the promise, faith actually receives the promise. For in grasping the promise faith holds to God, and that is the fulness of salvation. Faith therefore is the breakthrough of eternal life. "Wherever there is faith, eternal life has already begun."[17]

---

[12] Immediately after saying this, Luther asserts: "God does not require anything more of me than that I make him God. If his divinity is whole and uninjured, then God has whatever I am able to give him." *WA* 40^I, 360; cf. *LW* 26, 227.

[13] *WA* 30^I, 251; *BC*, 346.

[14] *WA* 40^{II}, 343; cf. *LW* 12, 322.

[15] *WA* 8, 8; *LW* 13, 6. *WA* 40^{II}, 342 f.; cf. *LW* 12, 322 f. "As you think about God, so He is." *WA* 37, 589.

[16] Matt. 8:13. According to Veit Dietrich's edition of Luther's lectures on Psalm 51, Luther himself refers to this passage. *WA* 40^{II}, 342; *LW* 12, 322.

[17] *WA* 31^I, 156; *LW* 14, 88.

Faith is the way in which, even while living in the midst of earthly life, we transcend it and live in God, in the fulness of salvation.

God Works Faith Through His Word

Although faith is an act of man which is oriented to the word of promise, it is not an act which he either should or can produce by himself; rather God creates it through the word. God the Holy Spirit works faith in a man through the preaching of the word. "Faith . . . comes only through God's word or gospel."[18] Luther thereby makes two points. First, it is not I but the word who works faith: in the word I experience the working of the Spirit. Second, no other authority except the word of God can provide the basis for my faith.

First, faith is not the result of human exertion; it is not man's own product but rather God's wonderful creation in him. Luther continually emphasizes that one must clearly distinguish genuine faith from self-made faith. Naturally, man, when he hears the gospel, is able to respond positively both intellectually and volitionally. He can do this "work" of giving assent. But such a faith has nothing to do with true faith. It is only a figment of the imagination, a "human fantasy" that a man can talk himself into. "The depth of the heart," however, knows nothing of this faith; that is, the whole man is not involved for he is not thoroughly grasped by the truth of the gospel. Such faith therefore also does not change a man's existence. Luther puts it this way in his *Preface to Romans* (1522): "Faith is not the human notion and dream that some people call faith . . . when they hear the gospel, they get busy and by their own powers create an idea of faith in their heart which says, 'I believe'; they take this then to be a true faith. But, as it is a human figment and idea that never reaches the depths of the heart, nothing comes of it either, and no improvement follows."[19] This "do-it-yourself faith," this "work of man," this "delusion" which a man can intentionally produce

---

[18] *WA*, DB 7, 7; *LW* 35, 368. *WA* 39¹, 83; *LW* 34, 153.
[19] *WA*, DB 7, 9; *LW* 35, 370. The contrast between do-it-yourself faith and that faith which has been created by God is discussed also in Luther's sermon on the wise and foolish virgins, preached in Erfurt October 21, 1522, where he says, "This faith is man's creation; therefore it is as useless as the foam on water or the scum on bad beer." *WA* 10ᵐ, 355.

proves particularly inadequate in death. In the serious times of life, in sin, in death, and in hell such faith fails.[20] That faith however which God awakens in the heart is powerful to oppose sin, death, and hell. Because God created it through his word, it has the same power as the word, yes, even as God himself; for God is truly present in his word. Like the word, this faith is "more powerful than any creature," than even the entire world; it is strong enough to overcome anything that threatens man's salvation. For this faith is the way in which the word, and therefore God himself, is present in a man. Faith is God's power, it is not a human capability. In faith man shares in the power of God. "Faith is omnipotent just as God himself is."[21] This is true of faith however only to the extent that God himself has worked it in the heart through his word. Fabricated faith "is nothing." Such faith is powerless. "God has nothing to do with such a delusion."[22]

Luther warns against such do-it-yourself faith but not simply because it fails and is powerless in the crises of life. He also sees man's attempt to produce faith on his own as terrible presumption over against God. For a man thereby presumes to bring about that which is within the creative power of God alone. Man must wait for God to act. Otherwise, man attacks God's glory as the only creator. Man's attempt to believe by his own power is therefore not only a delusion but also a sin against God.[23]

Secondly, only the word works faith and it does so by convincing a man of its validity. No other authority can be the basis of faith except the authority of the word, that is, of God himself in his word. This constitutes the big difference between "human" faith and "divine" faith. Human faith depends on the human person who speaks the word; it believes the word because of the

---

[20] *WA* 10III, 356 f.
[21] *WA* 10III, 214. "Suffering comes to the Christian so that the old Adam will really die. This demonstrates the power of the word and of faith; it makes certain that faith is more powerful than every other creature, for faith itself exists by the power of God and not by any human power." *WA* 17I, 73. Note that Luther here designates the power of the word as at one and the same time the power of faith, and the power of God.
[22] *WA* 10III, 356.
[23] "Let no one assume that he has faith by his own powers, as so many do when they hear about faith and then undertake to gain it by their own ability. They thus undertake a task which belongs to God alone, for having true faith is really a divine work." *WA* 12, 422 f.

speaker's person and authority, for example, because of the authority of the church, the clergy, the hierarchy, or some organization (such as a council of the church). Divine faith on the other hand depends solely on the word "which is God himself."[24] Such faith does not need earthly authorities to make the truth of the word certain but only the word itself. A man "feels that it is so certainly true that no one can ever tear him away from it." Luther illustrates this with a reference to the Samaritans in John 4:42. They first believe because of what the woman has told them; then, however, they recognize for themselves who Christ is. Not even the earthly person of Jesus and such things as his miracles are the ultimate ground of faith in the word; rather "the word itself without regard for the person must satisfy the heart and must so convince and grasp a man that he immediately feels compelled to admit that it is true and right even though all the world, all the angels, and all the princes of hell disagree; yes, even though God himself would immediately say otherwise."[25] (Luther is here thinking of those temptations in which God presents himself to us as the one who attacks and condemns us.) The word does indeed come to me through earthly witnesses and authorities, through the church and through its organs, and as in the case of the Samaritans, there is a preliminary stage in which I believe it on the authority of others. Ultimately, however, it is not they who guarantee the word for me; the word guarantees itself. True faith "rests on the word alone and is not influenced by any person."[26] The word, by the power of its own truth, is independent of all human authorities. Luther underscores that fact, together with the exclusive nature of the word's self-authentication, when he places the word of God in the same category as mathematical axioms which, independently of every human authority, immediately commend themselves to the human mind as sensible. They are so self-evident that no human authority can contradict them.[27]

---

[24] *WA* 10I,1, 129 f.
[25] *WA* 10I,1, 130.
[26] *WA* 10I,1, 131.
[27] "Therefore I allow no one to drive me away from that word which God teaches me. For example, it is certain and obvious that two and three add up to five. And if all the councils had decreed otherwise, I would still know that they were lying. One yard is more than half a yard and even if the whole world were to disagree I could still know that it was wrong. Who guarantees

Naturally, Luther can equate the evidence of the word of God with that of the mathematical axioms only in so far as the truth convinces by its own power without needing any other authorities. Otherwise their self-authentication is completely different. Viewed in terms of content, the word simply does not have the axiomatic character of mathematical principles. Therefore it does not make itself understood to every man by its own power; this occurs only when God himself speaks through the word to a man's heart and conscience (cf. p. 38). Self-authentication is not an "attribute" of the word; rather it exists only from moment to moment through God's presence and speaking in his word. The certainty that God's word is true is therefore something completely different from any axiomatic or a priori certainty. The self-certainty of reason, the evidential character of rational truths, is far removed from the "testimony of the Holy Spirit."

Luther's most central and characteristic thought about faith is that it is born when a man is inwardly and spiritually convinced by the living voice of God speaking to him in the word. The content of faith is determined accordingly: as the word is nothing less than God dealing with men in order to save them, so this same saving activity of God, and nothing else, is the content and object of faith. We dare not conceal the fact, however, that Luther could also speak of faith in quite different terms. At times he operates with a concept of faith quite like that which had become commonly accepted in the theology of his time. This view of faith accords with the fact that although Luther criticized the Bible in specific details, he nonetheless followed the tradition of his time and basically accepted it as an essentially infallible book, inspired in its entire content by the Holy Spirit. It is therefore "the word of God," not only when it speaks to us in law and gospel and thereby convicts our heart and conscience but also—and this is a matter of principle—in

---

that to me? No human being, but the truth which is altogether certain." *WA* 10ᴵᴵᴵ, 260 f. Luther here rejects the traditional Roman understanding of Augustine's statement, "I would not have believed the Gospel unless the authority of the universal church [*catholica ecclesia*] moved me to do so." *MPL* 42, 176. Luther says "that would be false and unchristian. Everyone must believe only because it is the word of God, and because he is convinced in his heart that it is true." *WA* 10ᴵᴵ, 90; *LW* 35, 151. Cf. *WA* 39ᴵ, 191, where Luther in interpreting Augustine's statement construes the "church," which is obediently believed, to be the apostles.

everything else that it says. Seen as a totality, its historical accounts, its world-view, and all the miracle stories are "God's word" given by the Holy Spirit; they are therefore all unquestionable truth, to be "believed" precisely because they are contained in the book.

Obviously, we are here confronted with a concept of the "word of God" quite different from that which we have met up to this point presented as Luther's concept, and hence also with a different concept of faith. If the word of God is understood in this way, as identical with the entire content of Scripture, including the historical and the cosmological material, we can no longer say that the word convinces the human spirit by its own power and validates itself—as we can when "word" describes God's speaking to us. Therefore that faith which has as its object the Bible in its totality can only be a faith that is almost identical with the "fabricated faith," which Luther elsewhere describes. This faith involves the compulsion to believe and to submit humbly to the written word as such. This understanding of faith resembles that faith which we have up until now presented as Luther's central concept insofar as it also gives God the honor due him. According to this understanding of faith, God commands us to believe the entire content of Scripture as though he himself were the author, and he insists that we abandon reason, and the questions and doubts it poses for us, in view of the fact that it is he who has said all this to us in his word, and in this case that means, in the Scripture.[*] On this single point of comparison, all resemblances cease. There is no getting away from the fact that these traditional concepts of the word and of faith contradict that understanding of the word and of faith which produced Luther's Reformation. In utilizing them at all, Luther brought about the infiltration of heteronomous and contradictory elements into the theonomous understanding of the authority of the word of God and of faith, and hence also into the relationship between faith and reason. The problem also had implications for that which was most fundamental in Luther's theology, namely, the clear distinction between law and gospel. The word which by the sovereign power of God's own Spirit attests and authenticates

---

[*] "Because God says it, I will believe that it is so; I will follow the word and regard my own thoughts and ideas as vain." *WA* 37, 39. Cf. *ibid.*, p. 40.

itself to me is the gospel; and the faith which is convinced by this word is truly evangelical faith. However, anything that I must believe simply on the grounds that it is set down in the Bible is law, and the corresponding faith is legalistic faith. Here is the point at which the clarity of Luther's own Reformation insight reached its limit. For it was at this point that Luther himself, in spite of everything, prepared the way for seventeenth century orthodoxy, and in so doing helped to bring about the difficult and perilous crisis which resulted when the new science of the Enlightenment rose up in opposition to the authority of the Bible which theology had both falsely understood and falsely asserted. Since theology had so closely connected this false legalistic authority of the Bible to its true authority as the bearer of the living word of God, the destruction of the former also damaged the latter. The same thing happened with respect to the ambiguous character of the concept of faith. Theology has had plenty of trouble in the past—and in many places still has—trying to repair this damage by distinguishing between the "Word of God" in the true sense and a false biblicism, and by differentiating what faith really is from the legalistic distortion of faith. In addition, as we have seen, it is also necessary for theology to distinguish within Luther himself between that which reflects the historical situation and tradition of his time, and that which belongs properly to the Reformation.

Luther also continues to use the [medieval] church's concept of faith in his approach to both the christological and trinitarian dogmas. His approach differs, however, in that for him these dogmas are established not primarily by the authority of the church but by that of Scripture ("what God himself says and teaches"). In this connection Luther says, "This must be believed; whoever will not believe it is a heretic."[*] These are thus articles which are to

---

[*] Speaking of the christological ("that God and man are one person") and the trinitarian dogmas, Luther says, "God does not want us to master it and fit it together, he wants us to believe it. He wants us to accord him the honor of admitting that he alone is wise and of letting ourselves be guided by his word . . . which simply means to tip your hat and say 'yes' to this and let it be true." *WA* 37, 44. Cf. *ibid.*, p. 45. "And even though reason is not able to grasp how this takes place still it must surrender itself into captivity under this word and believe it." (Note that Luther usually says that the word of God takes a man captive but here he says that reason must surrender itself into captivity.) *WA* 10^{I,1}, 152. Cf. *WA* I,1, 186, 191. Cf. *WA* 50, 273; *LW* 34,

be believed (*credenda*). Luther makes no distinction between the gospel itself, which calls us to faith and effects that faith by convincing our heart and spirit, and the doctrinal form which theological reflection has developed out of this faith in the gospel. This doctrinal form cannot itself become in turn the object of faith, it always remains merely the product of theological consideration and insight based on faith in the gospel. We take this distinction for granted today. It is a distinction, however, which Luther never made. He called men to believe in the theologically formulated dogma of the church in the same sense in which he called them to believe in the "word of God," the gospel.

I BELIEVE: THE PERSONAL NATURE OF THE CERTAINTY OF FAITH

The word authenticates itself to me—this is what we have been hearing up to this point. Now however we must also emphasize, as Luther does, that it authenticates itself to *me*. There is therefore within a man something to which the word bears witness that it is God's word. The word is something different from man's own inner life; it stands over against him; it speaks to him from the outside. It must be heard—no one can speak it to himself. When it is heard however, it enters into a man in such a way that it moves his innermost being; it convinces, convicts, and thereby proves to him that it is God's own truth. Luther refers to that within man to which the word bears convincing witness with the biblical terms of "the heart" or "the conscience." It is here that the certainty of faith exists.

I am "heart" or "conscience" however only as an individual, a completely unique and irreplaceable personal being. God's word speaks to me as an individual, and makes me an individual who is

---

216. "Here one must be silent and say: God has spoken it and I hear that there is one God and Three Persons; how that is possible I do not know." *WA* 39^{II}, 364. Cf. *ibid.*, 384. Referring to the trinitarian dogma Luther says, "We should therefore believe even those things which are hidden. . . ." *WA* 39^{II}, 279. Cf. *ibid.*, 280. Luther can also speak of such a faith as "believing the word." *Ibid.*, 279. "Word" is here not only the promise but rather everything which God "teaches" in Scripture. Faith "holds to Scripture which neither deceives nor lies." *WA* 10$^{\text{I,1}}$, 191. Speaking of the doctrine of the Virgin Birth Luther says, "Therefore we shall hold to the word in faith against all such temptations and speculations." *WA* 37, 55.

directly related to God. No other person or group stands between us. No one can take my place, no one can intervene and take away the grace and responsibility inherent in the fact that I stand alone and by myself before God. God's word and that irreplaceable "I-myself" belong together. The word makes me stand before God in the absolute uniqueness and loneliness of my own self and summons me to a faith which, being entirely my own, is both genuine and certain. Understood in this sense, faith is an unconditionally personal act.

This is all said by the same Luther who is very well aware of the reality of the Christian community, of the community in faith, and of the strengthening effect of the faith of the fathers and brethren on my own faith. "The faith of the church helps me out in my uncertainty."[20] In all this however one thing remains clear: The faith of others can only help me to believe for myself. No one can ever believe for someone else as though his faith were a substitute for the entirely personal faith of the other.[21] Each of us must believe for himself alone.[22] "A Christian is a person in his own right; he believes for himself and not on behalf of anyone else."[23] All the Christian community in the world and the rest of our vicarious intercessions on behalf of the others cannot remove this ultimate loneliness; on the contrary, it can only help us achieve it. Luther establishes the loneliness of faith by referring to death. In death each of us is completely alone and must die his own death; no one else can take your place; and no one else can struggle for you, that is, no one else can fight the fight of faith in death's great hour of trial and perplexity. If my faith is to stand fast at that moment, then it must be completely my own personal faith and my own most personal certainty. In this ultimate crisis all of the judgments of earthly authorities are of no help to me. I must be absolutely and personally certain for myself. Faith is therefore a deadly serious matter. I am lost if in dying I am not personally

---

[20] *WA* 6, 131; *PE* 1, 165.
[21] *WA* 10ᴵᴵᴵ, 306. 308. "My faith helps you only by encouraging and helping you to believe for yourself. Thus . . . everything depends on your own faith; the stronger it is, the more it receives and has; and the weaker it is the more it needs someone else's faith and intercession so that it may be strengthened." *WA* 10ᴵᴵᴵ, 310.
[22] *WA* 10ᴵᴵ, 90; *LW* 35, 151.
[23] *WA* 19, 648; *PE* 5, 59.

as certain of God's word as I am of my own existence. Only through such certainty does the conscience have peace."[54]

Thus we see that Luther regards the question about the certainty of faith as a most serious one. This is because salvation is a decidedly personal reality for him: it is fellowship with God—a fellowship, however, that is not actualized except in the very being of the man himself, in the "subjectivity" of his faith. As a result, Luther's question about salvation necessarily assumes the form of a question about the certainty of faith. This certainty of faith is more than a merely subjective condition of the person himself; that is, having this certainty is the same as being saved.

FAITH AND EXPERIENCE

Faith and Experience in Opposition: the Trials and Temptations of Faith

At this point we return to Luther's theology of the cross, for the meaning of faith can be fully understood only within this frame of reference.

Faith is directed toward the word of promise and at first has nothing except this word. The word offers a reality which is hidden and cannot be seen.[55] This reality therefore is not the object of

---

[54] This is particularly clear in the well-known beginning of the Invocavit sermons of March, 1522. "The summons of death comes to us all, and no one can die for another. Every one must prepare his weapons and armor to fight his own battle with death and the devil by himself, alone. . . . I will not be with you then, nor you with me." *WA* 10ᴵᴵᴵ, 1 ff.: *LW* 51, 70. Cf. *WA* 10ᴵᴵ, 23, *LW* 36, 248. "When I have to die, you [the pope] will not fight and answer for me; rather I must look out for myself. I must see to it that I am as certain of God's word as I am of the fact that you live—even more certain—so that you can stake your conscience on it. And even if all men—indeed the angels as well—come together and were to agree on this, still if you cannot judge and reach this conclusion for yourself, you are lost. . . . For if you on your deathbed would attempt to say that the pope has said it and the councils have decreed it and the holy fathers . . . have agreed on this, then the devil will immediately make a hole in your argument and break in by asking, 'And what if it is not true? Were they not able to err?' Then you have already been overcome. Therefore your knowing must be so far beyond the shadow of any doubt that you can say, "This is God's word and I'll stand on it.'" *WA* 10ᴵᴵᴵ, 259. "Well, then, let them decree and say whatever they want; you still cannot rest your confidence on it or console your conscience with it. It's your neck and your life that's at stake; therefore, God must speak into your heart, saying, 'This is God's word'—otherwise it remains uncertain. So it is that you must be certain in and for yourself quite apart from all men." *WA* 10ᴵᴵᴵ, 260.
[55] "His heavenly word has promised us that unseen help is available." *WA* 40ᴵᴵᴵ, 56. Cf. *ibid.*, p. 46

"experience" but something that can be grasped only through faith in the word. Faith thus stands in opposition to our experience and to our "seeing." Faith apprehends reality in a different way than seeing and experience do. Luther repeatedly quotes Hebrews 11:1, "Faith is the evidence of things not seen." Later, Luther translates, "Not doubting what one does not see." Because God himself is hidden, we have him and what his word promises only by believing in the word.[36] God's hiddenness and man's faith thus belong together. Yes, Luther can even say that God hides himself and his saving will precisely in order to make room for that faith to which he has called us. If faith is essentially concerned with concealed reality, then it is true that "it is necessary that everything which is to be believed be hidden so that there may be room for faith." And Luther continues, "It cannot be hidden any more deeply than when it appears to be the exact opposite of what we see, sense, and experience."[37] God and his salvation are thus hidden under their opposite. To the natural eye, God seems to be doing the opposite of that which he ultimately wills. He hides himself under the disguise of his antagonist, Satan. Faith must not only live without experience; it even has experience against it and must persevere and assert itself in opposition to experience.[38] For this reason, the believer is tempted and afflicted all his life by the empirical evidence of his senses. Thus the believer always struggles with doubt. Trial and temptation is not the exception but the rule in the life of the believer.

Luther describes the opposition between faith and experience especially by referring to the woes and troubles of this life and the great temptation to despair into which they plunge us. Our heart is afflicted by the present reality of severe trouble. The word of promise speaks of a redemption which lies in the future and is still hidden. Since we cannot see this hidden future, we cannot see the end of the present trouble either. We see only the beginning but

---

[36] "But this calls for faith. For the father, the judge, God, [cf. Ps. 68, 6] is present but cannot be seen. His dwelling is holy; that is, it is set apart and can be seen only with the eyes of faith. If you believe that he is your father, your judge, your God, then this is what he is." *WA* 8, 8; *LW* 13, 7.
[37] *WA* 18, 633; *BOW*, 101. *WA* 8, 22; *LW* 13, 22 f.
[38] "Stand fast, however, in such contradictory experience and nevertheless believe most constantly; for you wait for what cannot be seen." *WA* 40III, 55.

not the end. Our vision is too weak and too nearsighted; it is unable to comprehend that hidden salvation which cannot be seen. God however sees the end of our trouble; and it is he who speaks the word of promise to us. For this reason we must give heed to what he says in his word rather than to our own nearsighted heart.[39] Temporal trouble looks far different to God than it does to us. (Luther makes reference to Paul's statement in II Corinthians 4:17, "This slight, momentary affliction," and to Isaiah 54:7, "For a brief moment I forsook you.")[40] "God says, 'To me your trouble is only a point, a moment, a drop, a spark.' But reason converts a mathematical point into an infinite line, because it does not see the end of the affliction.'"[41] The Lord says, however, "I have better vision than you do." Reason is unacquainted with "the divine and heavenly mathematics," according to which all earthly trouble is only a moment, a mathematical point. To believe means to abandon the viewpoint of reason and of our own heart and take a chance on God's word and on his perspective.[42] Faith sees the reality of trouble as God sees it. Then the troubles and anxieties which seem so great and terrible to the natural eye become quite small, indeed nothing at all.[43] What are they compared with God and the reality of his eternal grace in Christ?[44] This is what the "divine and heavenly mathematics" teaches us.

Doubt and temptation are most grievous at the point where I am compelled to conclude that the troubles and difficulties of this life, which conceal God's purpose for my life and call it into question, are not only the "no" of Satan and of the world but also God's own "no" to me—and so regard my fate in the light of God's law. Luther made this situation unforgettably clear in his

---

[39] *WA* 40ᴵᴵᴵ, 59. Cf. also the printed text prepared by Veit Dietrich on the basis of Rörer's notes. "We should therefore look to the promise and not depend on ourselves." *Ibid.*, p. 61.

[40] *WA* 40ᴵᴵᴵ, 60, 63.

[41] *WA* 40ᴵᴵᴵ, 60 ff.

[42] "Faith must believe against reason, against its own feeling and intuition, and against its understanding which grasps and admits the validity only of that which is empirical." Cf. pp. 67 f. *WA* 40ᴵᴵᴵ, 61 (quoted in n. 38).

[43] "Let the devil and the world go, for here is God and here the Lord speaks. This makes all fear in my heart so small that it is hardly as big as a louse." *WA* 40ᴵᴵᴵ, 63.

[44] *WA* 40ᴵᴵᴵ, 64.

discussion of the story of the Syro-Phoenician woman. What makes this particular trial so grievous is the fact that Jesus Christ himself assumes a stance identical to that which our heart in its moment of perplexity and doubt ascribes to him. He himself speaks the "no" and our heart thinks of this "no" as absolutely final. But that is not the way it really is. "Therefore the heart must turn its back on such feelings and with strong faith in God's word grasp the deep and secret 'yes' that is under and above the 'no.' " This is what Christ's encounter with the Syro-Phoenician woman teaches us. The story is "written to instruct and comfort all of us, so that we may know how deeply God hides his grace and not think of him according to our own feelings and reactions but exactly according to his word."[45]

This all reaches its highest point when God's primary "no" is spoken directly to us by God's law. Our heart and conscience must agree with the law and its accusation of us. God is right when he condemns and damns us in his wrath.[46] Even then, however, the heart should hold God to his word of promise, which says that he will accept sinners, not the righteous. The deepest doubts and temptations arise from the fact that God's will and word come to us in the twofold form of law and gospel. Faith exists in the tension between law and gospel. Because the law and gospel are contrary to each other, whenever we believe the gospel we must do so in opposition to our own heart and conscience which are so determined by the law that our awareness of the law makes us doubt and despair of God's grace.[47] Here faith must do even more than merely break through that earthly reality which contradicts God's word; it must break through God's own word of law and

---

[45] Speaking of Christ's first reply to the Syro-Phoenician woman Luther says, "This sounds much more like 'no.' Actually there is nothing except 'yes' in it but the 'yes' is deeply hidden and appears to be a mere 'no.' This shows what our heart is like in moments of trial and temptation. Christ here assumes the stance which our heart feels he has taken. Our heart feels that there is nothing else than 'no' there and yet it is not true." *WA* 17ᴵᴵ, 203. . . . [Here follows the quotation footnoted in the text above.]" Luther treats the conversation between Jesus and Mary at the wedding of Cana in a similar manner. *WA* 17ᴵᴵ, 66.

[46] *WA* 6, 208; *PE* 1, 192.

[47] "When I believe, God saves me in opposition to the law." *WA* 39ᴵ, 219. The opposition to law implicit in this action of God has its counterpart in the opposition to law implicit in faith's believing the gospel.

through the wrath expressed in his law." The believer must also turn away from the feelings and condemnation of his own conscience and turn only to the gospel. We must fight with our conscience and must believe Christ and the gospel of the forgiveness of sins more than we believe our own conscience." Being tempted by the law not to believe the gospel remains part of our Christian experience as long as we live. Doubt is not constantly present but it always returns. The certainty which the Holy Spirit creates through the gospel and the doubt which the law works stand in conflict with each other throughout our lives. It is true that the certainty of faith always conquers through the help of the Spirit of God. But not until the life to come, will doubt be completely ended and certainty completely rule." So faith always takes a chance and the believer is always a hero. "A Christian is the sort of hero who constantly deals with absolutely impossible things."" But faith's "heroism" is always bound to the anguish of doubt and temptation. This is the situation in which it is "exercised."" It is in the struggle with temptation that the old man is supposed to die and faith experience the full power of God's word and so attain its own full strength. Consideration of Christ's own anguished death and of the grievous doubts and temptations of the Crucified helps faith to attain that end, to endure the most difficult troubles and anxieties without succumbing to despair. Only if Christ is with us, can we bear the worst troubles and anxieties without falling into despair."

"Coming to God is such a wonderful thing that we should break through his wrath, punishment, and displeasure as if we were breaking through a solid wall of thorns, indeed of spears and swords." *WA* 19, 224. Cf. *WA* 6, 208, 249; *PE* 1, 192 f., 249.

"So now turn from your conscience and its feeling to Christ who is not able to deceive; my heart and Satan, however, who will to drive me to sin are liars. . . . You should not believe your conscience and your feelings more than the word which the Lord who receives sinners preaches to you. . . . Therefore you are able to fight with your conscience by saying: You lie; Christ speaks the truth and you do not." *WA* 27, 223.

Cf. the statement in a disputation of 1542, *WA* 39ᴵᴵ, 163. "Thus the promise of the gospel always battles against the doubt of the law. Even though doubt is really engaged in battle with the promise, yet finally the promise shall win the field." *WA* 39ᴵᴵ, 200; *LW* 34, 318.

WA 27, 276.
WA 17ᴵ, 73.
Ibid.

Experience in Faith

Faith always struggles with the contradictions of natural experience. But faith and experience are not simply in absolute opposition to and conflict with each other. For there is such a thing as experience wrought by faith itself. It is different from the usual kind of empirical experience; it is experience in a new dimension.

First of all, faith experiences itself. As a human act, faith is simply the taking of a chance: I stake my life on the word. Our capacity to believe is so minimally involved that faith is not always aware of its own existence. Luther can even say that someone who is certain that he believes does not believe at all while someone else who seems to be completely bogged down in doubt and despair really believes most strongly.[54] To believe means to be certain of God's word; but this does not include faith's being certain of its own existence as faith. And yet faith is also an experience. I experience that God's word is powerful over me and that, as we have heard, it so convinces and grasps me that it takes me captive and does not let me go. This element must under all circumstances be considered in conjunction with the other element of blindly taking a chance on the word. As my own act, it may well be the taking of a chance in fear and trembling; but even this is something to which I am compelled by God's word and Holy Spirit. Remember Luther's distinction between false self-made faith and true faith. True faith is characteristically distinguished from do-it-yourself faith by the fact that it is created by the Holy Spirit through the word. And faith knows this too; it "feels" this much about itself. Someone admittedly may neither wish nor be able to speak of his own believing; he may even feel that he has no faith. Still he can bear witness to the power of the word of truth which does not let him go and which repeatedly overcomes his doubt. Luther uses a whole series of expressions to describe this element of experience in faith. The word "satisfies the heart," "convinces," "grasps" it, takes it "captive";[55] the heart "feels how true and right the word is"; it must "know," "feel," and "taste" (*sapere*—Luther

---

[54] "For it happens, indeed it is typical of faith, that often he who claims to believe does not believe at all; and on the other hand, he who doesn't think he believes, but is in despair, has the greatest faith." *WA* 26, 155; *LW* 40, 241.

[55] Compare the passages cited on p. 47.

uses this ancient expression for "direct awareness").[56] Thus faith in and of itself is an experience precisely because it merely holds to the word. In the fact that it repeatedly knows that it is based on the word, it has experienced the power of the word through the Holy Spirit.

Admittedly this experience of faith is not constant. Under the pressure of suffering it may even disappear. As Christ on the cross no longer felt his own deity, so the Christian according to his outer man may "no longer feel the faith" through which he is God's child. At such times faith "crawls away and hides."[57] Then the joy which faith gives ceases. Faith stands completely alone without experience. Nothing remains except to look to Christ on the cross. But things are not always this way. Luther knows that faith from time to time must pass through such moments of anguish, but that they in turn will pass and the experience of the joy of faith will return.

Not only does faith experience itself, it also experiences life. When the Christian believes the word, he experiences that Christ with his power to overcome sin, the devil, and the anxiety of death, is actually present with him. Admittedly, faith does not base itself on previous experience; the proper sequence is that faith always precedes experience, and this sequence must be preserved. We must believe the word even when we experience the opposite of that which it promises to us; that is, when we have no previous experience and even when experience contradicts the word. On the other hand, however, what we believe becomes an object of our experience.[58] Faith and experience are two different things. But the same faith which must and does believe in opposition to experience feels that in believing it gains experience of that which it believes. At first the Christian listens to the word and believes in the saving power of Jesus Christ, but then he experiences that power in

---

[56] "No one can correctly understand God or his word. unless he has received such understanding immediately from the Holy Spirit. But no one can receive it from the Holy Spirit without experiencing, proving, and feeling it." *WA* 7, 546; *LW* 21, 299. Cf. *WA* 10ᴵᴵᴵ, 261. "You yourself in your own conscience must feel Christ himself. You must experience unshakably that it is God's word, even though the whole world should dispute it. As long as you do not have this feeling, you have certainly not yet tasted of God's word." *WA* 10ᴵᴵ, 23; *LW* 36, 248.

[57] *WA* 17ᴵ, 72.

[58] *WA* 40ᴵᴵᴵ, 370.

his own heart.[58] He experiences the ethical power of the grace
which he receives in the word. Grace itself is hidden and therefore must be believed; its effects, however, do not remain hidden
but on the contrary are obvious and as such are a sign that grace
is present.[59] In such experience faith "exercises" and "strengthens"
itself. Therein it experiences the reality of redemption through
Christ. For this reason Christians are to be summoned, in keeping
with II Peter 1:10, to do what is right and thus gain confirmation
of the fact that they are saved, as they already believe.

Luther also explains the relationship between faith and experience in an Easter sermon on Mark 16:1-8, which Stephen Roth
has transmitted to us in the *Sommerpostille* of 1526.[61] We must
be cautious in using these sermons, since it has been proved that
Roth often reworked his notes with a very free hand.[62] However,
the thoughts on faith and experience which Luther presents in
this sermon bear the hallmark of his theology.

Luther here expresses very clearly the opposition between faith
and experience [he uses the term *"empfinden"* which means both
"experience" and "feeling"]. "Previously I have often said that
experience and faith are two different sorts of things. It is the
characteristic of faith that it does not seek experience but rather
lets reason fall aside, closes its eyes, and simply commits itself to
the word. It follows the word through death and life. Experience
is limited to what reason and the mind can grasp, that is, what
we hear, see, feel or recognize through the outward senses. For

---

[58] "At this point experience must enter in and enable a Christian to say:
'Hitherto I have heard that Christ is my Savior, who conquered sin and death;
and I have believed this. Now my experience bears this out. For I was often
in the agony of death and in the bonds of the devil, but He rescued me and
manifested Himself. Now I see and know that he loves me and that what I
believe is true (Cruciger's reconstruction).'" *WA* 45, 599; *LW* 24, 151. "Experience definitely confirms what many truly believe in their hearts. We must
stake life and limb on this word of God's almighty power and even experience
that the word is true in the midst of death and sin. Even the greatest saints
find this experience hard to bear." *WA* 19, 220.

[59] "God's grace is great, strong, powerful, and active. It is not what the
preachers of dreams imagine it to be: something which lies sleeping in the soul
and can be carried around as a painted board bears its color. No, it is not this
way at all. Rather, it bears, leads, motivates, conceives, changes, and works
everything in us so that it can really be felt and experienced. It is hidden but
its work is not hidden and the work and the Word show us where it is."
WA 10I,1, 114 f. In his *Preface to Romans*, Luther says something similar
about faith when he calls it a "living, busy, mighty, active thing." *WA, DB* 7,
11; *LW* 35, 370.

[61] *WA* 10I,2, 218 ff.

[62] Cf. G. Buchwald's comments, *WA* 21, pp. IX ff.

this reason, experience is against faith and faith against experience."⁶³ According to my "experience," my sins are still here—contrary to the gospel of the crucified and risen Christ. In response to this, I must "leave experience behind, fill my ears with the word, stuff my heart with it, and hold on to the word. Even though it does not seem that my sins have been taken away, since I still feel their presence, I must pay no heed to this feeling but instead constantly insist that death, sin, and hell have been conquered—even though I may still feel that I am stuck in death, sin and hell." It is this feeling above all that should drive us to believe.⁶⁴

Faith and "experience" are thus in conflict with each other. "So a battle begins in which experience struggles against the Spirit and faith, while the Spirit and faith struggle against experience," In this struggle the rule holds good that "the more faith, the less experience and vice versa." This, however, is according to God's will: sinfulness continues to remain in us in order to provide an opportunity for the exercise and the daily increase of faith. When this increase of faith occurs, experience decreases, that is, the sin which remains in the Christian and his bondage to death become less and less of a burden and trial to him. Luther can even say that we then receive "another insight, another experience." This does not happen completely until we die and are totally stripped of the old Adam. The experience of reason ceases completely only in eternity; faith, however, comes out of the conflict with reason to the vision of that redemption, which it believed. "Faith thus very quietly leads us through sin, death, and hell contrary to all experience and to all that reason can comprehend. Thereafter we shall see redemption before our eyes. Only then shall we be completely aware of what we have believed, that is, that death and all troubles have been conquered."⁶⁵ All this means that the tension between faith and experience remains throughout our life. It is not however always equally intense; instead faith wins more and more ground from experience. The tension will be fully resolved, however, only eschatologically—when believing becomes seeing in God's new heaven and new earth. "Until then, giving glory to God by believing he is good and gracious, puts our feeling to death and subdues the old man in us until all that remains is faith in God's goodness, faith alone without feeling."⁶⁶

---

⁶³ *WA* 10I,2, 222.
⁶⁴ *Ibid.*
⁶⁵ *WA* 10I,2, 223 f.
⁶⁶ *WA* 17II, 66.

8

REASON

LUTHER speaks of "reason" without defining it and without differentiating its various manifestations and possibilities.[1] He
always speaks of reason as a totality. In interpreting his statements however we must make distinctions. On the one hand, we
must distinguish reason in the earthly realm from reason in the
area of man's relationship to God. In addition, we must distinguish
between reason as a gift of God the Creator to man as he was
originally created, reason as it is found in man after his fall into
sin, and reason in the life of the regenerate Christian.

Reason is a gift of God, a dowry from the Creator to humanity.
God has given me my "reason and all the faculties of my mind."[2]
Luther speaks very forcefully of this gift of God and of its glory.
It is the essential and main earthly blessing and it stands far above
all other goods of this life as "the best and in a certain sense divine." It is reason that contributes the essential difference between
man and other living beings, indeed everything else. Through it,
man exercises that lordship over the earth which was given to him
in Genesis 1:28. Reason provides the light by which man can see
and administer the affairs of this world. Reason is the source and
bearer of all culture. It has discovered all arts and sciences, all
medicine and law, and it administers them. Reason makes itself
felt wherever wisdom, power, industry, and honor are found among
men in this life.[3] None of this is to be despised; rather all is to be
regarded and praised as the noble gift of God. Thus Luther, like
the humanists and unlike the scholastics, greets the new flowering
of the sciences in his time. He is, for example, very happy about

---

[1] Bernhard Lohse, *Ratio und Fides* (Göttingen: Vandenhoeck & Ruprecht,
1958).
[2] *WA* 30^I, 248; *BC*, 345.
[3] *The Disputation Concerning Man*, *WA* 39^I, 175; *LW* 34, 137. "All laws
have been produced by the wisdom and reason of men. . . . Human wisdom
or reason produces laws and determines what is right, just as all the other arts
which we have, have been born of human talent and reason." *WA* 40^{III}, 221.

the new art of printing books and praises it as the highest and final gift of God before the end of the world.[4] All of this was placed into creation and included in it by God. God the Creator has given men power to do all these things by originally implanting and creating them within him. This is a part of man's creation in the image of God, that is, so that he may rule over the earth.[5]

In evaluating reason's royal function Luther emphasizes what he calls its majesty, that is, that it serves this earthly life.[6] Reason has the task of ordering and developing this life. Therewith its limits are also indicated. Within this realm, however, that is, within "earthly government" in the broadest sense in which Luther can use that term, reason alone is the final authority; it contains within itself the basis for judging and deciding about the proper regulation and administration of earthly matters such as economics and politics. In these matters the Bible, Christian preaching, and theology have nothing to say. Holy Scripture and the gospel do not teach us how to make right laws or administer the affairs of state. This all is a matter of human reason which as such was originally given to men by the Creator. This is true not only of law and of government but also of all other arts. In these areas theology has no other task than to allow reason its place, to recognize it, and to testify that it is God's creation. As we shall presently observe, the reason of fallen man especially needs this affirmation of God's creation.[7]

Man after the fall did not lose his rational capacity to understand, regulate, and shape the world to some extent.[8] God did not take away the ruling position of reason.[9] Fallen man however mis-

---

[4] "Now all pictorial arts flourish." *WA,* TR 4, 4697. "It is marvelous to see how all arts now have equally returned to the light." *WA,* TR 2, 2772.
[5] After quoting Genesis 1:27 f. Luther says, "Here all law, science, economics, and medicine are implanted and created. . . . These are the strength and riches of the wisdom implanted in Paradise. Holy Scripture therefore is not troubled by but rather approves the laws which have been established and the arts which have been discovered." *WA* 40ᴵᴵᴵ, 222.
[6] "It is a sun and a kind of god appointed to administer these things in this life." *WA* 39ᴵ, 175; *LW* 34, 137. [Here follows Luther's reference to "majesty."]
[7] *WA* 40ᴵᴵᴵ, 221 f.
[8] *WA* 39ᴵᴵ, 375.
[9] "After the fall of Adam, God did not take away this majesty of reason, but rather confirmed it." *WA* 39ᴵ, 175; *LW* 34, 137. Luther finds it confirmed in God's covenant with Noah (Gen. 9:1 f.).

uses reason and its legitimate accomplishment in a twofold way. He is so conscious that he possesses reason and can do great things with it that he forgets the God who has given him all his gifts and works. He prides himself on his own achievements, saying, "This I have made," instead of—as would be right—humbly and thankfully confessing, "This I have received."[10] Man exalts himself, however, not only in the self-awareness and self-confidence whereby he takes away God's glory as creator and giver, but also in his own autonomous action and self-glorification. By following his own lusts and desires, he distorts the function which God has given him of caring for the world. He is concerned with his own satisfaction, his own advantage, his own honor rather than God's intentions for His world. Instead of being obedient to the will of the Creator he deals arbitrarily with the created world.[11] Reason as such with its logical, technical, and cultural capabilities is not destroyed by the fall but it is made to serve the sinful self-awareness and self-glorification of fallen man. At this point, the role of reason in the relationship between God and man becomes clear.

The reason of fallen man is "fleshly."[12] Luther can say the same things about "flesh," about "flesh and blood," about the "nature" of man, "natural reason," "sense," and the "free will," yes, even about "the entire world" that he does about reason.[13] All this belongs together and is to a large extent synonymous.[14] When Luther says in one of his hymns, "My free will hated God's judgment," any one of these other concepts could take the place of

---

[10] Speaking of fallen nature, Luther says, "After the fall of Adam we are so corrupted that we do not even think of these as gifts. The lawyer thinks that he has his ability of himself, etc., and he neither considers the source nor does he glorify God but rather says, 'I have done this.'" *WA* 40ᴵᴵᴵ, 222. "This is the vice of human nature: It does not consider these things to be creatures and gifts but rather says, 'This I have made.' Instead it should rather say: 'I have received and the Lord has given,' not 'man has made.'" *WA* 40ᴵᴵᴵ, 223. Cf. Veit Dietrich's edition, *ibid.*, p. 222 f. The "I have made it" which a man speaks over his own achievements is in painful contrast to the "I did not do it" with which sinful man ever since Adam and Eve excuses his sin and refuses to admit that it really exists. *WA* 39ᴵᴵ, 276.
[11] "Nature, however, is not able to obey with these gifts. Instead it says: I shall rule; I shall achieve my own goal; I shall seek my pleasure, glory, and convenience." *WA* 40ᴵᴵᴵ, 223.
[12] E.g., *WA* 18, 676, 688; *BOW*, 158, 174.
[13] *WA* 37, 46.
[14] ". . . reason or free will." *WA* 18, 766; *BOW*, 287. Reason refers not only to the natural man's intellect but also to his will.

"free will."[15] It is true of all of them that they are blind and unable to see God, man's actual nature and situation, and sin.[16]

In the area of man's relationship to God, reason has also received knowledge, both ethical and religious. Luther always emphasized that human reason possesses the natural law. No proclamation of God's will or of the law given to Moses would mean anything to men if the law were not written in their hearts. In the same way reason has a general knowledge of God and of what man owes him. "Reason knows that there is a God."[17] The use which man makes of this ethical and religious heritage shows, however, that reason has participated in the fall of man, that is, it is "flesh," and is possessed by the devil. As soon as a man's relationship to God is involved, reason stands in contradiction to the true God as he makes himself known in his word.

Reason is caught within the limits of this world.[18] Earthly realities and possibilities are its ultimate standard of judgment and it cannot set itself free of them. It rejects everything that does not accord with this standard. It recognizes only that which conforms to its evaluation of reality.[19] Reason therefore shuts out the word of God and faith. For the word proclaims God's hidden salvation. What it promises is unbelievable, impossible, and absurd; it lies beyond all possible experience, all natural ability to comprehend, and all reason. And faith is concerned precisely with these impossibilities. It "deals with impossible matters which will first be made possible in the future."[20] Faith transcends reason. Faith believes against reason, which is the same as saying against the "flesh," against "one's own heart," against one's own "feeling" and "experience."[21] God's word and reason—also faith and reason—are in

---

[15] *WA* 35, 423; *LW* 53, 219.
[16] Cf., e.g., *WA* 18, 673 f., 677, 766; *BOW*, 152 f., 158, 286. *WA* 39¹, 82; *LW* 34, 151.
[17] *WA* 19, 206.
[18] "Reason is not able to apply itself to invisible things." *WA* 40ᴵᴵᴵ, 51.
[19] "Reason judges on the basis of external appearances." *WA* 17¹, 68. "We are able to judge that such doctrines [. . . agreeable to natural reason . . .] are arrows of Satan, for they are so obvious and agree with the wisdom and righteousness of the flesh." *WA* 40ᴵᴵᴵ, 35 (the edited version).
[20] *WA* 27, 275. "Thus natural man deals with those matters which are possible. It is the office and art of the Christian, however, that he deals with impossibilities—which shall however be possible in the future." *WA* 27, 275.
[21] *WA* 40ᴵᴵᴵ, 54, 59 f. Cf. *WA* 17ᴵᴵ, 66.

sharp opposition to each other. What the word preaches and faith confesses to be reality, reason holds to be unrealistic nonsense.[22] Reason must contradict both the word and the faith which accepts the word. Reason cannot of itself produce faith. Only God can give faith, and that in opposition to reason and nature.[23]

The limitation of reason to the affairs of this world is at the same time a humanistic restriction which limits it to the concepts and postulates of man's own mind and righteousness. Reason thus demands that God act according to human concepts of righteousness. It attempts to prescribe what he must do if he wishes to remain God.[24] Reason therefore can neither see nor hear, nor understand God's wonderful activity,[25] the superhuman dimensions of his righteousness, the dialectic of his acting and ruling, and the paradox that he hides his righteousness and his goodness deep under their opposite. This is beyond reason's ability to comprehend, and reason takes offense at it.[26] The mystery of the incarnation, of the deity of Christ, and of the Trinity are also beyond reason's comprehension. Reason comprehends the unity of God but not the trinity of the Persons in unity. It is for this reason that the christological and trinitarian heresies in the history of doctrine are to be charged to the account of "natural reason."[27]

This humanistic limitation of reason is particularly obvious in the fact that reason is trapped in moralism. Reason thinks about the way to salvation in legalistic terms. The reason of sinful man

---

[22] "Faith, however, is the knowledge of things hoped for and not seen [Heb. 11:1]; this knowledge consists in the promise and word of God and like them it is divine even though it cannot be grasped or felt. The promise [of I Cor. 2:9] that no eye has seen into God's heart promises us absurd, unbelievable, and impossible things. . . . Nature is concerned with things that can be seen." *WA* 40ᴵᴵᴵ, 46. Cf. *WA* 40ᴵᴵᴵ, 34, 51. Luther describes Christ's rule: "He does not rule as reason teaches because he wills that his benefits, grace, and mercy should be known." *WA* 41, 675.

[23] "Flesh and reason . . . fight in our members [Rom. 7:23] against the word and faith." *WA* 40ᴵᴵᴵ, 46. "Reason despises faith." *WA* 39ᴵ, 90; *LW* 34, 160. "It is up to God alone to give faith contrary to nature, and ability to believe contrary to reason." *WA* 39ᴵ, 91; *LW* 34, 160.

[24] "It is the nature of reason that it seeks to understand and to measure God according to the law." *WA* 16, 140. *WA* 18, 729; *BOW*, 232.

[25] *WA* 41, 737.

[26] *WA* 18, 707 f. *BOW*, 201 f.

[27] *WA* 10ᴵ,¹, 191 ff. *WA* 37, 39, 42 ff.

is so corrupted and has become so blind through the fall that it simply can not think of any other way of justification than the way of work righteousness.[28] It constantly seeks to bring something to God to show how much it has accomplished.[29] It understands the law up to a certain point.[30] But it cannot understand the gospel and finds it repugnant. It knows and understands nothing of the unheard-of magnitude and power of God's mercy, whereby he accepts as righteous sinners who are and remain sinners.[31] Luther's *simul justus et peccator*, his notion that a man is "at one and the same time righteous and a sinner," is beyond reason's ability to understand or to believe; indeed reason finds the idea offensive. And what is true of the power of divine mercy is also true of the capability of faith to achieve salvation—it is finally one and the same thing. In matters concerning salvation therefore reason, the "wisdom of the flesh," is nothing else than foolishness, "death and darkness."[32] Reason must be miraculously renewed before it can believe the gospel.

All this is what Luther means when he calls reason a "whore" or a "prostitute," refers to it as "Frau Hulda," and ironically ad-

---

[28] "For human nature, corrupt and blinded by the blemish of original sin, is not able to imagine or conceive of any justification above and beyond works." *WA* 39I, 82; *LW* 34, 151.

[29] *WA* 40II, 452, 15; cf. *LW* 12, 397. *WA* 17II, 174.

[30] The judgment of the law and of reason coincide. Thus Luther can say: ". . . according to the law and our reason." *WA* 39I, 82; *LW* 34, 152. This is true however only of the superficial understanding of the law. The depth of the law's judgment over man's heart "goes incomparably far beyond natural reason." "You see, therefore, how incomparably the law transcends natural reason, and how bottomless is the sin of which it gives us knowledge." *WA* 8, 105; *LW* 32, 226.

[31] "For reason does not know nor understand the magnitude of divine mercy or how important it is and how effective faith is. . . . For they do not believe that incredible magnitude of God's power and mercy beyond all mercy. He who is righteous is willing to concede this, but he who is not righteous wants to consider himself righteous." *WA* 39I, 97; *LW* 34, 166 f. Luther discusses the fact that man is at one and the same time righteous and not righteous: "Note carefully that although reason which wants to know all about God's business and activities still cannot agree, two opposites can be present in one and same subject." *WA* 39I, 515. "The fact that someone like the author of Psalm 51 can both feel God's wrath and at the same time direct his prayer only toward God's mercy is not a theology of reason but supranatural theology." *WA* 40II, 342.

[32] *WA* 39I, 180; *LW* 34, 144. *WA*, TR 3, 2938.

dresses it as "Madam Reason."[**] He finds this reason in philosophy,[**] in scholastic theology, among the enthusiasts, and among the
heretics.[**]

But the conflict between God's word and reason or between
faith and reason is not the last word. Certainly, reason has gone
astray through its sinful vanity. But one must still distinguish in
reason, as in man himself, between the essence created by God and
the distortion of that essence. Indeed, we must not only distinguish
the two but also keep them separate from each other. Natural man
is admittedly not able to do this. It can be done only when a man
has first been enlightened through the Holy Spirit and made free,
that is, when he believes the word.[**] Then he rejects the distortion.
The distorted reason of unredeemed man must die. But at the same
time reason's God-given essence is brought to life and regenerated
through the word. In this process it remains one and the same
reason—even as I remain one and the same man—and still it becomes something entirely new, just as my tongue, for example,
after my regeneration is not destroyed, but converted, not done
away with, but enlightened.[**]

Whereas reason was previously opposed to and antagonistic
toward the word and faith, now that it is enlightened by the Holy
Spirit it allows itself to be determined by the word and by faith.
"It takes all of its thoughts from the word." It now serves faith
as an excellent tool and is useful as the gift of reflection or as the
gift of eloquent proclamation. It even becomes theological and

---

[**] *WA* 10^{I,1}, 326; *WA* 18, 164, 182; *LW* 40, 174, 192. "The greatest whore
that the Devil has . . ." *WA* 51, 126; *LW* 51, 374. *WA*, TR 6, 6889. *WA*
18, 674, 729; *BOW*, 154, 232.

[**] "Philosophy is a practical wisdom of the flesh which is hostile to God."
WA 39^I, 180; *LW* 34, 144.

[**] "The heretics depart from the word and assert those things which seem
to agree with reason." *WA* 40^{III}, 34. (The edited version.)

[**] "Faith, however, distinguishes the substance from the vanity. The body of
a prostitute is just as much God's creation as that of an honorable woman. We
should therefore distinguish the vanity and the foolishness from the essence
and the substance of the creature which God has created and given." *WA*, TR
3, 2938. "The substance remains, but the vanity is destroyed insofar as reason
is illuminated by the Spirit." *WA*, TR 1, 439.

[**] "It is put to death and made alive again. My tongue is now different than
it formerly was; now it is enlightened . . . and this is the regeneration which
the word brings as it flows into a person and his members." *WA*, TR 3, 2938.

helps faith properly to understand and explicate the Scripture.[38] Luther's own theology illustrates and proves that this can happen.

---

[38] "Before we come to faith and the knowledge of God, our reason is darkness; in the believers, however, it is a most useful tool. . . . Faith then is aided by reason, rhetoric, and language which were such great obstacles before [we had] faith. Enlightened Reason which is incorporated into faith receives gifts from faith . . . Reason in godly men is something different since it does not fight with faith but rather aids it." *WA*, TR 3, 2938. "Reason enlightened by the Spirit helps us to understand the Holy Scripture. . . . Reason, insofar as it is enlightened, serves faith in thinking about something. . . . Enlightened reason receives all of its thoughts from the Word." *WA*, TR 1, 439. Luther distinguishes "theological reason" from "human reason." *WA* 39¹, 180; *LW* 34, 144.

9

THE HOLY SCRIPTURE

FROM THE WORD TO SCRIPTURE

THE MEANS by which God encounters us is the word. For Luther the word is first and last the spoken word, that is, the living proclamation which takes place in any particular situation. But the living word is at the same time a limited word for its content is the apostolic word. Christ has commissioned the apostles to spread the news that he is the Savior and to preach the salvation he brings the world. For this purpose he has promised and has given them his Holy Spirit. Therefore the apostles are the legitimate and, in their proclamation of Christ, the infallible teachers of Christendom.[1] All Christian proclamation can only transmit and explain this apostolic word. The preaching of the apostles is the source and constant standard of the word which the church proclaims.

The proclamation of the apostles was originally also a spoken word. This corresponds to the nature of the gospel. For the gospel is not simply the communication of a truth which one might also learn by reading it; it is rather a summons to men. For this reason, its primal form is the spoken proclamation. The spoken word is not the inadequate preliminary form of the Scripture and of the printed word, and the Scripture and the printed word are not an advance over and beyond the living word. The spoken word always remains the basic form of the gospel. The Scripture has its source and exists for the sake of oral proclamation. It has come in between, as something which is necessary only because it is an indispensable aid in the proclamation of the word. Written Scripture is necessary because of the danger that preaching could be

---

[1] Cf. p. 5, n. 4. Luther says of Paul, "He was not only a man like Caesar or somebody else but he was destined and chosen by God." Luther describes the apostles as saying, "We have authority and power in this matter since we are God's apostles and have the Holy Spirit." *WA* 39^1, 296 f.

heretically distorted if the normative apostolic message were forgotten. Christendom therefore needs to have the "Scripture," the enduring memorial of the apostolic preaching, in written form. This also makes the congregations more independent of their teachers. For teachers can also fail and become false teachers. It is therefore necessary that congregations not be absolutely dependent on them, but have a standard by which they may criticize and correct their teachers. The Scripture provides this.[2]

For Luther the Old Testament and the letter, the New Testament and the living voice, belong together. Certainly both Testaments are now written Scripture, but that does not remove the basic difference in the significance of their being written: the Old Testament is originally and basically written material; the New Testament is written only in a derived sense. The fact that the New Testament is in writing is not essential to its basic character.[3]

---

[2] "In the New Testament era it is not really appropriate to write books about Christian doctrine. Rather good, learned, spiritual, diligent teachers should be everywhere available who are able without other books to draw the living word from the Old Testament and constantly to proclaim it to the people as the apostles did. For before they wrote they preached to the people with their physical voice and converted them. And this was their proper apostolic and New Testament work. The fact that it became necessary to write books reveals that great damage and injury had already been done to the Spirit. Books were thus written out of necessity and not because this is the nature of the New Testament. Instead of godly preachers heretics, false teachers, and all sorts of errorists arose who fed poison to the sheep of Christ. This made it necessary to attempt everything possible so that some sheep might be rescued from the wolves. And then they [the apostles] began to write and thus—insofar as this was possible—to lead the sheep of Christ into the Scriptures so that the sheep would be able to feed themselves and preserve themselves against the wolves when their shepherds did not feed them or became wolves." *WA* 10[I,1], 625 ff.

[3] "The gospel, however, is nothing else than the preaching and proclamation of the grace and mercy of God which Jesus Christ has earned and gained for us through his death. It is properly not something written down with letters in a book but more an oral proclamation and a living word: a voice which sounds forth into the whole world and is proclaimed publicly so that we may hear it everywhere." *WA* 12, 259. "Thus the books of Moses and the prophets are also gospel since they proclaimed and wrote about the Christ of whom the apostles later preached and wrote. And yet there is a difference between the two. For although both are written with letters on paper, the gospel or the New Testament should properly not be written but rather contained in the living voice which resounds and is heard everywhere in the world. It is therefore not at all necessary that it should be written. But the Old Testament is available only in writing and therefore it is also called 'a letter.' The apostles also call it 'the Scripture,' for it only pointed to the Christ who was to come. The gospel however is a living proclamation of the Christ who has come." *WA* 12, 275. This last passage shows that we simply cannot agree with Paul Schempp, *Luthers Stellung zur Heiligen Schrift* (Munich: Kaiser, 1929), pp. 33 f. when he says that for Luther, "law and the letter on one hand, gospel

CHRIST IS THE SOLE CONTENT
OF SCRIPTURE

Luther does not ignore the manifold character of Holy Scripture. He notes the different styles with which the apostles wrote and also the different ways in which they taught. He knows that the rich content of the Bible includes laws, historical accounts, prayers, proclamation, prophecy, etc. However, taken theologically, and that means in terms of its essential theme, Luther sees the Bible as a great unity. It has only one content. That is Christ. "There is no doubt that all the Scripture points to Christ alone."[4] "Take Christ out of the Scriptures and what more will you find in them?"[5] "All of Scripture everywhere deals only with Christ."[6] Christ is the incarnate Word of God. Therefore the Bible can be the word of God only if its sole and entire content is Christ.

This does not mean that the Holy Scripture contains exclusively gospel. According to Luther, its content is both law and gospel. And Christ is also the interpreter of the law. As far as the Scripture presents law, it drives men forward to Christ as the Savior. For the law is given as a preparation for Christ and drives men toward him. Thus the Scripture as law and gospel, indirectly and directly, bears witness to Christ. And it is in this sense that Christ is its sole and total content. Understood in this way, Scripture is a unity. Not everything in the Holy Scriptures is gospel, but it contains the gospel in all its parts; and where it is law it still directs men toward the gospel.[7]

---

and the proclamation of the word on the other hand each stand in the closest relationship." For in this passage, Luther clearly says that the Old Testament is also gospel and at the same time "letter." This means that we cannot simply identify letter and law. In any case, however, the letter is an inadequate and only temporary form of the gospel while it is an appropriate form of expression for the law.

[4] *WA* 10^{III}, 73; *LW* 35, 132.
[5] *WA* 18, 606; *BOW*, 71.
[6] *WA* 46, 414.
[7] Luther is concerned about the dangerous custom of referring to "four Gospels" and distinguishing the Epistles from them. As though there were more than *one* gospel which is proclaimed in the four Gospels, in the Epistles, yes, even by the prophets! "Just as there is no more than one Christ, so there is and may be no more than one gospel. Since Paul and Peter preach nothing but Christ, in the way we have just described, so their epistles can be nothing but the gospel. Yes even the teaching of the prophets, in those places where they speak of Christ, is nothing but the true, pure, and proper gospel—just as if Luke or Matthew had described it." *WA* 10$^{\text{I,1}}$, 10; *LW* 35, 118. Cf. *WA* 12, 259 f.

THE SCRIPTURE AUTHENTICATES ITSELF

Through this content the Holy Scripture authenticates itself. Since Christ is its content, this means that in the Holy Spirit Christ authenticates himself to men as the truth and thereby authenticates the Holy Scripture. Luther uses the Scripture's capacity to validate itself or to work faith in itself as an argument against the Roman Catholic thesis that it is only the church which has established the canon and therefore actually guarantees the authority of Scripture. According to this view, the canon is established by the decision of the church, and the church therefore stands above the Scripture. Luther replies that it makes just as much sense to say that John the Baptist stands above Christ because he bears witness to Christ by pointing his finger at him. No, the situation is exactly the opposite. (Luther here bases his position on what Paul says in Galatians 1:9.) The Holy Scripture is the queen which must rule over all and to which all must submit and obey. No one, no matter who he may be, is allowed to be the master and judge of the Scripture, rather all must be its witnesses, disciples, and confessors.[8] This means that no one is in a position to validate Scripture. Scripture validates itself. The church's witness to Scripture can never be anything more than the obedient recognition of the witness which Scripture bears to itself as God's word. The church's decision is never under any circumstances an authority standing above the word of God but only beneath it.[9] It is not the church which authorizes the Scripture, but quite the contrary: the Scripture validates the Church.[10] This is true of Scripture insofar as it is the word of God which convinces men of its truth. "The gospel is not believed because the church confirms it, but because one recognizes that it is God's word."[11] For Luther, however, the word of God is, as we shall see later,

---

[8] *WA* 40¹, 119; *LW* 26, 57. "This queen must rule, and everyone must obey, and be subject to her. The Pope, Luther, Augustine, Paul, or even an angel from heaven—these should not be masters, judges, or arbiters but only witnesses, disciples, and confessors of Scripture." *WA* 40¹, 120; *LW* 26, 58. Cf. *WA* 30¹¹, 420.

[9] *WA* 30¹¹, 420.

[10] *Ibid.*

[11] *WA* 30¹¹, 687. Cf., *ibid.*, p. 688.

not identical with the canon in its traditional form. What about
the authority of the canon as such? Here too Luther does not
recognize the church as the validating authority but only the word
of God itself. It is the word that decides whether a writing is
properly included in the canon or not (cf. pp. 82 f.)

The self-interpretation of Scripture corresponds to its self-authentication.[12]

SACRED SCRIPTURE IS ITS
OWN INTERPRETER

Luther observes the rule that all books are to be interpreted in
the spirit of their author.[13] Since the spirit of an author can nowhere be so directly and vividly recognized as in his writings, this
means that a writing must interpret itself.[14] If this is true of all
books, it is especially true of the Holy Scripture. For Scripture
ought to be the final authority and the highest judge. Its character as the final authority, which is grounded in and bears witness
to itself, precludes the possibility that the standard of its interpretation could somehow come from outside itself. It also includes
the fact that it interprets itself; and this self-interpretation is therefore the most certain, most easy, and most clear interpretation.[15]
If some other authority would explain the Scripture, then it would
also validate it. Thereby, however, Scripture would lose its character as the final authority. Its self-validation necessarily includes
its self-interpretation. "Scripture is therefore its own light. It is a
grand thing when Scripture interprets itself."[16] Luther uses self-interpretation of the Scripture and interpretation through the Holy
Spirit as a pair of synonymous expressions.

Luther asserts the basic principle that the Scripture interprets

---

[12] For a discussion of the fact that this doctrine of the self-authentication of
the Scripture is not an adequate response to the Roman Catholic antithesis because of the problem of establishing the historical authenticity of the Scripture,
cf. *CW*, p. 166. [Althaus points out that theology must examine the historical
basis for and validity of the church's decisions at the time the canon was established.—Trans.]

[13] Gerhard Ebeling, *Evangelische Evangelienauslegung: Eine Untersuchung
zu Luthers Hermeneutik* (München: Kaiser, 1942).

[14] *WA* 7, 97.

[15] *Ibid.*

[16] *WA* 10ᴵᴵᴵ, 238.

itself against both Rome and the enthusiasts. Each of these opponents claimed that something else than Scripture itself validates the interpretation of Scripture. In Rome, it was the teaching office of the church to which the Holy Spirit had been promised. Among the enthusiasts, it was the peculiar gift of the Spirit which is given to individuals apart from the Scripture. Luther also knows that only men who are moved by the Spirit of God can interpret the Scripture.[17] But the Spirit which enables them to interpret Scripture comes to them through the Scripture itself. If one expects it to come from outside Scripture and takes credit for such a spirit, the inevitable result will be that one "sets oneself above Scripture" and interprets it according to his own whims and subjects it to his own spirit.[18] Luther clearly recognized that Rome and the enthusiasts were in this respect both "enthusiasts."[19] They both subordinate the Scripture to an alien law.

The principle that Scripture interprets itself includes the rule that the Scripture is to be interpreted according to its simple literal sense. One may depart from this principle only when the text itself compels a metaphorical interpretation. In all so-called "spiritual" interpretation, however, each one can read his own spirit into the words. Scripture loses its clear meaning in the process. In all its parts Scripture has one and the same simple sense.[20]

The self-interpretation of the Holy Scripture presupposes that the Scripture is clear in itself.[21] The Roman assertion that the Scripture must be interpreted by the teaching office of the church is based on the presupposition that the Scripture is an obscure book. Luther had to disagree with this. He based his assertion that the

---

[17] "So listen now with the spirit to the prophet who speaks by the Spirit." *WA* 5, 42; *LW* 14, 305.
[18] Luther opposes both "those fanatics who subject the Scriptures to the interpretation of their own spirit . . . [and the papists who say:] 'The Scriptures are obscure and equivocal; we must seek the interpreting Spirit from the Apostolic See of Rome!' " In this way, he says, men have placed themselves above the Scripture. *WA* 18, 653; *BOW*, 124.
[19] Cf. n. 17 and the well known passages from the *Smalcald Articles*, *WA* 50, 245; *BC*, 312.
[20] *WA* 7, 711. *WA* 18, 700 f. *BOW*, 191 f.
[21] Luther discusses the clarity of Scripture particularly in *The Bondage of the Will*, *WA* 18, 609, 653 ff.; *BOW*, 71, 123-132. Cf. *WA* 8, 99; *LW* 32, 217. *WA* 10ᴵᴵᴵ, 236. In the same sense, Luther speaks of the "simplicity" and "sincerity" of the Scripture, *WA* 8, 112; *LW* 32, 236.

Scripture is clear and unequivocal on the Scripture itself. In view
of his doctrine of the Scripture, that is the only possible way. Just
as Scripture validates itself, so it alone can bear witness to its
clarity. Luther therefore proves the clear sense of Scripture from
Scripture itself; for example, since Jesus and the apostles argued
on the basis of Scripture it must certainly be clear. In addition, he
refers to many Bible passages, for example, II Peter 1:19 which
refers to the prophetic word as "a light shining in a dark place."
For Luther, the clear sense of the Scripture is therefore neither a
postulate which he establishes by his own authority nor is it proved
by experience. The voice of experience does not consistently speak
in favor of the clarity of Scripture. For many men the Scripture
is not clear at all; they either do not understand it at all or they
understand it wrongly. The reason for this, Luther explains, is that
the godless are held captive by Satan and that God allows even
godly men to err for a while so that he may in this way show
them that he alone is able to enlighten them.[22]

Luther's doctrine of the clarity of the Scripture, of course, remains true to his understanding of the relationship between the
word and the Spirit. This is illustrated by his distinction between
the "external" and the "inner" clarity of Scripture,[23] that is, between its objective and subjective clarity. Scripture in itself is clear.
Wherever it is preached, it illuminates everything with a bright
light and leaves nothing in the dark and open to misunderstanding. But this clarity "in Scripture itself as it lies there" (as Justus
Jonas puts it in his translation of this passage in Luther's *The
Bondage of the Will*) is to be distinguished from its clarity "inwardly in the heart." This latter clarity is first given through the
reception of the Spirit of God in the heart. Left to themselves,
all men have a darkened heart and could not see "one single iota
in Scripture." "For the Spirit is necessary to understand all of
Scripture as well as every part of it."[24]

---

[22] *WA* 18, 659; *BOW*, 133. The questions which remain to be asked today
concerning this point and those which are to be directed at Luther are out-
lined by R. Hermann, *Von der Klarheit der Heiligen Schrift* (Berlin: Evang.
Verlagsanstalt, 1958.
[23] *WA* 18, 609, 653; *BOW*, 73 f., 125.
[24] *WA* 18, 609; *BOW*, 74.

CHRIST IS THE LORD AND
KING OF SCRIPTURE[*]

For Luther the self-interpretation of Scripture through the Spirit
which speaks in it means that Scripture interprets itself in terms
of Christ as its center, that is christocentrically. In and of itself
that thought was not new in the church. Traditional theology also
knew that Christ is the center of Scripture. And Erasmus also
agreed with the principle that Scripture is to be interpreted christocentrically. What is really at stake here is the meaning of this
principle. One can do as Erasmus or the late medieval radicals in
their own way did, and understand Christ as a teacher of virtue
or as an ethical prophet and lawgiver. For Luther "Christ" means
the gospel of that free mercy of God in Christ on which alone
man's salvation depends. Luther finds that the Apostle Paul most
clearly understood and expressed this. Paul thus becomes Luther's
key to the New and Old Testaments. The Epistle to the Romans
is "a bright light completely adequate to illuminate the entire Holy
Scripture," that is, to shed light on the totality of Scripture.[*]
"Christ" for Luther means the Christ of the unified apostolic
proclamation, particularly of Paul and of John; the Old Testament also bears witness to this apostolic Christ.[*] He was certain that the on-going development of the entire Scripture was on
his side and that he had not therefore forced an alien hermeneutical principle on Scripture but rather had followed the one which
Scripture itself offered. One can formulate Luther's principle thus:
Scripture is always to be interpreted according to the analogy of
Scripture. And this is nothing else than the analogy of the gospel.
Christocentric interpretation for Luther thus means gospel-centered
interpretation, understood in terms of the gospel of justification by
faith alone.

---

[*] The expressions are found in *WA* 40¹, 458; *LW* 26, 295.
[*] *WA*, DB 7, 2; *LW* 35, 365 f. "According to Paul an understanding of
sin opens up all Scripture." *WA* 8, 107; *LW* 32, 229 f.
[*] "Therefore everything which a man preaches about Christ is a gospel even
though one describes it in a different way and with different words than another
man does. When we are concerned with the fact that Christ is our Savior and
that we are blessed, saved, and justified through faith in him without our own
works, there is only one word and one gospel." *WA* 12, 260.

On the basis of this position, Luther opposes that method of using Scripture which attempts to assert individual Bible texts or passages against the understanding of Scripture rooted in the gospel. In opposition to this he declares: "Christ is the Lord and not the servant; he is the Lord of the Sabbath, of the law, and of all things. And the Scripture must be understood in favor of Christ and not against him. For this reason every part of Scripture must either refer to him or not be considered true Scripture. Therefore, if our opponents attempt to use the Scripture against Christ we assert the authority of Christ against the Scripture."[28] These well-known theses from the year 1535 and other related statements contain the following thoughts. All of Scripture has a clear meaning in terms of the gospel. The interpretation of individual passages must be subordinated to this. Luther always begins with the hermeneutical principle that Scripture cannot be in conflict with Christ its head, that is, with the gospel. Only blindness and ignorance see what appear to be contradictions.[29] The interpreter has the right so to interpret all passages of Scripture that they agree with the gospel, the obvious center of the Scripture; that is, to apply Christ-centered and gospel-centered interpretation. If, for example, the opponents refer to the ethical imperatives of Scripture and moralistically argue that they are contrary to the gospel's "through faith alone," Luther answers: These imperatives first received their meaning from Christ. They are not to be taken as absolute but rather as relative, that is, as related to Christ. One must read "you should do this" and "you should do that" with the addition "in Christ," "in faith in Him." They are not to be interpreted as law but as gospel. For Christ is the Lord and the King of the Scripture, and

---

[28] *WA* 39¹, 47; *LW* 34, 112.

[29] "Even if you were to produce six hundred passages . . . I have the Author and the Lord of Scripture, and I want to stand on his side rather than believe you. Nevertheless, it is impossible for Scripture to contradict itself except at the hands of men who are blind and ignorant of Scripture. If you are not able to reconcile Scripture and yet stress Scripture . . . I shall stress the Lord; The King of Scripture who is the price of my salvation. There I shall remain. There you are safe [for] your heart remains fixed on the object of faith called Christ." *WA* 40¹, 458; cf. *LW* 26, 295 f.

the individual passages of Scripture are his servants. He is the Head and the Bible passages are his members. And one should not be loyal to the servants but rather to the Lord, not to the members but rather to the Head.[20]

Should it happen that a particular passage of Scripture is opposed to such evangelical interpretation and cannot be unified with the witness of all the rest of Scripture, then it simply does not have the authority of the word of God. This is the principle Luther applied to the doctrine of justification in James 2:21 ff. He explains that he had been previously accustomed to interpreting the Letter of James according to the meaning of the rest of Holy Scripture—for no one may derive any theological statement from it which conflicts with the obvious meaning of all Scripture. Since, however, some did not allow the validity of his interpretation of this passage, he simply said, "Away with James." "His authority is not great enough to cause me to abandon the doctrine of faith and to deviate from the authority of the other apostles and the entire Scripture."[21]

Thus if the text of Scripture is opposed to Luther's gospel-centered interpretation of Scripture, his interpretation becomes gospel-centered criticism of Scripture. Beside the statement that Scripture is its own interpreter we must, according to Luther, place the other (which he himself admittedly never expressed in just these words): Sacred Scripture is its own critic.

---

[20] "We have the Lord, they the servant; we have the Head, they the feet or members, over which the Head necessarily dominates and takes precedence." *WA* 39ᴵ, 47; *LW* 34, 112. Luther's use of the same imagery elsewhere makes it very clear that the "servant" is Scripture. "You are stressing the servant, that is, Scripture—and not all of it at that or even its most powerful part, but only a few passages concerning works. I leave this servant to you. I for my part stress the Lord, who is the King of Scripture." *WA* 40ᴵ, 459; *LW* 26, 295.

[21] Luther wrote this in 1543. *WA* 39ᴵᴵ, 219. In 1542, he wrote: "Up to this point I have been accustomed to deal with and interpret it according to the sense of the rest of Scripture. For you will judge that none of it must be set forth contrary to manifest Holy Scripture. Accordingly, if they will not agree to my interpretations, then I shall make rubble of it. I almost feel like throwing Jimmy into the stove, as the priest in Kalenberg did." *WA* 39ᴵᴵ, 199; *LW* 34, 317. (The pastor of Kalenberg used the wooden statues of the apostles for firewood when the Countess came to visit.) "It is flatly against St. Paul and all the rest of Scripture in ascribing justification to works." *WA*, DB 7, 384. Cf. *ibid.*, p. 386; *LW* 35, 396 f.

SACRED SCRIPTURE
IS ITS OWN CRITIC

Occasionally Luther practiced historical criticism in analyzing the biblical tradition, for example, by referring to contradictions or inaccuracies.[32] This is hardly reason, however, to consider him one of the fathers of historical criticism; for he makes such critical remarks only occasionally and he places no weight on them. What is decisive for him is that we have "the true understanding of Scripture and the genuine articles of faith." Compared with this, matters of historical criticism are of no significance. One can leave the remaining questions to deal with themselves, for example, the contradiction between Matthew and John about the time at which Jesus purified the temple.[33]

It was particularly within the canon that Luther practiced theological criticism of its individual parts. The standard of this criticism is the same as his principle of interpretation, that is, Christ: the gospel of free grace and justification through faith alone.[34] This is what Luther means when he says that the standard is "that which is apostolic." Luther's concept of apostolicity is based not only on a historical factor, that is, that Christ himself called and sent out a group of witnesses. Rather, it is determined by the content of a book. An apostle shows that he is an apostle by clearly and purely preaching Christ as Savior. "Now it is the office of a true apostle to preach of the suffering, resurrection, and office of Christ."[35] This shows that an apostle is inspired by the Holy Spirit; and this gives him his authority and infallibility. Since apostolic authority manifests itself in the gospel of the apostles, the church recognizes the authority of the Scripture as being based not on the person of the apostles but on the word of God or the gospel which bears witness to itself. The apostolic character of a New Testament author manifests itself in the content of his writing and in the clarity of his witness to Christ.

Luther now applies this standard or criterion to the canonical

---

[32] Cf. *GA* 1, 1574 ff. and Friedrich Loofs, *Leitfaden zum Studium der Dogmengeschichte* (4th ed.; Halle: M. Niemeyer, 1906), pp. 45 f.
[33] *WA* 46, 726; *LW* 22, 218 f.
[34] *WA* 12, 260.
[35] *WA*, DB 7, 384; *LW* 35, 396.

books. "All genuine books agree in preaching [*treiben*] Christ." He allows the canon to stand as it was established by the ancient church. But he makes distinctions within the canon. He evaluates the books according to the norm of their apostolic content. "This is the true test of all books, when we see whether or not they preach Christ. For all the Scriptures show us Christ [Rom. 3:21] and St. Paul will know nothing but Christ [I Cor. 2:2]. Whatever does not teach Christ is certainly not apostolic even though St. Peter or St. Paul teaches it. Again whatever preaches Christ would be apostolic even though Judas, Ananias, Pilate, or Herod were doing it."[36] If this characteristic is missing or inadequate in any of the canonical writings, as it is, for example in James, then the author cannot be an apostle.[37] For Luther, "preaching" Christ means proclaiming that the crucified and risen Christ is the Savior and that the salvation he brings is received through faith alone. Luther was so certain of this, as well as of the interpretation of Scripture, that he did not think of himself as approaching the canon with an arbitrary and autonomously chosen criterion but with the standard which Scripture itself offers in its on-going central proclamation ("St. Paul and all the evangelists"). Luther obtained this standard from nowhere else than the Scripture. To that extent it is the Scripture itself that criticizes the canon.

In his *Preface to the New Testament* of 1522 Luther applies this standard to determine which are "the true and noblest books of the New Testament."[38] He finds that these are the Gospel and First Letter of John, the letters of Paul, particularly Romans, Galatians, and Ephesians, and I Peter; these are "the heart and core of all the books. . . . For these do not describe many works and miracles of Christ but rather masterfully show how faith in Christ overcomes sin, death, and hell and gives life, righteousness, and blessedness." This section of the *Preface to the New Testament* was, however, omitted after 1534. The Christian is less concerned with the report of the historical miracles of Jesus than with the

---

[36] *Ibid.* Cf. Luther's evaluation of I Peter as a "true and pure gospel." "From this [that is, from the way in which I Peter teaches in agreement with Paul and all the evangelists] you can now form an opinion of all books and teachers and judge what is or is not gospel." *WA* 12, 260.

[37] *WA*, DB 7, 384; *LW* 35, 396.

[38] *WA*, DB 6, 10; *LW* 35, 361.

witness to the word which creates faith and the saving power of this faith.[39] For this reason, the Gospel of John which records many words of Christ but few of his miracles is "the true, genuine, and chief Gospel and is to be preferred over and more highly valued than the other three" because the other three do just the opposite. In the *Preface to James* in 1522 and still in 1543 Luther speaks of the "really main books." He cannot include the Letter of James among them because James preaches the law instead of the gospel. Luther recognizes that the intention of the epistle was good but James was not equal to his task. "He wanted to guard against those who relied on faith without works, but was unequal to the task. He seeks to bring it about by harping on the law while the apostles bring it about through encouraging people to love."[40] In discussing the Letter to the Hebrews, Luther emphasizes that it is later than the apostolic letters; and he praises it highly because of its witness to the priestly office of Christ and because of its interpretation of the Old Testament, even though "some wood, straw, or hay is mixed in with" the gold, silver, and jewels with which this letter builds on the apostolic foundation (I Cor. 3:12).[41] In 1522 Luther writes that he can find "no trace" of evidence that the Revelation of John "was written by the Holy Spirit," that is, inspired. He places it in a category with the Second Book of Esdras.[42] In accordance with this, Luther also changed the traditional order of the New Testament books. He placed those just named with Jude at the end of his Bible. "They have from ancient times had a different reputation" and do not belong to the "true and certain chief books of the New Testament."[43]

Luther did not intend to require anyone to accept his judgment, he only wanted to express his own feeling about these particular books.[44] This was already clearly expressed in the very sharply formulated introductions of 1522. After 1530, he even omitted

[39] Cf. *WA* 12, 260.
[40] *WA*, DB 7, 386; *LW* 35, 397. In *WA* 39ᴵ, 237, Luther explains that Paul and James each defend a different aspect of the gospel. In interpreting the Scripture we must always consider the particular conditions and the audience for whom the text was intended.
[41] *WA*, DB 7, 344; *LW* 35, 395.
[42] *WA*, DB 404; *LW* 35, 400.
[43] *WA*, DB 7, 344; *LW* 35, 394.
[44] *WA*, DB 7, 384, 404; *LW* 35, 395-400.

the sharpest phrases in the *Preface to James* (for example, "Therefore I do not want to have him in my Bible"). Luther therefore did not intend that the congregations should continue to read these judgments. For himself and in speaking before his theological students he maintained his judgment of James even later. In this however, he was for the most part more concerned with preventing his Roman opponents from continually using James as an argument against the Reformation gospel than he was about the letter as such. In 1530 he replaced the completely negative 1522 *Preface to the Revelation of St. John* with another which interprets the book in terms of the history of the church and shows its continuing value for the church.⁴⁵ But for the rest of his life, he continued to put a different value on the books which he had put together at the end of his Bible than on the "main books."⁴⁶

We shall not canonize Luther's individual opinions about the last books of the New Testament. They remain significant, however, simply because Luther distinguishes the word of God, or the Holy Scripture in its essential sense, from the canon and expressed theological criticism of the canon—precisely for the sake of the word and the gospel (including its relationship to God's law). He thereby established the principle that the early church's formation and limitation of the canon is not exempt from re-examination. At the same time, he thereby goes beyond the method of dealing with the Bible as if it were a legal document equally binding in all its parts. Within the canon itself, he distinguishes books in terms of their closeness to or distance from the center of the Scripture. Since these are distinctions in the clarity of the gospel, they also involve distinctions in the relative authority and significance of the book for the church. To this extent, the canon is only a relative unity, just as it is only relatively closed. Therewith Luther has in principle abandoned every formal approach to the authority of the Bible. It is certainly understandable that Luther's prefaces were eventually no longer printed in the German Bibles. However, the negative effect the omission of them had on the training of Christians for exercising proper freedom in the understanding

---

⁴⁵ *WA*, DB 7, 406 ff.; *LW* 35, 401-409.
⁴⁶ This term, *Hauptbüchern*, from the 1522 *Preface to the Letter to the Hebrews*, was still retained after 1530. *WA*, DB 7, 344; *LW* 35, 394.

and use of Scripture was unfortunate. The legalistic theory of
Scripture would hardly have infiltrated so deeply into Lutheranism
if Luther's prefaces had still been printed in the Bibles or even if
they had been replaced by a guide to the proper use of Scripture
in the spirit of Luther.

In all this, we should not overlook the fact that Luther expressed theological criticism within the canon only in the name of
that gospel proclaimed by Scripture. He was not critical, for example, in the name of reason or in the name of a scientific world-
view or the modern understanding of existence. Luther questions
that Scripture is the word of God only where he finds that the
gospel is obscured. As long as the decisive factor of "preaching
Christ" is not at stake, the Scripture always remains for Luther, as
it was in the tradition he received, the book written by the Holy
Spirit. As such it was an infallible authority to which everyone
had to submit and before which everyone had to abandon all objections of reason.⁴⁷ Luther's criticism is therefore strictly limited.
The problems of the relationship of the Bible to natural science,
to history, to anthropology, and to philosophy, which have become
such significant problems since the Enlightenment, did not yet
exist for him.

THE OLD TESTAMENT AND THE NEW

The position of the Old Testament in Luther's thought requires
special treatment.

The relationship of the Old Testament to the New Testament
is characterized by both unity and diversity.⁴⁸ For Luther the decisive distinction in the word of God is the distinction between law

---

⁴⁷ Cf. my essay, "Gehorsam und Freiheit in Luthers Stellung zur Bibel," in
Theologische Aufsätze I (1929), 140 ff. For example: Luther says that the
Holy Spirit speaks of "six days" in Genesis 1 and that we are to bow to his
authority: "Do the Holy Ghost the honor of realizing that he is more learned
than you are." *WA* 12, 440. In speaking of Jonah's spending three days and
three nights in the belly of the fish, Luther says, "Who would believe it and
not consider it to be a lie and a fable if it were not in the Scripture?" *WA* 19,
219. The Psalms were written by the Holy Spirit. *WA* 40ᴵᴵᴵ, 16. Luther was
troubled by Rom. 11:25 f. which speaks of the ultimate salvation of all
Israel: "I will, however, do the Holy Spirit the honor of saying—what I also
know to be true—that he is more learned than I." *WA*, TR 2, 1610.
⁴⁸ Cf. Heinrich Bornkamm, *Luther und das alte Testament*, (Tübingen: Mohr,
1948), pp. 69 ff

and gospel. The difference between the Old and the New Testaments however does not simply coincide with this distinction. Rather the distinction between law and gospel runs through both Testaments. The gospel is found in the Old Testament, that is, in the promises. And the law is found also in the New Testament, for example, in Jesus' interpretation of the law in the Sermon on the Mount. The Old Testament however contains more law while the New Testament contains more gospel. The content of the Old Testament is primarily "the teaching of laws, the denunciation of sins, and the demanding of good." The content of the New Testament is primarily "grace and peace through the forgiveness of sins in Christ."[49] Therefore the Old Testament may be characterized as a law book and the New Testament as a gospel.[50] This is the first way in which they are different from each other and indicates that a tension exists between them. Insofar as the Old Testament also contains the gospel, there is a basic unity between both parts of the Bible; the only difference is that the Old Testament promises Christ and salvation while the New Testament bears witness that his promise is fulfilled. The two Testaments are therefore related to each other as promise and fulfilment.[51]

There is, however, more to be said. Insofar as both Testaments contain the gospel, Luther's understanding of their relationship may be expressed in two theses: (1) The entire truth of the gospel is already present in the Old Testament, and for this reason the New Testament is based on the Old. (2) This truth is there, but it is hidden and must therefore first be made known and revealed, and this takes place through the word of the New Testament.

With regard to the first Luther can say, "Moses is a fountain of all wisdom and understanding, from which flows all that all the

---

[49] *WA*, DB 8, 12; *LW* 35, 237. "The New Testament, properly speaking, consists of promises and exhortations, just as the Old, properly speaking, consists of laws and threats." *WA* 18, 692; *BOW*, 180. (The following statements indicate that Luther understood these "exhortations" of the New Testament as the paraenetical admonitions directed to those who were already justified.)
[50] *WA* 10I,2, 159.
[51] "And what is the New Testament but a public preaching and proclamation of Christ, set forth through the sayings of the Old Testament and fulfilled through Christ?" *WA*, DB 8, 11; *LW* 35, 236.

prophets have known and said; moreover, the New Testament flows out of and is grounded in it."[53] Or, "The apostles have drawn everything which they taught and wrote out of the Old Testament; for it proclaims everything which Christ would do and preach in the future. It is for this reason that they base all their sermons on the Old Testament and that there is no statement in the New Testament that does not refer back to the Old Testament in which it was previously proclaimed."[53] Luther can even say that the "first chapter of Genesis contains the whole Scripture in itself."[54] In the same way, Luther finds the entire gospel is contained in the introductory words of the First Commandment, that is, in the promise, "I am the Lord your God." This is the source of the message of the prophets,[55] of the New Testament statements about sonship,[56] and even of the entire content of the Third Article of the Creed.[57]

However—and now we come to the second point—this meaning of the Old Testament and of the First Commandment must first be revealed. It is Christ who opens the New Testament for us. His word (Matt. 22:32) first reveals that God is a God of the living and not of the dead and that the First Commandment also bears witness to the resurrection of the dead.[58] Luther even can say that the New Testament basically has no other task than that of opening up the Old Testament and revealing the gospel hidden in it.[59] The New Testament proclamation is essentially an interpretation of the Old Testament. In this connection, Luther thought

---

[53] *WA*, DB 8, 29; *LW* 35, 247. Cf. *WA* 54, 2.

[53] *WA* 10I,1, 181. Cf. "We should learn to establish the New Testament on the basis of the Old. . . . Therefore we should ignore those useless babblers who despise the Old Testament and say that it is no longer necessary, for actually we still take the basis of our faith only from it." *WA* 12, 274.

[54] *WA*, TR 3, 3043.

[55] *WA* 14, 640; *LW* 9, 112. "We see this, however, that what is best in the Psalms and the prophets flows from the promise of the First Commandment, 'I am the Lord your God.'" (It should be noted that this is found only in Veit Dietrich's edition and not in Rörer's notes.) *WA* 40III, 165.

[56] *WA* 40III, 161 f.

[57] *WA* 31I, 154; *LW* 14, 87.

[58] *WA* 40III, 494 f.; cf. *LW* 13, 82 ff.

[59] "The New Testament is nothing more than a revelation of the Old." *WA* 10, 181. Paul in his letter to the Romans wishes "to prepare an introduction to the entire Old Testament. . . . Whoever has this epistle well in his heart, has with him the light and power of the Old Testament." *WA*, DB 7, 27; *LW* 35, 380.

it significant that Jesus wrote nothing at all and that the apostles wrote very little. They refer to and build on the "Scripture" which was already available to them in the Old Testament. They direct us to this "Old Scripture" just as the angels directed the shepherds to the manger and the swaddling cloths.[60] A statement of Luther's position on the relationship between the Old and New Testaments must therefore say both that the New Testament is completely grounded and even contained in the Old and that the Old Testament is first unlocked in the New and cannot be understood except through it.

All this is true of the Old Testament insofar as it contains gospel and thus treats of Christ. But that does not exhaust its content. The Old Testament is also the book of Israel: it presents the law given to Israel and the history of Israel. We must deal with both the book of Israel and the book of Christ. The Old Testament is both of these in one book.[61] But there are two completely different viewpoints involved and Luther's attitude toward the Old Testament varies accordingly.

THE OLD TESTAMENT AS THE BOOK OF ISRAEL

We shall speak first of the law of Israel.[62] Luther considers that law from different viewpoints. As contained in the Old Testa-

---

[60] "Here [in the Old Testament] you will find the swaddling cloths and the manger in which Christ lies, and to which the angel points the shepherds. Simple and lowly are these . . . cloths, but dear is the treasure, Christ, who lies in them." *WA*, DB 8, 12; *LW* 35, 236. "The prophets are opened up to us by the gospel . . . for in the New Testament the word ought to be preached publicly with a living voice and thus produce in speaking and in hearing that which previously was hidden in letters and in secret visions. This should especially be the case since the New Testament is nothing else than an opening up and revealing of the Old Testament." *WA* 10^{I,1}, 625 f. The apostles, who wrote, "do nothing more than direct us to the Old Testament." *WA* 10^{I,1}, 625. Cf. *WA* 10^{I,1}, 15; *LW* 35, 122.

[61] The men of the Old Testament stood under the law of Moses; but many of them such as Abraham and Isaac also had the proclamation of Christ. *WA* 39^{II}, 203; *LW* 34, 321.

[62] The basic sources are: The exposition of Exodus 19 and 20 written against the enthusiasts, *How Christians Should Regard Moses. WA* 16, 363-393; *LW* 35, 161-174. *Against the Heavenly Prophets in the Matter of Images and Sacraments. WA* 18, 75-214; *LW* 40, 79-223. *Wider die Sabbather* [*Against the Sabbatarians*]. *WA* 50, 312 ff. Cf. the detailed analysis of H. Bornkamm, *op. cit.*, pp. 104 ff. and Georg Merz, "Gesetz, Gottes und Volksnomos in Martin Luther," in *Luther-Jahrbuch*, 1934, pp. 51 ff.

ment, it is first of all the national law which God gave to Israel, binding and valid only for Israel; it is the common law of the Jewish people.[63] As such it has nothing to do with Christians and does not bind them. On this point, Luther strongly opposes the enthusiasts and the Anabaptists who based their position on Old Testament regulations—for, after all, this law of Moses is the word of God. Luther replies, "So what if it is the word of God? I must both know and take into consideration to whom this word of God was spoken."[64] "It is not enough simply to look and see whether this is God's word, whether God has said it; rather we must look and see to whom it was spoken, and whether or not it is addressed to you."[65] In this law, God spoke to Israel and not to Christians. "Moses is given only to the Jewish people and does not concern us Gentiles and Christians."[66] This is true not only of the Mosaic ceremonial and judicial codes but also—contrary to the far more usual distinction—of the Decalog. For the Decalog is the source and the center of all other laws of Israel. The ceremonial and judicial codes also "all depend on and belong to it." The Decalog's prohibition of images and the commandment to observe the Sabbath Day are "temporary ceremonies which have been abrogated by the New Testament." Jesus Christ is the end of this law.

The law of the Old Testament is, however, more than merely the law of Moses given only to Israel. It is at the same time also a particular expression of the natural law written in all men's hearts, that is, of the commandment to worship God and to love one's neighbor which, according to Luther, may be expressed in the rule of Matthew 7:12.[67] As far as the law of Moses agrees with this natural law it is also valid for and binding on us non-

[63] *WA* 16, 378; *LW* 35, 167. *WA* 18, 81; *LW* 40, 98.

[64] *WA* 16, 384; *LW* 35, 170. In speaking of the enthusiasts Luther says, "They want to include the political sword in Moses' law and with great assurance cry out, 'Here is God's word, God's word, God's word.' Just as though it were enough that God's word were there and it were not necessary to consider the differences between us and the people to whom it was spoken. . . . Therefore we must not ask whether it is God's word but rather whether this very same thing is said to us or not, and then either accept it or not." *WA* 19, 195.

[65] *WA* 16, 385; *LW* 35, 170.

[66] *WA* 18, 76; *LW* 40, 92. *WA* 31¹, 238; *LW* 14, 20.

[67] "For nature teaches—as does love—that I should act as I would like to be treated." *WA* 11, 279; *LW* 45, 128.

Jews. It binds us, however, not because it is the law of Moses but because it binds our conscience by being in our heart.[68] Moses is not the author but only the interpreter of those laws which are written in all men's minds.[69] If Christianity, in spite of this, continues to teach the law of Moses, that is, the Ten Commandments, it does so only because "the natural laws are nowhere else so clearly and orderly expressed as in Moses. Therefore, it is reasonable to follow the example of Moses."[70] But let it be emphasized once more, this is not true of the entire Decalog in its historical form; on the contrary, we must distinguish between what is binding and not binding in the Decalog. Whatever it contains above and beyond its excellent expression of the natural law is to be regarded as the ceremonial and judicial laws. "Therefore, let the law of Moses be the Jewish common law and do not confuse us Gentiles with it, just as France pays no attention to the Saxon common law and yet certainly agrees with it in natural law."[71]

This clear distinction between Moses' law as binding and as not binding for Christians does not exclude the possibility that certain things in Moses' law may also be exemplary for other nations without binding them. Luther explicitly names the tithe, the "sabbath of the land" (Lev. 25:8 ff.), the jubilee year (Lev. 25:2 ff.), and the divorce law (Deut. 24:1 ff.).[72] Luther thought that these and other regulations of the law of Moses should be accepted in secular affairs—not as though one were compelled to do all this by divine commandment but freely through rational insight—just as it occasionally happens in history that one nation adopts laws of another nation because it recognizes that they are good.[73]

---

[68] "Thus I keep the commandments which Moses has given, not because Moses gave the commandments, but because they have been implanted in me by nature, and Moses agrees exactly with nature." *WA* 16, 380; *LW* 35, 168. *WA* 39¹, 540 f. Luther discusses the divine law which concerns all of us in Moses' law and says, "I feel in my heart that I certainly owe this to God not because the Decalog is handed down and written for us but because we either know these laws within ourselves or have produced them in the world." *Ibid.*, p. 540.

[69] *WA* 39¹, 454.

[70] *WA* 18, 81; *LW* 40, 98.

[71] *Ibid.*

[72] *WA* 18, 81; *LW* 40, 98. *WA* 16, 376 f.; *LW* 35, 167. *WA* 31¹, 238; *LW* 14, 20.

[73] "There are also other extraordinarily fine rules in Moses which one should like to accept, use, and put into effect. Not that one should bind or be bound

The law of the Old Testament remains meaningful and significant for non-Jews. This is also true of the history of Israel as reported in the Old Testament. It is difficult to formulate briefly
what the Old Testament meant for Luther in this respect, and
what he learned and taught from it. Heinrich Bornkamm gives us
some impression of the way in which the Old Testament was for
Luther a "mirror of life," of political and secular affairs." Our
purposes do not require detailed discussion of this. We are concerned now only with Luther's explicit theological evaluation of
Old Testament history. For Luther the central point is that the
Old Testament is a book of examples of the way in which people
have both obeyed and disobeyed God's law and how God has re-
sponded to this with grace and wrath." Christianity is also concerned with this. The decisive elements of human life remain the
same at all times. In terms of his relationship to God, man is always concerned with the same or at least related questions and
decisions. For this reason, the history of the people of Israel has
exemplary significance for all other nations. We shall deal with
this again in the following section.

THE OLD TESTAMENT AS A
BOOK ABOUT CHRIST

The Old Testament bears witness to Christ in a twofold sense.
First, as law, the Old Testament is directed toward Christ. Second, as the promise and figure of Christ and of his church, the
Old Testament is full of Christ. Thus the Old Testament bears
witness to Christ through both the law and the gospel which it
contains.

Moses preaches the law so that he "might lead people not only
to recognize their illness and their dislike for God's law but also
to long for grace." He administers the "ministry of sin and of
death." This is necessary, for without such a ministry, human reason would not recognize man's sin and misery. "Moses' ministry is

---

by them, but . . . the emperor could here take an example for setting up a
good government on the basis of Moses." *WA* 16, 377; *LW* 35, 167. "This
occurs whenever a land follows examples from laws of other lands, as the
Romans took the Twelve Tables from the Greeks." *WA* 18, 81; *LW* 40, 98.
⁷⁴ *Op. cit.*, pp. 9-37.
⁷⁵ Cf. *WA*, DB 6, 2; *LW* 35, 358. *WA* 12, 275.

necessary to counteract this blindness and stubbornly impenitent presumption." This is why Moses must teach the law. "Nature must through this good law of God learn to recognize and feel its evil and to long for help in Christ."[76] This is "the real ministry of Moses." Luther can describe the ministry of Moses in this way because he understands the law of the Old Testament radically in terms of Jesus' interpretation of it. In all of this, Luther only renews the Apostle Paul's thoughts concerning the significance of the law in God's plan of salvation.

Through preaching the law, Moses leads people to Christ. And the prophets do just what Moses did. Luther recognizes that they proclaimed not only the promise but also the law. The same is true of the historical books. "They all fulfill the office of Moses. . . . They all have the common purpose of using the proper understanding of the law to convince the people of their unworthiness and to drive them to Christ, as Moses does. . . . Thus the prophets are nothing else than administrators and witnesses of Moses and his office, bringing everyone to Christ through the law."[77] The prophets provide us with "nothing but examples of how God has so strictly and severely confirmed his First Commandment."[78] For this reason the prophets' preaching is to be understood christocentrically even when they fulfill this ministry of Moses.

All this, however, is only one side of the Old Testament. It not only offers to lead men to Christ but is itself already filled with him. This is true first because Christ is always present in the God of the Old Testament, in his activity and promises, and in his relationship to the godly. For the people of the Old Testament are not confronted with a God apart from this world but with a definite "God of the fathers" who allows himself to be found in a particular place, under specific outward signs, and who gives promises to his people. These promises, ultimately are all promises of Christ.

---

[76] On this whole paragraph see Luther's *Preface to the Old Testament*, *WA*, DB 8, 10 ff.; *LW* 35, 235-251. The passages quoted here are from *WA*, DB 8, 20 ff.; *LW* 35, 241 f.

[77] *WA*, DB 8, 29; *LW* 35, 246 f. "The prophets rest on Moses and they have taken what he wrote and clarified it and expanded it with plainer words." *WA* 12, 275. Cf. *WA* 8, 105; *LW* 32, 225.

[78] *Preface to the Prophets*. *WA*, DB 11¹, 5; *LW* 35, 266.

The God who speaks in them is the God who is already at work fulfilling them and saving the world through Christ.[79] On this basis we can distinguish between the immediate significance of the promise and its prefiguration of Christ.[80]

Christ is promised in the prophets, in the Psalms, and in the well-known messianic passages of the historical books—but also in many places beyond these. As much as the prophets are concerned about their own time and even though they make many predictions about coming historical events—and they often erred in making these[81]—the decisive meaning and content of their proclamation remains the advance announcement of Jesus Christ and of his kingdom.[82] They are concerned to help their nation wait for the coming of this kingdom. Like the prophets, the Psalms are filled with prophecies of Christ, his person, his suffering, his death and resurrection, his ruling as king, the gospel, the kingdom, and Christianity or the church.[83] Not only the Psalms, however, are

---

[79] Although David does not refer to Christ in Psalm 51, "he speaks with the God of his fathers, with the promising God who includes Christ." *WA* 40II, 329; cf. *LW* 12, 312 f. "He spoke of the promising God who shows himself in external signs and places, including the promise of Christ." Thus Christ is not excluded. *WA* 40II, 387; cf. *LW* 12, 352.

[80] The following is only a sketch. A more extensive discussion will be found in H. Bornkamm, *op. cit.*, pp. 86 ff. 126 ff.

[81] *WA* 17II, 39.

[82] "All the prophets speak of the same thing. They all have the same concern: to see the future Christ or his future kingdom. All of their prophecies are centered in this and are not to be understood in terms of anything else although they sometimes mix in accounts both of contemporary and of future events; all of these, however, pertain to their declaration of the coming kingdom of Christ." *WA* 13, 88.
Luther says that Isaiah "is concerned altogether with the Christ, that his future coming and the promised kingdom of grace and salvation shall not be disregarded or be lost and in vain because of unbelief and great misfortune and impatience amongst his people." *WA*, DB 11I, 21; *LW* 35, 277. "This testament of Christ is foreshadowed in all of the promises of God from the beginning of the world; indeed, whatever value these ancient promises possessed was completely derived from this new promise that was to come in Christ." *WA* 6, 514; *LW* 36, 38. This means that all God's promises contained in the Old Testament are a prefiguration of the promise of the forgiveness of sins given in Christ and derive their validity from the forgiveness of sins in Christ.

[83] Cf. H. Bornkamm, *op. cit.*, p. 90. Bornkamm lists the psalms which Luther interpreted as prophetic psalms—there are no fewer than twenty-seven of them. But the other types of psalms are also filled with prophecy. Luther also finds a hidden proclamation of Christ and of his salvation in those psalms in which the psalmist turns to God as he confronts his earthly troubles and the inevitability of death. "At this point we should learn the rule that whenever in the Psalter and Holy Scripture the saints deal with God concerning comfort and

to be interpreted in a christological and prophetic sense but also much in the historical accounts of the Old Testament and in the books of Moses. There is more to Moses than his exercise of the function of the law; together with this, he "prophecies powerfully of Jesus Christ our Lord."[84] Moses thus preaches not only the law but also the gospel.

Besides such obvious and concealed promises expressed in words, the Old Testament offers figures of Christ and of his church. Luther finds these especially in the Levitical laws and priesthood, in the sacrificial system, and also in the monarchy. Here he follows the typology of the Letter to the Hebrews. "If you wish to have a proper and certain interpretation then keep Christ constantly before you, for he is the man to whom all this applies."[85] The high priest, the sacrifices, etc. are all "figures" which signify Christ. "The Old Testament pointed toward Christ. The New, however, now gives us what was previously promised and signified through figures in the Old Testament."[86] Christ, however, is already present in the "figures."[87] The Old Testament law and way of life must therefore be seen in two ways. On the one hand, it is a model which points far beyond itself to Christ; at the same time, how-

---

help in their need, eternal life and the resurrection of the dead are involved. All such texts belong to the doctrine of the resurrection and eternal life, in fact, to the whole Third Article of the Creed with the doctrines of the Holy Spirit, the Holy Christian Church, the forgiveness of sins, the resurrection, and everlasting life. And it all flows out of the First Commandment, where God says: 'I am your God' (Ex. 20:2). This the Third Article of the Creed emphasizes insistently. While Christians deplore the fact that they suffer and die in this life, they comfort themselves with another life than this, namely, that of God himself, who is above and beyond this life. It is not possible that they should totally die and not live again in eternity." *WA* 31¹, 154; *LW* 14, 87.

The interpretation of Psalm 90 draws a similar conclusion. The heading reads: "A prayer of Moses, the man of God." The fact that Moses prays when confronted by death directs our attention to Christ. For Moses' prayer fulfills the First Commandment. Whenever Scripture speaks of the First Commandment, Christ, the resurrection of the dead, and eternal life are proclaimed— this is Christ's own interpretation (Matt. 22:32). Praying in obedience to the First Commandment includes community with God and this always implies the victory over death. *WA* 40ᴵᴵᴵ, 484 ff.; *LW* 13, 76 ff.

[84] *WA* 54, 95.

[85] In the *Preface to the Old Testament. WA*, DB 8, 29; *LW* 35, 247.

[86] *WA* 12, 275. The concept of "figures" comes from the letter to the Hebrews. The Vulgate translates the Greek *hypodeigma* and *antitypa* with *figurae;* Luther translated "pictures," "examples," and "images" (Heb. 9, 23 f.; cf. I Peter 3, 21).

[87] *WA* 8, 87; *LW* 32, 200 f.

ever, it is set aside in Christ and is no longer binding for Christians.[88]

Luther calls such interpretation of the Old Testament "spiritual interpretation."[89] He definitely distinguishes it from the traditional allegorical interpretation practiced by Origen, Jerome, and others. They erred in ignoring the literal meaning of the words and the actual history of Israel; thus the spiritual meaning which they discovered is always something completely strange to the text.[90] Luther's "spiritual interpretation" is distinguished from all such allegorical interpretation by the fact that it is grounded in the history of salvation and that it interprets the texts in terms of their relationship to Christ. The allegorical interpreter goes beyond the literal meaning of the text because he is ashamed of the fact that it does not stand at the height of spiritual Christianity. As a result, he knows no other way of interpreting it than assuming that such texts are a secret code used to express something completely different from and unrelated to the situation described in the text. In opposition to this, Luther's "spiritual interpretation" discusses the meaning of prophecy in its particular historical context. It is the power of this prophecy which enables Old Testament history and institutions to point beyond themselves to Christ as the one in whom the history of the Old Testament actually reaches the goal which God has set for it. Allegorical interpretation is not concerned with what actually took place in the historical situation de-

[88] "For this reason the figures are now set aside; for they served the promises which are now completed, established, and fulfilled." *WA* 12, 275.

[89] *WA,* DB 8, 28; *LW* 35, 247.

[90] "They assert that only a spiritual sense is to be sought in the Old Testament." *WA,* DB 8, 11; *LW* 35, 235. For an overview of Luther's relationship to the allegorical method of scriptural exegesis, cf. *GA* 1, 553 ff. and G. Ebeling, *op. cit.* Cf. also H. Bornkamm, *op. cit.*, pp. 74 ff. In the controversy with Erasmus in 1525, Luther declares that we may interpret a passage of Scripture figuratively only if the context requires it or if the simple literal meaning would result in a contradiction that would damage the analogy of faith. *WA* 18, 700; *BOW,* 191. Luther makes the same point in opposition to Latomus. *WA* 8, 63 f.; *LW* 32, 167 f.

Luther applied allegorical exegesis as the sole method of interpreting a text only when he felt that a figurative interpretation was the only possibility. Otherwise, he frequently offers a literal and an allegorical interpretation of the same text. "Except in cases where it was obviously necessary, however, the allegorical interpretation never set aside the literal meaning of the text but often added the spiritual interpretation in terms of Christ and his kingdom to the literal meaning." Bornkamm, *op. cit.*, p. 81. Cf. the sermons on the Gospels in the Lenten series of 1525. *WA* 17^II^, 1-247, *pass.*

scribed by the text. Luther's spiritual interpretation is, however, particularly concerned with the meaning of the words; for the history which they describe is prophecy. Luther can thus place the original literal meaning and the spiritual interpretation beside each other and bring them into a vital relationship to each other through his concept of "sign" or "type."

An example: Christians should pray Psalm 111 as a psalm of thanksgiving for the holy Lord's Supper. At the same time, however, they should not forget its ancient and first meaning as a Passover song. "And yet it is good to have this psalm in its ancient and original interpretation as the dear fathers and prophets used it." Thus Luther first gives a "historical" interpretation of the psalm and then interprets it as a psalm of the New Testament church. The Old Testament Passover is ultimately "a sign and type" of our Easter festival. Israel has been robbed of that for which it once thanked God and can therefore no longer sing this psalm. Only Christians can sing it, "because they not only have such blessings (as the 'Turks and Tartars' also do) but also recognize them as God's blessings rather than human achievement. This psalm of thanks is now free to cover the whole world, wherever Christians are gathered together to celebrate the sacrament. It is no longer limited to the little land of Canaan and restricted to a small corner of the world; it has now become far greater and sounds out over greater distances."[61]

Luther did not intend his spiritual interpretation as an innovation. He was conscious of the fact that he was doing nothing else than the Lord and the apostles had done in their use of Scripture.[62] In his interpretation of John 3:14 ("As Moses lifted up the serpent in the wilderness, so must the Son of man be lifted up"), he says: "In this way the Lord shows us the proper method of interpreting Moses and all the prophets. He teaches us that Moses in all his stories and illustrations points and refers to Christ. His purpose is to show that Christ is the point and the center of a circle, with all eyes inside the circle focused on Him. Whoever turns his

---

[61] The interpretation of Psalm 111 is found in *WA* 31¹, 393 ff. The above quotations are from *WA* 31¹, 404; *LW* 13, 363.
[62] Cf. e.g., *WA* 10ᴵᴵ, 15; *LW* 35, 122.

eyes to Him finds his proper place in this circle of which Christ is
the center. All the stories of Holy Scripture, if viewed aright,
point to Christ."[93] This means that there is ultimately only one
hope—the hope of Christ. Wherever the Holy Scripture speaks of
hope, Christ is its ultimate point of reference. There is only one
real help against sin and death and that is Christ. If someone in
the Old Testament prays for God's help he is ultimately praying
for the coming of Christ.[94] In his explanation of Psalm 102, Luther
says: "This is a psalm of prayer in which the ancient fathers—
tired of the law, of sinning, and of dying—sigh from their very
hearts and cry out for the kingdom of grace promised to us in
Christ."[95] There is only one blessing: the overcoming of the curse
spoken to Adam. Every blessing promised in the Scripture ultimately refers to Christ. "For where Christ is not present, there
the curse remains which fell upon Adam and his children after he
sinned, so that all are completely subject to and the property of
sin, death, and hell."[96]

In all these promises and figures of Christ, he himself is already
present in the Old Testament. But if he is present, faith is also
there; for wherever God's promise is made known, it works
faith. Luther thus sees the Old Testament as full of "beautiful
examples of faith, of love, and of the cross" in the fathers beginning with Adam.[97] In this Luther follows Paul who, in Romans 4,
presents Abraham as the great example of true faith. And for
both Luther and Paul, this faith of the fathers is not an essentially different or pre-Christian faith but, because Christ himself
is already present in the Old Testament word of promise,
genuine faith in Christ; it is the one and the same faith which the
church today has. It is distinguished only by its "tense": that is, it
differs in terms of its temporal relationship to the Christ incarnate
in history. For the fathers it was faith in the promised Christ; for
us it is faith in the Christ who has already appeared. Then it was

[93] *WA* 47, 66; *LW* 22, 339.
[94] *WA* 38, 49.
[95] *WA* 38, 52.
[96] *WA*, DB 6, 7; *LW* 35, 359.
[97] *WA* 16, 391; *LW* 35, 173. Cf. Theses 1 ff., *WA* 39ᴵᴵ, 187. Conversely,
since the promise of Christ has been there since Adam's fall into sin, all sin
from the beginning is unbelief in and ignorance of Christ. *WA* 39ᴵ, 404.

faith in the promise; now it is faith in the fulfilled promise."[*] Faith in Christ is, however, justifying faith both before as well as after Christ's historical appearance. Thus justification has taken place since the beginning of the world—justification through faith in Christ.[*] The God of the fathers of the Old Testament is none other than the Father of Jesus Christ, the God of Christendom; he is one and the same God.[100] This also means that since the beginning of the world there has always been a church; it existed in the believers.

Luther here attempts to take seriously both the transcendent presence of Christ and of his salvation for those who believe, as well as the actual historical character of the history of salvation, the epochs introduced by Christ's coming in the flesh. He takes seriously both the essential contemporaneity of all believers before and after Christ, as well as the fact that they actually lived at different periods of history.

Thus the assertion that the church has existed since the beginning of the world, and therefore existed in the Old Testament, is accompanied by the parallel assertion that the church is prefigured in the Old Testament just as Christ is. Luther sees this in the destiny of the believers, especially as expressed in the Psalms; but he also finds it in the history of the people of Israel,

---

[*] "All the saints before the birth of Christ believed this same divine promise and thus were preserved in and saved through such faith in the coming Christ. . . . And this faith was the same as faith in Christ himself even though it comes before rather than after Christ; for both are trust in the seed of Abraham: the one before, the other after his coming." *WA* 10I,2, 4 f. "The fathers had the same faith and also the same Christ. He was just as close to them as he is to us, as Hebrews 13 says, 'Jesus Christ the same yesterday, today, and forever,' that is, Christ is present from the beginning of the world until its end and all are preserved through him and in him." *WA* 10I,2, 6. "The faith of all the ancient believers was faith in the coming Christ just as it is written, 'Christ yesterday and today.' They believed in God: they believed in the God who promised Christ and they looked forward to him." *WA* 39I, 64. *WA* 39II, 162. Cf. the parallel usage of "through faith in the promise" and "through faith in the fulfilled promise." *WA* 39II, 187, Theses 7 and 8; *LW* 34, 303.

[*] "For solely by faith in Christ, once promised, now delivered, the whole church is justified, from the beginning of the world to the end." *WA* 39II, 188; *LW* 34, 304. Cf. *WA* 39II, 197; *LW* 34, 313.

[100] "One and the same God has been worshiped from the beginning of the world in different ways through faith in the same Christ." *WA* 39II, 187; *LW* 34, 303. "In different ways" is also used but in a different sense, *WA* 10I,2, 6. "There always has been one and the same prayer and faith but the times have been different and thus there have also been other rites and ceremonies." *WA* 39II, 270.

particularly in their troubles and oppression by their enemies. He understands the Psalms first of all in their historical sense as hymns of the people of Israel and its believers. But their relationship to God and their fate once again has typological significance. "It is clear as day that everything which the people of Israel previously suffered physically from their enemies and surrounding neighbors is a symbol of the sufferings which the Church of Christ now endures from its enemies and neighbors, that is, from false brothers, false teachers and heretics. Thus these psalms and prayers remain to us under the very same titles and names, that we too may pray them against our enemies just as those others once prayed them against their enemies."[101] On this basis Luther establishes the propriety of applying the psalms in the Old Testament which deal with enemies of the psalmists to the contemporary struggles of the church. He puts their words into the mouth of Christ's community by means of his versifications of the Psalms.[102] Luther thus considers the Psalms the finest "book of examples for the saints on earth"; whoever recognizes himself and his experiences in the Psalms may be certain that "he stands in the community of the saints and that all saints have experienced what he experienced because they sing the same song that he does; this is particularly true because he can also speak these words to God as they have done; this can be done only in faith, for they are not to a godless man's taste."[103] The Christian finds in the Psalms not only the saints but also Jesus Christ, "the head of all the saints," with his suffering and resurrection.[104] (In psalms such as Psalm 22 and Psalm 69,

---

[101] *WA* 31¹, 29. "It is very beneficial to have words prescribed by the Holy Spirit which godly men are able to use in this danger." *WA* 40ᴵᴵᴵ, 16. Christians confronted with troubles similar to those of the psalmists thus can use the psalms preformed by the Holy Spirit as the text of their prayers.

[102] These are: "From Trouble Deep I Cry to Thee" (Psalm 130), *WA* 35, 419 f.; *LW* 53, 223 f. "Ah God, from Heaven Look Down" (Psalm 12), *WA* 35, 415 ff.; *LW* 53, 227 f. "Although the Fools Say with Their Mouth" (Psalm 14), *WA* 35, 441 ff.; *LW* 53, 230 f. "Would That the Lord Would Grant Us Grace" (Psalm 67), *WA* 35, 418 f.; *LW* 53, 234. "Were God Not with Us at This Time" (Psalm 124), *WA* 35, 440 f.; *LW* 53, 246. "Happy Who in God's Fear Doth Stay" (Psalm 128), *WA* 35, 437 f.; *LW* 53, 243 f.

[103] *WA*, DB 10¹, 98 ff; *LW* 35, 253, 256. *WA* 31¹, 57. Cf. *LW* 14, 79 f.

[104] *WA*, DB 10¹, 98; *LW* 35, 254. In his interpretation of Psalm 22 Luther says: "It is a prophecy of the suffering and resurrection of Christ and of the gospel. . . . It interprets Christ's suffering on the cross more clearly than any other Scripture." *WA* 38, 25.

the crucified Christ himself speaks.)[105] The experience of God's wrath and of his grace speaks in this book. For this reason, it is a contemporary book for Christians and presents them a picture of themselves.[106]

Again, Luther's interpretation is not arbitrary but rooted in a basic theological thought: in the final analysis all history is always one and the same. In spite of all change and variation in times, relationships, persons, and forms, men always remain the same insofar as they all must make the same great decision to believe or not to believe. They are always summoned to believe; this summons does not first arrive through the coming of Christ but through the promise of the coming Christ given to Adam, Abraham, and the other fathers. Faith and unfaith are at all times essentially the same. The Spirit of faith who lives in all members of the body of Christ from the beginning of the world to its end is one and the same Spirit. This makes it possible for every generation of the church to adopt the confession of the men of the Bible and apply it to itself.[107]

This understanding of the Old Testament determines Luther's method of translation. His rendering of the Bible into German is more than a "translation." It is a partial interpretation of the Scripture on the basis of Christ and of the Christian proclamation. He translates as one who believes the gospel. This is the standard by which he reproduces Old Testament texts. And, if a passage can be interpreted in more than one way, Luther deliberately chooses that interpretation and translation which "agrees with the New Testament."[108]

---

[105] *WA* 8, 86; *LW* 32, 200.

[106] *WA*, DB 10¹, 102; *LW* 35, 256 f.

[107] "For although in the course of time customs, people, places, and usages may vary godliness and ungodliness remain the same through all the ages." *WA* 5, 29 f.; *LW* 14, 290 f. "Times change, as to things, bodies, tribulations, but the same Spirit, the same meaning, the same food and drink abide in all and through all." Just before this, Luther says: "This same Spirit who was in Isaiah in the midst of his time of tribulation was also in Job, in Abraham, in Adam, and is still in all the members of the whole Body of Christ from the beginning to the end of the world, and is with each and everyone in his particular time and tribulation." *WA* 8, 69; *LW* 32, 176.

[108] *WA*, TR 5, 5533.

Emanuel Hirsch says: "At no religiously decisive place does Luther's translation of the Old Testament deny the fact that its words have passed through a Christian heart." Hirsch speaks of Luther's interpretation as "open toward the

We, today, cannot simply repeat the actual details of Luther's interpretation of the Old Testament, any more than we can repeat the interpretation of the early church. The development of historical exegesis stands between us and Luther, and we cannot simply go back to Luther as if it did not exist. This is what prevents us from interpreting the prophecies christologically. We have learned to understand their actual historical meaning and to recognize that this meaning has not been fulfilled in Jesus Christ. For us, then, the relationship of the Old Testament to Christ and to the New Testament is characterized by a much greater tension than it was for Luther. With Luther, however, we also confess that this book, like the history of Israel, points in the direction of Jesus Christ. And, to that extent we also attempt to interpret the Old Testament with reference to Christ, that is, christocentrically.[100]

New Testament." . . . Luther interpreted the Old Testament in the direction of the gospel." *Luthers deutsche Bibel* (Munich: Kaiser, 1928), pp. 46-49. Hirsch also gives the specific references to Luther's writings. Cf. also, Bornkamm, *op. cit.*, pp. 185 ff.

[100] Cf. *CW*, pp. 205 ff.; Bornkamm, *op. cit.*, pp. 104, 224; and R. Hermann, *op. cit.*, p. 38.

Part Two

GOD'S WORK

10

GOD IS GOD

IN USING *the phrase* "God is God" [*Gottes Gottheit*] as a heading for our presentation of Luther's theology, we are using a concept that Luther himself frequently uses.[1]

THE CREATOR WORKS ALL IN ALL

For Luther, being God and creating are identical. God is God because he and only he creates.[2] God creates and preserves everything. Nothing is and nothing continues to be without his activity. "All things must be God's, since nothing can be or become, if he would not bring it into existence; and when he stops, nothing can continue to exist." God's relationship to the world is quite different from a man's relationship to his work. Once done, man's work exists independently of the man who produced it. It thus continues to exist without him. The world is different: it cannot exist for even one moment unless God maintains it. God always works; and reality depends on his continuous and uninterrupted activity. "He has not created the world as though he were a carpenter: building a house that he could walk away from when finished and let stand the way it is. On the contrary, he remains with and preserves everything he has made. Otherwise it would neither hold up nor endure."[3] God's

---

[1] Luther finds the concept in the Bible in Romans 1:20 and Colossians 2:9. Apart from this he translates Paul's "depths of God" [*theou*] in I Corinthians 2:10 as "depths of deity" [*Gottheit*]. The quotations of this chapter will indicate how often this concept appears in Luther. Cf. *WA* 31¹, 126; *LW* 14, 74 where Luther says, "[It is] impossible . . . that he would forfeit his deity."

[I have used various forms of "God is God" to translate this term. The similarity to the title of Philip Watson's study of Luther's theology, *Let God Be God* (Philadelphia: Muhlenberg, 1948), is obvious. Althaus used Luther's phrase in the title of his essay, "Gottes Gottheit als Sinn der Rechtfertigungslehre Luther's," in *Luther-Jahrbuch* XIII (1931), 1-28. The German translation of *Let God Be God* uses this same phrase in its title: *"Um Gottes Gottheit."*—Trans.]

[2] David Löfgren, *Die Theologie der Schöpfung bei Luther* (Göttingen: Vandenhoek & Ruprecht, 1960).

[3] *WA* 21, 521. *WA* 46, 558; *LW* 22, 26.

105

constant preservation of creation at every point of space and time is also an on-going act of new creation.[4] In his sermons Luther explicates this with concrete examples from life—and one must note how much the certainty means to him that God's on-going creation and preservation is the ground of all reality. God is not yet finished creating but is still working at it. "Thus God creates throughout the entire world every day, even though he could have made all men at once."[5] He does not create everything at once, but bit by bit, without stopping. His creation is not a one-time but an on-going activity.

God is actively present, working and creating in all reality. Luther described God's creative presence in all reality especially forcefully in his book on the sacrament of the altar, *That These Words of Christ, "This Is My Body," . . . Still Stand Firm . . .* (1527). Here he develops his understanding of "right hand of God" in opposition to the opinions of Zwingli and his followers. God's right hand is not "a specific place" but rather "the almighty power of God, which at one and the same time can be nowhere and yet must be everywhere. . . . It must be essentially present everywhere, even in the tiniest leaf of a tree. The reason is this: It is God who creates, effects, and preserves all things through his almighty power and right hand, as our Creed confesses. For he dispatches no officials or angels when he creates or preserves something, but all this is the work of his divine power itself. If he is to create or preserve it, however, he must be present and must make and preserve his creation both in its innermost and outermost aspects. Therefore, indeed, he himself must be present in every single creature in its innermost and outermost being, on all sides, through and through, below and above, before and behind, so that nothing can be more truly present and within all creatures than God himself with his power."[6] God's creative power in all things is also his most immediate, comprehensive, and inwardly penetrating presence.

Although God's power is actively present in all things and com-

---

[4] "Daily we can see the birth into this world of new human beings, young children who were non-existent before; we behold new trees, new animals on the earth, new fish in the water, new birds in the air. And such creation and preservation will continue until the Last Day." *WA* 46, 559; *LW* 22, 27.

[5] *WA* 12, 441.

[6] *WA* 23, 133; *LW* 37, 57 f.

pletely enters into them, it still is not consumed in the reality of
the world. It continues to transcend the world. Luther says this at
the same place in his book on the Lord's Supper and in the same
breath with which he proclaims that God is creatively present in
all reality. The almighty power of God is necessarily present at
all places, and yet at the same time it need not be present at any
single given place. "The power of God cannot be so determined
and measured, for it is uncircumscribed and immeasurable, beyond and above all that is or may be."[7] His own divine nature
can be wholly and entirely present in all creatures and in every
single individual being, more deeply, more inwardly, more present
than the creature is to himself, and yet on the other hand may and
can be circumscribed nowhere and in no being, so that he actually
embraces all things and is in all, but no one being circumscribes
him and is in him."[8] God is in these creatures and is also beyond
them. "Nothing is so small but God is still smaller, nothing so
large but God is still larger, nothing is so short but God is still
shorter, nothing so long but God is still longer, nothing is so broad
but God is still broader, nothing so narrow but God is still narrower, etc. He is an inexpressible being, above and beyond all that
can be described or imagined."[9] God's power is thus transcendent
in the sense that it lies outside all of its own measurements, beyond all differences between large and small, etc. It has its own
unique dimension. It is in everything and at the same time outside of everything.

This living omnipresent working of God is the mystery of all
reality. God who causes all things is also the only causal agent.
For the agent who really works in all things is God, and not the
personal and impersonal powers of the world which we think of
as causes. God is the first or principal cause, all others are only
secondary or instrumental causes.[10] They are only the tools which
he uses in the service of his own autonomous, free, and exclusive
working; they are only the masks under which he hides his activity.

"All creatures are God's masks and disguises; he permits them

[7] *WA* 23, 133; *LW* 37, 57.
[8] *WA* 23, 137; *LW* 37, 60.
[9] *WA* 26, 339; *LW* 37, 228.
[10] *WA* 40ᴵᴵᴵ, 210 f., 215.

to work with him and help him create all sorts of things—even though he could and does create without their co-operation."[11] God does not need earthly agents. It is by his own free decision that he calls and uses them to work together with him. He commands us to perform our tasks with zeal and to fulfill the demands which our vocation and position in life make on us. We should do this because God has commanded it and because he will not give us his blessing unless we work. But we should not imagine that we are the real causes or rely on our own work as though it were we who make things happen. The success and the result are and remain God's doing. Our work does not cause the result and the blessing, but only the condition under which God wills to give things to us. Luther makes this clear with the example of children who fast and pray and hang up their clothes at night so that the Christ Child or St. Nicholas will give them presents. Their activity does not cause the gifts to come but is only a childish way of asking for them and an expression of their willingness to receive them. "What else is all our work to God—whether in the fields, in the garden, in the city, in the house, in war, or in government—but just such a child's performance, by which He wants to give His gifts in the fields, at home, and everywhere else? These are the masks of God, behind which He wants to remain concealed and do all things."[12] There is no immanent relationship and no causal necessity between what we do and the results that follow. Work and blessing are related to and bound to each other only through God's command and promise. God promises to bless our work. He waits to give until we work; but the worker must in turn wait for and ask for the gifts of his goodness. We should not depend on our work but on him. Here too, in respect of our own

---

[11] *WA* 17ᴵᴵ, 192. ". . . the course of the world, and especially the doing of his saints, are God's mask, under which he conceals himself and so marvelously exercises dominion and introduces disorder into the world [*in der Welt so wunderlich regiert und rumort*]. *WA* 15, 373; *LW* 45, 331.

This is true also of the preachers of the gospel. "Those who are now proclaiming the gospel are not those who really do it; they are only a mask and a masquerade through which God carries out his work and will. You are not the ones who are catching the fish, God says, I am drawing the net myself." *WA* 17ᴵᴵ, 262 f. "Creatures are only the hands, channels, and means through which God bestows all blessings." *WA* 30ᴵ, 136; *BC*, 368. Cf. *WA* 40ᴵ, 175; *LW* 26, 95.

[12] *WA* 31ᴵ. 436; *LW* 14, 114.

deeds, he alone is to be accorded the honor of having actually accomplished them.[12]

Human activity thus receives its necessary and limited place, its value, and its humble character within the context of faith in the Creator. It is both established and limited by God's creative will. All human activity is nothing else than a form of readiness to receive God's gifts. Without this active readiness, God will not give; but the preparedness expressed in the working does not produce the gift. At this point, God remains free to give.

God causes everything through his word. Luther knows this to be true from the creation story and from the entire Old Testament, as well as from Romans 4:17, "God calls into existence the things that do not exist." "God's command or speech is equivalent to creation." His word rules in nature and in history. By his word, God brings about the change of seasons. In all these, Luther does not see processes governed by natural laws, whose natural causes can be understood but simply the "great and wonderful deeds of

---

[12] "Man must and ought to work, ascribing his sustenance and the fulness of his house, however, not to his own labor but solely to the goodness and blessing of God. . . . God wants the glory as the one who alone gives the growth. . . . It behooves you to labor, but your sustenance and the maintenance of your household belong to God alone. . . . God wills that man should work, and without work He will give him nothing. Conversely, God will not give him anything because of his labor, but solely out of His goodness and blessing." *WA* 15, 366 f.; *LW* 45, 324 ff. "And so we find that all our labor is nothing more than the finding and collecting of God's gifts; it is quite unable to create or preserve anything." *WA* 15, 369; *LW* 45, 327. In his interpretation of Psalm 147; 13 ["For he strengthens the bars of your gates"], Luther says: "You should build and forge bars, fortify the city and arm yourself, establish order and laws the best you can. But once you have done this, see that you do not depend on it. . . . God could easily give you grain and fruit without your plowing and planting. But he does not want to do so. Neither does He want our plowing and planting alone to give you grain and fruit; but you are to plow and plant and then ask his blessing and pray; 'Now let God take over; now grant grain and fruit, dear Lord! Our plowing and planting will not do it. It is thy gift.' . . . He could give children without man and woman. But he does not want to do this. Instead, he joins man and woman so that it appears to be the work of man and woman, and yet he does it under the cover of such masks. . . . You must work and thus give God good cause and a mask." *WA* 31¹, 435; *LW* 14, 114 f. "Govern, and let Him give his blessing. Fight and let him give the victory. Preach, and let him win hearts. Take a husband or a wife, and let him produce children. Eat and drink, and let him nourish and strengthen you. And so on. In all our doings he is to work through us, and he alone shall have the glory from it. . . . Don't be lazy or idle, but don't rely solely on your own work and doings. Get busy and work, and yet expect everything from God alone." *WA* 31¹, 436 f.; *LW* 14, 115. On the relationship between working and praying for God's blessing, cf. *WA* 40ᴵᴵᴵ, 213, 216.

God."[14] God's miracles are done everywhere in the ordinary course
of nature rather than only in extraordinary events. God is no less
active through his word in political and sociological structures and
in historical developments. God himself rules the nations. God
must bring it about that the commandments of the princes have
authority among their subjects and that their subjects obediently
submit to such authority. Through his word, God gives effective
authority to the rulers and works reverence and obedience among
their subjects. God through his word thus preserves the effectiveness of the structures which order men's lives.[15] The word that does
this is not the word of the gospel but God's secret, creating and
preserving word.

Luther's understanding of God's omnipotence as not merely potential but constantly at work [*aktuell*] corresponds to this view of
divine creativity. God's omnipotence does not consist in having the
power to do what he actually does not do, but in the ceaseless
activity with which he works all in all.[16] Omnipotence means that
God works everything in everything that is. For Luther, it is "not
the infinite capacity for possibilities freely available to God but
that infinite power which is active in the formulation of the
existing world."[17]

The knowledge that God and God alone works everything has
immediate significance for faith. The unchangeableness and the
constancy of God's purpose as well as the trustworthiness of his
promises (and threats) depends on his being alone the one who
works all in all. Since he determines everything with his almighty

---

[14] *WA* 31¹, 445, 450; *LW* 14, 124, 128 f.
[15] "His word must be added in order to give force to the ruler's command
and respect and obedience to the subject." *WA* 31¹, 445; *LW* 14, 124. "Here
lords and princes, as well as subjects, should learn that the government of the
land and the obedience of the people are a gift of God—a gift bestowed out
of nothing but His pure goodness." *WA* 31¹, 79; *LW* 14, 52. Cf. *WA* 31¹,
81 f.; *LW* 14, 53 f.
[16] Luther interprets Luke 1:49 ["he who is mighty"]: "For the word
'mighty' does not denote a quiescent power, as one says of the temporal king
that he is mighty, even though he may be sitting still and doing nothing. But
it denotes an energetic power, continuous activity, that works and operates
without ceasing." *WA* 7, 574; *LW* 21, 328. "By the omnipotence of God I
mean, not the power by which he omits to do many things that he could do,
but the active power by which he mightily works all in all. It is in this sense
that Scripture calls him omnipotent." *WA* 18, 718; *BOW*, 217. The expression "works all things in all" is taken from I Corinthians 12:6.
[17] *GA* 1, 45.

working, I know that nothing and nobody can resist his will, change his mind, or restrict his activity. There is therefore no doubt that God is able to achieve the eternal purposes of his love as they are made known to me in his promises.[18]

Since God works all things everywhere, we are always in his hand. No matter where one goes, one can fall only into God's hands. "Where does a man who hopes in God end up except in his own nothingness? But when a man goes into nothingness, does he not merely return to that from which he came? Since he comes from God and his own non-being, it is to God that he returns when he returns to nothingness. For even though a man falls out of himself and out of all creation, it is impossible for him to fall out of God's hand, for all creation is surrounded by God's hand. So run through the world; but where are you running? Always into God's hand and lap."[19]

This inescapable living presence of God in all that exists is either the most blessed or the most terrible reality for a man, depending on what he knows God's relationship to himself to be. It is never neutral but is always either saving or damning. We are here confronted with the twofold character of God's dealing with men in the law and the gospel. The man who has peace with God through believing the gospel can be confident in the midst of the most terrible reality; for God is present even in such a situation and holds it in his omnipotent hand—whether it be death, hell, or hostile earthly powers. "He is present everywhere, even in death, in hell, among his enemies, yes even in their hearts. For he has made and rules everything so that it must do his will."[20] We should therefore fear and trust only in God and most certainly believe that nothing can destroy us; for God is Lord of all the powers that threaten us. We are in his gracious hand, no matter what happens. This is the believer's royal freedom and joy.[21] Ulti-

---

[18] *WA* 18, 619, 716; *BOW*, 84, 214.
[19] *WA* 5, 168.
[20] *WA* 19, 219. Cf. *WA* 18, 623; *BOW*, 88.
[21] "Therefore such a believer is so filled with joy and happiness that he does not allow himself to be terrified by any creature and is the master of all things; he is afraid only of God, his Lord, who is in heaven—otherwise he is afraid of nothing that might happen to him." *WA* 12, 442.

mately, he is always dealing with God himself and not with the creature: and he knows how he stands with God.[22]

The opposite is true when a man does not believe but stands in conflict with God. Then his guilty conscience turns God's effective presence in all creatures into a terrible reality, that is, into the vehicle of God's pursuing wrath.[23] If God who controls all creatures is against him, then he also experiences that all creatures are his enemies. He must be afraid of them all: even a rustling leaf falling from a tree frightens him (Lev. 26:36).[24] This does not mean that the creature which proceeds out of God's hand has changed; it is and remains good. The impression that it is our enemy does not come from the creature itself but from ourselves; and it is we ourselves who cause us to fear God and to flee from him. This is the guilty conscience which turns the world of God's creation into an arena of enmity and anxiety for us.[25] The very same presence and vital working of God in all creatures that signifies heaven to the believers means hell to the godless.[26]

Because of his almighty activity God also has each man completely in his hand. Like the whole creation of which he is a part, each man is surrounded and permeated with God's all-effecting activity.[27] God works everything in him. Luther therefore cannot even speak of man's freedom of the will in relation to God. God also works the will of men; their will is not free. Luther constantly asserts this against Erasmus, particularly in *The Bondage of the Will*. Free will is a divine attribute and is properly applied

---

[22] "They are afraid of nothing, for they know that God is on their side." *WA* 12, 443.

[23] *WA* 5, 213. "If you have no faith, your evil conscience sees the God whom you flee as present in every creature." *WA* 14, 101. Cf. *WA* 19, 226. "An evil conscience arms all of creation against us." *WA* 44, 546.

[24] *WA* 12, 443. *WA* 17¹, 72. *WA* 19, 226. *WA* 44, 500.

[25] *WA* 44, 546.

[26] *WA* 12, 443. "What, however, can serve as refuge if He becomes angry whose hand has made all things and who is able to do everything?" *WA* 40ᴵᴵᴵ, 512; *LW* 13, 93.

[27] "Whoever understands this [that God works all in all] soon becomes aware that he cannot make the smallest movement or even think unless God causes it: that his life is not completely in his own hand but solely and completely in God's hand. For, if I believe that he has made the entire world out of nothing and brought it into existence only by his word and commandment, then I must confess that I am also a piece of the world and of his creation. The consequence must be that I do not have the power to move a hand unless God works and does everything in me." *WA* 12, 442.

only to the divine majesty.* But over and above this the fact that
God works everything in a man means that a man must always
will and do something, for God works constantly and never rests.
Thus God is the constant mover and driving force in all his creatures. He allows no creature to rest, for he impels them with his
own dynamic energy.*

Again God's working all in all may be the most blessed or the
most terrible reality for a man, depending on his relationship to
God. For the believer it is a great comfort to know that God himself works faith in him. This takes salvation out of his own hand,
so that his weakness and tendency to fall into Satan's traps need
not destroy the unshakeable basis of his faith. The fact that God
works all things in my heart, that is, that my will is bound, makes
me certain of salvation.* For the godless, however, God's almighty working in the heart is a terrible reality. God works even
in Satan and in the godless. They too—just as they are—are
moved, driven, and pulled along by the energy of God's working
all in all. God may be compared with a rider who rides even
though the horse is lame, or with the carpenter who uses a jagged
and dull ax. God also constantly keeps evil people, his bad tools,
in restless movement. Thus the godless man cannot avoid sinning
because God works in him and he cannot "remain idle . . . [rather
he] wills, desires and acts according to his nature."* God thus binds
the godless man to his rebellious will and constantly permits him
to sin against God. More than this, God can even make the evil
man more evil. He may harden him and make him stubborn. Lu-

* *WA* 18, 636; *BOW*, 105. "So the foreknowledge and omnipotence of
God are diametrically opposed to our 'free-will.' " *WA* 18, 718; *BOW*, 217.
Cf. *WA* 18, 638, 662, 781; *BOW*, 107, 137, 310.
* "How incessantly active God is in all his creatures, allowing none of them
to keep holiday. . . . As the omnipotent Agent makes it act (as he does the
rest of his creatures) by means of his own inescapable movement, it needs must
actively will something." *WA* 18, 711; *BOW*, 206 f.
* *WA* 18, 783; *BOW*, 314.
* Luther points out that "The remnant of nature in the ungodly and in
Satan" is and remains God's creation and is therefore "subject to Divine omnipotence and action." God, however, uses them as "he finds them. . . . Since
they are evil and perverted themselves . . . they do only that which is perverted
and evil." *WA* 18, 709; *BOW*, 204. Luther repeatedly uses the terms *rapere*
and *raptus* in this discussion, e.g., *WA* 18, 709, 711; *BOW*, 204 ff. *Raptus* may
be translated as "impelling force."

ther illustrated this particularly with the person of Pharaoh." God's ceaseless movement and hardening of the godless is a means and demonstration of his wrath, but here too wrath is not an end in itself; God in his wisdom is simply using even his bad tool "so well that it works to His glory and our salvation."" This is also true in the case of Pharaoh—Luther refers to Exodus 9:16 and Romans 9:17. God hardens Pharaoh in order to use his hardness of heart to make room for His sign, to reveal His power, and thereby to strengthen the faith of His people." Ultimately, then, even such hardening of the heart serves God's plan of salvation.

In considering Luther's doctrine that God works all in all, we dare never forget that this is not all Luther says about God's basic relationship to men. Luther also knows that the man who is completely in God's hand and is at every moment moved by Him, at the same time stands before God as one who is responsible, guilty, and under God's judgment. Most important of all, however, Luther also sees this same man as the object of God's love: God summons him to an act of free surrender. Luther thereby sets a limit to the idea that God works all in all, a boundary which dare not be transgressed. Luther does not postulate the all-encompassing activity of God as absolute, he guards against drawing all the logical consequences that would imply. This is immediately clear from the fact that Luther, in spite of his assertion that God works even in Satan and in the godless, never attributes man's sin to God's will and working. In *The Bondage of the Will* he sharply distinguishes the fact that God works even in the godless so that they constantly must be that which they are, from the fact that they are what they are. God does not make them what they are; he moves them as they always are and as he has already found them. Thus Luther refuses to draw the conclusion which would logically follow from his basic idea that God works all in all. He thereby bears witness that we sinners who daily commit new sin are forbidden to draw the conclusion that God wills and works sin.

" *WA* 18, 710 ff.; *BOW*, 204 ff., 207 ff.
" *WA* 18, 711; *BOW*, 206.
" Luther quotes God: "Do not be terrified at Pharaoh's stubbornness, for I work that very stubbornness myself and I who deliver you have it under my control. I shall simply make use of it to work many signs and to declare my majesty, so as to help faith." *WA* 18, 714; *BOW*, 211.

That conclusion would relativize sin and guilt and thus remove the unconditional seriousness of man's position before God in judgment and in forgiveness.

Luther thus simply leaves the contradiction between these ideas that God works all in all and that man is responsible for his sin. In opposition to all rigidly logical theology, he bears witness to the mystery of God and of our existing through Him and under His judgment which is beyond all human knowledge, even human theological knowledge. For this reason one cannot consider that Schleiermacher, who declares that God has brought sin into existence, is superior to Luther. Schleiermacher speaks objectively about God's relationship to sin, as though he stood where God stands. Luther, however, at the decisive points speaks subjectively, as one who stands where the guilty and forgiven man stands.[*] To think as Schleiermacher does requires that we stand above our sin in order to think about it objectively. That, however, is the very thing which Luther says is impossible. We can rise above sin first and only through God's wonderful forgiveness and not through a theory which asserts that God has brought sin into existence. Theological thought dare not allow itself to be misled on this point.

GIVING LOVE

Viewed in relationship to men, God's creative activity is pure giving and helping. He thus demonstrates not only his divine ability but also that he is goodness and love, constantly engaged in giving. Whoever wishes to describe God as God, in terms of his "nature," cannot speak of him merely as the only and constant creator, but must also speak of him as love. God in the depths of his being is nothing else than love; and love is divine, for it is God himself.[*] "It is God's nature to do only 'good.'" This is his

---

[*] *WA* 18, 709, 711; *BOW*, 204, 206. Cf. above n. 31. Karl Holl apparently considers it a weakness in Luther's theology that he did not draw the conclusion that God produces the evil. This conclusion was first drawn by Friedrich Schleiermacher (*The Christian Faith*, ed. and trans., H. R. Mackintosh, J. S. Stewart, *et. al.* [Edinburgh: T. & T. Clark, 1928], § 83, pp. 341-345), who thought that "the only serious solution appears to be that God works the evil too; for if good and evil did not stand alongside each other too no decision and no conscience would ever be possible." See the note at *GA* 3, 55.

[*] "If I were to paint a picture of God I would so draw him that there would be nothing else in the depth of his divine nature than that fire and passion

glory: not receiving but constantly giving, freely without hope of gratitude, independently of man's attitude toward him, that is, in a completely different way than natural men do good. Thus God's goodness is "genuinely natural goodness." It "gladly loses its good deed on the unthankful."[87]

God demonstrates this love in various ways and in several stages.[88] First, as Luther says in his explanation of the First Article and as he so movingly and fluently pictures it in his sermons, God gives us life and preserves it. He nourishes and revives it through the gifts of nature; he allows all creatures to serve us and "does this all out of purely fatherly divine goodness and mercy."[89] In this we already experience God as "nothing but burning love and a glowing oven full of love."[40] In addition to all these temporal gifts God gives men eternal goods, his Son, and therewith himself. "He has poured out upon us both temporal and eternal goods and with them his own being; and he has poured himself out with everything he is and does for us who were sinners, undeserving enemies, and servants of the devil. He can neither do any more than this for us nor give us anything else."[41] Thus Christ and the fact that he is "for us" is the greatest gift of God's love. In this gift God gives himself. But God gives earthly goods not only because he is the good creator but also because of the mercy with which God in Christ turns favorably toward the sinner. Luther continually emphasizes that God gives earthly gifts in spite of all the unthankfulness and other evils of men, that is, with forgiving

which is called love for people. Correspondingly, love is such a thing that it is neither human nor angelic but rather divine, yes, even God himself." *WA* 36, 424.

[87] *WA* 31^I, 182; *LW* 14, 106.

"This is what it is to be God; not to take good things but to give, that is, to return good for evil." *WA* 4, 269. "It is his glory to be a benefactor to us." *WA* 56, 520; *LCC* 15, 411. "For the Divine Majesty is such that it gives to every man and helps in every anxiety and need. If I recognize that, I understand that I cannot help myself." *WA* 17^I, 233; *LW* 12, 187. "For God is he who distributes his gifts freely to all; and this is his praise of his own deity." *WA* 40^I, 244; *LW* 26, 127. "He is a loving, gracious, good and compassionate God, who continually does good and abundantly bestows his goodness upon us." *WA* 31^I, 68; *LW* 14, 47.

[88] "How has he loved us? Not only in the ordinary way of temporally preserving and nourishing us unworthy people together with all godless men on earth . . . but in the special way of giving his Son for us." *WA* 17^{II}, 205.

[89] Cf. *WA* 31^I, 69, 77; *LW* 14, 47 f., 51.

[40] *WA* 36, 425.

[41] *WA* 17^{II}, 205 f.

goodness; for "the fact that he neither becomes tired nor ceases to do good because of any evil really is, and deserves to be called, divine goodness."⁴⁸ In this sense, God already gives himself and his eternal goodness in his earthly gifts.

God "showers us with his own being." He gives us what he is. For Luther, God's sharing of himself is the highest expression of the fact that God is God. It means that the attributes of God are by their very nature creative and are not only his own and remain in himself but are also shared with men. Luther feels that this is true of all God's attributes. Luther first became aware of this in the biblical concept of the righteousness of God. At first, he understood it as God's judging and punishing righteousness until he discovered that the Scripture uses it as a synonym for grace. Then he recognized it as the righteousness with which God in his mercy makes men righteous through faith, that is, shares his own righteousness with them.⁴⁹ Starting here, he recognized that something comparable to this also holds true of the other concepts used to describe God's being: of his strength, for with it he makes us strong; of his wisdom, for with it he makes us wise; of his blessedness and glory, for he gives us a share in them.⁵⁰ All of God's

---

⁴⁸ *WA* 31¹, 77; *LW* 14, 51.
⁴⁹ Cf. the famous passage from Luther's *Preface to the Complete Edition of Luther's Latin Writings:* "At last, by the mercy of God, meditating day and night, I gave heed to the context of the words, namely, 'In it the righteousness of God is revealed, as it is written, "He who through faith is righteous shall live." ' There I began to understand that the righteousness of God is that by which the righteous lives by a gift of God, namely by faith. And this is the meaning: the righteousness of God is revealed by the gospel, namely, the passive righteousness with which the merciful God justifies us by faith, as it is written, 'He who through faith is righteous shall live.' Here I felt that I was altogether born again and had entered paradise itself through open gates. There a totally other face of the entire Scripture showed itself to me." *WA* 54, 186; *LW* 34, 337. " 'The righteousness of God' must not be understood as that righteousness by which he is righteous in himself, but as that righteousness by which we are made righteous by him." *WA* 56, 172; *LCC* 15, 18. Cf. *WA* 31¹, 331.
⁵⁰ "I also found in other terms an analogy, as, the work of God, that is, what God does in us, the power of God, with which he makes us strong, the wisdom of God, with which he makes us wise, the strength of God, the salvation of God, the glory of God." *WA* 54, 186; *LW* 34, 337. "It is to be noted that in this passage [Rom. 1:16], *virtus Dei*, is to be understood as 'potency' or 'power' . . . which does not mean that power by which he is powerful in himself but that power by which he makes powerful and strong." *WA* 56, 169; *LCC* 15, 15 f. "The wisdom and power of God are the life according to the gospel and the very rule of the Christian life, by which he makes and reputes us wise and strong before himself." *WA* 56, 173; *LCC* 15, 20.

attributes therefore describe an activity in which God shares himself with men and allows them to participate in his being. God brings this about in Christ. What is true of the righteousness of God, is also true of the righteousness of Christ—they are one and the same. His lordship consists in the fact that he makes those who are his become what he is.⁴⁸

JUSTIFICATION MEANS THAT GOD IS GOD

God is the only Creator; he gives simply and freely. This is true—as we saw in the previous section—not only of man's natural existence, as discussed under the First Article; it is true in the same strict sense of man's theological existence, his situation and value before God as discussed in the Second and Third Articles. It is faith in God the Creator that thoroughly determines man's understanding of himself—his salvation—no less than of his earthly life. For this reason, Luther can characterize faith in God the Creator as the ultimately decisive truth. In a sermon of 1523 he says: " 'I believe in God the Father, Almighty, creator of heaven and of earth' is, without a doubt, the highest expression of our faith. Whoever genuinely believes this has already been helped, has once again been set right, and arrived at the place from which Adam fell. Few reach the point of completely believing that He is the God who creates and makes all things. For such a man must have died to all things, to good and to evil, to death and to life, to hell and to heaven, and confess from his heart that he is able to do nothing by his own power.' "⁴⁹ Confessing faith in the Cre-

---

⁴⁸ In discussing Psalm 9:8 ("He judges the world with righteousness; he judges the peoples with equity"), Luther says: "We, however, ought to understand 'righteousness' and 'equity' not only as that within Christ which makes him righteous and equitable but also as that within his works by which he justifies the peoples and makes them righteous and as that within his grace by which he distributes justice and equity to them. . . . Thus the kingdom of Christ consists of truth, righteousness, equity, peace, and wisdom not only because he himself is these things but also because those who believe in him are, through him, made truthful, righteous, equitable, peacemakers and wise. . . . Justice and equity . . . are nothing else than the work of the mercy and judgment of God." *WA* 5, 301.

⁴⁹ *WA* 24, 18. The quotation is from the 1527 Cruciger edition, which was prepared on the basis of notes; a somewhat shorter version based on a special 1524 edition of the sermon is found in *WA* 12, 439.

ator thus means confessing one's own inability and that one expects everything from God alone.

At this point two elements of God's creative activity are to be emphasized. First, creating means creating out of nothing. Luther follows his theological tradition in emphasizing this "out of nothing," based on the *ex nihilo* of II Maccabees 7:28 and Romans 4:17. In Luther's revision of the Vulgate of 1529, Romans 4:17 reads, "Things which do not exist He calls into being [*vocat ea quae non sunt, ut sint*]." For Luther this is more than an assertion about the origin of the world. It is an all-inclusive characteristic of God's creating and working.[47] As such, it manifests itself also in the way in which God works men's salvation. In this too God creates everything out of nothing. He takes the man who is nothing before Him and clothes him with the worth of the righteous man.

As a second characteristic of God's creative activity, Luther emphasizes that God makes what he makes under the veil or form of its opposite, and therefore also *out of* its opposite. He creates life under the form of death, yes, by way of death. When he intends to exalt a man, he first humbles him. When he intends to give his gifts to us, he first of all destroys us and what we have and thereby creates room for his gift. Luther here refers to the words of Hannah's prayer (I Sam. 2:6 ff.), "The Lord kills and brings to life; he brings down to Sheol and raises up."[48] The fact that he deals in such a paradoxical way and hides his work under its opposite is also God's "nature." "You exalt us when you humble us. You make us righteous when you make us sinners. You lead

---

[47] "It is his nature to create all things out of nothing. And it is his own most proper nature that he calls those things into being which do not exist." *WA* 40III, 154. "Because He is God it is his [Christ's] proper office to create all things out of nothing." *WA* 40III, 90. Cf. *WA*, TR 6, 6515. "The material which our Lord God uses is nothing and everything." *WA* 39I, 470.

[48] "It is God's nature first to destroy and to bring to nothing whatever is in us before he gives us of his own . . . [here Luther quotes I Sam. 2:6, 7]. By this his most blessed counsel, he makes us capable of receiving his gifts and his works." *WA* 56, 375; *LCC* 15, 240. "For God's working must be hidden and we cannot understand its way. For it is concealed so that it appears to be contrary to what our minds can grasp." *WA* 56, 376; *LCC* 15, 242. "He himself makes nothing out of everything and everything out of nothing. These are the works of the creator and not our own. . . . God destroys everything and makes a man out of nothing, and then he justifies." *WA* 39I, 470. Cf. *WA* 8, 22; *LW* 13, 22.

us to heaven when you cast us into hell. You grant us the victory
when you cause us to be defeated. You give us life when you permit us to be killed."[48] Using the language of Isaiah 28:21, Luther
also describes the way God acts by saying that God does an alien
work [*opus alienum*] in order to come to his own proper work
[*opus proprium*].[50] Thereby God demonstrates that he is God and
shows the majesty of his creating activity which cannot be compared with any human work.

Luther's doctrine of justification must be viewed in the context
of these characteristics of God's creativity. The fact that God creates all things out of nothing and the fact that he works under
the form of the opposite are both applicable here. Luther expressly
includes justification as part of God's paradoxical creative activity.[51]
The justification of the godless appears as a special example of
God's way of doing things. The decisive basis for Luther's understanding of justification by faith alone lies in his understanding of
creation.

Why is a man not righteous before God through his "works,"
that is, through fulfilling the law of God? The first answer to
that question is certainly this: because no individual from the beginning of the world to its end, and not even a Christian, perfectly fulfills God's law.[52] Man's obedience is always imperfect and
blemished.

But this is not Luther's complete and final answer,[53] as is evident from a whole series of statements, many of which derive
from the years 1531 to 1533. Thus Luther explains in his exposition of Galatians 2:16 ("We . . . know that a man is not justified by works of the law") in the large commentary on Galatians.
Even though a man had fulfilled the basic commandments of the
law by fulfilling the double commandment of love, he still would
not thereby be righteous before God. For God simply does not

---

[48] *WA* 31¹, 171; *LW* 14, 95.
[50] *WA* 5, 63; *LW* 14, 335 and at many other places.
[51] "God enjoys bringing light out of darkness and making things out of
nothing, etc. Thus he has created all things and thus he helps those who have
been abandoned, he justifies the sinners, he gives life to the dead, and he saves
the damned." *WA* 40ᴵᴵᴵ, 154.
[52] *WA* 39¹, 51; *LW* 34, 117.
[53] No more than it is Paul's. Paul too says that a man neither can or should
achieve righteousness through the works of the law.

recognize the fulfilling of the law as the way to righteousness.[54] Whether a man attempts to fulfill God's law with his own powers or whether he achieves the righteousness of the law with the aid of God's power is not of decisive significance. Luther expresses this even more sharply than he did in the Galatians commentary in a conversational comment made about the same time in the fall of 1531. Here he comes to terms with Augustine's opinion that although man's attempt to fulfill the law with his own natural powers would not lead to justification, fulfilling the law with the help of the Holy Spirit would. Luther explains that what is at issue is really the validity of this latter righteousness. Luther denies its validity, "If a man were completely and absolutely to fulfill the law through the power of the Holy Spirit, he would still have to appeal for God's mercy; for God has determined that he will save men through Christ and not through the law."[55] Whatever significance the law continues to have, it is not intended to be used as a means to justification and salvation.[56] This means that God wills that under no circumstances is the relationship between himself and men to be determined by the law but solely and absolutely by his free grace received through faith. Man is not only unable to gain merit before God in fact, but he is also unable to do so in principle. In every case, he is dependent on God's unspeakable mercy for his salvation.

Any doctrine of grace or of the Holy Spirit therefore which

---

[54] "Therefore even if you were to do the work of the law according to the commandment, 'You shall love etc.,' you still would not be justified by this." *WA* 40ⁱ, 218; *LW* 26, 122. "Therefore even if it were possible that you could do a work that would fulfill the commandment 'you shall love the Lord your God with all your heart, etc.,' still you would not be righteous before God for this reason . . . for the law does not make righteous even if it is completely carried out and fulfilled (however, it is impossible for human nature to fulfill it)." *WA*, TR 6, 6720.
Since God has not commanded works as a means of being reconciled to him but rather as a way of serving our neighbor, doing works with the intention of reconciling God is not only useless but also an insult to God. "Not only is God not pleased by them, he is even offended." *WA* 40ⁱⁱ, 452; *LW* 12, 397.
[55] "It was Augustine's opinion that the law fulfilled by the powers of reason does not justify, so that moral works do not justify the heathen: but if the Holy Spirit is added, then the works of the law do justify. The question, however, is not whether the law or works of reason justify but whether the law done in the Spirit justifies. We answer that it does not and . . . [here follows the quotation footnoted in the text]." *WA*, TR 1, 85.
[56] "Even if anyone were to fulfill the law, he would nevertheless not thereby be righteous because the purpose of the law is something else than justification." *WA* 39ⁱ, 213.

sees the meaning of the grace of the Holy Spirit in the fact that it creates a supernatural capability of fulfilling the law and thus of earning merit completely misses the meaning of God's will. For this doctrine of grace still turns man's attention to the value of his works and ethical achievement, even though these things are carried out with the help of grace. The fact that there is justification only through Christ, that is, freely and through faith alone, is true independently of the fact that sinful man cannot fulfill the law. It is therefore also valid for someone who might be able to fulfill it with supernatural powers of grace, that is, for the Christian. Fulfilling the law avails as little for justification before God as the failure to fulfill it. God simply does not wish to deal with men in this way.[87]

---

[87] " 'For with you there is forgiveness' [Ps. 130:4]. You have decided that no one should come to you unless he hopes in grace. . . . Our thought should be 'Lord, let Thy mercy and grace lead us; since I am holy and accepted, nothing would help and I ought only to fear.' . . . He wants to be feared and to be given honor in his word that and nothing else." *WA* 15, 415. Cf. *ibid.*, p. 482. A similar view is expressed in the second verse of Luther's hymn, "From Trouble Deep I Cry to Thee":

> With thee counts nothing but thy grace
> To cover all our failing.

The similarity makes it seem likely that the hymn was written at about the same time as this sermon, that is, late in 1523 or early in 1524. Cf. W. Lucke's discussion of the dating of this hymn, *WA* 35, 101; [cf. a similar discussion by Ulrich S. Leupold, *LW* 53, 221.—Trans.] "With thee counts nothing but thy grace" corresponds to "You have decided" in the quotation from the sermon and the sermon's "because I am holy and accepted nothing would help and I ought only to fear" reappears in these lines of the hymn:

> The best life cannot win the race,
> Good works are unavailing.
> Before thee no one glory can,
> And so must tremble every man,
> And live by thy grace only.

Thus this hymn appears to express the same thought which we find in other texts, namely, that God has decided to deal with men only on the basis of grace and mercy even if they achieve the best life and completely fulfill the law—supposing that were possible. God's order of grace thus applies not only to the sinners but also to the righteous. "A man who does works, be he holy, wise, just or whatever he wills, if faith is lacking, he remains under wrath and is damned." *WA* 39[1], 48; *LW* 34, 113. "For God wills to give us life and righteousness but not apart from mercy." *WA* 39[1], 236. "God accepts no works but only faith which grasps the mercy promised in Christ. Therefore he has never at any time given nor wanted to give eternal life because of any works—no matter how glorious and great and how much they may correspond to the divine law—but only on account of his ineffable mercy. It is therefore neither safe nor wise for anyone to say: "I am worthy as I am, O God, and am what I ought to be.' " *WA* 39[1], 238. [These may be the words of one of Luther's students.] Cf. *WA* 6, 210 f.; *PE* 1, 195.

This will of God is rooted in his very nature and in the primal relationship which, as God, he bears to men. God's very deity consists in the fact that he is the creator and giver. The desire to bring "works" as achievements before God is the equivalent of a lie that dishonors God as the giver and creator. First, because man has received from God himself everything which he could thus bring. Taking one's stand before God on the basis of moral or religious achievements would therefore mean nothing less than forgetting that God is God, that is, forgetting the glory of the creator. At every moment, everything that man is and has are his only because God gives them. In such an attempt then, man would deny his total and constant dependence on God's giving. He would thus place himself in the false position of dealing with God as an equal partner, as if God gives something to man and man gives something to God. Such a reciprocal relationship would mean, however, that God is no longer God. Such a life would be an attack on God as God, because it is not at every moment understood and lived as life received from God. "Reason is so obviously foolish that it tries to make something great out of giving God what it has already received from him as a gift." Certainly man should bring to God what God has given him. But it is nonsense for him to bring it as though it were not God's gift and property but his own property and achievement. Bringing achievements before the creator of all gifts and of all powers in this way is an insult to God. There can be only one thing before God, the giving of thanks, and whatever we bring him can only be understood as an expression of thanks.⁵⁵ Thereby it loses its false tone. If a man, however, tries to bring his own achievements before God the

---

⁵⁵ "You cannot give me anything in return except only to thank, praise, and glorify me." *WA* 16, 444. "What is there in me, however, that is not his gift? . . . All things are from God . . . There is nothing left for us to do except to give God thanks; all that we are and have and our life itself are the gifts of God. 'Who has given him something in advance?' [Rom. 11:35]. That is the obvious stupidity of human reason that it accepts gifts and wills to do something great in return. You are not able to give anything to God that was not previously his own. . . . If you have all things from God yet wish to give him [something in return], then your reason condemns God as a robber." (Rörer's notes.) *WA* 40ᴵᴵ, 452; cf. *LW* 12, 397. "But we cannot return anything to God that is not already his own and that does not belong to him." *WA* 40ᴵᴵ, 433 (in Veit Dietrich's edition of Rörer's notes).

element of thanksgiving is lost.[59] In this connection, it should not be forgotten that no man gives thanks to the giver of all good things by his own power; rather this too is God's gift to us. He not only gives us the gifts for which we thank him, but he also gives us the gratitude.[60] Whenever man seeks to live before God on some basis other than forgiveness, no true fear of God remains. God, however, says, "I will remain God; I will be loved, honored, and feared!" And so that he may both remain God and be feared, he forgives man and orders him to live solely by this forgiveness. For this is what it means to fear God as God: to recognize him as the one who both gives us and wants to give us everything for nothing and who desires nothing else from us than that we allow him to do this giving.[61] Whoever will not accept the gifts of God's

---

[59] "These offerings of works spell the elimination of thank-offerings, which cannot exist alongside them." *WA* 31[I], 252; *LW* 14, 34. Cf. *WA* 6, 237; *PE* 1, 233, where Luther says of the unbelievers who do not want to need God's grace that they "will not let him be a God who gives to everyone and takes nothing in return." Another example of how in his doctrine of justification Luther is ultimately concerned for God's glory as the creator who creates *ex nihilo* is to be found in *WA* 40[I], 131; cf. *LW* 26, 66: "We take all righteousness from men and ascribe it to the Creator who creates out of nothing."
[60] *WA* 40[II], 453; cf. *LW* 12, 397.
[61] In his lecture on Psalm 130, Luther says: "It is good therefore that your righteousness consists in your forgiving and forbearing mercy, for thus you remain God; otherwise you would lose your divinity and be of no significance . . . if God would be lost and a new one created who would sit in his throne and think the sort of thoughts that the Carthusians think. Never let that happen. For what follows from the righteousness of the law is nothing else than true idolatry; and the righteousness of works is idolatry itself because it creates another God. In doing this I would do nothing but worship myself and say, as the Carthusians and all sorts of work righteous people do, 'I have preached and I have suffered many things.' So what? I am an idolator when I adore myself with my own works, because I think that God takes them into consideration. That imagination is an idol of my heart. Therefore the work righteous man is an idolator because he takes God away and God loses his divinity. There can therefore be no other results than that God through works loses his own being, name, honor, majesty, and great goodness. So it is that God says, 'I will remain God. I will be loved, honored and feared. And as for you, you ought to be justified by grace and not look down on me or exalt yourself above me in pride.' God has simply decreed that unless the doctrine of the forgiveness of sins, of grace, and of propitiation continues to stand, idolatry will reign; for he says '[There is forgiveness] with thee [that thou mayest be feared' Ps. 130, 4]." *WA* 40[III], 356. "Otherwise one simply cannot have a God; it is impossible to combine having a God and being righteous through the law. For fearing and honoring God on the one hand and wanting to be righteous through the law on the other are more antagonistic to each other than fire and water, than the devil and God. . . . Where there is no forgiveness there is no God, but idolatry pure and simple remains. The righteousness of works is in and of itself the purest idolatry. . . . But the chief art of Christians is to know that forgiveness remains with God and that it has gone out into all the

free grace for nothing takes away the glory of God's being God.[62] "It is presumptuous to bring to God, as though it were your own, something you have received from him. This is the worst sin of all."[63]

Whoever wishes to be righteous before God through his ethical achievement assumes the place of the creator. Creating righteousness, destroying sin, and giving life—these are all the work of the creator alone. "He has made us and not we ourselves"—this statement from Psalm 100 is not only true of the gift of earthly life in the first creation, it is equally true of the regeneration to eternal life in the second creation. For this reason, every synergistic doctrine is a completely distorted concept of God and of what our activity can and ought to mean. The idea that we should and could seek fellowship with God through our own achievement and thus gain eternal life is not only foolishness because we as sinners are not able to do it; it is also, as Luther expressly states, godlessness and blasphemy, because we thereby attack God's position as God. Man's claim to have brought something before God which secures his position with God means nothing less than that he puts himself in the place of God and makes himself his own god and creator. For he dares thereby to do what God has reserved for himself alone: to create righteousness and life. The desire to become righteous through one's own works is the equivalent of reversing the biblical word and preaching, "It is not God who made us but we ourselves"—both are equally blasphemous.[64]

---

world, so that God indeed remains if we believe that he is a redeeming and forgiving God." *WA* 40ᴵᴵᴵ, 358. Cf. the following statements from Veit Dietrich's edition of Luther's lecture: "For the prophet says that taking away grace also removes the fear of God [Ps. 130:4]. What does it mean to fear God except to worship and adore him and to know what his benefits are and how to obey him?" *WA* 40ᴵᴵᴵ, 358.

[62] "For God is he who dispenses his gifts freely to all, and this is his praise of his own deity. But he cannot assert his deity in dealing with self-righteous people who are unwilling to accept grace and eternal life from him freely but want to earn it by their own works. They simply want to rob him of the glory of his deity." *WA* 40ᴵ, 224; *LW* 26, 127 (Rörer's edition). "It is God's nature to give to everyone and help everyone; if I know this, I have the true God, but if I attribute anything to myself then I rob God of his honor." *WA* 17ᴵ, 233.

[63] *WA* 9, 462 f.

[64] *WA* 40ᴵᴵ, 466. Cf. Veit Dietrich's edition of this: "It is very comforting that God does not want sacrifices but condemns and rejects this highest act of worship if it is done with the purpose of turning away his wrath and making us righteous. Here the mercy of God is being commended to us, freely forgiv-

Luther's criticism of moralism is therefore characterized by its theocentricity. Its standard is the fact that God is really God. Moralism is regarded as idolatry and blasphemy. "Work righteousness is actually and essentially idolatry."[65] Man abandons the genuine reality of God and in its place sets the idol which he has made for himself. He constructs a picture of God's nature and will which corresponds to his own moral emptiness[66] but has nothing to do with what God really wants; it is the picture of an idol. The true God is the God of reconciliation through Jesus Christ, the God who alone gives and creates. The way of moralism is not only an ethical illusion, since no man can keep the commandments; it is primarily a religious fiction, because the God with whom one thinks he is dealing in this way is nothing but a figment of the imagination of one's own heart. God is robbed of his true deity and therewith set aside as God. The ethical man also practices idolatry insofar as he does not find his ultimate security in God but in himself and in his own achievements. In his eyes, these seem to possess an unconditional value which God must take into account. The ethical man therefore worships both himself and his achievements at the same time. He is his own idol.

---

ing sins and justifying us. Those who look for righteousness by their own works do nothing but try to become their own makers or creators. . . . Hence it is not only a false but a wicked notion to maintain that God can be so pleased by our works that he gives us eternal life or righteousness." *WA* 40ᴵᴵ, 456-57; *LW* 12, 402. "But they have not seen this at all and have made us sinners ten times worse than murderers. For they have attributed to me the work of the divine majesty: he alone destroys sin, makes righteous, and gives life. That is creating—and they tell me to do it. They thereby put me in the place of God and make an idol out of me—for they give me the works of the divine majesty himself." *WA* 40ᴵ, 442; cf. *LW* 26, 283. "Is this not a blasphemous and monstrous exaltation of our own works in place of and above God's grace? [The following sentence is not found in the English translation.] Is this not the same as taking God's divinity from him and denying Christ?" *WA* 31ᴵ, 244; *LW* 14, 26. In view of the fact that the righteous are called a new creation in Scripture (II Cor. 5:17) Luther asks, "But who can bear this blasphemy, that our works beget us or that we are the creatures of our works?" . . . In that case it would be permissible to say, contrary to the prophet, 'We have made ourselves and God has not created us.' [Ps. 100:3] . . . It is accordingly as blasphemous to say that a man is his own god, creator or producer, as it is blasphemous to say that he is justified by his own works." *WA* 39ᴵ, 48; *LW* 34, 114. "You see yourself but not God as trustworthy; that is blasphemy of God." *WA* 17ᴵ, 233; cf. *LW* 12, 187.

[65] "Grace cannot stand it when we want to give to God or establish merit or pay him with our works. This is the greatest of blasphemies and idolatries and is nothing less than the denial and even ridicule of God." *WA* 31ᴵ, 252; *LW* 14, 34.

[66] *WA* 40ᴵᴵ, 466.

Moralism and true fear of God thus exclude each other. "Desire for the righteousness of the law and having a God cannot possibly be combined. There is a greater contradiction between fearing or honoring God and wanting to be righteous according to the law than there is between fire and water or between Satan and God." This is the way in which Luther understood Psalm 130:4: " 'There is forgiveness with thee that thou mayest be feared,' that is, that you may remain God.'" This verse of the psalm constantly made Luther aware of the theocentric meaning of justification. This verse was his decisive scriptural basis. Ethical pride indicates the loss of the fear of God and hence also the denial that God is God.

The denial corresponds to the assertion. Not only Luther's criticism of moralism but also his evaluation of faith is theocentrically determined. As moralism is idolatry, so faith in God's promise in Jesus Christ is the true worship of God. Faith is the proper way of relating to God, not simply in the present because man necessarily breaks down along the way of works, but from the very beginning, because of what God is. "No one can boast before you," no one. This is true not only because everyone is a sinner but because God is God and man is man. We are to believe not only because nothing else remains for sinners but because God is God and man cannot honor him as God in any other way than by believing—because faith is the fulfilment of the First Commandment." Faith is the only attitude of man which corresponds to God's nature, God's deity. God's true godliness consists in the fact that he is the creator and that he creates out of nothing and even out of its opposite. Faith corresponds exactly to this. Faith expects something from God where nothing can be seen; it waits expectantly against all appearance. God's deity and man's faith correspond. Faith is completely directed to God as God; one can only completely believe and trust in him who is essentially God." Again, man cannot grasp, recognize, and honor God as God in any other way than with faith alone. Faith alone truly obeys and worships

---

" *WA* 40ᴵᴵᴵ, 360. "If I know that you forgive me then you remain, but if I do not know then I have lost the true God." *Ibid.*
" "Faith is the true worship and the main work of the First Commandment." *WA* 5, 394. Cf. *WA* 6, 516.
" *WA* 37, 42.

God as he really is. It is characteristic enough of the theocentric character of the doctrine of justification that Luther, like Paul, views faith in terms of obedience and the worship of God. It is the only form of worship which pleases God. Faith alone is the true fear of God."[70]

This theocentric understanding of justification and of faith is the decisive standard which Luther uses to distinguish between true and false religion. The religions known to him fall into two basic categories: One includes all the religions outside the gospel—including the Roman distortion of the gospel and even the God-commanded sacrificial system as the Jews understood it; the other includes only the gospel, the religion of faith. No matter how much religions of the first type differ from one another, they all agree that a man must bring something to God and that he dare not trust in unconditional reconciliation and justification. Luther places Judaism, Islam, the papacy, monasticism, the enthusiasts and the Swiss all in the same category as encouraging presumptuous human pride, idolatry, and contradicting genuine fear of God (in the sense of Psalm 130:4). God does not want this sort of false worship; the religion of unconditional faith in God's mercy is the sole possibility of truly worshiping God. Luther's theocentric viewpoint thus draws a line of division through all the religions of the world.[71]

Luther explicitly asserts that the theocentric character of his doctrine is the criterion of its truth. His doctrine is proved to be true by the fact that it lets God be God, magnifies his name, and

---

[70] "We are to sacrifice nothing else to God than to trust and hope in him." Then Luther discusses God's "nature" as the one who creates out of nothing and concludes, "Therefore whoever consents to this nature and follows it is a right man. He watches and hopes even if he does not see." *WA* 40ᴵᴵᴵ, 154.

[71] "The sacrifice to God, divinely instituted by Moses and approved by the prophets and the fathers, is of no value. . . . Distinguish, therefore, Christ from all the religions of the world. Christ is to be placed above Moses. The forgiveness of sins and grace are greater than the whole world's act of worship." *WA* 40ᴵᴵ, 451; cf. *LW* 12, 396 f.

"Papism, Mohammedanism, monasticism, the newest heresy, Zwingli, and Oecolampad are all idolatry." This is the order in Rörer's notes. According to Dietrich's edition, Luther included Judaism in the list. *WA* 40ᴵᴵᴵ, 359. "When a man loses Christ and the only Savior is no longer in his heart, then all faiths become one faith [*da wird aus allem Glauben ein Glaube*]. For they all agree in this one point that they do not have true faith and build on something else." *WA* 37, 59.

gives glory to him and not to man.[72] Luther finds this criterion in what Paul says in Galatians 1:10. Luther translates, "Am I now preaching in the service of men or of God?" Luther uses this criterion of the truth of a theology in order to validate his own. His theology exalts God and not man.[73]

Luther's doctrine of justification by faith alone is thus completely based on his principle that God alone is the creator. Only this understanding of justification treats the creatureliness of man with the full seriousness which Luther feels it demands.[74] The justification of the godless is the most sublime of all the specific examples of the way in which God creates out of nothing and under a contrary form.

---

[72] "I can say, 'Thus my teaching stands, and so it is correct.' It is a good teaching. This is evident from the fact that it builds upon the Lord Christ, it lets God be our Lord God, and it gives God the glory. This teaching is correct, and it cannot go wrong." *WA* 17^1, 32; *LW* 12, 187.

[73] In his exegesis of Gal. 1:10, Luther says: "Thus I make it obvious that by my preaching I am not seeking the favor or praise of men, but that I am seeking the grace and glory of God and to be reconciled with God." *WA* 40^1, 121; *LW* 26, 58. See also the sections following this quotation. "I still know this for certain, that what I teach is not from man but from God. That is, I attribute everything solely to God and nothing at all to men. . . . And it is true that the doctrine of the gospel takes away all glory, wisdom, righteousness, etc., from men and gives it solely to the Creator, who makes all things out of nothing. Furthermore, it is far safer to ascribe too much to God than to men." *WA* 40^1, 131 f.; *LW* 26, 66. Cf. *WA* 40^1, 589; *LW* 26, 387.

[74] "Where did I come from? Where did you come from? We certainly did not make ourselves since we didn't even exist. There must be someone who made us. And now we want to go to our Lord God and strike a bargain with him: We will sell him our work in exchange for his giving us heaven? Isn't it shameful that the creature exalts himself so high that he thinks that he can make a deal with his creator? And all this because we do not believe that God is the creator. If we believed that he were the creator we would proceed in quite a different way. But no one believes that he is the creator (even if he says he does) although our conscience convinces us that God is the creator of us all. Now if we had been created by another God then it would make sense for us to come before God and say, 'Lord God, accept me because of my works; for I come to you from someone else and you have not made me.' " *WA*, TR 5, 5492.

11

GOD'S WILL FOR MEN

THE TITLE of this section could also be "The Law of God." It is preferable, however, to reserve this title for our discussion of the relationship between law and gospel in view of sin. God's will for men, although expressed in the commandments, bridges the distinction between law and gospel. As a summons to salvation, it is at one and the same time gospel and law.

God's will confronts men in the commandments. The most important and decisive is the First Commandment. Luther considered the First Commandment one of the forms in which the gospel comes. He thought it very significant that the gospel immediately also confronts us in the form of a commandment of God. "I am the Lord your God," expresses the essence of the gospel. These words summon us to faith. "Let me alone be your God."[1] This summons has all the seriousness of a command. Luther understood and recognized that the statement of the gospel in the form of a commandment helps faith in every time of doubt and despair; and he used it in this way both for himself and for others. At the time of his inner spiritual struggles in the monastery, his confessor could give Luther's conscience no rest either through the absolution or through other comforts. Then his "teacher" replied to Luther's complaints about temptation by saying, "My son, what are you doing? Do you know that the Lord himself has commanded us to hope?" These words were the turning point. Luther reports, "I was so strengthened through this one word 'commanded' that I now knew I must believe the absolution."[2] The form of the commandment in which the gospel here confronted him helped him to believe. This experience remained determinative for his pastoral relationships to others. He constantly directs the doubting and the despairing to the First Commandment: God has commanded you

[1] *WA* 30ᴵ, 133; *BC*, 365.
[2] *WA* 40ᴵᴵ, 412; *LW* 12, 370.

to hope and to believe in him; if you doubt and despair, you are sinning against the First Commandment.[*]

The First Commandment is "the basic, the greatest, the best, from which all the others flow."[4] For this reason the "work" of the First Commandment, that is, "faith or trust in God's grace at all times" is the first, the greatest, and the best "work" from which all others flow. The First Commandment makes a claim on "man's whole heart and demands that he put all trust in God alone and in no one else." "Herein God is honored as God," that is, "This is the true honor and true worship which please God."[5] Whoever believes him when he promises and whoever hopes in him alone therewith trusts in him as God, in his power, his truthfulness, and his goodness.[6] The purity of heart which God wills consists in this faith. And this alone makes everything else we do pure. "Without faith no heart is pure; and without purity of heart no work is true and pure."[7] Fulfilling the First Commandment includes fulfilling all the others; and no other commandment is truly fulfilled unless the First Commandment is fulfilled.[8]

---

[*] "How are you acting? God does not want you to despair: rather he has commanded you to hope and to trust; he wills that you should worship and have confidence in his mercy. This is the First Commandment." *WA* 40^{III}, 343. "God wants you to hope in him and believe in Christ who has died and risen for you and he commands you through my mouth and the mouth of St. Paul to do this. . . . If you doubt this and despair, you sin against the First Commandment for God wants you to believe that he is your God." *WA* 39^I, 428.

[4] *WA* 6, 209; *PE* 1, 195. *WA* 28, 510. *WA* 30^I, 180, 324, 409.

[5] *WA* 30^I, 134; *BC*, 366. "The best and most appropriate worship of God is to trust and to believe; compared with this all outward worship is child's play. And he demands nothing more than a heart that believes in him." *WA* 37, 42. "You see that faith cannot be compared with anything else and that its power cannot be described, for it gives glory to God. . . . This is the highest thing that can be attributed to him. To attribute glory to God is to believe in him and to regard him as truthful, wise, righteous, merciful, and almighty, in short, to acknowledge him as the source and donor of every good." *WA* 40^I, 360; *LW* 26, 227. Cf. above, pp. 127 f.

[6] "Giving glory to God and worshiping him consists in sincere faith, sturdy hope, and perfect love of God. . . . Briefly summarized, worshiping God is nothing else than glorifying God. To glorify God is nothing else than to believe in him, to hope in him, and to love him; for whoever believes him treats him as true and through this ascribes truth to him. Whoever hopes in him believes that he is wise and good, that is, one who is able to help and to save; and through this attributes to God the power by which he is able, the wisdom by which he knows how, and the goodness by which he wills to help; this is what it means to truly be God and to truly have a God." *WA* 5, 103 f. Cf. *WA* 7, 25; *RW* 1, 362; cf. *LW* 31, 350.

[7] *WA*, *DB* 7, 186 (the marginal note to Gal. 5:3).

[8] *WA* 51, 204; *LW* 13, 150.

The faith in which we honor God as God expresses itself particularly in praise and thanksgiving. This is the sole sacrifice of the New Testament, the noblest and highest worship of God.*

Prayer, together with thanksgiving and praise, is the manifestation of our trust in God. Luther repeatedly says that we should bring our petitions to God because he commands us to do so. We are not free to choose whether we will or will not call upon God in both the external and internal troubles and needs of our lives. On the contrary, God wills to be honored and treated as God by our turning to him in our need.[10] Certainly, we need to call on God in every time of need and temptation. But the evil spirit tries to prevent that with all his power. He also tries to make us doubt that we are worthy to bring our requests before the sublime majesty of God. The only ultimate remedy against this is to remember that God not only promises to hear prayer but also commands us to pray on penalty of his "eternal wrath and displeasure." We must drive out the devil's suggestions with God's commandment; this and nothing else makes the devil stop. Courageous faith asks God for something because it trusts in his promise; it receives its final, decisive, and effective motivating power from obedience to God's gracious but very serious commandment. Luther expresses this most forcefully in his introduction to the Lord's Prayer in the *Large Catechism.* "It is our duty to pray because God has commanded it. . . . Prayer, therefore, is as strictly and solemnly commanded as all the other commandments, such as having no other god, not killing, not stealing, etc. . . . Call upon God in every need. This he requires of us; he has not left it to our choice. It is our duty and obligation to pray if we want to be Christians. . . . It is not left to my choice here whether to pray or not, but it is my duty and obligation . . . all our prayers must be based on obedience to God."[11]

"Faith manifests itself further in our desire to fulfill God's com-

---

* *WA* 31¹, 59. "We cannot perform a greater or finer deed, or a nobler service to God, than to offer thanks." *WA* 31¹, 76; *LW* 14, 51.

[10] *WA* 6, 223, 235; *PE* 1, 213, 230. "At His command and promise I kneel down, raise my eyes to heaven, and beg for comfort and help. Thereby he is honored as the true God, from whom I implore help and comfort; for a true God deserves that I so ask." *WA* 31¹, 98; *LW* 14, 61.

[11] *WA* 30¹, 193 ff.; *BC*, 420 f., 423.

mandments with joyful obedience. Faith makes us ready to suffer all evil for his sake and to risk body and life, property and honor, for him."[12]

The commandment to love our neighbor stands beside the commandment to love God. Basically these are not two commandments but one and the same. God directs me to my neighbor. He wants nothing from us for himself, only that we believe in him. He does not need our work for himself.[13] He does need it, however, for our neighbor.[14] Loving the neighbor becomes the way in which we love God; and in serving the neighbor we serve God himself. God is present for me in my neighbor. "You will find Christ in every street and just outside your door. Do not stand around staring at heaven and say, 'Oh, if I could just once see our Lord God, how I would do everything possible for him.' "[15] For Luther this is included in the incarnation of Christ. By taking upon himself the human form of a servant, Christ wished to take our love which is falsely directed up toward heaven and turn it completely downward in love to our neighbor. Our faith is not to seek

---

[12] *WA* 31^1, 433; *LW* 14, 111.

[13] "We . . . cannot deal with God otherwise than through faith in the word of his promise. He does not desire works, nor has he needed them; rather we deal with men and ourselves on the basis of works." *WA* 6, 516; *LW* 36, 42.

[14] "God is satisfied with my faith. . . . Therefore he wants me to do my works to benefit my neighbor. . . . He doesn't need my works at all. . . . God is rich enough himself without me and without my works. He lets me live on earth, however, so that I may show the same kind of friendship to my neighbor that God has graciously shown to me. . . . Thus God fuses the two commandments into each other so that there is only one work and only one love. Whatever we do for our neighbor by preaching, teaching, clothing him, and feeding him is all done to Christ himself." In Rörer's notes: "Therefore the love which I have toward God is the same which I have for my neighbor; for through his love, God directs us to our neighbor." *WA* 20, 513.

[15] *WA* 20, 514. In Rörer's notes we read, "The world is full of God." The printed text then reads: "If you wish to love me . . . help the poor by doing everything that you want done to yourself. . . . Then you have truly and completely loved me. But watch carefully that you do not forget about me; I will be close enough to you; I will be there in every poor man who needs your help and teaching—I myself will be present in him." *WA* 20, 515. "There [in the suffering and needy neighbor] we should find and love God; that is, we should serve the neighbor and do good to him, whenever we want to do good to God and serve him; thus the commandment to love God is fully and completely subsumed in the commandment to love our neighbor. . . . It was for this reason that he laid aside his divine form and took on the form of a servant so that he might draw our love for him down to earth and attach it to our neighbor. But we let our neighbors lie here and meanwhile stare into heaven and pretend to have great love for God and to serve Him greatly." *WA* 17^{II}, 99. "To love God is to love the neighbor" *WA*, TR 5, 5906.

God's deity in heaven but in the humanity of Christ; the same is true of our love. Since God has become man, our love for God should show itself as love for men. God is very close to us, that is, in men. This is true no less for our love than for our faith. Thus Luther's understanding of love is completely dominated by his faith in the incarnation.

Just as God neither needs nor wants me to offer anything directly to him except my faith, so I need do nothing else in order to receive salvation from God except that I receive his grace in faith; that is my salvation. I need nothing more for salvation. But my neighbor needs my works; he still does not have enough. For his sake—not for mine or the sake of my own salvation—I must use my life to serve my neighbor.[16] For this reason no one should live his life for himself. "Every man is created and born for the sake of others."[17] This means that everyone is born to love and to serve his neighbor. "Everything that we have must be used to serve. What is not used to serve is being stolen."[18] If I do not use everything that I have to serve my neighbor, I rob him of what I owe him according to God's will. For this reason, Luther on several occasions says it very sharply: "Cursed be the life which someone lives for himself and not for his neighbor. And again, blessed be that life which a man does not live for himself but for his neighbor, serving him with teaching, with admonition, with help, or whatever it may be."[19]

Love of the neighbor shares this characteristic of faith: The man who loves is outside of himself and lives in another. In faith he does not live for himself, does not rely on himself but on God's

---

[16] "Yes, you need do nothing as though it were necessary for your salvation, for the forgiveness of sins, or for the quieting of your conscience. You have all that you need in your faith. But your neighbor does not yet have all that he needs and he is the one you must help. It is for this reason that God lets you go on living . . . so that you with your life may serve not your sinful self but your neighbor." *WA* 10ᴵᴵᴵ, 168. "All that we do must be designed to help our neighbor, for each one has all he needs for himself in his faith. All our other deeds and the rest of our life are available so that we may use them in serving our neighbor out of unconstrained love . . . for I have enough of all things in Christ through my faith." *WA* 7, 35 f.; *RW* 1, 376 f.; cf. *LW* 31, 366 f.

[17] *WA* 21, 346.

[18] *WA* 12, 470.

[19] *WA* 10ᴵᴵᴵ, 98. Cf. *ibid.*, p. 168. "For cursed and condemned is every sort of life lived and sought for the benefit and good of self; cursed are all works not done in love." *WA* 11, 272; *LW* 45, 118.

mercy. In love he does not live for himself but for others. Thus the man who believes and loves lives in a particular form of "ecstasy."[20]

Luther finds the original pattern and standard of love and service to the neighbor in Christ, that is, in God's dealing with us in Christ. I should relate to my neighbor as Christ relates to me (Luther refers to Philippians 2:5). I should "become a Christ to my neighbor and be for him what Christ is for me."[21] This principle is to be followed in all of life and includes everything that is "necessary, useful and a blessing" to my neighbor.[22] It stretches from external help to the most heartfelt intercession.[23] All we own belongs to our neighbor insofar as it is not necessary for the bare maintenance of our own life. "In God's sight everything which a man has left over and does not use to help his neighbor is an illegal and stolen possession; for before God one ought to give, to lend, and to let everything be taken away from him."[24] Luther does not regard mere possession as theft. It can, however, become that when our possessions are not administered according to this rule. Every inner talent and capability, our own godliness and righteousness, and our own capacity in every sense of the word, also belongs to the neighbor. "For the sake of love we ought to help our neighbor in every situation. If he is poor, we ought to serve him with our possessions. If he is in dishonor, we should cover him with our honor. If he is a sinner, we should adorn him with our righteousness and piety. For this is what Christ has done for us."[25] Only then do we manifest that high quality of love which God demands. Everything that I have belongs to my neighbor. All

---

[20] "A Christian lives not in himself, but in Christ and his neighbor—in Christ by faith, and in his neighbor by love. By faith he rises above himself unto God; from God he stoops below himself by love, and yet remains always in God and in divine love." *WA* 7, 38; *RW* 1, 379; cf. *LW* 31, 371.

[21] *WA* 7, 35; *RW* 1, 376. "As our heavenly Father has in Christ freely come to our aid, we also ought freely to help our neighbor through our body and its works, and each one should become as it were a Christ to the other that we may be Christ to one another and Christ may be the same in all, that is, that we may be truly Christians." *WA* 7, 66; *LW* 31, 367 f.

[22] *WA* 7, 36; cf. *LW* 31, 367.

[23] *WA* 11, 76.

[24] *WA* 10[III], 275.

[25] *WA* 10[III], 217. "Let the virgin use her piety to serve the prostitute, the wise man to serve a fool, the pious man to serve a sinner, the righteous man to serve the erring." *WA* 10[III], 238. Cf. *WA* 11, 76 and *WA* 12, 470.

riches should flow toward those who are poor. Love eliminates the
distance between the righteous and the sinner. The righteous man
does not want to stand anywhere else than beside the sinner. Love
shares both property and burdens. I help my neighbor bear his
burden and thus give him a share in what God has given me.[26] My
proper place before God is beside the man who bears a heavy burden, who is fallen, and who is guilty; I even take his place for him.
Thus love is always completely involved in serving others with all
that I have. It thus becomes unlimited substitution, that is brotherly and vicarious participation in his condition. To sum it up, the
rule is: "Completely give yourself to and serve" your neighbor
"wherever he needs you and you are able," even to the point of
suffering and dying for him.[27]

God's commandment thus demands love. We should love—this
determines not only the act we are commanded to do but also its
personal reality in us. God's commandment furthermore demands
that our will be motivated *only* through God's good will, that is,
through pure pleasure in his law,[28] and that it be entirely our *own*
will.

God's commandment must therefore be fulfilled for its own
sake. Negatively stated, this means that obedience may not occur
as a means to an end but rather must be pure obedience, which
is meaningful because it corresponds to God's good will. Its basis
must thus be strictly theonomous and not heteronomous. Luther
thereby differentiates true obedience from that motivated by earthly
goals, for example, by considerations of honor and shame in human
society. Regardless of the fact that one may feel that the appeal
to honor and shame is necessary in training young people, such an
appeal is inconsistent with the essence of God's commandment and

---

[26] "Remember that all the good things of God should flow from one man
to another, and become common to all, so that each one may be as concerned
for his neighbor as for his own self. All good things come to us from Christ,
who has received us into His own life as if he had been what we are. From
us they should flow to those who are in need of them. This should be so completely true that I must offer even my faith and righteousness before God on
behalf of my neighbor, to blot out his sins, and take them upon myself. I must
act as if they were my own, just as Christ has done for us all. Indeed, that is
the nature of love if it is genuine." *WA* 7, 37; *RW* 1, 379; cf. *LW* 31, 371.
[27] *WA* 10¹,², 38.
[28] *WA* 5, 33; *LW* 14, 295.

the true obedience God wills. Whoever is concerned with true obedience does not need such a motive. He allows himself to be moved, or at least he should allow himself to be moved, through God's commandment itself, that is, through fearing, trusting, and loving God. Activity that is determined by concern for honor and shame may be good in the eyes of the world, but in God's judgment it is not good and counts for nothing.*

Obedience may not be used to gain salvation in the world to come. Luther's description of the children of God corresponds to God's commandment: "God's children do what is good because they want to and not for selfish reasons. They seek no reward except to be praised by God and to do his will. They would be willing to do the good even if—which is not possible—there were neither a heaven or a hell."³⁰ God will reward obedience; but whoever obeys because he desires this reward does not really obey and therefore loses the reward. Such people do not seek God's glory and will; they selfishly seek their own welfare even in relationship to God.⁸¹ How is it possible that such people could achieve the goal that is set for man, the kingdom of God and its blessedness? One neither can nor may understand and desire the kingdom of God as the fulfilment of his natural desire for happiness. The exact opposite is true. This kingdom itself is blessedness. ("We are blessed when God rules in us and we are his kingdom.") Therefore we must desire that God rule in us, which most certainly is our blessedness, for its own sake and not as a means to salvation. Otherwise we will receive neither the kingdom nor salvation. For the latter is only the result of the kingdom.⁸² Salvation is the other side of God's will. We cannot desire salvation for its own sake. To sum it up, we should be godly

---

* *WA* 6, 220; *PE* 1, 209.
⁸⁰ *WA* 18, 694; *BOW*, 182. "Moreover, this desire is the pure desire of the heart, and that pleasure does not ask what the Lord promises or threatens but only that the law is holy, just, and good." *WA* 5, 33; *LW* 14, 295.
⁸¹ "Indeed, should they do good works to obtain the kingdom, they never would obtain it, but would belong to the number of the ungodly, who with an evil, mercenary eye, seek the things of self even in God." *WA* 18, 694; *BOW*, 182.
⁸² *WA* 2, 98.

purely for the sake of being godly, and that means for God's sake.[33]

Luther expresses his sharp rejection of eudaemonism very clearly when he says: Whatever we do because we fear the punishment which the law threatens or because we desire the reward which the law promises is not our own work but rather the work of the law which has wrung it out of us with threatening or cajoling. Such activity does not express our own personal will but rather the psychological compulsion of the law insofar as it threatens or cajoles us.[34] Luther thus understands Paul's concept of "the works of the law" in a negative sense. We do not put our hearts into them. God, however, demands works that are really our own. "Everyone must be saved through his own works."[35]

Luther's interpretation of God's commandment is thus strictly opposed to all ethical eudaemonism, including the religious transcendental variety. The will of the man who does what the law commands must be completely and purely oriented to the good and to God's good will. His motivation must be pure and simple, he must not be seeking his own happiness out of the corner of his eye. Kant incorporated the severity of this demand into his practical philosophy: A man's activity should be determined solely by his respect for the moral law. But it is at this point that Kant and Luther go their separate ways. Kant knows that the heart and center of the Bible's moral law is the commandment to love God and the neighbor. And he explains that loving God means liking to do his commandments and that loving the neighbor means liking to do everything that is our duty to him. The law, however, cannot command us to like it but only to try to like it. "Liking it," however, is an ideal which we should strive to achieve in a

---

[33] "We ought not be devout in order to earn or to avoid something. All such are hirelings, servants, and paid workers; not willing children and heirs. These latter are devout and pure for the sake of godliness itself, for God's own sake. For God is the essence of righteousness, truth, goodness, wisdom, and sanctity. A man who does not seek the mere order [outward form] of religion, seeks and finds God himself. But the man who seeks gain, or flees pain, never finds God. He makes a God out of his gains. For the very aim or ground of a man's action is, in itself, his god." *WA* 7, 801; *RW* 2, 123.

[34] *WA* 2, 492; *LW* 27, 224. *WA* 10I,1, 450 f.

[35] *WA* 10I,1, 451.

constant but endless process of drawing closer to it.[36] But what is only an ideal for Kant (for a human being always requires "self-compulsion, that is, that he be innerly driven to do what he does not entirely like to do—but a creature can never achieve this high level of morality") is precisely what Luther sees as God's clear commandment to men. And it is commanded not as a goal toward which we are constantly to strive without ever reaching it but rather as what we should be right here and now. An ideal can wait, but a commandment cannot.

Kant thus modifies the sharpness of Jesus' commandment because he sees us as we actually are and that we fail to achieve the fulfilment of so high a demand. Luther lets the commandment say what it says even though no one is able to fulfill it. God demands that we should love today. This means that God's commandment should be obeyed with a joyful heart, in a spirit of freedom.[37] God does not accept "self-compulsion" as valid. The total man must obey with his feelings, his involuntary drives, and his emotional desires. God not only demands obedience in the conscious will but also in "the bottom of the heart."[38] We are not allowed to feel as if we would rather have never known the commandment and wish it did not exist. We must rather rejoice in it without even thinking about it. Whatever we do not do spontaneously with all our powers as though our doing it could be taken as a matter of course—that is, any moral actions which express only our conscious will in contradiction to what we secretly desire—has no value in God's sight. "How is it possible for a work which comes

---

[36] Kant says that the law which requires that we love God and neighbor is similar to "every moral prescription of the Gospel." It requires complete perfection; therefore although "as an ideal of holiness it is unattainable by any creature, it is yet an archetype which we should strive to approach and to imitate in an uninterrupted infinite progress." Immanuel Kant, *Critique of Practical Reason and Other Writings in Moral Philosophy.* Trans. and ed. by Lewis White Beck (Chicago: The University of Chicago Press, 1949), p. 190.

[37] *WA* 56, 205; *LCC* 15, 55. *WA* 2,500. *WA* 5, 564.

[38] *WA*, DB 7, 3; *LW* 25, 366. "If, now, there is no willing pleasure in the good, then the inmost part is not set on the law of God." *WA*, DB 7, 5; *LW* 35, 366. "But where the heart is not in the work, there is no faithfulness and no righteous work." *WA* 31¹, 421; *LW* 13, 381. "It is not as if God wanted these works done just for their own sake; he wants them done gladly and willingly. But if the gladness and willingness are absent, then, in God's sight the works are dead." *WA* 7, 800; *RW* 2, 123.

from a reluctant and recalcitrant heart to please God?"[38] "You must have as great a desire for chastity as you had for fornication."[40] That means that the good must become as natural for us as the evil was for our "old man." And we must move toward it with all our being and the same basic drives. Joy is a necessary part of doing right.[41]

---

[38] *WA*, DB 7, 7; *LW* 35, 368.

[40] *WA* 10ᴵᴵᴵ, 88.

[41] "They must be ready to do good works, in the sense that they do them with a willing mind." *WA* 56, 205; *LCC* 15, 55. Complete willingness presupposes that concupiscence has been completely extinguished. This first occurs fully in the life to come. But it begins now. "Works of peace and wellbeing . . . are done with the fullest ease and pleasantness after concupiscense has been extinguished—as will be the case in the life to come. Here there is only a beginning." *WA* 2, 493; *LW* 27, 224.

12

MAN AS A SINNER

MAN'S KNOWLEDGE OF SIN

MAN DOES not, by himself, understand his own sinfulness, at
least not in its real nature and depth. Admittedly he has
by nature a partial knowledge of sin. God's law is written by nature in his heart. Insofar as he accepts it, he also knows from it
that he transgresses it and sins.[1] But just as without the word and
the enlightenment of the Holy Spirit he cannot know the full extent of the demand God makes, so the sin in the depths of his
heart and his inner impurity also remain hidden. "Man's heart is
so deep that we cannot investigate it for ourselves." The psalmist
[Ps. 139:23] therefore asks the Lord to let him know his sin.[2] Sin
is infinitely great, especially sin against the First Commandment.
"What an abyss unfaith is!" How is it possible that a man could
plumb its depths and express it by himself.[3] By nature he perhaps
recognizes certain individual sins but not the "basic, main, and
really mortal sin," the primal or original sin which is essentially
unfaith toward God and his Christ, the sin against the First Commandment. Man also does not know where this sin comes from.
He can know of all those things only after God's word has told
him of them. The Scripture bears witness to him that he not
only sins here and there but that there is little good in his nature
and that whatever good there is is misused.[4] Man becomes com-

---

[1] *WA* 39ᴵᴵ, 367.
[2] *WA* 39ᴵᴵ, 323.
[3] *WA* 39ᴵᴵ, 366. "Then you shall know that you cannot make this sin great
enough, for absolutely no man can ever discover or comprehend his wickedness,
since it is infinite and eternal." *WA* 8, 115; *LW* 32, 240.
[4] "Radical sin, deadly and truly mortal, is unknown to men in the whole
wide world. . . . Not one of all men could think that it was a sin of the world
not to believe in Christ Jesus the Crucified." *WA* 39ᴵ, 84; *LW* 34, 154. "A
man by his own nature does not know where sin comes from nor does he even
know sin itself. A knowledge of sin, however, remains in man through the
word of God." *WA* 39ᴵᴵ, 365. Cf. *ibid.*, p. 366 and *WA* 8, 104.
[5] *WA* 39ᴵ, 86; *LW* 34, 156.

pletely aware of his sin only in the light of God's word and law.
But even then he sees the terrible and deadly power of sin only
from a distance and through a veil. "If anyone would feel the
greatness of sin he would not be able to go on living another moment; so great is the power of sin." Man can bear this knowledge
only when he stands under the promise of the gospel.[*]

Luther therefore repeatedly explains his doctrine of sin through
his interpretation of Bible passages and thus establishes a proof
from Scripture.[7] At the same time, however, he bases what he says
on experience. This is not a contradiction. Man learns to know
himself completely only by standing under the word of Scripture.
And conversely the words of Scripture, at least the confessions of
the psalmists and of the Apostle Paul to which Luther constantly
refers in support of his statements, describe the experiences of the
writers when they were encountered by God. Thus Luther's appeal
to Scripture is at the same time an appeal to men's experience of
their relationship to God. The word of Scripture is appropriated
in personal experience.[*] Luther finds that the biblical confessions
of sin are his own.

One of the decisive concerns of Luther's theology is to avoid
minimizing the greatness and seriousness of sin as though it did
not matter. At no other point has he fought against his opponents,
the scholastic theologians, with such passionate seriousness. We
need only think of his powerful attack on Latomus (1521). The
most important matter of all was at stake, that is, the recognition
of the infinitely great and marvelous glory of grace and of God's
saving activity in Jesus Christ. Making sin great is inseparably
connected with exalting and praising grace. For this reason Luther accuses those theologians who do not wish to admit the full
truth about the terrible reality of sin of not knowing anything
about Christ. The glory of God's mercy and of Christ, who re-

---

[*] "In all of this it becomes clear that we are not able to know the true definition of sin but only foggy and ambiguous terminology." *WA* 39[II], 210.

[7] Cf. particularly Luther's treatise *Against Latomus* (1521). *WA* 8, 59 ff.;
LW 32, 137-260.

[*] "Now look at your own experience and at the experience of other people
and you will find that no one can help him out of such a situation." *WA* 10[III],
245. Luther argues on the basis of "our own daily experience and that of all
the saints." *WA* 8, 98; *LW* 32, 216. Cf. *WA* 8, 109 f., 122; *LW* 32, 231,
235, 251 f.

deems us from sin, requires that the full seriousness of sin be recognized without any moderation. "We cannot make sin great enough" and "we cannot highly enough exalt the glory of grace"; each of these statements conditions the other and stands and falls with the other. The merciless seriousness and inflexible severity with which Luther speaks about sin are motivated by his concern to give all glory to God and Christ.[9]

CIVIL RIGHTEOUSNESS

Luther does not take a narrow view of man's moral capabilities. He knows that man is able to produce a kind of "righteousness." It is the righteousness which exists between men, the "moral," "civil," "external," and "civic" righteousness. It consists in fulfilling the demands which the civil or the moral law makes of men in their relationships with one another.[10] This is the essence of the civic virtues as these were taught by Aristotle and Cicero. The finest men of the classical period have provided outstanding examples of these virtues. And Luther praises these men in no uncertain terms.[11] This kind of righteousness may also be found among the heathen and the Turks. Luther finds this righteousness—he sometimes speaks of "heroic virtues"—frequently in the history and in the present affairs of nations.[12] Such virtues and deeds are necessary in order to preserve peace and order between nations. God wants and demands "civil righteousness," because he uses it in order to preserve peace and order in the world and to prevent the world from destroying itself. God therefore allows civic righteousness validity in its own area; indeed, he even rewards it and adorns it with the highest earthly goods.[13]

In the final analysis, however, this righteousness is valid only before men; it is honored only by men and not by God (Luther here develops what Paul says in Romans 4:2).[14] We must distin-

---

[9] *WA* 8, 108, 112, 115; *LW* 32, 230, 236, 240 f.

[10] *WA* 18, 767; *BOW*, 289. *WA* 39ᴵ, 459. *WA* 39ᴵᴵ, 289.

[11] *WA* 40ᴵ, 219; *LW* 26, 123. *WA* 40ᴵᴵ, 389; *LW* 12, 354. *WA* 18, 742; *BOW*, 251.

[12] *WA* 39ᴵ, 202.

[13] *WA* 8, 104; *LW* 32, 225. *WA* 39ᴵ, 82; *LW* 34, 151. *WA* 39ᴵ, 100 f., 202. *WA* 39ᴵ, 289. *WA* 40ᴵ, 393; cf. *LW* 12, 357.

[14] *WA* 39ᴵ, 82; *LW* 34, 51. *WA* 39ᴵ, 441.

guish between "two courtrooms," the "theological" and the "civil."
"God judges on a quite different basis than this world does." (The
judgment which a man's own conscience passes on him belongs in
the category of the world's judgment as long as his conscience has
not been illuminated by God's Spirit.)[15] "That righteousness which
justifies me before the civil judge is not to be identified with righteousness before God." When we stand under God's judgment, civil
righteousness does not help us.[16] It is not enough for God. Yes, as
God judges, it is only a false front, hypocrisy, and a lie. For the
"truth which God desires in our inward being" (Ps. 51:6) is missing. This means that an external act may, as such, be proper in the
political and civil realm. God however looks at the heart—and
that remains unclean in spite of and underneath civil righteousness.
For deep down man seeks only his own advantage and trusts in
himself.[17] It is particularly men's great achievements and "heroic
virtues" that are corrupted by this. Luther felt that the great men
of classical antiquity and of all nations were completely poisoned
by their desire for honor and fame. The desire for fame may be
considered honorable among men; as far as God is concerned, it is
the most shameful and terrible blasphemy, that is, robbery of God's
honor.[18] This shows how far man's judgment and God's judgment
are separated from each other. These same things are also true of
that moralistic self-security to which civil righteousness seduces us.[19]

SIN AS ROBBERY OF GOD

What is sin? Scripture, for the most part, does not use this
word to describe what men usually call "sins." In any case, it does
not refer only to them but particularly to the root from which the
deeds come.[20] "Sin, in the Scripture, means not only the outward
works of the body but also all that happens to move men to do
these works, namely, the inmost heart, with all its powers." The

---

[15] *WA* 8, 67; *LW* 32, 173. *WA* 39¹, 82; *LW* 34, 151.
[16] *WA* 39¹, 230.
[17] *WA* 40ᴵᴵ, 389; cf. *LW* 12, 354f. *WA* 39¹, 82; *LW* 34, 151. *WA*
39¹, 202, 212. *WA* 18, 767; *BOW*, 289.
[18] *WA* 6, 220; *PE* 1, 208. *WA* 18, 742 f.; *BOW*, 252. *WA* 40ᴵᴵ, 325; *LW*
12, 309. *WA* 42, 350; *LW* 2, 125 f.
[19] *WA* 39¹, 459. *WA* 2, 492; *LW* 27, 224.
[20] *WA* 8, 104; *LW* 32, 224.

Scripture "looks into the heart" and there finds "unfaith at the bottom of the heart" as the "root and source of all sin."[21] Luther can, however, also follow Augustine in describing egocentricity as the "beginning of all sin." Both come into existence at the same time. Egocentricity seeks its own, "takes from God and from men what belongs to them and gives neither God nor men anything of that which it has, is, and is capable of."[22]

Unfaith, the lack of fear, trust, and love of God, shows itself particularly in ingratitude. This is "the most shameful vice and the greatest contempt of God."[23] Luther learned this from Paul in Romans 1:21. Ingratitude in turn depends on egocentricity, self-satisfaction, trusting in ourselves and our own righteousness.[24] Even though men have received the goods of this life from God, they do not treat them as his gift. They are so concerned with the gift that they forget the giver. They take these gifts as though they were something which they obviously deserve or have made for themselves. "We use this gift as though we, not God, had made it."[25] But possessing God's gifts without recognizing them and treating them as his, that is, without giving thanks for them, is "the same as [possessing] stolen and plundered goods."[26] Whoever despises God by being ungrateful misuses the gifts both against God and against his neighbor. We misuse these gifts against God by constantly bragging, as though we had only ourselves to thank for everything; and we trust in such earthly gifts instead of committing ourselves to God. We misuse these gifts against our neighbor whenever we do not receive them from God's hand as a trust but instead use them for our own purposes and to hurt our neighbor, as "though we ourselves were God and lord here on earth." Thus contempt of God leads to contempt of the neighbor.[27]

Man constantly transgresses the First Commandment by not put-

---

[21] *WA*, DB 7, 6; *LW* 35, 369. "The main and real sin is unfaith, despising God, which is what takes place when a man does not fear, love, and trust in God as he certainly should." *WA* 31¹, 148; cf. *LW* 14, 84.
[22] *WA* 7, 212; *PE* 2, 364.
[23] *WA* 31¹, 76; *LW* 14, 51. *WA* 39¹, 580.
[24] *WA* 56, 178 f. *LCC* 15, 25 f.
[25] *WA* 31¹, 443; *LW* 14, 122. Cf. *WA* 56, 178; *LCC* 15, 26. *WA* 31¹, 433, 454; *LW* 14, 112, 133.
[26] *WA* 31¹, 454; *LW* 14, 133.
[27] *WA* 31¹, 438; cf. 434; *LW* 14, 115; cf. 113.

ting all his trust in God. Otherwise we would believe in God's love and praise him even in time of trouble. But we cannot do this. "When temptation comes or when I must die then I think that God is a devil; yes, even that He is a wrathful God who is angry with me."²⁸ In good times it is easy for us to imagine that we really love God. We can even produce quite a remarkable appearance of loving God and our neighbor. But we can do this only as long as we are not put to the test of suffering. "God has many lovers"—"in time of peace." Genuine and counterfeit love are so similar in peaceful times that they can be mistaken for each other; and genuine love is therefore hidden. The situation is however different "in time of war," that is, when God strikes and destroys men and when my neighbor injures me and is everything else but lovable. We find this same inconsistency in ourselves when we rejoice in God and give to our neighbor. "But just as the adherents of the flesh feign love in tranquil times, so it is with joy. They praise God and the gifts of God in men, but only until they are offended. Then the works of the flesh comes rushing forth. They disparage the gifts of God which they had formerly praised. They are saddened if their disparagement meets with no success and if the reputation of their neighbor is not diminished. For no one believes how deep the malice of the flesh is, so many does it send smugly to destruction, until they are tried and approved."²⁹ Outwardly a man is able to lead a "holy life." But inwardly the heart remains without faith, fears death, is full of pride, "and wherever there is room, all this breaks out."³⁰ True fear of God and trust in him must manifest themselves by making us independent of whether men think well or evil of us. But "we are the sort of people who are tickled when people like us. And that is a sign of an impure heart." (At this particular place, Luther applies this first of all to the preacher.)³¹

In all of this it becomes clear that man is not really committed to God but selfishly seeking his own advantage, even in relation-

---

²⁸ *WA* 31¹, 94; *LW* 14, 59. *WA* 46, 661; *LW* 22, 142.
²⁹ *WA* 2, 593; *LW* 27, 374.
³⁰ *WA* 17¹, 240; cf. *LW* 12, 190.
³¹ *WA* 17¹, 237; cf. *LW* 12, 188 f.

ship to God and with the help of God." "In everything which he does or does not do he seeks his own advantage, will, and honor rather than God's and his neighbor's. For this reason all his works, all his words, all his thoughts, and all his life are evil and not godly."** Luther expressed this most sharply in his lectures on Romans in 1515 and 1516. "Man is so self-centered that he uses not only the physical but also the spiritual gifts for his own advantage and seeks his own advantage at every opportunity." Human nature "is concerned only with itself, seeks only its own advantage, and always ignores anything that might get in its way. It even passes over God himself as though it did not even see him and is completely self-centered. . . . It puts itself in the place of everything else, even in the place of God himself and seeks only its own purposes and not God's. For this reason it is its own chief and most important idol."** It thus exploits God himself." It uses and administers even its obedience and subjection to God's will for its own purposes. Its eye is not fixed exclusively on God's will but also on secondary matters. Therefore it lacks the "joy, love, and happiness" with which God wants us to fulfill his will. It is "even godly against its will." It seeks its own "advantage and purpose in its devotion." No one is godly "purely for God's sake or because it is the right way to be. Nature both needs and likes to have some reason for being godly; it is neither willing nor able to be godly simply for the sake of godliness." In this way, man's natural religion constantly distorts and falsifies his relationship to God. He is ready to serve God only to the extent that God seems useful for his own purposes." He constantly sins against the First Commandment. What Feuerbach later characterized as the essence of religion is precisely what Luther sees as the constant form of actual

---

** "While a person is doing what is in him, he sins and seeks himself in everything." *WA* 1, 360; *LW* 31, 50. "Being so ingrown, I seek what is pleasing to me in God and in all creatures." Veit Dietrich's edition reads: "We do not seek the glory of God but our own glory in God and in all creatures." *WA* 40ᴵᴵ, 325, *LW* 12, 309.
** *WA* 6, 244; *PE* 1, 242.
** *WA* 56, 356 f.; *LCC* 15, 218 f.
** "They sin against the First Commandment because they do not seek the things of God but rather their own advantage in God himself and in his saints; and they thus do everything for their own ultimate purpose and are their own idol for they use God for their own benefit." *WA* 1, 425.
** *WA* 7, 800; *RW* 2, 123.

distortion. Godliness is reduced to a means to an end rather than
being recognized and desired as the highest good.

Man is self-seeking even in his ethos. It is his ultimate intention "to enjoy himself in his works and to adore himself as an
idol."[87] Thus pride, in addition to concupiscence, becomes an additional characteristic of self-love. This love of self is inflamed by
man's own ethical achievements. He can control his lower desires
through ethical effort but he cannot control pride for it arises from
his victories over error and from his ethical progress.[88]

This pride and self-satisfaction are rooted so deeply in man that
they can nourish themselves even on his humility and repentance.
This is naturally not true but rather the false and fabricated humility; for those who are truly humble are "themselves never aware
of their humility." "True humility never knows that it is humble
. . . for if it knew this it would become proud by thinking of so
fine a virtue. . . . It can neither see itself nor become aware of itself. . . . Humility is so tender and precious that it cannot bear to
see itself; only God is allowed to see it." Thus only God sees humility. If humility were to see itself it would become proud without even knowing it.[89] This happens to natural man precisely when
he takes humility seriously; his love of himself is nourished even
by such seriousness. These are the "hidden faults" (Ps. 19:12)
which are hidden from us because we fall into them precisely when
we think we can have a good conscience, for example, when we
humble ourselves, pass judgment on ourselves, and sacrifice ourselves. For then we please ourselves particularly in our self-hu-
miliation; we secretly think well of ourselves because of our repentance and self-accusation, and are proud of our self-contempt.
A man thus remains himself and takes his own part even when
he sits in judgment on himself and despairs of himself. He not
only asserts and enjoys himself in the security of ethical idealism
but also in ethical pessimism, the negative form which idealism
assumes when it has been disillusioned. How can man break away

---

[87] *WA* 1, 358; *LW* 31, 46.
[88] "For there are many who do not commit sins but do everything that is
good; and nevertheless, a most subtle pride is all that is born out of their very
virtues, and it pollutes them." *WA* 3, 292. Cf. *WA* 3, 486.
[89] *The Magnificat* (1520), *WA* 7, 561 ff.; *LW* 21, 315 ff.

from the routine of looking at himself and being pleased with what he sees?[40]

Pride makes all human activity sinful, especially "good works."[41] Expressed most sharply, "No one can be certain that he is not continually committing mortal sin, because of the most secret vice of pride." The pope condemned this statement in his bull excommunicating Luther, and Luther states it even more sharply in his defense in 1521. "Therefore I must retract this article, and I say now that no one should doubt that all our good works are mortal sins, if they are judged according to God's judgment and severity and not accepted as good by grace alone."[42] This is due not to the character of good works as specific individual acts but to man's pride which stains them all. The "glitter" of works, however, constantly misleads a man to such "false trust" as long as he does not look into the depths of God's commandment.[43]

All this means that a man sins against God not only because his own works always remain works of the law and he himself is not always totally involved personally in them, but just as much because—and this is the worst—he is involved in sin even when he takes everything seriously, attempts to establish his own righteousness, and thereby shuts himself off from that righteousness which God wants to give. Man thus sins even when he does the best he can, even with his best works. Luther learned this too from Paul; he bases his position on Romans 10:2, which he interprets to mean that even though the Jews are zealous for God and seek the righteousness of the law, still they transgress the law because they are not Jews "in spirit" but stiff-neckedly resist the righteousness of faith. "What other conclusion is possible than

---

[40] "Our flesh is so evil that it often deceives us in the very midst of tribulation and humility, so that we are pleased by our humility and disregard of ourselves, and by our own confession of sins; we become proud of accusing ourselves of being proud. This is the hidden presumptuousness and guilt of pride." *WA* 5, 564.

[41] "A righteous man sins in all his good works," *WA* 7, 433; *LW* 32, 83. "A good work, even though well performed is a venial sin according to God's merciful judgment, and a mortal sin according to God's strict judgment." *WA* 7, 438; *LW* 32, 86.

[42] *WA* 7, 445; *LW* 32, 91. "Every good work is a sin unless it is forgiven by mercy." *WA* 8, 93; *LW* 32, 209.

[43] "The 'works of the law' . . . are not only insufficient; but in their outward appearance they even give hypocrites false confidence." *WA* 2, 492; *LW* 27, 223.

that 'free will' is at its worst when it is at its best, and that the more it tries the worse it becomes and acts?"[44]

The will of God comes to men on the one hand in the "moral" commandments of the Second Table and on the other hand in the "religious" commandments of the First Table, particularly in the First Commandment. Accordingly man's sin is twofold. First, he does not fulfill the Commandments but trangresses them. And second, he sins against the First Commandment when he attempts to fulfill the commandments in order to win salvation, since he thereby sins against God as the only God and creator who alone gives righteousness to men. Man is guilty in relationship to God, not only when he does not care but also when he is very serious about morality. This seriousness allows him to fall prey to the most evil sin of all, religious sin, by trusting in himself. To trust in one's self rather than in God is blasphemy.[45] This main sin against the First Commandment is at its worst when men do not believe in the crucified Christ whom God has given to us as our Savior.[46] At every point Luther completely follows the lead of the Apostle Paul whose condemnation of man, in the form of the Jew, shares both these emphases.[47]

SIN AS ROBBERY OF THE NEIGHBOR

Pride and self-satisfaction, the sins against the First Commandment, not only rob God of his deity but also injure the neighbor. The Pharisee sins not only against faith but also against love.[48] It is a terrible thing to say, but he uses his brothers' failure in order to enjoy the feeling of being righteous in comparison with them. And in this self-righteousness he looks down upon the others. He does not concern himself with their ethical need, as love demands; instead he rejoices because he has such a dark foil for himself. Luther declares that no sin on earth is worse than this.[49]

This is particularly true of the Pharisee, that is, of the "right-

---

[44] *WA* 18, 760 f.; *BOW*, 278 f.
[45] *WA* 17¹, 233; *LW* 12, 187.
[46] *WA* 39¹, 84; *LW* 34, 154.
[47] Cf. my *Paulus und Luther über den Menschen* (3rd ed.; Gütersloh Bertelsmann, 1958), p. 49.
[48] *WA* 15, 673.
[49] *WA* 2, 606 f.; *LW* 27, 393 f. Cf. *WA* 15, 673.

eous man." It is, however, true of all men. God gives us gifts so that we might use them in the service of our neighbor. Instead of so using them, we misuse every gift which he bestows more upon us than upon others in order to raise ourselves above them. "Reason cannot keep from doing it. As soon as it finds that it has received more grace than others have, it turns up its nose at those who are not its equal."[50] According to the law of love, we should be concerned about our neighbor's need. Instead, however, men commonly rejoice at other men's troubles. "Where . . . are those who feel unhappy about it and do not enjoy seeing it? If you look at it in this way, the entire world is a mad dog with bloody teeth." This rejoicing at evil is already murder and a transgression of the Fifth Commandment.[51] No one fulfills this commandment as Jesus understood it. Here the assertion, "You can because you should," is simply not true; the fact of the matter is that "we must do it but we can't." What Jesus demands exceeds our powers and is contrary to our nature. Luther bases this assertion on the experience of every age and of his own heart. We cannot give orders to our heart. Anger against our enemy is ineradicable. Outwardly we can act friendly toward him. "However, we cannot give him our heart, try as we will, even though we should tear ourselves apart in the process." In this manner no one can pull himself up by his own bootstraps. God's commandments, as Jesus interprets them, are to be understood not as an ethical appeal to us men as we are or as an appeal to our free will; on the contrary, they show us our complete impotence. What they demand is nothing less than a completely new man, a rebirth. "Thou shalt not kill" ultimately means "you must be born again and become a different man."[52] In spite of every appearance of friendliness, deep down inside himself a man seeks his own advantage and therefore he is inwardly closed up against and an enemy of his brother.

Luther in no way denies the power of the moral will. This power enables a man to subject himself consciously to God's com-

---

[50] *WA* 10[III], 238.
[51] "If I say, 'It serves them right,' I am a murderer." *WA* 27, 264.
[52] *WA* 10[III], 243 ff., 247. "The laws of God, therefore, are only a mirror in which we see our weakness and evil; they bind us all in our sins so that we are not able to work our way out by helping ourselves and using our own free will; something else must come to help us." *WA* 10[III], 244.

mandment and to do works of the law; but the power of the will is limited to those activities controlled by his conscious will. This will has no power over the depths of the heart, its secret feelings, thoughts, and desires. For this reason, our acts are right in themselves, but we do not do them "from our heart." The conscious will is determined by the commandment and says "yes," but "the foundation of the heart," the seat of involuntary drives, often says "no" to this. Thus even our conscious surrender to God is crippled by our secret resistance. Since our love of God and neighbor must always first overcome this resistance—no matter how small it may be—whatever we produce is never so free and joyous as God would have it be. The movement of the conscious will is hampered by the weight of an inner not-willing. For this reason, willing is more or less difficult; it is not easy as love should be.[63] Not all of us, but only a part of ourselves is in the law of the Lord. Our actions lack the absolute integrity and genuineness, freedom and joyousness, which the commandment demands. To this extent, our morality is a façade of hypocrisy. Behind that façade lies something quite different from what meets the eye, namely, our sins.[64] This is true not only of man without Christ but also of the Christian man. For, although he has received the Spirit of God, he still remains "flesh" which resists God's will. For this reason he still sins even when he does what is right.

---

[63] "Since he never acts without reluctance, he never does good without its being corrupted. Therefore, he never completely fulfills the law of God. Since, as I have said, unwillingness to fulfill the law of God is always present in the flesh and because man also wills to do the law of God, he does good through his willingness and evil through his unwillingness. . . . The difficulty which impedes joyful and free love of the law hinders the full satisfaction of God's law. For that law is not fulfilled unless a man acts with a pure and free spirit. There is therefore just as much sin as there is unwillingness, difficulty, and reluctance in a man's heart and there is just as much merit as there is willingness, freedom, and joyfulness. These two are mixed in every life and in all our work. . . . There is, however, no integrated will in this life; therefore we always sin even when we do what is right; sometimes we sin more and sometimes we sin less, depending on how much our flesh assails us with its impure desires." *WA* 2, 412 f. Cf. *WA* 1, 367; *LW* 31, 61. "We are hindered by evil so that we are not wholly within His law, and a part of us which fights against us is opposed to His law." *WA* 8, 95; *LW* 32, 212.

[64] "For whatever is done out of concern for the law is sin because it is not done with a willing spirit but unwillingly and thus contrary to the law and truly sin." *WA* 7, 760.

THE FLESH

The pride and self-assertion which prevent a man from achieving genuine love either of men or of God is not an occasional distortion; it is the nature of fallen man. This means that sin is not only individual acts of commission and omission but the impurity of one's entire being. When we speak of sin, we may not, as Luther's opponents—the scholastic theologians—did, think only of the transgressions of the law in thoughts, words, and deeds. When we do that, we fail to understand the full depths of sin, that is, its root and the real sickness.[55] "Our weakness lies not in our works but in our nature; our person, nature, and entire being are corrupted through Adam's fall."[56] Man's acts reveal that his entire nature is impure, that is, there is simply nothing in us except sin.[57] The assertion of scholastic nominalists that "Nature is whole" must be corrected to read "Nature is corrupt."[58] Man is sinful before he thinks, says, or does anything. What he does flows from what he is.[59] This is "the real and most significant sin; if this were not present, there would be no real sin. This sin is not committed, as are all other sins; it simply is, it lives, and it commits all sin. It is the essential sin which sins not only for an hour or a little while but is present wherever and as long as a person exists. Only God sees this natural sin."[60]

Luther and Paul describe this condition by calling man "flesh." "Flesh" thus refers to the entire man insofar as he is in contradiction to God.[61] The distinction between "spirit" and "flesh" is completely different from the division of man into spirit, soul, and body which may be found in Scripture (I Thess. 5:23). This lat-

---

[55] *WA* 40II, 316; cf. *LW* 12, 304. "The radical ferment which bears fruit in evil deeds and works." *WA* 8, 104; *LW* 32, 224.

[56] *WA* 10I,1, 508. *WA* 8, 104; *LW* 32, 224 f.

[57] "In this deed [his adultery and murder of Uriah] David begins to know that he is totally sinful. . . . We too should therefore know that there is simply nothing in us that is not sinful." *WA* 40II, 322, cf. *LW* 12, 307.

[58] *WA* 40II, 323; *LW* 12, 307.

[59] "Define sin rather on the basis of this psalm as all that is born of father and mother, before a man is old enough to say, do, or think anything." *WA* 40II, 322, *LW* 12, 307. (This is from Veit Dietrich's edition.)

[60] *WA* 10I,1, 508 f.

[61] Luther is aware that the word "flesh" is used independently in Scripture to refer to the body and the physical nature of men. Where it is distinguished from "spirit" however, it refers to everything which is in opposition to "spirit." *WA* 18, 735; *BOW*, 242.

ter distinction is basically anthropological, the former is theological. It does not differentiate pieces or parts of human nature but
describes the quality of that nature's relationship to God. It thus
refers to the entire man, that is, to spirit, soul, and body at one
and the same time. On all three levels man can be either "spirit"
or "flesh," that is, either good or evil.[42] Medieval theology, under
the influence of Hellenistic dualism, inclined so to combine these
two distinctions that flesh was equated with man's physical being:
Man is "flesh" insofar as he participates in his physical desires
which are opposed to the spirit, which is called reason. In opposition to this, Luther declares with Paul that flesh is everything
which "is outside of the grace and the Spirit of Christ," everything which does not come from faith; "flesh" in this sense is not
just a part of man and certainly not merely his physical being, but
rather the whole man.[43] Man is "flesh" precisely in his spirituality,
in his "heart," soul, and in "his best and highest powers," that is,
particularly in his ethos and in his religiosity as a religious man.[44]
This is where the really terrible sin is. Man's self-satisfaction, his

---

[42] *WA* 7, 550; *LW* 21, 303.

[43] Commenting on Gal. 3:3, Luther says, "This makes it clear that 'flesh' is
to be understood not only in the sense of sensuality or the lusts of the flesh but
in the sense of everything that is outside grace and the Spirit of Christ. The
work righteousness of the Galatians is flesh. . . . Therefore, whatever does not
proceed from faith is flesh." *WA* 2, 509; *LW* 27, 249. "Paul uses 'flesh' for
everything that is not spirit, that is, for the whole man." *WA* 2, 610; *LW* 27,
399. Speaking of his opponents, Luther says: "The cause of their error is
that . . . they make a metaphysical distinction between flesh and spirit as
though these were two substances; however, it is the total man that is flesh
and spirit, spirit insofar as he loves the law of God and flesh insofar as he
hates the law of God." *WA* 2, 415. "I . . . do not completely separate flesh,
soul, and spirit. For the flesh experiences no desire except through the soul
and spirit by virtue of which it is alive. By spirit and flesh, moreover, I understand the whole man, especially the soul itself." *WA* 2, 585; *LW* 27, 363.
For further passages on the understanding of "flesh" and "spirit" in Luther,
cf. *WA*, DB 7, 12; *LW* 35, 371 f. "Everything that is done by the flesh is
'fleshly'—no matter how deeply it is hidden in the soul." *WA* 17ᴵᴵ, 8. "Everything that the old man is with his best and highest powers, both internal and
external—including the deep evil of his self-will, darkened understanding,
reason, wisdom, and pride in his good works, spiritual life, and whatever other
gifts of God may be in him [is 'flesh']." *WA* 17ᴵᴵ, 11.

[44] *WA* 18, 743 f.; *BOW*, 252 f. Luther cautions against interpreting "flesh"
in the sense of baser and gross affections, for the seat of ignorance and contempt is to be found "in the highest and most excellent powers of man in
which righteousness, godliness, and knowledge and reverence of God should
reign—that is, in reason and will, and so in the very power of 'free-will,' in
the very seed of uprightness, the most excellent thing in man!" *WA* 18, 761;
BOW, 280.

conceit, his insolence, his unfaith, his compulsion to assert his own righteousness against God are all something "spiritual," but it is precisely in and because of this that man is "flesh." All philosophy, all theology, all human wisdom which are "fleshly" do not teach faith.[65] However man is "spirit" and "spiritual" insofar as he loves God's law. Luther thus gives to the traditional concept of concupiscence a new meaning, corresponding to what it means in Paul's theology. Concupiscense is much more than sensuality lusting against reason as the higher part of man; rather it is the opposition of the entire man to God. This opposition is centered in man's soul and spirit. In all this Luther is conscious of restoring the genuine meaning of Paul's concepts, which were so badly misinterpreted in the theology of the early and medieval church.[66]

According to Luther, natural man is completely flesh. This does not mean that we are "so completely inclined toward evil that nothing at all remains in us which is inclined toward fulfilling the law." With one side of his being man wills to do the good; this is, however, only a "very tiny motion of his will."[67] Luther speaks of this when he uses the scholastic concept of the synteresis.[68] He places no emphasis on this, however. For Luther, only the Christian can be seriously described as "man in contradiction." Throughout the

---

[65] *WA* 2, 509; *LW* 27, 250.

[66] *WA* 2, 585; *LW* 27, 362 f. "Without such a grasp of these words, you will never understand this letter of St. Paul, nor any other book of Holy Scripture. Therefore beware of all teachers who use these words in a different sense, no matter who they are, even Origen, Ambrose, Augustine, Jerome, and others like them or even above them." *WA*, DB 7, 12; *LW* 35, 372.

[67] "Now it is true, I grant, that one can do and will some but not every good from such an attitude of mind, for we are not so thoroughly inclined toward evil that there is not left to us a portion which is affected toward the good, as is evident in synteresis." [*Synteresis*, a corruption of the Greek word for "conscience" was used by the scholastics to designate the soul's natural inclination toward the good.—Trans.] *WA* 56, 237; *LCC* 15, 88. "They said, namely, that when the will is subject to synteresis, it is, only slightly to be sure, 'inclined toward the good.' And this tiny motion toward God [of which man is naturally capable] they imagine to be an act of loving God above everything!" *WA* 56, 275; *LCC* 15, 130. Cf. my *Paulus und Luther über den Menschen,* pp. 59 f. *GA* 1, pp. 61 f. cites references from *Against Latomus* as proof for the double character [*Doppelheit*] of the flesh and the 'better ego' in man. *WA* 8, 119 f.; *LW* 32, 247 ff. In view of Luther's understanding of Romans 7:14 ff., however, these references do not describe a man without Christ but apply only to the Christian.

[68] For Luther's doctrine of the conscience, see Emanuel Hirsch, *Lutherstudien* 1 (Gütersloh: Bertelsmann, 1954).

life of a Christian good and evil are mixed in every act.[69] Luther
does not understand the inner conflict described by Paul in Romans 7:14 ff. as a description of the natural man without Christ
and the Holy Spirit but as a description of the Christian to whom
the Holy Spirit has been given. Man as a whole, without Christ, is
full of lusts in spite of that "very tiny motion" toward the good.[70]

THE BONDAGE OF THE WILL

Man is flesh. This includes the fact that he can neither escape
from his moral condition nor overcome it by his natural powers.
Luther here stands in sharp opposition to Aristotle and the theological tradition influenced by him. That tradition referred to the
significance of discipline. Luther replies that love, chastity, and humility are not achieved through discipline.[71] That requires a rebirth
through faith. Without such a rebirth man's will remains enslaved
and bound. Man stands under the inescapable necessity of sinning
in everything that he is and does. This, however, does not remove his responsibility and guilt. A man is not forced to sin
against his own inner will. Rather it is in his will that he experiences the inescapability of sin. He is necessarily a sinner but he is
also a sinner voluntarily. "We do not sin against our will but
rather according to our will."[72] Man is, however, unable to change
his basic will. And he himself is bound within it as a person.[73] He
cannot handle his lack of freedom to do good and his subjection

---

[69] *WA* 2, 413 (quoted in n. 53).
[70] "And now look at man as he actually is, and see how his whole person is
full of these sinful desires (and how that little motion has no effect at all)."
WA 56, 275; *LCC* 15, 130. This is the continuation of the passage quoted in
n. 67.
[71] "Here Thomas errs in common with his followers and with Aristotle who
say, 'Practice makes perfect': just as a harp player becomes a good harp player
through long practice, so these fools think that the virtues of love, chastity, and
humility can be achieved through practice. It is not true." *WA* 10[III], 92 f.
[72] "Lust is born into us; and we do not act involuntarily but with the greatest
will and desire both in the act of sinning and in the source of sinning [*in pec-
cato originali*]. We are not able to sin involuntarily." Another set of notes
reads: "Adam sinned willingly and freely and from him a will to sin has been
born into us so that we cannot sin innocently but only voluntarily. But this is
our evil." *WA* 39[I], 378.
[73] "But for those who do good and evil willingly, even though they cannot
alter their will by their own strength, reward and punishment follow *naturally*
and *necessarily*." *WA* 18, 693; *BOW*, 181. "He wills to sin and he sins voluntarily, not under compulsion or innocently, even though he cannot choose to
change his will through himself." *WA* 39[I], 379.

to the evil as though it were his fate or a natural condition of his existence that could be separated from himself as a person. His will is bound, but it is and remains *his* will. He repeatedly and voluntarily acts according to it. For this reason, the inescapability of sin does not cast doubt on the fact of man's guilt. Luther always asserted both at one and the same time. A man is and remains guilty in his sin, because he has been given that law in which God makes his good will known to him. Since the sinner constantly acts contrary to the law, his action is evil and he is guilty.[74]

It is God who imprisons man's will. This is the punishment of sin. God has passed sentence on man and condemned him to forfeit his original freedom to do good. He is now the slave of his own sin. Therewith God has also subjected him to slavery to Satan (cf. pp. 161 ff.). Man is a slave of his own sin and is also under the power of Satan. Now he no longer has the power to turn to the good.[75] He can, however, be turned by God. He retains this capacity. Luther here adopts the scholastic concept of a passive aptitude to be turned. Even though a man has lost every capacity to do good in matters concerned with his relationship to God, this passive capacity still remains: he can be grasped by grace and by God's Spirit. Sin does not destroy this capacity. For it remains true that God has created and intended man for eternal life —as well as for the possibility of eternal death.[76]

ORIGINAL SIN

Sin is personal sin, and personal sin is at the same time "natural sin," that is, we receive it together with our nature. It does not first become our fate through the individual decisions of life; it is "born with us" and "innate within us." It "is called inherited sin [*Erbsuende*] because we have not committed it but bring it with us from our parents; and it is no less imputed to us than if

---

[74] *WA* 16, 143.

[75] *WA* 18, 636, 670; *BOW*, 104, 148 f.

[76] "Human beings [are] fit subjects to be caught up by the Spirit and touched by God's grace, as creatures made for eternal life or eternal death." *WA* 18, 636; *BOW*, 105.

we ourselves had done it." It comes to us through our parents from Adam's fall.[77]

Adam fell into sin. God did not create him as a sinful being. Luther follows ecclesiastical tradition in teaching a primeval state. Adam was "created by God as a righteous, godly, and holy man" without any inclination to evil but only to good.[78] Why did he fall? Here Luther confronted a problem which cannot be solved by theology but must remain a riddle. On the one hand, Luther is certain that God is not the originator of sin. The holiness and righteousness of God which we know from the seriousness of his commandments preclude that possibility. "The causes of sin are the devil and our will."[79] On the other hand, however, Luther finds that his doctrine that God works all in all compels him to bring God as close to sin as possible without making him the cause of sin. Even though God did not cause Adam's fall into sin, he still allowed it.[80] Satan sinned when God forsook him.[81] And since Satan has now become evil, God incites him to further evil; he even incites him to bring man to sin.[82] Luther makes a sharp differentiation between the fact that God is not the author of sin since he does nothing evil, and the fact that God's desertion [*deserante Deo*] and stimulation [*incitari*] are directly involved in the source of satanic sin and therefore, through Satan, indirectly involved in human sin.

Luther finds himself compelled to assert that God both forsakes and incites to sin—though neither of these is intended to signify

---

[77] *WA* 17[II], 282. *WA* 40[II], 379 ff.; *LW* 12, 347-351. "This is original sin born in us after Adam's fall, and not only something personal but also natural." *WA* 39[I], 84; *LW* 34, 154.

[78] *WA* 17[II], 282. *WA* 40[II], 323; cf. *LW* 12, 308.

[79] *WA* 39[I], 379.

[80] *WA* 18, 712; *BOW*, 209.

[81] God did not create Satan's will to be evil. "It became so by Satan's sinning and God's withdrawing; God now carries it along by his own operation and moves it where he wills." *WA* 18, 711; *BOW*, 206. "The ungodly man is a creature of God, but one which, being perverted and left to itself without the Spirit of God cannot will or do good." *WA* 18, 710; *BOW*, 204. The problem lies in the relationship between the "withdrawing" and the "sinning" in the first quotation, the "being perverted" and "left to itself" in the second. Which comes first; God's forsaking a man and leaving him to himself—or, man's turning away from God and sinning? Or are they so closely intertwined that it is not legitimate to ask which comes first?

[82] *WA* 16, 143.

that God is the author of sin. But what does this mean? Does it mean that God's will is in contradiction with itself? He gives us the law and wants us to fulfill it and yet he incites the devil to seduce us to sin? There is a real conflict between these two and theology cannot resolve it. Luther finally is able to say nothing more than "This is too deep for us. God's will is involved, but I am not supposed to know how this all happens."[88] Luther here already confronts the problem which appears in *The Bondage of the Will* under the form of the distinction between the hidden and the revealed God. And the pastoral advice which he gives to Christians faced by this problem entirely corresponds to his advice to those confronting the problem of the hidden God who works all things and the mystery of predestination. The Christian is to hold fast to God's will as revealed in law and gospel. That tells him what he should do. He ought to hold in abeyance the question why God acts as he does, for example when he incites to sin. When the Christian has been trained through law and gospel then he will also understand those things about God's will and activity which now seem so obscure to him.[84]

Luther responds in the same way to anyone who asks why God permitted Adam to fall when he could have prevented it. Luther's first answer is to reject the question. God is God and that means that we dare not seek a reasonable explanation for what he wills, since the fact that God wills it is the ultimate explanation. God's allowing Adam to fall belongs to "the mysteries of His majesty" which we are not to investigate but only to adore.[85] In spite of this, however, Luther can even find a twofold meaning in God's dealing with Adam. He can say that in Adam God has given us a terrible example of what man's "free will" is able to do when God leaves it to itself and does not constantly and increasingly motivate and strengthen it with his Spirit. If this is true of Adam before he fell, is it not even more true of us who are fallen sinners?

---

[88] *WA* 16, 143. The quotation in the text is from Aurifaber's edition of the sermon. Rörer's notes read: "But this is so deep that no answer is possible except that this is what pleases God."

[84] *WA* 16, 143.

[85] *WA* 18, 712; *BOW*, 209.

Thus Adam's fall should destroy our moralistic pride.[86] It should sharpen our awareness that the grace of the Holy Spirit is absolutely indispensable. The second meaning which Luther finds in God's permitting Adam's fall is that it is a "blessed guilt" [*felix culpa*]. "If someone at the last judgment were to ask God: 'Why did you permit Adam to fall?' God would answer, 'So that it might be known that I like the human race so much that I would give even my Son to save men!'" Luther adds that we would then say, "Let the whole race fall all over again so that Thy glory may be made manifest!" This means that without mankind's fall in Adam, without sin and guilt, we would never have experienced and learned to know the full greatness of God's mercy.[87]

According to Psalm 51:5, sin perpetuates itself through the natural process of conception.[88] Although God wills the sexual act as such and it is well pleasing to him, it has lost its primeval purity and become sinful through lustful desire.[89] Even though this is the case, sin its not perpetuated through this sinfulness of the marriage relationship and of the act of conception as if these acts were sinful in themselves, but through the sinfulness of the seed. God creates men out of Adam's seed which has become sinful.[90] His reason for doing this is his secret and we cannot find out why he does it. We are thus sinners through our descent from Adam. As far as the origin of the individual soul is discussed, Luther inclines to follow Augustine's theory of traducianism without wishing to make a dogma of it.[91]

---

[86] "By the dreadful example of that first man, it was shown us, with a view to breaking down our pride, what our 'free-will' can do if it is left to itself, and is not continually moved and increased more and more by the Spirit of God." *WA* 18, 675; *BOW*, 156.

[87] *WA*, TR 5, 5071.

[88] *WA* 40ᴵᴵ, 380 ff.; *LW* 12, 347-350 Cf. *WA* 37, 55.

[89] *WA* 2, 167. "If it could still happen that a woman could conceive without the male seed, then such a birth would also be pure. This is why Christ was born of a virgin." *WA* 12, 403.

[90] *WA* 18, 784; *BOW*, 314. Cf. *WA* 37, 55.

[91] *WA* 39ᴵᴵ, 341, 349 f., 354 f., 358 f., 390 ff.

13

MAN BETWEEN GOD
AND SATAN

W HEN Luther wants to designate the power to which every
man is subject in his sinfulness, he speaks of "flesh," of
"the world," and of "the devil." He repeatedly places these three
concepts together. Each of the three powers seduces men to sin
and holds them captive in it; all three are opposed to God, to his
word, and to faith. The effect of these powers on us cannot be
completely differentiated. Both the devil and "the world" persecute God's truth; and our "nature," "flesh," and fleshly reason, together with the world and Satan, are cut off from and enemies of
the word and faith.[1] The devil works through our "flesh" and
through "the world." He is the lord of this world, as both Luther
and the Bible say. Though the three powers are still quite distinct,
all three concepts represent that unified will which surrounds us on
every side and is opposed to God. It is in us, around us, and over
us. For Luther, evil is much more than a power which grasps all
mankind. It is both the effect and the realm of a personal will
which grasps not only the will of the individual but also the joint
will of all mankind; it is a superhuman will directed against God,
one that has its own existence.

Luther presents a doctrine about the devil on the authority of
the Holy Scriptures and in continuity with ecclesiastical tradition.
What he says about the devil, however, and the way in which he
says it, goes far beyond biblicism and traditionalism. He does not
merely develop further a piece of theological and popular tradition; rather, on the basis of his own experience, he bears witness to
the reality and the terribleness of the power of the devil. He does

---

[1] On "the world," cf. WA 18, 766; BOW, 287. The world hates and persecutes the righteousness of God proclaimed in the gospel. Luther often says that
the devil does the same.

this in utter seriousness and with deep personal conviction.[2] It is
not simply to construe this part of his theology as something inherited from the Middle Ages, even though some of its specific
details are determined by the traditional belief in devils and demons. Luther takes the devil much more seriously than the Middle
Ages did. "Luther's devil has, one might say, more hellish majesty
than the medieval devil; he has become more serious, more powerful, and more terrible."[3] This is undoubtedly due to the new clarity
of Luther's understanding of the lordship of God and of Christ,
which brought with it a new and deeper insight into both the nature of the power opposed to God and the sharpness and depth of
the universal battle between God and the rebel powers. Here again
Luther returns to the view of Jesus and of the ancient church.
What he says about the devil is inseparably connected to the center of his theology. The following sketch is intended only to give
an over-all impression. It will not display the full richness of what
Luther said and thought about Satan.[4]

The devil is the great opponent of God and of Christ. For this
reason Luther can see him at work in everything that particularly
contradicts God's own ultimate will for his creation and for men.
The devil therefore is also at work in unhappiness, in sickness and
other troubles of life, and in death. According to Hebrews 2:14,
he has the power of death.[5] What is decisive, however, is that the
devil, God's first and most powerful opponent, always opposes
God. In opposition to God, he established his kingdom of sin and
disobedience. He misled the first men to sin and is still the one
who misleads and pushes men into sin. In the course of history
he acts in opposition to God and Christ, to truth, and to the gospel. He hates Christ and persecutes him in his church.[6] It is the
devil who stands behind all enemies of the word, behind the misinterpretation of Scripture, behind all false doctrine and sects, and

---

[2] "No matter which way you look at it, the devil is the prince of this world."
WA 23, 70; *LW* 37, 18. "By the grace of God, I have learned to know a great
deal about Satan." *WA* 26, 500; *LW* 37, 361.
[3] Reinhold Seeberg, *Lehrbuch der Dogmengeschichte* (2nd and 3rd eds.;
Leipzig, 1917) IV¹, 172.
[4] Cf. *LT* 1, 18 and H. Obendieck, *Der Teufel bei Martin Luther* (Berlin,
Furche: 1931).
[5] *WA* 40ᴵᴵᴵ, 68.
[6] *WA* 37, 50. *WA* 39ᴵ, 420.

behind philosophy.[7] He cannot bear the pure word and the true doctrine and attempts to falsify them: particularly to falsify their decisive content, justification through faith alone.[8] He does everything possible to do away with the doctrine of justification.[9] He blinds men to God's clear word; and he causes their reason to be scandalized by it.[10] He hardens men so that they no longer fear God's judgments and do not realize their miserable condition.[11] His work is found in security, conceit, and dullness, as well as in hopeless despair of the mercy of God and of Christ.[12]

Every man is threatened by the devil at all times and is subject to his temptation. For the devil shares this one dimension of divine being, that he is near to everyone everywhere.[13] Thus the power of God and the power of the devil are opposed to each other and necessarily in the most severe conflict with each other. This conflict continues through all of history and keeps it in unrest: the devil against God, God against the devil, the true God against anti-God.[14] For the devil too wants to be God. He is the "ruler of this world" (John 12:31; 14:30) and the "god of this world" (II Cor. 4:4).[15] God and the devil are fighting for men,[16] for humanity, and for the lordship. Here there is no neutrality, no buffer state. Whatever is not in the kingdom of God and of Christ is in the devil's kingdom.[17] Man has no freedom in matters pertaining

---

[7] *WA* 39^{I}, 180; *LW* 34, 144.

[8] *WA* 18, 764; *BOW*, 284. Cf. *WA* 39^{II}, 266.

[9] *WA* 39^{I}, 420, 489.

[10] *WA* 18, 659; *BOW*, 133. Cf. *WA* 37, 58.

[11] *WA* 39^{I}, 429. *WA* 18, 679; *BOW*, 162.

[12] *WA* 37, 47. *WA* 39^{I}, 426. *WA* 40^{II}, 338; cf. *LW* 12, 318.

[13] ". . . our teachers and authors . . . who do not consider that the devil is round about them with all his venomous flaming darts . . ." *WA* 23, 71, *LW* 37, 17. "Against the devil, who is ever around us, lying in wait to lure us into sin and shame, calamity and trouble." *WA* 30^{I}, 142; *BC*, 374, Cf. *WA* 30^{I}, 146; *BC*, 378, 100. The devil is especially close to theologians. He inspires them with "the most beautiful thoughts adorned with Scripture" and they do not notice that they are errors from the devil. *WA* 23, 70; *LW* 37, 17.

[14] "The world and its god cannot and will not bear the word of the true God, and the true God cannot and will not keep silent. Now these two gods are at war; so what else can there be throughout the world but uproar?" *WA* 18, 626; *BOW*, 91. Cf. *WA* 18, 627, 782; *BOW*, 93, 312. *WA* 39^{I}, 420.

[15] *WA* 23, 70; *LW* 37, 17.

[16] *WA* 18, 635; *BOW*, 103.

[17] "And if it is a stranger to God's kingdom and Spirit, it follows of necessity that it is under the kingdom and spirit of Satan. For there is no middle kingdom between the kingdom of God and the kingdom of Satan, which are ever at war with each other." *WA* 18, 743; *BOW*, 253. Cf. *WA* 17^{II}, 217. Cf. *WA* 18, 659; *BOW*, 133.

to his relationship to God and to his salvation or destruction. He is always in the power either of God or of Satan.[18] "So man's will is like a beast standing between two riders. If God rides, it wills and goes where God wills. . . . If Satan rides, it wills and goes where Satan wills." So man's will cannot select his rider or run to him; "but the riders themselves fight to decide who shall have and hold it."[19] Satan, when he has gained control over man, does what God does: he gives him no rest or peace, but through the dynamic of his will drives him forward along the evil way.[20] Whoever has not been grasped by Christ and is not under the power of His spirit, is under the power of the devil. And no other power can take a man away from the devil except the Spirit of God; this Spirit is the stronger man who according to Jesus' parable [Luke 11:21 f.] overcomes the strong man.[21]

God in Christ wrests men out of the power of the devil. A man receives a share of this freedom from Satan through baptism.[22] But this freedom can be asserted only in a lifelong battle with the devil.[23] We have only two alternatives: either fight against the devil or fall into his power.[24] The weapon in this battle is the word of God.[25] This is true both of the individual Christian and of the church as a whole. Through its proclamation of the word of God the church must kill the devil with teaching.[26] Since he, in spite of this, remains powerful in the world and in history—for not everyone believes—the church anxiously awaits the Last Day, when Christ will come again and finally destroy the power of the devil.

The devil stands in opposition to God. Although his power and

---

[18] "However, with regard to God, and all that bears on salvation or damnation, he has no 'free-will,' but is a captive, prisoner, and bound slave, either to the will of God or to the will of Satan." *WA* 18, 638; *BOW*, 107.

[19] *WA* 18, 635 f.; *BOW*, 103 ff.

[20] "Their god, the devil, goads them on and does not let them rest or relax as long as they can move. . . . As the devil goads them and drives them on, they scramble and storm and bluster in his service. They cannot cease or pause." *WA* 31¹, 119 f.; *LW* 14, 70 f. *WA* 40ᴵᴵᴵ, 35.

[21] *WA* 17ᴵᴵ, 218, Cf. *WA* 18, 782; *BOW*, 312.

[22] *WA* 30¹, 217, 222; *BC*, 441, 446.

[23] *WA* 39¹, 420.

[24] "Choose, then, whether you prefer to wrestle with the devil or whether you prefer to belong to him. . . . If you refuse to be his, defend yourself, go at him!" *WA* 23, 70; *LW* 37, 17.

[25] *WA* 30¹, 127; *BC*, 359. *WA* 30¹, 146; *BC*, 379, 100 f.

[26] *WA* 30¹, 129; *BC*, 361.

his claim are so great that he can be called the "god of this world," there is never any doubt that only the true God is God. Luther holds dualism within the boundaries set by God's omnipotence, which works all in all. Satan and his evil work are also subject to God's almighty activity." This means that the devil must still serve God's will for men and for the world—in spite of the fact that his will and activity are directed against God. God keeps him in his service and uses him for his own work. He uses him primarily as the tool of his wrath." What God's wrath does and what Satan does frequently appear to be one and the same. The devil is "God's devil." And yet at the same time he remains the devil, the enemy of God, who wants the opposite of what God wants. What then, according to Luther, is the relationship between the willing and working of Satan and the activity of God, particularly God's wrath? This is a particular form of the larger question of how God's working in general so relates to the activity of his creatures as to comprehend that activity and still not be identical with it.

The tension in the relationship between God's activity and the working of his creatures is especially high when the powers involved threaten and wish to destroy a man's life in body and soul. For example, what happened to Job was truly the work of the devil." And yet Scripture ultimately attributes it to God (Job 2:3). What does this mean? How is it to be understood? "God does not do it through himself but through means or instruments."³⁰ Here two things are asserted: First, that it is God himself who is working through the instruments; and second, that with respect to any particular event that brings evil to a man's life, we must distinguish between what God does and what his instruments do.

First, among the instruments God uses there is, of course, Satan. But Luther also puts the law into this category. The law then becomes a power inimical to God as well as man. Yet God uses the

" *WA* 18, 710; *BOW*, 204.
" "God indeed uses the devil to afflict and kill us. But the devil cannot do this if God does not want sin to be punished in this way." *WA* 40ᴵᴵᴵ, 519; *LW* 13, 97. [This is from Veit Dietrich's edition.]
" *WA* 40ᴵᴵ, 416; cf. *LW* 12, 373.
" *WA* 40ᴵᴵ, 416; cf. *LW* 12, 373 f.

law." We should know then that in everything bad that happens to us it is God himself who is at work through instruments. Luther not only emphasizes that Satan has the power of death (cf. Heb. 2:14)," but he is no less concerned to remind us that according to Psalm 90:3 it is God himself who lets us die: "Thou causest men to die."" In death man has to do with God. Under no circumstances may he attribute misfortune and death to some other demonic power. To do that would be to deny the unity of God and of faith as the Manichaeans did." It is simply not possible for us to accept as coming from God's hand only the good in our lives and not the bad as well." It is God himself who is always dealing with us, whether in his wrath or in his grace. Man cheats himself out of his encounter with God in wrath and in grace when he thinks of misfortune and death as coming to him not from God but from some other power. He shirks the experience of the wrath of God and does not take it seriously as such; instead he thinks he can deal with death by despising it, as the men of classical antiquity, for example, tried to do." But in doing this he also fails to recognize that misfortune and death are means in the hands of God's grace. God uses misfortune, suffering of body and soul, and death in order to humble those who belong to him and to lead them from trust in something earthly to trust in him alone." We do not confront God in good times and someone else in bad times; rather we always deal with one and the same God. He remains true to himself with unshakable consistency, not friendly for a while and then angry for a while, but always the merciful God even when he strikes me." Admittedly, believing that God is mer-

---

" *WA* 40ᴵᴵ, 417; cf. *LW* 12, 373 f.

" "That long he has been the prince of death." *WA* 31ᴵ, 149; *LW* 14, 84.

" *WA* 40ᴵᴵᴵ, 514 ff. (especially pp. 517 f.); *LW* 13, 94-99 (especially p. 96).

" *WA* 40ᴵᴵ, 417; *LW* 12, 374. *WA* 40ᴵᴵᴵ, 516 f.; cf. *LW* 13, 96. "But this is to imagine that there is another god and not to remain in the simplicity of the faith that there is one God." *WA* 40ᴵᴵ, 417; *LW* 12, 374. Cf. *WA* 40ᴵᴵ, 418; *LW* 12, 375.

" *WA* 40ᴵᴵᴵ, 517; cf. *LW* 13, 96. " 'Who has incited this evil against us?' The righteous answer, 'The devil, for God is righteous, and he would not do it.' But God has indeed done it for otherwise he cannot be known." *WA* 16, 138.

" *WA* 40ᴵᴵᴵ, 517; cf. *LW* 13, 96.

" *WA* 40ᴵᴵ, 417; cf. *LW* 12, 374.

" "Nor is God cruel, but he is 'the Father of comfort' (II Cor. 1:3). Because he delays his help, our hearts make a wrathful idol of God, who is always like himself and constant." *WA* 40ᴵᴵ, 417; *LW* 12, 374.

ciful when we experience his blows in time of misfortune, "is an art" which only the Holy Spirit gives.[39] For God hides himself and gives us a distorted picture of himself when he deals with us through his instruments.[40]

Ultimately then man deals only with God. And yet Satan or the law still remain instruments that work in our lives. We should therefore not only see God's work and Satan's work as one; we should at the same time also distinguish them. As we have already heard, God does not through himself do the things which destroy our life. But how is it still possible to distinguish between the work of the devil which Satan does and the activity of God when he lets Satan have a free hand, as he did with Job? Luther answers this question clearly. God and Satan are both involved in what happens to a man, yet in effecting one and the same deed they are poles removed from each other so far as their intentions are concerned. Luther asserts that even as Satan tempts us to despair of God, so does God himself.[41] God is angry, and Satan makes God's wrath so great and terrible for a man, for example in the hour of death, that man can do nothing else but despair.[42] Both launch a heavy attack against man. God, however, does it to save man, in order to set him free of himself and of all trust in himself and drive him into God's merciful arms. Satan does it in order to tear a man completely and finally loose from God. These then are two completely different things; yes, there is even an infinite difference and an absolute contradiction between Christ and the devil when they terrify a man with the law. One does it to save him, the other to put him to death. The devil wants men to despair of the forgiveness of sins; Christ wants them to despair of themselves and take refuge in God's mercy in Christ.[43] Thus temptation always has two faces and two purposes: God's and the devil's. And these are in opposition to each other. It is the task of faith to overcome the Satanic purpose in temptation by trusting in the unquestionable mercy of God hidden under the distress of that

---

[39] *WA* 40ᴵᴵ, 418; *LW* 12, 374.
[40] "God dissimulates . . ." *WA* 40ᴵᴵ, 417; cf. *LW* 12, 374.
[41] Luther says this about Satan, *WA* 40ᴵᴵ, 416; *LW* 12, 373 f. He says it about Christ in *WA* 39ᴵ, 426.
[42] *WA* 31ᴵ, 147, 159; *LW* 14, 84, 89.
[43] *WA* 39ᴵ, 426 f.

temptation. Faith thus frustrates Satan's purpose in a given affliction by trusting God's intention in that same affliction—and so
brings it to realization. God's purpose is thereby accomplished. Luther thus indicates that a man may, in the difficulties of his external
and inner fate, encounter the possibility of a demonic purpose opposed to God. Man can know God's purpose only when he gives up
hope of knowing it; for God waits for man to grasp him in faith
and man can do this only when he is struggling against the feeling
that God is opposed to him.

Luther also expresses all this by saying that God uses Satan for
his "alien work" (*opus alienum*) but in so doing is always aiming
at his proper work (*opus proprium*). (Isa. 28:21, cf. p. 120). For
God this alien work is only a means through which he accomplishes something else; for Satan, however, it has the goal and
purpose of destroying life. Thus Luther can regard Satan both as
the instrument and as the enemy of God. God uses him but at the
same time also fights against him and redeems us from him.

14

MAN UNDER THE
WRATH OF GOD

THE BASIS AND THE REALITY
OF GOD'S WRATH

A s THE holy God, God cannot respond to man's sin in any
other way than with enmity and wrath.[1] Referring to Paul,
Luther says, "God is the enemy of sin, just as sin is the enemy of
God."[2] Luther uses several concepts, which all say essentially the
same thing, to express this necessity in God's being. He can refer
to the righteousness of God; every sin insults and injures God for
sin injures righteousness. Since God loves righteousness and himself is righteousness, sin strikes and injures him in his very being.[3]
In relationship to sin therefore God's righteousness necessarily expresses itself as wrath. Since Luther finds all commandments included in the First, he can also see the real nature of sin as an
attack on God as God, and find a corresponding basis for God's
wrath in his determination to remain God. God is the "jealous"
God and preserves his glory as the only God with holy jealousy—
Luther here uses Old Testament terminology. He cannot stand idly
by and allow men to have some other lord apart from him, and
love something else instead of him or more than him, for precisely this is the nature of sin.[4] This jealousy necessarily becomes
wrath in response to sin. He has both the will and the power to
punish.[5]

God's wrath is a terrible reality which man cannot bear.[6] God's
wrath is co-extensive with his majesty; like God himself, it is eternal, omnipotent, and infinite.[7] God in his wrath is really "a de-

---

[1] Theodosius Harnack, *Luthers Theologie* (*LT* 1) remains the best presentation of Luther's doctrine of the wrath of God.
[2] *WA* 10I,1, 472.
[3] *WA* 5, 50; *LW* 14, 316. *WA* 6, 127; *PE* 1, 157.
[4] *WA* 10I,2, 361.
[5] *WA* 28, 582.
[6] *WA* 22, 285.
[7] *WA* 39II, 366. Cf. *WA* 40III, 513, 567; *LW* 13, 93 (cf. 125).

vouring fire" (Deut. 4:24) and that means that he destroys completely and absolutely.[8]

Luther could also say quite different things about the wrath of God, and these statements appear to be in irresolvable contradiction to what has just been said. He sometimes declares that God's nature is nothing else than pure love; he is not a God of wrath and of anger but only of grace.[9] The wrath of God then appears to be a figment of man's imagination. Man sees not the true God but an idol, not God as he is in reality but only a dark cloud covering God's face. This cloud, however, exists in man's heart and is therefore not objectively but only subjectively present. It exists only in the false thinking about God to which Satan constantly seduces man.[10] Luther in this connection constantly repeats his basic rule: God is—is for you—the kind of God you think and believe he is.[11] In addition, he can even say that Scripture when it speaks of the wrath of God only reflects our own subjective impression of God and does not intend to say that God is really wrathful.[12]

How are we to understand these statements, conflicting as they

---

[8] *WA* 28, 557, 581.

[9] *WA* 36, 428. *WA* 40ᴵᴵ, 363; cf. *LW* 12, 336.

[10] "Anyone who regards Him as angry has not seen Him correctly, but has pulled down a curtain and cover, or even more, a dark cloud over His face." *WA* 32, 328; *LW* 21, 37. Cf. *WA* 40ᴵᴵ, 417; cf. *LW* 12, 374. *WA* 31ᴵ, 147 ff., 159; *LW* 14, 84 f., 89.

[11] *WA* 17ᴵᴵ, 66. "As you think, so God is. If you believe that God is angry, he is. . . . Thus our thoughts have a great effect. For God will be toward me as I think he is. So that even though the thought that God is angry is false, it will nevertheless be so, although false." *WA* 40ᴵᴵ, 342. [The edition of these notes prepared by Veit Dietrich on the basis of these notes of Georg Rörer reads: "The thought of God's wrath is false even of itself, because God promises mercy; yet this false thought becomes true because you believe it to be true. However, the other thought, that God is gracious to sinners who feel their sins, is simply true and remains so. You should not suppose that it will be this way because you believe this way. Rather be assured that a thing which is sure and true of itself becomes more sure and true when you believe it. On the other hand, if you believe that God is wrathful, you will certainly have him wrathful and hostile to you. But this will be a demonic, idolatrous, and perverse thought, because God is served if you fear him and grasp Christ as the object of mercy." *LW* 12, 322.—Trans.]

[12] "In the Scripture you must often take the rule into account that Scripture speaks of God as we feel him to be. For as we feel him to be, so he is for us. If you think that he is angry and unmerciful then he is unmerciful. Thus when Scripture says that God is wrathful this means nothing else than that we feel he is wrathful." *WA* 24, 169 (edited by Cruciger). "The Holy Spirit speaks out of our feeling. For we think that he is truly wrathful when we are corrected by the Lord." *WA* 25, 320. Cf. I Cor. 11:32 in the Vulgate, where, to be sure, it reads "accused" [*corripimur*] instead of "corrected" [*corrigimur*].

seem to Luther's other strong expressions about the reality of God's wrath? We must begin with Luther's statement that God's wrath is his "alien work," against his nature. Human evil forces him to it.[13] This implies both that God's own nature is love and that wrath is essentially alien to him, and yet wrath, as God's reaction to sin is a reality—although it is admittedly not the final reality. This conflict between Luther's own statements would in fact be unbearable if the second group of statements were intended to say that the wrath of God which a man claims to feel is a mere fiction. However, that is not at all what Luther is saying. What he intends to say is that it is false to speak of God's wrath as though it were an essential part of God's true being. Wrath is deceptive to that extent, but whenever anyone thinks wrath is an essential part of God's being, wrath is the undeniable reality between God and him. Sinful man, who is so bound to his sin that he cannot believe and because of this unfaith thinks of God as wrathful, really experiences the wrath of God. This human delusion about God is in itself a manifestation of the wrath of God. For the wrath of God rests upon him who does not believe.[14]

The apparently contradictory statements are intended to be understood in terms of the dialectic of God's alien work and his proper work, of law and gospel. Christ is the dividing line. Apart from Christ man stands under wrath.[15] Where Christ is, that is, where there is faith in Christ, the wrath of God is no longer present and God's alien work is recognized as God's proper work of love. For Christ has reconciled wrath. One must, however, constantly keep in mind both the persons to whom Luther says there is no wrath in God and Luther's purpose in saying this. He says it to those who think they must first reconcile the wrath of God through all sorts of achievements. He says it to terrified consciences whom he wishes to encourage to really take a chance on the love of God which has appeared in Christ. And conversely, when Luther says that God's wrath is a terrible reality and no fig-

---

[13] "Wrath is truly God's alien work, which he employs contrary to his nature, because he is forced into it by the wickedness of man." *WA* 42, 356; *LW* 2, 134.

[14] Cf. the "he is," *WA* 40ᴵᴵ, 343. This is quoted in n. 11.)

[15] *WA* 28, 117.

ment of the imagination, he says it to those who are secure and deceive themselves about God's seriousness. To such he cannot say that God's wrath does not exist. The gospel of God's love can be spoken only to someone who has feared God's wrath. To such a person we may and must preach that there is no wrath in God. Neither of these statements is "absolutely" valid itself; each is only relative, that is, always addressed directly to a man in terms of his specific spiritual condition.

It is thus the dialectic of law and gospel that is expressed in Luther's two series of statements about God's wrath. Accordingly the certainty that God is not wrathful does not result simply from abandoning a false concept of God. The message about God's love without wrath does not come as enlightenment but as proclamation; and faith in God's love is constituted not by deeper insight into God but by running a risk and taking a chance on this proclamation. In faith the heart moves from fear of the manifest wrath of God to confidence in his love. Faith is not an intellectual breakthrough from appearance to reality; it is a breakthrough gained by courageously venturing to trust that a reality which the conscience has experienced is not the final reality in God.[16] All statements which deny the wrath of God are assertions of faith. And faith always has a "nevertheless" character about it. For Luther, faith means "against God [to] force its way through to God and call upon God, . . . to break through to God through his wrath, through his punishment, and through his disfavor."[17] Thus faith always has the character of a battle: Man struggles to drive out from within himself the image of God's wrath and to grasp the image of his mercy.[18] He cannot, however, do this by his own power. God's grace and Spirit must give it to him.[19]

The faith that calls upon God changes the "wrath of severity"

---

[16] Cf. *LT* 1, 296 (in the second edition, 1927, p. 226).

[17] "Nature cannot lift itself above such wrath by its own bootstraps or leap over its own feelings and thereby against God force its way through to God and call upon God." *WA* 18, 223.

[18] *WA* 40ᴵᴵ, 342; *LW* 12, 321.

[19] "First God gives grace and his spirit to comfort the heart so that it remembers his mercy and abandons its thoughts of wrath and turns itself from God the Judge to God the Father. But this is not done by human power." *WA* 19, 229.

into the "wrath of mercy."[20] Wrath is then understood as God's "alien work" which prepares for his "proper work" of love. God's blows are then no longer understood as a final rejection but as fatherly discipline administered by a love which seeks to educate and renew us. The fact that God's wrath stands in the service of his love is not a universal and self-evident truth. The conscience which has been struck by God's law does not know this truth and does not have it available. It is only in faith in the gospel that the heart can look backward and recognize God's loving intention in his wrathful activity.

THE EXPERIENCE OF WRATH

God's wrath takes its most terrible form when God does nothing at all, when he remains silent and does not punish the sinner but allows him to go his evil way. By comparison, it is a sign of God's mercy when he does not let a man alone but strikes him with severe punishments.[21] Our reason thinks that exactly the opposite is true. This is why the natural man does not by himself know that he stands under the wrath of God. As long as God does not send men a hard fate, get in their way, and knock them down, they go their way hardened and secure. In his interpretation of the prophet Jonah, Luther sets forth a penetrating illustration of this. The storm has begun but Jonah sleeps below in the ship. This is an illustration of the sleep of sin into which man falls even while he stands under God's judgment.[22] No man feels God's wrath by himself. God must awaken him.

---

[20] *WA* 3, 69. Luther distinguishes the "wrath of indignation or the wrath of anger," or "wrath of severity" from the "wrath of goodness and the rod of the father." *WA* 56, 196; *LCC* 15, 44 f.

[21] *WA*, TR 6, 5554, 6690. "When God speaks, shows his wrath, is angry, punishes, gives us into the hands of our enemies, sends plague, hunger, the sword and other troubles, it is a certain sign that he is gracious to us and seeks our welfare. If, however, he says, 'I will no longer punish you but be silent, withdraw my wrath from you, and let you go on and do whatever you want as you think best,' this is a sign that he has turned away from us. But the world and our reason turn this upside down and think that the opposite is true." *WA*, TR 1, 1179.

[22] "Because God remains silent, does not punish and does not prevent sin, or at least does not take immediate action, it is the natural character of sin to so blind and harden a man that he becomes secure and no longer fears God but lies down and sleeps without seeing what a terrible storm and misfortunes are about to come upon him." *WA* 19, 209.

God sends hard fates upon men. He strikes them through his creatures with every sort of misfortune and trouble and finally with death. "All creatures are God's rods and weapons when he wishes to punish."[23] But even then man does not feel the wrath of God. He still does not understand that the blows and the bad luck are God's judgment, and they do not lead him to fear God.[24] God must first open man's eyes. He does this through the law. Through the law God strikes man's conscience and leads him to an experience of his wrath.[25]

The law was originally not a means of God's wrath.[26] In the primeval state man could still fulfill it. Therefore it was not a burden for him but a joy.[27] Since the fall, however, everything is different. Man is no longer able to fulfill the law. For this reason the law which for men was once a means of community with God, now becomes the instrument of God's wrath.

Admittedly, not all men immediately experience it as such. Luther distinguishes a twofold attitude toward the law and defines two corresponding groups of men or even two stages in the relationship to the law.[28] One group understands the law in its obvious gross sense. Thinking that they can keep it, they lead a respectable life and believe that they have thereby done enough; they are proud of their righteousness. They imagine that they love God's law. In truth, however, they do not love it from their heart but hate it in their inmost being. The outward fulfilment conceals the impurity of the heart. Thus it is that their supposed fulfilment of the law is hypocrisy, self-deception, and a lie.[29] They sin against the law in a twofold way. First, they do not fulfill it in its true sense and depth. Second, being blind to the law's true meaning,

[23] *WA* 17ᴵᴵ, 59.
[24] *WA* 40ᴵᴵᴵ, 567; cf. *LW* 13, 125.
[25] *WA* 19, 210. "For the conscience also feels that every trouble which comes upon us is the wrath of God, and the whole world thinks or feels that God is jealous and wrathful." *WA* 19, 226.
[26] See Luther's doctrine of law and gospel, pp. 251 ff.
[27] *WA* 39ᴵ, 364.
[28] *WA* 5, 447 ff. *WA* 10ᴵᴵᴵ, 89. *WA* 39ᴵ, 50; *LW* 34, 116. *WA* 46, 659 f.; *LW* 22, 141 f.
[29] *WA* 17ᴵ, 240; cf. *LW* 12, 192. "They seem to themselves to be fulfilling the law and doing the works of the law but this is a great deception since without grace neither the heart nor the body can be innocent." *WA* 2, 514. Cf. *WA* 5, 557. *WA* 5, 33; *LW* 14, 294. *WA* 39ᴵ, 569.

they pretend that the appearance of obedience is real obedience and are satisfied with themselves; indeed they even boast of their pretended fulfilment of the law and thus establish their own righteousness.[30] So it is through the law that their sins become really sinful. To be sure, they are not conscious of experiencing God's wrath through the law, but they do in fact suffer it. That they thus become guilty through the law, that is the wrath of God.

The man to whom the Spirit of God has opened the deep spiritual meaning of the law is in a different situation.[31] He realizes what God's holy demand really is. It seems to him to be gigantic. He feels that he cannot fulfill it. He experiences how the man who begins to try to fulfill God's commandment is tortured with relentless and constantly new demands that completely exhaust him. The more he works to fulfill it, the more guilty he becomes. The law thus presses in on him and tortures him, makes him tired and depressed, and produces resistance and antagonism in him.[32] He must hate the law. For it constantly forbids the satisfaction of his own desires opposed to God; he still cannot give up his own desires. He must therefore necessarily begin to hate the law.[33] At the same time he despairs of God and of his mercy and of his own salvation. For he recognizes that God makes unfulfillable demands on him and is now inescapably opposed to him.[34] There is, however, no greater sin than despairing of God's mercy.[35] Despair of God's mercy, of necessity, becomes hatred against God for having put man into such a hopeless situation through his law.[36] It also leads to rebellion, blasphemy, and to the passionate wish that there were no God, no law, and no eternity. Man would really like to

---

[30] *WA* 5, 557.

[31] *WA* 5, 557. "When a man really begins to feel this force, with the Spirit reproving him, he soon despairs of God's mercy." *WA* 39ᴵ, 50; *LW* 34, 116.

[32] "For the letter kills and burdens the heart since the heart feels that it cannot satisfy the law's demands by its own strength and works; the more it exerts itself and works, the more indebted it knows itself to be." *WA* 5, 556. "For the law is not satisfied with works; rather it exhausts the workers by its infinite demands and in various ways brings it about that they fall into self pity or become recalcitrant, self-centered, and unwilling workers, working against their wills." *Ibid.* "Thus the law exhausts and tires them until it consumes them eternally." *Ibid.*, p. 559.

[33] *WA* 5, 557.

[34] See n. 1. Cf. *WA* 39ᴵ, 557, 559.

[35] "But despair of God's mercy is the greatest sin and is unforgivable unless grace cancels it in suitable time." *WA* 39ᴵ 50; *LW* 34, 116.

[36] *WA* 39ᴵ, 558.

kill God if he could."[37] The net effect of the law is thus to make
man constantly more evil.[38] This is a manifestation of God's wrath
against sin. God, through his law, forces man continually deeper
into sin. "A man never sins more terribly than in that moment
when he begins to feel and to understand the law."[39] Luther refers
to Paul's assertion in Romans 7 that the commandment makes sin
"sinful beyond measure" (Rom. 7:13) and that sin kills man
through the commandment (Rom. 7:11).[40] This is what Luther
always taught about the work of the law. He expressed it most
forcefully in his interpretation of Psalm 19:9 in his lectures
[*Operationes*] on the Psalms of 1519-1521. But he repeats the
substance of these statements and even the same words in the disputations of the 1530's (as can be seen from the references which
we have given as proof for our presentation).[41]

Thus two things can happen to a man under the law. Either
he can ignore the seriousness of the law and think he is able to

---

[37] "They hate the testimonies of the Lord and they do not wish to be bound
in these matters. . . . They would prefer you to think that whatever cannot be
seen does not exist." *WA* 5, 556. "And they who despise and do not notice
God but choose the impurity of their own hearts would prefer that it were
possible not to fear." *WA* 5, 560. "You do not do this [that is, what the law
demands] and for that reason you are angry with and blaspheme God—wishing that both God and the law would be cut down." *WA* 39¹, 560. "And I
wished that there were no God." *WA* 46, 660; *LW* 22, 142. 'He blasphemes
the most high majesty when he so strongly wishes that it did not exist and that
he could end its existence—if he were able." *WA* 5, 210. "The more strongly
a man feels the power of the law, the more he turns away from and hates
God." *WA* 39¹, 382.
[38] *WA* 5, 557.
[39] *WA* 39¹, 50; *LW* 34, 116.
[40] *Ibid.*
[41] It is precisely Luther's references to Paul which demonstrate the differences
between them—in spite of the fact that they share the same basic thought.
Paul establishes only that sin becomes sinful beyond measure through the law.
He probably thought of the way in which the commandment forces man's selfish
drives to become conscious resistance to God. That is also Luther's final conclusion. Luther, however, provides a psychological description of man under
the law, describing in detail the law's effect in the sinner's soul. Paul does not
give such detailed descriptions. Furthermore, Paul is concerned only with the
fact that the law makes man a conscious rebel against God. Luther adds to
this and shows how a man who feels that God's law demands too much of
him falls into despair and hatred which are the worst sin against God. Paul
says nothing about that. In Romans 7:7 ff. Paul describes not man's subjective
awareness of his situation under the law without Christ but man's objectively
hopeless situation—which a man can understand only later and from the viewpoint of faith in Christ. Cf. my commentary on Romans, *Römerbrief, Das
Neue Testament Deutsch*, (9th ed. Göttingen: Vandenhoeck & Ruprecht,
1959), p. 71. R. Bultmann, *Theology of the New Testament*, trans. Kendrick
Grobel (New York: Scribners, 1951), 1, 267 f.

fulfill it, in which case he falls into godless conceit and self-satisfaction, or he can recognize the depth of the law and understand
that he is not able to fulfill it, in which case he falls into despair
and hatred against God. There is no third possibility. In both
cases the wrath of God drives man deeper into sin.[42]

The second possibility is nothing other than hell.[43] For it means
that God's wrath uses the law to strike man's conscience and turn
it into a bad conscience. A bad conscience, however, is the real
trouble and punishment of hell. "Hell will be nothing else than a
bad conscience itself. If the devil's conscience were not imprisoned
in guilt, he would be in heaven. Such a conscience ignites the
flames of hell and awakens the most fearful tortures and memo-
ries in the heart . . . the wrath of God is the hell of the devil and
of all the damned."[44] Hell first becomes hell through the wrath of
God, which strikes a man inwardly in the form of an evil conscience. This means that hell is just as much a present and inner
reality as a bad conscience and man's experience of God's wrath
through the law striking his conscience. "Everyone carries his own
hell with him wherever he is, as long as he does not feel the final
disasters of death and God's wrath."[45] Hell is thus primarily not a
particular place but an inner condition of man. After the last day
it will become a particular place to which a man will go with
body and soul.[46]

The real torture of hell, as it already begins to be felt in this
life, comes when a man feels in his conscience that God is against
him and he cannot endure to be close to God. He tries to run
away from God and cannot get away. For the omnipresent God
meets him everywhere in his conscience and is close to him with
his wrath. The omnipotent God holds man in his hands. He tries
to run from God but cannot get away. This is the terrible condition of the man whose conscience is awakened and now experiences the wrath of God. He burns with hatred against this God

---

[42] "Briefly, it is necessary either to despair when one, ignorant of the grace
of God, understands the law, or, one must trust in oneself, not understanding
the law and despising the wrath of God." *WA* 39¹, 50; *LW* 34, 116 f.
[43] *WA* 39¹, 345, 477.
[44] *WA* 44, 617. Cf. *ibid.*, pp. 500.
[45] *WA* 19, 225.
[46] *WA* 19, 225. *WA* 10ᴵᴵᴵ, 192.

who so painfully holds him prisoner in his wrath.[47] Nor does he find the only way out into freedom, namely that he, being under the wrath of God, should turn to this same God and call on him in prayer. If he would only turn to *this* God, fleeing from the wrathful God to the gracious God, he would be helped. "For God can do nothing else; He must help the man who cries and calls. . . . For hell would neither be nor remain hell if someone who is in it were to call out to God for help."[48] But sinful man is not able to do that. He is not able to rise above his experience of God's wrath.[49] In his terrible bondage to himself which makes him hate God, he can neither see nor believe God's mercy, nor can he produce trust in it.[50] Thus he looks elsewhere for help against God's wrath and, precisely for this reason, remains helplessly lost under the wrath of God.[51] Only God himself can open this prison by confronting man with the gospel and opening his heart to faith through his Spirit.

---

[47] "For he seeks an escape and does not find it; then he is very soon involved in the most ardent hatred of God." *WA* 5, 209, cf. 509, 603. "Thus nature is constantly fleeing without ever getting away and so is necessarily condemned in wrath, sin, death, and hell. And here you can see very much of what hell is and what it is like for sinners after this life, namely, that they flee from God's wrath without ever escaping it and yet they do not cry to him and call upon him." *WA* 19, 223. "But real terror arises when the voice of the wrathful God is heard, that is, when it is felt by the conscience. Then God, who previously was nowhere, is everywhere. Then He who earlier appeared to be asleep hears and sees everything; and His wrath burns, rages, and kills like fire." *WA* 42, 419; *LW* 2, 222 f. "If God is angry, there is no escape. This is what eternal punishment will be: they will try to flee and will not be able." [I Thess. 5:3] *WA* 40^{III}, 512; cf. *LW* 13, 93.

[48] *WA* 19, 222.

[49] See n. 17.

[50] *WA* 5, 209.

[51] "No one can believe how difficult it is thus to call upon and cry to God. . . . It is impossible for nature alone or for a godless man to do this and to bear up under this burden [of the evil conscience which feels God's wrath] and at the same time call for help upon that God who is angry and punishes and not to run to someone else for help. It is rather the character of nature to run away from God—to say nothing of turning to him and calling upon him—when he is angry or punishes; it always looks for help somewhere else and does not want to have this God and cannot bear him." *WA* 19, 222.

15

GOD IN JESUS CHRIST

THE RECEPTION OF THE ANCIENT DOGMAS

I BELIEVE in Jesus Christ: this is the confession of faith in the Christian tradition which Luther received.[1] Luther felt that the words "I believe" by themselves assert that Jesus Christ is God. For faith is a relationship to God. "If I should say to someone, 'I believe in you and I place my trust and the confidence of my heart in you,' that one must be my god."[2]

Luther understands the confession that Christ is God in terms of the christological dogma of the ancient church. He expressly accepts the great ecumenical creeds of Greek and Latin theology. Apart from individual concepts he expresses no criticism of the traditional christological dogmas. He agrees with Athanasius and rejects Arius. His Christmas song, "All Praise to Thee, O Jesus Christ," adores the miracle of the incarnation of the Eternal Son in the style of Greek christology.[3] He particularly emphasizes that no power of reason is able to comprehend the paradox of the incarnation. The Creator has become a creature.[4] Luther without reservation uses the traditional terminology of the "two natures" and of their unification in the one person of the Lord to describe the mystery of Jesus Christ. He adopts the ancient doctrine of the communication of attributes, that is, of the exchange of attributes between the two natures in the person of Christ and expands it in his doctrine of the Lord's Supper. He is as much concerned with the true deity of Christ as Athanasius or Anselm was and in the same sense as they. "If Christ is divested of his deity, there re-

---

[1] On Luther's christology, see Ernst Wolf, *Die Christusverkündigung bei Luther* (1935). Reprinted in *Peregrinatio* (Munich: Kaiser, 1954), pp. 30 ff. Erich Seeberg, *Christus, Wirklichkeit und Urbild* (Stuttgart: Kohlhammer, 1937). P. W. Gennrich, *Die Christologie Luthers im Abendmahlsstreit 1524 bis 1529* (Göttingen: Vandenhoeck & Ruprecht, 1929).
[2] *WA* 37, 42.
[3] *WA* 53, 434 f.; *LW* 53, 240 f.
[4] *WA* 37, 43 f.

mains no help against God's wrath and no rescue from his judgment."⁵ "We Christians must know this: If God himself is not
involved and does not add his weight to the scale, our side of the
balance will sink to the ground. By this I mean that if it were
true that it was not God but only a man who died for us, then we
would be lost. But when God's own death and the dead God lie
in the balance pan of the scale it falls down and we are lifted up."⁶
    Luther also follows the traditional way of establishing the true
deity of Christ. The word of God, the Holy Scripture, as well as
Jesus' own witness to himself (here the accounts in the Gospel
of John are decisive), and the miracles which have been reported
to us all teach that Jesus Christ is true God.⁷ The authority of
Scripture thus guarantees the true deity of Christ. There is the additional consideration that the kind of works attributed to Christ
and even now experienced as coming from him are not merely
human but divine works. Furthermore, Christ could not be our
redeemer if he were not the true and eternal God. The proof
from Scripture, however, remains decisive and primary. Everything
new which Luther has to say in christology presupposes the certainty of Christ's deity and incarnation in the sense of the ancient
dogmas. Faith in Christ to this extent rests on the recognition of
the authority of God's word, of the Holy Scripture. And to this
extent Schleiermacher calls on Luther for support when he maintains: "The authority of the Holy Scripture cannot establish faith
in Christ; rather this faith must be presupposed in order to grant a
particular authority to Holy Scripture."⁸ One may not modernize
Luther at this point.

⁵ *WA* 46, 555; *LW* 22, 22.
⁶ *WA* 50, 590. In *WA* 49, 252, Luther also speaks of the "weight" of the
Deity. "The Word [that is, the Son of God] who was in the beginning must
do it Himself; He is the weight who tramples sin and death under foot and
eternally devours them."
⁷ E.g., *WA* 10I,1, 181. *WA* 37, 40. Additional references in Johannes von
Walter, *Die Theologie Luthers* (Gütersloh: Bertelsmann, 1940), pp. 212 f.
and *LT* 2, 164, 169 ff. Theodosius Harnack correctly observes, "Luther holds
these dogmas . . . especially the deity of Christ, not merely as honorable relics
of the ancient church or for the sake of their source, but partially because he
sees that these dogmas are clearly and firmly based in the Holy Scriptures and
partially because they are a postulate of faith and absolutely necessary for faith."
⁸ *The Christian Faith*, ed. and trans. H. R. Mackintosh, J. S. Stewart, *et. al.*
(Edinburgh: T. and T. Clark, 1928), p. 591. [The translation is my own.—
Trans.]

THE NEW ELEMENT IN
LUTHER'S CHRISTOLOGY

There is a new emphasis in Luther's doctrine of Christ, even though he accepts the old doctrine. With all orthodox theologians of the church, he accepts the deity of Jesus Christ. However, he gives new and deeper insight into the meaning and significance for man of the fact that Jesus Christ is true God. No other theologian since the time of the New Testament has so deeply and powerfully expressed the meaning and significance of this fact. Luther's new approach to christology depends on the search for salvation which brought him to Christ.

That is, of course, also true of the earlier forms of christology. Ancient Greek Christianity was particularly motivated by concern for the immortal life of God which redeems from corruption and from death. For this reason, Greek christology thinks of Christ primarily as the One who through his incarnation and resurrection shares the immortal life of God with human beings. This understanding of salvation corresponds to the statements made about Christ. Western Christianity has been determined by the search for freedom from the guilt and the power of sin. The decisive statements about Christ therefore speak of him as having atoned for sin and now through the sacraments, granting the power of grace for a holy life.

Luther also knows these emphases in the doctrine of salvation; and for this reason the corresponding forms of christology continue to be living elements in his own thought. At the center of his theology, however, the concern for salvation assumes a new form. What does God intend to do with us sinful men? What is his relationship to me? How does he feel about me? This is therefore no longer a concern about God's incorruptible and unfading life, his power, his atoning and saving grace; rather Luther is concerned about God Himself, his will, and his heart. For Luther everything depends on the answer to this question about salvation. He finds the answer in Jesus Christ. For this reason, the decisive thing about Christ is that God has opened his heart to us in the person, activity, and history of Jesus Christ and thus gives us certainty about how he feels about us and what he intends to do with us. This is the new meaning and importance of the deity of Jesus Christ for Luther. Christ is "the mirror of God's fatherly heart,"⁹ in whom God himself appears to us. We can say that before Luther, the church and its theologians were primarily concerned with the divine in Christ. They looked for his divine nature, his divine life, and for the divine significance of his satisfaction. Luther, however, looks and finds God the Father himself in person in Jesus Christ.

Thereby Luther's christology takes on Johannine characteristics. The great words of Christ recorded in John such as, "Whoever sees me has seen the Father" [14:9] are the ultimate text of his christology. Luther, however, views Paul and John as in perfect agreement at this point. "This is the knowledge in which St. John, an outstanding evangelist with regard to this thesis, and St. Paul instruct more than the others do. They join and bind Christ and the Father so firmly together that we learn to think of God only in Christ."¹⁰

Luther finds the Father in the man Jesus Christ and nowhere else. The will of the Father is revealed to him in the attitude and activity of the historical Jesus. The coming of the Christ "in our poor flesh and blood," that is, the incarnation, is part of Christ's activity. From this deed Luther learns Christ's attitude toward us and therewith God's feeling about us. For Luther, Christ's coming into the world and his activity and life in this world are inseparably bound together; they are a totality. But in terms of this totality, meditation on the earthly life of Jesus, the consideration of what he did as a man receives new and decisive meaning. The medieval church also looked at the man Jesus, also meditated on his suffering, and also viewed him as an example. Bernard of Clairvaux, in particular, placed the Lord's humanity in the center of his piety and practiced devotional meditation on His suffering. The essential characteristics of this association with the humanity of Christ were deep love of him, suffering with him, and following in the steps of his poor life. Luther's primary concern, to meet

⁹ *WA* 30¹, 192; *BC*, 419, 65.
¹⁰ *WA* 45, 519; *LW* 24, 61. For a study of Luther's relationship to John, cf. Walther von Löwenich, *Luther und das Johanneische Christentum* (Munich: Kaiser, 1935), pp. 20, 35 ff.

the Father in the man Jesus, receded far into the background. No emphasis was put on this. Augustine was Luther's closest forerunner in this; but for Augustine it is only one point among many others, whereas it becomes the heart and center of Luther's view of Christ. In 1519, Luther wrote a well-known letter to his friend Spalatin in which he says, "Whoever wishes to think about or to meditate on God in a way that will lead him to salvation must subordinate everything else to the humanity of Christ."[11]

Luther never tired of centering his own attention and, through his sermons, his congregation's attention on the humanity of Christ. More than half of all his sermons are based on texts from the first three Gospels. He treats the individual details of Jesus' relationships with men and of his life history with unusual love and devotion; and thereby he produces a very living and concrete picture of the man Jesus.[12] Unlike the "Jesus-piety" of the latter nineteenth and early twentieth centuries, Luther is not interested in Jesus as a great "religious personality" but in recognizing the Father in his Son, in knowing God himself. Jesus is the Son of the Father. And God himself stands in the same relationship to us as Jesus did to men, for example, as he did to the Syro-Phoenician woman. We ascend from the viewing of Jesus to the Father, that is, "through the heart of Christ to the heart of God." Augustine in his sermons also urged his congregation to make such an ascent from Jesus to the Father. "Know Christ and then rise through the man to God."[13] We may assume that Luther had either direct or indirect knowledge of this quotation from Augustine. He himself uses it very often.[14] It became one of his decisive descriptions of

---

[11] *WA*, Br 1, 329. Luther says the same thing in a sermon on John 6:47. "If you can humble yourself, hold to the word with your heart and hold to Christ's humanity—then the divinity will indeed become manifest. Then the Father, the Holy Spirit, and the entire Godhead will draw you and hold you." *WA* 33, 154; *LW* 23, 102. Cf. *WA* 33, 156; *LW* 23, 103.

[12] Cf. Walther Köhler, *Wie Luther den Deutschen das Leben Jesu erzählt hat* (Leipzig: Haupt, 1917). Walther von Löwenich, *Luther als Ausleger der Synoptiker* (Munich: Kaiser, 1954), pp. 132 ff.

[13] *Sermo*, 81, 6. Cf. F. Loofs, *Leitfaden zum Studium der Dogmengeschichte* (4th ed., 1906), p. 396, n. 2.

[14] In his *Treatise on Meditating on Christ's Holy Passion* [*Sermon von der Betrachtung des heiligen Leidens Christi*] (1519) Luther instructs us not to stop with looking at the suffering of Christ which terrifies us and leads us to repentance but to "penetrate into the center" [*hindurchzudringen*] and to "see his friendly heart, so full of love for you, which compels him to bear the heavy burden of your conscience and your guilt. After that ascend through

the meaning of believing in Jesus Christ. Luther can speak of
"penetrating" as well as of "ascending"; what counts is that we
do not stop with the humanity of Christ but that, through knowing Jesus as a man, we penetrate [*durchdringen*] to the heart of
God.[15] Both concepts say the same thing. The "logic" of this "ascent" and "penetration" is this: Because Jesus Christ is the Son of
the Father, his activities in relationship to men (as described in
the Bible) are nothing else than what the Father himself wills
and does. Therefore his activity is the basis on which we know
the will of the Father.

Since this certainty about the Father's will is so decisive for
Luther's understanding of salvation, everything ultimately rests on
the will and the attitude toward men that is made known through
Jesus' coming and activity. Naturally the "facts of salvation" as
such are also important for Luther: the wonder of Christmas, the
incarnation, the cross, and Christ's bearing our sin and our need
through his vicarious suffering. However, after reverently treating

---

Christ's heart to God's heart and see that Christ could not have shown this
love to you if God, whom Christ obeys, had not willed it in eternal love."
WA 2, 140. After speaking of Christ's loving vicarious substitution for us
sinners, Luther says, "When I realize this then I must love him and must be
committed to such a man. Then by way of the Son, I climb up to the Father
and see that Christ is God and that he gave himself into my death, into my
sin, and into my misery, and at the same time he gives me his grace. Likewise
I here also recognize the gracious will and the great love of the Father which
no heart can experience; thus I grasp God where he is most tender and think,
'Ah, this is God; ah, this which God has done for me in Christ is God's will
and is well pleasing to him.' And in this vision I experience the great and unspeakable mercy and love of God who has given his dear Child into disgrace,
shame, and death for me. This gracious appearance and loving face of God
preserves me." *WA* 10ᴵᴵᴵ, 154.
[15] Luther discusses the way in which we must "penetrate" to the heart of
God in a letter which he wrote to Spalatin in 1519. Part of this letter is quoted
above, See n. 11. The letter continues: "However, he should keep this [human-
ity of Christ] before his eyes, either while it is suffering or while it is nursing,
[*sugenten*] until the sweetness of its goodness fills him. He should not stop
with this, however, but should penetrate it and think: 'Behold at this time and
at that time, he did not do his own will but the will of God the Father.' Then
the will of the Father, which he shows to us in the humanity of Christ, begins
to be pleasing and acceptable to us." *WA*, Br 1, 329.
Emanuel Hirsch, *Hilfsbuch zum Studium der Dogmatik* (Berlin: de Gruyter,
1937), p. 27. Hirsch has translated *sugentem* as though it meant that the humanity elevated itself. But Luther uses *sugentem* not *surgentem* and *sugere*
means "to nurse." Luther therefore advises us to look to the infant Jesus as
he nurses at his mother's breast. The manger and the cross are placed beside
one another as two images for the way in which Christ emptied himself.

the great wonder of the incarnation and its significance for our salvation he ends a Christmas hymn with the verse beginning:

> All this for us did Jesus do,
> That his great love he might show.[16]

Luther felt that everything in the incarnation of the Eternal Son ultimately shows his love and therewith also the Father's love. This personal dimension in everything which took place at Christmas and later in the life and suffering of Jesus is, for Luther, the real depth of our salvation. It is the one thing which finally matters: God is for us! Luther can therefore characterize the difference between true faith in Christ and a merely historical faith which knows the history of Jesus Christ by saying that true and saving faith recognizes the love of God the Father and his will to save me.[17]

We dare not confuse Luther's method of beginning with the man Jesus and then ascending from him to God with what modern theology has characterized as "christology from below toward above [*von unten nach oben*]." It would be equally dangerous to confuse it with Ritschl's attempt to overcome the doctrine of the two natures by beginning with the man Jesus on the grounds that his earthly, historical life reveals to us the characteristics of God. First, Luther's beginning with the man Jesus does not mean that he needs his human characteristics to reassure himself of the fact that Christ is really God or that God is present in him. For Luther, the deity of Christ is assured through the witness both of Scripture and of the church. When Luther leads us to look at the man Jesus, he is not concerned with showing us that Jesus is God but with showing us what He is, that is, with giving us certainty about the character and the heart of God. One may not therefore quote Luther in support of the modern method of coming to know the deity of Christ.

Second, Luther's view of the man Jesus goes far beyond anything that modern theology would understand under that phrase. Particularly, Luther presupposes the dogma that the Son has become man and that he bears the sins of mankind on the cross—

---

[16] *WA* 35, 435; *LW* 53, 241.
[17] This faith which apprehends Christ "understands the love of God the Father who wants to redeem and save you through Christ, delivered up for your sins." *WA* 39^1, 45; *LW* 34, 110.

several of the passages quoted in the footnotes to show this. Luther thus thinks of something else, or in any case, something more
than the "historical [*geschichtliche*] Jesus" of modern theology. He
thinks of the entire history of Christ which begins in heaven with
the pre-existence of the Eternal Son. It is in his coming in our
flesh and blood that the love of Christ and of God is to be recognized. The so-called "metaphysical" christology is thus already included or presupposed in the humanity of Christ. And the mere
historical fact of the cross does not, as such, reveal the love of
Christ and of God, but does so only within the "word of the cross,"
that is, when it is interpreted in the dogma of the cross. This is
the sense in which Luther's summons to look to the humanity of
Christ is to be understood. The distance between Luther's theological situation and task and our own is obvious. The primary
christological problem and task confronting us is to establish the
deity of Christ; this is completely and clearly decided for Luther
by the witness of the Holy Scripture.

Luther also directs us to follow in the way "from below to
above" in order to know Christ, that is, God in Christ. This way
leads from Christ as a man to Christ as God and thereby to God.
This does not, however, mean that acquaintance with the man
Jesus makes us certain of his deity (Luther never says anything at
all like that), but that we should encounter in Christ God's saving power. When we thus encounter God, we experience his love
and his mercy toward us men. The God who presents himself to
us in the earthly human life of Christ does not kill us earthly and
sinful men but is present to save us. This is the lowest rung on
the ladder to heaven which God has placed for us so that we may
come to him. It stands on the earth—and it is here on earth that
we should find the Son of God and not in heaven. If we begin
with the lowest step, then we will certainly climb into heaven, that
is, to the knowledge of God himself.[18]

Two particularly impressive passages from Luther's sermons
show how he sees the real meaning of the history of Jesus Christ

---

[18] "Scripture begins very gently by leading us first to Christ as to a man
and afterwards to the Lord of all creation and finally to a God. Thus I come
in easily and learn to know God. Philosophy and the wise men of this world,
however, want to begin at the top and have become fools in the process. One
must begin at the bottom and afterward rise up." *WA* 10^{I,2}, 297.

in the revelation of his gracious will for us. One of the gems among Luther's sermons on texts from the life of Jesus is the sermon on the baptism of Jesus preached on the Festival of the Epiphany, 1526.[19] In this sermon Luther develops the end of the story of the baptism according to Matthew, who reports the Voice speaking down from heaven, "This is my beloved Son with whom I am well pleased." This word thus bears witness that Jesus is God's Son and that he pleases him. "With these words God gives a joyous and happy heart to all the world and fills all creation with divine sweetness and comfort. How so? Well, if I know and am certain that the man Christ is God's Son and pleases him —as I must be certain because the divine majesty from heaven itself says this and it cannot lie—then I am also certain that everything the man says and does is the word and the work of that dear Son which must please God best of all. So then, I mark this and hold it fast. . . . Now how could God pour out more of himself and offer himself in a more loving or sweeter way than by saying that his heart is pleased because his Son Christ speaks so friendly with me, is so heartily concerned about me, and suffers, dies, and does everything with such a great love for me. Do you not think that a human heart, should it actually feel that God is so well pleased with Christ when he serves us in this way, must shatter into a hundred thousand pieces because its joy is so great? For then it would peer into the depths of the fatherly heart, yes, into the inexhaustible goodness and eternal love of God which he feels and has felt toward us from eternity."[20]

Luther's sermon for Palm Sunday on Philippians 2:5 ff., published in the Lenten Sermons of 1525, expresses the same thoughts. After interpreting Paul's statements about Christ's emptying and humbling himself, Luther seeks the motive for Christ's action and puts his finger on these words of the text: " 'He was obedient' . . . [Christ did all this] to obey the Father." And now Luther continues: "Thus Paul opens the heavens with one word

---

[19] "This order must be carefully preserved. We are not to ascend to the study of the divine majesty before we have adequately comprehended this little infant. We are to ascend into heaven by that ladder which is placed before us, using those steps which God prepared and used for this ascent. The Son of God does not want to be seen and found in heaven. Therefore he descended from heaven to this earth and came to us in our flesh. He placed himself in the womb of his mother, in her lap, and on the cross. And this is the ladder which he has placed on the earth and by which we are to ascend to God." *WA* 40ᴵᴵᴵ, 656.

[20] *WA* 20, 228. Cf. "Thus this word ['This is my dear Son'] leads you to see God's good pleasure and his entire heart in Christ in all his words and works, and again you see Christ in the heart and good pleasure of God so that the two are in every way most inimitably joined together." *WA* 20, 229.

and clears the way for us to look into the depths of the divine majesty and see the gracious will and love of his fatherly heart for us, which cannot be expressed in words. Paul wants us to feel that God has from all eternity been pleased with what that glorious person Christ should do and has done for us. Whose heart does not simply melt for joy at hearing this? Who can fail to love, praise, and give thanks and not only become a servant of the whole world but gladly become even less—less important than nothing—when he sees that God himself values him so highly and so richly pours out and proves his fatherly will in the obedience of his Son."[m]

All of these passages describe the ascent from Christ to the Father in different ways, each determined by the particular text. For Luther, our thinking can make this ascent only by treading on the step that is made by the fact to which the Holy Scripture bears witness: This man Jesus, together with everything he does for our sake and all that he shows us of himself is God's son; therefore, he is God and at one with the will of the Father. The deity and sonship of Christ are now of decisive importance for Luther because he knows that Christ's will is God's will and that Christ's work takes place according to God's will and under his good pleasure. Since Luther's ultimate concern is completely personal, that is, he is concerned with God's gracious will for us, he also emphasizes that Christ's person is God and is united with God. This unity is found in the unity of his will with God's will and in the Son's obedience to the Father. The words with which "St. Paul opens heaven" are "He was obedient." Heaven is opened by the statement about obedience and not by the reference to Christ's eternal deity—according to Luther, Christ does not give up his deity but retains it even in his humiliation.

Through all this, Luther changes the basic character of "knowing Christ." As far as the objective knowledge of Christ is concerned, Luther includes everything that the ancient dogmas say about the two natures of Christ and their union in him, as we have already said. Luther denies none of it and it is also important for him. For Luther, however, the understanding of the deity and humanity of Christ found in the ancient christological formulas is

_____

[m] *WA* 17ᴵᴵ, 244.

not yet the decisive thing about Christ's deity; and such knowledge is not yet true knowledge of Christ but only its presupposition. Luther says it very clearly in his explanation of the Second Article of the Apostles' Creed. "I believe that Jesus Christ, true God begotten from the Father from eternity, and also true man, born of the Virgin Mary, is my Lord."[22] The great christological theses of the dogma are present, not however as the sole content or object of "I believe," but in apposition to "Jesus Christ." The content of faith in Jesus Christ for Luther is that "He is my Lord" or, in other words, not what Christ is in and for himself, but rather what he is for me.

We might also express this by saying that the true knowledge of Christ consists in recognizing and grasping God's will for me in Christ's will for me and God's work to save me in Christ's work for me. This is how Luther says it in one of his sermons on John 14 and 15 which was preached in the year 1537 (Cruciger wrote it down and published it in 1538). "The first and foremost point about Christ's being in the Father is this, that I do not doubt that everything this Man says and does, stands and must stand in heaven before all the angels, in the world before all tyrants, in hell before all devils, in the heart before every evil conscience and my own thoughts. For if I am sure that everything he thinks, says, and wants reflects the will of the Father, I am able to defy anyone who would be wrathful and angry with me. In Christ I have the Father's will and heart."[23] Luther thus interprets John 14:20. His interpretation of John 14:24, part of the Gospel lesson for Pentecost, follows as transmitted in Cruciger's *Sommerpostille* of 1544). "The devil can still stand it when a man grasps only the man Jesus and does not go beyond this. Yes, he even permits the statement that Christ is truly God to be spoken and heard. He struggles, however, to prevent the heart from joining Christ and the Father so closely and solidly together that it certainly concludes that Christ's word and the Father's word are one and the same word, heart, and will. Hearts that do not understand think, 'Yes, I certainly hear the friendly and comforting words which Christ speaks to the troubled conscience; who knows, however, how I

---

[22] *WA* 30[1], 295; *BC*, 345.
[23] *WA* 45, 589; *LW* 24, 141.

stand with God in heaven?' This means that such a heart does not unite God and Christ but fabricates one kind of Christ and another kind of God for itself and thus misses the true God, who does not will to be found and grasped any place else than in this Christ."[34]

The devil, who wants to snatch men away from the true God, is thus quite willing to allow two things to happen: (1) He allows men to honor and love the man Jesus, and to relate to him in their piety, for example, in "Jesus mysticism" without looking for and finding the Father in him; (2) He allows men to be convinced of the orthodox doctrine of Christ's eternal deity. From the viewpoint of Satan these two attitudes are still neutral and harmless and not a matter of concern. For as long as Jesus does not mean more than this to a man he has not yet found the one true God—and that is what Satan wants to prevent. Christological orthodoxy is not yet true faith in Christ. True knowledge of Christ begins only when the heart sees Christ and the Father as completely one, when it takes them together and thus recognizes and grasps the presence of the Father with his word, heart, will, in the word, heart, will, of Jesus Christ. Such a man becomes completely certain of the heart of God through and for the sake of Jesus. The devil cannot bear that. For such a man has really found God and is now completely removed from the power of Satan. Mere christological orthodoxy did not yet have this effect. The ancient dogma was concerned with the unity of the two natures in Christ. Luther teaches this as the tradition does. But it is not the "metaphysical" unity of the two natures but rather the personal unity of the Son with the Father, of the man Jesus with the eternal God, that is ultimately decisive in the matter of salvation. We earthly men know how God thinks about us and how he relates to us only in the earthly reality of someone who is like us, that is, in the human will and activity of Jesus. For this reason, the primary and the only saving truth is that God himself is present for us in the humanity of Jesus Christ. God the Father himself is present and not merely the "divine nature." In this sense it is true that the reality of God for us is Jesus Christ "and there is no other God."

---

[34] *WA* 21, 467.

"I know of no other God except the one called Jesus Christ."* To be certain of this is to believe in Jesus Christ. This unity of Jesus with God and of God with Jesus, the presence of the heart and will of God in Jesus, is the "deity of Christ" in the fullest sense.

Thus Luther involved the deity in the humanity with a boldness previously unheard of in theology. More accurately, it is not merely the deity or divine nature but God himself who is personally involved. The fact that Luther views God and man outside of Christ as "further apart than heaven and earth" did not hinder him. God is this man, and this man is the presence of God for us. Basically, Luther thereby transcends the doctrine of the two natures as inadequate. It says far too little and does not say what is decisive. Luther is ultimately concerned not with the relationship of the divine and the human nature but with the relationship of the person of Jesus to the person of the Father. Luther thus takes the deity of Christ and his incarnation more seriously than anyone since the New Testament writers themselves.

According to Luther, this also means that the knowledge of God's metaphysical attributes is not ultimately decisive for a man who is seeking salvation (as essential as these attributes are to God's deity); the ultimate decisive factor is knowledge of God's personal nature and activity. "God is truly known not when we are aware of his power or his wisdom which are terrible, but only when we know his goodness and his love."* God's deity is—as we saw earlier—centered in the fact that it is God's nature to give, to bestow, to sacrifice himself, and to have mercy. Faith can read these divine characteristics in the picture of Jesus and places its trust in them. God opens his personal being to us only in the human person of Jesus.

The significance of this for the subjective side of our knowledge of Christ is: Subjective knowledge of Christ does not consist in intellectual and theoretical character, but like its content, is the completely personal, practical, existential, and vital grasping of Christ with the "heart" and with the whole person. It is not

---

* "There is no other God apart from this Christ who has become our light and sun. . . . He and no one else is the true God. It is he, I say, who has enlightened us through his gospel." *WA* 31¹, 63.
* *WA* 2, 141.

enough to accept the eternal deity of Christ because of the authority of Scripture and the church. Accepting the Second Article of the Apostles' Creed as true and repeating the content of the text is also not yet faith in Christ. Such faith is present only when "I believe that he is my Lord." "We find many people who say, 'Christ is a man, Son of God, born of a pure virgin, has become man, died, and is risen again from the dead, etc.'—that is all nothing. The fact that he is Christ means that he was given for us without any of our works. He gained the Holy Spirit of God for us and made us children of God without our merits, so that we might have a gracious God, become Lord with him over everything that is in heaven and earth, and in addition have eternal life through him. That is faith and that is what it means to really know Christ."[37] I thus begin to seriously believe in Christ and really recognize him only when I know that he has been given for my salvation and with heartfelt confidence let him be for me what he wills to be and should be according to God's will. This means that true faith in Jesus Christ is characterized by the fact that it relates Christ and his work to the believer's own existence with its "for me" and "for us." This is what distinguishes true faith from a merely theoretical, historical, and metaphysical faith, which holds that the historical facts of the history and the deity of Christ are true without relating them to a man's own existence.[38] Only saving faith therefore is true faith in Christ. Christology is basically soteriology. Christ is known only in his works and I know his work only when I know it has taken place for me. Thus according to Luther, the doctrine of the person of Christ and the doctrine of his works cannot be separated from each other; they are one in such a way that I can grasp the meaning of Christ's work only in its significance for me. Faith in Christ is thus one and the same as justifying faith.[39] Salutary knowledge of Christ is thoroughly personal not only in terms of its content, that is, of God's personal relation-

---

[37] *WA* 17[1], 365.

[38] *WA* 39[1], 45 f.; *LW* 34, 110 f. "You do not yet have Christ, even though you know that he is God and man. You truly have him only when you believe that this altogether pure and innocent person has been granted to you by the Father as your High Priest and Redeemer, yes, as your slave." *WA* 40[1], 448; *LW* 26, 288.

[39] "The papists therefore have not called upon the Son of God in true faith, that is not as the one through whom alone we have forgiveness of sins and

ship to me, but also according to its method. I know only when I am personally involved in grasping and in accepting Christ as my Lord and only when I risk everything on him. The only significant knowledge of Christ does not precede being overcome and brought to complete trust in him but first comes into existence in and with such trust.

This understanding of Jesus Christ presupposes and is bound to the fact that he is present for us. He is present for us through the word about him. We have him in no other way, for he is now in heaven with the Father. He does not come down to us in person but only in the gospel. And this gospel does not merely bring him to us but also teaches us to know him for what he is. Christ's humanity is as such also a veiling of the deity. If he would come to us today in his historical reality we would not recognize him as the Son in his deity. This must first be revealed to us. And this takes place through the gospel. We need the apostolic word about him which bears witness to who he is. We have him only in faith in his presence in the gospel. Thus the basis of faith is not the "historical Jesus" by himself (Christ's "flesh") but that Christ who is preached in the apostolic witness. Luther does not know Christ apart from the witness of faith which Scripture and Christianity give to him.[20] This is so indispensable for the knowledge of Christ that Luther can say, God wishes the spoken word to be revered more than Christ's humanity.[21]

THE TWO-NATURE CHRISTOLOGY IN LUTHER

As we have already pointed out, Luther adopts the traditional dogmatic doctrine of the two natures. In agreement with it he teaches the full unity of the deity and the humanity in the person

---

eternal life. Since they trust also in their works, they do not pray to the true God." *WA* 39^{II}, 278.

[20] *WA* 10^{III}, 349, *LW* 51, 114. (This is quoted in Chap. 6, n. 1.) "Christ is known only through his word. Without the word, his flesh would be of no benefit to me even though it came today." *WA* 10^{III}, 210. "Thus He comes to us through the gospel. Yes, it is far better that he comes through the gospel than that he would now enter in through the door; for you would not even know him even though he came in. If you believe then you have; if you do not believe then you do not have." *WA* 10^{III}, 92.

[21] *WA* 17^{I}, 5.

of Jesus Christ, the full participation of the humanity in the deity and of the deity in the humanity. "God has suffered; a man created heaven and earth; a man died; God who is from all eternity died; the boy who nurses at the breast of the Virgin Mary is the creator of all things."[33] Luther teaches the impersonality of the human nature of Christ (*an-* or *enhypostasis*).[33]

How is it possible for Luther to maintain the true humanity of Christ under these circumstances? He teaches that Jesus Christ, according to his human nature, also possessed the attributes of the divine majesty, that is, that even the child Jesus was omniscient, omnipotent, and omnipresent. Luther thus does not understand Christ's emptying himself in the incarnation to mean that he left his deity or essential characteristics of it in heaven. Luther does not agree with the exegetes of the early church who understood Philippians 2:6 f. ("He emptied himself") as describing an act of the pre-existent Christ at the time of the incarnation; rather he understands it as describing the attitude of the incarnate earthly Christ.[34] Christ did not empty himself once for all; rather he constantly emptied himself throughout his entire earthly life. He did not give up the "form of God" and take on "the form of a servant" once for all at the time of the incarnation; rather the man Jesus possessed the form of God at all times and could have used it and brought it to bear, but at every point he laid it aside and made himself the servant of all rather than their Lord. "The 'form of God' is wisdom, power, righteousness, goodness—and freedom too; for Christ was a free, powerful, wise man, subject to none of the vices or sins to which all other men are subject. . . . [Christ] relinquished that form to God, the Father, and emptied himself, unwilling to use his rank against us, unwilling to be different from us. Moreover, for our sakes he became as one of us and took the form

---

[33] "The union of the humanity and the divinity of Christ is one Person, not two, and whatever is attributed to one is properly assigned also to the other." *WA* 39^{II}, 280. The material quoted in the text follows. On the communication of attributes, cf. *WA* 39^{II}, 93 (theses 2 f.).

[33] *WA* 39^{II}, 93 f. (Thesis 11 f., 116 ff.) Luther rejects Augustine's formulation: "The divine Person assumes a man" (otherwise there would be two persons in Christ); instead he says: "The divine Person assumes the human nature." Cf. Loofs, *op. cit.* p. 286, n. 9.

[34] Luther's interpretation is followed by Calvin, by the older Lutheran exegetes until J. A. Bengel, also by modern exegetes, e.g., A. Schlatter, and by dogmaticians such as A. Ritschl and Werner Elert.

of a servant, that is, he subjected himself to all evils. And although he was free . . . he made himself servant of all [Mark 9:35], living as if all the evils which were ours were actually his own."[35] The opposite of Christ is the Pharisee. He commits "robbery," that is, he keeps what he has for himself, does not give it back to God, and does not use it to serve his brother.

Luther's understanding of Christ's emptying of himself in the Philippians passage reveals the full depth of his christology. The act of the will with which the Eternal Son became man is constantly repeated throughout his entire life in new ways. One can say that the incarnation is a progressive event, an always new act of Christ. Here we are dealing with the fact that he gave up not only the use of the so-called metaphysical attributes which the divine nature communicated to the human nature but also that he did not draw the conclusions from his ethical superiority of righteousness, and goodness. Unlike G. Thomasius, the nineteenth century kenotic theologian, Luther does not distinguish between different kinds of attributes but takes them all together as the form of God. Christ's emptying of himself consists in an on-going act of giving himself for sinful men in a particular situation, that is, Christ wished to be equal to men, entered into the difficulties resting upon humanity, and took them upon himself even though he in the form of God was free of them all. The incarnation is completed in the cross of Christ. It is thus no longer only the metaphysical presupposition of Christ's work of salvation but the completion of that work itself. The work of salvation is not something different from an emptying which had previously taken place, but occurs in Christ's on-going emptying of himself. Christ's emptying is continued in Christians. Christ's attitude and activity is their example.[36] Thus Luther's understanding of the incarnation and of the emptying determines and permeates his ethics.

Luther illustrates his understanding of the emptying in his sermon in the Lenten series of 1525 on Philippians 2:5 ff. with a particularly well-formed illustration.[37] He distinguishes between

[35] *WA* 2, 148; *LW* 31, 301.
[36] *WA* 2, 147 f.; *LW* 31, 300 ff.
[37] *WA* 17^{II}, 237.

the deity and the "form of divine majesty." The fact that Christ
empties himself of the latter does not mean that he lays it aside
and gives it up; rather he retains it; however, he "does not make
use of it and boast of it against us but uses it to serve us."
He "thus remains God and in the form of God. That is, he was
God, did all the divine works, and spoke all the divine words for
our good and thus serves us as our servant."[38] Christ's emptying
of himself thus consists in serving us with his "divine form" and
using it for us and not for himself.[39] Luther can thus use Christ's
emptying of himself as an example even for a prince. The prince
should give up his power not outwardly but "in his heart." This
means that he should not exploit it for himself but use it to
serve his people. "Let a prince then empty himself of his power
and supremacy in his heart and concern himself with the needs
of his subjects as though they were his own needs. For this is
what Christ has done for us, and this is a genuine work of Christian love."[40]

However, all our admiration of this understanding of Christ's
emptying of himself, cannot keep us from asking whether Luther's
presupposition that the man Jesus had the attributes of the divine
majesty available to him can be reconciled with the biblical picture of the historical Christ, or even with the strong emphasis on
the Lord's' true humanity which we find elsewhere in Luther's own
theology. In some of his statements Luther, in spite of everything,
seeks to preserve the true humanity of the historical Jesus. An example is his interpretation of Luke 2:40 and 52, "Jesus increased
in wisdom." (This is Luther's translation after 1530.) How can
this passage be reconciled with the dogmatic thesis that Jesus from
the beginning was true God and thus also possessed the Spirit of
God. Luther explains: Certainly the Spirit was in Christ from the
time of his conception; but as he grew in body and increased in
reason "the Spirit descended more and more upon him and moved
him more as time went on." Luke's statement that Christ became
strong in spirit is to be taken seriously. Furthermore, the Spirit of
God did not move Christ constantly and equally at every time but
from time to time, "at one time he awoke him to this, at another

---

[38] *WA* 17ᴵᴵ, 243.
[39] *WA* 11, 76. *WA* 12, 469 ff.
[40] *WA* 11, 273; *LW* 45, 120.

time to that.["] There is no question that Luther with these thoughts
stands in the tradition of Antiochian christology.["] These ideas do
not, however, agree very well with his acceptance of the doctrine
that human nature did not have its own human person (*anhypos-
tasis*). For these thoughts presuppose an independent personal life
of the man Jesus which is more and more moved by the Spirit of
God. On the other hand, taken as dogmatic statements they are
only a very small concession. The contradiction between Luther's
understanding of the *genus majestaticum* [the doctrine that Jesus,
according to his human nature, possessed all divine power and attributes at his birth] as the presupposition of Christ's emptying himself within history remains for the most part in contradiction to
the genuine picture of the man Jesus.

And yet the *genus majestaticum* is not Luther's final christological statement.["] He transcends it when he makes statements which
point in the direction of a *genus tapeinoticon* [the doctrine that
God in Christ shared the weakness, suffering, and humiliation of
Jesus]. Luther holds that the deity of Christ, because of the incarnation and of its personal unity with the humanity, enters into
the uttermost depths of its suffering. God suffers in Christ. However Luther did not teach "patripassionism" [that the Father suf-
fered], as the modalists did, but "deipassionism" [that God suf-
fered].["] He always regarded God's suffering as an incomprehensible mystery. It is a constant stumbling block to reason and even
the angels cannot fully understand it. For it means nothing else
than that God is at once completely above and completely below.
He is the creator and the Lord and yet at the same time the
lowest creature and a servant subject to all men, yes, even to the

---

["] *WA* 10I,1, 446.

["] Cf. Luther's position with that of Theodore of Mopsuestia, particularly the
citations in Loofs, *op. cit.*, p. 282. Theodore also teaches that the indwelling
of the Logos became more perfect in the course of Jesus' ethical development.
There is also precedent in Theodore for Luther's description of Christ's humanity as the "tool and house of the Deity." *WA* 10I,1, 447. Cf. Loofs, *op. cit.*,
pp. 280, 282 and R. Seeberg, *Lehrbuch der Dogmengeschichte* (3rd ed.;
Leipzig." Deichert, 1933) II, 187 ff.

["] For an evaluation and criticism of Luther's christology, cf. *CW*, pp. 450,
459.

["] In a disputation of 1540, Luther on the basis of his understanding of the
communication of attributes, rejects the opinion that the deity did not suffer
in Christ. "What Christ has suffered should also be attributed to God for they
are one." *WA* 39II, 121.

devil. This man Jesus who bears the wrath of God, the sin of the
world, all earthly trouble, yes, hell itself, is at the same time the
highest God.[45] The mystery of Christ cannot be expressed without
these paradoxes. This is especially true of Christ's suffering on the
cross. The deity itself is present with its power in the sufferings.
It is with his humiliation and particularly with his suffering on the
cross that Christ has overcome the devil and hell—that, however,
is the work of God himself.[46]

At the same time, Luther had to come to terms with Christ's
assertion on the cross that he was forsaken by God. In a sermon
of 1537, he understands it in this way: The deity has certainly not
departed from the humanity (deity and humanity are inseparably
united in Christ); but "the deity withdrew and hid . . . the humanity was left alone, the devil had free access to Christ, and the
deity withdrew its power and let the humanity fight alone."[47] Elsewhere Luther says that Christ on the cross did not feel his deity
but suffered purely as a man.[48] This second statement can be reconciled with Luther's thought that the deity suffered in Christ but
the former cannot, at least not in the form that the deity "withdrew." This does not do justice to the mystery of the suffering of
the deity in the sufferings of the man Jesus Christ; that can be
expressed only in paradoxical terms. The deity of Christ specifically did not withdraw while the man Jesus was suffering but is
present in him both in his suffering and victory.

Luther's basic christological confession (that the Father's heart
and will are present in Christ) will always be significant. However, his dogmatic theory which describes Christ as true God and
true man is not unified within itself but displays contradictions.
Theology had to go beyond it.

---

[45] *WA* 39ɪɪ, 279, 340. *WA* 43, 579 f.
[46] *WA* 43, 579.
[47] *WA* 45, 239 f.; *LW* 12, 126 f. The text is edited by Aurifaber but the
decisive words are supported by Rörer's notes.
[48] *WA* 17ɪ, 72.

16

THE TRINITY

LUTHER accepts the orthodox doctrine of the Trinity because he knows that it is supported by the Scripture—not only by the New but also by the Old Testament.[1] He emphasizes the "one-ness" and the "three-ness" equally.[2] God is one and three. His unity exceeds the one-ness of any creature and of any mathematical concept. For this reason Luther has no love for the concept "threefoldness" [Dreifaltigkeit] for "there is most sublime oneness in the deity."[3] But this one-ness is at the same time the three-ness of distinct "persons." One God in three persons—every person is the entire deity and yet no person exists as the deity for itself without the other two.[4] This all is based on the Scripture. Reason admittedly finds all this talk about one-ness and three-ness in God a stumbling block. But since it is based on clear Scripture, reason must be silent at this point and we must believe.[5]

The concepts used to express this mystery may very well be inadequate. Scripture does not speak of the "Trinity." But one must teach in this way for the sake of the weak and in order to instruct at all. Whoever wants to use some other expression in place of that of the three persons is free to do it, but he must be very careful to preserve and express the substance which is at stake.[6] That substance, however, is these two factors which are both with-

---

[1] "Scripture thus cleverly proves that there are three persons and one God. For I would believe neither the writings of Augustine nor the teachers of the church unless the New and the Old Testaments would clearly show this doctrine of the Trinity." WA 39II, 305.
[2] WA 39II, 287 (theses 5 ff.).
[3] WA 46, 436.
[4] WA 39II, 287.
[5] WA 10I,1, 152. "Here faith and not all sorts of sharp speculation is needed." WA 10I,1, 157, 186. "If natural reason does not comprehend this, it is proper that faith alone should comprehend it; natural reason produces heresy and error but faith teaches and holds the truth for it sticks to the Scripture which does not lie or deceive." WA 10I,1, 191. Cf. p. 186 of this volume and WA 37, 44.
[6] WA 39II, 305, 287.

out doubt founded in the Scripture: the one-ness and the three-ness in this one-ness.[7]

Since Luther found that the Scripture bears witness to God's Trinity, he thought about it just as seriously as about the other basic Christian truths. Several of his series of theses and disputations deal with it;[8] and he presented it in his sermons when the christological texts used in the Christmas season, such as John 1 and Hebrews 1, demanded it.[9] He was well aware of the medieval discussion of the doctrine.[10] However, he rejects the "subtleties" of the scholastics who wanted to derive the Trinity from the nature of God and thus make it understandable to reason. He wishes to stick to and remain with the word of Scripture.[11] In his interpretation of Scripture, he uses traditional concepts such as the eternal birth of the Son or that the works of God directed outside of himself are indivisible.[12] Here, as elsewhere in the basic form of his doctrine of the Trinity, Luther follows the trail blazed by Augustine; for example, Luther says that the three "persons" cannot be theologically distinguished from each other by anything else than their respective relationships to one another as Father, Son, and Spirit.[13]

---

[7] Luther translates the Latin word *trinus* by saying that God is a *"Gedritts"* in one essence. *WA* 49, 239.

[8] *WA* 39[II], 287 f.; 293, 305, 339 f.

[9] *WA* 10[I,1], 152 ff., 180 ff. *WA* 37, 38. *WA* 49, 238 ff.

[10] *WA* 39[II], 287 f.

[11] *WA* 10[I,1], 181, 185. "The scholastic teachers have attempted to make this understandable with very great subtleties." *WA* 10[I,1], 181. "Instead of this, one should stick to the simple, clear, powerful words of Scripture." *WA* 37, 41.

[12] "Christ is eternally and without ceasing born from the Father." *WA* 10[I,1], 154. Cf. *WA* 39[II], 293 and *WA* 49, 239.

[13] *WA* 37, 41.

17

JESUS CHRIST AS THE
RECONCILER AND REDEEMER

G OD'S FEELING toward us sinners can be known in Christ. In him the heart of God is revealed. As the chapter on christology [Chapter 15] showed, Luther places decisive emphasis on this point. God makes his feeling known in the history of Jesus Christ. This history of Jesus Christ also has its own value as an event between God and humanity, and between God and the powers to whom his wrath has surrendered humanity. In accord with Christian tradition since the time of Paul, Luther understands the history of Jesus as the event of reconciliation and redemption. The wrath of God rests on sinful humanity. Through Jesus Christ, the crucified and risen, a new situation is created. Christ becomes our Lord in place of the powers of wrath. He is "a Lord of life, righteousness, and of all good and blessedness." Through his work we become his own and are so ruled by him that he gives us a share in his life in "righteousness, innocence, and blessedness"— this is his lordship.[1]

All this is God's work in and through Christ. It is he who sends the Christ to do his work.[2] But Christ acts in the name and in the power of God in such a way that he not only deals with humanity and the powers to which it has succumbed but also with God himself. He acts also in relationship to God; he "reconciles" God, or we may also say, he reconciles humanity with God.[3] God in Christ deals also with himself, in himself, and in an inner trinitarian relationship.

---

[1] Cf. the explanations of the Second Article in Luther's *Small* and *Large Catechisms. WA* 30¹, 295 f. and 185 ff.; *BC,* 345 and 413 ff.

[2] *WA* 17ⁱⁱ, 293.

[3] *WA* 8, 519; *LW* 36, 177. *WA* 10ⁱⁱⁱ, 136. As these and other passages show, Luther uses the expression interchangeably: God is reconciled; we are reconciled with God the Father; we are reconciled with God.

CHRIST'S WORK AS
SATISFACTION TO GOD

God cannot simply forget about his wrath and show his mercy
to sinners if his righteousness is not satisfied.[4] Luther, like Anselm, views Christ's work in terms of satisfaction. Christ must bring
a satisfaction to God for our sins.[5] Certainly the grace of God is
given to sinners freely without their own merit and assistance.
From another viewpoint, however, it does not take place for nothing. It costs us nothing but "it has still cost someone else very
much for us."[6] This is true because satisfaction can occur only
through substitution. Jesus Christ takes our place.[7] In a "wonderful exchange" he takes upon himself all men's debts and guilt before God.[8] He achieves that satisfaction which men were not able

---

[4] "All this does not take place for nothing or without the satisfaction of God's
righteousness; for mercy and grace cannot be thought of as being effective over
us and in us or as helping us to eternal blessings and salvation unless God's
righteousness has previously been completely satisfied . . . for no one can come
to God's rich grace unless he has absolutely and completely satisfied God's
commandments." *WA* 10[I,1], 121.
  "Now although God purely out of grace does not impute our sins to us, still
he did not want to do this unless his law and his righteousness had received a
more than adequate satisfaction. This gracious imputation must first be pur-
chased and won from his righteousness for us." *WA* 10[I,1], 470.

[5] The concepts "satisfy" [*genugtun*] and "satisfaction" appear frequently in
Luther. Cf. "If he was to be priest and to reconcile us with God according to
his priestly office then he had to satisfy God's righteousness for us." *WA* 10[I,1],
720. Cf. *WA* 10[III], 49; *LW* 51, 92. *WA* 17[II], 291. *WA* 29, 578 f.
WA 30[I], 187; *BC*, 407, 313. *WA* 40[II], 405; *LW* 12, 365. *WA* 31[II], 339.
WA 39[I], 46. At the same time, however, Luther felt that the term "satisfaction" was not adequate to express the full significance of Christ's work and of
his saving power to redeem us from death and the devil, and to establish the
eternal kingdom of his grace. Satisfaction, he says, "is still too weak to fully
express the grace of Christ and does not adequately honor his suffering." *WA*
21, 264.

[6] *WA* 10[I,1], 471.

[7] "Christ, the Son of God stands in our place and has taken all our sins upon
his shoulders. . . . He is the eternal satisfaction for our sin and reconciles us
with God, the Father." *WA* 10[III], 49; *LW* 51, 92. "Christ has taken our
place." *WA* 29, 578. Christ became "obedient for the sake of all of us." *WA*
39[I], 53; *LW* 34, 119.
  Cf. the beginning of the third verse in Luther's hymn, "Death Held Our
Lord in Prison":

> Jesus Christ, God's only Son,
> Into our place descending . . .

WA 35, 443; *LW* 53, 257.

[8] *WA* 31[II], 339 (Luther's comment on Isa. 43:24).

to produce for themselves. He is driven to this by his love; and in his love is God's love and mercy toward sinners.[*]

Christ makes satisfaction for sinners in a twofold way. He fulfills the will of God expressed in the law; he suffers the punishment of sin, the wrath of God. Both are done in our place and for our benefit.

Christ has completely fulfilled the law. "For he has loved God with his whole heart, with his whole soul, with all his powers, with his whole mind, and his neighbor as himself." He loved God by obeying him (Phil. 2:8), by becoming man, and carrying out everything the Father gave him to do. He loved his neighbor, for everything he did on earth had no other purpose than to serve men up to and including giving his life.[10]

Christ has not only fulfilled the law, but he has also suffered the punishment which the law pronounces over transgressors. Only this fully satisfies God's righteousness. For Anselm, there were only two possibilities, either punishment or satisfaction. For Luther, satisfaction takes place through punishment, not of the sinner but of Christ.[11] The punishment of sin consists in God's wrath together with all that this wrath brings upon men. So Christ stands under God's wrath. He suffers it in his passion. He dies the death of a sinner. But, unlike us sinners, he suffers and dies an "innocent and pure death." Thereby he has "paid God" and brought it about that God takes his wrath and his eternal punishment away from us.[12]

Luther's understanding of Christ's suffering on the cross was determined primarily by the biblical texts, particularly the fourth word from the cross [Matt. 27:46] and Galatians 3:13;[13] he was,

---

[*] See the hymn "Dear Christians, Let Us Now Rejoice," especially vss. 4 and 5, "Then God was sorry on his throne . . ." and "To his dear Son he said: 'Go down. . . .' " *WA* 35, 423; *LW* 53, 219 f. Cf. *WA* 39ᴵ, 45; *LW* 34, 110.
[10] *WA* 17ᴵᴵ, 291.
[11] On the relationship between Luther's and Anselm's doctrine of reconciliation, cf. my *Grundriss der Dogmatik* (3rd ed.; Gütersloh: Bertelsmann, 1949), 11, 32.
[12] *WA* 37, 59. Cf. *WA* 8, 519; *LW* 36, 177.
[13] The main sources are: "Treatise on Meditating on the Holy Suffering of Christ" [*Sermon von der Betrachtung des heiligen Leidens Christi*] (1519), *WA* 2, 136 ff.; "Treatise on Preparing to Die" [*Sermon von der Bereitung zum Sterben*] (1519), *WA* 2, 685 ff.; the interpretation of Psalm 22 in Luther's lectures [*Operationes*] on the Psalms (1521), *WA* 5, 598 ff.; the interpretation of Galatians 3:13 in the large commentary on Galatians (1535), *WA* 40ᴵ,

204 The Theology of Martin Luther

however, also influenced by his personal experience of the temptations which a Christian experiences.[14] It was in these experiences
that the real meaning of the biblical statements was opened up for
Luther. Christ's suffering and the Christian's temptations belong
together. They belong together in a twofold way. First, the Christian's experience of his own temptations gives him a concept of
Christ's personal agony. Second, Christ's sufferings must be understood also in terms of his entering into the deepest inner needs of
men—otherwise, Christ could not be our Savior in these specific
needs.

Christ's sufferings are completely human. He suffers as an "absolutely genuine man." Even though the depth of his personal
agony on the cross cannot be measured, the fact that he suffers
completely like any other man means it is still an analogy between
the temptation which the godly experience in their conscience under God's wrath and the passion of Christ.[15] He is a man who is
tempted to the point of despair. He suffers God as his conscience
bears the burden of the consciousness of guilt. For this reason, he
is able to understand us men in the total depth and burden of our
need under God and help us in it.[16] We must take the fourth word

---

432 ff.; *LW* 26, 276 ff.; the sermon on the fourth word from the cross (1521),
WA 17¹, 67 ff.

[14] Erich Vogelsang, *Der angefochtene Christus bei Luther* (Berlin: de
Gruyter, 1932). We may not, however, so simply and easily treat Scripture
and the temptations as two opposite poles in Luther's thought. For Scripture
also plays a role in the experience of temptation—at least insofar as Luther
understands temptations in the light of the experience of godly men as these
are recorded in Scripture—especially in the Psalms. Cf., e.g., *WA* 5, 603.
Luther constantly maintains that we can only partially understand the affliction of Christ's crucifixion on the basis of the affliction of our own temptations;
on the other hand, however, we can first fully understand the affliction of our
own temptations, which is otherwise hidden from us in our godlessness, on
the basis of Christ's suffering the wrath of God. It is thus necessary to say
both: We partially understand Christ's sufferings on the basis of our own experience, but on the other hand we arrive at a full understanding of affliction
under God only through viewing Christ's suffering as the Scripture testifies
to it. "We do not know ourselves and we do not know in what a shameful
condition we are. . . . All things which Christ bore are therefore to be applied
to our own being; thus as we can more clearly see Christ's suffering, we shall
better see our own damnation." *WA* 17¹, 71.
[15] "We must allow Christ to be a mere man. . . . He was a man like any
other. . . . This is what happens to righteous men. . . . He felt everything as
a man." *WA* 17¹, 68 f. These are references to Rörer's edition; corresponding passages from Roth's notes are found on the same pages.
[16] "For no trouble and suffering is so great that we cannot bear it provided
we have this comfort that we have a gracious God; then let our troubles assume

from the cross and what Paul says in Galatians 3:13 ("Christ . . . was made a curse for us . . . cursed is everyone who hangs on the tree") in their radical seriousness and not explain them away." Christ really was forsaken by God; he was removed from the experience of his fatherly closeness, and in its stead he was surrendered to the experience of wrath and hell. According to Isaiah 53, God strikes him because of our sins and punishes him with our punishment. This, however, does not consist only in physical death but "also in the anxiety and terror of a terrified conscience, which feels God's eternal wrath as though it would be forsaken and rejected by God for all eternity." Christ therefore also had to "endure the anxiety and the terror of a frightened conscience which feels eternal wrath."[17] Thus Christ is, even in his own eyes, as one who is cursed. We may not in any way reduce the meaning of "cursed" in Galatians 3:13 but must with Paul, in all seriousness, accept its full validity in reference to Christ. The same is true of Isaiah 53:6. "God does not play with the words of the prophet."[18] Whoever does not take this completely seriously—because he finds it unbearable to say that Christ has borne our punishment and our curse—robs us of the sweetest comfort.[20]

Christ has thus fully endured the horror of the anxiety of death, of being forsaken by God, and of being under God's wrath. Luther gives a detailed description of the absolutely terrible hopelessness of this situation.[21] Christ's suffering is, however, distinguished from our experience of wrath and of being forsaken by God by the fact that he does not suffer all this for himself but for us. He lovingly enters into the entire need of the sinner under God. "He was moved both by his own desire and by the will of the Father to be

---

any form. Here however God is against him [Christ]. . . . He had to be mangled so that he might be like us and know how to help us. This is our comfort when we are in trouble; then we can think: 'You, too, have been in the hospital.' Those who have some experiences are good people to confess to. Christ therefore understands us right away and knows how to help us. For he has also experienced trouble. And this is a most certain comfort." *WA* 45, 370 f.

[17] *WA* 40^{I}, 432; *LW* 26, 276.
[18] *WA* 5, 602 f.
[19] *WA* 40^{I}, 434; *LW* 26, 278. Cf. *WA* 8, 33; *LW* 13, 35.
[20] "This knowledge of Christ and most delightful comfort, that Christ became a curse for us, to set us free from the curse of the law—of this the Sophists deprive us." *WA* 40^{I}, 434; *LW* 26, 278.
[21] *WA* 5, 602.

a friend of sinners."[20] Thus he is forsaken by God and suffers God's wrath in our place. He takes our sins upon himself as though they were his own.[21] In this way, he stands before God as a sinner among sinners and God treats him as such. Our salvation depends on Christ's thus taking our sins upon himself.[22]

However, even though Christ suffered as a sinner in our place still he himself did not sin, even when he suffered. This distinguishes his pure sufferings from our sufferings in which we cannot escape sinning through murmuring, defiance, despair, and blasphemy. The fourth word from the cross admittedly sounds as though Christ were complaining against God. In truth, however, it is only the creature's natural resistance to the terror of death—like the cracking of an overloaded beam. The truth is that Christ even in the depths of his temptation always loves God with all his powers.[23] In the midst of the most terrible experience of being forsaken by God and cursed, he is not at odds with God but surrenders to him in love and obedience. Thus the highest joy and the greatest sorrow, the greatest helplessness and the greatest power, the worst disturbance and the deepest peace, absolute death and absolute life, all dwell together in Christ paradoxically; for Christ is both forsaken by God and still not forsaken. Luther finds both in the fourth word from the cross. Christ calls on the same God he feels has forsaken him. No one who knows that he has been completely forsaken calls on God saying, "My God."[24]

Christ does not stop loving God above all things even though he fully experiences being forsaken by God, being under God's wrath, and the hell of being far from God. He thereby overcomes wrath and hell and destroys the power of judgment. The rest of us so stand under God's wrath that we become angry with God and sin all over again because we seek our own benefit. Christ is completely different. Certainly he feels as the damned feel. He trembles before God and would like to flee from him; but, at the same

---

[20] *WA* 40[1], 434; *LW* 26, 278. On the love with which Christ for our sake took everything upon himself, cf. *WA* 17[1], 70 f.

[21] *WA* 5, 603. "Whatever sins I, you, and all of us have committed or may commit in the future, they are as much Christ's own, as if he himself had committed them." *WA* 40[1], 435; *LW* 26, 278.

[22] *WA* 40[1], 435; *LW* 26, 278.

[23] *WA* 5, 604 f.

[24] *WA* 5, 602.

time, he is able to love him." This is how Luther expresses it in
his *Sermon von der Bereitung zum Sterben*, "Treatise on Preparing
to Die." Christ is the heavenly image of one who, although forsaken by God as damned, has yet overcome hell through his omnipotent love; and he bears witness that he is the dearest Son and
offers this same status to us as our own if we believe."[28]

We need not dwell on the fact that this understanding of the
suffering of Christ lies beyond all psychology. Psychologically it is
hardly possible to imagine how Christ in the midst of being forsaken by God still continues to love God, and therefore lives in
the peace of God even in the midst of anxiety. This is a theological conclusion which Luther draws from the twofold content
of the fourth word from the cross and from the doctrine of the
sinlessness of Christ.[29]

Christ suffers hell and the wrath of God and overcomes them
with the power of his love of God. This is how Luther understands the Article of Christ's descent into hell. It is part of Christ's
death agony. Through it Christ gains the victory over hell. Luther took this position in all stages of his writing.[30] Beside it
stands a somewhat different explanation. On the basis of Scripture
passages such as Psalm 16:10 and Acts 2:24-27 and in view of
the sequence of the Articles in the Apostles' Creed (where the descent into hell follows his death) Luther also teaches a descent of
Christ into hell after his death. This two-sidedness brings him into
difficulty.[31] In spite of this, there is no doubt that Luther's own
personal understanding of Christ's descent into hell relates it to the
passion, Gethsemane, and Golgotha. Calvin adopted this understanding and it was accepted in some confessions of faith of the
Reformed Church. In distinction from Luther, Melanchthon understood the descent into hell as Christ's triumphal victory march into
hell. Christ terrifies the devils and the damned by showing them
his power. Lutheran orthodoxy developed this idea. The descent

---

[27] *WA* 5, 605.
[28] *WA* 2, 691.
[29] "For Christ was neither able to sin nor to do any evil—although those
things which he did would really have been sin if we had done them." *WA* 50,
604.
[30] Cf. the evidence in my article; "Niedergefahren zur Hölle," *Zeitschrift für
systematische Theologie*, XIX (1942), 371 ff.
[31] *Ibid.*

into hell is the first stage of Christ's exaltation. Thus Luther's deep understanding is abandoned. Lutherans, for the most part, opposed the Reformed understanding of the descent into hell as part of the humiliation without realizing that they were also polemicizing against Luther.

Luther's doctrine of the cross transcends all earlier theology through the radical seriousness with which he allows Christ to suffer both hell and being totally forsaken by God. In his understanding of the incarnation and of the cross, he cannot involve Christ deeply enough in our humanity. The reason for this lies in the fact that, as we have already emphasized, Luther consistently treats Christ's passion in relationship to man's suffering [*Anfechtung*] under the wrath of God; and from this viewpoint, he must be able to understand and recognize this passion as the completely adequate help in his own distress. He who wills to be our Savior must also have suffered our own hell. This hell is not a future condition or place but a present reality which a terrified conscience experiences under the wrath of God. Christ who has experienced both hell and being forsaken by God is directly involved in the distress of all men under the wrath of God and their distress is directly involved in his passion.

CHRIST'S WORK AS A BATTLE WITH THE DEMONIC POWERS

As Luther's understanding of the descent into hell already indicates, he describes the work of Christ not only as the satisfaction of God—as the suffering and overcoming of wrath, of being forsaken by God, of the curse and of hell—he describes it also as Christ's battle against the demonic powers which God's wrath uses in its service and to which God has surrendered humanity.[85] Luther personifies these powers. Sin, the essence of all the sin of humanity, appears and seeks to damn Christ as it does all other men. But here, in the form of a man who takes our place as "the worst, the greatest, and the only sinner," it confronts a person of eternal and unchangeable righteousness;[86] it confronts Christ's "uncon-

---

[85] Our main source is the large commentary on Galatians, *WA* 40^{1}, 432 ff.: *LW* 26, 276 ff. and Luther's sermons.

[86] *WA* 40^{1}, 438; *LW* 26, 281.

querable obedience."[34] This duel can have no other outcome than that "all of sin is conquered, put to death and buried." Christ's righteousness swallows up sin.[35] The law which condemns and seeks to pass judgment on Christ, as it does on the rest of us, has no right and no power over him, for he has fully and completely fulfilled it.[36] Death, the omnipotent tyrant of the entire world, tries its hand on him, but it meets immortal life.[37]

> That was a right wondrous strife
> When Death in Life's grip wallowed
> Off victorious came Life,
> Death he has quite upswallowed.
> The Scripture has published that—
> How one Death the other ate.[38]

"Christ is nothing else than pure life"; therefore he smothers death with his own life.[39] Satan and hell seek to swallow him, but they have no right to him; rather, they themselves are swallowed up by him, for he lives in perfect love of God.[40] Instead of speaking about Satan and hell, Luther can also speak of the curse of God's wrath as a power which, in Christ's passion, does battle with the power of blessing over Christ. The curse attempts to destroy the blessing, but it is not able to do so; for the blessing is divine and eternal. It is characteristic that Luther here places the curse of divine wrath together with powers of sin and death and lists it as one of "those monsters" with which Christ fights.[41] This is an indication of the fact that the powers with which Christ must do battle are ultimately to be understood theocentrically.

---

[34] "He is the picture of God's grace against the sin which he has taken upon himself and conquered through his invincible obedience." *WA* 2, 691. Cf. the line, "My innocence shall bear thy sin," in vs. 8 of "Dear Christians, Let Us Now Rejoice." *WA* 35, 425; *LW* 53. 220.

[35] Sin "did indeed attack him but he was too powerful for it; he swallowed it and it was extinguished in him like a spark of fire which falls into the great ocean, for he was nothing but righteousness." *WA* 17ᴵᴵ, 291.

[36] *WA* 17ᴵᴵ, 291.

[37] *WA* 40ᴵ, 439; *LW* 26, 281.

[38] *WA* 35, 444, *LW* 53, 257.

[39] *WA* 2, 689; Cf. *WA* 17ᴵᴵ, 292.

[40] *WA* 17ᴵᴵ, 292. *WA* 2, 691.

[41] *WA* 40ᴵ, 440. *LW* 26, 282.

God's wrath is one of them and is the real threatening and killing power in them all."

This battle is of all inclusive significance and yet, according to Colossians 2:15, it took place "in him," that is, in the one and only person of Christ." The man Jesus survived all this. Without his deity, however, he could not have conquered in this fearful struggle against these mighty enemies." Luther has strongly emphasized that the deity of Christ is simply indispensable for this. Anyone who denies that Christ is God, as Arius did, must, if he is consistent, also deny that we are redeemed by Christ. "For to conquer the sin of the world, death, the curse, and the wrath of God in himself—this is the work, not of any creature but of the divine power. Therefore it was necessary that he who was to conquer these in himself should be true God by nature . . . to abolish sin, to destroy death, to remove the curse in himself, to grant righteousness, to bring life to light, and to bring the blessing in himself; that is, to annihilate these and to create those—all these are works solely of the divine power."" Similarly, since Christ has conquered and killed the law in his own person, he must really be God for he must be above the law as only God is."

In everything that he says about Christ's battle with and victory over the powers, as well as wherever he treats the work of Christ theocentrically, Luther constantly holds Christ's death and resurrection closely together, just as the Apostle Paul does. Good Friday and Easter belong inseparably together." It is characteristic

---

"Luther does not hesitate to use the word "satisfaction" in speaking of Christ's conflict with the demonic powers and thus uses the same expression as he does in describing the way in which Christ satisfied God's righteousness. He speaks of the law in the same way. *WA* 17ᵤ, 291. *WA* 40ᵢ, 503; *LW* 26, 325.

" *WA* 40ᵢ, 440; *LW* 26, 282.

" During his inner struggle in the garden of Gethsemane, Christ was preserved through divine power. "Otherwise he could not have conquered." *WA* 10 ᵢᵢᵢ, 74. "For if the person who sacrificed himself for us were not with God, the fact that he was born of a virgin and even suffered a thousand deaths would be meaningless and of no help before God. But the fact that the seed of Abraham is also true God, who gives himself for us brings us the blessing and the victory over all sin and death." *WA* 17ᵤ, 236.

" *WA* 40ᵢ, 441; *LW* 26, 281.

" *WA* 40ᵢ, 569; *LW* 26, 373.

" Luther distinguishes the saving significance of Christ's suffering from that of his resurrection, just as Paul does in Romans 4:25: "In his suffering Christ makes our sin known and puts it to death; but through his resurrection he

of this fact that Luther did not write a single Lenten hymn of the type composed by later Lutherans. His song about Christ's work of salvation is an Easter hymn, "Death Held Our Lord in Prison."[48] The explicitly formulated Lenten hymns of seventeenth century Lutheran poets are modeled after medieval Catholic examples. Luther did not prepare the way for such hymns. Reconciliation has taken place in the death and resurrection of Christ together. Our certainty of the accomplished reconciliation depends on Christ's resurrection. To believe the resurrection of Christ means to be certain of reconciliation through Christ.[49]

Christ's work was done at a particular time in history. But in God's sight it has existed from all eternity. It is in this sense that, according to Revelation 13:8, Christ was crucified for the sins of all mankind "before the foundation of the world." For the gospel and the promise are there from the beginning and these include Christ and his work. Thus all men of all times who believe the promise, and thereby are blessed, live from the work of Christ—even though this actually first took place on Golgotha. The work of salvation is, however, based on God's eternal will to save;[50] and its significance therefore transcends time.[51]

THE CONTEMPORANEITY OF CHRIST'S WORK IN THE WORD AND IN FAITH

Christ's work took place "outside of us" and therefore without us. It is always given to us and thus it is "objective." At the same time, however, Luther emphasizes as strongly as possible that Christ's work does us no good without faith; it helps us only in

---

makes us righteous and free of all sins." *WA* 2, 140. Cf. ". . . he conquers it through his resurrection." *Ibid.*

[48] *WA* 35, 444; *LW* 53, 257.

[49] "Believing in the resurrection of Jesus Christ is nothing else than believing that we have someone who reconciles us with God and that this is Christ who maks us acceptable to the Father and godly. . . . Faith in Christ's resurrection is when we believe . . . that Christ took our sins and the sins of the whole world as well as the Father's wrath on his shoulders and that he has drowned them both in himself so that we are thereby reconciled to God and become completely righteous." *WA* 10ᴵᴵᴵ, 136 f.

[50] Cf. I Peter 1:20.

[51] "Furthermore, Christ died for the sins of the whole world from the beginning of the world. . . ." *WA* 39ᴵ, 49; *LW* 34, 115. "Christ was not in reality slain from the foundation of the world, except in promise only." *WA* 39ᴵᴵ, 197; *LW* 34, 313. Cf. *WA* 18, 203; *LW* 40, 214.

so far as we take Christ into us through faith.[62] This cannot happen unless his work is proclaimed to us. This characteristic of Christ's work also characterized in totality the person and history of Jesus Christ. Only the proclamation brings them to us and lets us understand their significance for us. (Cf. p. 193.)[63] The statement that no other work or faith can help us before God remains valid without exception even in reference to Christ. Although he is the Savior of the whole world, he does not help me as long as I do not believe.[64] In his person Christ has won the victory over the demonic powers. But his victory is of benefit to me only when Christ lives and rules in me; and this occurs in faith. Thus the assertion that our faith is the victory which overcomes the world (I John 5:4) remains inseparably joined to the assertion that Christ has personally triumphed over the demonic powers.[65] Christ's victory is not a metaphysical event of the kind which would enable us to say that since the time of his victory the demonic powers are no longer present. Rather, it is a victory in the sense that the victory depends on him and that the enemies are overcome and no longer present when he is present. We may describe the reality of his victory only with this spatial image of "where he is present" and not with the temporal image of "since" as though the world has, since Golgotha and Easter, been changed in a metaphysical sense. The demonic powers, including the wrath of God and the law, are all still there, but they are overcome in Christ; and therefore they are overcome for those in whom Christ lives through

---

[62] "To the extent that Christ rules by his grace in the hearts of the faithful, there is no sin or death or curse. But where Christ is not known, there these things remain. And so all who do not believe lack this blessing and this victory. 'For this,' as John says, 'is our victory, faith.'" *WA* 40[I], 440; *LW* 26. 282. Luther repeatedly uses expressions such as "to the extent that we believe" when he speaks of the work of Christ.

[63] "If Christ had been crucified a hundred thousand times and no one had said anything about it, what good would the fact of his crucifixion be?" *WA* 26, 40. Cf. *WA* 10[I,2], 7.

[64] "Let no one undertake to be saved through the faith or works of someone else. Yes, you cannot be saved through the work and faith of Mary or even of Christ himself without your own faith. For God will not permit Mary or even Christ himself to take your place and thus make you righteous and godly, unless you yourself believe and are godly. . . . Otherwise no alien faith or work is of any use at all, even if it is Christ's who is the Savior of the whole world; his benefits and his help are of no use to you unless you believe and are enlightened." *WA* 10[III], 306, 308.

[65] Cf. n. 52. Luther describes genuine faith as "that which shall make Christ effective in us against death, sin, and the law." *WA* 39[I], 45; *LW* 110.

faith. For this reason, Christ's work of reconciliation and redemption is not a material achievement which would be valid and effective even without our knowing it and without personal sharing with Christ. In this sense it is definitely not "objective." It demands "subjective" appropriation in faith; it actually works salvation only for and in faith. When salvation is at stake, God deals with men always and only in a personal way, that is, through faith. Thus faith belongs to the work of Christ.

In faith Christ's work becomes our own. Luther feels that it must be expressed thus: Christ in his love has made himself one with man. Now man in faith makes himself one with Christ. Christ takes everything which is ours, our sin, the agony of our death under the wrath of God and in the power of the devil, upon himself and gives himself and everything which belongs to him, his innocence, righteousness, and blessedness to us as our very own. This is the "wonderful exchange."[56] Faith, however, is the way in which a man allows this "wonderful exchange" to take place in him; through faith he holds himself to it and risks his life on it. Christ says to man, "Your sin is mine and my innocence is yours." Faith says to Christ, "My sin lies on you and your innocence and righteousness now belong to me." Thus this blessed exchange takes place only through faith. Faith is the wedding ring through which Christ's marriage with the soul and therewith the "wonderful exchange" takes place. Through it Christ and the soul become "one body" and along with this the sharing of property and of suffering is also effected. Faith is thus a part of reconciliation itself.[57]

Faith can, however, appropriate Christ's intercession for us

---

[56] *WA* 7, 25; *RW* 1, 363. *WA* 7, 54; *LW* 31, 351. This concept appears much earlier. *WA* 1, 593; *LW* 31, 189 ff. "This is the mystery of the riches of divine grace for sinners; for by a wonderful exchange our sins are now not ours but Christ's, and Christ's righteousness is not Christ's but ours." *WA* 5, 608. "Now the wonderful exchange takes place and Christ gives himself and his benefits to faith and takes upon himself the heart and whatever lies heavy upon it and makes it his own." *WA* 10ᴵᴵᴵ, 356, 358. "See the wonderful exchange. One man sins, another man makes satisfaction. One man has peace coming to him and another man receives it." *WA* 31ᴵᴵ, 435 (interpretation of Isa. 53, 5).

[57] " 'The subjective appropriation' of reconciliation is not something which follows an 'objective' work of God but is itself a part of this 'objective' work of God without which this could not be accomplished and without which 'satisfaction' would not have taken place." (Regin Prenter, *Schöpfung und Erlösung*, trans. Christiane Boehncke-Sjöberg [Göttingen: Vandenhoeck & Ruprecht, 1960] II, 365.)

through his cross only by allowing itself to be drawn into Christ's
suffering and death. Like Paul, Luther also speaks of dying with
Christ. Dying with Christ is not an event which takes place only
once. (Luther understands Galatians 2:19 to mean "I am crucified with Christ" rather than "I have been crucified with Christ.")
He thus equates it with the on-going act of the crucifixion of the
flesh (Luther translates Paul's "crucified your flesh" in Galatians
5:24 in the present tense).[58] Luther here uses a distinction made
by Augustine: Christ's passion is both a "sacrament" and "an example." Luther understands this to mean: Christ's passion is a
sacrament insofar as sin is basically killed through it; it is an example, insofar as we should follow after Christ by suffering and
dying physically. As a "sacrament" Christ's passion is an event
which "took place for my benefit"; as an "example," it means
that "I, too, must suffer according to my old Adam."[59] "Christ's
sufferings must be dealt with not only in terms of words and appearances but honestly in terms of life."[60] Luther says that the letters of Paul and of Peter are full of such statements. And he especially emphasized this thought in his doctrine of baptism. It is
an inseparable part of his understanding of the vicarious work of
Christ. The substitution is to be understood not as though it were
merely exclusive but also as inclusive. Christ not only suffered for
us but wishes thereby to draw us into his sufferings.[61]

Christ's sufferings were both a battle with and a victory over
the demonic powers. Faith appropriates this side of his sufferings,
too, in such a way that Christ's battle and victory are actualized
in the Christian. Luther echoes John in calling faith the victory.
Christ's battle and victory, his cross and resurrection, are thus con-

---

[58] From 1522 to 1527, Luther properly translated Paul's text as "have crucified"; after 1530, however, he uses the present tense. This is of the same significance for his theological relationship to Paul as his use of Romans 6 in the
fourth question on baptism in the *Small Catechism.* Cf. pp. 353 and *CW*, p.
561.

[59] *WA* 2, 141. 501. *WA* 17[1], 74.

[60] *WA* 2, 141.

[61] In Rudolf Bultmann's existential theology, the connection between both
sides of the matter is broken, and they are placed in opposition to each other.
"Believing in the cross means taking Christ's cross upon oneself as one's own
and allowing oneself to be crucified with Christ." *Offenbarung und Heilsge-
schehen* (Munich: Kaiser, 1941), p. 61. For Luther this is the second event
and happens after the "for us." For Bultmann this is all there is.

temporary events, present to us in the battles and the victories of the individual Christian. Christ in his person definitely conquered the demonic powers, law, Satan and death in principle, once for all." But empirically they are still in the world and exercise their tyranny where Christ does not rule." They will not be completely abolished until the end of the world." Until then they continue to fight against Christ whom they hate; now, however, they fight against him in the form of his Christendom, the church." To this extent Christ's battle is—in spite of his victory—still not ended."

Christians, because they still have the old man, and sinners remain subject to the attacks of the demonic powers. They are threatened and tempted by them in their conscience; and such attacks do not cease. Therefore Christ must now wage the battle in the hearts of his people through word and sacrament—even though he has already won the battle on the cross and at Easter. The Christ for us must become the Christ in us through faith. Thus he once again becomes a warrior." He fights this battle with the demonic powers in the hearts of his people on the basis of his victory. But his victory is a real and present factor for his people only in constantly new battles. Christ's confrontation with the de-

---

⁶² *WA* 17ᴵ, 71.

⁶³ *WA* 19, 140.

⁶⁴ "This is the masterful way in which death and sin are conquered: not by forcibly destroying them in a moment so they are never again felt, but by first taking their power and authority and condemning them with an authoritative judgment to destruction. Now even though they continue to rage and make themselves felt before they are completely destroyed, it makes no difference; for judgment has been passed upon them: they have neither power nor authority but shall and must soon cease and come to their end." *WA* 19, 141. Cf. *WA* 8, 92; *LW* 32, 207.

⁶⁵ According to Psalm 110, Christ's kingdom dominates "in the midst of his enemies." Christ's kingdom is a kingdom of the sort which "is constantly in battle position." *WA* 34ᴵᴵ, 68.

⁶⁶ "These tyrants [the demonic powers] have in one day been defeated on the cross through blood; and He still constantly gives them a beating because he proclaims that all who believe in him shall be free from the law, sin, and death. The same battle still goes on today through the word and the sacraments." *WA* 49, 24.

⁶⁷ "Christ is the Lord Sabbaoth, that is, a God of the hosts or of the armies, who constantly wages war and takes up his battle position within us." *WA* 30ᴵᴵ, 621. Immediately before this Luther asserts the same of faith, "Thus faith and the spirit are busy and restless, must always have something to do, and always remain in battle position." *WA* 30ᴵᴵ, 621. "Scripture calls Christ . . . the Lord of hosts, because his Christians constantly carry on the conflict through the gospel and always engaged in battle against the devil, world and flesh." *WA* 8, 13. Cf. *WA* 8, 123; *LW* 32, 252, and cf. *WA* 37, 50.

monic powers is constantly renewed in every Christian.[68] The Christian conquers in this battle by holding fast to the victory of Christ proclaimed to him in the gospel.[69] He fights and he conquers by the power of Christ's victory and in view of his faith in it. Thus new temptations constantly come through the demonic powers but are repeatedly overcome. These demonic powers thus lose both their authority to accuse man (which they have by themselves) as well as the power to mislead and corrupt him.

The battle against these accusing powers is waged by the conscience, that is, by Christ in the conscience. Since God's wrath strikes man in his conscience, it must also be overcome in the conscience; it is overcome when the conscience grasps Christ in faith.[70]

Faith in Christ sets man free from the demonic powers and makes him "a free lord of all things." For the demonic powers have, because of Christ, lost their power to separate the man who believes in Christ from God and from his salvation. On the contrary, they must now serve men as a means and a help to true life exactly as they served Christ himself. "Nothing can now damage a man's salvation; yes, all things must be subject to him and help him to salvation," (according to Romans 8:28). This is "the freedom of the Christian," "the precious freedom and power of the Christian."[71] This freedom comes from Christ through his cross and resurrection and becomes the Christian's very own; but the Christian has it only as he constantly receives it in faith from the presence of Christ and lives in it.

Thus as Luther tries to understand the cross of Christ in terms of the temptations of the Christian, he also interprets the temptations and distress of a Christian attacked by the powers of wrath in terms of the cross and resurrection. Christ's battle and victory

---

[68] *WA* 17ᴵᴵ, 291 f. Note Luther's description of Christ's encounter with the demonic powers, his description of the encounter of Christians with the demonic powers, and the attack of the demonic powers on the Christian.

[69] "Christ has conquered sin, death, hell, and the devil. This has also taken place in him who grasps this, firmly believes, and trusts; in Christ Jesus he becomes a conquerer of sin, death, hell, and the devil." *WA* 10ᴵᴵᴵ, 356. "See, Christians must thus arm themselves with Christ's victory and beat back the devil with it." *WA* 36, 694 (Cruciger's edition). "If the earth itself cries out against me; I shall not fear because I know that Christ has conquered all the things that confront me." *WA* 17ᴵ, 71.

[70] "The conscience conquers when Christ helps; for then grace and the victory are present in us." *WA* 39ᴵᴵ, 170.

[71] *WA* 7, 27 f. *RW* 1, 365 f.; cf. *LW* 31, 354 f.

are thus made fully contemporary, and the Christian is contemporaneous with the event of the cross and of Easter which happened once for all but which affects the lives of all. The Christ who fought then still fights today. He who once arose from the dead constantly and increasingly rises from the dead in his Christians."[73] Luther's Christ is both the historical and the risen and living Christ. He is a person by himself, before us and for us; and yet he envelops all things with his living spiritual power and is present in all. Christ lives completely in his community. His work transcends the distinction between what has happened and what is happening, between history outside of us and before us and history within us, and thus also between past history and the Spirit who today works and creates faith. All this belongs to the theology of the work of Christ. It is a reality before us, for us, and in us. With this perspective Luther has gone far beyond all previous interpretations of the work of Christ. He has reached back behind them to the New Testament itself and completely renews the Apostle Paul's basic understanding of Christ's work.

Luther found still another wonderfully simple expression to sum up the work and the effect of Christ. Jesus Christ, as true man, has passed through our entire life, activity, and suffering. He has experienced everything in life that we have, yet in a completely different way than we have, that is, without sin. Our way through life and death is always sinful; everything becomes sin for us and hurts us. But the path of Christ's life was completely pure. Thereby, he has sanctified everything life brings whether we suffer or act. And he does this in a twofold sense. First, our life which is in itself impure becomes pure and holy in God's eyes and judgment because of Christ's sinless way through life. Second, Christ's pure passage through life takes the curse out of all the relationships of life and out of death itself; it makes all of these things a blessing to us and a means of God's grace. In this twofold sense Christ's pure life and death sanctifies our entire life and death; it even sanctifies the whole world so that we need no longer become sinful in it. In so far as we are baptized and stand in faith in Christ, nothing can make us impure because he has passed through it all.

---

[73] "Christ is not yet completely revived in his believers but in them, as the first fruits, he begins to be revived from death." *WA* 39¹, 356.

Here the entire work of Christ, his life and death, is all summed up into one and expressed as simply and as meaningfully for our life as one can imagine.[73]

GUSTAF AULÉN'S UNDERSTANDING OF CHRIST'S WORK

Our presentation of Luther's doctrine of the work of Christ is, in substance, an implicit rejection of a modern interpretation which puts Luther's accent at a different point. According to this modern interpretation, the decisive factor in Christ's work is not its relationship to God's righteousness and wrath but to the demonic powers which threaten men. Albrecht Ritschl asserted, "Luther understands the satisfaction wrought by Christ as something rendered not to God but to those demonic powers."[74] Although Theodosius Harnack, on the basis of the sources, proved that this thesis is a distortion of Luther's thought,[75] the Swedish dogmatician Gustaf Aulén has again asserted it.[76] Aulén distinguishes three types of

---

[73] *WA* 37, 53 ff. "Through his holy and pure life Christ has sanctified our shameful and sinful life." *WA* 37, 53. "He has purified everything through his body, so that because of him everything which belongs to our natural birth and this life does not damage us; but it is considered to be as pure as what belongs to him, because through baptism and faith I have been clothed with his birth and life. Therefore everything I do is pleasing to God and is properly called a holy walking, standing, eating, drinking, sleeping, and waking, etc. In every Christian this becomes a pure and holy thing, even though he still lives in the flesh and is definitely impure in himself; through faith, everything about him is pure. Thus it is an alien holiness, however, and yet our own, because God wills to see nothing which we do in this life as impure in itself; but everything becomes holy, precious, and acceptable to him through this Child who makes the whole world holy through his life." *WA* 37, 57. "The Lord Christ goes through our entire life from birth on: he has experienced, lived through, and done everything just as we do; and by thus laying his own hand on life has consecrated it and made it holy. . . . Now everything connected with both Christ's life and death is our treasure, which makes us thoroughly holy and in which we have everything, although we no longer have or are anything here upon earth, cut off from this life by death. And yet we are so holy in him that even in death we are not dead before him but death itself must become a life for us." *WA* 37, 59 f. Cf. *WA* 37, 62. Christ with his purity touches "my life and death, my walking, standing, my suffering, trouble and temptation, all of which he has borne, carried and passed through. . . ." *WA* 37, 62.
On the way in which Christ's pure obedience to the Father when he died transforms our death, see the Good Friday sermon of 1532. *WA* 10ᴵᴵᴵ, 75 ff.
[74] *Die christliche Lehre von der Rechtfertigung und Versöhnung* (3rd ed.; Bonn: Adolph Marcus, 1889), I, 224.
[75] *LT* 2, 70 f., 342.
[76] *Christus Victor*, trans. A. G. Herbert (London: S. P. C. K., 1931), "Die Haupttypen des Christlichen Versöhnungsgedanken," *Zeitschrift für System-*

the doctrine of reconciliation in the history of the doctrine: the "classical," the "Latin," and the "ethical" type—the ethical type does not concern us at this point. The classical type is characterized by the interpretation of reconciliation as a result of battle and victory. In Christ, God himself fights against the powers of corruption, the "tyrants" under whom humanity is kept in chains; God thereby reconciles himself with the world. Aulén asserts that reconciliation is thus consistently understood as an act of God and specifically as an act of his love. The love of God breaks through the relationship of justice between God and man. Aulén finds this classical type in the New Testament, in ancient Greek theology, and in Luther.[77]

The Latin type is opposed to this. It treats reconciliation "legalistically," in the context of a consistent relationship of justice. For this reason, reconciliation is only partially an act of God, for it is also necessary that the demands of God's righteousness be fulfilled. Reconciliation is then not interpreted positively as a victory, as in the classical type, but basically in a negative sense as the remission of punishment because of the act of Christ. Anselm's theology gives the best examples of this view. Luther's doctrine of the cross would, according to Aulén, thus stand in sharp opposition to that of Anselm. Aulén demands that the traditional doctrine of reconciliation which has been determined by the combined influence of Anselm and classical Protestant dogmatics be revised on the basis of the New Testament and of Luther.

It must be noted, however, that Aulén's interpretation of Luther is not substantiated by the sources. The assertion that Luther provides the basis for Aulén's own dogmatic acceptance of the "classical" type is not true. Luther places the emphasis elsewhere. Certainly, Luther often liked to describe Christ's work as a struggle with the demonic powers; he used drastic mythological pictures not only to interpret Christ's work to the ordinary congregation

---

atische Theologie, VIII (1930/31), 501 ff. For a critique of Aulén's position, cf. my essay "Das Kreuz und das Böse" in *Zeitschrift für Systematische Theologie* XV (1938), 165 ff. and especially O. Tiililä, "Das Strafleiden Christi," *Annalen der Finnischen Akademie der Wissenschaften* (Helsinki, 1941).

[77] Other Lundensian theologians do the same, e.g., Ragnar Bring, *Dualismen hos Luther* (Lund: Hakan Ohlsson, 1929) and Philip Watson, *Let God Be God!* (Philadelphia: Muhlenberg, 1948).

220   *The Theology of Martin Luther*

but he even used them with the intention that these statements be
taken in complete seriousness theologically without detriment to
their illustrative character. We find them not only in his sermons
but also in his lectures. In his hymn, "Dear Christians, Let Us
Now Rejoice,"[78] Christ's work of salvation is treated from the viewpoint of his battle with the devil ("For he would catch the devil,"
etc.) And yet we must repeat and confirm what Theodosius Harnack[79] and more recently O. Tiililä[80] have demonstrated and emphasized on the basis of Luther: The powers with which Christ struggled had their power and authority only through God's wrath.
They are his instruments against the sinner. Luther says that the
devil "has the wrath of God which we fear on his side."[81] We
must note that Luther speaks not only of the might but with equal
frequency of the authority of these powers.[82] They have this authority, however, only through God's wrath and only so long as
this is not stilled—although they at the same time are, and remain, God's enemies. We must, in addition, point out that the
law occupies a special position among these powers. On the one
hand, Luther can, in the deep dialectic of his doctrine of the law,
characterize this law as an enemy not only of man but also of
God.[83] On the other hand, it is that one of all the powers which
most directly and obviously carries out God's work and will and
functions as an instrument of his wrath and judgment. The mere
fact that Luther places it in a category with the other powers and
tyrants illustrates how God's wrath is the authority of all of them.
This is why Luther in discussing Christ's work, places primary emphasis on its relationship to God's wrath and thus to our guilt
rather than on its relationship to the demonic powers.[84] The satisfaction which God's righteousness demands constitutes the primary
and decisive significance of Christ's work and particularly of his
death. Everything else depends on this satisfaction, including the
destruction of the might and the authority of the demonic powers.

---

[78] *WA* 35, 493 ff.; *LW* 53, 219 f.
[79] *LT* 2, 66 ff.
[80] *Op. cit.*, pp. 215 f.
[81] *WA* 20, 609.
[82] *LT* 2, 75.
[83] *WA* 40ᴵ, 565; *LW* 26, 370. *WA* 40ᴵᴵ, 417; cf. *LW* 12, 374.
[84] *LT* 2, 70 f.

It is simply not permissible to declare that the concept of Christ's battle and victory over the evil powers is decisive for Luther, but that the concepts of satisfaction and stilling the wrath of God do not express his own position and instead reflect the form of the question put to him by his opponents.[85] Luther himself has explicitly stated the way in which the two elements of stilling the wrath of God and setting men free from the demonic powers are related to each other. Therefore "the freedom by which we are free from God's wrath forever is indescribable; it is greater than heaven and earth and all creation. From this there follows the other freedom by which we are made safe and free through Christ from the law, from sin, death, and the power of the devil, and hell."[86] It is self-understood that Luther does not mean that this second freedom "follows [*folgt*]" the first as though it came at a later time than the first freedom. The second freedom from the powers is given in and with the freedom from wrath, as the other side of the same coin. However, the expression "follows" indicates that the purification of man's relationship to God is the decisive thing and that the theocentric relationship of Christ's work is primary and of greater significance than the relationship to the demons.

Luther distinguishes the unified twofold meaning and result of Christ's work in terms of his being priest and king. As king,

---

[85] Watson, *op. cit.*, pp. 119 ff., 144, n. 130. The passage cited by Watson is from *WA* 21, 251 (equivalent to WA 34ᴵ, 301, 303). "We do not permit the word satisfaction to be used in our schools and sermons" refers only to the moralistic use of the word in the sense of penances brought by men. Luther uses it to describe Christ's work—and he does not use it only for polemical reasons. The passages cited, p. 203, adequately refute that idea. The assertion that the concept of satisfaction is not essential to Luther's thought (Watson, *op. cit.*, p. 120) is an assumption that the texts do not confirm. Luther also uses synonymous expressions, such as, "Christ has paid for us." *WA* 30ᴵ, 187; *BC*, 414. *WA* 37, 59. In his hymn on the Lord's Supper," Let God Be Blest," Luther says:

> Of our debt paid the sum,
> That God gracious is become.

WA 35, 515; *LW* 53, 254. Are we to believe that Luther did not use such theological expressions seriously? Unfortunately Watson did not adequately consider Tiililä's work. Watson says "the Penal Theory implies a fundamentally legalistic conception of God's character and of His dealings with men." Therefore Luther, "who is otherwise so implacable an opponent of legalism" could not seriously have held it. On this point we must join Tiililä in reminding Watson and Aulén that they have failed to distinguish between "legalistic" and "legal": between a false legalism and any form of applying the concept of law to the work of reconciliation.

[86] *WA* 40ᴵᴵ, 4, 11: *LW* 27, 4.

Christ is "a lord of death, of hell, of the Devil, and of all creatures," as priest, Christ through his mediations between God and
us bring us that "which is absolutely necessary for us. Through his
kingdom and lordship he protects us from all evil in all things;
through his priestly work he protects us from all sins and the
wrath of God, intercedes for us, and sacrifices himself in order to
reconcile us to God." Luther expressly adds, "Now he makes us
so secure in relationship to God and gives peace to our conscience
that God is no longer against us, or we ourselves. This is a far
greater act than making the creatures harmless for us; for guilt and
sin are far greater than pain and death."[87] We note that all the
powers which press in upon us and damage us are only "God's
creatures," even Satan and the law.[88] As such they are not ultimately to be taken seriously. It is only God's wrath which makes
them serious. Everything depends on the fact that God has been
reconciled.[89]

It is therefore a significant misinterpretation of Luther to classify
him one-sidedly as a representative of the "classical type" as the
Lundensians do. On the contrary, Luther combines the classical
and the Latin concepts—to use Aulén's term—but in such a way
that he decisively follows the Latin line.[90] Luther agrees with the
doctrine of the Greek theologians and of the early church when
he understands the crucified and risen Christ as the conqueror of
those powers of corruption which presently destroy men; he agrees
with Anselm in putting Christ's work decisively in relationship to
God. Both concepts are unified in Luther's thought by the fact that
he, together with Paul, treats the law as one of the powers of corruption, and that he sees the wrath of God which we feel in our
conscience as that which ultimately threatens us in and behind the

[87] *WA* 10[I,1], 717 f.
[88] Luther refers to the law as a "creature." "This was truly a remarkable duel
where the law a creature came into conflict with its creator." *WA* 40[I], 565;
LW 26, 370.
[89] Cf. a passage such as *WA* 10[III], 136, where Luther completely applies
Christ's incarnation and cross to the overwhelming of the enmity between God
and man, to the "drowning" of sin and wrath, and to reconciliation.
[90] "Luther's understanding of Christ's objective work essentially follows along
the path of the medieval theory of satisfaction." (Fr. Loofs, *Leitfaden zum
Studium der Dogmengeschichte* 4th ed.; 1906), p. 778. Tiililä says that Luther
"can be considered as having renewed and deepened the 'Latin' understanding
of the atonement." *Op. cit.*, p. 226.

demonic powers. At the same time, Luther stands closer to the Greeks than to Anselm insofar as he is not so much concerned with turning away the wrath which is to come, as with suffering and overcoming the wrath of God which is present. Thus Luther's understanding of Christ's work combines the elements of contemporaneity and a strictly theocentric relationship.

18

RIGHTEOUSNESS IN FAITH

THE DOCTRINE of justification[1] is not simply one doctrine among others but—as Luther declares—the basic and chief article of faith with which the church stands or falls, and on which its entire doctrine depends. The doctrine of justification is "the summary of Christian doctrine," "the sun which illuminates God's holy church." It is the unique possession of Christianity and "distinguishes our religion from all others." The doctrine of justification preserves the church. If we lose this doctrine, we also lose Christ and the church; for then no Christian understanding remains. What is at stake in this doctrine is the decisive question as to how man can continue to stand before God. This doctrine "consoles our conscience before God." Luther repeatedly expresses this in the strongest terms, as though he were under oath.[2] "Nothing in this article can be given up or compromised, even if heaven and earth and things temporal should be destroyed . . . on this article rests all that we teach and practice against the pope, the devil, and the world. Therefore we must be quite certain and have no doubts about it. Otherwise all is lost, and the pope, the devil, and all our adversaries will gain the victory." That is how Luther expresses it in the *Smalcald Articles*.[3] In the same year, 1537, Luther admonishes his pupils in the introduction to a disputation: We cannot emphatically and often enough sharpen our thinking on this doctrine. We must devote ourselves to it with the greatest theological diligence and seriousness. For neither reason nor Satan is so opposed to anything else as they are to this. No other article of faith is so threatened by the danger of false

---

[1] Rudolph Hermann, *Luthers These Gerecht und Sünder zugleich* (1st ed., 1930; 2nd ed., 1960; Gütersloh: Mohn) and Hans Joachim Iwand, *Glaubensgerechtigkeit nach Luthers Lehre* (3rd ed.; Munich: Kaiser, 1959).

[2] *WA* 40[III], 335, 352. Cf. *WA* 39[I], 205. *WA* 25, 330.

[3] *WA* 50, 199; *BC*, 292.

teaching.⁴ Thus with the single exception of the doctrine of the Lord's Supper, Luther throughout his life devoted more theological work, strength, and passion to this doctrine than to any other.

Luther says the same things about the doctrine of Jesus Christ that he says about the doctrine of justification. The doctrine of Christ is the essence of all Christian knowledge; it is the decisive element of Christianity which distinguishes it from all other religions. In it "rest all our wisdom, salvation, and blessedness." All Christian certainty depends on this doctrine. It is the criterion by which all matters of doctrine and life are to be judged. The entire Christian faith stands or falls with this doctrine.⁵ The fact that Luther could say the same thing about both doctrines shows that they belong very close together and are interdependent in his theology. Justification through faith alone is not a second or a new element in relationship to faith in Christ; rather it is precisely this faith itself, understood in its radical seriousness and related to man's quest for salvation. The sentence from the *Smalcald Articles* quoted in the previous paragraph refers to Christ's work and justification as one and the same thing. The doctrine of justification is nothing else than faith in Christ, when this is properly understood. This faith has comprehensive and exclusive significance. It excludes all self-trust in matters of salvation.⁶ Thereby faith exactly corresponds to the essential content of the doctrine of justification. Thus Luther can say that the Evangelicals⁷ were called heretics by their opponents because of their doctrine of the Lord Jesus Christ. We are condemned, Luther says, because we "so clearly and powerfully teach and proclaim the doctrine that Christ alone is the only valuable possession we have and our only reason for being called Christians. We wish to know no other Lord, no other righteousness, no other holiness."⁸ Luther turns this around and accuses his Roman

⁴ *WA* 39ᵡ, 205.
⁵ *WA* 37, 71 f. *WA* 30ᴵᴵ, 186. *WA* 32, 348; *LW* 21, 59.
⁶ *WA* 39ᵡ, 46; *LW* 34, 111. Adding trust in one's own works "destroys faith and the entire Christ. For it is Christ alone who counts and I must confess this . . . by saying: 'since Christ does it, I must not do it.' For Christ and my own works cannot tolerate each other in my heart; I can, therefore, not put my trust in both of them, but one of them must be expelled—either Christ or my own activity." *WA* 37, 46. Cf. *ibid.*, p. 48.
⁷ [The name the Reformers preferred to apply to themselves. It derived from the Greek word for "gospel."—Trans.]
⁸ *WA* 37, 71.

opponents of confessing Christ with their mouths but in their doctrine denying what he is.[9] In the *Small Catechism* Luther nowhere expressly speaks of justification and even the concept is completely missing; but the explanation of the Second Article implicitly contains the entire doctrine of justification through faith in Christ alone. Conversely, this relationship between faith in Christ and justification indicates that Luther under no circumstances thought of separating justification from faith in Christ; we cannot therefore construe Luther's doctrine a-christologically. Justification depends on faith in Christ, is constituted by it, and is only the form (although not the only form) of faith in Christ.[10]

Luther uses the terms "to justify" [*justificare*] and "justification" [*justificatio*] in more than one sense. From the beginning, justification most often means the judgment of God with which he declares man to be righteous [*justum reputare* or *computare*].[11] In other places, however, this word stands for the entire event through which a man is essentially made righteous (a usage which Luther also finds in Paul, Romans 5),[12] that is, for both the imputation of righteousness to man as well as man's actually becoming righteous.[13] Justification in this sense remains incomplete on earth and is first completed on the Last Day. Complete righteousness in this sense is an eschatological reality. This twofold use of the word cannot be correlated with Luther's early and later theology; he uses "justification" in both senses at the same time, sometimes even shortly after each other in the same text.[14] Theoretically, then, jus-

---

[9] *WA* 37, 36. *WA* 46, 6. *WA* 39[II], 188; *LW* 34, 304.

[10] Cf. H. J. Iwand, *Rechtfertigungslehre und Christusglaube* (Leipzig: J. C. Hinrichs, 1930).

[11] E.g., in the lectures on Romans, *WA* 56, 39, *pass.*, likewise in the first lecture on Galatians, *WA* 2, 490; *LW* 27, 221. Luther uses the same words later in his life, e.g., in 1536, cf. *WA* 39[I], 46; *LW* 34, 111. "The term 'to be justified' means that a man is considered righteous." *WA* 39[I], 98; *LW* 34, 167. In *WA* 39[I], 443, Luther distinguishes between justification and fulfilling the law.

[12] *WA* 39[II], 202; *LW* 34, 320.

[13] "He has begun to be justified and to be healed. . . . Meanwhile, however, while he is being justified and healed, the sin that is left in his flesh is not imputed to him, etc." *WA* 2, 495; *LW* 27, 227. In this passage Luther distinguishes "justifying" from "not imputing." *WA* 39[I], 83; *LW* 34, 152. "Then at last we shall be made perfectly righteous." *WA* 39[I], 98; *LW* 34, 167. "Our justification is not yet completed." *WA* 39[I], 252.

[14] Cf. the *Disputation Concerning Justification* of 1536. "We are justified daily by the unmerited forgiveness of sins and by the justification of God's

tification in the sense of a judgment could be interpreted in either of two ways. One possible interpretation is that a man is declared righteous by God on the basis of his having fulfilled the law.[15] The other possible interpretation is that God would declare the sinner righteous in spite of the fact that he did not fulfill the law. Both possibilities are "forensic."

ALIEN RIGHTEOUSNESS

Luther's doctrine of justification is directly related to Paul's. Together with Paul (Rom. 4:1 ff.) Luther ordinarily understands justification as God's act of crediting, imputing, or recognizing (*imputare, reputare*) as righteous, that is, as the act through which God grants a man value in relationship to him. In the case of the gospel, it is the act by which God considers and receives the sinner who is unrighteous before him as righteous. This means, first, that justification consists in the fact that God does not impute sin but forgives it (cf. Ps. 32:1). God treats a man's sins as though they were not present: "He does not know them any more."[16] Described positively, the forgiveness of sins or the nonimputation of sin is the imputation of righteousness. The righteousness of Christ is imputed to the sinner. God sees the sinner as one with Christ. He forgives his sin and considers the sinner to be righteous for Christ's sake.[17] Thus the righteousness granted to the sinner is not his own produced by himself but an "alien" righteousness belonging to Jesus Christ. Righteousness is not a quality of man as philosophy and the scholastic theology determined by it thought it to be; rather it consists in being righteous only through God's gracious imputation of Christ's righteousness, that is, it is a righteous-

---

mercy." *WA* 39I, 98; *LW* 34, 167. "For we perceive that a man who is justified is not yet a righteous man, but is in the very movement or journey toward righteousness." *WA* 39I, 83; *LW* 34, 152.

[15] Cf. Luther's comment on Romans 2:13 in *WA* 56, 22; *LCC* 15, 50.

[16] "Nor is any sin . . . imputed to us, but as if it were nothing, [is] removed in the meantime by remission." *WA* 39I, 83; *LW* 34, 153. "A man is so absolved as if he had no sin, for Christ's sake." *WA* 39I, 97; *LW* 34, 166. "Because our righteousness is divine ignorance and free forgiveness of our sins." *WA* 40III, 350.

[17] "We are considered righteous on account of Christ." *WA* 39I, 83; *LW* 34, 153. Cf. *WA* 39I, 97; *LW* 34, 166. *WA* 40I, 229; *LW* 26, 130.

ness "outside of" man.[18] Man cannot earn this for himself but can
only permit it to be granted and given to him through God's free
grace for Christ's sake.[19] The situation with our righteousness is no
different from our entry into heaven on the Last Day. Christ will
take us from earth and put us into heaven (I Thess. 4:16), and
we will not do it for ourselves. We are completely passive in this
process and cannot do anything toward it. The same is true here.
Something happens to us; and we can only let it happen to us,
without being actively involved in it in any way. The righteousness of the sinner is, accordingly, not an "active" righteousness but
a "passive" righteousness which he can only "suffer" and receive.[20]
This all is contained in the statement that Christ personally is the
sinner's righteousness, that is, the crucified, risen, and ascended
Christ (according to Romans 8:34).[21] When Christ makes himself
one with man, this "alien" righteousness becomes man's own and
makes him righteous before God.[22] A man lives before God

---

[18] *WA* 2, 145 f.; *LW* 31, 297 ff. "All become righteous by another's righteousness." *WA* 2, 491; *LW* 27, 222. "Christ or Christ's righteousness is outside of us and alien . . . to us." *WA* 39[I], 83; *LW* 34, 153. "This is spiritual
theology, which philosophers do not understand, since they call righteousness
a quality." *WA* 39[I], 99; *LW* 34, 169. Cf. *WA* 46, 43 f., especially 44; *LW*
24, 345-349, especially 347. "You are righteous through mercy and pity. That
is not my own condition or a quality of my heart but something outside myself, that is, divine mercy." *WA* 40[II], 353; cf. *LW* 12, 328. Cf. *WA* 40[II],
356, 407; *LW* 12, 330 f., 367.
[19] "To be outside of us means to be beyond our powers. Righteousness is our
possession, to be sure, since it was given to us out of mercy. Nevertheless, it is
alien to us, because we have not merited it." *WA* 39[I], 109; *LW* 34, 178. Cf.
WA 39[I], 235.
[20] "Thus I am justified just as though I were a piece of material and I suffer;
I do not do anything." *WA* 39[I], 447. "The righteousness which comes from
us is not Christian righteousness. Christian righteousness is just the opposite;
it is passive and we receive it; we do nothing for ourselves but allow someone
else, namely God, to work in us." *WA* 40[I], 41; cf. *LW* 26, 4 f. "As far as
we are concerned, the whole procedure of justification is passive." *WA* 40[II],
410; *LW* 12, 368. Cf. *WA* 54, 186; *LW* 34, 337.
[21] *WA* 17[I], 245. *WA* 40[I], 47, 229; *LW* 26, 8 f., 130. *WA* 46, 44; *LW* 24,
347. In his second series of lectures on Galatians, Luther explicitly says that
God's righteousness "is called the resurrection of the dead." Luther is primarily
referring to Christ's resurrection on the basis of what Paul says in Romans
4:25. *WA* 40[I], 64; *LW* 26, 21. Cf. *WA* 39[II], 237.
[22] *WA* 2, 495; *LW* 27, 227. "It is thus an alien holiness and yet it is still
our own holiness, for God does not consider everything which we do in this
life in terms of its being impure in and by itself, but sees everything as holy,
precious, and acceptable through this child who makes the entire world holy
through his life." *WA* 37, 57. "This is a peculiar righteousness: it is strange
indeed that we are to be called righteous or to possess a righteousness which
is in us but is entirely outside us in Christ and yet becomes our very own, as
though we ourselves had achieved and earned it." *WA* 46, 44; *LW* 24, 347.

throughout his whole life on the basis of this "alien" and "passive" righteousness—not only at the moment when he begins to be a Christian in baptism. This means that passive righteousness is not more and more replaced and limited by an active righteousness, the alien righteousness is not more and more replaced by man's own. Man, including the Christian man, remains a sinner his whole life long and cannot possibly live and have worth before God except through this alien righteousness, the imputation of Christ's righteousness. This takes place in the daily forgiveness of sins.[²³]

Luther can say both that our righteousness is Christ's righteousness and that our righteousness consists in God's mercy.[²⁴] Each says that righteousness comes to a man from outside himself and is not a quality of his heart. Each is the opposite of being justified through our own works and achievements. It is important to maintain the fact that this grounding of righteousness in God's mercy does not, for Luther, exclude that it happens "for Christ's sake" [*propter Christum*], as is so often asserted in modern theology. On the contrary, precisely this is included, for God's mercy comes to us for Christ's sake.

God reveals the "unbelievable greatness of His power and mercy" in his relationship to men by accepting the man who is not righteous as righteous. "This imputation is not something of no consequence but is greater than the whole world and all the holy angels."[²⁵] The fact that God declares the unrighteous to be righteous transcends all human understanding and reason. God's judgment contradicts the judgment of man and each man's judgment of himself. A man condemned as a sinner both by himself and by other people is declared righteous.[²⁶] God deals with men in this wonder-

---

[²³] "For the forgiveness of sins begins in baptism and remains with us all the way to death, until we arise from the dead, and leads us into life eternal. So we live continually under the remission of sins." *WA* 39ˣ, 95; *LW* 34, 164. "We are justified daily by the unmerited forgiveness of sins and by the justification of God's mercy." *WA* 39ˣ, 98; *LW* 34, 167. "I daily live under tolerance." *WA* 40ᴵᴵᴵ, 348. Cf. *The Holy and Blessed Sacrament of Baptism* (1519), *WA* 2, 731; *LW* 35, 34.

[²⁴] Cf., e.g., *WA* 40ᴵᴵ, 340; cf. *LW* 12, 320. "The mercy of God alone is our righteousness, not our own works." *WA* 39ˣ, 48; *LW* 34, 113. "Righteousness is not situated in those qualitative forms, but in the mercy of God." *WA* 8, 92; *LW* 32, 208.

[²⁵] *WA* 39ˣ, 97; *LW* 34, 166 f.

[²⁶] *WA* 39ˣ, 82; *LW* 34, 151 ff.

ful way. Luther liked to refer to Psalm 4:3: "Understand that the
Lord wonderfully leads his saints."[27] Reason simply cannot comprehend the paradox of God's judgment and the hiddenness of the
righteousness which he imputes. But it is also a constantly new
temptation for the believer, since even the godly cannot easily believe that the sinner is justified.[28]

Man receives justification only through faith, that is, by believing in Jesus Christ. To believe in him is to recognize and grasp
the love of God the Father in the history of Jesus Christ.[29] A man
believes when he accepts God's gracious judgment over him. He
takes the risk of living before God on no other basis than that
righteousness of Christ which God's mercy imputes to him. This
justifying faith is thus more than merely being convinced that the
facts of salvation are true without being personally related to them.
It includes this, but what has happened must be appropriated as
having happened "for me" and "for my sake." This "for me" is
the decisive and essential factor in justifying faith which definitely
distinguishes it from everything else which we otherwise call faith
and especially from a mere "historical faith."[30] Luther sees the essence of justifying faith in the fact that it grasps Christ. It is a
"grasping" and appropriating faith (*fides apprehensiva*).[31] In addi-

---

[27] *WA* 39¹, 82; *LW* 34, 151. Cf. *WA* 39¹, 515. Cf. Luther's interpretation
of this passage *WA* 5, 107 ff., especially 108. Luther also quotes the Vulgate
version of Psalm 68:35, which in the Vulgate is Psalm 67:36, "God is wonderful [*mirabilis*] in his saints." *WA* 56, 296; *LCC* 15, 125. *WA* 57, 164;
cf. *LCC* 15, 125. *WA* 8, 124; *LW* 32, 254. [The RSV translation of these
passages from the Psalms emphasizes different elements of the original text
than the Vulgate and Luther do. —Trans.]

[28] *WA* 39¹, 82; *LW* 34, 151. *WA* 40¹, 41; cf. *LW* 26, 14. *WA* 40¹¹, 420;
LW 12, 376. *WA* 46, 44; *LW* 24, 347.

[29] *WA* 39¹, 45; *LW* 34, 110.

[30] "Accordingly, that 'for me' or 'for us' if it is believed, creates that true
faith, which distinguishes it from all other faith, which merely hears the things
done. This is the faith which alone justifies us. . . ." *WA* 39¹, 46; *LW* 34,
110. On historical faith, see also *WA* 37, 45.
Luther also describes the elements of faith. It arises through the renewal of
the mind so that it assents to God's word as well as through the conversion of
the will so that it relates itself to the promise with the assent of trust. A twofold assent is thus involved. *WA* 39¹¹, 243.

[31] "Faith apprehends [or takes hold of] Christ." *WA* 39¹, 45; *LW* 34, 110
(cf. also theses 18-25). Luther also says that faith "comprehends [or grasps]
Christ." *WA* 39¹, 83; *LW* 34, 153. "Apprehends" is also found elsewhere,
e.g., *WA* 40¹, 228 f.; *LW* 26, 129 f. "Our faith is the power which takes hold
[*virtus apprehensiva*]." *WA* 39¹¹, 319.

tion to being an intellectual act, it is also an effective act of trusting in the mercy God offers to us in Christ.[32]

It is not enough, however, to say either that faith receives justification or that man receives justification *in* faith. Luther's thought must be expressed more definitely. Justification is received *with* faith, that is, in the form of faith. Faith is the work and gift of God. God justifies a man by giving him faith. Christ is the righteousness of men and to this extent this righteousness is outside of us. But Christ is my righteousness only if I appropriate him and make him my own. Faith is the only way in which Christ can give himself to me. Only the Christ who is appropriated in faith, that is, the Christ who lives in my heart through faith is my righteousness.[33] Christ is not only the "object" of faith but is himself present in faith. Through faith Christ is present with and in a man.[34] The believing heart holds fast to Christ just as the setting of a ring grips the jewel: we have Christ in faith.[35] Only in faith are Christ and man so joined together, so made one, that man in God's judgment participates in Christ's righteousness. Thus in matters of justification, Christ and faith cannot be treated as two different things and set in opposition to each other. Christ is what he is for me in God's judgment only in that faith in which I "grasp" him; and faith is meaningful in God's judgment only because Christ is present with a man. Luther therefore means the same whether he says that we become righteous on account of Christ or that we become righteous on account of faith in Christ.[36] It is the same when Luther, on the one hand, emphasizes the greatness of God's power and mercy in justification as when he, on the other hand, emphasizes the greatness and effectiveness of faith.[37] Faith is powerful only because it grasps the power of God's mercy in Christ and because it rests on Christ's own righteousness.[38]

In Luther's first lectures on Galatians, faith is also related to the "name of God" on which it calls in prayer. In substance, this

[32] *WA* 40[1], 228; *LW* 26, 129.
[33] *WA* 40[1], 229; cf. *LW* 26, 130.
[34] *WA* 2, 502; *LW* 27, 239. *WA* 40[1], 228 f.; *LW* 26, 130.
[35] *WA* 40[1], 165, 233, 235; *LW* 26, 89, 132, 134.
[36] *WA* 40[III], 351. *WA* 39[II], 214.
[37] *WA* 39[1], 97; *LW* 34, 166.
[38] *WA* 8, 114; *LW* 32, 239.

is not different from faith's relationship to Christ. For the name
of God sums up his mercy and truth which are nowhere more
clearly revealed than in Christ. Luther here asserts that the Lord's
name and the heart become one and hold to each other through
faith, as Christ lives in the heart through faith and Christ and the
believer become one through faith. The heart participates in the
purity, holiness, and righteousness, which belong to the Lord's
name. The meaning remains unchanged when Luther, shortly afterward, says that Christ's righteousness and the Christian's righteousness are one and the same thing bound together in an inexpressible way.[39] Luther says basically the same thing in *The Freedom of a Christian* when he decribes the mystery of a man being
justified through his connection to the word which he grasps in
faith. "When the soul is united with the word, it becomes like
the word—just as iron becomes red like the fire in which it is
heated."[40] The sermon Luther preached on August 15, 1522[41]
makes the same point. Thus Luther can use different concepts to
express one and the same thing. It should also be noted that according to these passages, the word not only declares that man is
righteous but also gives him a new being.

As we have already seen, faith makes us righteous because it
grasps Christ. "Faith justifies because it takes hold of and possesses this treasure, the present Christ."[42] Faith therefore does not
justify by itself but only because Christ makes himself present in
us through it. Faith is, as the later dogmaticians said, significant
only as the means or the instrument by which we receive. It is
comparable to the open hand which a man must have if he is to
receive.[43]

---

[39] *WA* 2, 490 f.; *LW* 27, 220 ff.

[40] "Through faith and by God's word, the soul will become holy, righteous,
true, peaceful, free, and entirely good, and he will become a true child of God."
WA 7, 24; *RW* 1, 362; cf. *LW* 31, 349.

[41] "Faith thus results in the complete unification of the soul with the word;
its fire and its goodness so penetrates the soul that it takes on the nature of the
word, and just as we may not criticize the word, so also we may not criticize
the conscience, since its substance now is a combination of the word and faith."
WA 10ᴵᴵᴵ, 271. "Whoever becomes one and the same thing as the word is
righteous and beyond reproach." *WA* 10ᴵᴵᴵ, 273.

[42] *WA* 40ᴵ, 229; *LW* 26, 130.

[43] The later Lutheran dogmaticians speak of faith as a "receptive organ"
[*organon receptivum* or *leptikon*]. "Faith is the only means and instrument
whereby we accept Christ and in Christ obtain the righteousness which avails
before God." *Formula of Concord* (*Epitome* III, 5), *BC*, 473. The picture of
the hand and the treasure is found in Hollaz among others.

Luther, however, also evaluates faith as a human attitude worked by the Holy Spirit. Faith includes the fact that a man is no longer satisfied and pleased with himself." Such a man expects nothing from God because of what he is and he brings nothing of his own before God; rather he completely and unreservedly commits himself to God's mercy and trusts—then he is ready to receive from God. Thereby faith becomes the real fulfilment of the First Commandment; it is the only way in which man recognizes that God is God and properly honors him as the only creator of life and salvation. Faith makes the heart pure. Faith itself is purity of heart." Only in faith is man completely what he ought to be before God." Faith is thus "the work of the First Commandment." Luther uses this formula in his *Treatise on Good Works* when he describes the proper fulfilment of the Ten Commandments." Later, however, he did not like to hear this definition used in theology. He had his doubts about characterizing faith as a work." That could perhaps be permitted in a certain context but strictly speaking, this usage should be avoided as not scriptural. Luther felt this, because according to Scripture faith is not our work but God's work. Primarily, however, he felt that the concept "work" belongs together with the law; faith, however, has nothing to do with the law but with God's promise." Under no circumstances, however, is it permissible to characterize faith as a work within the doctrine of justification. If one speaks of faith as a "work," then it is true of it as of every work that it does not justify insofar as it is man's work. "We ought to let every work remain in its own category so that the question is not thrown into a complete jumble."[150] The description of faith as the "work of the First Commandment" may have its place within an ethical exposition of the fulfilment of the commandments, but it does not belong in the theology of justification.

" *WA* 56, 157 f., 199; *LCC* 15, 3 f., 48.

" *WA* 2, 514, 563; *LW* 27, 257, 331.

" *WA* 5, 104.

" *WA* 6, 209; *PE* 1, 194.

" "I do not willingly hear faith called a work." *WA* 39¹, 98; *LW* 34, 167.

" *WA* 39¹, 90; *LW* 34, 159 f. *WA* 39¹, 207.

" *WA* 39¹, 91; *LW* 34, 160.

THE BEGINNING OF THE NEW CREATION

Although faith is not to be considered as a "work" in relationship to our justification, it remains the source and fountain of "good works." As such it is the beginning of a new righteousness which a man has because he is actually righteous. This is implicit in the fact that faith justifies through Christ, that is, it brings Christ into the heart or, expressed in other words, it is worked by the Holy Spirit and "brings (this Spirit) with it."[61] This means—as Luther says in his first lectures on Galatians—that God's name, his holy, pure, and divine nature as revealed to us in Christ, so joins itself to our heart in faith that it makes our heart like itself. Thus our heart itself becomes righteous, not only because it is accepted as such through the imputation of Christ's righteousness, that is, of God's own righteousness; but it also becomes righteous because God's Holy Spirit is poured into the heart and he brings love and new obedience with him.[62] Christ, whom faith brings into the heart, is not only a man's "alien" righteousness before God because of Christ's own righteousness; he is, at the same time, also an effective power, the power of God himself, in the believer, and able to draw a man's heart into his own life and being.[63] Luther also expresses this by saying that Christ fulfills the law in relationship to us in a twofold way. First, he fulfills it for us outside of us. Second, he fulfills it in us through his Holy Spirit who enables us to follow Christ.[64] Faith in Christ is thus the only way in which God transforms a sinful man so that he becomes like God.

Faith looks only and solely to the Christ for us, toward his righteousness "outside of us"; yet it thereby becomes the presence

---

[61] *WA*, DB 7, 10; *LW* 35, 370.

[62] "Therefore just as the name of the Lord is pure, holy, righteous, true, good, etc., so if it touches, or is touched by, the heart (which happens through faith), it makes the heart entirely like itself." *WA* 2, 490; *LW* 27, 22. Cf. *WA* 39¹, 482.

[63] "The righteous man himself does not live; but Christ lives in him, because through faith Christ dwells in him and pours his grace into him, through which it comes about that a man is governed not by his own spirit, but by Christ's." *WA* 2, 502; *LW* 27, 238. "He who believes in Christ empties himself and no longer busies himself with his own works, in order that Christ may live and work in him." *WA* 2, 564; *LW* 27, 332. *WA* 8, 6; *LW* 13, 5.

[64] "Our empty law is ended by Christ who fills the vacuum first by being outside of us, because he himself fulfills the law for us; then he also fills it with the Holy Spirit who begins this new and eternal obedience within us." *WA* 39¹, 435, 483, 383, 388.

and the power of Christ in us. One and the same faith in Christ gives both forgiveness of sins and the triumph over sin.[55] In faith a man becomes a new man. Justifying faith means being born again from God. The certainty of God's forgiving mercy makes me glad in God, and brings the slavish service under the law to an end, works a new, free, and joyful obedience to God's will, places me in the line of battle against the sin of the old man, creates the readiness to serve someone else in love and to suffer "in love and praise of God." Luther, with overflowing joy, constantly proclaims this ethical fruitfulness of faith.[56] He fully and concretely describes the rich meaning of the fact that Christ is powerful in man and that the Holy Spirit lives in him and makes him alive.

The two effects of faith in Christ are: It receives the forgiveness of sins and therewith the imputation of righteousness; it also establishes a new being and makes a man righteous in himself. These two effects of faith are inseparably joined together in Luther's theology. When he speaks of that righteousness which faith is and gives he sees both together: the righteousness imputed for Christ's sake, and man's transformation to a new obedience.[57] "Justification" in the full sense of the word consists in both of these together. The basic and decisive factor is that man is forgiven and receives new worth before God. The second kind of righteousness, which a man has within himself, comes only through the power of

---

[55] "The start of a new creature accomplishes this faith and the battle against the sin of the flesh, which this same faith in Christ both pardons and conquers." *WA* 39ᴵ, 83; *LW* 34, 153. Cf. *WA* 39ᴵᴵ, 236.

[56] Especially in the *Preface to Romans:* "Faith is a divine work in us which changes us and makes us to be born anew of God, John 1[:12, 13]. It kills the old Adam and makes us altogether different men, in heart and spirit and mind and powers; and it brings with it the Holy Spirit. Oh, it is a living, busy, active, mighty thing, this faith. It is impossible for it not to be doing good works incessantly. . . . Faith is a living, daring confidence in God's grace, so sure and certain that the believer would stake his life on it a thousand times. This knowledge of and confidence in God's grace makes men glad and bold and happy in dealing with God and with all creatures. And this is the work which the Holy Spirit performs in faith. Because of it, without compulsion, a person is ready and glad to do good to everyone, to serve everyone, to suffer everything, out of love and praise to God who has shown him this grace." *WA,* DB 7, 10; *LW* 35, 370 f. Cf. also the following note.

[57] "Righteousness, then, is such a faith. It is called 'the righteousness of God' because God gives it, and counts it as righteousness for the sake of Christ our mediator, and makes a man to fulfill his obligation to everybody. For through faith a man becomes free from sin and comes to take pleasure in God's commandments. . . ." *WA,* DB 7, 11; *LW* 35, 371.

the first kind of righteousness."[58] It remains equally true, however, that God's forgiveness aims beyond itself to give a man new being and new obedience. If this goal of mortifying the old man were not achieved, "the gospel, faith, and all else would be useless."[59] God would, under no circumstances, declare man to be righteous if he did not also intend to make a new man out of him and if he had not already begun to do this with the gift of justifying faith. To this extent, God's forgiveness, his justifying judgment over sinful man, has an eschatological dimension. Just as God aims beyond forgiveness and the new worth he gives to man toward man's really becoming new, so God also moves the believer toward this goal. The believer does not rest in security on the forgiveness of his sins, as though sin were no longer of any consequence, but he is completely involved in fighting to gain the victory over sin every day.[60]

Thus the Christian's righteousness exists in the present and at the same time is still coming in the future. It exists in the present as the righteousness which man has through God's imputation, as what he is before God for Christ's sake, and also as the beginning of the essential righteousness created through Christ's effective presence in faith. The Christian righteousness comes in the future as the righteousness he will have when he is a completely new being. The already present righteousness is a promise of and waits for the righteousness coming in the future. The already present righteousness is both a complete and a partial righteousness, depending on the way in which it is viewed. It is complete when viewed as acceptance by God and as participation in Christ's righteousness;[61] Christ's righteousness is a totality and the believer participates in it totally. It is partial as man's new being and new obedience.[62] God's acceptance of us must be described in the perfect tense: we have been made righteous and we are now righteous. The condition of being righteous in ourselves can be de-

---

[58] "However, the first foundation is the stronger and more important, for although the second amounts to something, it does so only through the power of the first." *WA* 8, 114; *LW* 32, 239.

[59] *WA* 8, 26; *LW* 13, 22.

[60] *WA* 39¹, 353.

[61] "This is, however, true, that by divine imputation we are in fact and totally righteous." *WA* 39¹, 563. Cf. *WA* 8, 106 f.; *LW* 32, 227 f.

[62] *WA* 39¹, 241. Cf. *WA* 2, 498; *LW* 27, 232.

scribed in the present tense only as having begun, but its completion lies in the future: we are only becoming righteous.[ω] In this sense the Christian still waits for righteousness. Here too Luther agrees with the Apostle Paul in Romans 8:24 and Galatians 5:5.[ω] After 1530, Luther translates the latter passage: "We wait, however, in the spirit through faith for the righteousness for which we must hope." And he interprets it to mean, "We are not yet made righteous—yet we are already made righteous, but our righteousness still rests on hope."[ω] The expression that the righteousness of the Christian has its reality not yet here and now but in hope is found in both commentaries on Galatians.[ω]

It is from this viewpoint that the relationship between Luther's twofold usage of justification as the forgiveness of sins and as the new being in the Christian life can be understood. The Christian too is and remains a sinner who daily depends on God's forgiveness and on the imputation of Christ's righteousness. But God has already begun his new work of creation in the same faith with which the Christian receives forgiveness.[ω] With this faith God has already begun his new creation. Luther frequently uses the expression from James 1:18 which the Vulgate translates "a kind of beginning of his creation" [*initium aliquod creaturae ejus*].[ω]

[ω] "For we understand that a man who is justified is not already righteous but moving toward righteousness." *WA* 39ᴵ, 83; *LW* 34, 152. "Our justification is not yet complete. . . . It is still under construction. It shall, however, be completed in the resurrection of the dead." *WA* 39ᴵ, 252. Luther can also express it thus: "Christ is awakened from death in his people; but he has only begun to do this for he is not yet completely awakened in us." *WA* 39ᴵ, 356.
[ω] Luther refers to both, *WA* 40ᴵᴵ, 24; *LW* 27, 20 f. [The English edition does not explicitly identify the reference to Gal. 5:5.—Trans.]
[ω] *WA* 40ᴵᴵ, 24; cf. *LW* 27, 21.
[ω] *WA* 2, 495; *LW* 27, 227. *WA* 40ᴵᴵ, 24; *LW* 27, 20.
[ω] "That newness of life has miraculously begun . . ." *WA* 39ᴵ, 98; *LW* 34, 167.
[ω] *WA* 39ᴵ, 83; *LW* 34, 152. "We are the first fruits of creation only insofar as we receive and have the first fruits of the Spirit in this life." *WA* 39ᴵ, 235. "Only the beginning of the new creation." *WA* 39ᴵ, 204, cf. 252, 356. In his German Bible Luther understood "the first of his creatures" to mean that the believers and the community are the beginning of God's new creation which will go far beyond them. Here, however, he understands them to mean that the new creation which God proposes to bring about in us has only started in us and is not yet completed. Cf. the sermons on this verse, *WA* 45, 80. *WA* 41, 587.
In his revision of the Latin Vulgate of 1529 Luther substitutes *primitiae* for *initium*; this corresponds to his German translation *Erstlinge*. Luther thus interpreted this passage in various ways.

This beginning of the new creation is not a matter of indifference for God's justifying judgment. More than once Luther, in his early as well as in his later years, emphasizes that God justifies and bears with his people because of the new creation begun in them and in consideration of this beginning.[69] Together with the "because of Christ" stands an "on account of the beginning of his creation in us." This makes what we have already recognized absolutely clear: God's justifying judgment and his activity in man belong inseparably together, not only because God begins to make a man new when He accepts him into sharing with Him, but also in that God accepts a sinful man as righteous because He, at the same time, begins to renew him and to make him inherently righteous. God's justifying verdict over the sinner includes within it a divine "as if." God accepts the sinner as though he were righteous, as though he had fulfilled the law.[70] But this "as if" exists in order to be abolished; and this abolition begins at the very moment in which God's mercy accepts the sinner by forgiving him, that is, when he takes him into sharing with him. Thus God's acceptance of the sinner and His justification of him through faith alone also has an eschatological dimension. God knows that this new work of creation, or this "healing" (as Luther likes to say, remembering the Good Samaritan with whom he compares Christ[71]), which be-

---

[69] "God does not hold this against us whatever sin is still to be driven out, because of the beginning that we have made in godliness and because of our steady battle against sin which we continue to expel. . . ." *WA* 7, 343; *LW* 32, 28. "He sustains and supports them on account of the first fruit of his creation in us, and he thereupon decrees that they are righteous and sons of the kingdom." *WA* 39^{I}, 83; *LW* 34, 152. "We are thus held in God's arms as the beginning of the new creation until we are made perfect in the resurrection of the dead." *WA* 39^{I}, 204. "And God really takes sin in such a way that it does not remain sin, because he begins materially to purge and to forgive completely." *WA* 39^{I}, 98; *LW* 34, 167. This causal relationship is also found in *WA* 2, 497; *LW* 27, 230 f.

"And yet because the Christian is involved in the work of cleansing and sanctifying and constantly allows the Samaritan to heal him and no longer increasingly corrupts himself with uncleanness, all this is graciously imputed and given to him for the sake of the word through which he allows himself to be sanctified and cleansed; he is forgiven and must be called clean." A reference to John 15:3 follows, "You are already clean because of the word which I have spoken to you." *WA* 51, 520. Cf. *WA* 56, 272. *WA* 57, 165; cf. *LCC* 15, 127. *WA* 8, 107; *LW* 32, 229.

[70] *WA* 39^{I}, 242.

[71] Luther uses "to be justified" and "to be healed" synonymously. *WA* 2, 495; *LW* 27, 227 and *WA* 51, 520. Luther especially refers to the parable of the Good Samaritan in his lectures on Romans. *WA* 56, 272, 513; *LCC* 15, 127, 402. *WA* 57, 165; cf. *LCC* 15, 127.

gins when God accepts man, will achieve its goal. And God declares such a man already righteous in view of the fact that the man in God's new creating hand is already moving along the way to that goal. Luther constantly expresses this eschatological dimension of the forgiveness of sins and of justification by speaking of an "interim," an "in between," "meanwhile," and "for the time being." He uses all these to describe the way in which God forgives the man who is still a sinner. This means that God forgives him, even though he still is a sinner, still is not yet completely renewed, still stands in between his new relationship to God and being completely new, and is still only moving toward being righteous in himself. "Meanwhile" means until God has made him completely righteous.[72]

This concern for the beginning of renewal and of faith's battle against sin does not replace concern for Christ. "On account of the beginning of the new creation" does not compete with and certainly does not substitute for "on account of Christ." Luther emphasizes both in one and the same connection and in the same sentences.[73] His refusal to allow the "on account of Christ" to be replaced or even overshadowed by "on account of the beginning of the new creation" may not be interpreted as bondage to his

---

[72] "Meanwhile, however, while he is being justified and healed, the sin that is left in his flesh is not imputed to him. . . ." *WA* 2, 495; *LW* 27, 227. Cf. *WA* 39¹, 204. [Cf. n. 68 above.] ". . . Meanwhile forgiving . . ." *WA* 39¹, 98; *LW* 34, 167. "Meanwhile . . ." *WA* 7, 345; *LW* 32, 28.
The lectures on Romans especially emphasize the eschatological dimension of God's verdict pronouncing man righteous by characterizing this verdict as a promise of perfect healing and salvation in the life to come. "God's promise and act of reputing [him to be righteous] make the just certain that he shall be freed from these things until he is completely healed." *WA* 56, 272; *LCC* 15, 127. Luther also speaks of ". . . righteousness by faith in the promise and by the hope that it will be fulfilled." *WA* 57, 165; *LCC* 15, 127.

[73] "Therefore, because righteousness and the fulfilling of the law have been begun through faith, for this reason what is left of sin and falls short of fulfilling the law is not imputed to them, for they believe in Christ." [Note that "because" and "for they believe in Christ" *(propter Christum)* are co-ordinated.] *WA* 2, 497; *LW* 27, 231. Luther establishes two "reasons" why God does not impute sin to Christians: "First, because we believe in Christ, who through faith takes our place and covers our sin with his innocence; second, because we battle unceasingly against sin to destroy it. Where these two reasons are not present, sin is imputed, is not forgiven, and condemns us eternally." Luther is thus able to place "on account of Christ" and "on account of the beginning of righteousness" simply beside each other as the two indispensable bases of conditions for God's forgiveness. *WA* 7, 345; *LW* 32, 28.

tradition. On the contrary, it is theologically necessary. The beginning of the new creation and the battle against sin in the Christian in no way changes the fact that he still remains a sinner. And this means more than that he is not yet righteous: he is guilty before God. God could put up with a mere "not yet," in consideration of the full renewal that is coming; guilt, however, remains guilt and future righteousness does not make up for it. Thus God's forgiveness cannot, at this point, mean that he bases his verdict on seeing and recognizing the coming righteousness. On the contrary, this is the place for "on account of Christ."[74]

The Christian daily needs forgiveness of sins. For this new righteousness is only a fragmentary beginning. The Christian is not yet completely the man of faith in whom Christ lives; he still remains the old man, the man of "flesh." For this reason he cannot stand in God's judgment even with his new being. For he constantly has the old man beside him, and thus even with his new obedience remains completely a sinner and damnable before God. For this reason, even a man who is in the process of being made holy can stand in God's judgment only through God's gracious forgiveness and imputation.[75] He is forgiven, however, only for the sake of Christ. Christ must therefore still constantly intercede for his Christians so that he covers and increases the value of their imperfect and fragmentary righteousness with his own perfect righteousness.[76] The "works" of the Christian insofar as he is still

---

[74] Cf. my essay, "Zum Verständnis der Rechtfertigung," *Zeitschrift für systematische Theologie*, VII (1930) reprinted in *Theologische Aufsätze* (Gütersloh: Bertelsmann), II (1935), 31 ff.

[75] *WA* 39¹, 228, 230, 235, 204, 211. *WA* 39¹¹, 207, 225.

[76] "The sin that is left in his flesh is not imputed to him. This is because Christ, who is entirely without sin, has now become one with his Christian and intercedes for him with the Father." *WA* 2, 495; *LW* 27, 227. "Moreover, God forgives and is merciful to us because Christ, our advocate and priest, intercedes and sanctifies our beginning in righteousness. His righteousness, since it is without defect and serves us like an umbrella against the heat of God's wrath, does not allow our beginning righteousness to be condemned." *WA* 39¹, 83; *LW* 34, 153. "For this reason, he has given us a bishop, namely Christ, who is without sin and who is to be our representative until we, too, become entirely pure like him [Hebrews 7:26; Romans 8:34]. Meanwhile the righteousness of Christ must be our cover. His perfect godliness must be our shield and defense. For his sake, the sin that remains in those who believe in him, may not be charged against them." *WA* 7, 345; *LW* 32, 28. *WA* 8, 111 f. *LW* 32, 235 f. Cf. *WA* 50, 250; *BC*, 315. *WA* 39¹¹, 214, 289 (theses 39 ff.).

an old man are always "works of the law.'"[77] For he does not as a matter of course obey as God's child whose faith bears this fruit of obedience but as a slave; and as such his obedience is not good in God's judgment but is sin and damnable. But God's forgiving mercy increases the value of the works of the law.[78] Just as God accepts a man's person as righteous even though he is sinful, so He also accepts the "works" in which that person is involved. Just as God accepts the sinner for Christ's sake, so he also accepts this broken, halfway, and blemished obedience; he accepts it as total obedience.[79]

The preceding paragraphs implicitly state our opinion of Karl Holl's understanding of Luther's doctrine of justification.[80] The truth of Holl's position lies in his strong emphasis on Luther's "on account of the beginning of the new creation," that is, the thesis that God forgives man and declares him to be righteous because he both wills to renew him and has already begun to do so. This association is, in fact, an essential condition for God's forgiveness in Luther's thought. Holl, however, takes this indispensable condition and makes it the sufficient basis for God's verdict of justification: God declares the sinner to be righteous now, because God, being eternal, already sees man as what God's renewing power will make him be at the last judgment. God's verdict is understood in proleptic-analytical terms: God now declares that man to be righteous who will be righteous at some time in the future. Thereby Holl abandons the "on account of Christ" in the sense of the imputation of Christ's "alien" righteousness. According to Holl, this verdict is valid only in the sense that God justi-

---

[77] The works of the law "which man's will does apart from faith under the pressure and motivation of the law" are distinguished from the works of grace "which the regenerated will of a man does in faith under the motivation of the Holy Spirit." *WA* 39¹, 202. Cf. *WA* 2, 492; *LW* 27, 224.

[78] *WA* 8, 69, 77, 78; *LW* 32, 175, 186, 189. "Insofar as they are in the flesh . . . they do the works of the law, that is, they are neither righteous nor do they do good works . . . but these works of the law are in God's judgment, not considered as works of the law even though that is their natural character." *WA* 39¹, 204.

[79] *WA* 39ⁱⁱ, 238.

[80] "Die Rechtfertigungslehre in Luthers Vorlesung über den Römerbrief . . ." *GA* 1, 111 ff. "Die Rechtfertigungslehre im Licht der Geschichte des Protestantismus," *GA* 3, 525 ff. "Zur Verständigung über Luthers Rechtfertigungslehre," *Neue kirchliche Zeitschrift*, XXXIV (1923), 165 ff. On the entire problem, see my essay, "Zum Verständnis der Rechtfertigung," *Zeitschrift für systematische Theologie*, VII (1930), 727-741. Reprinted in *Theologische Aufsätze*, II (1935), 31 ff.

fies the sinner for God knows that the renewing power of Christ is already working in him. This latter factor is indeed also significant in understanding Luther's justification. It dare not, however, limit and replace the former meaning of the "on account of Christ." For Luther, justification is based on reconciliation through Christ's satisfaction. This basis is missing in Holl. The "on account of Christ" is dissolved in the "on account of the beginning of new creation."[81] This, however, contradicts Luther. Holl's construction constitutes an ethical rationalization of justification. It overlooks the fact that God judges man not only in terms of his moral being, but also and primarily in terms of his guilt. And that guilt is not changed by his future righteousness. How can the fact that God forgives sinners today and wipes out their guilt be understood proleptically and analytically? God's love transcends all ethical insight and is not understandable in these terms.

AT ONE AND THE SAME TIME A RIGHTEOUS MAN AND A SINNER

We can now understand the meaning of Luther's famous formula which describes the Christian as at one and the same time a righteous man and a sinner, *simul justus et peccator.*[82] He is righteous through the forgiveness of sins, that is, through the judgment of God who accepts him as righteous for Christ's sake; and he is a sinner in himself, that is, as he now exists as a human being. "A righteous man and a sinner": each of these is valid in a different dimension.[83] This one is true in terms of God's stern judgment; the other is true in terms of God's great mercy; or—and this is the same for Luther—the one in terms of myself without Christ and

---

[81] This is also true of E. Hirsch, *Luthers Gottesanschauung* (Göttingen: Vandenhoeck und Ruprecht, 1918), p. 19.

[82] This formula appears in the lectures on Romans, e.g., *WA* 56, 70, 272; *LCC* 15, 127. "At one and the same time a righteous man and a sinner: a sinner in fact but a righteous man through faith in the promise and through hope of its fulfillment." *WA* 57, 165; *LCC* 15, 127. It appears also in the first lecture on Galatians. "Those who have been justified in Christ are not sinners and are sinners nevertheless . . . at one and the same time, therefore, both righteous and a sinner." *WA* 2, 496 f.; *LW* 27, 230 f. [Cf. also, "Even though I am indeed a sinner yet I am not a sinner."] *WA* 38, 205. "No Christian has sin, and all have sins." *WA* 40ᴵᴵ, 352; cf. *LW* 12, 328. Cf. *WA* 8, 67; *LW* 32, 173. Cf. R. Hermann, *op. cit.*, and Wilfried Joest, *Gesetz und Freiheit* (Göttingen: Vandenhoeck und Ruprecht, 1951), pp. 55 ff.

[83] *WA* 39ᴵ, 492, 521, 564.

the other in terms of Christ who intercedes for me." "In myself outside of Christ, I am a sinner; in Christ outside of myself, I am not a sinner."" This double character remains through all of life. Both are always true of me at one and the same time. This is the great paradox of Christian existence. Neither reason nor legalistic thinking can understand the contradiction involved in the fact that one and the same man is at one and the same time both a righteous man and a sinner:" and he is both completely; it is not as though he were partially righteous and partially a sinner but rather he is completely a sinner and completely righteous." Such is the wonderful way that God deals with his people."

This contradiction involved in being a righteous man and a sinner "at one and the same time" does not cease in this life but continues until death. Yet it is not a static relationship but is constantly in movement between these two opposing poles. For as we have already seen, Christ is drawn into the heart together with that faith which receives forgiveness. From this position, Christ now begins the battle against the old man." Thus Luther's "at one

---

" "You will therefore judge yourselves one way in accordance with the severity of God's judgment, and another in accordance with the kindness of his mercy. Do not separate these two perspectives in this life." *WA* 8, 96; *LW* 32, 213. "You know that we are certainly righteous, pure, and holy even though we are sinners, unrighteous and damned. We are, however, righteous in terms of the imputation or mercy of God promised in Christ, that is, on account of Christ in whom we believe. . . . According to our own form and substance, however, we are unrighteous and damned. . . ." *WA* 39ᴵ, 492. "A man who believes in Christ is righteous and holy by divine imputation. . . ." *WA* 39ᴵ, 21. "With reference to Christ our Lord and the forgiveness of sins in Christ, we are truly holy, innocent, and righteous . . . with reference to myself and my flesh, however, I am a sinner." *WA* 39ᴵ, 552.

" *WA* 38, 205.

" *WA* 39ᴵ, 507. "We are his children, and yet we are sinners." *WA* 6, 216; *PE* 1, 203.

" *WA* 39ᴵ, 563 f.

" "God deals so wonderfully with his saints that he constantly brings it about in the church, that the church is holy and nevertheless not holy, that someone is righteous and at the same time not righteous, that another is blessed and at the same time not blessed." *WA* 39ᴵ, 515. " 'God is wonderful in his saints,' who are at one and the same time righteous and not righteous." *WA* 57, 164; cf. *LCC* 15, 125.

" "So both sin and righteousness are present in us. . . . Faith fights against sin. . . . Sin fights against faith." *WA* 39ᴵ, 376. "When this faith has been born, you see, its task is to drive what is left of sin out of the flesh. . . . So that in this way the law of God gives pleasure and is fulfilled not only in the spirit and in the heart but in the flesh that still resists faith and in the spirit which loves and fulfills the law." *WA* 2, 497; *LW* 27, 231. Cf. *WA* 40ᴵᴵ, 352; *LW* 12, 328.

and the same time a righteous man and a sinner" has still another dimension of meaning. As long as Christ works powerfully in a man through faith and this man, through the power of the Holy Spirit, fights against himself as the old man, he is righteous.[90] So far as he, however, at the same time remains "flesh" which is to be struggled against and given into death, he remains a sinner.[91] Understood in this way, "at one and the same time a righteous man and a sinner" does not describe things that are both completely true of a man at one and the same time, but describes the tension and conflict involved in the coexistence of the righteous man and the sinner within the individual. The boundary and the battle lines between these two run through the individual. Luther based this picture of the Christian as a man in contradiction on Romans 7. In his judgment, as well as in that of the other reformers, Romans 7:14 ff. does not describe the man without Christ but the Christian man.[92] Thus the phrase "at one and the same time a righteous man and a sinner" characterizes not only the paradoxical theological and empirical togetherness of the divine verdict and a man's actual condition, but also the anthropological conflict within the Christian man. "Righteous man" and "sinner" are here not total but partial dimensions of man.

The twofold sense of "at one and the same time a righteous man and a sinner" corresponds to two other things that are true about the inner movement of the Christian life. On the one hand, the Christian is involved in a daily renewed surrender of himself in faith to God's totally merciful judgment of life and death as a daily new reception of judgment and of the grace of justification.[93] On the other hand, the constant renewal of my surrender to

---

[90] Luther repeatedly emphasizes that forgiveness of sins and justification for the sake of Christ are valid for those who fight against sin, and that they are bound to such a struggle. *WA* 8, 95, 114; *LW* 32, 212, 239 f. His specific biblical basis for this is Romans 8:1 where the *textus receptus* inserts the words, "those who do not live according to the flesh but according to the spirit" after "those who are in Christ Jesus."

[91] *WA* 2, 497; *LW* 27, 231. Cf. *WA* 39ᴵ, 494.

[92] In addition to the interpretation of Romans 7 in Luther's lectures in Romans, cf. *WA* 2, 497; *LW* 27, 231. Cf. also Luther's *Against Latomus*, *WA* 8, 112, 118 ff.; *LW* 32, 237, 245 ff. and *WA* 39ᴵᴵ, 221. On Romans 7:15 ff.: "Therefore, I am at one and the same time a sinner and righteous because I do evil and hate the evil that I do." *WA* 56, 70.

[93] Cf. *WA* 39ᴵ, 95, 98; *LW* 34, 164, 167. *WA* 40ᴵᴵᴵ, 348. *WA* 2, 731; *LW* 35, 34.

God's working in me results in the progressive death of the old man and the resurrection of the new man.[94] The former is total; the latter is only partial. We might say that the death of the old man occurs in the vertical dimension of life and the resurrection of the new man occurs in the horizontal dimension of life.[95] Christ's form takes shape within us through a lifelong on-going event. Having received justifying grace means that I am blessed right here and now for Christ is with me, for me, and in me—but precisely this means that I am in the process of becoming and have not yet become.[96] In this process of becoming I move forward toward perfection. Luther, however, did not understand this perfection as an ethical high point but as the depths in which a man loses all trust in himself and purely and strongly desires to be completely free from sin and to be completely one with God's will. that is, he is ready and willing to die.[97]

FAITH AND ITS FRUITS

Justification, and therewith all of salvation, is given to men through faith alone, *sola fide*. For justification and salvation depend only on God's mercy; and this can be received only in an act of faith. Man's ethical activity and "works" have no place

---

[94] *WA* 30[I], 225; *BC*, 449. "In the life to come, we shall be perfectly formed as righteous men. In this life we are in the process of becoming." *WA* 39[I], 251. "Since holiness has begun and is increasing daily . . ." *WA* 30[I], 190; *BC*, 418. "Christians increase daily in spiritual stature, always possessing the peace of a good conscience." *WA* 8, 20; *LW* 13, 20. Cf. *WA* 2, 147; *LW* 31, 301. *WA* 8, 7, 12; *LW* 13, 5, 11. *WA* 8, 111; *LW* 32, 235. *WA* 40[II], 355-358; cf. *LW* 12, 329-331. *WA* 39[I], 432. 439.

[95] "For Christ is constantly formed in us and we are formed according to his own image while we live here." *WA* 39[I], 204.

[96] "Our justification is not yet finished. It is in the process of being made; it is neither something which is actually completed nor is it essentially present. It is still under construction." *WA* 39[I], 252. "This life, therefore, is not godliness but the process of becoming godly, not health but getting well, not being but becoming, not rest but exercise. We are not now what we shall be, but we are on the way. The process is not yet finished, but it is actively going on. This is not the goal but it is the right road. At present, everything does not gleam and sparkle, but everything is being cleansed." *WA* 7, 337; *LW* 32, 24.

[97] *WA* 17[II], 13. God "frightens our conscience, and afflicts us with all kinds of troubles, so that our sinful old Adam becomes mellow and soft. Finally, through our death, our pride, trust, and confidence in our own efforts and knowledge will completely die." *WA* 31[I], 169; *LW* 14, 94.

here. They can neither cause nor preserve salvation for us. It is only through faith that we are preserved to eternal life.[98]

As we have seen, however, righteousness and certainty of salvation, once experienced, lead, with inner necessity, to "works," to new obedience, and to joyfully serving God by serving the neighbor. These works are born out of faith. That, however, does not exhaust their relationship. This new obedience depends on faith. But conversely, this new obedience is for this very reason significant for faith, as the hallmark of the fact that it really is faith.[99] If faith is the actual basis of the work, then the work becomes the basis for knowing we have faith. Such a basis is needed, because not everything that claims to be faith is genuine faith.[100] There is an imagined and counterfeit faith. In this counterfeit faith man has not really encountered God's love in Christ and not seriously grasped Christ, and Christ therefore has not entered his heart. That hallmark, however, which distinguishes genuine from counterfeit faith and living from dead faith is the "work" of the new obedience, the battle against sin.[101] Here Luther asserts the validity of the thoughts contained in the Letter of James and in the First Letter of John just as seriously as he emphasizes the Pauline "by faith alone." He also constantly confirms his agreement with II Peter 1:10, "Be zealous to confirm your call and election."[102] He also agrees with James that if no works follow it is certain that true faith in Christ does not live in the heart but a dead, imagined, and self-fabricated faith.[103] Indeed, Luther explains, God's justifying for-

---

[98] *WA* 39[I], 255 f.

[99] "We must therefore most certainly maintain that where there is no faith there also can be no good works; and conversely, that there is no faith where there are no good works. Therefore faith and good works should be so closely joined together that the essence of the entire Christian life consists in both." *WA* 12, 282.

[100] *WA* 47, 789.

[101] "True faith is not idle. We can, therefore, ascertain and recognize those who have true faith from the effect or from what follows." *WA* 39[I], 114; *LW* 34, 183.

[102] E.g., *WA* 6, 217; *PE* 1, 205. *WA* 10[III], 95, 226. *WA* 14, 22. *WA* 32, 423; *LW* 21, 149. *WA* 39[I], 204.

[103] "Accordingly, if good works do not follow, it is certain that this faith in Christ does not dwell in our heart, but dead faith." *WA* 39[I], 46; *LW* 34, 111. Cf. *WA* 39[I], 92; *LW* 34, 161. *WA* 12, 289. "When no work is there then faith has been completely lost." *WA* 39[II], 248. "For that faith which lacks fruit is not an efficacious but a feigned faith." *WA* 39[I], 106; *LW* 34, 176. *WA* 39[I], 114; *LW* 34, 183.

giveness is partially dependent on man's having taken up the battle of the Spirit against the flesh.[104] If this battle is missing and a man persists in gross sins, then he is not a Christian and he does not stand under God's forgiveness.[105] Accordingly, Luther declares positively that new obedience, the battle with sin, good works, and love make us and others certain that our faith is true and thereby that we are saved.[106]

The fifth petition of the Lord's Prayer and the addition to it in Matthew 6:14 f. provided Luther with the clearest biblical basis for these assertions. He speaks emphatically in his interpretation of this passage. He even speaks of a twofold forgiveness: the inner forgiveness which the heart received through faith in God's word and the outward forgiveness received in the "work," that is, in the act of forgiving the neighbor. As a sign and seal the latter is placed almost on a level with the sacraments through which God wills to strengthen our faith.[107] Thus the Holy Spirit, through the works which he works in us, both inwardly and outwardly bears witness that we are saved.[108] The certainty of salvation does

---

[104] *WA* 7, 343; *LW* 32, 28.

[105] *WA* 39ᴵ, 92; *LW* 34, 161.

[106] "Works are a certain sign, like a seal on a letter, which make me certain that my faith is genuine. As a result if I examine my heart and find that my works are done in love, then I am certain that my faith is genuine. If I forgive, then my forgiving makes me certain that my faith is genuine and assures me and demonstrates my faith to me." *WA* 10ᴵᴵᴵ, 225. "Works assure us and bear witness before men and the brethren and even before our own selves that we truly believe and that we are sons of God in hope and heirs of eternal life." *WA* 39ᴵ, 292. Cf. *WA* 39ᴵ, 293. "If this beginning is truly present, it shows itself through good works and thus makes our calling certain." *WA* 39ᴵ, 204, 8. "Love is evidence of faith and gives us firm and certain confidence in the mercy of God; thus we are commanded to make our calling certain by good works (II Pet. 1:10). When works follow it becomes apparent that we have faith. . . ." *WA* 39ᴵᴵ, 248.

[107] "The forgiveness of sins takes place in two ways: first inwardly, through the gospel and the word of God which is received by faith in the heart toward God; second, outwardly through works, about which II Peter 1[:10] says in its instructions regarding good works: 'Dear brethren, be zealous to confirm your calling and election.' He means to say that we should confirm our possession of faith and the forgiveness of sin . . . the outward forgiveness that I show in my deeds is a sure sign that I have the forgiveness of sin in the sight of God. On the other hand, if I do not show this in my relations with my neighbor, I have a sure sign that I do not have the forgiveness of sin in the sight of God but am still stuck in my unbelief. . . . He takes the work and puts a promise on top of it, so that it might quite appropriately be called a sacrament, a means of strengthening faith." *WA* 32, 423 f.; *LW* 21, 149 f. Cf. *WA* 14, 627; *LW* 9, 86.

[108] *WA* 40ᴵ, 577; *LW* 26, 379.

not depend solely on the Christian's new experience of obedience, that is, on his experience of Christ's power to renew men, but it is, however, partially dependent on that.

In view of Jesus' words to the adulterous woman (Luke 7:47), Luther can speak both of a twofold righteousness and of a twofold forgiveness of the Christian. He distinguishes the "inner" righteousness before God, which we receive in faith in Christ through the forgiveness of sins, from the "external" righteousness before men, which manifests itself in that love which is born out of justification. The former is "hidden in the spirit"; the latter is revealed for the sake of others and makes known to them that we have forgiveness of sins and are thus righteous before God or, what is the same, that we have faith.[109]

All of this becomes a second pole in Luther's theology of justification. Does it constitute a danger for the first and the decisive pole of faith alone? Does it contradict it?[110] The tension seems to be great. "By faith alone" means that the Christian should not attempt to answer questions about his salvation on the basis of his works, sins, and omissions but listen only to God's gracious word in the gospel that He accepts us without any merit or worthiness on our part and in spite of all our sins. Does Luther retract at this point? He now requires the Christian to consider what he has done or not done. And his activity or nonactivity strengthens or endangers his certainty of salvation. And yet there is no contradiction here. For the consideration of what he has done and not done, of his works and of his sins, has a completely different meaning in each case. The Christian should not take these things into consideration in the sense that he is not to depend on his works as the basis of his salvation and should not bring them before God as achievements. He should take them into consideration as giving him a "certain sign" of true faith. They can neither gain nor guarantee salvation; but as the fruits of faith they provide a posteriori certainty of it. This has nothing at all to do with "meriting" salvation. For that purpose, works would have to be without spot and

[109] *WA* 39¹, 92 f. 96; *LW* 34, 161 f., 165.
[110] In my first book *Die Prinzipien der deutschen reformierten Dogmatik* (Leipzig: Deichert, 1914), p. 198, I concluded that the "basic position of the Reformers was therewith destroyed."

blemish and be perfect. However, even in their imperfection they are able to serve as a sign of the salvation which has been given to us. The Christian feels that God's Spirit compels him to love; and he is thus made certain of his sharing with Christ, even though the end result is never a completely pure work but always bears the marks of the old man. In the same way, taking or not taking one's own sins and failures into consideration means something completely different in each case. There is no contradiction involved in telling a man who has been terrified into repentance by God's law and who now asks about his salvation not to take his sins and failures into consideration before God but to believe the word of justification in spite of them! It is, on the other hand, something quite different from this when the Christian is, in view of the possibility of an imagined and counterfeit faith, warned not to feel secure in his "faith" but to allow himself to be so disturbed and frightened by his sins and failures that he asks whether he really believes and thus really is saved. Both elements have their necessary place in the life of the Christian. And the second does not in any way detract from "by faith alone."

Luther has expressed what needs to be said at this point in a very meaningful way. He says that good works, the "works of grace," are necessary. At the same time, he refuses to characterize them as necessary for salvation or for justification. They are necessary as a witness of faith (and therewith they give glory to the heavenly Father and serve the neighbor).[111] They are not, however, necessary "for salvation." Such a teleological significance would set aside the "by grace alone" and "by faith alone" of justification and of salvation.[112] Luther thought that the expression that works or the new obedience are necessary to salvation raises thoughts about merit and guilt and that such questions are unbearable in the discussion of salvation.[113] The expression "works are necessary to salvation" is thus equivocal and to be avoided in theology as

---

[111] *WA* 39¹, 224, 254: Cf. *WA* 39ɪɪ, 241.
[112] "Our renewal [*novitas*] is thus necessary but neither for our salvation nor for our justification. The only thing which is necessary for salvation and justification is the mercy of God which is received by faith." *WA* 39¹, 225. Cf. *WA* 39ɪɪ, 241.
[113] *WA* 39¹, 214 f., 254, 257.

improper.[114] "We must keep this doctrine [of justification] pure."[115]
At the most, Luther can agree to a pedagogical use of the expression "for the sake of the hypocrites" in order to sharpen their awareness that faith must be active. In that case, however, we must very definitely assert that although "works are necessary to salvation, they do not work salvation, for faith alone gives life."[116] Or, new obedience, the necessary fruit and activity of faith, "occurs with reference to salvation but it does not earn salvation."[117] The fact that it "occurs with reference to salvation" is to be understood in terms of the final revelation of this salvation. The assertion that new obedience occurs in connection with and in reference to salvation implies that the Christian already has salvation in faith and in hope; and that precisely in this hope, he reaches out toward the revelation of this salvation. The Christian's holiness and new obedience are the practical form of hope appropriate to the condition of waiting between already and having salvation and not yet having it. The new obedience flows from the certainty that salvation is already present and is oriented to its future revelation. It has its source in the fact that the believer has it and at the same time eagerly expects to receive it.[118]

---

[114] *WA* 39^1, 224 f.
[115] *WA* 39^1, 215.
[116] *WA* 39^1, 96, cf. 104; *LW* 34, 165, 172.
[117] *WA* 39^1, 254.
[118] *Ibid.*

19

LAW AND GOSPEL

IN PREVIOUS chapters we have repeatedly spoken of law and gospel. Luther's doctrine of justification in particular completely expresses his understanding of law and gospel and their relationship to each other. These two themes of his theology are very closely connected. This is the appropriate place then, immediately following our discussion of justification, to present Luther's doctrine of law and gospel as a whole. Many things already specifically referred to or only hinted at will be discussed once again.[1]

The word of God comes to men in the twofold form of law and gospel. According to Luther, the preservation of pure doctrine absolutely depends on the accurate theological statement of the nature and meaning of both law and gospel; they must be carefully distinguished and their true relationship to each other must be rightly understood.[2]

OPPOSITION IN UNITY

Man has known God's law since his creation. God's finger has written it into the heart of every man through creation, that is "by nature." Luther teaches this, agreeing with and referring to what Paul says in Romans 2:14. Even if God had never given the written law through Moses, the human spirit still would know naturally that he should worship God and love his neighbor.[3] The revelation and knowledge of God's will thus antedates Moses' Decalog and differs from it as the "living" law in man's heart.[4] Its content is the same as Moses' law and as the moral admonitions of the gospel, that is, the rule in Matthew 7:12 which commands us to love our neighbor as ourselves. "There is thus a single law, effective in all

---

[1] Cf. Gerhard Heintze, *Luthers Predigt von Gesetz und Evangelium* (Munich: Kaiser, 1958.)
[2] *WA* 7, 502. Cf. *WA* 18, 680; *BOW*, 163. *WA* 39¹, 361 f.
[3] *WA* 39¹, 374, 454, 478, 539, 540. *WA* 17ᴵᴵ, 102.
[4] *WA* 39¹, 352, 402.

ages and known to all men because it is written in everyone's heart. From the beginning to the end no one can excuse himself [for] the Spirit never stops speaking this law in the hearts of all men."[5]

But this light "which dwells in and illumines everyone's reason" has, since the fall, been darkened by man's sinful desires. God was therefore compelled to give a written law to the people of Israel through Moses in order to remind men of the natural law in their hearts.[6] Moses thus is not really the author of the Decalog. He has a more modest rank. Properly understood, he only interprets and clarifies the natural laws written in men's hearts.[7] "Natural law is clearly and exactly summarized on Mt. Sinai—in a much better way than the philosophers have done it."[8] Christ, too, only interprets the law. He, also, is not a lawgiver but only wants to make clear to us what the law written in our hearts, or respectively, the Decalog, really demands.[9]

We must speak about this law in a twofold way. The law, seen only as the summary of the eternal will of God, has one set of implications; and as the law which confronts the sinner, it has a quite different significance. Or we could say that we must distinguish the content of God's law from the form in which this content confronts the sinner.[10]

In terms of its content, the law is the eternal will of God and man's salvation lies in fulfilling it. It says only that man should let his God and Lord be precisely that which God offers to be for man, that is, man's gracious God. To that extent, the law expresses God's love and gives a man a share in the life of that love. The fact that God is God can save only the man who holds to it and actively grasps its offer, "I am the Lord thy God." In

---

[5] *WA* 2, 580; *LW* 27, 355. Cf. Luther's lectures on Romans, *WA* 56, 197; *LCC* 15, 46.

[6] "But evil desire and love darken this light and blind a man so that he does not look at such a book in his heart and does not follow such a clear commandment of reason. One must therefore curb and drive him back with external commands, books, with the sword and by force, and remind him of his natural light and place his own heart before his eyes." *WA* 17[II], 102. *WA* 39[I], 539. "And so the law is renewed." *WA* 39[I], 540. Cf. *ibid.*, 549.

[7] *WA* 39[I], 454, 478.

[8] *WA* 49, 1.

[9] *WA* 39[I], 387.

[10] *WA* 39[I], 455.

this sense, Luther can, on the basis of Paul's statement in Romans 7:10, say that the law is given "for good," "for life," and as a "doctrine and word of life."[11] The law in this sense confronted man before the fall and will, as such, still remain valid in the world to come; it will be completely fulfilled in the world to come just as it was already fulfilled before the fall into sin.[12] Thus the law's content, although not the outward form which it has in relationship to sinners, shows what man was before the fall and what he shall be in the future; it has both protological and eschatological meaning.[13] Before the fall, man could fulfill it; and he did fulfill it joyfully and was totally committed to it. The law made him glad.[14] This inner relationship to the law must now be restored to us by Christ through his Holy Spirit and will be fully restored only in the life to come.[15] This, then, is blessedness. For "that is what it means to be blessed: God rules in us and we are his kingdom."[16]

Through Adam's fall, however, we have fallen from our original condition, and the life to come is not yet here. The fall into sin changed the very basis of the law's relationship to man as God's eternal will. God's eternal will for men has now become "law" in its specific sense for the sinner. Luther explains the meaning of this in his doctrine of the "office [*Amt, Officium*]," "function [*Brauch, usus*]," or "meaning [*Sinn, sensus*]" of the law.[17]

The law has a twofold function.[18] One function is the "civil" and the other the "theological," "spiritual," or "holy" meaning and function.[19] The first function of the law is to hinder gross transgressions and crimes in this world of sin which is controlled by the devil. It thus preserves public peace and makes possible the education of the young and, particularly, the preaching of the gospel. The law does this in the form of the God-instituted offices of government, parents, and teachers, as well as through the civil

---

[11] *WA* 46, 658, 661; *LW* 22, 140, 143.
[12] *WA* 39ᴵ, 413.
[13] *WA* 39ᴵ, 204, 454.
[14] *WA* 39ᴵ, 364.
[15] *WA* 39ᴵ, 365, 374.
[16] *WA* 2, 98.
[17] [In the following *Amt* is often translated with "function." —Trans.]
[18] *WA* 39ᴵ, 441. Cf. *WA* 40ᴵ, 429; *LW* 26, 274.
[19] *WA* 26, 15. Cf. *WA* 40ᴵ, 429 f. *LW* 26, 274, 308 f.

254 *The Theology of Martin Luther*

laws." Man is basically able to fulfill these laws and therefore also God's law in its civil sense, that is, he can produce civil righteousness, acceptable to the world.

The second meaning and function of God's law is different from this. The law has another dimension and accordingly another function than that expressed in its civil function." The law has a second function insofar as it is not simply understood in its civil or in its "political" sense but also in its spiritual sense; and this latter is its true and genuine meaning." Jesus shows what this is in the Sermon on the Mount. His interpretation of the law radically sharpens its demands." The law of God demands a pure heart, perfect obedience, perfect fear and love of God. The law is not satisfied by mere outward fulfilment." Paul illustrates the breadth and depth of the law in the same way that Jesus does." This, however, makes it clear: The law understood in this sense both could be and was fulfilled before the fall into sin; sinful man, however, simply cannot fulfill it." Now the law does not help a man to become righteous. On the contrary, it reveals his sinfulness and increases it." It constantly accuses him" and delivers him up to God's wrath, to judgment, and to eternal death." This is the law's power. All men know something about God's law without being at all aware of or feeling its power." This happens through the preaching of the law. It intends to, and actually does, awaken men out of their unawareness, make them feel the power of the law, recognize their sin, experience God's wrath, and be led to repent-

20 *WA* 40[I], 479; *LW* 26, 39. Cf. *WA* 11, 250; *LW* 45, 89 f.

21 "Thus the law is twofold and is to be known in a twofold way." *WA* 39[I], 460.

22 *WA* 39[I], 460.

23 *WA* 39[I], 533, 570.

24 *WA* 39[I], 387, 404, 461.

25 *WA* 39[I], 388, 393.

26 *WA* 39[I], 364, 374.

27 *WA* 39[I], 557 ff. Sin begins to increase on the level of morality, in violation of the commandments of the Second Table, according to the rule: "We seek that which is forbidden." *WA* 39[I], 556, 559. This increase becomes fully apparent, however, in our violation of the commandments of the First Table; for the knowledge that we cannot fulfill the law produces hatred against God and despair.

28 "The strength of sin is the law which constantly accuses and puts to death." *WA* 39[I], 412. Melanchthon's assertion that "the law always accuses" [*Apology of the Augsburg Confession*, BC, 150, 285], is thus also found in Luther.

29 *WA* 39[I], 383.

30 *WA* 39[I], 345, 366, 404 f.

ance."ª At all of these points, Luther accepts the doctrine of the
Apostle Paul.

The law was originally an expression of God's love; now it is
the tool of his wrath. The law once made man rejoice; now it
has become a terrible thing for him.ª A detailed description of
what the law in the hands of God's wrath does to man and the
problems into which it leads him has been given in the chapter
on God's wrath (cf. pp. 174).

This is then the theological or spiritual meaning and function
of the law. It shows man, who without this function of the law is
blind and unaware, his sin and thereby reveals to him God's wrath,
death, and hell.ª Anyone who tries to interpret and use it as a
means of achieving righteousness before God therefore completely
misunderstands and misuses it. That is neither its function nor its
goal. And it is completely incapable of achieving this purpose.ª
On the contrary, the law works the opposite of justification. That
is the function which God himself has given to it.

There is thus no doubt that the law is God's own word. It is
even "spiritual"; that is, it comes from God and is "written with his
own finger." It is truth; and all truth comes from the Holy Spirit.
Whoever does not wish the law to be preached refuses to hear the
truth of God.ª It is significant that Luther opposes the antinomians and emphasizes that the law is spiritual and comes from
God—even though he at the same time distinguishes this working
of the Spirit in the law from the working of the Spirit whom
Christ sends from the Father.ª Luther speaks of God's Spirit

ªª *WA* 8, 103; *LW* 32, 224. Cf. *WA* 39ˣ, 401.
ªª "Those who stand outside of Christ find the law's demands painful, hate-
ful, and impossible." *WA* 39ˣ, 365, 374.
ªª *WA* 18, 677, 766; *BOW*, 158 f.; 287. "The function of the law is to
show sins, to create sorrow, and to lead into hell." *WA* 39ˣ, 477, cf. 347 f.
ªª "The purpose of the law is something other than justification." *WA* 39ˣ,
213. "Not only is the law not necessary for justification but it is obviously of no
possible use at all . . . for the law is given neither so that it might justify and
make alive nor that it might help anyone to righteousness but that it might
show sin and work wrath, that is, make the conscience guilty." *WA* 39ˣ, 347.
"The law ought to be separated from justification just as far as heaven is from
the earth." *WA* 39ˣ, 348.
ªª *WA* 39ˣ, 349.
ªª "When the Holy Spirit is God in his nature, he is the author of the law
without whom the law does not convict anyone of sin. When, however, he is
that gift which is given us through Christ, he is the one who makes us alive
and sanctifies us." *WA* 39ˣ, 391; cf. 370, 389, 484.

in a twofold way. This corresponds to the twofold character of God's word as law and gospel. The Holy Spirit is, insofar as he is the author of the law, to be distinguished from God's gift through the gospel of Jesus Christ. The former is "God in his nature," the latter comes from God as revealed in Jesus Christ." Accordingly, when God's Spirit speaks through the law, his work in the heart is quite different and even opposite to what he does when he speaks through the gospel. The Spirit speaking through the law terrifies, kills, and is a consuming fire for the conscience. Through the gospel, however, he is the Comforter who makes a man holy and alive. Therewith, we have made the transition to the gospel.

The law is not God's entire word. The gospel stands alongside it. Law and gospel have completely different and even opposite functions. The law demands that something be done or not be done; it accuses and condemns us because we have acted or failed to act in a way contrary to its demands. The gospel contains God's promise in Christ. It proclaims that all the law's demands have been met in Jesus Christ, that is, it preaches the forgiveness of sins. "The gospel is the preaching of forgiveness of sins through the name of Jesus Christ."" Luther adopts Paul's characterization of the gospel as "promise." Like Paul (II Cor. 3:6 ff.), he also places law and gospel in opposition to each other and describes the law as the ministry of death and the gospel as the ministry of the Spirit." The law leads into death; the gospel proclaims eternal life by the power of Christ's redemption. The law places a man under the wrath of God; the gospel brings grace."

Law and gospel thus are opposed to each other. The law demands a pure heart and complete obedience. The gospel proclaims that the sinner and the unclean man are accepted for Christ's sake. The gospel thus abrogates the law's power. The sinner is justified contrary to the law; and the gospel must be believed against the

" *WA* 39¹, 370.
" *WA* 2, 466; *LW* 27, 184. "The proper definition of the gospel is that it is the promise of Christ, which frees us from the terrors of the law, sin, and death, and brings grace, forgiveness of sins, righteousness, and eternal life." *WA* 39¹, 387. Cf. *WA* 46, 665; *LW* 22, 145.
" *WA* 39¹, 447.
" "The true and proper function of the law is to accuse and to kill; but the function of the gospel is to make alive." *WA* 39¹, 363; cf. *ibid.* p. 382. Cf. *WA* 8, 108; *LW* 32, 230.

law. Since the law confronts a man in his conscience and determines the character of his conscience, he must believe against the accusations of a conscience determined by the law and against the doubt and belief that the law works in his conscience. Paul teaches that justification takes place "without the law" (Rom. 3:21). Luther, in substantial agreement with the apostle, sharpens the expression to read "against the law."[41]

In all this, however, law and gospel are not only contrary to each other but are, in this opposition, related to each other. They are to be sharply distinguished but not to be separated from each other.[42] They may not be mixed together with each other (for example, by converting the unconditional grace of God proclaimed by the gospel into a grace conditioned by human achievement),[43] but they also may not be separated from each other. For they are inseparably bound together with and connected to each other. Thus both statements are valid: Justification takes place "against the law"; and also, "do not think that law and gospel are in conflict with each other!"[44] For this reason both must be preached.[45] There is thus difference and opposition and also an inseparable connection, antithesis and also harmony between the law and the gospel. How is this to be understood?

The gospel presupposes the law and its proclamation. For the gospel brings the forgiveness of sins. This, however, presupposes sin itself.[46] Sin, however, exists and is recognized only under the law. For this reason, Luther in his battle with the antinomians can assert that abolishing the law means abolishing sin: "But if sin is abolished, then Christ has also been done away with for

---

[41] "Thus I am indeed above the law and I do not care about it. For God saves the believer, even contrary to the law which wills that no one should be saved except righteous people. But God saves the unrighteous. Thus the law is abrogated, that is, the condemning and justifying law." *WA* 39^1, 219.

Speaking of the blind man along the road to Jericho, Luther says, "He struggles not only with his conscience which without doubt made him feel that he was not worthy of this . . . also fights his way through and wins and does not allow the whole world or even his own conscience to separate him from his confidence." *WA* 17^{11}, 177.

[42] "The law and the gospel neither can nor should be separated; just as repentance and the forgiveness of sins should not be separated. For they are so closely bound together and involved in each other." *WA* 39^1, 416.

[43] *WA* 18, 680; *BOW*, 163 f. Cf. *WA* 46, 663, 665; *LW* 22, 145, 147 f.

[44] *WA* 39^1, 566.

[45] *WA* 39^1, 382.

[46] *WA* 39^1, 416.

there would no longer be any need for him."⁴⁷ We can not understand or desire to hear the gospel that Christ's saving work redeems from sin unless we have stood under the law. Apart from
the law, we cannot recognize the greatness of what Christ
does for us and to us.⁴⁸ The gospel is thus directly related to the
law. The proclamation of the law is the indispensable and necessary presupposition for the preaching of the gospel.⁴⁹ Without the
law a man would not recognize his own sickness but would remain
secure and proud of his own moral capacity as he thinks of it.⁵⁰
Only the law teaches us to recognize our actual sinful condition
and places us under condemnation, under God's wrath and judgment, and thereby prepares us for the gospel.⁵¹ It teaches us to
long for our Savior. It leads us to repentance and thus opens us
to receive the comfort of the gospel. Thus the preaching of the
law is directed toward the gospel and wants to lead us toward it.
This was Christ's intention when he interpreted the law.⁵² Through
the law, God works his alien work so that he may begin his
proper work.

The law must therefore be preached. The proclamation of the
law by itself is not able to lead a man to true repentance and to
faith in the gospel. Many hear it without its making any impression. They do not yet feel the power of the law. Its threats and
terrors do not move them. God's Spirit must work together with
the preached word in the case of the law as well as of the gospel.⁵³

However, even when God gives his Spirit to the proclamation

---

⁴⁷ *WA* 39¹, 546, 348 f., 371, 535, 546.
⁴⁸ *WA* 39¹, 424, 465, 534.
⁴⁹ "The teaching of the law ought always to have a place in the doctrine of
redemption." *WA* 39¹, 466; cf. 348.
⁵⁰ *WA* 39¹, 348.
⁵¹ "The gospel . . . most beautifully follows the law. The law introduces us to
sin and overwhelms us with the knowledge of it. It does this so that we may
seek to be freed and desire grace." *WA* 8, 105; *LW* 32, 226. If the teaching
of the law really touches the heart "then the whole wide world becomes too
small for us and there is no help anywhere except in Christ." *WA* 39¹, 456.
⁵² *WA* 39¹, 533.
⁵³ "Many hear the law and yet are not moved by its threats and terrors because they do not feel the force of the law. Therefore I do not convert anyone
by the power of my preaching unless God is present and his Spirit works together with what I preach." *WA* 39¹, 368. "The law does not convince of sin
without the Holy Spirit." *WA* 39¹, 371; cf. 389 f. This is why Luther can
use either the Spirit or the law itself as the subject of "terrifies" and "kills";
the Spirit works through the law. *WA* 39¹, 484.

of the law, it does not necessarily lead a man to true repentance. Rather, two things can result. When the law convicts a man of his sin and reveals God's wrath, it leads him to despair. If a man has only the law, his despair cannot be healed. Despair leads him into the new sin of hating God.[54] This situation can be changed only if a man not only has the law but also hears the word of the gospel. Then he recognizes that the law is not God's final word and that its threats, judgment, and condemnation are not the goal but the means in God's hands.[55] Then man's despair becomes a salutary despair, that is, he does not despair of God's mercy but of himself and of his own capability so that he expects everything from Christ. The law is to be interpreted through the gospel; and its intention is to be understood on the basis of the gospel. Admittedly, the law will still—as it should—lead a man into the terrors of conscience and these can be demonic or "evangelical." Demonic terrors result in godless despair which, if it remains alone, is evil and death itself. The evangelical terrors lead to proper "evangelical despair" and to Christ.[56]

When the law strikes home to a man he stands between God and the devil. Each intends to use the terrors of the law to achieve exactly opposite goals. The devil seeks to bring man to destruction and death. God, however, wills that he should be blessed and live.[57] In the first case, the law itself becomes a devil to the conscience like a highway robber who intends only to kill him. In the other case, the law under the consolation of the gospel becomes a "disciplinarian that drives a man to Christ." This, however, "is a comforting word and a true genuine and immeasurably joyful purpose of the law." Luther confesses: "I feel great comfort and consolation, when I hear that the law is a disciplinarian to lead me to Christ rather than a devil or a robber that trains me not in discipline but in despair."[58] The law by itself without the gospel has

---

[54] "For the law by itself is able only to induce terror and to drive a man down to hell." *WA* 39¹, 445.

[55] "But then the gospel comes and pulls out the law's sting and makes it a disciplinarian [*paedagogum*]." *WA* 39¹, 445.

[56] *WA* 39¹, 442; cf., 430.

[57] *WA* 39¹, 440.

[58] "And so the law ought to be interpreted by the gospel and to be led back through that which is impossible to that which is salutary; it ought to be

no healing power. With the gospel, however, it works salvation. By itself alone, it leads a man into hell; together with the gospel, however, and understood on the basis of it, it leads a man to Christ.

All this means that we reach a true understanding and grasp of the gospel only by passing through the law. At the same time, however, a salutary understanding and use of the law is possible only on the basis of the gospel.[59] Thus law and gospel belong together as "God's two Testaments, ordained for our salvation, so that we may be freed from sin."[60] For our salvation, it is necessary both that we become aware of our sickness, of our sin through the law—that is "a great blessing"—and that we seek and find healing in the gospel.[61] For this reason the ministry of the word must proclaim both law and gospel. This is God's will and commission.[62] Christ also preached both.[63] It is not permissible to preach the law without the gospel or the gospel without the law; one alternative is just as dangerous as the other.[64] God places us under both law and gospel and wants us to believe both: to believe the law that we are sinners and have rightly deserved the punishment of eternal damnation; and to believe the gospel that we should not doubt God's mercy but, in contrition and terror over our sins and his righteous judgment, flee to his mercy in Christ.[65] Both belong together and both must be preserved in the church: anxiety and pain under the law, and comfort and joy under the gospel.[66] These two together constitute true evangelical repentance. Evangelical repentance is thus worked by the law and the gospel together.[67] In this process the law precedes the gospel.

---

brought back to Christ and the gospel, which by its power makes a disciplinarian out of a robber and takes the man who was killed by the law and brings him back to Christ; this is what the law cannot do." *WA* 39¹, 446; cf. 441, 445.

[59] "It is very difficult to understand either Moses or Christ without the other." *WA* 39¹, 547, cf. 445.

[60] *WA* 8, 103; *LW* 32, 223.

[61] *WA* 39¹, 517.

[62] *WA* 39¹, 428; cf. 430, 382.

[63] *WA* 39¹, 533 f.; cf. 538.

[64] *WA* 39¹, 430.

[65] *WA* 39¹, 428.

[66] *WA* 39¹, 430.

[67] *WA* 39¹, 345, 414, 452, 471.

LAW AND GOSPEL AS FUNCTIONS OF ONE AND THE SAME WORD

All this does not exhaust Luther's doctrine of law and gospel. We have shown what law is and how it works and what gospel is and how it works as well as the way in which they conflict and belong together. But where do we find law and where gospel? Luther's controversy with the antinomians led him to consider this question. This answer opens the full depth of his doctrine of law and gospel.

First, it is self understood—as we have already heard—that Luther finds the law not only in the Old Testament, that is, in Moses in the narrower and wider senses, but also in the proclamation of Jesus, in "the gospel." (Luther frequently uses the word "gospel" in its broader sense. It thus designates the total proclamation of Jesus and the apostles.)[68] Christ also preaches the law. He confirms the law of Moses and interprets it. "Law" is everything that makes us realize our sin and accuses and terrifies the conscience, regardless of whether one finds it in Christ or in Moses.[69] "Law" is furthermore not only those words which are expressly imperative, accusatory, or judgmental, but also prayerful such as, for example, the Lord's Prayer. It is "full of the doctrine of the law." Whoever prays it seriously confesses that he sins against the law and needs to repent. Everything we pray for in the first three petitions: that God's name be hallowed, that his kingdom come, and that his will be done is demanded of us by God's law. And if we pray for all this, we thereby bear witness that we have not yet fulfilled it. In this way the Lord's Prayer also carries out the work of the law on us.[70] It does the same thing to us that the law always does. It shows us that we do not have what we unconditionally ought to have.[71]

Luther goes still a step further in his struggle with the antinomians about the question: should repentance be preached on the basis of Moses' law or with reference to the gospel, since men sin by not believing in the Son? The antinomians hold the latter

[68] *WA* 39¹, 535, 351, 542.
[69] *WA* 39¹, 348, 535, 351.
[70] *WA* 39¹, 351.
[71] *Ibid.*

position. Luther rejects this either-or. He declares that a man can be led to repentance even through Christ's cross and death." How could he deny that when he reads what Paul says in Romans 2:4, "Do you not know that God's kindness is meant to lead you to repentance?"" His sole concern in the controversy with the antinomians is that they should not declare the law to be useless since repentance can also come and grow from the gospel." He leaves room for both: for that repentance which comes from the knowledge of the law as well as for that repentance which comes from the knowledge of the cross of Christ and salvation; and accordingly, he also leaves room for the proclamation of the one as well as for the other. The law and gospel do indeed lead to repentance in different ways. Luther speaks of the "rhetoric" of the gospel. On the one side, we hear the hard voice, accusing, convicting, condemning, and showing us down into hell. On the other side, we hear the encouraging and alluring voice freely offering forgiveness of sins and eternal life in the word of the Good Shepherd. But whether we are led to repentance along one path or the other, we finally arrive at the same place. "Let it take place through whatever it will, it makes no difference." There are therefore several ways to be called to Christ. God does not lead all men to him along the same path."

In all this, Luther also transcends this either-or of repentance, either through the law or through the gospel. He shows that this question does not present a genuine either-or of law and gospel. On the contrary, the gospel bears the law within itself and the

---

" *WA* 39^x, 405.
" *WA* 39^x, 400, 536.
" *WA* 39^x, 407. Luther agrees that in the first period of the Reformation he preached in exactly the way that the antinomians wanted to preach and that he used the same words in discussing repentance which they were using. He simply intended to preach the gospel powerfully. That was necessary at that time and correct, for under the papacy men had been more than sufficiently terrified. Now, however, the situation is quite different; men are secure, fresh, and Epicureans who fear neither God nor man. The different spirit of the times requires a different kind of preaching. For this reason it was not proper for the antinomians to cite Luther's earlier practice in support of their position and to claim to be his genuine pupils. *WA* 39^x, 571-574. This passage in the *Third Disputation Against the Antinomians* is very important for understanding Luther's rejection of Agricola. ["Antinomians" is used in many senses; as used here, it refers to those who reject the use of the law in leading men to contrition and repentance.—Trans.]
" *WA* 39^x, 407.

proclamation of the gospel itself is also proclamation of the law. This is true in a twofold way. First, it is clear that the proclamation of Christ as our example has the character of the proclamation of the law. For it shows us the will of God which we are to fulfill.[76] The proclamation of Christ as redeemer is, however, in itself also a preaching of the law since redemption presupposes the fact of sin. The statement that Christ is my Savior thus leads me to a knowledge of sin. Everything, however, that shows me my sin is law.[77] The proclamation of the gospel thus also becomes a preaching of the law.[78] Secondly, the gospel bears witness to God's mercy and Christ's benefits. As a man becomes aware of what he owes to God in love and obedience, however, he is filled with shame because he has been unthankful and despised God's goodness. In the first case, the gospel causes a man to recognize sin which precedes it and is presupposed by it. In the second case, it leads him to recognize his sin against the gracious God of the gospel.

Knowledge of sin can therefore come either from the law in the narrower sense or from the gospel of the goodness of God and of redemption through Christ. In the latter case the gospel is law.[79] Whatever shows me what I ought to do and that I remain in guilt is always law. Indeed, Luther concludes that no law can strike so deeply and so into our heart and cause such fearful pain as the vision of God's goodness in the gospel. No knowledge of a sin against the First or the Second Table of the law can torture us

---

[76] *WA* 39[I], 464.

[77] This is also true of the gospel which is proclaimed in the promise of the First Commandment. *WA* 40[II], 370.

[78] "Thus even when we say that Christ is set before us as an example or as the Redeemer, we teach the law. And this is a true preaching of the law. For if he comes to you as your Redeemer and Savior, you must have sinned; redemption itself presupposes sin." *WA* 39[I], 464. We must note, however, that here too, Luther wishes to make a sharp distinction between the function of the law and the function of the gospel. Even though a man learns to know his sin through the gospel, still condemnation is not properly a concern of the gospel but of the law. For this reason, Luther says that it is not the gospel itself which accuses us of sin; but the gospel shows us the law and this law accuses us of sin. *WA* 39[I], 388.

[79] "The proclamation of the law, however, reveals sin . . . but this can be done even by showing the benefits of Christ who had to suffer such great things for you and for your sins. It is all the same whether this is done by preaching the benefits of Christ or the law; it makes no difference, it is all law." *WA* 39[I], 535.

so painfully as the opening of our eyes to the fact that we have thanklessly despised the gracious God of the gospel. Whoever becomes aware of this can easily fall into despair.[80] How can such a man be helped, however? Certainly not through the law but also apparently not through the reference to God's goodness—he has sinned against this goodness and remembering it can only make him despair still more.[81] We can express Luther's position by saying: The message of the gospel can be a more terrible law for man than the real law itself. This side of the gospel is a potential law. In this whole presentation, Luther obviously uses the concept "law" in a twofold sense. On the one hand, it characterizes that law which is to be strictly distinguished from the gospel and, on the other hand, it expresses the law-character which even the gospel itself can have for the sinner.

For Luther, then, God's word can, in the final analysis, definitely not be categorized into law and gospel. The one and the same word strikes sinful man both as law and as gospel. Even the center of the gospel, the word about the cross, carries out the function of the law. It reveals man's sin and lost condition in a deeper and more painful way than any "law" in the narrower sense can do. Still no other advice and help can be given to a man who is in this situation of knowing his sin in relation to God's love in Christ than to refer him to this same word, to the crucified Christ, to the Lamb of God who bears the sin of the world, to that Jesus Christ who proclaims the gospel to the poor.[82] The same Jesus Christ against whom we always sin in unthankfulness is still proclaimed to us as the Savior, the mediator, the comforter of the disturbed and the troubled, who has come to rescue the lost.[83] This

---

[80] *WA* 39¹, 536, 580.

[81] "How can the man who has been made a pauper be helped? Certainly not by the law and not by the goodness of God which makes the situation even more serious for him than the law itself does." *WA* 39¹, 537. The traditional text reads "Certainly not by law, *but* by the goodness of God. . . ." The *but* is an error, however; the complete context and particularly the following sentences require *not* rather than *but*: "I ask then how we can heal the man whom *neither* the law *nor* the goodness of God is able to help, but only thoroughly terrify him. For the more you emphasize God's goodness, the more such a man despairs because he has either neglected or despised such great goodness." *Ibid.*

[82] *WA* 39¹, 537.

[83] *WA* 39¹, 538. On the basis of *ibid.*, p. 537 it could appear that Luther distinguishes the goodness of God against which we have sinned from the good-

one and same gospel leads to repentance and to faith, to despair and to peace. The fact that it both can and should still lead me away from despair to faith, even though it also carries out the function of the law on me, can only be explained in this way: the crucified Christ also bears my sin when I sin against his cross. Or also: The fact that I become and remain guilty of sinning against his love does not change the fact that he has come to save guilty men. Thus the pain of repentance is both preserved and set aside in the joy of faith. This, however, does not take place once for all but is a transition which we must risk over and over again. For we because of our lukewarmness and unthankfulness do not cease sinning against Christ's self-sacrificing love.

Law and gospel thus each have a completely different and opposite function. But these two functions are functions of the same word. They always take place concurrently. Faith, however, moves from the law to the gospel. And this movement is irreversible. The gospel constantly carries out the work of the law on a man by making him guilty. But because this gospel is the word of comfort for the guilty, faith's movement always comes to rest in the gospel. The law is both set aside and preserved in the gospel; but the reverse is never true. The gospel transcends the law; the law never transcends the gospel. For the God and Lord against whose mercy I am and remain guilty does not therefore cease being the merciful God. Faith then means that when I hear the gospel I place it above the law and even set it in opposition to the law.

Such faith in the gospel, in spite of the law, fulfills the law in its deepest sense. For the decisive element in the law is the First Commandment. This, however, rests fully on the gospel, that is, in the offer and promise: I am the Lord your God "who both can and will save all who call on him." For this reason we should not have other gods and should not despair but fear, trust, and hope in God.[54] The First Commandment of the law thus demands only that we believe the gospel, especially since we are the kind of men

---

ness of God revealed in the crucified Christ; the latter would rescue us in our despair over having sinned against the former. But statements such as those at *ibid.*, p. 536 show that Luther viewed the goodness of God and the benefits of Christ as a unity; this means that the cross of Christ, too, both makes us guilty and rescues us.

[54] *WA* 39^1, 531, 581.

who are guilty of sinning against God's law. The First Commandment, when it is fulfilled in faith in Christ, expresses the unity of
law and gospel. The opposition between law and gospel in the life
of sinful man is only a transitional stage between their original
unity and their paradoxical Christian unity in the Christian life.
This paradoxical Christian unity consists in the fact that the Christian has not fulfilled God's law and stands under its accusation
and condemnation; yet he believes the gospel in spite of it and
thus in the midst of his sinful existence fulfills God's First Commandment.

THE LAW IN THE CHRISTIAN'S LIFE

Justification completely transforms man's relationship to the
law. Christ is the end of the law. This means that the law is
abrogated for the justified man in so far as it makes demands,
forces, accuses, and condemns him.[65] For Christ has through his
obedience completely fulfilled the law and has himself borne the
curse of the law as one who was accused and damned by the law;
and he has done this all for us. God imputes this fulfilling of the
law through Christ to us. Christ has given us his innocence and
righteousness.[66] Through Christ, the justified are freed from the demands, from the compulsion, from the accusation and condemnation of the law. They have been transferred from "the kingdom
of the law" into Christ's kingdom.

This does not mean, however, that the law is no longer valid
as God's will for men. Christ has freed us from the power of the
law, that is, the power to force, to accuse, to damn, and to deliver
man to wrath and death.[67] In distinction from this, the content of
the law, that is, God's good will for men, remains unchanged. Indeed, according to Paul in Romans 8:4,[68] justification should set a
man free from his inability to do God's will so that he may fulfill it. The law is, in one sense, then fulfilled through Christ and
the Christian is no longer concerned with it. At the same time,

---

[65] *WA* 39¹, 219, 250, 374, 380, 392, 579. *WA* 2, 477; *LW* 27, 202. *WA*
39ᴵᴵ, 274.
[66] *WA* 39¹, 219, 250, 366, 375, 380, 435 f., 478 f.
[67] *WA* 7, 760.
[68] *WA* 39¹, 367.

however, it is to be fulfilled as God's holy will.⁸⁹ Yet this will of God no longer confronts the justified as the demand of the law, that is, in the form of the law. For Christ and his Spirit live in them through faith. Therefore they do what the law wants of themselves. Christ does it in them.⁹⁰ The Spirit has produced new drives within them in the form of loving God and his laws and hating evil.⁹¹ They now rejoice in God's law (Psalm 1 and Romans 7:22—Luther interprets these passages as referring to a Christian man). When I have been enlightened by the Holy Spirit, then "the grace of God, which Christ has bestowed on me because I believe in him, makes the First Commandment a pleasure for me." I therefore no longer stand helpless and despairing before this commandment of God but in faith in Christ I know that I can fulfill it. Indeed, in faith I have already begun to fulfill it.⁹²

The law thus "begins to be a joyous thing," and the Christian becomes willing to fulfill it and is at least able to make a beginning in fulfilling it.⁹³ He no longer stands under a demand but is joyfully moved toward God's law by the power of the Holy Spirit. Christ leads man out of his condition under the law back to that joyous obedience of the law, which men knew before the fall into sin.⁹⁴ The Christian conforms to the law freely, not because the law demands it but because he loves God and righteousness.⁹⁵ He no longer acts with the assistance of the law to say nothing of being compelled by it but in the spirit of freedom. His activity is spontaneous.⁹⁶ Thus his works are no longer "works of the law" forced out of him by the law, but free "works of grace."⁹⁷ The

---

⁸⁹ *WA* 39¹, 203 f.

⁹⁰ *WA* 39¹, 46. "But having been justified by grace . . . we then do works, yes, Christ himself does all in us." *WA* 39¹, 46; *LW* 34, 111.

⁹¹ *WA* 39¹, 395.

⁹² *WA* 46, 662. "I sense that I can do it; I have started with the lesson and have already mastered the ABC's. . . . Formerly I found that I had no delight in the law. But now I discover that the law is precious and good, that it was given to me for my life; and now it is pleasing to me. Formerly it told me what to do; now I am beginning to conform to its requests, so that now I praise, laud, and serve God." *WA* 46, 662; *LW* 22, 144. Cf. 39¹, 373. *WA* 2, 492; *LW* 27, 224.

⁹³ *WA* 39¹, 373 f.

⁹⁴ *WA* 39¹, 375.

⁹⁵ *WA* 7, 760. *WA* 39¹, 434.

⁹⁶ *WA* 7, 759. *WA* 39¹, 250, 354.

⁹⁷ *WA* 2, 492; *LW* 27, 224.

law thus no longer has anything to do with the believer; it neither demands (for he does that which is commanded by himself) nor does it accuse him. To this extent the law is no longer active in his life but rather is powerless.[98]

And yet the law continues to have significance, even for justified Christians. (No mention need be made of the fact that the civil function of the law is indispensable and must remain effective in the world.) For the Christian is not yet completely a man "in Christ" and a believer but a "double being," partially already holy (through faith in Christ), partially still a sinner, partially already in the spirit, partially still in the flesh.[99] He is partially holy, partially a sinful man—this refers not to the togetherness of God's gracious judgment, which views man as righteous and holy and man's own empirical sinful existence but to the existence of Spirit and flesh, of the new and the old man alongside each other in the justified person (cf. p. 242). The old man or the flesh struggles against the new man and his joy in God's law.[100] As long as the Christian is still "flesh" and "old man," the law is not abrogated for him as it is for the new man (according to I Timothy 1:9).[101] On the contrary, he still stands under the law.[102] "Whoever knows how to distinguish that well is a good theologian."[103] Since the Christian here on earth is both new and old man, righteous and sinner, he lives without the law as well as under the law, and the law has both lost its power over him and remains in force.[104] Of course, the decisive element has been abrogated for the whole man. He is justified as an entire person. The law can no longer damn him and lead him to despair.[105] And yet, on account of the flesh, it still has a task to carry out in him.[106] What is this?

---

[98] *WA* 39¹, 433, 435.
[99] *WA* 39¹, 542.
[100] *WA* 39¹, 373, 375, 432.
[101] *WA* 39¹, 249.
[102] *WA* 39¹, 204, 552, 575. Luther also expresses the opposition between the Spirit and the flesh in the Christian in another way. "Insofar as Christ is made alive in us, we are without the law, sin, and death. But insofar as he is not yet made alive in us, we are to that extent still under the law, sin, and death." *WA* 39¹, 356; cf. 511.
[103] *WA* 39¹, 552.
[104] *WA* 39¹, 433.
[105] *WA* 39¹, 373 f.
[106] *WA* 39¹, 374.

Insofar as the Christian is still an old man, the law must still carry out its spiritual function on him and show him his sin. The law convinces the justified that the old man also remains in him and that he is still a sinner.[107] Thereby it summons him to participate in the battle which the spirit must wage with the flesh, the new man with the old man, throughout his life until the old man is completely given up into death (cf. pp. 214, 242).[108] In this battle the law still has a task to fulfill. The Holy Spirit and the new man of faith impress the law on the flesh and the old man.[109] Otherwise the Christian is in danger of becoming secure and lazy, of going to sleep instead of going out to do battle. The law exhorts and drives him to battle.[110] For the Christian as for anyone else, this means that the law terrifies him and gives him into death just as it did before he believed the gospel. And yet the terrifying and killing which now takes place in the Christian are quite different than they were before the gospel.[111] It now takes place in the context of justification and forgiveness instead of under the destructive curse of the law as it did without Christ. The lifelong repentance in which the law keeps the Christian[112] is clearly distinguished from the effect of the law without Christ. The death which the law inflicts is now "bearable," and it no longer leads to despair and damnation but to righteousness. The law and its terrors are greatly "moderated" in the context of justification.[113] Thus the Christian's repentance is not unpleasant and difficult as it once was, but easy and joyful; for Christians already have the Spirit.[114] The heavy yoke of the law is replaced by the light and easy yoke of Christ.[115]

Even though this process of sanctification and purification from

---

[107] *WA* 39¹, 497, 514.

[108] On innumerable occasions Luther emphasizes that this struggle, and that includes repentance, must continue throughout our life. Cf. *WA* 39¹, 350, 394 ff., 398, 474. The first of the 95 theses: "When our Lord and Master Jesus Christ said, 'Repent' [Matt. 4:17], he willed the entire life of the believers to be one of repentance." *WA* 1, 233; *LW* 31, 83.

[109] *WA* 39¹, 412.

[110] *WA* 39¹, 356, 432, 474, 500, 510, 513.

[111] The law is "able to accuse and terrify even the believers, but it is not able to drive them to despair and damn them." *WA* 39¹, 367.

[112] *WA* 39¹, 399.

[113] *WA* 39¹, 412, 474.

[114] *WA* 39¹, 398.

[115] *WA* 39¹, 381.

sin progresses, the struggle does not completely reach its goal in this earthly life. The law is only in the process of being fulfilled; it is, however, not yet fulfilled.[116] Certainly it has been fulfilled for us through God's imputation of Christ's fulfilment but it still must be actually fulfilled in us and by us.[117] This will happen fully only after the resurrection.[118] Only then will the law completely accomplish its work and come to its end.[119]

Does this mean that the law no longer has any significance for the Christian insofar as he is a new man? Luther explicitly declares that the law is not preached for the new man, the man of faith, for he has the spirit of God which is freely subject to the law (according to Romans 8:1).[120] As such he no longer needs the law. He does not need the law's demands and warnings as a motive for what he does and does not do. Being moved by the Spirit of God, he does what the law wants him to do by himself. But is what is true of the motivation of Christian activity also true of the knowledge of what is to be done? Doesn't the Christian need the law as an expression of God's will to inform him of what God's will is? Luther said two things on this point. First, the Christian who is moved by the Holy Spirit is not dependent on the Decalog. He can—in the power of the Holy Spirit—establish new decalogs for himself just as Jesus and the apostles have already done. He thus does not need written regulations; rather, the Spirit teaches him what he is to do in each specific situation.[121] Second, however, Luther immediately limits this statement by pointing out that not every Christian has the Spirit to such an extent. The flesh still struggles against the Spirit within him and thus restricts his clear judgment about what is to be done. Luther was alerted to this by his observation of the way in which the enthusiasts claimed and asserted that they had received private revelation through the Spirit even without the biblical word. Thus it is necessary for the

---

[116] *WA* 39¹, 374, 380.

[117] *WA* 39¹, 431, 434 f., 456.

[118] *WA* 39¹, 375.

[119] Luther gives an excellent explanation of repentance under the gospel in terms of the relationship between fear and love in the life of the Christian, as described in I John 4:18. *WA* 39¹, 437 ff., 565.

[120] *WA* 39¹, 374.

[121] *WA* 39¹, 47; *LW* 34, 112 f. Cf. *WA* 2, 478 f.; *LW* 27, 204 f. "All of us are given the dangerous liberty of doing either good or evil." *WA* 7, 760.

Christian to abide by the apostolic imperatives in the New Testament. For only in this way will the unity of ethical judgment be preserved in Christianity.[122]

Luther here is not speaking of the "law" but of the apostolic "commandments"—to use the terminology of the New Testament. However, according to Luther's broad concept of the law, the New Testament commandments are also "law." Then, however, the Christian as a new man is still dependent on the law. Is that still the theological function of the law as we learned to know it? Hardly—although Luther also bases the necessity of paying attention to the apostolic directives on the fact that the Christian's flesh still struggles against the Spirit. The theological function of the law for the Christian is concerned with the battle against the sin that still lives in his flesh. But Christian life does not consist merely in that battle against sin but, according to Luther, also in the positive activity of doing the "good works" commanded by God as the "fruits of righteousness and of the Spirit which have been given to us." The New Testament instructions (the law—according to Luther's usage of the concept) thus are therefore significant beyond the law's theological function in helping a man recognize and fight against sin and can no longer be understood in terms of the law's theological function. The commandments also serve the Christian who has received the Spirit by helping him to a true understanding of "good works" and by summoning him to action.[123]

---

[122] *WA* 39¹, 47; *LW* 34, 113.

[123] Luther has explained that the New Testament consists of promises and exhortations. He then states what the gospel is and goes on to say that exhortations should follow with an intent of stirring up "those who have obtained mercy and have been justified already, to be energetic in bringing forth the fruits of the Spirit and of the righteousness given them, to exercise themselves in love and good works, and boldly to bear the cross and all the other tribulations of this world." *WA* 18, 693; *BOW*, 180. Obviously, Luther is not speaking of a function of the law but of the exhortations which come from the gospel. His intention in this is the same that has moved some of us modern theologians to distinguish between "law" and "commandment." We are concerned to find terminology that will distinguish the imperatives that flow out of the gospel from those that come from the law as the sinner experiences it. Cf. W. Joest, *Gesetz und Freiheit* (Göttingen: Vandenhoeck & Ruprect, 1951) and my *Gebot und Gesetz* (Gütersloh: Bertelsmann, 1952).

Luther, after discussing the theological function of the law, asserts that it is the law's function "to order that sort of new life which those who have become saints and new men ought to enter upon." *WA* 39¹, 542. Elsewhere, Luther says: "In the New Testament, all those things are shown which ought to be done and not to be done." *WA* 7, 760. He also says of the believers that

This is true also of the Decalog. This is the sense in which Luther interprets it in his catechisms—admittedly applying it freely and creatively and extending it on the basis of the totality of biblical admonition. Luther saw the commandments not only as a mirror in which he recognizes sin—although they certainly are and remain that even for the Christian—but beyond this as instruction about the "good works" God wants; and such instruction is necessary and wholesome for the Christian.[124] The commandments are all this—to say it once more—only as they are supplemented from the totality of biblical teaching and understood in the light of the gospel. Accordingly, Luther structured his *Treatise on Good Works,* which was designed to describe the Christian life, as an interpretation of the Decalog. The Ten Commandments have their place not only "before" but also "after" justification; thus they not only exercise the Christian in the theological function of the law but also lead him to a right knowledge of the good he ought to do according to God's will.[125]

"they are now taken out of the kingdom of the law and placed into the kingdom of Christ. Therefore the law is to be retained by the believers so that they might have a pattern for doing good works." *WA* 39[II], 274. The reason given for which the justified should retain the law is that they are in the kingdom of Christ. The law gives them instruction in good works. This passage completely guarantees the passage: "The law is to be retained so that the saints might know what sort of works God requires and in what things they should practice obeying God." *WA* 39[I], 485. Since this last passage is missing from most of the manuscripts Werner Elert labeled it as a forgery, copied into Luther's works out of Melanchthon's later *Loci* [*Corpus Reformatorum* 21, 406]. Elert, *Zwischen Gnade und Ungnade* (Munich: Evang-Presseverband, 1948), p. 162; see new Elert, *Law and Gospel,* trans. Edward H. Schroeder ("Facet Books—Social Ethics Series," 16; Philadelphia: Fortress Press, 1967), pp. 38 ff. As the above passage shows, however, the content of *WA* 39[I], 485 is not foreign to Luther's thought.

[124] In Luther's hymn on the Ten Commandments, he says:

> To us come these commands, that so
> Thou son of man, thy sins mayst know,
> And make thee also well perceive,
> How before God man should live.

Here he expressly distinguishes "learning" how to live properly before God on the basis of the commandments from learning to know our sin from them. *WA* 35, 428; *LW* 532, 279. Elsewhere he says that the Ten Commandments give us a summary of divine teaching on what we are to do to make our whole life pleasing to God. "They are the true fountain from which all good works must spring, the true channel through which all good works must flow." *WA* 30[I], 178; *BC*, 407, 311.

[125] Under no circumstances therefore may one interpret the position of the Decalog in Luther's catechism as meaning that it has a place only before "justification." And it is equally incorrect to assert that the position of the Decalog in the *Heidelberg Catechism*—after "Redemption" and under "Gratitude"—is

Luther does not use the expression "the third function of the law [*tertius usus legis*]." Melanchthon did use this expression and it was then adopted in the *Formula of Concord,* in Lutheran orthodoxy, and by nineteenth century theology. In substance, however, it also occurs in Luther. As we have seen, Luther does not consider the form which God's law assumes over against the sinner to be the first and therefore also not the only possible form and meaning of the law. Since he knows of a law of God before man's fall into sin, why should he not also recognize it in the life of a Christian—not only in its theological function and thus not only intended to lead the old man to know his sin and cleanse him of it, but also in its function of training the Christian in good works.

---

specifically Reformed rather than Lutheran. It is well known that the order of the chief parts in the *Heidelberg Catechism* occurs in a Lutheran catechism as early as 1547.

20

THE FREEDOM OF THE GRACIOUS GOD

THE HIDDEN GOD AND THE REVEALED GOD

FOR LUTHER the assertion that God is God implicitly includes the fact that God alone works all in all together with the accompanying foreknowledge (cf. p. 105).[1] This determines not only man's outward but also his inner fate, his relationship to God in faith or unfaith, in obedience or disobedience. Here too man is completely in God's hands. Luther finds the biblical basis for this particularly in I Corinthians 12:6, "God works all in all." Luther expands the sense of this passage far beyond Paul's meaning in its original setting. It appears very frequently in Luther's thought.[2]

The Bible in addition bears witness, and experience confirms the fact, that men actually relate themselves differently to the word of God. Some are open to faith; others remain closed to it. Accordingly, the Bible expects human history to end in a twofold way. Not all will be blessed; and many will be lost. Luther can, in the context of his assertion that God works all in all, find the ultimate cause in God himself, in his intention, and in his working. This decision is not made by man's supposedly free will, but only by God's willing and working. He chooses some to be saved and rejects the others without an apparent reason for either choice. He gives faith to one through the working of His Spirit; and he refuses to give faith to others so that they are bound in their unbelief. Salvation and destruction thus result from God's previous decision and his corresponding twofold activity. God's choice is not based on the individual's condition; it establishes this condition.

---

[1] *WA* 18, 719; *BOW*, 218.
[2] Cf. the following statements in *The Bondage of the Will: WA* 18, 614, 685, 709, 732; *BOW*, 78, 170, 204, 236.

This means an unconditional, eternal predestination both to salvation and to damnation.[*]

Luther does not reach this conclusion on the basis of philosophical speculation about God, but finds it in the Scripture. He experienced it in God's relationship to him personally; and the God whom he thus personally experienced is the very same God who speaks and is proclaimed in the Scripture. Paul especially testified to Luther that God makes this twofold decision and that he hardens those who are lost: "God has mercy upon whomever he wills, and he hardens the heart of whomever he wills" (Rom. 9:18). Paul illustrates this with the picture of the potter making vessels of honor as well as dishonor out of the same clay (Rom. 9: 20 ff.). In addition, Paul quotes Malachi, "Jacob I loved, but Esau I hated" (Rom. 9:13). And Paul specifically refers to God's treatment of Pharaoh (Rom. 9:17).[*]

The position Scripture thus presented to Luther was also the inescapable result of his understanding of God. He even cites man's innate rational concept of God as an additional proof.[*] It seems blasphemous even to think that God does not work man's decision to believe or not to believe, as though God could be surprised by man's choice and men might be saved or lost without God knowing it. Whoever so thinks denies that God is God and makes fun of Him as though he were a ridiculous idol.[*] Whoever speaks seriously of God must necessarily teach his foreknowledge and his unconditional determination of all things.

Luther thus finds a twofold will of God in the Scripture. Together with statements about God's all-inclusive grace are other statements which express another willing and working of God which stands with his willing and working of salvation. Together with grace stands wrath, a wrath which rejects and which is no

---

[*] What Luther reads in Romans 9-11 is his own confession: "God's eternal predestination out of which originally proceeds who shall believe or not, who can or cannot get rid of sin—in order that our salvation may be taken entirely out of our hands and put in the hand of God alone." *WA*, DB, 7, 23; *LW* 35, 378.

[*] *WA* 18, 631, 690, 700, 716, 720, 724; *BOW*, 98, 177, 190, 214, 218 f., 224.

[*] *WA* 18, 709, 718 f.; *BOW*, 203, 216, 218.

[*] *WA* 18, 706, 718 f.; *BOW*, 200, 216, 218. "God should cease to be God." *WA* 18, 712; *BOW*, 208.

longer a part of love; and this is found not only in the Old but also in the New Testament. Luther did not draw a two-sided picture of God from his own imagination, but he saw it already present in Scripture. The God of the Bible is not unequivocally the God of the gospel. The God of the Bible is not only the God of all grace but is also the God who, if he wills, hardens and rejects. This God even treats a man equivocally: he offers his grace in the word and yet refuses to give his Spirit to bring about his conversion. He can even harden a man—in all this Luther does not go in substance beyond the difficult passages of Scripture which describe God as hardening a man's heart.

Luther, however, summarized the substance of such scriptural statements in the sharpest possible expressions. In *The Bondage of the Will* he teaches that God has a double will, even a double reality. The God revealed and preached in the gospel must be distinguished from the hidden God who is not preached, the God who works all things. God's word is not the same as "God himself." God, through his word, approaches man with the mercy which (according to Ezekiel 33) does not seek the death of the sinner but that he turn and live. But the hidden will of God, the will we must fear, "determines for itself which and what sort of men it chooses to enable to participate in this mercy offered through the proclamation." God "does not will the death of the sinner, that is, according to his word; he does, however, will it according to his inscrutable will." God revealed in his word mourns the sinner's death and seeks to save him from it. "God hidden in his majesty, on the other hand, does not mourn the sinner's death, or abrogate it, but works life and death in everything in all. For God has not limited himself to his word but retains his freedom over everything. . . . God does many things that he does not show us through his word. He also wills many things his word does not show us."[7]

Luther discussed this hidden God (the expression comes from Isaiah 45:15) in the early period of his development, for example, when he developed his theology of the cross in the *Heidel-*

---

[7] For this entire section, see *WA* 18, 664, 684, 686, 698; *BOW*, 139, 619 ff., 175 f.

berg Disputation of 1518.[8] There, however, the concept has a completely different meaning than it has in *The Bondage of the Will*:
God is hidden in his revelation and is revealed to us not directly
but paradoxically in the cross and in suffering.[9] He can reveal himself to us sinful men only when he is thus hidden. The hiddenness Luther describes in *The Bondage of the Will*, however, is not
the coincidence of revelation and of hiddenness but God's hiddenness behind and beyond revelation in the mystery which forms
the background of his almighty double-willing and double-working
of salvation and damnation. "God himself" is to be found behind
and beyond the word and not in it. Luther also bases this dictinc-
tion between the hidden and the revealed God on Scripture, that is,
on what Paul says in II Thessalonians 2:4.[10] The antichrist is described as the one who sets himself above everything "that is
preached and honored as God." (Luther's translation of this passage is probably based on the Vulgate.) Here Luther finds the
preached and worshiped God. It is said that the antichrist can set
himself above this God. Luther concludes that Paul distinguishes
between this God who is preached and worshiped and another God
of whom these two qualifications are not true—although there is no
basis for this in the text. No one can raise himself above this latter God, because everything is under his powerful hand.

Paul's statement does not contain what Luther finds in it. There
is no basis here for the distinction between the hidden and the
preached God. Beyond this, we must ask whether that distinction
is even substantially scriptural. Certainly the Bible is aware of a
dark mystery of God's hardening a man's heart. For the Bible,
however, this remains only the dark border which surrounds the
bright light of God's will to save men. For Luther on the other
hand—at least in *The Bondage of the Will*—this knowledge of the
hidden God lies like a wide shadow across the picture of God's revealed will. In comparison to the Bible, a shift in emphasis has
taken place. It is one thing not to hide the sobering fact that God
also hardens men's hearts and in the fear of God, to take it seri-

[8] Cf. W. von Löwenich, *Luthers Theologia Crucis* (4th ed., Munich: Chr.
Kaiser, 1959), pp. 21 ff.
[9] Cf. p. 25.
[10] *WA* 18, 685; *BOW*, 170.

ously as the Bible does; it is, however, quite another thing to take—
as Luther does—the mystery that confronts us in the history of
God's dealing with men and with peoples, a mystery which certainly conflicts with God's will to save as we know it, and develop
it into a full-blown doctrine of God's double will, of the duality
and extensive opposition between the hidden and the revealed God.
It is one thing when Paul discusses God's hardening of men's
hearts without immediately understanding it as a final rejection;
and it is quite another thing when Luther no longer understands
this hardening as a transition to mercy (as Paul does in Romans
11) but interprets it as final rejection. Luther's doctrine of the
hidden God, although he bases it on the Scripture, certainly goes
beyond Scripture both in its form and in its content.

We must furthermore ask whether Luther's doctrine of the hidden God as it is presented in *The Bondage of the Will* does not
abrogate the rest of his theology as we have come to know it.[11]
Luther generally appeals from that speculation about God which
seeks to investigate God-as-he-is-in-himself to the God who has limited himself in his word,[12] yet here in *The Bondage of the Will* he
teaches that God has not limited himself in his word and demands
that we distinguish "God himself" from the God who is revealed
in his word, and thus from that word itself. Is this not immeasurably dangerous, even deadly, to man's trust in the word of promise?
It actually asserts that God, according to his secret will, to a great
extent disagrees with his word offering grace to all men. The will
which stands behind the word is for many a different will than
that expressed in the word. God deals with part of humanity in
a way which is contrary to the will to save revealed in his word.
God is apparently free even in relationship to the gospel. How can
the man who hears that still, without reservation, trust in the word
which offers him God's mercy?

Luther always maintained that God's saving activity hides itself
under its opposite and that God in this way makes room for faith
which always deals with what cannot be seen (cf. p. 55). It is

[11] Cf. Martin Doerne, "Gottes Ehre am gebundenen Willen," *Luther-Jahrbuch*, XX (1938), 45-92. Also *CW* 63, 616-621.
[12] *WA* 40^{III}, 386, *LW* 12, 352.

the nature of faith that it breaks through God's "alien work" to his proper work. With this reference to the nature of faith, Luther tried to make the proclamation of the hidden God meaningful; he simply placed the hidden God alongside the hiddenness of God's proper works under his alien works. In the same breath in which he speaks of the latter, he also speaks of the former. After speaking of the paradox of God's activity (He makes alive by putting to death; he justifies by making us guilty, etc.), Luther continues, "Thus God conceals his eternal mercy and loving-kindness beneath eternal wrath, his righteousness beneath unrighteousness." Thus for Luther, the utmost in faith is believing God is merciful, though he "saves so few and damns so many; believing that he is just, though of his own will he makes us perforce proper subjects for damnation."[12] The second sentence goes far beyond the first and speaks of something completely different. Here we are no longer concerned with the tension between God's alien and proper work. In the latter case, there is no question that God shows both grace and wrath to one and the same man and that both types of activity are directed to an unequivocal goal of salvation. God's saving activity is merely hidden under an apparent nonsaving activity. However, Luther's doctrine of the hidden God as presented in *The Bondage of the Will* speaks of an activity of God that does not aim at salvation and that consequently stands completely outside of and beside God's saving activity. As such, it is purely nonsaving activity, carried out not in relationship to those whom God wishes to save but to those whom he does not wish to save. How can this side-by-side existence of saving and nonsaving activity still have the purpose of making room for the moment of faith and for the tension in which faith's "nevertheless" stands? At this point, saving activity is no longer hidden in what appears to be nonsaving activity, but on the contrary, saving activity is limited by nonsaving activity.

We must then ask whether or not this contradiction in God's activity belongs, as the paradox of his dealing graciously does, to the temptations of faith, in which faith truly becomes faith and thereby conquers such temptations. Or, must it not result in faith

---

[12] *WA* 18, 633; *BOW*, 101.

being broken and destroyed by this contradiction in God?[14] How does Luther know that God eternally damns men whom he himself has made guilty and damnable? From the Scripture? Is this a necessary thesis of faith? Does it not rather indicate that Luther has drawn an improper theoretical conclusion on the basis of his doctrine that God works all in all—a conclusion which, however, no longer has any basis in the legitimate theological meaning of that doctrine and is far removed from it?

THE MEANING OF THE DOCTRINE OF GOD'S HIDDEN WILL

The critical questions could not be avoided. We can, however, not stop with them. Even though the form of Luther's doctrine of God's twofold will cannot be theologically established and maintained, it is still possible that it expresses an intention which is a necessary part of the proclamation of the gospel. We must now ask whether it actually does so. Luther has clearly expressed his feelings as to why theology must discuss God's hidden will and how the Christian should relate himself to this dark background of the gospel. We begin our discussion with the latter.

First of all, Luther says to the Christian: We should not concern ourselves at all with God insofar as he has hidden himself. God does not want us to know that much about him. He does not want us to confront him "in his own nature and majesty." Rather he wants to come to us "clothed . . . in his word." "We must keep in view his word and leave alone his inscrutable will; for it is by his word and not by his inscrutable will that we must be guided."[15] We should not attempt to penetrate the mysteries of his majesty but "concern ourselves with the God who has become flesh," with

---

[14] Cf. M. Doerne, *op. cit.* pp. 79, 89 f. "Luther here twists the genuine paradox of faith into the distortion of a logical contradiction. The believer does indeed experience that God hides his goodness behind his wrath. The assertion that God damns innocent men, however, is not an assertion of faith, but the witness of faith becoming so rigid in its rational character that it contradicts itself. . . . Under no circumstances does the 'theology of temptation' [*Theologie der Anfechtung*] lead to a doctrine of predestination. . . . What takes place here is . . . a misinterpretation of the mystery of God." Doerne's excellent analysis and criticism discusses the total range of problems involved in Luther's *The Bondage of the Will* in a more comprehensive and intensive manner than the above description does.

[15] *WA* 18, 685; *BOW*, 170 f. Cf. *WA* 43, 463.

"the crucified Jesus in whom are all the treasures of wisdom and of knowledge—even though hidden."[16] As Luther's hymn says of God, "Jesus Christ it is . . . and God but him is none." In his lectures on Genesis, Luther expressly reminds his hearers of this line from "Our God He Is a Castle Strong."[17] This means that the Christian should not stare into the abyss of predestination of the hidden God with the tortured question whether or not he is chosen; but he should hold to that predestination which is revealed in Christ and to his calling as he has received it in his baptism and through the proclamation of the word. He may be certain of his salvation by looking to Christ and hearing the word. He should therefore not approach the mystery of predestination with "why" questions: Why does God reject men at all? Why does he bind men in sin and then impute this to them as guilt? Or, why does he not use his power over men's hearts to convert the resisting wills of all?[18] We are prevented from asking this sort of question by our feeling of awe before the mystery of God which he has reserved for himself. He does not allow anyone to look into it. "You must let God be God: he knows more about you than you do about yourself."[19] It is therefore senseless even to ask these questions, for these are mysteries into which we cannot enter. And apart from that, it is deadly dangerous; for it leads either to despair or to cynicism.[20] Luther constantly gave this advice and this warning. He repeats it in his *The Bondage of the Will* and in later writings with great emphasis.

Does this mean that Luther has limited his most difficult teachings for pedagogical reasons?[21] Luther would hardly have felt that way. He does not advise us to hold to the will of God revealed in Christ and the word or to avoid brooding over the mystery of God's secret willing and working as though we were to forget the dark background of this hidden God. No, the Christian should

---

[16] *WA* 18, 689; *BOW*, 176.

[17] *WA* 43, 463. Cf. *WA* 35, 457; *LW* 53, 285.

[18] *WA* 18, 690; *BOW*, 176. Cf. *WA*, DB 7, 23; *LW* 35, 378. *WA* 43, 463. *WA* 18, 696, 712; *BOW*, 184, 208.

[19] *WA* 2, 69. "He has kept it to himself and forbidden us to know it." *WA* 18, 684; *BOW*, 169.

[20] *WA*, DB 7, 25; *LW* 35, 378.

[21] Thus F. Loofs, *Leitfaden zum Studium der Dogmengeschichte*[4], p. 760.

know that this background is there. He should fear and adore the mystery of the hidden God. To do that, however, he must remain aware that this God exists. God wants us to refer publicly to the fact that God wills and works many things in secret. And Paul makes such reference in Romans 9.[22]

Reverently adoring God in his secret willing and working excludes the possibility that we men might be allowed to argue with God and accuse him of unrighteousness.[23] Luther, like Augustine before him, accepts Paul's rejection of man's murmuring against God (Rom. 9:20). To our human way of thinking, God's act of choosing one and rejecting another, even though he himself works everything in them, seems to be simply unrighteous and arbitrary. But Luther reminds us that we may not judge God's activity by the law and the human standards that determine what is right for us. We must consider the distance between God and man. God's righteousness is, because it is God's, necessarily superhuman and therefore not available to us for examination and evaluation; our reason cannot comprehend it. If we could understand it, it would not be divine righteousness. "How incomprehensible are his judgments," the Apostle Paul says.[24] Unlike men, God is under no law. If he were, he would not be God but would be subject to another authority over him. He himself, however, is the highest authority and the final court of appeal, "the rule for everything." He himself is his own law.[25] He does not will and act arbitrarily but according to the norm of his holy nature. Since this is the essence of all goodness, whatever he wills must be good, for he wills it out of his own being. His will is the highest good. There is therefore no doubt of his righteousness. For the present, admittedly, we must simply believe it. But at the end, he will reveal his glory and let us see that he was and is righteous in all he does. The gospel as the "light of grace" solves the riddle and removes the

---

[22] "It is enough simply to know that there is in God an inscrutable will." *WA* 18, 686; *BOW*, 171. Cf. *WA* 18, 631 f., 684, 716; *BOW*, 98 f., 169, 214.

[23] *WA* 18, 690; *BOW*, 176.

[24] *WA* 18, 784; *BOW*, 315.

[25] *WA* 56, 396; *LCC* 15, 268. Cf. *WA* 16, 140. "Whoever does not know that God is subject to no law, let him be silent; in God there is nothing but will, will, will." *WA* 16, 148. Cf. *WA* 18, 712; *BOW*, 209.

stumbling block which the apparently unrighteous distribution of earthly destinies provides. It unveils their righteousness and meaning to us. At some future time, "the light of glory" will likewise lead us beyond the problem of God's apparent unrighteousness in choosing and rejecting and reveal its deeper meaning to us. Until then we should believe and take courage from what the light of grace, the gospel, has already revealed of God's eternal goodness."

Whoever considers these statements of Luther will, in spite of all that Albrecht Ritschl has said, no longer conclude that his doctrine of God expresses the nominalists' idea of a God who is unlimited in arbitrariness. He will, however, still ask whether this expectation of the light of glory and of the final self-illumination of the riddle of divine activity can cover the thesis that God damns innocent men and make it bearable for faith."

Luther's assertion that theology must speak also of the hidden God is based not only on the fact that God wants this. He also tries to show that this is necessary and good for us Christians. As we have already seen, Luther here once again repeats the thought— always so important to him—that the hiddenness of God's grace under the terrible reality of rejection creates room for faith and for its character as a risky "nevertheless." Faith fully becomes faith only when confronted by temptation through its knowledge of the hidden God." Beyond this: The knowledge that God has man's salvation and damnation completely in His hand and that he chooses and rejects by his own free will, completely frees a man from the delusion that he could contribute something to his own salvation. This teaching of God's hidden will and activity serves to "humble our pride and lead us to know God's grace." Only this can destroy man's final self-trust before God. When he completely despairs of himself, is made nothing, he becomes ripe for faith, that is, ready to throw himself without reservation into the arms of God. Preaching about the hidden God thus leads to despair and Luther testifies that this condition is terrible; at the same time, however, he asserts that it is salutary and "very close to grace." For God has promised to be gracious precisely to the despairing. This is revealed "that

---

" *WA* 18, 632, 731, 784 f.; *BOW*, 100, 234 f., 315 ff.
" Doerne, *op. cit.*, p. 90.
" *WA* 18, 633; *BOW*, 101.

those who fear God might in humility comprehend, claim, and receive his gracious promise."[29]

Faith needs to be helped to humility in still another way. Luther puts his finger on the unusual fact that we speak of God's unrighteousness when he rejects men who have not deserved it, but we do not complain when he accepts and saves unworthy people by grace. We glorify and praise God for the latter act but argue with him about the former. As though God's dealing in both cases were not equally "unrighteous" (according to human standards) or equally righteous! This betrays the absolute roguishness of the human heart. Even in his relationship to God, man is so completely egocentric that he thinks only of his own interest and makes it the standard by which he judges God. He agrees with God insofar as God promotes man's own advantage. Thus he seeks his own advantage from God and is not concerned about God.[30] The fact that he does not object to God's choosing and saving unworthy people but finds this completely in order, betrays the fact that he obviously takes God's saving grace for granted. This conceals the implicit demand that God ought to save everyone. When man demands this, he forgets that God's mercy on sinners is an act of divine freedom which could not have been expected and is an unheard-of wonder. For this reason, by not giving it to all, God shows us that his grace cannot be taken for granted. God demonstrates the freedom of the mercy he shows us by demonstrating that he is free not to have mercy but to reject. He is really free in his grace. We cannot demand it. We have no rights in relationship to God; on the contrary, he has every right to do what he wants. He owes nothing to us men. "He has received nothing from us [compare Rom. 11:35] and has promised nothing but what he wills and is pleased to do."[31] In everything, he retains his majestic freedom of initiative. We should consider that God could also pass me by and should praise his free grace. We men seem to need this dark background, the stark opposite of election, to both become and remain completely humble in receiving grace: completely aware of the royal freedom and greatness of the mercy

[29] *WA* 18, 632; *BOW*, 101.
[30] *WA* 18, 730; *BOW*, 234.
[31] *WA* 18, 717; *BOW*, 216.

granted us. If grace were completely universal, we would interpret this universality by taking it for granted. Faith would then be
separated from the fear of God and get a swelled head. Thankfulness for and adoration of grace achieve completeness and full depth
only in view of the opposite.[32]

All this means that the hidden God, his secret will, and his almighty working in man must be preached so that the faith of
Christians will really remain faith that humbly fears God. If we
had only the picture of the "preached God" and of his all-inclusive will to save, human reason could control God. The doctrine
of the hidden God, however, eliminates this possibility. Now reason cannot control God; on the contrary, man knows that he is in
the hand of God who in free grace controls him. This is the end
of all presumption and security. The certainty of salvation still belongs to the humble man who receives God's mercy as a pure
miracle.

And yet Luther did not require all Christians to think about the
hidden God. He distinguishes stages in the Christian life. Just as
the first eight chapters of Paul's letter to the Romans preceded
chapters nine, ten, and eleven which treat "predestination," so also
the Christian should first hold completely to the revealed God,
steep himself in law and gospel, and practice bearing the cross
and suffering with Christ. Only then can he consider predestination without damage but be comforted and strengthened in his
certainty of salvation.[33] Luther knows, however, that a Christian
can, in spite of this, be tempted by the anxiety that he has not
been chosen and thus can fall into very great inner difficulty and
despair. He deals pastorally with such people. Those who are
anxious about this should rejoice because God promises to be especially concerned for those who are anxious and in despair. And
God does not lie. Anyone who feels this anxiety should courageously rely on this "and he will be saved and chosen."[34]

---

[32] In its own way, the *Formula of Concord* has preserved these thoughts of
Luther. *Solid Declaration,* 2, 60; *BC,* 626.
[33] "The old Adam must first die before he can tolerate this thing and drink
the strong wine. Therefore beware that you do not drink wine while you are
still a suckling. There is a limit, a time, and an age for every doctrine." *WA,*
DB 7, 23 f.; *LW* 35, 378. Cf. *WA* 16, 143.
[34] *WA* 56, 387; *LCC* 15, 254.

Luther describes a still higher stage of the certainty of election. In his lectures on Romans he speaks of men whose love of God is so free of all selfish desires and is so pure that they are prepared even to go to hell and eternal death if God wills it—so that his will may be completely accomplished. This readiness to accept rejection, if that is God's will, is actually salvation, for God is well pleased with and loves anyone who completely submits himself to God's will and wills what God wills. This is salvation. For such a man hell is heaven.[35] Luther thus picks up the idea of "resignation to damnation" which the mystics, as well as Staupitz, had taught.[36] Luther does not explicitly repeat this thought in his later writings. His later theology, however, continues to be characterized by the theocentric understanding of salvation he always advocated: Salvation is based on and consists in the will of our oneness with God's will.

Finally, we remind ourselves again that Luther declares that the hidden God and his secret activity must be discussed *for the sake of the elect!*[37] In the final analysis, Luther does not establish a theoretical doctrine of double predestination as Calvin does. In spite of all appearances to the contrary, his theology is at this point completely untheoretical and pastoral. His idea of the hidden God, finally intends only to purify Christians' faith from all secret claims and all self-security by proclaiming the freedom of God's grace. In this he agrees with Paul in Romans 9-11. He has just as little independent interest in an eternal rejection as Paul does.

---

[35] *WA* 56, 388, 391, 397; *LCC* 15, 255, 262, 268.
[36] Cf. *GA* 1, 149 ff. and Ernst Wolf, *Staupitz und Luther* (Leipzig: Heinsius, 1927), pp. 107 ff. Holl also discusses the relationship between Luther and the mystics in the treatment of this doctrine.
[37] *WA* 18, 633; *BOW*, 100.

21

THE PEOPLE OF GOD

LUTHER'S Reformation took place in conflict with the church of his time. He was opposed not only to its empirical reality but also to the Roman concept of the church. He did not wage this battle, however, in the name of a churchless and individualistic piety but in the name of his own clear concept of the church derived from his understanding of the gospel.[1] Luther thankfully and humbly knew he was a member of the church. He not only sang, "Our God He Is a Castle Strong," but he could also boldly confess: "The church shall be my fortress, my castle, and my chamber." He spoke these words in German in the midst of his Latin lectures on Genesis.[2] He sang a hymn in praise of the church based on Revelation 12:

> To me she's dear, the worthy maid,
> And I cannot forget her . . .[3]

He directs the man who wishes to find Christ to the church: "Whoever seeks Christ must first find the church. Now the church is not wood and stone but the group of people who believe in Christ. Whoever seeks the church should join himself to them and observe what they teach, pray, and believe. For they certainly have Christ among them."[4] The reality of the church is thus an essential part of man's relationship to Christ. A man's relationship to the church obviously precedes even his relationship to Christ and does not follow that relationship as Schleiermacher

---

[1] Cf. especially Karl Holl, "Die Entstehung von Luthers Kirchenbegriff," *GA* 1, 288-325. On Luther's doctrine of the church, see Wilhelm Walther, "Das Erbe der Reformation," *Luthers Kirche*, No. 4, (1917); E. Kohlmeyer, "Die Bedeutung der Kirche für Luther," *Zeitschrift für Kirchengeschichte*, XLVII, *Neue Folge* X, (1928), 94 ff.; Martin Doerne, "Gottes Volk und Gottes Wort," *Luther-Jahrbuch*, XIV (1932), 61 ff.
[2] *WA* 44, 713.
[3] *WA* 35, 462; *LW* 53, 293.
[4] *WA* 10I,1, 140.

taught in his addresses, *On Religion.*[5] Luther clearly does not speak of an "invisible church" but of a recognizable "group [*Haufe*]" which one can "join." This means that the church was for Luther no less real and important and no less a historical reality than it was for Roman Catholicism. The difference between them lies in their respective understandings of the nature and, accordingly, the visibility of the church.

Luther feels that the church is defined by the Apostles' Creed as a "communion of saints." Luther does not understand this as a separate doctrine, but translates it as the "community[6] [*Gemeine*] of saints" and as an appositional phrase explaining "one holy Christian church."[7] He does not like the word "church." It is "not German and conveys neither the meaning nor thought of this article."[8] The church is thus essentially this community [*Gemeinde*]. Luther prefers to speak of a "Christian community or gathering" or of "holy Christendom" or "the holy Christian people of God." This means the sum total of all on earth "who hear the voice of their shepherd," that is, all the believers.[9] Thus an institutional concern is, at this point, missing from Luther's descriptions of the "church."[10] This concern is, however, not excluded but included. The community is "called together by the Holy Spirit," who "has called me through the gospel" (*Small Catechism*).[11]

The church is thus the group which has been gathered together

[5] Friedrich Schleiermacher, *On Religion*, trans. John Oman (New York: Harper Torchbook, 1958), pp. 157-180 and 190-193.

[6] [See the note on the translation of this term at the beginning of the next chapter, p. 295. —Trans.]

[7] "The church of Christ is the community of saints [*communio sanctorum*]." *WA* 7, 712.

[8] *WA* 50, 624. Cf. *WA* 30[I], 189; *BC*, 416-48. Luther uses the word *Kirche* [church] only a few times in his translation of the Old Testament. With the exception of Genesis 49:6, it refers to the holy place in which God is worshiped. In the New Testament, Luther translates the Greek and Latin *ecclesia* with *Gemeinde* [community]. The word *Kirche* does not appear in the explanation of the Third Article in the *Small Catechism;* rather, Luther speaks of "the entire Christendom on earth" [*die ganze Christenheit auf Erden*]. *WA* 30[I], 296; *BC*, 345. The same is true in his hymn on the creed. *WA* 35, 452; *LW* 53, 273.

[9] The most important passages for the description of the church are *WA* 7, 219; *PE* 2, 373. *WA* 26, 506; *LW* 37, 367. *WA* 30[I], 190; *BC*, 417, 51. *WA* 50, 250; *BC*, 315.

[10] Luther, however, can also say: "The church is the number or the gathering of the baptized and the believers under one pastor, whether this is in one city or in one province or in the whole world." *WA* 30[II], 421.

[11] *WA* 30[I], 190; *BC*, 417. *WA* 30[I], 294; *BC*, 345.

through the gospel and therefore is also gathered around the gospel.[12] Since the community is gathered together through and preserved by the word, this word necessarily becomes the decisive characteristic which identifies this gathering of people as the community and "the holy Christian people of God." Luther always immediately adds the sacraments of baptism and the Lord's Supper to the word. In *On the Councils and the Churches* he adds the office of the keys, the presence of ministers and offices in the church, prayer, the public praise of God, and finally the "shrine of the holy cross," that is, inner temptation and outward persecution as characteristics.[13] But the decisive characteristic remains the word of God, together with the sacraments. "The whole life and nature of the church is in the word of God."[14] It is "the chief holy thing because of which Christian people are called holy." Luther refers to the "external word proclaimed through the mouths of men," that is, the preaching of the gospel.[15] Luther here coins the double thesis: "God's word cannot exist without God's people and God's people cannot exist without God's word." He bases the first part of his statement on the "certain promise" of Isaiah 55:11, "My word shall not return to me empty."[16] On the basis of this promise, faith dares to

---

[12] "For since the church owes its birth to the word, is nourished, aided and strengthened by it, it is obvious that it cannot be without the word." *WA* 12, 191; *LW* 40, 37.

[13] *WA* 50, 628 ff.; PE 5, 269 ff.

[14] "The external marks by which we can know where this church is in the world are baptism, the Lord's Supper, and the gospel." *WA* 6, 301; PE 1, 361. "By what sign therefore can I recognize the church? For some visible sign ought to be given by which we may gather together in one group in order to hear the word of God. I answer: A sign is necessary and we have it, namely, baptism, the bread, and most important of all the gospel; these three are the symbols, seals and marks of Christians. For wherever you find baptism, the bread, and the gospel, in whatever place and whatever persons, do not doubt that the church is there." *WA* 7, 720. Luther again emphasizes that the word is of more importance than the sacraments and a mark of the church: "For the gospel is the unique, the most certain, and the most noble sign of the church—more so even than the bread and baptism; for it is through the gospel alone that the church is conceived, formed, nourished, born, trained, fed, clothed, cared for, strengthened, armed, and preserved—in short the entire life and substance of the church is in the word of God." *WA* 7, 721. Therefore do not forget that God's people are best identified and best comforted by their possession of God's word." *WA* 31¹, 456, *LW* 14, 135. Cf. *WA* 11, 408; *PE* 4, 75.

[15] *WA* 7, 721. "We are speaking however of the external word which is preached by men like you and me. For this is what Christ left behind himself as an external sign, by which we should be able to recognize his church or his Christian holy people in the world." *WA* 50, 629; PE 5, 270 f.

[16] *WA* 11, 408; PE 4, 75. Cf. *WA* 50, 629; PE 5, 271.

be certain that God's preached word is powerful. "Wherever you hear this word being preached and observe people believing, confessing, and acting according to it, have no doubt the true and holy catholic church must be present and that they are a holy Christian people even though they are very few in number, for God's word does not remain without effect." Thus the preaching of the word always points forward and backward to God's people. It points forward because the word creates God's people; and it points backward, for preaching and listening to preaching presuppose God's people are already there."

This connection between God's word and God's people means that the church lives and is essentially held together by the preaching of the word about Christ. At the same time, however, only the proclamation of the word is necessary to create the church—this is its freedom. The church is not bound to a particular denomination, for example, "not bound to Rome" but only to the proclamation of the word." The church is nothing else than the miracle of the power of the word constantly appearing in a new form.

All the great predicates of the confessions of the ancient church are properly applied to this church. It is one and as such "catholic," that is, universal, and found in all the world." It is one because of its faith in the one gospel." It is all-inclusive in the temporal sense. It was from the beginning, has been here from the time of Adam, and will remain to the end of the world." Christ's promise in Matthew 28:20 gives faith the certainty that God's people will remain to the end of time." This church is holy

---

¹⁷ *WA* 50, 629; *PE* 5, 271.

¹⁸ *WA* 6, 300; *PE* 1, 361.

¹⁹ "I believe that there is no more than one holy catholic [*gemeine*] Christian church upon earth anywhere in the world; and this is nothing else than the community or gathering [*Gemeinde*] of the saints, the righteous and believing men upon the earth." *WA* 7, 219; *PE* 2, 373. "The holy church is not bound to Rome, but is gathered in one faith throughout the whole world." *WA* 6, 300, *PE* 1, 361. Cf. *WA* 26, 506; *LW* 37, 367.

²⁰ *WA* 7, 721.

²¹ "The church has always existed; there has always been a people of God from the time of the first person Adam to the most recently born infant. . . ." *WA* 40ᴵᴵᴵ, 505; *LW* 13, 88. "The church is the name of the holy Christian people not only at the time of the apostles but until the end of the world so that there always will be a holy Christian people living upon earth." *WA* 50, 625; *PE* 5, 266.

²² *WA* 50, 628, *PE* 5, 269 f.

because it believes in Christ and has the Holy Spirit. It is holy
not because it is without sin, either in its individual members
or as a whole, but the holy word of God from which it is constantly born again through the Holy Spirit makes it holy.[²³] It is
an apostolic Church for it lives from the apostolic gospel and thus
stands in the true apostolic succession.[²⁴] It is also true of this
church that there is no salvation outside the church. "I believe
that no one can be saved who is not part of this community and
does not live in harmony with it in one faith, word, sacrament,
hope, and love."[²⁵] "For outside the Christian church there is no
truth, no Christ, and no salvation."[²⁶]

The Church is visible because it can be recognized by its marks.
Only faith, however, can recognize its existence. "The church is
a so deeply hidden thing that no one can see or know it but can
only grasp and believe it in baptism, the Lord's Supper, and the
word."[²⁷] The eyes of the world cannot see that it is the church of
Christ. It shares this hiddenness with the entire content of faith
and thus with God's revelation generally and with Jesus Christ.
Here Luther's theology of the cross once again makes itself felt.
As God meets us "hidden in the sufferings" of Christ, so the
church is also "veiled in the flesh" and hidden under its opposite.[²⁸]
Reason therefore is not able to recognize the church as such. One
can, and must, be scandalized by it in the same way that one is
scandalized by Christ. For its "holiness is in heaven where Christ
is and not visible in the world like merchandise in the market-
place." It is hidden under many errors and failures, under heresies,
divisions and offenses—just as the individual Christian can see only
failure and unholiness in himself and is thus even hidden from
himself as a Christian. For this reason, the article about the church

---

[²³] "There is one holy Christian people which believes in Christ and is therefore called a Christian people and has the Holy Spirit who daily sanctifies it."
WA 50, 624; *PE* 5, 265. "The most important holy possession of the Christian people, because of which it is called 'holy,' is the holy word of God."
WA 50, 629, PE 5, 270.

[²⁴] *WA* 39¹, 191. Cf. *WA* 39ᴵᴵ, 176.

[²⁵] *WA* 7, 219, 6: *PE* 2, 273. "Outside this Christian church there is no
salvation or forgiveness of sins, but everlasting death and damnation." *WA* 26,
507; *LW* 37, 368.

[²⁶] *WA* 10ᴵ,¹, 140.

[²⁷] *WA* 51, 507.

[²⁸] *WA* 39ᴵᴵ, 161.

is no less an "article of faith" than all the others. The church
cannot "be discovered but must be believed." Faith, however, is
always concerned with what cannot be seen.[29]

The church is also invisible because it is the community of believers. No one can see faith. Christ, the good shepherd, is the
only one who knows his sheep. No one else can look into another's heart.[30] The soul which Christ receives with joy as he did
Zacchaeus "is a hidden temple known only to the Holy Spirit"—
and neither man nor the devil knows about it. Luther here uses
the daring illustration, "God does not want the world to know
when he sleeps with his bride."[31] Faith is given only by the Holy
Spirit and his work is hidden. Luther argues this invisibility of
faith together with the hiddenness of the true church against
Rome's hierarchical claims to rule Christendom and particularly to
exclude people from it through excommunication. No earthly
power can draw the boundaries of the church and decide who belongs to it and who does not. Only Christ, who gives faith to the
heart, knows this; and only he sees this faith. Ecclesiastical discipline can exclude from the community of the outward church but
never from the "inward, spiritual, invisible [community] in the
heart" which is given together with faith.[32] The Christian existence
of the individual is beyond the reach of every ecclesiastical organization.

---

[29] "This article, 'I believe in the holy Christian church,' is as much an article
of faith as the rest. This is why natural reason cannot recognize it, even if it
puts on all its glasses. The devil can cover it over with offenses and divisions,
so that you have to take offense at it. God too can conceal it behind faults and
shortcomings of all kinds, so you necessarily become a fool and pass false judgment on it." *WA*, DB 7, 418; *LW* 35, 410 [*Preface to the Revelation of St.
John* (1530)]. Cf. *WA*, DB 7, 420; *LW* 35, 411. *WA*, DB 7, 710, 722.

[30] *WA* 21, 332.

[31] *WA* 17[II], 501, 510.

[32] *WA* 1, 639. Luther, speaking of spiritual community, says: "No man is
able either to give or take away this community—whether he is a bishop, the
pope, an angel or all creation. God alone gives it through his Holy Spirit by
pouring it into the heart of the believer . . . here no excommunication is of
any effect." *WA* 6, 64. "How can a man rule over something he neither
knows nor understands? And who can however know whether a man truly believes or not?" *WA* 6, 298, *PE* 1, 357. "This word of Christ, 'I know my
own,' overthrows . . . Judaism with its law and priesthood and also our papacy
and all that goes with it; he takes away from them all authority to rule and
judge his flock and does not want them to rule his church. He rejects and condemns every judgment which attempts to establish who are Christians and
the people of God and who are not." *WA* 21, 333.

Even though Luther, in opposition to Rome's hierarchical claims, so strongly emphasizes the invisibility of faith and the hiddenness of the church, these doctrines are not valid in an absolute sense.[33] They are stated in such absolute form because of their antithesis to a tyrannical hierarchy. When Luther is not fighting against this, he does not hesitate to assert that we indeed can recognize that someone else believes. He never intended his thesis of the invisibility of faith and of the unavailability of Christian existence for examination by ecclesiastical authority to dissolve the community of the church—as the Roman polemic accused him of doing. There is no hint of a theological solipsism in which the Christian would be certain only of his own faith and his belonging to the church. For Luther says that the Christian is hidden even from himself.[34] However, he believes that he is a Christian because of the word and the sacraments which have called him. The same is true of his relationships to other Christians. Where the word is present, I both may and should conclude that those gathered around the word are Christians and members of Christ's flock. Luther distinguishes between the faith of the heart and the confession of the mouth—as Paul does in Romans 10:10. Admittedly we cannot see faith but believers can be recognized by their confession of faith. "The community is visible because of its confession of faith."[35] Thus the church of Christ is not a hidden reality in every sense of the word, rather it is also in the public eye. Luther does not distinguish a visible church from an invisible church but teaches that the one and the same church of Christendom is both invisible and visible, hidden and at the same time revealed—in different dimensions.[36]

---

[33] Cf. my book, *Communio Sanctorum* (Munich: Kaiser, 1929), pp. 86 ff.

[34] "All his people are hidden and concealed even from themselves." *WA* 9, 196. "A Christian is even hidden from himself; he does not see his holiness and virtue, but sees in himself nothing but unholiness and vice." *WA*, DB 7, 420; *LW* 35, 411. Luther, however, also says: "If this faith were present in you how could you possibly not be aware of it?" *WA* 2, 458; *LW* 27, 173.

[35] *WA* 39^{II}, 161.

[36] For a discussion of Luther's temporary use of a "polemical spiritualism," see Werner Elert, *The Structure of Lutheranism*, trans. Walter A. Hansen (St. Louis: Concordia, 1962), I, 258 f.

22

THE CHURCH AS THE
COMMUNITY OF SAINTS

LUTHER'S UNDERSTANDING OF
"THE COMMUNITY OF SAINTS"

WE HAVE seen that Luther interprets *comunio sanctorum*, commonly translated "the communion of saints," in the Apostles' Creed in apposition to "the holy Christian church,"[1] that is, it explains what the church is.[2] This is decisive for Luther's understanding of this doctrine.

The main question in interpreting this doctrine is whether the word *communio*, commonly translated into English as "communion," means a congregation, group, community, gathering, and assembly, [*congregatio, Haufe, Gemeinde, Sammlung, Versammlung*] or refers to "participation" [*Gemeinschaft*] in the ordinary sixteenth century use of the term,[3] that is, to being bound together with, participating with someone, an act of common participation, and having a common right to something. In the first case, "saints" (*sanctorum*) is a subjective genitive; in the latter case, it is an objective genitive and may be interpreted either in a personal sense so that *communio* means participating together with someone, or, in an impersonal sense, participation in a material object. If it is a subjective genitive, *sanctorum* would be masculine; and if it is an objective genitive, it could be either masculine referring to saints, that is, holy people, or neuter, meaning "holy things." Thus there are three possibilities. Within this framework, we could distinguish two interpretations in Luther.

Luther's understanding of *communio sanctorum* as being in apposition to the statement about the church is closest to an un-

---

[1] *WA* 2, 190, 415. *WA* 6, 606. *WA* 11, 53. *WA* 30ᴵ, 92; *LW* 51, 166. *WA* 30ᴵ, 189; *BC*, 416 f. *WA* 50, 624.

[2] Luther explains that this article was originally probably a gloss which did not actually belong to the text of the creed. Luther refers to Rufin's explanation of the creed. In the course of time, it then became part of the text. *WA* 2, 190. *WA* 30ᴵ, 189; *BC*, 416, 47.

[3] Cf. *WA* 30ᴵ, 189, n. 3 and Grimm's *Deutsches Wörterbuch* 4ᴵ, 3266.

derstanding of this *communio* as made up of saints, "a community of the holy,"" "a community only of holy people," perhaps best expressed as "a holy community" or "a holy people."⁴ Luther criticizes the common German translation of *communio* as *Gemeinschaft* as an inaccurate rendering of *communio* into bad German.⁵ He understands *communio* as a summary or collective concept, but the modern usage of the German word *Gemeinschaft* in the sense of understanding or trusting one another is unknown to him. The classical example of this interpretation is his treatment of the Third Article in the *Large Catechism*.⁷

Elsewhere, Luther interprets *communio* in the traditional sense of participation. In this case, the question is whether the objective genitive *sanctorum* ["of the holy"] is personal or impersonal, that is, whether it refers to participation in the benefits of grace or whether it means participating together with the saints. If the first were the case, it would mean that Luther sometimes understood the word *sanctorum* in a personal and sometimes in a neuter sense. This itself is not very probable. And all the pertinent passages confirm this suspicion.⁸ Luther understands *communio* in this sense

---

⁴ [I have usually used "community" to translate *Gemeine* and *Gemeinde*. "Congregation" is also a possible translation, but I have used it only infrequently because both its derivation and ordinary connotations in common usage differ from Luther's term. "Community" seems to me to present fewer problems—Trans.]

⁵ *WA* 50, 624 ff.; *PE* 5, 264 ff. Cf. T. Pauls, "Gemeinschaft der Heiligen bei Luther, das Wort und die Sache," *Theologische Studien und Kritiken* CII (1930), 31 ff.

⁶ *WA* 30¹, 189; *BC*, 417. Sometimes, however, Luther uses the term, e.g., *WA* 2, 756; *LW* 35, 70. *WA* 7, 218; *PE* 2, 373.

⁷ *WA* 30¹, 189; *BC*, 416 f. and 47-50. This understanding of the term is also presupposed in *WA* 2, 190, 415. "As Wittenberg is a community [*communio*] of citizens so the church is a name given to all believers who are in the world. . . . It is called a 'community of saints' [*communio sanctorum*] because it is made holy by God. . . ." *WA* 11, 53. This later quotation makes it clear that Luther understands *sanctorum* as masculine; the interpretation is the same as it is in the *Large Catechism*. For Luther, however, *communio* is more than an inclusive gathering, for he also thinks of it as a unity. "For this position is outside the *communio* [community] of saints who are of one heart in the Lord." *WA* 2, 169.

⁸ For a discussion of *WA* 4, 401 which could, at first glance, seem to support the interpretation of this word as a neuter, cf. my book, *Communio Sanctorum* (Munich: Kaiser, 1929), p. 39, n. 8. The following quotation illustrates the use of *sanctorum* in a personal sense: "What does it mean that we believe in the holy church but that we believe in the *sanctorum communio*? But what do the saints have in common? Not only blessings, but evils; all things belong to all." *WA* 6, 131; *PE*, 1, 166. In addition, see all those passages in which the German translation *Gemeinschaft der Heiligen* appears in

as the sharing of goods among the believers, the giving and receiving of the members to and from each other, the becoming one
with all others, and working for one another. Certainly, Luther
was also directed to this understanding by the Vulgate text of Romans 12:13, "communicating (contributing) to the needs of the
saints [*necessitatibus sanctorum communicantes*]."[*] *Communio* and
the ideas of participation and contribution [*communicare*] were
closely associated in Luther's thinking. "To share and participate"
always has both a personal and an impersonal object. We participate with the brethren in the benefits of nature and of salvation
as well as in their needs.[10] The expression, *communio sanctorum*,
by itself, however, does not yet define the impersonal object. And
yet, the personal object expresses everything—for to share with the
brethren who have both received grace and are burdened means
that we share in their grace and in their burden.

Does Luther actually hold two different interpretations? Viewed
linguistically and grammatically, he does indeed. For sometimes,
he equates *communio* with the Latin *congregatio* (later used in the
Augsburg Confession) and describes *Gemeinde* as a *"Sammlung,"*
"Versammlung," or *"Haufe"* ["gathering," "group," or "assembly"].[11] At other times, he uses it to describe the act of mutual
sharing [*communicare*]. It is decisive for Luther, however, that
the latter is implicit in the former because the community involved
is the assembly of those who believe in Christ. The German *Gemeine* used by Luther in the sense of "community" to translate
communio in the Apostles' Creed also expresses a living give-and-
take relationship. It is the nature of this gathering or community

the context of a description of the sharing of goods in the church. The most
important are those in *The Blessed Sacrament of the Holy and True Body of
Christ. WA* 2, 743, 756 f.; *LW* 35, 50 ff., 70, 72.

[*] Luther with his understanding of the *sancti* [saints], could not read this
text without immediately thinking of the *communio sanctorum* [community of
saints] and interpreting it on this basis. *WA* 56, 470; *LCC* 15, 351. *WA* 6,
131; *PE* 1, 166.

[10] In the *Large Catechism* Luther says: "I am also a part and member of this
community [*Gemeine*], a participant and co-partner in all the blessings it
possesses." *WA* 30[1], 190; *BC*, 417.

[11] "Gemeine oder Sammlung der Heiligen" [community] or assembly of the
saints." *WA* 7, 219; *PE* 2, 373. *"Gemeinschaft der Heiligen,* that is, 'a group
or assembly of such people as are Christians and holy.' " *WA* 50, 624; *PE* 5,
264.

[*Gemeine*] that everything is held in common.[12] Whoever belongs to this is a member not only of a group of people but also of a body.[13] Luther never thinks of the gathering together of the many in the unity of the community without understanding the unity in terms of membership in the body and thus as sharing [*Gemeinschaft*] with one another.

THE NEW UNDERSTANDING OF "COMMUNIO"

Luther inherited the idea of the church as a *communio sanctorum*.[14] And theologians long before him understood *sanctorum* in personal terms. For example, Thomas places understandings of *sanctorum* [the holy] in terms of the gifts conveyed in the sacraments alongside the personal understanding of *sanctorum* as "holy people." On the one hand, *communio sanctorum* describes participation in the benefits of salvation and in the merit of Christ through the sacraments (in this case *sanctorum* is understood as a neuter); on the other hand, it also means participating in the saints as holy people, that is, in their merits: for through the power of love the good works of the saints benefit the other members of the church. The church's love thus expresses itself in the sharing of goods. Compared with the New Testament, however, the traditional concept is limited and distorted in two ways. First, it is of decisive importance for the doctrine which Luther found in the church of his time, that the earthly church be related to, and connected with, both the heavenly church and the church suffering in purgatory. This takes place through the veneration of the saints and the use and application of merits. In contrast to this, sharing [*Gemeinschaft*] within the earthly church is not particularly important especially since the biblical meaning of "saint" was pushed into the

---

[12] "I believe that in this community or Christendom all things are held in common." *WA* 7, 219; *PE* 2, 373. Luther thus never speaks of the community without being reminded of their sharing goods and suffering in common; even when he uses *Gemeinde* [community] only in the sense of *Sammlung* [an assembly], this other sense of having all things in common is always implied.

[13] *WA* 28, 149.

[14] On the understanding of the *communio sanctorum* in the Middle Ages, cf. my *Communio Sanctorum* (1929), pp. 10 ff. For the usage of this term in the early church, see Werner Elert, *Abendmahl und Kirchengemeinschaft in der alten Kirche hauptsächlich des Ostens* (Berlin: Lutherisches Verlagshaus, 1954).

background by the ordinary medieval meaning of that term. Second, the sharing [*Gemeinschaft*] with the saints was materialized and egocentrically distorted through moralism; Luther calls it "workism" [*Werkerei*]. Both of these characteristics are closely connected. We look up to the heavenly church because it possesses the treasury of merits. And the ordinary medieval concept of the "saints" is in itself moralistic.

At this point Luther begins to renew the concept of *communio sanctorum*.[15] He gives it a new meaning in two ways. First, Luther brought down the community of the saints—in which he knew that he himself was a member of this community—out of heaven and down to earth. As early as 1513, even before his first lectures on the Psalms, he rediscovered the fact that the saints in the New Testament, and particularly in Paul's letters, are not a particular group in the community but all its members, that is, all who believe in Christ are saints.[16] Scripture uses the word "holy," not as it is commonly used in ecclesiastical terminology to denote the blessed, the perfected ones, but specifically to describe the living.[17] Saints are to be found not only in heaven but here among us on earth throughout the community. Thus we no longer distinguish between saints and ordinary Christians but only between the saints who have died and those who are still alive. We are obligated to serve not those who are dead but those who are alive. The service of the saints is accordingly completely from previous practice: formerly a man thought he ought to serve the saints staring into heaven; now he looks about himself right here on earth for the lowliest brothers of Christ.[18] The life of the departed is hidden

[15] Cf. Karl Holl, "Die Entstehung von Luthers Kirchenbegriff," *GA* 1, 288 ff., especially 320 ff.; and "Luther als Erneuerer des christlichen Gemeinschaftsgedankens," *Deutsch-Evangelisch*, (1917), pp. 241-246.

[16] *WA* 56, 469; *LCC* 15, 351. *WA* 17ᴵᴵ, 50. For a discussion of Luther's early understanding of the "saints," cf. L. Pinomaa, "Die Heiligen in Luthers Frühtheologie," *Studia Theologica*, XIII (1959), No. 1. Pinomaa describes the process by which Luther moved from the traditional medieval understanding of the "saints" to the evangelical concept advocated by the Reformers.

[17] *WA* 17ᴵᴵ, 50.

[18] "Whatever it is that you want to do for the saints, turn your attention away from the dead toward the living. The living saints are your neighbors, the naked, the hungry, the thirsty, the poor people who have wives and children and suffer shame. Direct your help toward them, begin your work here, use your tongue in order to protect them, your coat in order to cover them and to give them honor." *WA* 10ᴵᴵᴵ, 407 f. Cf. *WA* 17ᴵᴵ, 50.

from us.[19] The "sharing" is to be realized here on earth among the living.

Luther's purification of the thought of helpful sharing is closely related to this. Medieval theology moralistically distorted the significance of the saints for the church militant in two ways. The concept was materialized; and rather than leading away from the atmosphere of religious egoism, it is itself completely permeated with it. In the final analysis these two are one and the same distortion.

The materialization of the sharing between the saints finds expression in the doctrine of the treasury of the church: the totality of the merits of Christ and of the saints which the church claimed to administer through its office of the keys in order to enable sinners to balance their lack in good works and penitential satisfactions. In the fifty-eighth of his *Ninety-five Theses* and in the *Explanations* defending it, Luther expresses sharp disagreement. "No saint has adequately fulfilled God's commandments in this life."[20] Yet the saints have a vital and contemporary significance for the church. This does not lie in their moral achievements, for they too were sinners. We may therefore not use their achievements to prove the truth of the gospel. Nor are their lives fit to be summarized in a rule and imitated as a legalistic example. They are examples in a different sense: through their "teaching," that is, through their certainty and knowledge of God. Their agreement with us in these serves to confirm our knowledge of God. In the history of their lives we can see how God deals with his people in free grace. And this awareness can help to strengthen our confidence in his mercy. The saints are our examples through their faith and obedience, through their humility and through the pa-

---

[19] "Let the dear saints rest where they are and take care of those whom we have with us; for we have enough to take care of with ourselves if we are to live as Christians should. Therefore let them be, and let God take care of them. We can neither know nor understand how they live in the world beyond. That world is quite different from this one." *WA* 17ᴵᴵ, 255.

[20] *WA* 1, 605 ff.; *LW* 31, 213

tience in suffering which God has granted them.[21] The vital power
of faith proceeds from them. Luther speaks of the significance of
the saints in the way the Epistle to the Hebrews does. Whoever
has watched the long series of witnesses to the faith described in
Hebrews 11 pass by was strengthened in the seriousness and the
courage with which Paul said, "Therefore let us also" (12:1). We
may certainly speak of a treasury of the church here but in a completely different sense than the medieval theory does. The lives
of the saints are a treasury not because of the merit they produced but because Christians live, suffer, and do everything for
each other as members of one body. And this is the community
of the holy [*communio sanctorum*].[22]

Luther's understanding of God and of justification shattered the
medieval catholic conception of the saints. Since our salvation depends only on God's free mercy, the transfer of merits[23] in the
heavenly bank from one account to another has lost all meaning.
Merit is replaced by serving one another. No one can, in the strict
sense of the word, help another in God's judgment—either through
substitutionary achievement or through meritorious intercession.
(For God deals with each man by himself and no one can believe
or obey or die for another. Insofar as we can speak of vicarious or
substitutionary activity, we can never do that but we can only help
the faith and life of the man for whom we intercede.)[24] Even the

_____

[21] *WA* 15, 789. Cf. Luther's *Preface to the Psalms.* "There again you
look into the hearts of all the saints . . . this also serves well another purpose.
When these words please a man and fit his case, he becomes sure that he is in
the community of saints, and that it has gone well with all the saints as it goes
with him, since they all sing with him one little song." *WA, DB* 10ᴵ, 102; *LW*
35, 256.

[22] Therefore this part of the thesis is proved, that is, that the merits of the
saints cannot act as a treasury for us since the saints themselves considered them
deficient; unless someone should think that they are a treasure for us, not because they are surplus merits, but because the church is a community of saints
in which each one works for the other, as members one of another." *WA* 1,
607; *LW* 31, 215 f. Luther once illustrated this for us by using the example
of poor Lazarus. God permitted Lazarus to serve the whole world through his
poverty and his misery; through his life namely he aids us in bearing our suffering with the same patience. "This is the powerful character of a man who
believes. He has fed us with his hunger, clothed us with his nakedness, and
comforted us with his suffering by giving us all an example so that we may
follow after him." *WA* 10ᴵᴵᴵ, 185 f.

[23] "A certain transference of works." *WA* 1, 606; *LW* 31, 212.

[24] "The fact that we are all priests and kings means that each of us Christians may go before God and intercede for the other, asking God to give him
his own faith. Thus if I notice that you have no faith or a weak faith, I can

intercession of the saints means something different for Luther than it does for medieval theology. God remains free to hear or not to hear these intercessions, for man finally lives only from God's free grace.[25] All intercessory prayers are thus really significant not because they achieve something before God[26] but for just the oppo-

---

ask God to give you a strong faith. I do not ask that God would give you my faith or my works but that he would give you your own faith and your own works so that Christ may be able to give you all of his works and salvation through your faith just as he has given them to us through our faith." *WA* 10ᴵᴵᴵ, 308. "See to it that no one proposes to be saved through someone else's faith or works; indeed you cannot be saved through the work and faith of Mary or of Christ, unless you have your own faith, for God does not permit Mary or Christ himself to take your place and to make you faithful and righteous, unless you yourself are faithful and believing." *WA* 10ᴵᴵᴵ, 306. "No one can fulfill God's law for someone else; each one has to fulfill it for himself. . . . [Luther quotes Gal. 6:5 and II Cor. 5, 10.] That is why the commandment says: You, you, you, ought to love. It does not say you should let someone else love in your place. For although we can and should pray for one another that God should be gracious and help, no one will be saved unless he has fulfilled God's commandment for himself. Therefore we should pray not that God would permit someone else to go unpunished, as those rascals who sell indulgences pretend, but that he would become godly and keep God's commandment." *WA* 17ᴵᴵ, 100. Luther thus wants to interpret Gal. 6:2 in such a way that Gal. 6:5 ["each one must bear his own burden"] is not set aside. The intercession of the saints cannot mean that we have no burden but that they help us to bear our own burden. Cf. what Luther says against the use of the merits of the saints in order to set someone free from divine punishment: "However, the punishments of the martyrs and saints should be instead an example for us in bearing punishments." *WA* 1, 607; *LW* 31, 215. All substitution therefore is inclusive, not exclusive. And it is from this viewpoint that we must understand Luther's doctrine of reconciliation.

[25] "God nudges us just a little harder when he not only rejects our own person but also takes away from us the only comfort which we have left, namely the comfort and intercession of godly and holy men. For our last resort when we feel that God is not gracious to us or whenever we suffer some sort of trouble is to seek advice and help from godly spiritual men who are willing to give it to us as love demands, but nothing comes of it, prayers also are not answered, and things get worse for us." *WA* 17ᴵᴵ, 202.

[26] The Roman Catholic *Kirchenlexikon*, ed. Wetzer and Welte (2nd ed.; Freiburg im B.: Herder, 1882-1903), V, 1622, and Scheeben-Atzberger, *Dogmatik* (Freiburg im B.: B. Herder, 1889-1903), IVˢ, 885, find it inconsistent that the Reformers "deny the intercession of the saints or at least the propriety of calling on them for help" but yet permit the living to pray for one another. They, however, overlook the fact that Luther warns against prayer to the saints because it is so closely connected with the idea of meritorious intercession; this concept was much less likely to be present in the brotherly intercession of the living for one another. Beyond this, however, the concept of the brotherly intercession of the dead recedes into the background of Luther's thought because the condition of those who have died is hidden from us. Even in the *Smalcald Articles*, Luther did not deny the possibility that they pray for us. "Although angels in heaven pray for us (as Christ himself also does), and all those saints on earth, and perhaps all those in heaven, do likewise," there is still no reason for the religious veneration of the angels and the saints—just as little as we pray to and venerate the brethren here upon earth

site reason—because they are God's gracious working in us. He draws me to himself by having my brothers serve me.

The distinction between the Lutheran and the medieval doctrines of community can be expressed thus: Exclusive and materialized intercession is replaced by inclusive and personal. This is true also of the understanding of the work of Christ. This is the difference between Anselm and Luther. We can clarify the distinction in terms of substitutionary self-denial. According to the medieval position, self-denial is meaningful as an ascetic achievement which a man brings about by himself apart from any relationship to the actual life of the brother. It thus becomes a merit which can be credited to the brother. For Luther, as for Paul, self-denial is substitutionary participation in the brother's situation and is meaningful only as identification with his particular burden and a means to his freedom from it. In the Roman doctrine, men are thought of as a society in which measurable values can be transferred. In the Lutheran doctrine they are involved in the community of men really living together with one another.

Therewith, we touch the second point at which Luther restored the purity of the idea of *communio*. The medieval church simply could not understand the church as a real community because it was dominated by the moralistic principle that everyone must first of all take care of himself. "Love begins at home."[27] And even where love acts for and in the life of another, its final goal is to secure one's own salvation. Luther relentlessly exposed this

---

who are able to pray for us. Luther says, "There are other ways than this in which I can honor, love, and thank you in Christ." *WA* 50, 210, *BC*, 297. Luther clarifies our thinking about the saints in heaven by pointing out that our relationship to them is no different than our relationship to the brethren here upon earth. The concept of the community of saints was thus purified by the fact that Luther applied the title of "saints" to the brethren here upon earth; conversely it was religious egotism which limited the title of "saints" to those who were in heaven. "It serves us right that we who neglected the living saints, who were in need of our help, had to make pilgrimages and seek out the dead saints in order to try to fulfill our own needs through them." *WA* 17ᴵᴵ, 49.

[27] Cf. Luther's lectures on Romans, *WA* 56, 390, 517; *LCC* 15, 262, 406. Duns Scotus and Gabriel Biel both asserted that "charity begins at home." *WA* 56, 390; n. 3: *LCC* 15, 262, n. 4. Thomas Aquinas also teaches this. *GA* 1, 165. And as Holl elsewhere points out the idea is found in Augustine himself. *GA* 3, 87, 109.

connection. Moralism is selfish in its very essence, because it does not allow the community of saints to come into existence. Instead of establishing this community, moralism destroys it. The drive to produce outstanding ascetic achievements creates religious classes. The equality of all believers in their membership in the body of Christ is broken—most obviously by the haughty claim of some to serve as mediators for the ordinary Christians which resulted in work righteousness.[28] The gospel destroys the foundation of this whole world of pious selfishness and leaves it in ruins. Luther knows that only the gospel of justification by free grace through faith can really create genuine community. Faith in the gospel places man's salvation completely in God's hands and frees man from that selfish concern for his own eternal destiny which had determined all his activity; it thus sets him free to active service of his brethren.[29]

Roman Catholicism also describes the nature of the church in terms of Paul's concept of the body; and it too knows that love is the law by which the church lives. Augustine proclaimed this especially well. All this, however, is distorted by moralism and pious selfishness. The community becomes a means by which each individual achieves salvation. For Luther, sharing in the community is important for its own sake. It realizes the "law of Christ." Love has no goal outside itself. It is God's own life.

---

[28] "Those who trust in their own work righteousness had to establish divisions and differences among Christians. The priests wanted to be better than the laity, and the monks wanted to be better than the parish priests, the virgins wanted to be better than married people, and those who prayed and fasted often wanted to be better than those who worked, while those who lived austere lives wanted to be more than those who simply lived normal lives. . . . So it was that the attention of simple people was drawn away from the work of faith and the calling which comes to the believer. . . . Finally these people reached the point of wanting to pray for poor Christians and to be intermediaries between God and these Christians and thus despised other conditions of life as of no value at all." *WA* 17ᴵᴵ, 33.

[29] "It is enough for me that I am a member of his body and have as many rights and as much honor as all others. Therefore I neither may nor will work so that I may become a member of and participate in his body. For this I already have and it is enough for me. My works ought rather to serve the body and its members, namely my dear brethren and comrades, and I will not take upon myself any unusual work, lest I create division and dissension." *WA* 17ᴵᴵ, 37. "I shall have enough of the food of salvation, so that all things which I have in my own life may be used for the benefit of others." *WA* 15, 607.

COMMUNITY AS GIFT AND AS TASK

The church is the *communio sanctorum*, community of saints.[30] "I believe that there is only one holy common Christian church on earth throughout the whole world. This is nothing else than the community or gathering of the saints and of the godly, believing men on earth which the Holy Spirit gathers, preserves, and rules. ... I believe that in this community of Christendom all things are common, that the goods of each one belongs to the other, and that no one possesses anything that is his own. As a result all prayers and all good works of the entire community help me and every believer; they all stand by and strengthen each other in every time of life and of death so that each one bears the other's burden, as St. Paul teaches." This is the way in which Luther puts it in the *Short Form of the Ten Commandments* of 1520 and in his *Little Prayer Book [Betbüchlein]* of 1522.[31]

Community rests upon the fact that Christ's sacrifice of love makes the believers one body or "one loaf" with Christ and therefore also with each other.[32] The Holy Spirit makes each one who believes the word a member of the body of Christ. Existence for one's self ceases; it is replaced, however, not by mystical absorption into each other but rather by full sharing [*Gemeinschaft*] of life through love.[33] No individual has strength or weakness, right-

---

[30] The most important sources for Luther's doctrine of the church as *communio* are: *Treatise on Preparing to Die, WA* 2, 685-697. *The Blessed Sacrament of the Holy and True Body of Christ and the Brotherhoods* (1519), *WA* 2, 742 ff.; *LW* 35, 49-73. The lectures on Galatians of 1519 (especially on Gal. 6:1 ff.), *WA* 2, 601 ff.; *LW* 27, 387 ff. *The Fourteen of Consolation* (1520), *WA* 6, 130 ff.; *PE* 1, 164-167. *The Freedom of a Christian* (1520), *WA* 7, 49 ff.; *LW* 31, 333-337. Several sermons preached between 1522 and 1524, *WA* 10^{I,2}, 67. *WA* 10^{III}, 217, 238. *WA* 12, 486. *WA* 15, 494.

[31] *WA* 7, 219; *PE* 2, 373. *WA* 10^{II}, 394.

[32] *WA* 10^{III}, 218. *WA* 12, 490. *WA* 15, 607. *WA* 28, 149. "By faith in Christ, a Christian is made one spirit and one body with Christ. 'For the two shall be one flesh' [Gen. 2:24]. 'This is a great mystery, and I take it to mean Christ and the church' [Eph. 5:31 f.]. Therefore, since the Spirit of Christ dwells in the Christians, by the means of which brothers become co-heirs, one body, and citizens of Christ, how is it possible for us not to be participants in all the benefits of Christ? Christ himself has all that belongs to him from this same Spirit." *WA* 1, 593; *LW* 31, 190.

[33] Luther speaks of "faith, hope, love, and other gifts and graces, which through love become the common property of all." *WA* 6, 131; *PE* 1, 165. "The church is ... the divine, the heavenly, the noblest brotherhood; ... the community of saints in which we are all brothers and sisters, so closely united that a closer relationship cannot be conceived for here we have one baptism, one Christ, one sacrament, one food, one gospel, one faith, one spirit, one

eousness or sin, peace or trouble, without all being involved." The marvelous transaction, the "joyful exchange,"" the "sharing of goods"" between Christ and men also means that there is a complete exchange, an unconditional sharing of life, of goods, and of troubles by his people among themselves." The body lives *one* life. This is the nature of Christ's love. Christ himself lives from this spirit of love. All that he is and has is nothing else than what the Father has given him as a share in all that the Father himself is and has."

Participation in this community involves every member of the church in a simultaneous gift and task, grace and calling." Luther summarizes the gift of this participation: All the goods of Christ and the saints are my goods; my burden, trouble, and sin belong to Christ and all the saints." This participation means that Christ's righteousness atones for man's sins and that "Christ and his saints intercede for us before God so that our sins may not be imputed to us according to God's strict judgment." It also includes the fact that Christ and the community "fight for us" against sin, suffer with us, and bear the burdens of one another." The others' faith, purity, and prayer is a powerful help to me in the poverty and weakness of my own Christian life. In life or in death I am never alone, for Christ and the church are with me." Whatever

---

spiritual body [Eph. 4:4 f.], and each person is a member of the other [Rom. 12:5]." *WA* 2, 756; *LW* 35, 70.

"" "Of this community I also am a part and member, a participant and co-partner in all the blessings it possesses." *WA* 30¹, 190; *BC*, 417.

"" "Indeed, this most present participation in the benefits of Christ and joyful exchange of life do not take place except by faith." *WA* 1, 593, *LW* 31, 190 f.

"" "Notice that we thus so become one loaf [*Kuchen*] with Christ that we enter into a community with him in which we share his possessions and he enters into a community with us in which he shares our possessions." *WA* 12, 486.

"" "It is a community and a gracious exchange or blending of our sin and suffering with the righteousness of Christ and his saints." *WA* 2, 749; *LW* 35, 60. Cf. *WA* 6, 131; *PE* 1, 166 (cf. n. 7).

"" Cf. the last sentence of the quotation in n. 31.

"" Luther distinguishes these two aspects very clearly in *The Blessed Sacrament of the Holy and True Body of Christ and the Brotherhoods* (1519), *WA* 2, 744 ff: *LW* 35, 52 ff.

"" *WA* 1, 593; *LW* 31, 190. Cf. *WA* 6, 131, *PE* 1, 165 and often elsewhere.

"" *WA* 2, 744; *LW* 35, 53.

"" *WA* 1, 333. *WA* 2, 745; *LW* 35, 53 f. A wonderful passage from *The Fourteen of Consolation* reads: "Therefore, when I suffer, I suffer not alone, but Christ and all Christians suffer with me. . . . Even so others bear

concerns one member of the body concerns the whole body. Luther finds the biblical basis for this certainty particularly in Paul's statements about the law of Christ (Gal. 6:2) and about the participation of the members of the body in each other's lives (I Cor. 12:22 ff. and 26) which he so frequently quotes. Luther repeatedly requested such intercessions for his own battle with Satan and felt that he needed them particularly in his great temptations of 1527. Luther was greatly comforted by knowing that the brethren were fighting with him.[43] Luther mentions the intercessions of the brethren as the means through which this participation benefits the individual as well as the helping, admonishing, warning, and consoling pastoral word, "the mutual conversation and consolation of the brethren" as he puts it in the *Smalcald Articles*.[44] The fact that Luther spoke of the church only with great joy and overflowing thankfulness is to no small extent based on his certainty of this community of the saints.[45]

In this connection, Luther thought not only of the conscious intercession of the brethren for each other. The help the brethren give to each other extends far wider than they themselves know or consciously intend. Their lives are examples and sources of power for us in our own struggle. God has placed them with their most personal problems with which they struggle and suffer in themselves, in the service of his community without their even knowing it or willing it. In this sense too it is true that none of us lives for himself.[46]

This community is thus never merely a gift to faith but always a task for love.[47] Each one should take the burden of Christ and

---

my burden, and their strength becomes my own. The church's faith supports my fearfulness, the chastity of others bears the temptations of my flesh, the fastings of others are my gain, the prayer of another pleads for me. . . . Who, then, could despair in his sins? Who would not rejoice in his pains? For it is not he that bears his sins and pains; or if he does bear them, he does not bear them alone, but is assisted by so many holy sons of God, even by Christ himself. So great a thing is the community of saints, and the church of Christ." *WA* 6, 131; *PE* 1, 165 f.

[43] Cf. Luther's correspondence in 1527. *WA*, Br 4.

[44] *WA* 50, 241; *BC*, 310. Cf. *WA* 40III, 343.

[45] This is true particularly of confessions made to the brother and the proclamation of the absolution received from him. Cf. pp. 316 ff.

[46] This is true of Lazarus, *WA* 10III, 185 (quoted in n. 22). Luther expresses the hope that his own struggle with Satan will prove of advantage to many. *WA*, Br 6, 235.

[47] *WA* 2, 745-750, 757; *LW* 35, 55-61, 72.

his church upon himself as his own burden. The shame of Christ, the contradiction of his word, the troubles of the church, the unjust suffering of the innocent, the guilt and shame of the sinner, the needs of the poor: all these he must feel in his heart, not with some sort of cheap sympathy but by actively bearing the burden and suffering. Each Christian should "defend, act, pray"; each Christian should struggle for truth, fight off injustice, work for the renewal of the church and its members, use his possessions for the poor, give his own life for the sick,[48] and intercede before God and men for the sinner with his own righteousness.[49] In brief, all Christians must share all their external and internal goods,[50] with one another in all the troubles, whether these troubles come from the natural course of life or because they are Christians. All our possessions are "the form of God" (Phil. 2:5). We are to empty ourselves of them just as Christ did. They must be transformed in us to the form of a servant[51]—just as Christ in his love took our form upon himself. "We should be so transformed by this love that we make the weaknesses of all other Christians our own; we are to take their form and neediness upon ourselves and give them all

---

[48] *WA* 20, 713. *WA* 23, 352 ff. These passages discuss the duty of remaining during an epidemic of the plague in order to care for the sick and to proclaim the word to them. Luther himself practiced what he preached.

[49] *WA* 2, 606; *LW* 27, 393. Cf. n. 50.

[50] "As Christ has become the common possession of us all . . . we should also become the common possessions of one another." *WA* 10I.2, 89. "If you are learned [*sanus* appears to be an error and should be read *doctus*] you should not use your teaching for your own advantage but to serve your brethren. If you are healthy and your neighbor is weak, see that you strengthen him. If you see a husband [*mirabilem*] who is disagreeing with his wife make peace between them. If you do not do this, you do not have the mind of Christ. If you are rich and see that your neighbor is poor, serve him with your possessions; if you do not do this you are not now a Christian. This is what we are to do with all our possessions both spiritual and material." *WA* 11, 76 [Rörer's notes; cf. the printed text *WA* 12, 470]. Cf. *WA* 17ᴵᴵ, 327 f.

[51] "Behold, Christ is like men, that is, like sinners and weak men. And he displays no other nature and no other form than that of a man and a servant, since he does not despise us, though he is in the form of God; but he takes our form and bears our sins in his own body." *WA* 2, 603; *LW* 27, 389. "These are the forms of God of which we must empty ourselves in order that the forms of a servant may be in us [Phil. 2:6], because it is with all these qualities that we must stand before God and intervene with him on behalf of those who do not have them, as though clothed with someone else's garment. . . . But even before men we must with the same love serve our opponents, even the violent ones." *WA* 2, 606; *LW* 27, 393. Cf. the letter to George Spenlein of April 8, 1516. *WA*, Br 1, 35; *LW* 48, 13.

our good so that they may profit from it."[53] The lives of the members of the church should be shaped not by the lordly form of ownership but by the form of a servant engaged in sacrificial service, by becoming one with all trouble, shame, and guilt. "All we have should be used in service and whatever is not used in service has been stolen."[53] Every gift, every power, all health, peace, and purity belong to love and to the brethren.[54] "You should bear your cross not to save yourself but so that your neighbor might benefit by seeing it and by being encouraged to bear his cross."[55] Because the question of our own salvation has been solved in justifying faith, and because a man expects everything from God and nothing from himself, he is now completely free to use all he has, can do, and suffer to serve his brother. He no longer in any way lives for himself but rather completely for the community of saints. "Every man has been created and born for the sake of the other."[56]

Luther repeatedly emphasized the significance of the law of love for the external goods of life.[57] But this was of minor importance to him in comparison with bearing the weakness and sin of the brother.[58] He distinguishes three stages of community:[59] first, the

---

[53] *WA* 2, 748; *LW* 35, 58. We should imitate Christ who took off his own clothes when he washed his disciples' feet, that is, he did not insist upon his own superiority and holiness in his relationships with his disciples. *WA* 15, 507.

[53] *WA* 12, 470.

[54] "Furthermore, if there is anything in us it is not our own; it is a gift of God. But if it is a gift of God, then it is entirely a debt we owe to love, that is, to the law of Christ. If it is a debt owed to love, then I must serve others with it. Thus my learning is not my own; it belongs to the unlearned and is the debt I owe to them. My chastity is not my own; it belongs to those who commit sins of the flesh, and I am obligated to serve them through it by offering it to God for them by sustaining and excusing them, and thus, with my respectability veiling their shame before God and men. . . . Thus my wisdom belongs to the foolish, my power to the oppressed. Thus my wealth belongs to the poor, my righteousness to the sinners." *WA* 2, 606; *LW* 27, 303. "Indeed this gift is given to me that it may become the common property of the others. . . . I shall have enough of the food of salvation and everything in my life and possessions are to be used for the benefit of others." *WA* 15, 607.

[55] *WA* 10III, 119.

[56] *WA* 21, 346 [Cruciger's edition].

[57] E.g., *WA* 24, 409.

[58] *WA* 10III, 97. "Now it seems to be a great work of love when we let our possessions become the servants of someone else. But the greatest of all is when I give up my own righteousness and allow it to serve my neighbor's sin." *WA* 10III, 217. "You have heard that we should trust in God and love men

sacrifice of "temporal possessions" and physical service to men; second, service through doctrine, consolation, and intercession; the highest, however, is bearing the weakness of the brother and the sharing of those to whom God has been gracious and protected with sinners, of the "healthy people" with "sick people." Here he felt the pulse of the innermost heart of Christ's love and therefore also of Christian love. He repeatedly described the example of Christ, particularly on the basis of Philippians 2:5,[60] Romans 15:1 ff.,[61] and the washing of feet,[62] and described the nature of such substitutionary love by interpreting the parables of Luke 15[63] and the story of the Pharisee and the publican.[64]

The places at which Luther speaks thus are the particularly high points in his sermons. He especially condemns selfish Christians. "They watch out for themselves, puff themselves up and never get around to being gracious to sinners. They do not even know that they should become servants and that their religiosity should serve the others."[65] The Pharisee—and Luther knows that he lives right in the middle of Christendom—sins not only against God but also against his brother."[66] He injures not only faith but also love. When he says, "Lord, I thank thee, that I am not like other people," he condemns himself as a liar. He thinks he does not steal but does precisely that when he acts as though he were the only righteous one and thus robs his neighbor of his honor before God. Beyond this he ought to pray for, admonish, and help his sinful brother out of his sin. God lets some men in the community fall, so that the others may have the opportunity to demonstrate their evangelical, brotherly concern for them."[67] Instead of this, however, the Pharisee feeds on his brother's sin and rejoices when

---

with our external possessions; this is the least we can do. Beyond this we can allow our righteousness to serve a sinner and this is the greatest thing of all, that the highest does not withdraw from the sinner but rather appears to be just as poor as the greatest sinner." *WA* 10[III], 238.

[59] *WA* 15, 499.

[60] *WA* 2, 603; *LW* 27, 389. Cf. *WA* 7, 65; *LW* 31, 366. *WA* 10[III], 217, 219.

[61] *WA* 2, 603; *LW* 27, 389. Cf. *WA* 10[I,2], 67 ff. *WA* 20, 715.

[62] *WA* 15, 507.

[63] *WA* 10[III], 217 ff.

[64] *WA* 10[I,2], 349 ff. *WA* 15, 671 ff.

[65] *WA* 10[III], 218.

[66] *WA* 15, 673.

[67] *WA* 20, 715.

his soul falls into eternal death. He uses his brother's weakness and failure to feed his own self-confidence.[68] Luther judges that there is no more terrible sin.[69] This is a hatred greater than any which can be found among the heathen. "When I am stuck in my sins, he should weep bloody tears and come to my help; instead he rejoices and says 'I am righteous in God's sight!' "[70] Luther seldom preached with such terrifying seriousness as he did at this point. We sense that he is concerned with what is, for him, the most decisive issue at the very heart of the gospel. The good news of God's glory bears witness against all work righteousness and also protects the honor of men against the robbing and murdering lovelessness of the "righteous." Luther sees the basic connection: moralistic pride dishonors both God and the neighbor. It treats neither God as God nor man as man.[71] Instead of taking his place in the community as a poor sinner like all the others, the proud man destroys them.[72]

What does it mean, however, to be concerned about the sinner and his sin and to share it with him? Luther thinks primarily of what is decisive in Christ's dealing with the sinners. Christ covers our sin and intercedes for us with his righteousness. This is the pattern which we too should follow. What counts is putting our own righteousness to work to help the sinner.[73] Every typically Roman interpretation of this is—as we have already seen—to be kept out of this. What is at stake is nothing else than this: "I stand under grace not only for myself and not alone; rather at

---

[68] *WA* 2, 598; *LW* 27, 383, 603 f., 607.

[69] *WA* 10[III], 221. Cf. *WA* 15, 673.

[70] *WA* 15, 673. *WA* 32, 321; *LW* 21, 28.

[71] *WA* 15, 673.

[72] Speaking of the Pharisee, Luther says: "If he had only said, 'O God, we are all sinners; and this poor sinner is also one just as I and the others are.' If he had only thus included himself in the common group and said, 'O God, be merciful to us,' then he would have fulfilled God's commandment." *WA* 10[I.2], 351.

[73] *WA* 10[III], 220. "This is what you must do: the virgin must place her wreath [the symbol of virginity] upon a prostitute, a virtuous wife must give her veil to an adultress, and we must let everything we have become a covering for the sinners. For every man will have his own sheep and every woman will have her own coin [Luke 15:3-10]. All of our gifts must however become the property of someone else." *WA* 10[III], 238. Cf. *WA* 7, 37; *RW* 1, 377: cf. *LW* 31, 368-371. "Now we shall speak of the great work of love in which a godly man uses his righteousness for the sinner and a virtuous woman uses her honor for the benefit of the worst adultress." *WA* 10[III], 217.

every moment I take my brother into it with me. I stand by him and will not be anything else than he is even as I cannot be anything else in God's sight. For I am capable of every sin which another does; today I stand, but tomorrow I may fall because the flesh can do nothing good."[74] "And it is God and not my merit that protects me when I do not fall into my neighbor's sin."[75] I establish solidarity with my brother as one who actually is standing in solidarity with him. "The children of God do not want to go into heaven alone but rather wish to bring along the most sinful people if they are able."[76] Before God, they stand nowhere else than beside their brothers, or more correctly, in their place. Truly substitutionary love is, for the sake of the brother, able even to relinquish the salvation which God has given and like Moses and Paul to pray to God to reject me and make my brothers blessed in my place.[77] This substitution is not some sort of cheap forbearance of sin. Not sin but the sinner is suffered and carried along; and his sin is to be condemned in such a way that we remain in love and in solidarity with the brother—Luther here refers to Matthew 18. We enter into the brother's filth and shame in order to help him out of his sins by the power we have because God has protected us. We become his fellow prisoners so that he may be free, and we become companions in his fall so that he may stand up and walk.[78]

---

[74] The same thought appears in Thomas à Kempis, *De imitatione Christi,* Book 1, at the end of Chapter 2.

[75] *WA* 15, 674.

[76] *WA* 1, 697.

[77] In Luther's lectures on Rom. 9:3 (*WA* 56, 389 ff; *LCC* 15, 260-265), the emphasis is primarily on giving up one's self rather than explicitly on giving up one's self as a sacrifice for the brethren. Luther places much more emphasis on the hatred of one's own self than on love of the brethren. This latter characteristic of Pauline thought recedes into the background. However, in his important sermon preached on the Third Sunday after Trinity, 1522, Moses' prayer in Exod. 32:32 and Paul's statement in Rom. 9:3 are given as examples of intercession for sinners. "Note that Moses was a man who knew that God loved him and had written his name in the Book of Life. And still he said, 'Lord I would prefer it if you would damn me and save the people.' The same is true of Paul who obviously condemns the Jews most severely even calling them 'dogs' and other such names, but yet he falls down and says, 'I have desired that I might be damned and eternally rejected if only the people could be helped.' Reason is not able to understand this statement for it is beyond it." *WA* 10ᴵᴵᴵ, 219.

[78] "I must be the sinner's friend and love him; but I must also hate his vice and heartily condemn it; yet I must so love him in my heart that I cover his sin with my righteousness. I must be so opposed to him that I cannot stand

Luther particularly required ministers of the church to practice such sharing. Authority can exist only where there is solidarity, and lordship only where there is service. Hierarchical majesty must learn "to take off its vestments" as Jesus did when he washed the disciples' feet. The real substance of every ecclesiastical office is its pastoral care of sinners through the proclamation of the gospel to individuals.[79]

The rule of sharing [*communio*] with sinners, however, determines our relationship not only to individuals but also to the entire church.[80] For it too can sin.[81] Then, it is also necessary to fulfill the "law of Christ" and to take the burden of the church upon one's self. If the church degenerates, and if popes and priests fail, love and community must be preserved. Such a time does not therefore call for division and separation—Luther declares most sharply that the Hussites' separation from the Roman Church in order to establish a community of holy people was inexcusable, godless, and against the law of Christ;[82] on the contrary, such a situation demands the closest connection and participation. This is not the time to run away from but, on the contrary, to run to

---

him; and I should love him so much that I run after him like a shepherd seeking lost sheep or a housewife looking for a lost coin. [Luke 15:3-10]." *WA* 10[III], 217. "God now enters into the situation and passes judgment saying that such people ought to humble themselves and take the sinners on their shoulders and bear them, thinking of themselves as helping the others out of their sins through their own righteousness and godliness. . . . These are the genuinely Christian works: that we fall into and get as deeply involved in the quicksand in which the sinner finds himself, and that we take his sins upon ourselves and work our way out with them—acting just as though they were our own. We should admonish him and deal with him most seriously, but we should not despise him, rather we should love him most heartily. . . . These are the genuinely great works which we ought to practice." *WA* 10[III], 218. Cf. *WA* 10[I,2], 68 f.

[79] In a sermon on the washing of feet preached in 1524, Luther says: "If the bishops say, 'If we were to disguise ourselves then our power would come to an end.' [But I say to you] 'If the bishops would disguise themselves and would take care of poor people [*Episcopos* does not seem to fit the context and should probably be read as *pauperes*] in an institution then the whole world would be converted' . . . but they do not care anything about this as long as they preserve their majesty. You will not be able to rule over Christians until you do as Christ did and lay aside your garments. This means that those who hold the pastoral office ought to spiritually wash people's feet, that is to concern themselves with the sins of their neighbor, and to comfort him when he sins." *WA* 15, 507. Cf. *WA* 1,2, 306.

[80] *WA* 2, 605; *LW* 27, 391 f.

[81] "The appearance of the church is the appearance of a sinner." *WA* 45[II], 560; *LW* 12, 263.

[82] *WA* 2, 605; *LW* 27, 392 f.

the church and to work within the church for its renewal.[83] Luther thereby describes the road he himself wished to follow in his relationship to the Roman Church. Did he not have reason enough to break off community with the degenerated church? In 1519 his answer was a passionate "perish the thought!" He will accuse, rebuke, threaten, plead—but the unity of the church should not for this reason be broken. Let love be above everything! For the sake of love we must accept not only the loss of external goods of this life but also the abomination of sin. That love which accepts only advantages from the other but will not bear burdens is an imaginary love.[84] Thus, for Luther, community includes the duty of preserving the unity of the church in spite of sin and degeneracy within it. He himself would never have separated himself from Rome if Rome had not impenitently thrown him out. But even after the separation, community must not cease. Luther constantly felt himself responsible for the one church. This was the significance of his polemical writings against Rome up to the very end of his life.

THE EVANGELICAL PRIESTHOOD

Luther can also express his entire understanding of the church as the community of saints by describing priesthood as the law of the church's life. When Christ bears our burden and intercedes for us with his righteousness, he does the work of a priest: mutual bearing of burdens and substitution in Christianity is also priestly activity.[85] The church is founded on Christ's priesthood. Its inner

---

[83] "For if the bishops or priests or any persons at all are wicked, and if you were aglow with real love, you would not flee. No, even if you were at the ends of the ocean, you would come running back to them and weep, warn, reprove, and do absolutely everything. And if you followed this teaching of the apostle [Gal. 6:2] you would know that it is not benefits but burdens that you have to bear." *WA* 2, 605; *LW* 27, 392. Cf. *WA* 2, 456; *LW* 27, 169.

[84] "We who are bearing the burdens and the truly intolerable abominations of the Roman curia—are we, too, fleeing and seceding on this account? Perish the thought! Perish the thought! To be sure, we censure, we denounce, we plead, we warn; but we do not on this account disrupt the unity of the spirit, nor do we become puffed up against it, since we know that love rises high above all things, not only above injuries suffered in bodily things but also above all the abominations of sins. A love that is able to bear nothing but the benefits done by another is fictitious." *WA* 2, 605; *LW* 27, 392 f.

[85] It is for this reason that Luther refers to the priesthood of Christ in connection with the apostolic admonition to fulfill the law of Christ by bearing the sinful brethren. *WA*, Br 1, 61.

structure is the priesthood of Christians for each other. The priesthood of Christians flows from the priesthood of Christ. As Christ's
brothers, Christians receive a share in his priestly office, namely,
through baptism, regeneration, and the anointing with the Holy
Spirit.[86] The priesthood means: We stand before God, pray for
others, intercede with and sacrifice ourselves to God and proclaim
the word to one another.[87] Luther never understands the priesthood
of all believers merely in the "Protestant" sense of the Christian's
freedom to stand in a direct relationship to God without a human
mediator. Rather he constantly emphasizes the Christian's evangelical authority to come before God on behalf of the brethren and
also of the world.[88] The universal priesthood expresses not religious
individualism but its exact opposite, the reality of the congregation as a community. The individual stands directly before God,

---

[86] "Through baptism we have all been ordained as priests." *WA* 6, 407;
PE 2, 66. "We are all priests as long as we are Christians." *WA* 6, 564; *LW*
36, 113. "Here [John 16:26 f.] he has crowned, ordained, and anointed us all
with the Holy Spirit so that all of us together are priests in Christ, exercise a
priestly office, come before God and intercede for one another. Thus all of
us may say, 'Christ has become the high priest and he has prayed for me and
gained for me faith and the Spirit; for this reason I am also a priest and should
continue to pray for the people of the world that God would also give faith
to them.'" *WA* 10[II], 309. Cf. *WA* 11, 411; *PE* 4, 79 f. "Since he is a
priest and we are his brethren, all Christians have the power and must fulfill
the commandment to preach and to come before God with our intercessions
for one another and to sacrifice ourselves to God." *WA* 12, 308. Luther speaks
of "their spiritual priesthood," which is the "common property of all Christians . . . who are anointed inwardly in their hearts with the Holy Spirit." *WA*
17[II], 6. "Christ is a priest together with all his Christians. . . . This priesthood
cannot be made or given by ordination. Here no one is made a priest. He
must be born a priest and bring it with him as the inheritance with which he
has been born. The birth of which I am speaking is the birth of water and the
Spirit. Through this all Christians become priests of a great high priest, children of Christ and fellow heirs with him." *WA* 17[II], 6. *WA* 12, 178 f.; *LW*
40, 19 f. Luther also cites John 6:45, Ps. 45:7, I Pet. 2:9, Rev. 5:10. Cf. *WA*
6, 407 and *WA* 11, 411; *PE* 4, 79 f.
[87] In addition to the passages cited in the previous footnote, cf. *WA* 7, 28,
57; *RW* 1, 366 f.; *LW* 31, 354 f. In his book, *Concerning the Ministry*,
(1523), Luther enumerates the seven rights of the universal priesthood: to
preach the word of God, to baptize, to celebrate the sacrament of the altar,
to minister the office of the keys, to pray for others, to sacrifice, to judge doctrine and to distinguish spirits. *WA* 12, 180 ff.; *LW* 40, 21, 32. The same
three points which are made in this citation from *WA* 12, 308 in the previous
footnote are repeated in *WA* 12, 309, 318 and in *WA* 41, 183 ff. "It is the
fourth duty of a priest to bear the sins of his brethren just as Christ has borne
our sins." *WA* 10[III], 107. (There is admittedly some doubt about the re-
liability of the text of this sermon.)
[88] *WA* 10[III], 309 [quoted in n. 85] indicates that Christians are to exercise
their priestly function not only toward one another but also toward the
"world."

he has received the authority of substitution. The priesthood means "the congregation" and the priesthood is the inner form of the community of saints.[89] This characteristic distinguishes Christians from the rest of humanity. They are a priestly generation, a royal priesthood.[90] Luther also says that the teaching that "Christ has born our sins" makes "a great and eternal distinction between the religion of all other men on earth and our religion." For Luther, Christ's priesthood and the Christian's priesthood belong together, as reconciling faith in Christ and the community of saints together constitute the nature of the church. In the final analysis, the Christian's priestly sacrifice is nothing else than Christ's own sacrifice. For the life of Christians is Christ's life. All sacrifice through which the community exists is an offering with and in Christ in that one sacrifice which took place once but is yet everywhere present, which cannot be repeated but lives on in the reality of the community.[91]

Two manifestations of this priesthood must be treated in particular: (1) the preaching of God's word and (2) the administration of absolution and discipline. The priesthood of all believers means that they have the right and duty to confess, to teach, and to spread God's word.[92] This is the highest priestly office.[93] Luther admittedly limits the public preaching of the word within the church to those who have been called through the community (cf. p. 329) and permits an individual who has not been called to preach publicly only in genuine mission territory or in time of trouble when the called teacher fails or errs.[94] Within these limitations, all have been called to proclaim God's word to one another. The community as a whole possesses the power and the unlimited authority and duty of such preaching. Whoever believes can do nothing else. "I believe, therefore I speak."[95] Luther recog-

---

[89] Cf. *GA* 1, 320 and especially the phraseology in the table of contents, p. VII, "The universal priesthood as the condition for the establishment of a genuine community in the church."

[90] *WA* 2, 606; *LW* 27, 394.

[91] *WA* 17ᴵᴵ, 6.

[92] *WA* 7, 57; *LW* 31, 355. Luther points out "that a Christian not only has the right but the duty to teach the word of God; and he fails to do so at the risk of his own salvation." *WA* 11, 412; *PE* 4, 80.

[93] *WA* 12, 318.

[94] *WA* 6, 408; *PE* 2, 68. *WA* 11, 412; *PE* 4, 80 f.

[95] *WA* 10ᴵᴵᴵ, 234, 311. Cf. *WA* 12, 318. *WA* 45, 540; *LW* 24, 87.

nizes no community which is not a preaching community and no community in which all have not been called to be witnesses. Each one is to care for his brother with the consolation of the word which he needs in his trouble.[96]

A special form of such preaching of God's word to each other is speaking the forgiveness of sins. "What is the difference between saying 'Thy sins are forgiven thee' and preaching the gospel?"[97] For Luther, the greatest good which the community possesses is that forgiveness of sins is to be found in it. In his *Short Form* of 1520, he follows the progression of the Third Article of the Creed by proceeding directly from a description of a sharing of goods within the community and directly to the forgiveness of sins. "I believe that the forgiveness of sins is to be found in this community and nowhere else."[98] The entire community and every one of its members has received the authority to proclaim and bring this home to the brother from Christ himself (according to Matthew 16:19 and 18:18).[99] "The whole church is full of the forgiveness of sins."[100] This is the community's glory.[101] We experi-

---

[96] *WA* 40III, 342. *WA* 40III, 543; *LW* 13, 111. Cf. *WA* 49, 139.

[97] *WA* 10III, 395. "For what is it to loose, if not to announce the forgiveness of sins before God, what is it to bind, except to withdraw the gospel and to declare the retention of sins?" *WA* 12, 184; *LW* 40, 28.

[98] *WA* 7, 219; *PE* 2, 373. Thomas Aquinas also established a relationship between the forgiveness of sins and the *communio sanctorum* but how differently than Luther does! *Opusc.* 6, *expositio* Symboli, art. X. [Thomas emphasizes that the members of the church receive forgiveness through the seven sacraments. He would thus in this respect interpret *sanctorum* as a neuter—Trans.] Cf. my *Communio Sanctorum* (1929), p. 15.

[99] "For any Christian can say to you, 'God forgives you your sins, in the name,' etc., and if you can accept that word with confident faith, as though God were saying it to you, then in that same faith you are surely absolved. . . . Now this authority to forgive sins is nothing other than what a priest, indeed, if need be, any Christian, may say to a brother when he sees him afflicted or afrighted in his sins. He can joyously speak this verdict, 'Take heart, your sins are forgiven' [Matt. 9:2]. And whoever accepts this and believes it as a word of God, his sins are surely forgiven." *WA* 716, 722; *LW* 35, 12, 21 (from the year 1519). *WA* 10III, 215 f., 394 ff. "Whoever has faith and is a Christian also has Christ, and all that belongs to Christ is his; thus he also has the power to forgive sins. . . . This means that I possess the authority of Christ . . . for whoever has faith also has everything that belongs to Christ; and if a Christian has the power to forgive sins, he also has the power to do everything that a priest can do." *WA* 10III, 394 f. "But this office of the keys belongs to all of us who are Christians." *WA* 12, 183 f.; *LW* 40, 26 f.

[100] *WA* 2, 722; *LW* 35, 21.

[101] "The great thing about the Christian is that God cannot be fully loved and praised if we are no longer given to hear more than one man speaking this to us. Now the world is full of Christians, yet no one pays any attention to this or gives God thanks." *WA* 2, 723; *LW* 35, 22.

ence this in private confession and absolution "when one privately confesses to the other, speaks into his ear whatever troubles him so that he may hear a comforting word from him."[102] Luther rejects the ecclesiastical rule which requires confession. It cannot be made a law, but is an indispensable form of the gospel. It its therefore not a requirement but rather a gift which we cannot do without.[103] To hear confessions is a priestly service which I may request from every brother.[104] Even when I turned to the called servant of the word—and Luther usually thinks of him—I ask for a brotherly service. Luther sees the priest as the brother who when he hears confession also always shares the burden of sin.[105] This stands under the promise given in Matthew 18:18.[106]

The community cannot get along without such private confession

---

[102] Luther does not cite James 5:16 as we might expect him to. He interprets this passage—as does Erasmus—as referring to the request for forgiveness for an injustice done against the brother. Cf. my essay, "Bekenne einer dem andern seine Sünden," *Festschrift für Theodor Zahn* (Leipzig: Deichert [Scholl] 1922), pp. 176 ff.

[103] "Nevertheless I will allow no man to take private confession away from me, and I would not give it up for all the treasures of the world, since I know what comfort and strength it has given me. No one knows what it can do for him except one who has struggled often and long with the devil. Yea, the devil would have slain me long ago, if the confession had not sustained me." *WA* 10^{III}, 61; *LW* 51, 97 f.

[104] "This means that I may go to my good friend and say to him, 'Dear friend, this is the trouble and the difficulty which I am having with sin,' and he should be free to say to me, 'Your sins are forgiven, go in the peace of God.' You should absolutely believe that your sins are forgiven as though Christ himself were your father confessor—as long as your friend does this in the name of God." *WA* 10^{III}, 395. "So when your conscience troubles you, go to a godly man and tell him of your problems; if he forgives you accept it; he needs no authorization from the pope to do this." *WA* 10^{III}, 398, 35.

[105] "Furthermore I admonish you not to confess anything privately to a priest because he is a priest but only because he is a brother and a Christian." *WA* 8, 184. "If I ask my brother for advice and the devil deceives me in this way or in that, nevertheless brotherly love has begun and this helps me." *WA* 15, 487. In this entire sermon, Luther seems to be thinking of confession to a priest. However, he often speaks simply of confessing to the "brother." *WA* 15, 488. J. Köstlin pointed out that Luther "often deliberately speaks of the priest as our neighbor or our brother," *Theology of Luther*, trans. Charles E. Hay (Philadelphia: Lutheran Publication Society, 1897) II, 529. Luther rejects the hierarchical understanding of the priestly office as contrary to the gospel.

[106] Referring to Jesus' promise, Luther says: "Therefore let us freely and with a good conscience proceed on the basis of his clear words and confess, take counsel with, and ask one another for help in everything which is a matter of private concern to us, whether it is sin or trouble and in no wise doubt this clear promise of God." *WA* 8, 184. It is significant that in this and in other passages confession and absolution are not mentioned simply as isolated acts but belonging together with counseling and helping.

to the brother. Strong faith in God's forgiveness, however, does not
need the brother, for the Christian is then able to confess only to
God. But how many have such strong faith?[107] And should we not
gratefully use every way of hearing the gospel? "God has been so
gracious to us that he has stuffed every corner of the world full
with God's word" that is, in the form of brethren, fellow Christians in the community. We should not throw this to the wind,
but rather receive it with thanks.[108] "The gospel shall without ceasing sound and resound through the mouths of all Christians; therefore we should joyfully accept every possibility of hearing it, lift
up our hands and thank God, because we can hear it everywhere."[109]
This seems to be the greatest thing about the community for Luther: God's word, the gospel, is always near and present to me so
that I am everywhere surrounded by its sound and do not need to
ask for it. It is close to me in every brother, for he may, in God's
name, speak it to me in my trouble.[110]

THE SACRAMENT OF COMMUNION

Luther found that the sacrament of the Lord's Supper both expresses and guarantees the reality of the church as the community
[*communio*] of saints.[111] In a sermon on the Lord's Supper

[107] *WA* 10III, 63; *LW* 51, 99.

[108] *WA* 15, 486, 488.

[109] *WA* 15, 486. (The present form of this passage may not be the work
of Luther himself.) "To whom else will you confess your weakness except to
God? But where can you find him except in your brother? Your brother can
strengthen and help you with his words." *WA* 15, 488.

[110] We refer again to Luther's emphasis on the "mutual conversation and consolation of brethren," in the *Smalcald Articles*. *WA* 50, 241; *BC*, 310.
Luther's "and also" places it alongside of and co-ordinates it with preaching,
baptism, the sacrament of the altar, and the office of the keys as one of the
means through which God gives us strength and help against sin. He distinguishes "mutual conversation" from the "power of the keys"; J. Köstlin,
op. cit., II, 528 ff., interprets this "mutual conversation" as the total association
of the Christian who is in need of comfort and advice with his brethren." It
cannot however be separated from the absolution. The *Wittenberg Concordia*
describes absolution as the goal of the conversation. And the consolation of the
sinner consists in communication of the forgiveness of sins. [The text is in the
St. Louis edition of *Luthers Sämmtliche Schriften*, XVII, 2089. Cf. *WA* 15,
508.]

[111] The sources of this evaluation of the Lord's Supper as the sacrament of the
community of saints were written between 1519 and 1524. The most important is *The Blessed Sacrament of the Holy and True Body of Christ and the
Brotherhoods* (1519). *WA* 2, 742-758; *LW* 35, 49-73. See also, *The Adoration of the Sacrament* (1523). *WA* 11, 431-456; *LW* 36, 275-305. Also

preached in 1519, he developed his understanding of the church as community. Augustine and Thomas had already dealt with the Lord's Supper as "the sacrament of love."[112] For Luther, however, this heritage becomes something new, because he understands *communio* in a new way. In the Lord's Supper we receive "a sure sign of community and incorporation into Christ and all the saints."[113] Just as community is both a gift and a calling, so the Lord's Supper also has a unified double sense.[114] It guarantees me the priestly sacrifice and intercession of Christ and the whole church on my behalf.[115] At the same time, however, I am obligated to priestly sacrifice for the brethren.[116] We may not have the comfort of the sacra-

---

sermons from 1522-1524. *WA* 10^{III}, 55 ff.; *LW* 51, 92-96. *WA* 12, 485 ff. *WA* 15, 497 ff.

[112] *WA* 2, 745; *LW* 35, 54. Cf. Augustine's comment "O symbol of unity! O chain of love!" In *Joann.* 26, 13, *MPL* 35, 1613. Thomas Aquinas calls the Eucharist the "sacrament of love . . . the bond of perfection, as it is called in Col. 3:14." *Summa* III, ques. 73, art. 3. Cf. Bernhard Bartmann, *Dogmatik* (4th and 5th ed.; 1920), II, 342: "The Eucharist is the sacrament of love." Luther finds the same symbolism in the elements: bread is made when the individual grains of wheat give up their individual shape and form and are mixed together in the flour to become one loaf; in the same way the grapes lose their individual existence in becoming wine; and in eating and drinking, we transform the bread and the wine in us. In all of these Luther finds that "love is described." *WA* 2, 748; *LW* 35, 58. Cf. *WA* 11, 441; *LW* 36, 287. *WA* 12, 488. *WA* 15, 503. *WA* 19, 509, 511; *LW* 36, 352. This thought appears very frequently in the ancient fathers of the church, e.g., in the letters of Cyprian (*ad Caecilium*, ep. 63, and *ad Magnum*, ep. 76) and in Augustine. Cf. also Johann Gerhard, *Loci Theologici*, ed. Preuss (Berlin: Schlawitz, 1867), V, 13. In all this however the constant point of comparison is that the many become one. But what is most important in Luther's interpretation is missing in the fathers', that is, the grains of wheat and the grapes lose their own form— just as Christ takes our form upon himself and we take his form and that of other Christians upon us.

[113] *WA* 2, 743; *LW* 35, 51. Cf. "The significance of or effect of this sacrament is the community [*Gemeinschaft*] of all the saints." *WA* 2, 743; *LW* 35, 50. When the priest gives me the Holy Body of Christ, "whether I am worthy of it or not, I am still a member of Christendom; this is what the sacrament says and demonstrates." *WA* 2, 694. Cf. *WA* 6, 63; *PE* 2, 38.

[114] "This community consists in this, that all the spiritual possessions of Christ and his saints are shared with and become the common property of him who receives this sacrament. Again all sufferings and sins also become common property; and thus love engenders love in return and this mutual love unites." *WA* 2, 743; *LW* 35, 51. Cf. *WA* 2, 745; *LW* 35, 53 f.

[115] "In this sacrament, therefore, we are, through the priest, given a sure sign from God himself that he is thus united with Christ and his saints and has all things in common with them, that is, that Christ's sufferings and life are his own, together with the lives and sufferings of all the saints." *WA* 2, 744; *LW* 35, 52. Cf. *WA* 2, 745; *LW* 35, 53 f.

[116] "When you have partaken of this sacrament, therefore, or desire to partake of it, you must in turn share the misfortune of the community [*Gemeine*], as has been said. . . . Your heart must go out in love and learn that this is a

ment and forget the duty. If we are so concerned about what we get out of it, the sacrament does not help us. For the fruit as well as the basis of the sacrament is love.[117] Luther is well aware that such statements strike against not only the usual egotistical practice but also the individualistic doctrine of the Lord's Supper. The Lord's Supper was no longer understood in its genuine sense.[118] Many masses were held, and "still the Christian participation which should be preached and practiced and displayed in Christ's example was completely disappearing." Things were different in the ancient church. Luther contrasts the early Christian Lord's Supper with the individualistically distorted celebration of the sacrament common in his time.[119] And his doctrine of the Lord's Supper in the decisive years of the Reformation actually does rediscover the early Church's "participation in the Body of Christ" in the sense of I Corinthians 10:16 ff. Together with the New Testament understanding of the church as community, Luther had at the same time regained the sacrament of Holy Communion [*communio*] as such. Luther thinks of the Lord's Supper as the proper sacrament of the church as community. It stands in the center of its life, and it expresses and

---

sacrament of love. As love and support are given you, you in turn must render love and support to Christ and his needy ones." *WA* 2, 745; *LW* 35, 54.

[117] *WA* 10[III], 55; *LW* 51, 95. Cf. *WA* 15, 497 ff., 500. Luther also refers to the Lord's Supper within a completely different context, when he wishes to exhort his hearers to love; he points out that many receive the sacrament without bearing fruit. *WA* 11, 76. In *The German Mass,* the Collect after the Communion says, "And we beseech thy mercy to strengthen us through the same in faith toward thee, and in fervent love among us all. . . ." *WA* 19, 102; *LW* 53, 84. As far as I can see there is no pattern or parallel to this in the Roman mass: the section of this collect beginning "to strengthen us through the same . . ." was written by Luther himself; the first part is based upon the Collect after Communion for the Eighteenth Sunday after Pentecost; cf. P. Drews, *Beiträge zu Luthers liturgischen Reformen* (Tübingen: Mohr, 1910), pp. 95 f.

[118] *WA* 2, 747; *LW* 35, 56. Speaking to the Christians in Wittenberg, Luther said: "You are willing to take all of God's goods in the sacrament, but you are not willing to pour them out again in love. Nobody extends a helping hand to another, nobody seriously considers the other person, but everyone looks out for himself and his own gain, insists on his own way, and lets everything else go." *WA* 10[III], 57, *LW* 51, 96. "What a terrible blasphemy against God that we all take the sacrament and want to be good Christians, but none of us is willing to stoop down and serve our neighbor." *WA* 12, 470.

[119] *WA* 2, 747, *LW* 35, 57. Luther also describes the Lord's Supper as the sacrament of the community [*Gemeinde*] in other ways. He reminds us that in the early church, Communion was the confession and sign by which Christians recognized one another and which brought persecution and death upon them." *WA* 15, 491.

guarantees the "law of Christ" and his love from which the church does and ought to live.

Luther takes this understanding of the Lord's Supper very seriously. This is shown by the fact that he dares to co-ordinate the Christians' eating and drinking of one another, through their sharing goods and troubles in love, with the eating of Christ through the believing reception of the sacrament.[120] As Christ is our food and drink in the Lord's Supper, so we also become food and drink for each other. This means that I give everything which I have to my neighbor who needs it and conversely that I allow him to help and to serve me in my poverty. However, Luther clearly limits this correlation between the "eating" of Christ and the eating of the neighbor. The correlation is true only of the spiritual eating of the Christ, that is, of the reception of Christ in believing his "for you." Beyond this, Luther teaches a physical eating of the body of Christ; there is, however, nothing in the relationship of Christians to each other which corresponds to this.[121]

These thoughts, as well as the entire evaluation of the Lord's Supper as the sacrament of the community of saints [*communio sanctorum*], later recede into the background of Luther's thought and he is primarily interested in the real presence and the reception of the heavenly body and blood of Christ. These thoughts of 1519 are to be found—as far as I can see—only up to the year 1524. It is significant that they cease at the very point at which

---

[120] "And just as one member serves another in such an integrated body, so each one eats and drinks the other; that is, each consumes the other in every drink, and each one is food and drink for the other, so that we are simply food and drink to one another, just as Christ is simply food and drink to us." *WA* 11, 441; *LW* 36, 287. "Through believing the word which the soul takes and receives into itself, we eat the Lord. My neighbor in turn eats me together with my possessions, my body and my life; I give him this and everything that I have and let him make use of everything in all his needs. In the same way when I in turn am poor and in trouble and need my neighbor, I'll allow myself to be helped and served. And in this way we are made part of one another so that one helps the other just as Christ has helped us. This is what it means that we spiritually eat and drink one another." *WA* 15, 503; cf. 498. 14. Cf. also the close of Luther's hymn on the Lord's Supper written in 1524, "Jesus Christ, Our Lord and Savior";

> Fruits of faith therein be showing
> That thou art to others loving;
> To thy neighbor thou wilt do
> As God in love hath done to you.

WA 35, 437, *LW* 53, 251.
[121] Cf. the clear distinction which Luther makes, *WA* 23, 179; *LW* 37, 85 f.

the battle about the real presence begins. There can be no question that this development restricted and impoverished the doctrine of the sacrament of the Lord's Supper and the celebration of this meal in the Lutheran Church compared with its fulness among primitive Christians. Luther did not restore the Lord's Supper to the dominant position in the life of the church as a community that it had among the first Christians. As celebrated in our church, it is certainly the high point of the individual Christian life; but it is not equally the center of the community's life of sharing as the body of Christ. In this respect Luther's earliest writing on the sacrament of the Lord's Supper (the treatise of 1519) stands far above all those that follow. We today must once again take up his thoughts.[122]

Luther's doctrine of the community of saints represents an extremely vital conception of Christ's presence in the community. Christ is present in a twofold way: in giving and in taking. Christ himself is present in the word of concern and of comfort which the community or the brother speaks to me in God's name, in his intercession for me, and in his bearing and helping.[123] And in this sense we both may and should become a Christ to the others— emptying ourselves and taking on the "form of a servant."[124] At the same time, however, Christ is, according to his own word in Matthew 25:40, present in the needy, in the sinners, and in the burdened.[125] Whatever is done to the lowliest of the brethren is done to Him. He wills to be loved and served in them all. This is Christ's presence in the community.

---

[122] Cf. Paul Philippi, *Abendmahlsfeier und Wirklichkeit der Gemeinde* (Berlin: Evang. Verlagsanstalt, 1960).

[123] *WA*, Br 4, 238.

[124] *WA* 7, 35; *RW* 1, 376; cf. *LW* 31, 366. "I will therefore give myself as a Christ to my neighbor, as Christ offered himself to me . . . we ought . . . each one of us to become as it were a Christ to the other that we may be Christs to one another and Christ may be the same in all, that is, that we may be truly Christians." *WA* 7, 66; *LW* 31, 367 f.

[125] *WA* 12, 333. Cf. especially the sermon preached on September 30, 1526, *WA* 20, 514. The printed text of the sermon corresponds to the substance of Rörer's notes. "So it is that all the world is full of God. You can find Christ in every street outside your door; don't stare up into heaven. . . ." Cf. also *WA*, Br 4, 15.

23

THE OFFICE OF THE
MINISTRY

IN HIS *On the Councils and the Churches,* Luther lists the signs of the church's presence. Among these he includes the fact that the church has offices and calls men to fill them.[1] Now Luther does list this particular sign in the fifth place. It is preceded by God's word, baptism, the Lord's Supper and the office of the keys. But precisely these four "healing powers" of the church make it necessary that the church, "the Christian holy people," have offices and "servants of the church" who administer these saving remedies.[2] Luther describes a double basis for the necessity and authority of this official ministry. On the one hand, he proceeds from the priesthood of all the baptized. By the power of the priesthood they are authorized and called to serve through the word and the sacrament. It would not, however, be possible for every member of the community to publicly administer the word and sacrament to the entire community. That would lead to a deplorable confusion.[3] To avoid this the community must commit this public ministry to some one person who administers it "for the sake of and in the name of the church." The necessity of and authority of this office is, however, "much more" derived from its institution by Christ. According to Ephesians 4:8-11 he has "given gifts to men" and appointed some to be apostles, prophets,

---

[1] *WA* 50, 632; *PE* 5, 275. Cf. W. Brunotte, *Das geistliche Amt bei Luther* (Berlin: Lutherisches Verlagshaus, 1959.) H. Lieberg, *Amt und Ordination bei Luther und Melanchthon* (unpublished dissertation, University of Erlangen, 1960).

[2] *WA* 50, 632; *PE* 5, 275. *WA* 11, 411; *PE* 4, 79. *WA* 39ᴵᴵ, 287.

[3] "Otherwise, there might be a shameful confusion among the people of God." *WA* 12, 189; *LW* 40, 34. "For the whole group cannot do this but must either themselves order someone or permit someone to do it. Otherwise what would be the result if everyone wanted to preach or to administer the sacrament and no one would give in to anyone else? One individual must be appointed and he must do the preaching." *WA* 50, 633; *PE* 5, 275 f.

evangelists, teachers, etc. This institution does not only refer to the
first generation of Christians. For the Church will remain until the
end of the world. For this reason, when the first Christian apostles
and other ministers were no longer living it was necessary for
others to take their place and to "teach God's word and carry out
his work."[4] Thus God himself has "commanded, instituted, and
ordered" the office of preaching.[5]

Luther without hesitation co-ordinates these two derivations of
the office of the ministry—the one from "below" and the other
from "above." He sees no contradiction in them. There are, however, two different lines of development. In the first, he bases the
office on the presupposition of the universal priesthood and thus
describes it as a mediated office. In the second, he derives it directly from its institution by Christ without reference to the universal priesthood. In the latter case, it is an office which Christ
gave to the preachers of the gospel from the very beginning. Both
derivations presuppose that the gospel must be preached and the
sacraments administered as long as the world stands, so that the
church may endure. However, when we ask who should do this,
we come to a fork in the road. One chain of thought replies:
"Everyone" concludes that it is necessary to entrust this office to
an individual only on the basis of rational and sociological considerations. The other feels that the Lord has directly given and
instituted this special office. But even when based on the universal priesthood, God ultimately wills the office not directly however, but only indirectly; for God desires order in the community.

Luther cannot base this office only on its direct institution by
Christ. That would obscure the fact that all baptized Christians
have received this priesthood from Christ the Priest and that they
have both the power and the duty of exercising all the functions

---

[4] *WA* 50, 633 f.; *PE* 5, 275 f.
[5] *WA* 50, 647; *PE* 5, 292. Additional passages asserting that the office of
the ministry was instituted by God or Christ are: *WA* 30ᴵᴵ, 598. *WA* 37, 269,
192. Cf. Werner Elert, *The Structure of Lutheranism*, trans. by Walter Hansen
(St. Louis: Concordia, 1962), 1, 344. "The offices of the ministry and sacrament are not our property but belong to Christ. For he provided for these
and left them with his church so that they might be used and administered till
the end of the world." *WA* 38, 240. Luther, in his *Confession Concerning
Christ's Supper* (1528), lists the office of the ministry together with marriage
and government as "holy orders," "institutions," and "estates" established by
God. *WA* 26, 504; *LW* 37, 364.

of the priest, described by Luther.[6] They all have the authority of the ministry of the word and sacrament.[7] Since the special office does not abrogate the priestly office of all Christians which, as far as Luther is concerned, is the community's law of life, he must provide a foundation of the special office which takes the universal office into account. He does this by deriving the special office from the universal. He thereby distinguishes the exercise of the priestly office between brother and brother, and in case of necessity from the public exercise of the office in the administration of the ministry of the word for the entire congregation.[8] The special office is necessary for the sake of order; Luther cites Paul (I Cor. 14:40). Everything in the community should be done in an orderly way.[9] For this reason, the community must call an individual to this special office of the ministry of the word and sacrament.[10] The authority which the entire congregation, and every individual in it, possesses is thereby delegated to the one whom they choose from their midst or who is called by a superior. Precisely because the authority of the ministry of word and sacrament has been given to the entire community, no individual may presume to exercise it on his own initiative. He must be called to this office and the community must consent. Then he administers his office in the place of all and as the representative of the entire community.[11]

---

[6] Cf. p. 313.

[7] *WA* 6, 566; *LW* 36, 116.

[8] "For it is one thing to exercise the right publicly; another to use it in time of emergency. Publicly one may not exercise a right without consent of the whole body or of the church. In time of emergency each may use it as he deems best." *WA* 12, 189; *LW* 40, 34.

[9] *WA* 12, 189; *LW* 40, 34.

[10] *WA* 6, 440; *PE* 2, 119.

[11] For Luther's derivation of the office of the ministry from the universal priesthood of all believers, cf. especially: *An Open Letter to the Christian Nobility.* *WA* 6, 404-469; *PE* 2, 61-164. *The Babylonian Captivity of the Church.* *WA* 6, 497-573; *LW* 36, 11-126. *Concerning the Ministry, WA* 12, 169-195; *LW* 40, 7-44. *The Right and Power of a Christian Congregation or Community to Judge All Teaching and to Call, Appoint, and Dismiss Teachers, Established and Proved from Scripture* (1523). *WA* 11, 408-416; *PE* 4, 75-85. *On Private Masses [Von der Winkelmesse und Pfaffenweihe.]* *WA* 38, 195-256. "Let everyone, therefore, who knows himself to be a Christian, be assured of this, that we are all equally priests, that is to say, we have the same power in respect to the word and the sacraments. However, no one may make use of this power except by the power of the community or by the call of the superior. (For what is the common property of all, no individual may arrogate to him-

The pastor is the representative of the community and does everything in its name, both in preaching and in the liturgy. Luther has dealt with this masterfully in describing the evangelical mass as the "true Christian mass." The pastor "sings Christ's ordinance instituting the Lord's Supper," that is, the words of institution; the community kneels beside, behind, and around him. All of them are "true and holy priests," as the pastor himself is. "We should not permit our pastor to speak Christ's words by himself as though he were speaking them for his own person; rather, he is the mouth of all of us and we all speak them with him in our hearts."[11] We see that the representative activity of the pastor does not exclude but rather includes the co-operation of the community. The same is true of the proclamation of the word. For Luther, public preaching by ministers of the word does not release the members of the community from their priestly duty of speaking God's word to each other.

For Luther, the special office to which an individual is called out of the community of universal priests has no other content and also no other authority than the priesthood of all the others. The bearer of the church's office acts in the name of Christ. His word is Christ's word; and he stands before the members of the community in Christ's place.[12] All of this is, however, true of every Christian whose brother requires him to serve as a pastor by hearing his confession or in some other way. Because he is a priest through Christ, every Christian may say, "Christ's authority is

---

self, unless he is called." *WA* 6, 566; *LW* 36, 116. "Since we are all priests in this same way no one of us may, without our consent and election, put himself forward and undertake to do what is in the power of all of us. For without the will and the command of the community, no one dare to take upon himself what is common to all." *WA* 6, 408, cf. 407, *PE* 2, 68, cf. 66 f. "The ministry of the word, therefore, is common to all Christians." *WA* 12, 180; *LW* 40, 21. Cf. *WA* 12, 189; *LW* 40, 34.

Luther frequently expresses his understanding of the delegation of powers to representatives, e.g.: he speaks of one man "exercising the power on the behalf of others." *WA* 6, 407; *PE* 2, 67. He speaks of the pastor as one who "preaches and teaches in the stead of and by the commission of the rest." *WA* 11, 412 f.; *PE* 4, 81 f.; "The rights of the community demand that one, or as many as the community chooses, shall be chosen or approved who, in the name of all those who possess these same rights, shall perform these same functions publicly." *WA* 12, 189; *LW* 40, 34. Cf. *WA* 38, 230.

[12] *WA* 38, 247.

[13] "It is a wonderful thing that the mouth of every pastor is the mouth of Christ." *WA* 37, 381. "Therefore you ought to listen to the pastor not as a man but as God." *WA* 49, 140.

mine.'"[14] When his brother requires him to hear his confession of his need and sin, he too stands before his brother in the name of and with the authority of Christ.[15]

Christ's relationship to the communiy and all its members appears in the relationship of the ministry to the community and to every member—but no more than it appears in the relationship of every Christian to his brother when he has to speak the word of God, the comfort of the gospel and of forgiveness to him. Thus the only distinction between the ecclesiastical office of the ministry and the universal priesthood is the public character of the official ministry of the word and sacrament to the entire community. The individual Christian has been entrusted with his neighbors; the bearer of the office of the ministry has been entrusted with the entire community. Some recent Lutheran theologians have made a basic distinction between the authority of the ministry and of lay Christians; they have attributed a greater and more certain effectiveness to the sacrament when it is distributed by an official minister than when it it administered by a layman. All this has nothing to do with Luther, although he did feel that the sacrament should normally be administered by the special ministers of the word. He speaks of the ministry of the word, the office of preaching, as the "highest office in the church.'"[16] This refers, however, not only to the special office but also to that office granted and committed to all Christians with their priesthood.[17] Christ has instituted the one as well as the other. For Luther, the question of who carries out the ministry of the word is of secondary importance in comparison to the question of whether it is carried out.

---

[14] *WA* 10^{III}, 394.

[15] In spite of Luther's struggle with those who "sneak around and preach in corners," he continued to maintain this position in his later years with the same definiteness as in his basic Reformation writings. Thus in his interpretation of John 20:21 ("As the Father has sent me even so I send you"), he says: "I give you this command everywhere until the end of the world so that you may know you do not act by your own authority but by the command of him who sends you, and so that you may know that you do not do these things by human power. . . ." Then Luther expressly says: "I speak not only of you who are ministers but of all Christians." This means that the passage refers also to Christians who have no ecclesiastical office but who comfort and console one another by the command and with the authority of Christ. *WA* 49, 139.

[16] *WA* 11, 415; *PE* 4, 84. *WA* 12, 181; *LW* 40, 23.

[17] "The ministry of the word is the highest office in the church, it is unique and belongs to all who are Christians, not only by right but by command." *WA* 12, 181; *LW* 40, 23.

Everything depends on the function; in comparison to this, the question about the person is of only secondary importance.[18]

All this denies Roman doctrine and practice at several points. First, the bearer of ecclesiastical office is not a "priest" in the traditional sense. The title of "priest" is the property of all Christians and may therefore not be claimed as the exclusive property of the bearer of the office. In the New Testament there is no place for a special priesthood ordained through a liturgical rite but only for the "innate" priesthood of all the baptized.[19] Accordingly, the New Testament does not attribute the name of priest to any apostle or to any other office of the church but only to all Christians in common.[20] The fact that the church had priests later was due to the influence of pagan worship or of the Old Testament tradition: a paganization and Judaization which caused great damage in the church.[21] The ecclesiastical office, called the priesthood up until Luther's time, consists in nothing else than in the service [or ministry] of the word.[22] For this reason one should not call the clergy priests but perhaps "servants" or "ministers" as the Apostle Paul does (I Cor. 4:1).[23] Second, this means that the call to an office in the church does not convey a special Christian status but only the special ministry of word and sacrament to the community. There is no indelible character. There is a distinction between the called clergyman and the layman only because of the office: not because of what they are but because of what they do.[24] Since the rite of ordination to the priesthood has no scriptural basis, it is not a sacrament but only a liturgical rite through which the preacher of the gospel is called.[25] And it is this calling which is

---

[18] Cf. Elert, *op. cit.*, pp. 343 ff.

[19] "The New Testament knows of no priest who is, or can be [made a priest, by being] anointed externally. . . . For priests, especially in the New Testament are not made but born, created, not ordained." *WA* 12, 178; *LW* 40, 19.

[20] *WA* 38, 230.

[21] *WA* 12, 190; *LW* 40, 35.

[22] "The priesthood is properly nothing but the ministry of the word." *WA* 6, 566; *LW* 36, 116. Cf. *WA* 38, 239.

[23] *WA* 12, 190; *LW* 40, 35.

[24] "The sole difference between a priest and a layman is his ministry." *WA* 6, 567; *LW* 36, 117.

[25] *WA* 6, 560 ff.; *LW* 36, 106 ff. "A sacrament of ordination can be nothing else than a certain rite by which the church chooses its preachers." *WA* 6, 564; *LW* 36, 113. "Ordination is not a sacrament, but a rite and ceremony by which an individual is called to the ministry of the church." *WA* 54, 428; *LW* 34, 357.

the decisive act. This was Luther's opinion not only in his early years but as late as 1541.

THE CALL

No individual Christian can assume the office of the ministry for himself. It is given to him through an orderly call. Luther has good reason to emphasize this in opposition to the many sectarian enthusiasts who gathered a small group around themselves. He distinguishes two ways in which God calls man into the ministry: one is the inner, direct call such as God gave, for example, to the prophets and the Apostle Paul; the other is the outer, indirect call which comes to a man through other men.[26] The former must prove itself with "outward signs and witness." Luther constantly demanded this of Müntzer and the peasants.[27] He was open to the possibility that God would somehow break through the historically established order, but that would have to be confirmed by signs and wonders (although caution was necessary even here since Satan can also do signs and wonders!). The other, the outer call through men, however, requires no such signs. It takes place when others request an individual to preach, that is, to accept the office. The commandment of love requires him to accept. Love is commanded by God, however, and therefore whoever is called by men into this office is called by God himself. He requires no certification through signs and wonders. Luther emphasizes this particularly with reference to his own ministry in Wittenberg.[28]

---

[26] *WA* 16, 32 f. (Aurifaber's edition). *WA* 17ᴵᴵ, 254. *WA* 12, 460. *WA* 31ᴵ, 210 ff.; *LW* 13, 63 ff. *WA* 38, 493. *WA* 40ᴵ, 59 ff.; *LW* 26, 17 ff.

[27] E.g., *WA* 18, 304; *PE* 4, 227.

[28] "I am called by God since man urges me . . . [the man who says this] ought to be heard, because he says, 'Love your neighbor as yourself.'" *WA* 16, 33. "I am able to preach without any signs at all and nevertheless preach according to God." *WA* 16, 35. Luther explicitly asserts that the rule that no one ought to preach without having been called in an orderly way holds true only within the Christian community; among non-Christians, however, it does not hold—in that situation one should not wait to be called but like the apostles preach without having been explicitly called. *WA* 11, 412; *PE* 4, 80 f. Cf. *WA* 16, 35. This means that what holds true within Christendom and within the community does not hold true in mission territory. This rule is also not effective even in a time of emergency, that is when a group of Christians obviously has no true teacher. *WA* 11, 412, 414; *PE* 4, 81 f. Cf. *WA* 12, 189; *LW* 40, 34. "I cannot establish [my right to preach] by showing that I have been called to the office of the ministry by a vision of God but by the fact that I have been compelled to do this by other people and must do it

Luther considers it important that the preacher be called in an orderly way, not only for the sake of order in the church but also for the preacher personally. He tells us this was true for himself in his reforming activity. In the midst of the great tasks, and in view of the difficulty of the responsibility, the temptations, and the struggles which his work brought to him, Luther found strength and comfort in the fact that he had not sought his office but had been called into it, yes, even "forced" into it, that is, through his doctor's degree in theology. "For I would surely in the long run break down and despair under the great and heavy burdens which lay upon me, if I had begun this task by sneaking into the work without being called and commanded to do it."∞ This is true, however, not only of Luther personally but of every preacher. "It is not sufficient if a man has the word and the pure doctrine. He must also have the assurance of his call," otherwise "God will not prosper his work." How can a man who is not certain of and insecure in his calling stand his ground in those battles and assaults of Satan which the office of the ministry must endure?∞ To force one's self into the office of preaching on one's own authority is disobedience against God and such disobedience "makes all one's works evil"; such a man works with a bad conscience and he sins against the word to whose proclamation he has forced his way.∞ With all this Luther places the thesis, "What does not take place on the basis of a call is sin," as a rule for pastors and preachers on a level with Paul's statement that "what does not proceed from faith is sin" [Rom 14:23]. "This call and command makes pastors and preachers . . . for it is God's will that nothing be done as

---

for the sake of other people. Thus I have the authorization of the Spirit of love which does not seek its own but is diligent in seeking the welfare of others. I personally have nothing from it but trouble; I would much prefer to stay at home in my room, but this is the duty which has been laid upon me by the Spirit of love." *WA* 20, 222.

∞ *WA* 30ᴵᴵᴵ, 522; *LW* 40, 387 f. Cf. *GA* 1, 393. Speaking of the fact that he had written books which "the whole world" read, Luther says: "I have never wanted to do it and do not want to do it now. I was forced and driven into this position in the first place, when I had to become Doctor of Holy Scripture against my will." *WA* 31ᴵ, 212; *LW* 13, 66.

∞ *WA* 40ᴵ, 62; *LW* 26, 19 f. "Therefore, we who are in the ministry of the word have this comfort, that we have a heavenly and holy office; being legitimately called to do this, to prevail over all the gates of Hell. On the other hand, it is dreadful when the conscience says: 'You have done this without a calling!'" *WA* 40ᴵ, 62; *LW* 26, 20.

∞ *WA* 40ᴵ, 63; *LW* 26, 20.

a result of one's own choice or decision, but everything as a consequence of a command or a call. That is especially true of preaching."[32]

Luther knows that the self-consciousness of those who consider
themselves talented to preach, rebels against this strict rule. They
think that God needs them and that they can accomplish a great
deal through their preaching. To them Luther says, "If God needed
you, he would certainly call you"—and they may confidently wait
for that to happen![33] Only he bears fruit who is called to teach
without his own will. Whoever teaches without being called damages both himself and his hearers, for Christ is not with him.

It is not necessary for our presentation of Luther's theology to
deal with the details of who has the right to call and the proper
way to issue a call.[34] We are concerned only with presenting the
main lines of Luther's thought.[35] Luther recognizes no single method as unconditionally necessary. The way in which the call is ex-
tended depends on the individual situation and its needs and is not
a matter of divine right. For Luther it is always of decisive importance that the community has the authority to choose and to
call its servants of the word. At the same time, however, he follows the example of the New Testament described in Acts and the
pastoral epistles by wanting the bishops, if they are genuine bishops, to participate. They may not, however, call without the approval of the community. No call may be issued without the con-

---

[32] *WA* 31¹, 211; *LW* 13, 65.

[33] "Who has called you? Wait for him who calls. Meanwhile be untroubled.
In fact, even if you were wiser than Solomon himself and Daniel, still, if you
are not called, avoid spreading the word more than you would shun hell itself.
If God needs you, he will call you. If he does not call you, you will not
burst with your wisdom. As a matter of fact, it is not true wisdom either; to
you it only seems to be. And it is very foolish for you to imagine what fruit
you are able to produce. Nobody produces fruit by means of the word unless
he is called to teach without wishing for it. For one is our teacher, Jesus Christ
[Matt. 23:10]. He alone, through his called servants, teaches and produces
fruit. But the man who teaches without being called does so to his own harm
and that of his hearers, because Christ is not with him." *WA* 2, 454; *LW* 27,
167.
Roth includes this section of Luther's commentary (in translation) in a
sermon which he assembled from various writings of Luther and attributed to
Luther. *WA* 17¹¹, 258.

[34] Cf. Elert, *op. cit.*, pp. 346-351. Also the literature cited above p. 323, n. 1.

[35] Cf. *The Right and Power of a Christian Congregation or Community to
Judge All Teaching and to Call, Appoint, and Dismiss Teachers, Established and
Proved from Scripture* (1523), *WA* 11, 413 ff., *PE* 4, 81 ff.

sent of the community.[36] Luther distinguishes normal situations from emergency situations. In an emergency situation, for example, the government may call a preacher[37] or an individual may even take the office upon himself, if a community does not exist which would be in the position to call a pastor for itself. But all of these are exceptions. Luther formulated the norm once more in a thesis of 1545: "A call is properly issued by the church," but he can never think of the church as acting without the co-operation of the community.[38] A call issued through the church, however, is a call from Christ himself.

Being called by a community was so decisive for Luther that he is not particularly interested in a special liturgical act of ordination—the expression he adopted from the medieval church. He clearly distinguishes it from the Roman ordination to the priesthood. "Ordination should and can basically be nothing else (if things are done in the right way) than a call or command to carry out the office of the ministry or of preaching."[39] Ordination as an ecclesiastical act thus is basically a form and also a public confirmation of the call.[40] It does not have absolute character but is meaningful only in terms of the ordinand's service in a specific community. Luther uses the terms *call* and *ordain* synonymously. This is also indicated by the formula for ordination of 1535.[41] It does not follow the Roman rite for the ordination of priests but the New Testament example.[42] Luther freely composed the formula for ordination which consists in the reading of Scripture, prayer, and the laying on of hands.[43]

---

[36] *WA* 11, 413 f.; *PE* 4, 81 f.
[37] *WA* 11, 415; *PE* 4, 82.
[38] *WA* 54, 428.
[39] *WA* 38, 228, 238. Cf. *WA* 15, 721.
[40] *WA* 38, 428; *LW* 53, 125, especially n. 5.
[41] *WA* 38, 423 ff.; *LW* 53, 124 ff.
[42] *WA* 38, 228.
[43] Luther advocated the laying on of hands as early as 1523, *WA* 12, 193; *LW* 40, 40. On Luther's understanding of ordination, see particularly Drews' introduction to the Order of Ordination, *WA* 38, 401 ff.; cf. *LW* 53, 122 f., and also the literature cited p. 323, n. 1. In addition see Peter Brunner, *Nikolaus von Amsdorf als Bishof von Naumburg* (Gütersloh: G. Mohn, 1961), p. 60 ff.

24

THE TRUE CHURCH
AND THE EMPIRICAL CHURCH

THE AUTHORITY OF TRADITION
AND ITS LIMITATION

FOR LUTHER the Christian church is, without detriment to its spiritual nature, a historical reality, which constantly existed through all the centuries from the time of the apostles till his own time. The Evangelicals are not another and a new church but "the true old church, one body with the entire holy Christian church, and one community of saints."[1] In spite of all his heartfelt criticism of the Roman Church, Luther remained certain that God had, in spite of everything, miraculously preserved the true church even in the midst of its Babylonian captivity.[2] The Evangelicals received the great Christian inheritance from the hands of the pre-Reformation church—for this inheritance was not lost even under the papacy. "We on our part confess that there is much that is Christian and good under the papacy; indeed, everything that is Christian and good is to be found there and has come to us from this source. For instance, we confess that in the Papal Church there are the true Holy Scriptures, true baptism, the true sacrament of the altar, the true keys to the forgiveness of sins, the true office of the ministry, the true catechism in the form of the Lord's Prayer, the Ten Commandments, and the articles of the Creed."[3] The things which Luther lists are, with the exception of the last, "the articles of the Creed," all biblical material. The fact that he names these together with materials taken directly from the Bible leads us to conclude that he, in spite of many concerns about details, received the creeds of the ancient church as essentially corresponding to biblical truth.[4] He found genuine Christian content in the Ro-

---

[1] *WA* 51, 487.
[2] *WA* 38, 220.
[3] *WA* 26, 147; *LW* 40, 231 f. Cf. *WA* 40ᴵ, 69; *LW* 26, 24. At this place Luther specifically mentions the church in the city of Rome. Cf. *WA* 51, 501. *WA* 39ᴵᴵ, 167
[4] Cf. p. 7.

man mass together with what was contrary to the gospel. He expressed this position also in his German mass.[*] In the same way, he adopted a by no means small number of collects which had been written in the Middle Ages. (His translation of them into German was admittedly often a creative reconstruction).[*] And since he includes "many good songs and hymns both Latin and German" in the evidence proving that God preserved the substance of Christianity even in the ancient church,[*] he also introduced these into the German service of worship and into the worship of the evangelical communities. He translated a number of the best Latin hymns and other accepted musical texts from the liturgy and composed them in the form of German songs. ("We are determined to preserve the best Latin songs for particular festivals. They certainly have our heartfelt approval.") In addition, he took the most powerful German songs of the Middle Ages, purified them from unevangelical thoughts, and added some verses to them.[*]

Thus Luther thankfully received not only biblical substance in the direct sense of the term from the hands of the ancient and medieval church but also elements of ecclesiastical tradition. Not the least of these was the church's custom of baptizing children. Since, in Luther's judgment, it is not expressly commanded in the Holy Scriptures, his opposition to the Anabaptists' rejection of infant baptism gave him an opportunity to express himself basically about the authority of tradition in the church.[*] Luther asserts: The consensus of the entire church in a doctrine or a custom is binding insofar as it is not contrary to Scripture. He opposes the spiritualistic interpretation of the Lord's Supper by declaring: "The witness of the entire holy Christian church (even if we had nothing else) should be enough for us to maintain this doctrine and neither to listen to nor tolerate any sectarian objections. For it is dangerous and terrible to hear or believe anything contrary to the common witness, faith, and doctrine which the entire holy Chris-

---

[*] *WA* 19, 72; *LW* 53, 61.
[*] Paul Althaus d. Ä. [Sr.], *Forschungen zur evangelischen Gebetsliteratur* (Gütersloh: Bertelsmann, 1927), pp. 195 f. Cf. *LW* 53, 129-146.
[*] *WA* 38, 221.
[*] Paul Althaus d. Ä. [Sr.], *Luther als Vater des evangelischen Kirchenliedes* (Leipzig: Deichert, 1917), pp. 29 ff. Cf. *LW* 53, 191-309.
[*] Cf. pp. 359 ff.

tian church has maintained from the beginning until now—for more than 1500 years throughout all the world."[10]

Luther did not, as is obvious, in any sense advocate an absolute biblicism. He did not absolutize the Bible in opposition to tradition. He limits neither Christian dogma nor the ethical implications of the gospel to what is expressly stated in Scripture. He does not demand that the truth of Christianity be reduced to biblical doctrine. The Holy Spirit led not only the apostles but also Christendom since the time of the apostles. Luther, however, strongly emphasized the difference between the two cases. This establishes the right and the validity of the Christian tradition. It is to be tested only as to whether or not it contradicts the truth of the gospel clearly contained in Scripture. Whatever passes this test should be preserved.

In this sense then, Scripture is the standard of what can and cannot claim to be good tradition of the church. Since Luther emphatically asserts the validity of this standard, his basic affirmation of the church's tradition cannot be unconditional. Rather, it contains the possibility of disagreement. This "no" to tradition is not a basic and universal "no," but is always spoken in a specific situation and based on Scripture. We cannot, however, avoid such rejection of tradition whenever it cannot be harmonized with Scripture because it obviously contradicts it.

Luther himself tells us that he found it bitterly difficult to express this "no." For his confidence in the continuity of the church and the uninterrupted leadership of it through the Holy Spirit were an indispensable part of his faith. His opponents argued against him: "The church, the church: Do you suppose that God is so merciless that he would reject his whole church for the sake of a few Lutheran heretics? Do you suppose that he would leave his church in error for so many centuries?"[11] "Do you really imagine that you are the only one who is wise?"[12] Every rejection of an essential part of the tradition placed the entire historical development of the church, even the entire dogma of the church in

---

[10] *WA* 30ᴵᴵᴵ, 552.
[11] *WA* 40ᴵ, 54 f. (Rörer's printed edition and notes); *LW* 26, 15. Cf. *WA* 40ᴵ, 130; *LW* 26, 65.
[12] *WA* 46, 22; *LW* 24, 323.

question. "The church, the church"—the rallying cry of the pope
and of his followers caused Luther considerable inward difficulty.
"That blow really strikes home," that is, this constant insistence
upon the reality of the church and the power of its truth. As late
as 1538 he discusses this temptation in a sermon.[13] The Roman
Church claims that it is the true church. And Luther himself cannot deny what he constantly recognized: "The papacy has God's
word and the office of the apostles, and we have received the Holy
Scriptures, baptism, the sacrament, and the office of preaching from
them." Does this not mean that whoever opposes the Roman
Church also opposes the church of Christ and Christ himself? This
is what the opponents ask and Luther feels it is extremely difficult
to deprive them of this argument and to talk them out of it. "Yes,
we ourselves find it difficult to refute it. . . . Then there come rushing into my heart thoughts like these: Now I see that I am in
error. Oh, if only I had never started this and had never preached
a word! For who dares oppose the church, of which we confess in
the creed: I believe in a holy Christian church. . . ."

Luther overcame this difficult temptation and decisively attacked ecclesiastical tradition. "No one likes to say that the church
is in error; if the church teaches anything in addition to or contrary to God's word, we must say that it is in error."[14] At this
point a new problem admittedly arises. What is "God's word?"
Luther had to experience opposition to his doctrine and his criticism of tradition that itself was based on Scripture passages. A formal legalistic biblicism would not have been enough to get at his
opponents. Luther's ultimate authority and standard was not the
book of the Bible and the canon as such but that Scripture which
interpreted itself and also criticized itself from its own center:
from Christ and from the radically understood gospel. For Luther
the authority of Scripture is strictly gospel-centered.[15] One may
characterize his attitude in this way: The canon itself was, as far
as Luther was concerned, a piece of ecclesiastical tradition and
therefore subject to criticism on the basis of God's word. Roman

---

[13] *WA* 46, 5 f. [edited by Cruciger]; *LW* 24, 304.

[14] *WA* 40ᴵ, 132; *LW* 26, 66 f.

[15] Cf. p. 82.

Catholic theology has, up until the present day, frequently condemned Luther's method of approaching and validating the authority of Scripture as subjective and arbitrary. But Luther is as far as the heaven is from the earth in determining the center of Scripture by himself and self-confidently presenting his theology as this center. Rörer in his notes on the lectures on Galatians of 1531 has preserved the Reformer's remark that he constantly found within himself contradictions against the gospel as he understood it.[16] But he also knew that he was always overcome and compelled by the witness of the Apostle Paul, and he found Paul's basic melody in the entire Scripture—anything within the canon which did not agree with this was an exception and could make no claim to the authority of God's word.[17]

In all of this Luther maintains a decisive thesis as the material criterion of his theology. This basic principle was the theocentric character of the gospel and the preservation of God's honor as he who creates out of nothing. Luther tells us that Staupitz once comforted him in his doubts by pointing out that Luther's doctrine gave all honor to God and not to men. "One cannot give too much to God." Luther accepted this criterion and used it to overcome the temptation which came to him because he contradicted tradition. "I still know this for certain, that what I teach is not from men but from God (cf. Gal. 1:10). That is, I attribute everything solely to God and nothing at all to men . . . it is far safer to ascribe too much to God than to men."[18] "My teaching . . . lets God be God and it gives God the glory . . . therefore it cannot be wrong."[19] But even this criterion for the truth of his interpretation of the gospel was not something which he arbitrarily established. It was given to him by the Apostle Paul in Romans 4:17, "Abraham believed in the God who calls into existence the things that do not exist."

---

[16] *WA* 40ᴵ, 131; cf. *LW* 26, 65 f. It should be noted that the printed text [on which the English translation is based] tones down Luther's explicit statement, "and I also often think contrary to this teaching [*ego qui saepe sentio contra hanc doctrinam*]."

[17] Cf., e.g., *WA* 40ᴵ, 458; *LW* 26, 295. For Luther's statement on James, see *WA* 39ᴵᴵ, 199.

[18] *WA* 40ᴵ, 131 f.; *LW* 26, 66.

[19] *WA* 17ᴵ, 232; *LW* 12, 187.

THE AUTHORITY OF SCRIPTURE AND
THE AUTHORITY OF THE CHURCH

For Luther, there is no unconditional authority in the church parallel to and apart from the word of God. Whenever anyone refers to the "opinion of the church" on matters of Christian faith and life, we must ask what this means. Is it the true opinion of the church which can be recognized by the fact that it stands in and is based on Scripture or is it a self-fabricated opinion "found outside of Scripture" which someone only claims to be the true opinion of the church. Only the former has authority, because it alone is based on Scripture and agrees with Christ's will and command. "The church believes and thinks nothing except what Christ has thought and commanded, much less something contrary to what he thought and commanded." Such an opinion of the church cannot err any more than God's word can.[20] It is only in this sense, then, that we can and may cite the authority of the church. It is relative to and dependent on the Holy Scripture.

The authority of the church as such, of its fathers, of its traditions, of its officials and organs cannot be an unconditional authority. For the church can err, as the Lord himself predicted (Matt. 24:24). For this reason we cannot simply cite the church fathers to establish our position. "We can neither rely nor build very much on the life and works of the fathers but only on God's word."[21] The Old Testament, through the examples of David and Nathan, shows that the church can err. The New Testament presents no less evidence of this, since even the apostles "often sinned and failed," for example, Peter erred, as Paul reports in Galatians 2:11 ff.[22] For this reason, the church, without prejudice to its holiness, must daily pray the fifth petition of the Lord's Prayer which asks for forgiveness. This must be prayed not only by individual members of the church but also by the church as a whole.[23] The church "remains an obedient sinner before God until the last day and is holy only in Christ her Savior through grace and the for-

---

[20] *WA* 38, 203, 216 ff. Cf. *WA* 51, 518.

[21] *WA* 38, 206.

[22] *WA* 38, 208. Cf. *WA* 12, 417, 419.

[23] *WA* 38, 208, 216. Cf. *WA* 40^I, 132; *LW* 26, 66. *WA* 39^I, 351. *WA* 40^{III}, 506; *LW* 13, 89.

giveness of sins."[24] For this reason a Christian cannot unconditionally obey the church. We owe Christ unconditional obedience, but we pass judgment on the apostles, the church, and even on angels according to the standard of God's word. (For this reason, the apostles must also permit us to measure them by the standard of Christ's word even though they have greater authority than the church does.) "We obey the apostles and the church insofar as they bear the seal of that man [Christ]," that is, if they preach the gospel according to Christ's commission in Matthew 28:19 f. "If they do not bear this seal we do not pay any more attention to them than St. Paul did to Peter in Galatians 2." Paul did not listen to Peter but rebuked him because he had deviated from the gospel. Under such circumstances, an appeal to the authority of the church carries no weight.[25] The authority and thereby also the duty to obey is based on and limited by the gospel, that is, because and insofar as the church bears true witness to the gospel and thus demonstrates that it has been sent by Christ.

The Christian's obedience to the church must therefore take the form of obedience to Christ. But these two can be different. It can happen that, for the sake of obeying Christ, we must refuse to obey the church. And there is also an obedience to human authority that is disobedience against God. In a memorable statement, Luther expressly names the church among such human authorities. "Let all obedience be damned to the depths of hell which obeys the government, father, mother, or even the church in such a way that it disobeys God. At this point I know neither father, mother, friendship, government, or the Christian church."[26] The church thus occupies no special place in relationship to the other earthly authorities which are named. All are embodied in men and "to err is human." Luther emphasizes this particularly with reference to the church.[27] The church is exempt neither from

---

[24] *WA* 38, 216. "The appearance of the church is the appearance of a sinner." *WA* 40ᴵᴵ, 560; *LW* 12, 263.

[25] *WA* 38, 208.

[26] *WA* 28, 24.

[27] Luther points out that the fathers of the church have also erred as do all men. *WA* 7, 711. Luther declares that the true interpretation of Paul's doctrine of justification cannot be determined on the basis of what the recognized fathers of the church said. "Were they not equally blind? Did they not ignore Paul's clear and understandable statements?" *WA* 18, 771; *BOW*, 294. *WA* 39ᴵ, 185.

humanity nor sinfulness. Both of these factors forbid any of these
authorities from claiming unconditional authority and demanding
unconditional obedience. But doesn't the church occupy a special
position among all authorities since the Holy Spirit has been promised to it? Luther deals with this question, too—we will come to
it in the following.

Luther concretized these thoughts about the limits of the
church's authority and its capacity for error by specifically applying them to the councils." A council as such does not possess unconditional spiritual authority any more than the church and its
tradition do. The councils have constantly claimed that they as-
semble in "the name of Christ" and thus that they are not able
to err—according to Christ's promise in Matthew 18:20 ("Where
two or three are gathered together in my name . . ."). Luther
points out that the mere claim to have gathered in the name of
Christ does not yet mean that a council really has done so and
possesses Christ's authority. "If they have come together in the
name of Christ, they will show that by acting according to Christ
and not contrary to the gospel." Thus the content of the council's
decrees will determine whether a council has actually gathered in
the name of Christ. "Even though saints are present at the council, even though there are many saints, and even though angels are
there, still we do not trust personalities but only God's word, since
even saints can make mistakes. There is no excuse for saying that
a man was a saint and is therefore to be believed. Most certainly
not; Christ says just the opposite, believe him only if he speaks
correctly about me." This is not a majority decision; rather "if I
see someone who thinks correctly about Christ I ought to kiss
him, throw my arms around his neck, and let all the others
who think falsely alone." Thus the pure truth of the gospel gives
genuine authority to the men of the church who witness to Christ.
Luther asserts the same thing when he says that only those have
assembled in the Holy Spirit who bring the "analogy of faith" and
not their own thoughts."

" Cf. the *Disputation on the Authority of a Council* (1536), *WA* 39¹,
189 f. Cf. Theses 12 ff., *WA* 39¹, 185 f. In addition, Luther's criticism of the
councils in his *On the Councils and the Churches* (1539), *WA* 50, 509-624;
PE 5, 157-263.
▪ *WA* 39¹, 186.

When a council does not err but bears witness to the truth, we should not take it for granted. Such a council does not necessarily witness to the truth because it is ecumenical or because of its formal authority; when a council does so, that is an empirical and "accidental" fact (in distinction from that which can be taken for granted). Each such instance is a particular sign of Christ's grace toward his church, whether he uses an individual "saint" in the council or the voice of the entire church. As has been said, this is a particular grace and does not simply follow from the council's authority. Truth is not guaranteed by the authority of the council, but Christ's free gift of truth in a specific instance gives a council its authority.[30] The mere fact that a council "represents" the church also does not mean that it itself is the church, the true church. This is, as has been said, not something to be taken for granted and not simply given with the assembling of the council, but is a purely empirical and "accidental" fact.[31]

Luther recognizes that the Holy Spirit has been promised to the church of Christ. But this is not necessarily promised to the gathering of the bishops or the council. This means that no council can cite the promise of the Holy Spirit to prove its decrees and derive binding authority for its canons from this promise of the Holy Spirit.[32] The ecclesiastical legitimacy of such a gathering does not necessarily include its spiritual legitimacy. This latter depends completely on the apostolicity of its doctrines and resolutions.[33] We hardly need mention that Luther would say the same about the claim of the highest teaching office of the church. The First Vatican Council's dogma that the pope's teaching *ex cathedra* is infallible is subject to the same criticism as the dogma that the council is infallible.

THE HOLY SPIRIT IN THE HISTORY OF THE CHURCH

Luther's evaluation of the councils clarifies the distinction between the Roman and the evangelical understanding of how the

[30] *WA* 39¹, 185.
[31] *WA* 39¹, 186 f.
[32] *WA* 39¹, 186.
[33] *WA* 39¹, 187.

Spirit leads the church. The difference is not that the Roman Catholic Church recognizes the leadership of the Spirit and evangelical
thought does not recognize it. Luther is as sure and confident as
his opponents are that Christ remains with his church through
his Holy Spirit and that he guides and leads it into all truth. He
can say, "We, too, confess that the church does everything right."[34]
And although he definitely denies that any one individual in the
church after the time of the apostles can claim to be infallible in
matters of faith, he is equally certain that the universal church
can not err.[35] But where is the church of which all this is true
and what sort of church is it? At this point, Luther's theology
of the cross once again enters the picture. It determines his understanding of the church of Christ. It says that the true church of
Christ and historical Christendom are not identical. The true
church is hidden[36] and not to be identified with the official church
and its history—the official church has not even recognized the
true church as church. This true and hidden church is ruled by
Christ's Spirit; it cannot err, even in the smallest article of faith;
for Christ has promised to remain with it until the end of the
world. It is the "pillar and bulwark of the truth" (I Tim. 3:15).[37]
His promise is, however, not automatically valid for the entire organization of the church and for the official church. The apostolic
succession of its bishops, which the official church claims for itself, does not necessarily imply the succession of truth and of the
genuine apostolic gospel as something which can be taken for
granted. The former is not inseparably connected with the latter.[38]

A theory of church history formulated in terms of the organic development of the church cannot simply explain the decisions and
development of the empirical church by assuming that the Holy

---

[34] *WA* 7, 713.
[35] "Hence, after the Apostles no one should claim this reputation that he cannot err in the faith, except only the universal church." *WA* 39¹, 48; *LW* 34,
113. Cf. *WA* 6, 561; *LW* 36, 108. *WA* 6, 615.
[36] "The church is hidden away, the saints are out of sight." *WA* 18, 652,
BOW, 123. This is true in the Old Testament. The true people of God are
hidden and not to be identified with the Jewish religious community. On the
contrary, in the Old Testament the true church is always opposed by those who
pretend to be the church, but who persecute the true church; cf. the references
in H. Bornkamm, *Luther und das alte Testament*, pp. 176 ff.
[37] *WA* 18, 649; *BOW*, 120. Cf. *WA* 51, 511.
[38] *WA* 39¹, 191. Cf. *WA* 39ᴵᴵ, 176 f.

Spirit has led the church. Luther can understand the history and the reality of the empirical ecclesiastical organization only by assuming that it also stands under God's wrath.[*] Or to use other words, Luther, in a thesis that is sharply and polemically formulated, declares that we must always ask whether the papal and other official decrees and regulations of Rome came from the Holy Ghost or from Satan.[40] Certainly, Luther's statements about the differences and contradictions between the official and the hidden church are conditioned by his struggle with Rome, and thus, by the concrete polemical situation. We may not, however, ignore the fact that the basis and meaning of these statements extend far beyond this situation. Luther finds that this law which describes the church's nature is also present in the Old Testament, for example, at the time of Elijah and in the entire history of God's people since then. He applies this principle to the entire history of the church. It has always been true "that some were called the people and saints of God who were not, while others, who were among them as a remnant, were the people and saints of God, but were not so called."[41]

The official and the secret church are identical at the point of the gospel, sacraments, office of the keys, etc. Luther finds all these present also in the official church. This assures him that the hidden church is not a Platonic ideal. According to Luther, it has historical reality. The theology of the cross which says God's people, the community of Christ, are not identical with the historic form of the official church but are hidden under it, is complemented by the theology of the resurrection. According to the theology of the resurrection God has always preserved his church, even under a church organization such as the papacy which erred in many ways. He has done this by marvelously preserving the text of the gospel and the sacraments; and through these many have lived and died in true faith. This remains true even though they were only a weak and hidden minority within the official church. Luther repeatedly says this.[42] Thus he sees a line of truth

---

[*] *WA* 5, 43; *LW* 14, 306.
[40] *WA* 7, 713.
[41] *WA* 18, 650; *BOW*, 121. On the hiddenness of the true church, see also *WA* 40ᴵᴵᴵ, 504 f.; *LW* 13, 88 ff.
[42] *WA* 18, 651; *BOW*, 121. *WA* 39ᴵᴵ, 167 f. *WA* 40ᴵᴵᴵ, 505; *LW* 13, 89.

in the actual history of the church along which the promise that the Holy Spirit will lead the church has again and again been fulfilled.

In this sense, the true church is the object not only of "nevertheless" faith but also of historical experience; it is part of an obvious historical continuity which Luther always recognized. But this continuity of leadership through the Spirit and of the preservation of the true church is definitely not identical with and is not guaranteed by the official tradition and supposed apostolic succession of the ecclesiastical structure." In every age, God chooses his witnesses to the truth how and where he wills. Luther, as we have seen, points out that in a specific situation in the church, one single individual might have the truth; he then must constantly maintain it against the authorities of the official church. This prevents us from understanding the Holy Spirit's leadership in hierarchical or supernatural evolutionistic terms. God allows the official church to err in order to destroy the ever present danger that men trust in the church rather than in God's word alone." Then, however, God again sends the church witnesses to his truth.

" *WA* 39ᴵᴵ, 176.
" *WA* 12, 418.

25

THE SACRAMENT

GOD CONFRONTS us in his word. We receive and accept his word in faith. God deals with men within the context of this correlation between the promise of the gospel and faith. And Luther understands the sacraments within this context.[1] This determines the evangelical character of his doctrine of the sacraments. We shall demonstrate this first in terms of the sacrament's relationship to the gospel and then in terms of its relationship to faith.

THE SACRAMENT AND THE GOSPEL

For Luther, a sacrament consists in the combination of the word of promise with a sign, that is, it is a promise accompanied by a sign instituted by God and a sign accompanied by a promise.[2] This means, first, that a sign or a symbol by itself is not yet a sacrament. Luther explains that every visible act can naturally mean something and be understood as a picture or an analogy of invisible realities. This is not enough, however, to make a symbolic act into a sacrament.[3] The symbolic act must be instituted by God and combined with a promise. Sacramental character ultimately depends on the presence of a divine word of promise.[4]

---

[1] "For it is not a sacrament unless it is expressly given with the divine promise which demands faith, since apart from the word which promises and faith which receives we are not able to enter into any kind of relationship with God." *WA*, Br 1, 595; *S-J* 1, 264.

[2] "But our signs are sacraments as well as those of the fathers, and have attached to them a word of promise which requires faith and cannot be fulfilled by any other work." *WA* 6, 532; *LW* 36, 65. *WA* 6, 572; *LW* 36, 124. Luther frequently quotes Augustine's rule: "When the word is added to the element it becomes a sacrament [*Accedat verbum ad elementum et fit sacramentum*]," e.g., *WA* 30¹, 214; *BC*, 438.

[3] "We have said that in every sacrament there is a word of divine promise, to be believed by whoever receives the sign, and that the sign alone cannot be a sacrament . . . but figures or allegories are not sacraments, in the sense in which we used the term." *WA* 6, 550; *LW* 36, 92.

[4] "For to constitute a sacrament there must be above all things else a word of divine promise, by which faith may be exercised." *WA* 6, 550; *LW* 36, 92.

Where this is missing, as in marriage or confirmation, one cannot speak of a sacrament. On the other hand, however, there are realities and deeds in the Christian life such as prayer, hearing and meditating on the word, and the cross, to which God has attached a promise. But they lack the characteristic of a sign or a symbol. This is the case, for example, in the so-called sacrament of penance. Strictly speaking therefore there are only two sacraments in the church of God: baptism and the Lord's Supper. For only in these is there both a sign instituted by God and the promise of the forgiveness of sins.[5]

The decisive element in the sacrament is accordingly the word of promise.[6] The sacrament is nothing without the word.[7] It has no other content and no other effect than the word of promise does. The promise, however, is always the promise of the forgiveness of sins. Luther expressed all this very clearly in the answers to the third and fourth questions on baptism and the Lord's Supper in the *Small Catechism.*[8] Thus Luther does not recognize various sacramental graces but always only the one and the same complete grace which brings forgiveness of sins, life, and salvation.

Since the sacrament is a form in which the word comes to us, this form has its unique nature and significance beside the oral proclamation. The sacrament gives man a guarantee, a pledge, and a seal of God's promise.[9] This should strengthen faith and help it in its struggle with doubt.[10] For this purpose the sacraments were instituted. In 1520, Luther classified the Lord's Supper, including the real presence and the reception of the true body and blood of Christ, under this definition of the sacrament as a sign for faith. For the gift of Christ's body and blood is a sign which assures us of the promise of the forgiveness of sins. Later, the emphasis on

[5] *WA* 6, 571 f.; *LW* 36, 124.

[6] *WA* 40ᴵᴵ, 411; *LW* 12, 369 f.

[7] "We baptize with the word." *WA* 12, 180; *LW* 40, 21. "The majesty of the word of God reigns in baptism." *WA* 12, 182; *LW* 40, 23.

[8] "It is not the water that produces these effects, but the word of God connected with the water . . ." *WA* 30ᴵ, 310; *BC*, 349. "The eating and drinking do not in themselves produce them, but the words 'for you' and 'for the forgiveness of sins'." *WA* 30ᴵ, 317; *BC*, 352.

[9] *WA* 2, 694, 692, 686. *WA* 7, 323; *LW* 32, 15. *WA* 10ᴵᴵᴵ, 142.

[10] In addition to the passages cited in n. 9, cf.: "All the sacraments were instituted to nourish faith." *WA* 6, 529; *LW* 36, 61.

the real presence of the body and blood of Christ admittedly led him beyond this evaluation of the sacrament of the altar as a sign. (See the discussion of the doctrine of the Lord's Supper in chapter 27.) But even then, the forgiveness of sins remains the real gift of the Lord's Supper and the body and blood of Christ are still understood as a "sure pledge and sign" of it.[11]

Luther also sees the peculiar significance of the sacrament and its advantages over the spoken word in the fact that the preached word is directed to all in general, whereas the sacrament conveys the content of the word to a particular individual.[12] This element is closely connected with what we have been discussing. For the fact that the sacrament is given to me as an individual strengthens my faith that this promise is also valid for me. Preaching leaves this question unanswered, at least for the man who is under temptation. For public preaching cannot speak to the individual specifically as individual.

The sacrament is unique also because of its physical character. The sacraments are physical acts, done to our bodies, and in which we participate through our bodies. For Luther this physical character of the sacraments signifies particularly that the sign or pledge which the sacrament contains as a help for faith is available to, and appropriated by, the senses. It can be grasped with the senses and thus appropriated by the heart.[13] In addition to this, however, the fact that the sacraments are an act which affects our bodies and in which our bodies participate means that the promise which comes to us in the form of the sacrament is valid also for our bodies. Through its physical character the sacrament assures us that our bodies also are intended for eternal life and blessedness. This is

---

[11] *WA* 30¹, 225; *BC*, 449.

[12] "However, a distinction has to be made here. When I preach his death, it is an open and public proclamation, in which I am addressing myself to no one individually; whoever grasps it, grasps it. But when I distribute the sacrament, I designate if for the individual who is receiving it; I give him Christ's body and blood that he may have forgiveness of sins, obtained through his death, and preached in the Christian community. This is something more than the public sermon; for although the same thing is present in the sermon as in the sacrament, here there is the advantage that it is directed to definite individuals. In the sermon I do not point out or portray any particular person, but in the sacrament, it is given to you and to me in particular, so that the sermon comes to be your own." *WA* 19, 504 f.; *LW* 36, 348 f.

[13] "Yes, it must be external so that it can be perceived and grasped and thus brought into the heart." *WA* 30¹, 215; *BC*, 440.

true of baptism." In the doctrine of the Lord's Supper, the supernatural and physical character of the gifts of the body and blood of
Christ are added to the physical nature of the elements and of the
act which takes place through them. Luther thinks that the supernatural and physical character of the gift is a more significant
pledge of the promise that the body is also intended for eternal life than the physical nature of the elements is." There is
nothing corresponding to this in baptism.

THE SACRAMENT AND FAITH

This understanding of the sacrament as a sign of the promise
offered in the word establishes an insoluble relationship between
the sacrament and faith. For the sacramental form of the word,
like the word itself, is present for faith; it depends on faith and
contributes nothing to a man's salvation without faith. Luther
constantly emphasizes this in opposition to Roman sacramentalism.
According to the Roman doctrine, the sacrament gives grace to
everyone who does not "lock the door against it" with a mortal sin.
In opposition to this, Luther declares, "It is heresy to hold that the
sacraments . . . give grace to those who place no obstacle in the
way."" The papal bull which proclaimed Luther's excommunication condemned this sentence. Luther always maintained it. It is
the necessary correlate of the recognition that the sacrament com-
municates the divine promise of acceptance. Such an offer from
one person to another must be grasped and accepted in a personal
act of faith." As the word itself, so the sacrament is always God's

---

[14] "I have the promise that I shall be saved and have eternal life, both in
soul and body. This is the reason why these two things are done in baptism:
the body has water poured over it, though it cannot receive anything but the
water, and meanwhile the word is spoken so that the soul may grasp it. Since
the water and the word together constitute one baptism, body and soul shall
be saved and live forever: the soul through the word in which it believes, the
body because it is united with the soul and apprehends baptism in the only
way it can." *WA* 30^I, 217; *BC*, 442.
[15] Christ gives us his own body to eat "in order that with such a pledge he
may assure and promise us that our body, too, shall live forever, because it
partakes here on earth of an everlasting and living food." *WA* 23, 155; *LW*
37, 71.
[16] *WA* 1, 544; *LW* 31, 106 f. Cf. *WA* 7, 317; *LW* 32, 12.
[17] "When one deals with words and promises, one needs faith even between
men here on earth. . . . Now, as we can plainly see, God deals with us in no
other way than by his holy word and sacraments, which are like signs or seals

personal encounter with man. It is therefore true that "God's works are salutary and necessary for salvation; and they do not exclude but rather demand faith, for without faith they could not be grasped."[18]

In opposition to Roman sacramental doctrine and piety, Luther can even declare that faith can do without the sacraments, especially baptism. Referring to Mark 16:16, where Christ says only, "He who does not believe will be condemned," and not, "He who does not believe and is not baptized will be condemned," Luther concludes that Christ thus shows that faith is so necessary to the sacrament that it can even preserve a man to eternal salvation without the sacrament.[19] If we can be baptized, we should be; for we should not despise the sacrament of baptism. If baptism is, however, not available or if it is denied, we shall still be saved if we only believe the gospel. "For wherever the gospel is, there is also baptism and everything that a Christian man needs."[20] This means, then, that baptism is only a special sealing of the gospel. Its con-

---

of his words. The very first thing necessary, then, is faith in these words and signs, for when God speaks and gives signs, man must fully and wholeheartedly believe that what he says and signifies is true." *WA* 7, 321; *LW* 32, 15. Since every sacrament contains a divine word and promise in which God offers and pledges us his grace, it is truly not enough to 'put away the obstacles' as they call it, but there must be an unwavering, unshaken faith in the heart which receives the promise and sign and does not doubt that what God promises and signifies is indeed so." *WA* 7, 323; *LW* 32, 15. "Hence to seek the efficacy of the sacrament apart from the promise and without faith is to labor in vain and to find condemnation." *WA* 6, 533; *LW* 36, 67.

[18] *WA* 30ᶦ, 216; *BC*, 441.

[19] "He shows us in this word that faith is such a necessary part of the sacrament that it can save even without the sacrament." *WA* 6, 533; *LW* 36, 67. Luther makes the same assertion in *WA* 7, 321; *LW* 32, 14, where he refers to Mark 16:16 and also to Rom. 1:17 ("The righteous will live by faith"): "He does not say that the righteous shall live by the sacraments, but by his faith, for not the sacraments, but faith together with the sacraments, gives life and righteousness." Immediately after this, he refers to Romans 10:10, where Paul speaks not of the sacraments but of faith. "He does not say that it is necessary that he receive the sacraments, for you can become righteous by faith without the bodily reception of the sacraments (so long as you do not despise them)." *WA* 7, 321; *LW* 32, 15. Cf. *WA* 2, 694. In 1533, Luther still maintains this relationship between word and sacrament. "For the word can exist without the sacrament, but the sacrament cannot exist without the word. And in case of necessity, a man can be saved without the sacrament, but not without the word; this is true of those who desire baptism but die before they can receive it." *WA* 38, 231.

[20] In 1522, Luther says, "You can believe even though you are not baptized, for baptism is nothing more than an external sign which reminds us of the divine promise." The quotation in the text follows. *WA* 10ᴵᴵᴵ, 142.

tent is nothing else than the gospel itself and, accordingly, baptism is contained within the gospel. This means that the content of baptism is present and effective for faith even without the actual administration of baptism.

The Council of Trent condemned this doctrine of the sacraments, especially the thesis that faith may under some circumstances get along without them.[21] Admittedly, Roman Catholic doctrine also recognizes that a relative substitute for baptism is possible under certain circumstances. This substitute is the "baptism of desire," which consists of an act of perfect love combined with the desire to receive baptism by water.[22] Here, too, Bernard's principle that "it is not the absence but the contempt of the sacrament that damns" always remains valid. This does not, however, even come close to Luther's position. For Luther does not make the desire for baptism, but only faith in the gospel, a condition of salvation. Whoever has the gospel has everything.

Luther held this position in his controversies with the Roman Catholic doctrine. Later during his battle with the Anabaptists and the Spiritualists, he was called to open a second front in his discussion of the sacrament. In opposition to these people, other elements of the doctrine of the sacraments had to be emphasized. For just as they considered the external word of little value in comparison with the inner word, so they also despised the "outward sign" of the sacraments. They took everything they had learned from Luther about the fact that faith alone saves and used it to devaluate the sacraments. They turned the principles which Luther used to validate the sacraments against the sacraments. In opposition to this Luther now had to emphasize that God has instituted and commanded the sacraments and that he wills to do his work in us through such an "external order." He does this for our sakes so that we who are related to the world through our

---

[21] *Canons and Decrees of the Council of Trent. Sessio* VII, *De sacramentis,* canon 4 (Denzinger, No. 847).

[22] *Ibid. Sessio* VI, canon 4, (Denzinger, No. 196). Michael Schmaus, *Katholische Dogmatik* (3rd. and 4th eds.; Munich: Max Hüber, 1952) IV[1], 158, points out that "the baptism of desire" conveys justification but not an "indelible character" and the "conformity to Christ [*Christusgepräge*]."

senses may receive his word into our hearts through these same senses. "For just as the entire gospel is an external spoken proclamation" which may not be separated from faith, so one may not separate faith and the "external action" of the sacraments. The ultimate reason for this is that since God has explicitly bound and joined himself to these external acts by placing his word into them and binding it to them, he now wills to deal with us in this way. Certainly, everything depends on faith but faith must "have something to which it may cling and on which it may stand."[23]

Moreover, the Spiritualists went beyond Luther's correlation of the sacrament and faith; they completely falsified it when they denied the priority of God's action through the sacrament and made the administration of the sacraments dependent on the condition of faith. Thus baptism was changed from a sign and an assurance of God's promise to a sign of man's faith, and consequently lost its significance for salvation. Here, too, Luther abandons nothing of the indissoluble relationship of the sacraments to faith. Now, however, he emphasizes that God's activity in the sacrament precedes faith, calls a man to faith, and establishes faith. Certainly, the sacrament does not work salvation without faith; but yet it is valid within itself without reference to a man's atti-

---

[23] "It is of the greatest importance that we regard baptism as excellent, glorious, and exalted. It is the chief cause of our contentions and battles because the world now is full of sects who proclaim that baptism is an external thing and external things are of no use. But no matter how external it may be, here stand God's word and command which have instituted, established, and confirmed baptism. What God institutes and commands cannot be useless. It is a most precious thing even though to all appearances it may not be worth a straw." *WA* 30¹, 212; *BC*, 437. "Our know-it-alls, the new spirits, assert that faith alone saves, and that works and external things can contribute nothing to this end. We answer: It is true, nothing that is in us does it but faith, as we shall hear later on. But these leaders of the blind are unwilling to see that faith must have something to believe—something to which it may cling and upon which it may stand. Thus faith clings to the water and believes it to be baptism in which there is sheer salvation and life, not through the water . . . but through its corporation with God's word and ordinance and the joining of his name to it. . . . Now, these people are so foolish as to separate faith from the object to which faith is attached and bound on the ground that the object is something external. Yes, it must be external so that it can be perceived and grasped by the senses and thus brought into the heart, just as the entire gospel is an external, oral proclamation; in short, whatever God affects in us he does through such external ordinances. No matter where he speaks—indeed, no matter for what purpose or by what means he speaks—their faith must hold." *WA* 30¹, 215; *BC*, 440, 28 ff.

tude toward it or to whether he rightly uses or misuses God's gift.[34] Faith does not make the sacrament but receives it. The sacrament is thus given to man before faith, as an act of God to which a man may confess himself in faith. Luther particularly explicated this in his arguments in favor of infant baptism against the Anabaptists.

In this discussion the emphasis is placed on a different point, than in the discussion of the Roman doctrine. But Luther's basic understanding of the sacraments was not changed in the process.

---

[34] "The sacrament is not vitiated if someone approaches it with an evil purpose." *WA* 30^I, 219; *BC*, 443. [*BC* interprets "sacrament" as referring to the sacrament of the altar.—Trans.] "Therefore, only presumptuous and stupid persons draw the conclusion that where there is no true faith there also can be no true baptism. Likewise, I might argue, 'If I had no faith, then Christ is nothing.' . . . Is it correct to conclude that when anybody does not do what he should, the thing that he misuses has no existence or no value?" *WA* 30^I, 218; *BC*, 444.

26

BAPTISM

BAPTISM AND THE CHRISTIAN LIFE

B APTIZING with water is, at first glance, a human act. Men do not, however, baptize in their own name but in God's name. And men have not invented and discovered baptism; rather it is instituted and commanded by God, and it is God himself who acts in it: "To be baptized in God's name is to be baptized not by men but by God himself. Although it is performed by man's hands, it is nevertheless truly God's own work."[1] Through its institution, baptism is "water used according to God's command and connected with God's word."[2] God's word, however, "contains and conveys all the fullness of God."[3] This word of God, that is, the command to baptize, and the promise connected with baptism (in his *Small Catechism* Luther refers to Matthew 28:19 and Mark 16:16), gives baptism its power and makes it "a washing of regeneration" according to Titus 3.[4]

This means, however, that baptism conveys all of salvation. The assertion of the *Small Catechism* that it "effects forgiveness of sins, delivers from death and the devil, and grants eternal salvation to all who believe"[5] is constantly repeated in similar form by Luther. Through baptism, "I am promised that I shall be saved and have eternal life, both in body and in soul." Baptism does not give a particular grace, not only a part of salvation, but simply the entire grace of God, "the entire Christ and the Holy Spirit with his gifts."[6] The total gift of baptism is meaningful throughout the

---

[1] *WA* 30¹, 212 f.; *BC*, 437. The basic sources for this chapter are *The Holy and Blessed Sacrament of Baptism* (1519), *WA* 2, 727-737; *LW* 35, 29-43, and *The Babylonian Captivity of the Church* (1520), *WA* 6, 497-573; *LW* 36, 11-126, and the catechisms. *WA* 30¹, 308-313 and 212-222; *BC*, 348 f. and 436-446.

[2] *WA* 30¹, 308; *BC*, 348.

[3] *WA* 30¹, 214; *BC*, 438.

[4] *WA* 30¹, 215; *BC*, 440.

[5] *WA* 30¹, 310; *BC*, 348 f.

[6] *WA* 30¹, 217; *BC*, 442.

Christian's life and remains constantly valid until he enters into eternity. He lives from no other grace than from that promised and conveyed to him through baptism, and he never needs new grace. That repentance which is proper when we have fallen away from our baptism into sin is not a new means of grace, but only a return to our baptism and to faith together with the promise and the power which are given to us through it. "For the truth of the promise once made to us remains unchanged; it waits to receive us with open arms when we repent."[7] Thus the Christian throughout his entire life must constantly grasp and reappropriate that which baptism has promised to him once for all. Once for all it makes us "God's own."[8] Thus baptism is a unique act, but at the same time it is a constantly present and meaningful reality in the Christian life.

Luther demonstrates in terms of Romans 6 the way in which baptism is constantly present and meaningful throughout our life. Like Paul, he begins his discussion with the external act of baptism, that is, the act of immersing and once again bringing up the man who is baptized. The meaning of this is that the old man is put to death and the new man is raised from the dead.[9] This has taken place in a "sacramental" way, permanently in the fact of baptism; in the reality of life, however, it must be constantly and repeatedly re-enacted in faith.[10] The "Christian life is nothing else than a daily baptism, once begun and constantly lived in."[11] The "significance" of the external act of baptism must thus always be increasingly realized; this is what the *Small Catechism* means when

---

[7] *WA* 2, 733; *LW* 35, 38. *WA* 6, 528; *LW* 36, 59. "Therefore, when we rise from our sins or repent, we are merely returning to the power and the faith of baptism from which we fell, and finding our way back to the promise then made to us, which we deserted when we sinned." (The quotation in the text follows.) *WA* 6, 528; *LW* 36, 59. Cf. *WA* 6, 535; *LW* 36, 69. "Therefore baptism remains forever. Even though we fall from it and sin, nevertheless we always have access to it so that we may again subdue the old man." *WA* 30¹, 221; *BC*, 445 f. The quotation is from *BC*, 446.

[8] *WA* 30¹, 222; *BC*, 446.

[9] *WA* 6, 534; *LW* 36, 67 f. *WA* 30¹, 220; *BC*, 444 f. *WA* 30¹, 312; *BC*, 349.

[10] *WA* 2, 728, 730; *LW* 35, 30 f. "Thus, you have been once baptized in this sacrament, but you need continually to be baptized by faith, continually to die and continually to live." *WA* 6, 535; *LW* 36, 69.

[11] *WA* 30¹, 220; *BC*, 445.

it says that baptizing with water signifies "that the old Adam in us together with all sins and evil lusts, should by daily sorrow and repentance be put to death, and be drowned, and that the new man should come forth daily and rise up, cleansed and righteous to live forever in God's presence." All the sanctification of the Christian is thus nothing else than a completion of baptism. "We must always be baptized more and more until we fulfill the sign of baptism [that is, the symbol of dying and rising again which is found in the fact of baptism] perfectly at the last day."[12] Or with other words, we might say that the death of our physical bodies fulfills the meaning included in baptism. The sooner we die, the sooner the meaning of baptism becomes an actuality. The more we must suffer, the more properly we conform to our baptism. Baptism and death, baptism and suffering, baptism and martyrdom, belong together.[13]

Throughout our lives, God helps us to arrive at the fulfilment of baptism through the dying of the old man and the resurrection of the new man. In the act of baptism, he makes a new covenant with us and gives us the assurance that he will forgive us our sins throughout our entire life and at the same time that he will put our sins to death—this is how Luther describes it in his treatise on *The Holy and Blessed Sacrament of Baptism of 1519.*[14] Through baptism, God begins to carry this out; and throughout our life he uses the tasks which our position and calling bring to us and all sorts of suffering to train us to become free of sin and strong in faith.[15] He trains us for that death in which sin finally dies.[16] In the act of baptism, however, a man obligates himself to realize this meaning of baptism: "To submit himself into the sacrament of baptism, to participate in God's gracious work in him by fighting against sin and killing it until he himself dies."[17] Thus the

---

[12] *WA* 30[1], 312; *BC*, 349.

[13] "You will understand, therefore, that whatever we do in this life which mortifies the flesh or quickens the spirit has to do with our baptism. The sooner we depart this life, the more speedily we fulfill our baptism; and the more cruelly we suffer, the more successfully do we conform to our baptism." *WA* 6, 535; *LW* 36, 69.

[14] Cf. n. 1.

[15] *WA* 8, 11 f.; *LW* 13, 9, 11.

[16] *WA* 2, 729 ff.; *LW* 35, 32 f.

[17] *WA* 2, 730 f.; *LW* 35, 33 ff.

entire Christian life is lived in the power and under the obligation of baptism.

Luther thus places baptism in the center of the Christian life.
His understanding of baptism exactly expresses his doctrine of justification. Through the sacrament of baptism we are "sacramen-
tally" or "because of the sacrament," made completely pure and
innocent in God's gracious judgment, that is, we are "children of
grace and justified persons."[18] God now wills to take us, who remain sinners throughout our lives, and actually make us what we
are in his gracious judgment. The same word of judgment which
makes us innocent also puts us, that is, our old man increasingly
to death so that we may become pure.[19] In baptism we are immediately given complete forgiveness of sins and purity in God's
judgment. The man who is baptized may, and should, at every
moment of his life cling to the totality of this in faith. At the
same time, however, this becomes the basis of a movement of our
lives which comes from God: the process by which God is continually at work throughout our entire lives establishing actual
newness and purity in us. Baptism is a sign to us; it assures us
of God's covenant with us by which he makes us pure through
forgiveness and now also wills to purify our nature. Both of these
elements are inseparably joined together in his doctrine of baptism
just as they are in his doctrine of justification. His doctrine of baptism is basically nothing else than his doctrine of justification in
concrete form.

In his understanding of baptism Luther refers, as we have seen,
to Paul and especially to Romans 6. It is, however, worth noting
that Luther in both the *Small* and *Large Catechisms* first begins
to speak of the meaning of baptism as a dying and being raised
again, at the end of his discussion. In the *Small Catechism* he
mentions it first in connection with his fourth question. And only
then does he make the connection to the external act of baptism.

---

[18] *WA* 2, 728; *LW* 35, 30.

[19] "So you understand how in baptism a person becomes guiltless, pure, and
sinless, while at the same time continuing full of evil inclinations. He can be
called pure only in the sense that he has started to become pure and has a sign
and covenant of this purity and is ever to become more pure. . . . A person is
thus pure by the gracious imputation of God, rather than by virtue of his own
nature." *WA* 2, 732; *LW* 35, 35 f. Cf. *WA* 8, 93, 96; *LW* 32, 208 f., 213.

It is thus possible for Luther to describe the basic nature of baptism without reference to Romans 6 and without speaking of death and resurrection.

This makes us aware of a basic difference between Luther's doctrine and Paul's. For Paul, a dying and also a being raised again have already taken place in and with baptism (cf. Col. 2:12 f.). Admittedly, a man must constantly reaffirm this by putting his old man to death and seeking what is above (Col. 3:5); such imperatives are based upon the indicatives "you have died," and "you are raised with Christ" (Col. 3:3). The old man has been put to death in baptism and the new man has been raised. As far as I can see, there are no statements corresponding to this in Luther. His use of Romans 6:3 ff. in the *Small Catechism* is a characteristic example. The symbolic act in baptism, according to Luther, does not signify something which has taken place once in the past but something which must continually take place. The old man "should" be drowned, etc. Luther thus applies Paul's statement about the meaning of baptism not to the initial act of baptism but to the lifelong realization of the meaning of baptism.[20] We could say (and the position of Romans 6 in the *Small Catechism* clearly shows this) that Romans 6 with its theology of baptism in terms of death and resurrection belongs, as far as Luther is concerned, not in the dogmatic treatment of baptism but in the discussion of its significance for ethics. This explains its position at the close of his explanation.

I can find no single passage in Luther corresponding to Paul's statement that we have died with Christ in baptism. He does say that the man who comes out of baptism is pure and innocent;[21] but he never says that he is dead. He always says that God has promised this dying in baptism and that since it has begun, it must continue throughout life until completed in death and resurrection. Paul uses present perfects (cf. the aorists in Romans 6 and Colossians 3) whereas Luther uses a progressive present [*praesens perpetuum*] which is certainly signified by the single act of baptism and even begins with it, but which has not yet taken place as a totality. Luther does indeed say that baptism is nothing else than a dying into eternal life;[22] the baptismal act

---

[20] Luther describes the power and work of baptism as "the slaying of the old Adam" and the "resurrection of the new man." However, he says nothing of a dying and resurrection in the act of baptism itself but immediately speaks of the fact that "both of these actions must continue in us our whole life long." *WA* 30^1, 220; *BC*, 445.

[21] *WA* 2, 730; *LW* 35, 32.

[22] *WA*, Br 5, 452.

itself does not bring about this death, but: "Whoever is baptized is condemned to death." The deviation from Paul is particularly clear when Luther explicitly interprets the apostle's statements. Thus in his *Third Disputation against the Antinominans* of 1539 he occasionally says that "to be dead and die in relationship to sin are Paul's expression for fighting with sin and not allowing it to rule in us."[*] We might say that while Paul in Romans 6 bases the twelfth verse on the eleventh, Luther equates vs. 11 ("that you have died to sin") with vs. 12 and thus interprets the fact of having died to sin in terms of the on-going will to struggle with sin. In *The Babylonian Captivity of the Church*, Luther does indeed say with Paul that the sinner dies and rises through baptism with Christ; but here again, he immediately makes the transition to the thought that baptism is a matter of all of life.[*] There can be no question that Luther places the emphasis at a different point than Paul does.

The distinction between Paul and Luther on this point has its roots in the basic distinction between their two theologies and their understandings of Christian existence. The apostle thinks in terms of the missionary situation; Luther is concerned with the situation within the Christian church.[*] This means: Paul speaks of baptism as baptism of conversion and as the great point of distinction which clearly divides what a man once was from what he now is. Luther is concerned with infant baptism in which the great decision and the clearly marked boundary line in one's life are missing. Instead of that, Luther must deal with the problem of that sin which remains in the life of the baptized. For this reason, Paul places the emphasis on what has taken place in baptism while Luther places it on the fact that baptism must be realized throughout our lives. We must then ask whether this does not result in a difference in the doctrine of the sacraments as such. Luther once said, "When we begin to believe we also begin to die to this world and to live to God in the life to come."[*] Dying with Christ is thus not identified with the act of baptism as such but with faith. Faith actualizes that which the act of baptism signifies: dying and rising with Christ.

In all of this, however, the question remains whether or not Paul connected dying and rising with Christ to baptism in all his theological thought as he did in Romans 6. In Galatians 2:19 and

[*] *WA* 39[I], 551.
[*] *WA* 6, 534; *LW* 36, 68 f.
[*] Cf. my *Paulus und Luther über den Menschen* (3rd ed.; Gütersloh: Bertelsmann, 1958), pp. 80 ff.
[*] *WA* 6, 534; *LW* 36, 68.

II Corinthians 5:14, he speaks of a dying with Christ without any reference to baptism. But even if we feel that this is important, the decisive fact remains: for Paul dying with Christ is something that has already happened (without denying that it must be constantly repeated in life) whereas Luther understands it solely as a matter of the entire life and as a task to be fulfilled.

INFANT BAPTISM

In establishing the right of infant baptism against the Anabaptists, Luther places the common Christian tradition in the foreground of the discussion.[27] To use the terms of the early Lutheran church we could call it the "catholic" (universal) reality of infant baptism. That is certainly not Luther's last word on the subject, but it is certainly his first.

Infant baptism has been "practiced since the beginning of the church," and it comes to us "from the apostles and has been preserved ever since their time." It is therefore "catholic" in terms of both time and space. It was practiced in all centuries and is "accepted among all Christians in the whole world." Through this uninterrupted acceptance of the validity of infant baptism in all centuries and in all places, God has already given it his approval. Luther here argues on the basis of his theology of history: God will not permit something wrong to continue so long from the beginning to the present day. He certainly does not cause all Christians in the world to accept something wrong. God has permitted all the heresies which arose much later than infant baptism to perish. But he has always and everywhere preserved infant baptism; such a miracle of God shows that infant baptism must be right. Such an argument from the theology of history is, however, only conditionally valid: being valid only if the institution under discussion is not contrary to Scripture. If it meets this condition, however, the argument is valid. The preservation of infant baptism through all centuries and all parts of the church is a miracle and the work of God. "For where we see the work of God, we should yield and

---

[27] The basic sources are: The sermon on Matthew 8:1 ff. from the Lenten sermons in *WA* 17[II], especially 78 ff. *Concerning Rebaptism, WA* 26, 144-174; *LW* 40, 229-262. The sermons on baptism preached in 1528, *WA* 27, 32 ff. and 49 ff.; and the *Large Catechism, WA* 30[I], 218 ff.; *BC*, 442-444.

believe in the same way as when we hear his word, unless the plain Scripture tells us otherwise."[28] God has in every period of the church's history unmistakably shown his approval of infant baptism in still another way; he has obviously given his Holy Spirit to many who were baptized as infants and sanctified them right down to the present day. At this point Luther does not shy away from referring to clear experience. He evidently feels that the presence of the Holy Spirit in a man cannot be mistaken. The Spirit is recognized by his gifts in teaching and in life. God's Spirit is at work wherever men are able to interpret Scripture and to recognize Christ, and wherever "great things are done in the church" by men. Luther names St. Bernard, Gerson, John Huss, as examples. However, he also cites contemporary examples. "Even today there are many whose doctrine and life attest they have the Holy Spirit. Similarly by God's good grace, we have been given the power to interpret the Scriptures and to know Christ—which is impossible without the Holy Spirit."[29] It also must be said that if infant baptism were false and contrary to God's will, then there would have been no true baptism and thus also no church for more than a thousand years. For without baptism there is no church. This necessary conclusion, however, is an irreconcilable contradiction of the article of the creed, "I believe . . . one holy Christian church" and of this faith's certainly that the church cannot perish until the end of the world. If the church continues to exist in spite of this, then infant baptism must also be proper. For the church has the true gospel and the sacraments. If the church's clearly proved and uninterrupted practice of infant baptism were false, then it would have erred in a decisive point and could no longer be the "holy" church. In brief, there would then have been no true church for more than a thousand years—something which is impossible to reconcile with our confession of faith.[30]

However, as we have already said, Luther does not intend such arguments to provide an unconditional and ultimately valid foundation for his position. The traditions of both the ancient and the

---

[28] *WA* 26, 155, 167 f.; *LW* 40, 241, 255 f. Cf. *WA* 27, 52.
[29] *WA* 30ᴵ, 218; *BC*, 442. Cf. *WA* 26, 168; *LW* 40, 256.
[30] *WA* 26, 168; *LW* 40, 256. Cf. *WA* 27, 52. *WA* 30ᴵ, 218; *BC*, 442 f.

universal church have only limited authority: "We should not discard or alter what cannot be discarded or altered on clear scriptural authority. God is wonderful in his works. What he does not will, he clearly witnesses to in Scripture. What is not so witnessed to there, we can accept as his work. We are guiltless and he will not mislead us."[81] Thus the unanimous witness of tradition points beyond itself to the testimony of Scripture. The decision about infant baptism must be made on the basis of Scripture. What kind of scriptural proof is necessary? The above statement by Luther answers that question. Luther is not a puritanical biblicist. He does not demand that the validity of every doctrine and practice be established by an explicit command of Scripture. The church can, in the course of its history, be granted knowledge which is not expressed in Scripture. Everything depends, however, on the fact that such knowledge is not contradicted by Scripture but is in accordance and in harmony with Scripture. This does not mean that Luther constructed this theory to fit his needs—as though his inability to produce scriptural proof in the strict sense of the term, for infant baptism forced him to revise his scriptural principle so that it made only the more moderate demand that infant baptism not be contrary to Scripture. Rather, Luther required that everything taught and done in the church, and not merely infant baptism, be compatible with Scripture.

Luther freely admitted that infant baptism is neither explicitly commanded or explicitly mentioned in Scripture. There are no "specific passages" referring to infant baptism.[82] The direct witness of Scripture is by itself not strong enough to provide an adequate basis for beginning infant baptism were it not already practiced. On the other hand, however, the witness of Scripture is so clear and strong "that at the present time no one may with a good conscience reject or discontinue infant baptism which has been practiced for so long a time"—especially since God has obviously preserved it. This is the significance of Luther's individual arguments in support of infant baptism. (1) According to the gospel of the children in Matthew 19, Mark 10, and Luke 18, Christ

---

[81] *WA* 26, 167; *LW* 40, 255.
[82] *WA* 26, 167, 169; *LW* 40, 255, 258.

allows the little children to come to him and says that the kingdom of God belongs to them. "Who can bypass this test? Who
dares act contrary to it by forbidding little children to come to
baptism or by not believing that Christ blesses them when they
come?"[33] In addition to this blessing of the children, Luther also
refers to the saying about children in Matthew 18:10. (2) Luther also cites the command to baptize. Admittedly, children are
not expressly named in that command. But then neither is any
other age group or sex designated. The command to baptize simply
refers to "all nations" in general and "excludes none." The children
are also included. Accordingly, the Acts of the Apostles and the
letters of Paul frequently report the baptism of entire "houses."
Obviously "they baptized all who were in the houses." "Children,
however, are certainly a substantial part of the household." Since
the apostles, in speaking of other matters in their letters, so often
emphasize that there is no respect or difference of persons among
Christians, they would certainly have explicitly mentioned it if
they had received such a distinction in matters related to baptism.[34]
The undifferentiated universality of the command to baptize, which
apparently corresponded to the apostolic practice of baptism, is
only an expression of the universalism of the gospel. And this is
the decisive point for Luther.[35] Luther ultimately bases the right
and necessity of infant baptism on the basic meaning of the gospel. Other scriptural passages such as I John 2:12 or Luke 1:41
(John the Baptist already believed in his mother's womb.) are still
quoted but all take a secondary position in relationship to this. For
the most part, Luther knew that the opponents of infant baptism
would not accept scriptural proof as refuting their individual arguments. Nor was that his purpose. It is enough to show that the
Scripture is not opposed to infant baptism, that it does not expressly exclude children from baptism, and that it does not command that only adults be baptized.

The scriptural witnesses cited show in any case that infant baptism is not opposed to but according to Scripture. This means that
the Anabaptists have no solid foundation for their attack on in-

---

[33] *WA* 17[II], 83, 88. Cf. *WA* 26, 157, 169; *LW* 40, 243, 257.
[34] *WA* 26, 157-158; *LW* 40, 243-245.
[35] *WA* 26, 169; *LW* 40, 252.

fant baptism. It is clear that the biblical material gives no certain answer. That in itself, however, means that they acted incorrectly. "For in divine matters one should act on certain and not on dubious grounds."[36] The Anabaptists are the innovators. And it is they and not the adherents of infant baptism who have the duty of proving their position. They need a clear scriptural basis for their rejection of infant baptism. For those who maintain infant baptism, it is enough that Scripture is not against infant baptism, but that infant baptism is compatible with Scripture. They have the consensus of the church of all times on their side. And even more, they know that God has with this agreement bound them to continue the practice as long as Scripture does not explicitly speak against it.

As we review the basis which Luther asserted for infant baptism, we must emphasize that the Reformer demonstrated the right of infant baptism in terms of the basic thoughts of his theology, based on his understanding of the gospel and his high evaluation of the universal tradition of the church. He uses no concepts in discussing baptism which he does not use elsewhere in considering other questions and other decisions. For example, he also asserted the binding character of the consensus of the entire church, insofar as it cannot be attacked on the basis of Scripture, in defending the doctrine of the Lord's Supper against a spiritualistic interpretation.[37]

---

[36] *WA* 26, 159, 169; *LW* 40, 246, 252.

[37] *WA* 30ᴵᴵᴵ, 552. Karl Barth expresses the opinion that the real and decisive basis for infant baptism in the minds of its proponents is that they do not wish to abandon the practical identification of membership in the nation with membership in the church. *The Teaching of the Church Regarding Baptism*, trans. Ernest A. Payne (London: S.C.M., 1948), pp. 52-55. That is most certainly not true of Luther. Otherwise we would have to expect that Luther's use of the concept of a gathering of those who seriously wanted to be Christians, in his preface to *The German Mass* of 1526, would have led him to consider the possibility of changing the church's practice of infant baptism. However, he says nothing of that. And although he proposes limitation of membership to those who wish to affiliate voluntarily with the church, the very serious exercise of church discipline according to Matthew 18, and an extensive reduction of the church's liturgy, he does not even begin to draw the conclusion that baptism must now be based on a previous conscious decision and confession of the person to be baptized. He merely says: "Here one could set up a brief and neat order for baptism and the sacrament." *WA* 19, 75; *LW* 53, 64. However, he does not in any way reject infant baptism. He has no "extraneous" reasons for doing this, as Barth would imply. Everything depends upon the witness of the church's tradition and of Scripture.

THE PROBLEM OF INFANT BAPTISM:
BAPTISM AND FAITH

One of Luther's decisive Reformation theses asserts that the
sacraments save only when they are received in faith (cf. p. 348).
Naturally, this is true also of baptism. In Mark 16 Christ says,
"He who believes and is baptized will be saved."[38] "He puts faith
before baptism; for where faith is not present, baptism does no
good." This is why Christ immediately adds, "He who does not
believe will be condemned" even though he is baptized, for it is
not baptism, but faith in baptism, that saves."[39] Even in arguing
with the Spiritualists and the Baptists about the value of the baptismal act which has been instituted by Christ, Luther does not
in any way deny that faith is necessary for baptism.[40] This, however, creates a problem for infant baptism. Do children below the
age of reason have faith when they are baptized?

Luther's thoughts about this are not always constant but are in
a process of development. At first (and as late as 1521) Luther
declares that children are baptized on the basis of the faith and
the confession of the sponsors, who in the baptismal liturgy are
asked to answer in the place of the child being baptized whether
he believes.[41] However, in 1522, Luther gave up this idea in order to preserve the insight that we are saved not through someone else's faith but only through our own. "Baptism helps no
one and is to be administered to no one unless he believes for
himself. No one who does not personally believe is to be baptized. . . . Faith must be present either before or in baptism itself,
otherwise the child is not freed from the devil and his sins."[42]
This is nothing more than the consistent application of the basic

---

[38] *WA* 6, 533; *LW* 36, 67.

[39] *WA* 7, 321; *LW* 32, 14.

[40] *WA* 26, 154; *LW* 40, 240. Cf. *WA* 30ᴵ, 216; *BC*, 440 f.

[41] *WA* 7, 321; *LW* 32, 14.

[42] *WA* 17ᴵᴵ, 19 ff., 81. Luther expresses this as early as his sermon of
September 7, 1522. *WA* 10ᴵᴵᴵ, 306 ff. Speaking of children at the time of
baptism, he says: "When we baptize, then we see the faith of children; when
the children stand there completely naked in body and soul, they are without
faith and without works. Now here comes the Christian church and prays that
God would pour faith into them. The intention is not that our faith or our
works should help the child, but that the child should receive his own faith."
WA 10ᴵᴵᴵ, 310.

Reformation insight into the indissoluble connection between the sacraments and faith.

As a result, Luther begins to teach infant faith: Children below the age of reason believe when they are baptized. Before tracing the specific details of Luther's position, we must emphasize that he never bases the validity of infant baptism on the presence of the child's faith. Rather, he does just the opposite: Insofar as he maintains that children have faith, he bases his assertion on the institution and therewith the validity of infant baptism. Children are to be baptized not because it can be proved they believe, but because infant baptism is scriptural and the will of God. For this reason, Luther brings no empirical proof for the faith of infants. And he most sharply rejects the attempt to determine whether or not an adult believes, particularly in the form in which it was practiced by the Baptists. He is certain that children believe because infant baptism is right and valid—and for no other reason. Thus Luther does not even consider demonstrating that such faith really existed but defends the possible existence against the polemical attacks of the Baptists.

We shall now trace the detailed development of Luther's doctrine. Our source for the year 1525 is his Lenten sermon on Matthew 8:1 ff.[44] He rejects the Roman position that children are baptized on the faith of the church. He also clearly rejects the opinion of the Waldensians, who baptized children in view of the faith they would have in the future.[45] Children must believe for themselves and must believe at the time of baptism. The fact that they do so is not to be doubted. Since Christ both promises the kingdom of heaven to children and says, "He who does not believe will be condemned," who can maintain that the children he receives into his kingdom do not believe?[46] If the church seriously practices infant baptism as a means of salvation, it thereby necessarily confesses that children can believe. Otherwise baptism of infants would not save and be "a game and a blasphemy."[47] How does faith come into existence in children? God works it "through

---

[44] *WA* 17ᴵᴵ, 78 ff.
[45] *WA* 17ᴵᴵ, 79, 81.
[46] *WA* 17ᴵᴵ, 83.
[47] *WA* 17ᴵᴵ, 82.

the intercession of the sponsors who bring the child to be baptized in the faith of the Christian church. This is the power of someone else's faith. Such faith cannot save the child but through its intercession and help the child may receive his own faith from God; and this faith will save him."[47] "Children are not baptized because of the faith of sponsors or of the church; rather the faith of sponsors and of the church gains their own faith for them and it is in this faith that they are baptized and believe for themselves."[48]

The Baptists object that children below the age of reason cannot believe because they do not understand and have no reason. Luther answers that just the opposite is true. Reason always "most strongly opposes faith and God's word." And reason always stands in the way of faith. Since children do not have reason "they are more fitted for faith than older and more rational people who always trip over their reason and do not wish to push their swelled heads through the narrow gate."[49] Is it true that little children do not hear the word? Luther answers, "Even though they do not hear the word through which faith comes in the same way that older people do, they still hear it as little children do. The older people grasp it with their ears and their reason but often without faith; children, however, hear it through their ears without reason and with faith. And the less reason one has, the closer faith is."[50] Children who are brought to be baptized hear the word because the baptism they experience is in itself nothing else than the gospel. And they hear this gospel in a very powerful way "because Christ, who has commanded that they be brought, takes them into his arms."[51]

We have many objections to raise against these theses of Luther. Luther uses the concept "reason" in a different sense than the opponents intended it. Those who object to infant baptism intend to say that faith is a personal act. Luther does not understand reason in this formal sense but immediately interprets it in

---

[47] *WA* 17[II], 82.
[48] *WA* 17[II], 83.
[49] *WA* 17[II], 84 f.
[50] *WA* 17[II], 87.
[51] *WA* 17[II], 87.

terms of its content as the summary of our sinful, rebellious, and unbelieving thoughts. In this way, Luther places faith and reason in simple opposition to each other. However, this does not yet answer the objection that the infant lacks that kind of "reason" which is necessary in order to believe, that is, the personal character of being in which I submit to God's grace. Certainly I do not do this "by my own reason," but I do it with my reason. It is also true, however, that we do not need to argue this point with Luther. For he himself restricts his concept of infant faith by declaring: We, with a good conscience, baptize adults who come to be baptized, simply because they come, even though we do not know whether they have genuine faith; so we may and should also baptize children, because Jesus has commanded that they be brought. The matter of their faith may be placed into the hands of him who has commanded that they be brought. The faith of those who do not come by themselves but are brought is to be put in the hands of him who has commanded that they be brought; and they are to be baptized because he has commanded it. We can only say, "Lord, you have brought them here and commanded that they be baptized. You will certainly take responsibility for them. I depend on your doing also."[63] With these statements Luther does not abandon his thoughts about infant baptism. The context of the last quoted passage clearly indicates this. But neither does Luther assert the possibility and the presence of infant faith as though it were ultimately decisive for our attitude toward infant baptism. What is decisive is that the Lord receives children and commands that they be brought to him. We baptize them on the basis of his will and of his word. Whatever the character of their faith may be, we leave it to him. The situation is no different when we baptize adults. Certainly the adult brings himself to baptism. But is this more reason for baptizing joyfully and with a good conscience than that the Lord commands that children be brought? For all his emphasis on infant faith, Luther does not depend on it but only on Jesus Christ. We do not have to take responsibility for baptizing on the basis of our uncertain, and controversial, certainty about the faith of children or of adults; he

[63] *WA* 17ᴵᴵ, 85 f.

who commands that children be brought to him takes the responsibility.

In 1528 Luther takes another step in this direction. He continues to presuppose infant faith. Scripture demonstrates that children can believe; for example, John the Baptist who believed while in the womb of his mother "when Christ came and spoke through the mouth of his mother."[53] The Baptists' assertion that children cannot believe is contrary to Scripture.[54] No one can prove that children below the age of reason cannot believe.[55] Nor can anyone prove with scriptural passages that infant faith is present. We are certain, however, that children can believe when they are baptized because no one else than Jesus Christ himself speaks to them and deals with them in baptism. They are with him, and his word and work passes over them. And that must have results![56] It is Christ himself who works faith in children through his speaking and acting. The fact, or at least the possibility, of infant faith is established. The "how" is to be left in the hands of God[57]—for we do not know what it is. In any case, however—and Luther clearly expresses this—infant baptism is not based on the certainty that the baptized person believes and thus is not based on infant faith. "For even if I were not sure that they believed, yet from my conscience's sake I would have to let them be baptized," because infant baptism comes from the apostles. If I should neglect and refuse to baptize children I would become responsible for their being lost since we certainly believe that baptism saves![58] Indeed, and here Luther goes a step further, baptism certainly should be received in faith. Baptism is, however, valid as an act of God in and by itself. Anyone who does not believe or falls away from faith misuses baptism—but such misuse does not invalidate baptism. Everything is in order if the baptized person sooner or later comes to or returns to faith.[59] "If faith appears, ten years after baptism, what is the need of a second baptism, since bap-

[53] *WA* 26, 159; *LW* 40, 245.
[54] *WA* 26, 156; *LW* 40, 242.
[55] *WA* 26, 156; *LW* 40, 241 f.
[56] *WA* 26, 156, 159; *LW* 40, 243, 246.
[57] *WA* 26, 157, 169; *LW* 40, 243, 259.
[58] *WA* 26, 166; *LW* 40, 254.
[59] *WA* 26, 159; *LW* 40, 246.

tism is now completed and everything is in order? For now he believes, as baptism requires."[60] "When faith then comes, baptism is complete." Just as the validity and power of baptism are not changed "even if the Christian falls from faith or sins a thousand times a year" and thus becomes a baptized person without faith, "why should not the first baptism be adequate and proper if a person truly becomes a believing Christian?"[61] Luther thus considers that it is possible for a Christian to think of infant baptism as a baptism without faith and that it is only later grasped in faith.

In the *Large Catechism* of 1529 Luther limits infant faith even more. Here too he still maintains that children believe.[62] In complete opposition to the statements of 1525, Luther now says that it is not decisive for baptism whether the baptized person believes or does not believe; that does not make baptism invalid but everything depends on God's word and commandment. "When the word accompanies the water, baptism is valid, even though faith be lacking. For my faith does not constitute baptism but receives it."[63] Baptism must be grasped in faith. Whoever does not believe misuses it. But that does not change the fact that baptism itself "always remains proper and essentially perfect." It is not baptism that needs to be changed but we ourselves. "If you have not believed, believe now." Baptism summons me to faith, and its reality and validity does not depend on my faith. This is true also of adult baptism. Those who come to baptism in faith cannot rest on the fact that they believe "but I rest on the fact that it is your word and commandment." The same is true also of infant baptism. "We bring the child to be baptized because we think and hope that it will believe, and we pray that God will give it faith; we do not baptize it because of this, however, but only because God has commanded it."[64]

This is Luther's final position. In all his later statements on the subject he maintains that little children receive the Holy Spirit

---

[60] *WA* 26, 160; *LW* 40, 246.
[61] *WA* 26, 160 f.; *LW* 40, 246, 248.
[62] *WA* 30¹, 219; *BC*, 443 f., 55 ff.
[63] *WA* 30¹, 218, 220; *BC*, 443 f. and 56 f. *WA* 30¹, 220; *BC*, 444.
[64] *WA* 30¹, 219; *BC*, 443 f. and 55 f.

when they are baptized and believe with their own faith." But he also repeats the other assertion that the propriety and the validity of infant baptism does not depend on their faith and that infant baptism is thus proper even though the children should not be-lieve (which is certainly not the case)."

LUTHER'S REJECTION OF THE ANABAPTISTS

Luther not only defended the validity of infant baptism against the attacks of the Anabaptists; he also attacked their baptismal practice and showed it to be impossible on the basis of the gos-pel." Luther's rejection of the Anabaptists is thus not merely the self-evident result of his positive attitude toward infant baptism but has its own content and significance. Luther's rejection of the demand that only adults be baptized therefore protects and strengthens his acceptance of infant baptism. The Anabaptists wanted to baptize a man only when he had come to personal faith. Luther raises two main objections.

First of all, making baptism dependent on the faith of the per-son baptized always leaves us uncertain about any particular bap-tism. For we can never know definitely whether the candidate for baptism really believes. There is no unmistakable symptom of such faith, not even that he comes to baptism and confesses his faith. The Baptists' position has no certain basis and is thus an act of uncertainty. That, however, is sin. A few quotations: "Have they now become gods so that they can discern the hearts of men and know whether or not they believe?" "The Anabaptists cannot be certain that their rebaptism is valid. For their rebaptism presupposes that the person baptized has faith. They can never be certain of such faith, however, and their rebaptism is thus an act of uncertainty. Whoever is uncertain about and doubts divine mat-

---

" Cf. the evidence presented by Karl Brinkel, *Die Lehre Luthers von der fides infantum bei der Kindertaufe* (Berlin: Evan. Verlagsanstalt, 1958), pp. 60 ff.

" See *WA* 37, 281. *WA* 45, 170. *WA* 46, 152.

" The basic sources for this section are *Concerning Rebaptism, WA* 26, 144-174; *LW* 40, 229-262, and the sermons on baptism preached in January and February of 1534. Rörer's notes are found in *WA* 37, 258 ff.; the printed edition of these sermons is found in *WA* 37, 627 ff.

ters, sins against God and tempts him." "Whoever bases baptism on the faith of the one to be baptized can never baptize anyone."[68] The person being baptized cannot base the validity of baptism on his faith any more than the person baptizing him can.[69] "For he is not sure of his own faith."[71] The right and the validity of his baptism will therefore always remain uncertain as long as he wishes to base baptism on his faith. At any time the devil can make me doubt whether the faith in which and on the basis of which I have had myself baptized was genuine faith. Thus he makes me doubt my baptism, and in this way I constantly remain uncertain of my salvation.

Second, baptizing and allowing oneself to be baptized on the basis of faith not only make us uncertain but are also idolatry.[72] By depending on faith in this way, I make it a "work." The Baptists' practice is thus nothing else than a new work righteousness. They speak about faith, but they actually emphasize human activity and work. "There is, however, a devil who promotes confidence in works among them. He feigns faith, whereas he really has a work in mind. He uses the name and guise of faith to lead the poor people to rely on a work."[73] The Baptists want to reduce baptism and the Lord's Supper, "which are God's word and institution to mere human works. . . . They do not want to be made godly through baptism, but instead want to make baptism good and holy through their own piety." They deny the character of baptism as a communication of the grace of Christ which alone makes us holy and, on the contrary, wish "to make themselves holy" before baptism. They thus reduce baptism to an unnecessary sign that identifies them as pious people.[74]

Luther certainly does not argue against the attempt to make baptism dependent on the faith of the person baptized on the basis of a sacramental objectivism which cares nothing about the faith

---

[68] *WA* 26, 154, 164, 171 f.; *LW* 40, 240, 252, 260. Cf. *WA* 17ᴵᴵ, 85. *WA* 37, 667.
[69] *WA* 26, 154; *LW* 40, 239 f.
[70] *WA* 26, 155; *LW* 40, 240.
[71] *WA* 26, 154; *LW* 40, 240.
[72] *WA* 26, 165; *LW* 40, 252.
[73] *WA* 26, 161; *LW* 40, 248.
[74] *WA* 31ᴵ, 257; *LW* 14, 39.

of the person baptized, but precisely because he knows what faith is. Faith is corrupted and destroyed when it becomes its own object. Luther sharply and clearly distinguishes between believing and believing in faith itself. "It is true that we should believe when we are baptized; but we should not receive baptism because we believe. It is one thing to have faith and something completely different to rely upon faith and to receive baptism because one has it."[75] Even the believing adult who comes to baptism cannot receive baptism because he believes but only because God has commanded it. "If an adult wants to be baptized and says, 'Sir, I want to be baptized,' you say, 'Do you believe?' . . . Then he will not blurt out and say, 'Yes, I intend to move mountains by my faith.' Instead he will say, 'Yes, sir, I do believe, but I do not build on my faith. It might be too weak or uncertain. I want to be baptized because it is God's command that I should be, and on the strength of this command I dare to be baptized. In time, let my faith become what it may. If I am baptized on his commandment I know for certain that I am baptized. Were I to be baptized on my own faith, I might tomorrow find myself unbaptized, if I fell from faith or were tempted to think that I might not really have believed yesterday.'"[76] If a man must speak in this way when he is baptized as an adult, then he can also trust his baptism if he has received it as an infant. "I thank God and am happy that I was baptized as a child, for thus I have done what God commanded. Whether I believed or not, I have followed the command of God and been baptized. My baptism was correct and certain, whether God today grants me certain or uncertain faith. I should take care that I believe and am certain. Nothing is lacking in baptism; something is always lacking in faith. No matter how long we live, we always have enough to learn about faith. It can happen that faith fails, so that it is said, 'See, he had faith but has it no more.' But we cannot say about baptism, 'See, baptism was there but is no longer present.' No, it remains, for the command of God remains, and what is done according to his command stands and will ever remain."[77]

---

[75] *WA* 26, 164; *LW* 40, 252.
[76] *WA* 26, 165; *LW* 40, 253.
[77] *WA* 26, 165; *LW* 40, 253 f.

It should be understood that Luther does not say that the baptism received by an adult who decides he wants to be baptized cannot be a genuine Christian baptism according to the commandment and will of Jesus. He knows that such a person can answer the baptismal question, "Do you believe?" with all seriousness, "Yes, Lord, I believe."[78] But everything is distorted and turned upside down when that simple question is replaced by the concern of whether he has enough faith to be baptized. And abandoning infant baptism and making a law of adult baptism must inevitably lead to this. For, although Luther does not explicitly say so, his decision is based on the unspoken presupposition that the situation within the church is different than it is in mission territory. For it is one thing when a man who has turned away from the world, from paganism, or Judaism to Jesus Christ is simply asked about his faith in such a moment of decision. But it is something completely different when a man who has grown up in the Christian congregation, and who has lived in faith since he was a child is asked whether his faith is now adequate, mature, and conscious enough for him to decide to be baptized and confess his faith—it is especially so when he must ask himself this question. This converts the simple confession of faith into trust in his own faith. This is, however, exactly the opposite of faith. For then a man looks, "trusts, and builds," says Luther, on "his own," "that is, on a gift which God has given him and not on God's word alone"; that, however, is an idolatrous denial of the gospel.[79] Being baptized for the second time because one rejects infant baptism and the Christian existence and righteousness which it gives as "inadequate," means that the transition from the righteousness of faith to the righteousness of works has been made. For in all this, the second baptism ends up as the "better righteousness." Luther sees this as a repetition of the Galatians' apostasy from the righteousness of faith. "We Germans are and remain true Galatians"; this is the devil's masterpiece; he could not permit the Germans to "truly recognize Christ through the gospel," that is, the righteousness of faith. For this reason he sent the Anabaptists.[80]

---

[78] *WA* 26, 165; *LW* 40, 253.
[79] *WA* 26, 165; *LW* 40, 252.
[80] *WA* 26, 162; *LW* 40, 249.

Luther's concern for the purity of justifying faith is thus his ultimate reason for rejecting a second baptism and opposing the replacement of infant baptism with a generally required adult baptism. One of his greatest passages illustrates the depth of his understanding of the essence of faith. We may not base baptism on faith because neither the one who baptizes nor the one who is baptized are certain of faith. In any case they stand in the danger and temptation of their uncertainty. "For it happens, indeed, it even seems to happen consistently in this matter of faith that the man who thinks he believes finally does not believe at all, and the man who thinks that he does not believe and despairs actually believes most of all." For really believing and "knowing that one believes" are two quite different things. Faith is not self-consciousness. Jesus says, "He who believes . . ." and not "He who knows that he believes." "One must believe but we neither should nor can know it for certain."[81] Luther had experienced the temptation of not knowing any more whether he believed at the very time when he possibly believed most genuinely. Since faith is this way, we neither can nor dare make baptism dependent on the certainty that the person baptized really believes. Neither the person being baptized nor the person baptizing needs to have such certainty.

----

[81] *WA* 26, 155; *LW* 40, 241.

27

THE LORD'S SUPPER

I N DISCUSSING Luther's doctrine of the Lord's Supper we cannot avoid distinguishing the different forms through which it
passed before reaching its final form.[1] The controversies with Karlstadt, the Swiss, and Schwenckfeld led Luther far beyond his earlier teaching on the Lord's Supper. In this process, earlier emphases receded into the background. Luther certainly did not simply abandon them. However, he did not repeat them and they
were thus de-emphasized and perhaps even lost their place in his
total theology of the Lord's Supper. And yet they remain an essential part of his total understanding of this sacrament. We may,
therefore, neither simply ignore them nor can we fit them into the
final form of his theology of the Lord's Supper. Rather we must
discuss them individually before presenting Luther's doctrine as developed in his great writings on the Lord's Supper.

THE DEVELOPMENT UNTIL 1524

In viewing the total development of Luther's doctrine of the
Lord's Supper, we must distinguish between two stages. The dividing point is the beginning of the controversy about the real presence in about 1524. In the first stage, Luther is opposed to Rome;
in the second stage, he is opposed to the Enthusiasts and the Swiss.
In the first stage, Luther is fighting to preserve the genuine meaning of the sacrament as a gift of God in opposition to the doctrine
of the sacrifice of the mass. In the second stage, Luther empha-

---

[1] For this entire chapter, cf. Hans Grass, *Die Abendmahlslehre bei Luther
und Calvin* (2nd ed.; Gütersloh: Bertelsmann, 1954) and Ernst Sommerlath,
*Der Sinn des Abendmahls nach Luthers Gedanken über das Abendmahl 1527-
1529* (Leipzig: Dörffling, 1930). [The reader who is limited to English will
find two books helpful: Hermann Sasse, *This Is My Body: Luther's Contention
for the Real Presence in the Sacrament of the Altar* (Minneapolis: Augsburg,
1959), and Jaroslav Pelikan, *Luther the Expositor: Introduction to the Reformer's Exegetical Writings* (St. Louis: Concordia, 1959), pp. 137-260. Sasse,
op. cit., pp. 233-272, reconstructs the Marburg Colloquy.—Trans.]

sizes the bodily presence of the body and the blood of Christ in
the bread and wine over against its abandonment in the symbolic
theory.

Luther teaches the "real presence" in the first stage of this
process. It was part of the theology he inherited from the ancient
Church and he unquestioningly accepted it as a biblical statement.
The only change which he made was the replacement of the ecclesiastical doctrine of transubstantiation with the concept of con-
substantiation. He first does this in his treatise on *The Babylonian
Captivity of the Church*. In doing this, Luther followed the tradition of nominalism. He asserts that Christ's body and blood are
present in the untransformed bread and wine.[2] Luther did not,
however, particularly emphasize this change. In 1520, he was still
saying that anyone who wanted to could continue to hold the
doctrine of transubstantiation. Somewhat later, he rejected it without any particular emotion; speaking to the Swiss, he could even
emphasize his agreement with Rome in the question of the real
presence. He explicitly declares, "Before I would drink mere wine
with the Enthusiasts, I would rather have pure blood with the
Pope."[3] Certainly Luther had his own inner struggles about the
real presence. In his letter to Strassburg in 1524 he confesses that,
at the time of his decisive confrontation with the papacy, he was
greatly troubled by the temptation to interpret the words of institution in a purely symbolic sense and abandon the real presence

---

[2] Luther rejected the dogma of transubstantiation. He felt that the church
had in this dogma confused a metaphysical scholastic theory about the miracle
of the real presence with an article of faith; furthermore, the metaphysical
theory in the dogma of transubstantiation was completely dependent on the
philosophy of Aristotle. Luther sees this as a "captivity" of the sacrament.
WA 6, 508; *LW* 36, 28 ff. Such is also true of every other theory which
would attempt to describe the way in which the real presence takes place, as
soon as that theory would become dogma. In content, the dogma of transubstantiation is different from the doctrine of the gospel because it asserts the
transformation of an earthly substance into a heavenly substance. *WA* 6, 511;
LW 36, 34. The real presence must be understood in exact analogy to christology, that is, the deity dwells in the complete and untransformed human nature.
Just as we cannot speak of a transformation of the human nature in the incarnation, so we cannot speak of such a transformation in the sacrament.
"Thus, what is true in regard to Christ is also true in regard to the sacrament."
WA 6, 511; *LW* 36, 35.

[3] "I have often enough asserted that I do not argue whether the wine remains wine or not. It is enough for me that Christ's blood is present; let it be
with the wine as God wills." *WA* 26, 462; *LW* 37, 317. The quotation in
the text follows.

of Christ's body and blood in the elements so that he could do the greatest damage to the Roman structure. But in the face of that temptation—as well as at every other time when his natural desire to get rid of this difficult article of faith was a problem ("I am unfortunately all too inclined to do this whenever I feel my old Adam.")—he was always held in line by the clear text of the words of institution.[4]

It is characteristic of this first stage of Luther's thought that although the real presence remains an essential part of his doctrine of the Lord's Supper, he neither particularly emphasizes nor fully utilizes it in his total understanding of the Lord's Supper.

Within the first stage, we must now distinguish two clearly differentiated subphases. The first is particularly characterized by *The Blessed Sacrament of the Holy and True Body of Christ and the Brotherhoods*, (1519). The second begins with *A Treatise on the New Testament, that is, the Holy Mass*, (1520).[5]

The treatise on the Lord's Supper of 1519 holds a unique place in the development of Luther's thinking about the sacrament. As in his doctrine of baptism, Luther begins by referring to the external sign, the bread made from many grains of wheat and the wine made from many grapes. When we eat the bread and drink the wine we transform them within us. Luther sees this as a twofold sign of the "community." In the sacrament, the Christian is assured that Christ and all his saints will intercede for him; and he also is obligated to intercede for the benefit of Christ and his people. It is thus the "sacrament of love," the *communio*, as it was for Augustine and Thomas. Luther's concept of the church as the community of saints was developed on the basis of this understanding of the sacrament.[6] But what is the significance of the presence of Christ's body and the blood? First, it means a "perfect sign."[7] The transformation of bread and wine into Christ's body and blood completely assures us, as bread and wine and our reception of them have already done, that we are transformed and incorporated

[4] *WA* 15, 394; *LW* 40, 68.
[5] *WA* 2, 742-758; *LW* 35, 49-73. *WA* 6, 353-378; *LW* 35, 79-111. Cf. Reinhold Seeberg, *Lehrbuch der Dogmengeschichte* (3rd ed.; Leipzig: Deichert, 1917), IV¹, 323 ff.
[6] Cf. pp. 304.
[7] *WA* 2, 749, 751; *LW* 35, 59, 62.

into Christ's spiritual body and the community of love. The presence of body and blood thus has only symbolic significance. It is not particularly important that the body and blood are received but only that they are present and thought about. Luther does not emphasize the eating of the body but only the eating of the bread: This symbolically assures us we are united with Christ and with all the saints. In this context, there is no place for the real presence commensurate with its significance. The reference to it appears to be an afterthought and in no way necessary. For this reason, the treatise of 1519 could not be the final form of Luther's doctrine of the Lord's Supper. Luther had yet to find the organic relationship between the real presence and the "significance" or the "work" of the sacrament. He also had to move beyond this formulation of his doctrine, because the words of institution have no significance in the entire treatise. In spite of this, however, one must agree with Reinhold Seeberg that "Luther probably never again came so close to the genuine meaning of the Lord's Supper as he did in this writing." Further development was not simply progress. Insofar as the thoughts of this treatise recede into the background—and they continue to appear in his sermons until the middle of the twenties[*]—his understanding of this sacrament was impoverished.

Luther progressed to the second phase of the first stage of his doctrine—a stage at which his thinking was not yet determined by the controversy about the Lord's Supper—by clarifying his concept of the sacraments in general. This he did in 1519 and 1520. Luther now emphasizes that the essential factor in the sacrament is the expressly stated divine promise, which is always a promise of the forgiveness of sins.[*] In accordance with this, the words of institution and the forgiveness of sins offered in them now occupy the central place in Luther's thinking about the Lord's Supper. In his *A Treatise on the New Testament, that is, the Holy Mass.*[10]—the title is indicative—Luther teaches that the words of institution in the Lord's Supper are Jesus' last will and testament. "Everything depends . . . on the words of this sacrament. These are the words of

---

[*] Cf. the passages cited p. 321.
[*] *WA* 6, 513; *LW* 36, 38.
[10] *WA* 6, 353 ff.; *LW* 35, 79-111.

Christ.["] The content of this testament is forgiveness of sins and eternal life.["] Accordingly everything on our side depends on the faith which grasps the words of the testament. By his death Jesus seals "these promises to us as irrevocable"; he gives his body and blood for this purpose and leaves us both as a sign.["] This sign helps our faith. The significance of the real presence of Christ's body and blood consists therefore in the fact that they are signs certifying the promise of the forgiveness of sins. Also at this point emphasis is put on the fact that the body is eaten. Here again we must say that the concept of the real presence has not yet received its full significance within the doctrine of the Lord's Supper. Understanding Christ's body and blood as signs that his promise is true obviously establishes an artificial and inadequate connection between these two thoughts. Luther says we need a sign because we are sensible beings. For this reason, it must also be an "external" sign.["] But are Christ's body and blood really a sign that is accessible to our senses? Only bread and wine are that kind of sign! However we must believe the real presence. How can it then be a sign, that we can receive through our senses, which demonstrates the truth of the promise? The limited extent to which the real presence occupies an organic and necessary place in Luther's concept of the Lord's Supper is apparent also from his explicit declaration that the signs can be missing as long as we have the words. We can be saved without the sacrament (and thus also without the real presence) but not without the testament. "Christ is more concerned about the word than about the sign."["]

The further development of Luther's thought is determined by the necessity of defending the real presence against its attackers. We now enter into the second stage of this doctrine. It was unavoidable that the real presence, now that it was no longer taken for granted as an undisputed part of the doctrine of the Lord's Supper, should be much more strongly emphasized and of much greater significance for Luther's total understanding of the Lord's

---

[11] *WA* 6, 360; *LW* 35, 88.
[12] *WA* 6, 358 f., 361; *LW* 35, 85-89.
[13] *WA* 6, 358 ff.; *LW* 35, 85 ff. *WA* 6, 515, 518; *LW* 36, 38, 44. Cf. *WA* 10ᴵᴵᴵ, 351; *LW* 51, 116.
[14] *WA* 6, 359; *LW* 35, 86.
[15] *WA* 6, 363, 373 f.; *LW* 35, 91, 106.

Supper. Reinhold Seeberg put it very well when he said that the characteristic element in the first phase of this doctrine as we have discussed it, was "seeing" while in the second phase it was "hearing" the words of institution. Now, however, because of the controversy about the real presence, the "eating" is emphasized. Luther was conscious of the shift of emphasis in his doctrine of the sacrament caused by the beginning of the controversy about the real presence. In 1526 Luther says that up until then he has said very little about the object of faith, that is, the sacramental presence of Christ in the bread and wine. His attention had been concentrated on the subjective element, the proper faithful use of the sacraments, which must be known for each sacrament, and "which is also the best thing to know." Now, however, he must turn his attention to the objective character of the sacrament because the real presence is under attack.[16]

The words of institution are therefore now treated in a new manner. They are no longer considered only as the vehicle for the promise of the forgiveness of sin but are understood also as the promise of the real presence. Luther strikes a new note as early as 1523 when he says that the word "brings with it everything of which it speaks, namely, Christ with his flesh and blood and everything that he is and has."[17]

But Luther did not arrive at his position of 1527/28 all at once. During the first years of the controversy the special significance of the real presence and its relationship to the word of the gospel is by no means certain. The proof of this is Luther's treatise *Against the Heavenly Prophets*, which so strongly asserts the real presence as the true meaning of the words of institution. Luther, using excellent illustrations, there teaches that the forgiveness of sins gained on the cross is "given and distributed through the word" in the Lord's Supper just as in the gospel, where it is preached. The sacrament is simply described as "gospel." "I find in the sacrament or gospel the word which presents, offers, distributes and gives to me that forgiveness which was won on the cross. . . . Whoever has a bad conscience from his sin should go

---

[16] *WA* 19, 482 f.; *LW* 36, 335.
[17] *WA* 11, 433; *LW* 36, 278,

to the sacrament and obtain comfort, not because of the bread and wine, not because of the body and blood of Christ, but because of the word which in the sacrament offers, presents, and gives the body and blood of Christ, given and shed for you."[18] This formulation is especially interesting. It shows that the forgiveness of sins stands in the center of Luther's thinking as the special gift of the sacrament. Second, the real presence is fitted into this thought. What is at stake is not the presence of body and blood as such, but the offering to me in the word of the body and blood given for me on the cross. The cross thus stands in the center of the discussion. The emphasis is placed on the body given into death for us.

If, however, everything depends only on the fact that the words of institution with their "for you" open and convey to us the treasure gained by Christ,[19] then the real presence of the body and the blood which have gained forgiveness of sins for us is not absolutely necessary. This is especially true in view of Luther's concept of the power of the divine word. Luther also drew this conclusion: "Even if only bread and wine were there present, as they claim, as long as the word, 'Take, eat, this is my body given for you,' etc., is there, the forgiveness of sins would, because of this word, still be present in the sacrament."[20] At this point Luther explicitly refers to the analogy of baptism. Later his doctrine of the content and effect of the Lord's Supper goes far beyond this analogy.

Here again one sees that the doctrine of the Lord's Supper is not yet complete. The proper emphasis on the real presence—Luther became more and more conscious of this during the struggle about it—does not yet really fit into that understanding of the sacrament which was oriented to the promise of the forgiveness of sins. Luther, to obey the Scripture, strictly maintained the real presence; but from now on, he was more definitely and more consciously interested in the real presence for its own sake. However the influence of his basic concept of a sacrament still does not enable him to utilize fully the real presence. We might say that the

[18] *WA* 18, 204 f.; *LW* 40, 214 f.
[19] *WA* 18, 203; *LW* 40, 214.
[20] *WA* 18, 204; *LW* 40, 214.

general concept of a sacrament is now struggling with Luther's
understanding of the real presence in the Lord's Supper; the lat·
ter goes beyond the general concept of a sacrament. In 1525 his
concept of the sacrament is still the stronger factor—as the pre·
viously quoted passages have demonstrated. But what direction will
the development take? If the full significance of the real pres·
ence is taken into account, must it not lead Luther beyond the
understanding of the sacrament centered in the promise of forgiveness, either complementing or even replacing it with a more realis-
tic understanding? With this question in mind, we turn to Luther's doctrine of the Lord's Supper as it was fully developed in
this controversy, that is, particularly to his writings of 1527 and
1528, as well as to the statements he made in Marburg.

THE DEVELOPED FORM OF THE DOCTRINE

The Authority of the Words of Institution

What were the decisive motives which led Luther to his doctrine
of the Lord's Supper and bound him so unshakeably to it? Luther
himself, at every decisive point, refers to the clear text of the
words of institution. Obedience to the words of the Lord compelled
him to teach what he taught. The christological concepts with
which he tried to make the real presence of the body of Christ
understandable in his great polemical writings were first developed
in answer to the objections of his opponents. It is characteristic
that since Luther's opponents in the Marburg colloquy do not mention their localization of Christ in heaven,[a] he does not develop
his own doctrine of the right hand of God but constantly refers
back to the simple text. But this reference should not be interpreted as biblicistic stubbornness. Luther is bound neither by a
theory of verbal inspiration of the Scripture nor through grammar.
Upon occasion he did respond to Karlstadt's remarks about grammatical points by saying: "Something higher than rules of grammar must always be present when the grounding of faith is
concerned . . . if my faith had to rest on Donatus [a Latin gram-
mar] or the primer, I would be in a bad way. How many new

---

[a] Cf. Osiander's report, *WA* 30^{III}, 148.

articles we would have to establish, if we were to master the Bible in all passages according to grammatical rules?"[22] In fact, "We must ask why Luther did not handle the Scripture more freely in discussing the real presence."[23] The only possible answer is that the substance of the words of Scripture themselves compelled him to take the position he did and that his entire understanding of Christ and of the gospel—in which he was certain that he was obedient to Scripture—bore witness on behalf of his exegesis. Accordingly, we describe the situation adequately only when we speak of the mutual conditioning of Luther's exegesis and of the substantive concerns connected with basic elements of his understanding of the gospel. His thinking was determined neither by text alone nor by the subject alone but by one with and in the other. As he still inwardly struggled about and with the subject itself, the text bound him—as he confesses in a *Letter to the Christians in Strassburg* of December 15, 1524, and also elsewhere.[24] In the controversy about the meaning of the text, however, it was his feeling for the subject itself which made him certain that his exegesis was correct.

We shall therefore first discuss Luther's exegesis and then the content of his doctrine of the Lord's Supper and its connection with his total theology.

In dealing with Luther's exegesis of the words of institution, we

---

[22] *WA* 18, 157; *LW* 40, 167.

[23] Ernst Sommerlath, *Luthers Lehre von der Realpräsenz im Abendmahl* in *Das Erbe Martin Luthers* (Leipzig: Dörffling, 1928), p. 335. Cf. also Karl Barth, "Ansatz und Absicht in Luthers Abendmahlslehre," *Zwischen den Zeiten* (1923/4), pp. 50 f., also published in *Die Theologie und die Kirche* (Munich: Kaiser, 1928), pp. 26 ff. Barth correctly characterizes one aspect of Luther's thought when he says: "Everything which Luther produced as evidence for this thesis . . . is only a paraphrase of 'this is my body'; for Luther, this completely settled the matter." Barth then continues, and what he says is equally correct: "Thus it was written and thus it had to be written. Luther would have said this in a completely different way than Zwingli even though he had not found the problematical 'is' in the Bible."

[24] "But I am a captive and cannot free myself. The text is too powerfully present, and will not allow itself to be torn from its meaning by mere verbiage." *WA* 15, 394; *LW* 40, 68. Cf. *WA* 18, 166; *LW* 40, 177. This means that we cannot agree with Karl Barth, when he says: "Luther's exegesis of the words of institution does not raise the problem of the source of his doctrine but only of the subsequent proof of his doctrine." *Loc cit.* This oversimplifies the relationship between Luther's exegesis and his relationship to the substance of the matter in a way in which his letter to the theologians in Strassburg does not permit.

must point out that Luther first became certain of their meaning on the basis of what Paul says in I Corinthians 10 and 11. The words of institution were his final fortress in battle. However, it was Paul who gave him the keys to the fortress.

On two different occasions, in 1525 and in 1528, Luther asserts that Paul's statement in I Corinthians 10:16 ("The cup of blessing which we bless, is it not a participation in the blood of Christ? The bread which we break, is it not a participation in the body of Christ?") is the real confirmation of his position. In 1525 he explicitly refers to his "temptation," that is, to his inner struggle about the question of the real presence and the temptation to abandon it of which his letter to Strassburg speaks. "That is a verse which is a thunderbolt on the head of Dr. Karlstadt and his whole party. This verse has also been the life-giving medicine of my heart in my trials concerning this sacrament. Even if we had no other passage than this we could sufficiently strengthen all consciences and sufficiently overcome all adversaries."[28] And in 1528 he says, "This text I have extolled, and I do so still, as my heart's joy and crown, for it not only says, 'This is Christ's body,' as we read in the Lord's Supper, but mentions the bread which was so broken and says, 'The bread is Christ's body,' indeed, 'The bread which we break is not only the body of Christ but the distributed body of Christ.' Here, now, is a text so lucid and clear that the fanatics and the whole world could not desire or demand anything more."[29] The importance of Paul's statement for Luther personally and for the objective content of his doctrine cannot be expressed more clearly. Admittedly, Luther also had to contend for this passage in controversy with the Swiss and with Schwenckfeld. His own interpretation of the passage reads: "Now Paul speaks thus: 'The bread which we break is a participation in the body of Christ,' i.e., whoever partakes of this broken bread, partakes of the body of Christ as a common possession distributed among many; for the bread is this common body of Christ, says Paul. This is stated in clear and distinct terms, which no one can understand differently without

28 *WA* 18, 166; *LW* 40, 177.
29 *WA* 26, 487; *LW* 37, 348.

changing the words."[27] The opponents wanted to interpret the "participation in the body" of which Paul speaks as "spiritual" and based their opinion on the following verse [17]: "Because there is one loaf, we who are many are one body because we all partake of the same loaf." Since the "participation in the body of Christ" also means belonging to the spiritual body of Christ, that is, the church, the "participation" itself must also be understood as a spiritual one. Thus, even in vs. 16, Paul was not speaking of a physical eating of the body of Christ. However, Luther did not admit the validity of this argument. According to Luther, Paul here speaks of a bodily participation in the body of Christ in which even Judas and the unworthy share because they too break the bread.[28] "Body" and "blood" cannot be understood as tropes at this place. Over against this attempted interpretation Luther points particularly to I Corinthians 11:27 and 29, "guilty of the body and the blood of the Lord because he does not distinguish the body of the Lord."[29] In these verses the tropological understanding is impossible. Paul here does not speak of a symbol of the body but rather the body itself. "How does one sin against the body of the Lord by eating, if His body is not present in the eating or the bread?"[30] On this basis Luther reaches a decision also about I Corinthians 10:16 and on this basis about all passages dealing with the Lord's Supper. "If body and blood in this passage . . . are not a trope but rather refer to the true body and blood of Christ as our doctrine holds, then they also can not be tropes in other passages referring to the Lord's Supper."[31]

---

[27] *WA* 26, 490; *LW* 37, 353 f. Luther's interpretation of vs. 17 emphasizes that Paul does not say that we are the body of Christ but simply that we are a body and assembly, a community. *WA* 26, 491; *LW* 37, 355. This assertion is untenable. But Luther's opponents are equally wrong. Whereas Luther attempts to understand vs. 17 on the basis of vss. 16 and 18, his opponents attempt to do just the opposite and understand vss. 16 and 18 on the basis of vs. 17. However, they do not succeed in interpreting vss. 16 and 18 in such a way that the "bodily" relationship to the body of Christ disappears. The relationship of vs. 17 to vss. 16 and 18 is a very difficult exegetical problem.

[28] "So this verse of Paul's stands like a rock and forcefully requires the interpretation that all who break this bread, receive, and eat it, receive the body of Christ and partake of it. As we have said, it cannot be spiritual, so it must be a bodily participation." *WA* 18, 172; *LW* 40, 181.

[29] *WA* 26, 481, 486, 498; *LW* 37, 341, 347, 358.

[30] *WA* 18, 173; *LW* 40, 183.

[31] *WA* 26, 489; *LW* 37, 351. *WA* 26, 498; *LW* 37, 359 f. is especially significant.

Thus Paul's statements open up the clear meaning of the words of institution. They show that the words of institution must be understood as they read without any tropological interpretation. The general principle which Luther frequently states would have led to this position in any case. Every passage of Scripture is to be understood according to its simple literal meaning unless a recognized article of faith compels us to another interpretation. "In Scripture we should let the words retain their natural force, just as they read, and give no other interpretation unless a clear article of faith compels otherwise."[32] However, there is no need to interpret the words of institution in such a non-literal way. Furthermore in spite of all the differences in the accounts about the institution of the Lord's Supper—and Luther very seriously deals with the details of these differences[33]—the decisive words, "This is my body," are common to them all.[34] These are clear words and they are God's words. This text, " 'This is my body' . . . comes not from men but from God himself, spoken by his own lips and set down in these very letters and words."[35] "Our text is certain and it shall and must remain as the words say; for God himself has placed it where it is, and no man may dare add or take away a single letter."[36]

All interpretations, however, come from men and are uncertain, as the existence of several interpretations among the opponents shows.[37] Even though such an exegetical interpretation may be good in itself, it is of no use when such great matters of faith are at stake. "What becomes of my conscience, which would like to have a good,

---

[32] *WA* 26, 403; *LW* 37, 270. *WA* 18, 147; *LW* 40, 157. "For anyone who ventures to interpret words and the Scripture any other way than what they say, is under obligation to prove his contention out of the text of the very same passage or by an article of faith." *WA* 23, 93; *LW* 37, 32. In Marburg, Luther said: "The ultimate nature of faith demands of us that we do not edit our dear God's word unless some absurdity [resulting from a literal translation] contrary to faith or the articles of faith compel us." *WA* 30ᴵᴵᴵ, 122; cf. Sasse, *op. cit.*, p. 243.

[33] *WA* 26, 454 ff.; *LW* 37, 310 ff.

[34] *WA* 26, 459; *LW* 37, 314.

[35] *WA* 26, 446; *LW* 37, 304.

[36] *WA* 26, 446, 448; *LW* 37, 304, 307. "I see the clear, distinct, powerful words of God which compel me to confess that the body and blood of Christ are in the sacrament." *WA* 18, 166; *LW* 40, 176. Cf. *WA* 23, 83, 87; *LW* 37, 25 f., 28 f. At Marburg, Luther said: "My dear sirs, since this text of my Lord Jesus Christ, 'This is my body,' continues to stand, I really cannot possibly get around it but must confess and believe that the body of Christ is there." *WA* 30ᴵᴵᴵ, 116, 137; cf. Sasse, *op. cit.*, pp. 237, 257.

[37] *WA* 26, 446; *LW* 37, 304.

sure foundation? Is it supposed to stand on this hungry, thirsty, needy comment?"[38] Such interpretations not only show a lack of reverence for God's clear word, but they are also an unmerciful act against a conscience seeking a certain basis for its faith. God is glorified and the conscience firmly established when a man simply obeys God's words as they stand. Thus one of the decisive elements of Luther's piety and theology enters into his doctrine of the Lord's Supper: obedience to the clear word of God contrary to all thoughts of vain reason. Luther felt his opponents were rationalists who wanted to learn to understand God's clear word with their human thoughts and in terms of their concepts of what is possible and impossible, useful and not useful.[39] The question is not whether Luther's evaluation of his opponents in the controversy on the Lord's Supper was accurate. At present we are not concerned with passing judgment on the controversial situation between the opponents, but with understanding Luther's position.

God's clear word must be obeyed; and this obedience is demanded completely independently of whether we can understand how Christ's body and blood are present in the bread and wine. Luther constantly and strongly emphasized that this "how" of the real presence is and should be hidden from our reason.[40] God is greater than we are able to understand; and what he does must be beyond our ability to comprehend.[41] That demonstrates that it is God's activity.[42] The christological thoughts which Luther used in the controversy on the Lord's Supper therefore cannot be used and were not intended to be used to remove the stumbling block for reason; they cannot enlighten reason on the way in which the

---

[38] *WA* 26, 483; *LW* 37, 344. "For if we must depend on simple naked words, we would rather depend on the simple naked text which God has spoken to us, than on the simple naked interpretations made up by men." *WA* 36, 497.

[39] *WA* 23, 123; *LW* 37, 51. "This is the rancor and hatred of natural reason, which wants nothing to do with this article and therefore spits and vomits against it, and then tries to wrap itself in Scripture so that it may avoid being recognized." *WA* 23, 127; *LW* 37, 53. Cf. *WA* 23, 161; *LW* 37, 137 f.

[40] E.g., *WA* 18, 206; *LW* 40, 216. *WA* 23, 87, 145, 209, 265; *LW* 37, 28 f., 64, 103, 139.

[41] "But God's word and works do not proceed according to our view of things, but in a way incomprehensible to all reason and even to the angels." *WA* 26, 318; *LW* 37, 207 f. Cf. *WA* 30ᴵᴵᴵ, 119; Sasse, *op. cit.*, pp. 239 f.

[42] "If we knew his ways, he who is most wonderful would no longer be incomprehensible." *WA* 30ᴵᴵᴵ, 119; Sasse, *op. cit.*, pp. 239 f.

real presence occurs. Their purpose is only to remove our small, narrow, human thoughts about God's presence and to remind us that God's possibilities constantly exceed our capacity to comprehend them. Luther brings the incomprehensible closer to human reason only insofar as he refers us to the wonderful and incomprehensible events which already surround us in our natural lives. We live in and from them without understanding how they happen."

The obedient man asks God neither "how" nor "why" He is doing what he has promised. Luther therefore rejects his opponents' questions about the purpose of the real presence as the presumption of human reason against God. The opponents asked what use the presence of Christ's body and blood in the Lord's Supper could serve. Luther did indeed answer this question, as we shall see. He does not, however, give this answer to those who demand to see the usefulness before they believe God's clear word; he gives it to those who reverently and humbly believe God's words. Luther at this point emphasizes the nature of faith as strongly as possible. Everything is at stake here. To believe means abandoning our own thoughts and wishes and blindly submitting to God's word and will. "A believing, God-fearing heart does this: It asks first whether this is God's word. When it hears that it is, it smothers the question about why it is useful or necessary. For it says with fear and humility, 'Dear God, I am blind; truly I do not know what is or what is not useful to me, nor do I wish to know it. But I believe and trust in you as knowing and intending the very best for me according to your divine goodness and wisdom. I am happy and satisfied to hear your simple word and be informed of your will.'" Luther here is concerned with nothing less than the sovereignty of God's word and will, in opposition to all human claims to insight into the religious necessity and meaningfulness of what God does. Whatever God's word says and gives is good for us. We may not, however, turn this standard around and measure and control God's word by asking how useful it is. On the contrary, for that would

---

" "I shall not mention the fact that they ought to know how they see, hear, speak, and live physically. All such things we feel, and we are daily involved in them, and yet we do not know how they occur. Yet they want to know how Christ is present in the bread." *WA* 23, 266; *LW* 37, 139.

" *WA* 23, 247, 249, 253; *LW* 37, 127 f., 131.

be an expression of the original sin of human self-assertion which reverses the relationship between God and man. If a man makes his subjection to God's word dependent on his insight into the usefulness of God's word, he actually places himself above God. "For he who asks why something which God says and does is necessary surely is trying to elevate himself above God and be wiser and better than God." Luther feels that such pride is a terrible thing. "A man's heart might burst at such insolent prattle of the hellish devils and his fanatics." "If they had any understanding of faith, however, and ever felt a spark of it, they would know that faith's highest single virtue and quality and glory is the willingness not to pry into the benefit or necessity of what one believes. It refuses to circumscribe God or demand to know the purpose or what is the necessity of that which he commands or enjoins, but is perfectly happy to be ignorant, to give God the glory and believe his simple word."⁴⁴ In Marburg, Luther expresses the same thought in a very drastic form: "If God told me to eat manure I would do it and be certain that it was wholesome for me."⁴⁵ In all of this, there is no mention of ultimately surrendering ourselves to a meaningless and arbitrary will. As all the quoted passages show, Luther not only always maintained that everything God does is really useful and necessary for us, but he also attempted to demonstrate the usefulness of the real presence. He is concerned only about one point: We should not base our faith on our understanding of God's thinking and should seek understanding only in faith. For meaningfulness is not the standard by which God's word is evaluated; rather God's word is the source and standard of meaningfulness. God wills to make his meaning known to us through the Holy Spirit. The Spirit, however, gives himself only to the man who is obedient—and obedience is always heteronomous. The way to a theonomous understanding of God's purpose leads through blind and heteronomous obedience.

If we once begin to raise rational objections against an article of faith based on God's word there is no place to stop. Then the other articles of faith also fall. "If it disapproves this one, it

---

⁴⁴ *WA* 23, 265; *LW* 37, 139.
⁴⁵ *WA* 30ᴵᴵᴵ, 116; Sasse, *op. cit.*, p. 237. "The servant should not inquire about the will of his Lord. He ought to close his eyes." *Ibid.*

also disproves all articles. For God's word is always folly to reason, I Corinthians 1 [:18]." It is "difficult and even impossible" to believe not only this doctrine but also, for example, the doctrine that Christ is both God and man. "The only exception are the saints who not only find it easy but also find joy and happiness, yes, even life and salvation in believing all of God's words and works."[47]

Luther's passionate and unshakeable commitment to the literal words of institution is thus also deeply related to his understanding of the relationship between God and man, between divine truth and reason, between the word and faith. One of the finest passages from Luther's 1528 *Confession Concerning Christ's Supper* will make us aware of that.

"First, when we are dealing with the works and words of God, reason and all human wisdom must submit to being taken captive, as St. Paul teaches in II Corinthians 10 [:5]. They must allow themselves to be blinded and led, directed, taught, and instructed, lest we presume to sit in judgment over God's words. We shall surely lose out when we try to judge his words as Psalm 51 [:4] testifies. Second, if we surrender to him and confess that we do not comprehend his words and works, we should be satisfied. We should speak of his works simply using his words as he has pronounced them for us and prescribed that we speak them after him; and we should not presume to use our own words as if they were better than his. For we shall surely go wrong unless we simply repeat his words after him as he pronounces them for us, just as a young child repeats the creed or the Lord's Prayer after his father. Here we need to walk in the dark with our eyes closed, and simply cling to the word and follow. For since we are confronted by God's words, 'This is my body'—distinct, clear, common, definite words, which certainly are no trope, either in Scripture or in any language—we must embrace them with faith, and allow our reason to be blinded and taken captive. So, not as hairsplitting sophistry dictates but as God says them for us, we must repeat these words after him and hold to them."[49]

[47] *WA* 23, 127; *LW* 37, 53.
[48] *WA* 23, 161; *LW* 37, 75.
[49] *WA* 26, 439; *LW* 37, 296.

For one moment Luther confronts the possibility that the text and the literal understanding of the words of institution would be uncertain and obscure—even though they were not for him—even the possibility that the man who believed in the real presence on the basis of the words of institution might have fallen into an illusion because God, in reality, intended these words to mean something else. But even if this were a real possibility (although it is not even a possibility for Luther), Luther feels that it would be better to follow the literal meaning than human interpretations. For in any case, God has given the text in this way. If it is obscure then it is obscure because Christ wills it to be; and he forgives our failure to understand and our misunderstanding just as he forgave the disciples' failure to understand his prophecies of his passion. "If I must have an uncertain, obscure text and interpretation, I would rather have one from the mouth of God himself than one spoken by men. And if I must be deceived, I would rather be deceived by God (if that were possible) than by men. For if God deceives me, he will take the responsibility and make amends to me, but men cannot make amends to me if they have deceived me and led me into hell."[60]

Even someone who feels that the exegetical problem is not as simple as it appears to be in Luther's writings,[61] yes, even that his understanding of the words of institution does not express their biblical meaning (for example, "body" and "blood"), must still admit that Luther's attitude is a dynamic expression without parallel of the greatest thing that God permitted him to express with his words and his life, that is, absolute obedience and dependence on God's word alone. For this reason alone, Luther's writings in the controversy about the Lord's Supper are a particularly precious legacy to the church.

LUTHER'S OBJECTIVE INTEREST IN THE REAL PRESENCE

Luther's interpretation of the words of institution in obedience to their clear literal meaning also expresses his objective concern.

---

[60] *WA* 26, 446; *LW* 37, 305.
[61] Cf. my criticism of Luther's and Lutheran orthodoxy's exegesis of the words of institution in *CW*, pp. 563-588, §§ 57 f.

We now ask what it was in his total theology that led him to the concept of the real presence and bound him to it. We ask, for example, how his doctrine of the Lord's Supper is connected with and fits into his total understanding of the gospel and how it influences individual doctrines, for example, christology, in Luther's theology.

Luther's primary concern is always that which he maintained against Rome: The sacrament is really to be understood as God's gift. As a gift it is indeed present for faith, but it also exists independently of and prior to faith. Human activity adds nothing to it. The first fault which he found with the enthusiasts and the Swiss was that they failed to recognize that the Lord's Supper is God's gift to the man who is struggling to achieve the joy of faith. Their conception of the sacrament as primarily a meal of remembrance not only despised the clear words of Christ, but was also a merciless act toward man in his actual situation. Certainly Luther also remembered the death of Christ when he celebrated the sacrament. He had every right to ask, "Who knows more about this than we do?"[52] However, more than this was involved. The understanding of the Lord's Supper as a meal of remembrance is ultimately nothing else than a doctrine of work righteousness which does not lead man out of his trouble. Instead, it actually leads him deeper into his trouble because it requires that he climb out by genuine remembrance and love, which he must create by his own powers. "But suppose your knowledge and remembrance of Christ were pure passion, pure heart, pure ardor, pure fire . . . What would come of it? What would be gained? Nothing except new monks and hypocrites who would with greater devotion and earnestness stand before the bread and wine (if everything went well), as hitherto the sensitive consciences stood before the sacrament." "Even if I . . . practiced the remembrance and knowledge of Christ with such passion and seriousness that I sweated blood and became feverish, it would be of no avail and would be all in vain. For it would be pure work and commandment, but no gift or word of God offered and given to me in the body and blood of

---

[52] The quotation above is from Rörer's notes, *WA* 19, 504. Cf. the context, *WA* 19, 503 f.; *LW* 36, 347 f.

Christ."⁵³ The meaning of the celebration of the sacrament is not that we lift ourselves up to Christ by our own thoughts but that Christ lowers himself to us. Luther does not base the service and worship of God on the fervor of our devotion or meditation on Christ's sufferings, for how could a certain and joyful worship of God ever be possible under such circumstances? Rather, he bases it on the presence of Christ who bears and forgives our lack of devotion.

All of Luther's thought is dominated by this concern. In it, Luther now grasped the biblically founded thought of the real presence which tradition offered him. The real presence means that we are here dealing with a genuine gift which is present for us in bodily form and is most obviously independent of all human attitudes and all "spiritual" capabilities. Zwingli's symbolic understanding of the sacrament was connected with an explicit activism: "The Eucharist is never the bread or the body of Christ but the act of giving thanks."⁵⁴ Luther, however, felt that the essential character of every confrontation of God with man is passive and all man's activity is purely receptive in character. Luther thought that this empasis was a necessary part of any non-symbolical understanding of the Lord's Supper and of the real presence.

Luther also found that the basic character of all God's activity in saving men was present in the real presence in still another way. The real presence means that Christ is bodily present. Luther knew that the Lord is personally present even in the oral proclamation of the word. In the Lord's Supper, however, Christ's own word promises that he will be present bodily. Luther did not consider this something special and unique. Rather, this has occurred in the history of God's saving activity always and everywhere.

The Word became flesh [John 1:14]—to Luther this also means that it became body. This bodiliness is not insignificant. It is identical with genuine historicity. History always takes place in the body. The fact that Christ was in the body means that he was near and comprehensible to men. God deals with them in a physi-

---

⁵³ *WA* 18, 195, 203; *LW* 40, 205 f., 213.
⁵⁴ Zwingli, *Opera,* ed. Schuler and Schulthess (Zurich: Schulthess, 1832) 3, 542.

cal and spiritual totality. Jesus' contemporaries were able to enter into a spiritual and at the same time a physical relationship to him. Mary gave birth to him both spiritually and physically. The shepherds and Simeon were allowed to see him both spiritually and bodily. We are to have just as much. He wishes "to be just as close to us bodily as he was to them." He does this today in another and a supernatural way so that he can be so close to all the world; this would not be possible if he appeared visibly. Thus he is definitely present in a bodily but hidden way.[85] In faith we are permitted to grasp him totally according to his soul and body. Should such a bodily presence of Jesus be something unimportant? Was it of no importance to his work of redemption during his earthly life? To be sure, it was good when he walked on earth and helped anyone whom he touched with his flesh. Through his body, with his physical voice, he called Lazarus from the grave [John 11:43]. He touched the leper and made him clean [Matt. 8:3]. He walked on the sea and stretched forth his hand to the sinking Peter and drew him to the land [Matt. 14:31], and all his acts were miracles and good deeds. (Luther's references are only to physical acts.) It is also his character and nature to do good wherever he is. Why should he now not help us in the bread when it is the same flesh, the same word, and the same nature, and must be altogether good and useful?"[86]

If Christ's flesh is useless when it is eaten bodily, why is it "not also useless when it is physically conceived and born, laid in the manger, taken up in one's arms, seated at table at the supper, hanging on the cross, etc.? All these are outward modes and uses of his flesh as truly as when he is physically eaten. Is it better when it is in his mother's womb than when it is in the bread and in the mouth? If it is of no help here, it can be of no help there either; if it helps there, it must also help here. For nothing more can be made out of this than that Christ's body is dealt with physically and outwardly, whether it is eaten or conceived, born or carried, seen or heard. And in all these instances, it is not the spiritual eating that helps but only the physical using or handling."[87] Because the

---

[85] *WA* 23, 193, 173, 175; *LW* 37, 81, 94 ff.
[86] *WA* 23, 256; *LW* 37, 133 f.
[87] *WA* 23, 177; *LW* 37, 85.

word became flesh, Christ's flesh is full of God's word. It is something completely different from our flesh and blood. "It is God who is in this flesh. It is God's flesh, the Spirit's flesh. It is in God and God is in it." Death tried to gain power over this flesh without success. "This food was too tough for death and has devoured and digested that glutton" when he tried to eat it.[88]

The Swiss did not have the slightest understanding of what Luther was saying. And this indicates the true depth of the opposition between them. The difference lies in the way in which Luther and the Swiss understood the concepts of flesh and spirit.[89] Luther's opponents based their position on Christ's statement, "the flesh helps nothing" (John 6:63). They are concerned with spiritual things. And spirit arises only out of spirit. Spirit has an effect only on spirit. What is the sense then of the real presence and of the bodily eating of Christ?[90] Such ideas are incompatible with the spirituality of God and of our relationship to him. The sacrament may be understood only as the symbol which illustrates a spiritual reality that faith is able to experience; in this case, it is Christ's sacrificial death.

Luther's penetrating insight recognized that the concept of flesh and spirit underlying this kind of thinking was different from the biblical concept. In fact, Zwingli and his followers were teaching the dualism and the spiritualism of late classical antiquity. They understand spirit as the opposite of flesh in the sense of bodiliness. For Luther, however, spirit is the opposite of flesh in the sense of sinfulness. For this reason, it is meaningless to consider the bodiliness in the sacrament unimportant and unworthy of God in order to assert the Spirit's interests. Bodily eating is itself a "spiritual" eating when it takes place in faith. For everything which is done in faith is spiritual. "Everything that comes from the Holy Spirit is spirit, spiritual, and an object of the Spirit, in reality and whether it is physical or material, outward or visible; similarly, everything which comes from the natural power of the flesh, without Spirit is flesh and fleshly no matter how inward and

---

[88] *WA* 23, 243; *LW* 37, 124. Cf. *WA* 23, 201, 253; *LW* 37, 98, 130 f.; *WA* 26, 351; *LW* 37, 236 f.

[89] Cf. the important descriptions by Erich Seeberg, *Der Gegensatz zwischen Zwingli, Schwenckfeld, und Luther* (Leipzig: Deichert, 1929).

[90] *WA* 23, 173, 199; *LW* 37, 81, 97.

invisible it may be."[61] Christ's flesh is therefore "spiritual" because
it comes from the Spirit, and the bodily eating is spiritual because
it is done in faith in God's word. To eat "spiritually" does not
mean that we receive something that is merely spiritual; rather we
receive a reality that comes from the Holy Spirit and that must
be received and enjoyed in a spiritual way, that is, in faith."[62]

On this point, Luther's position is far superior to that of his
opponents. He breaks through their idealistic equation of the
world of the Holy Spirit with the sphere of inwardness in which
there is only "spirit." He preserves the relationship of the Holy
Spirit to the totality and the significance of reality, of sharing with
God, association with God for all of life. All of these are not
only spiritual but also bodily in nature. We need only consider
what sort of Bible passages Luther's opponents quote against him.
Apart from the John 6 passage already mentioned, they particularly quote II Corinthians 5:16, "We no longer know Christ according to the flesh," and Colossians 3:1 f.: "Seek the things which
are above. . . . Set your minds on things that are above, and not
on things that are on earth."[63] Not to seek that which is upon
earth—is that really to be used as a proof against the emphasis
on the real presence? Luther's reply is powerful. "But suppose I
ask why they attend preaching and seek the gospel, and why they
observe the Lord's Supper? Why do they love and serve their
neighbor? Our father, mother, master, servant, and neighbor are all
on earth; all right, let us not seek them, nor honor, obey, serve,
or love anyone! Wouldn't this be fine? But all this is on earth.
And St. Paul says that we must not seek that which is on earth."[64]

At first glance it may appear that Luther is unfairly reduc-

---

[61] *WA* 23, 203; *LW* 37, 99. Cf. "Lifting a piece of straw by divine command is a spiritual act . . . what matters is not what is said but who says it."
WA 30ᴵᴵᴵ, 115.

[62] *WA* 23, 183, 189, 191; *LW* 37, 88, 92, 93 f. Cf. the reports of the
Marburg Colloquy: "If God would present me with horse manure to eat, I
should eat it spiritually. For wherever the word of God is present, there is a
spiritual eating." *WA* 30ᴵᴵᴵ, 116, 118. On spiritual and physical eating, cf.
WA, Br 6, 156.

[63] *WA* 26, 306 ff.; *LW* 37, 199-203. Melanchthon and Luther made an excellent comment on "according to the flesh" at Marburg. "Melanchthon: that is
according to our flesh. Luther: that is according to our flesh, in the sense of
knowing in a fleshly way, namely to know without the spirit and without
faith." *WA* 30ᴵᴵᴵ, 132.

[64] *WA* 26, 306; *LW* 37, 199.

ing his opponents' argument to absurdity. This answer, however, very clearly indicates what it was that most deeply separated Luther from the Swiss. For Luther, God's Spirit does not confront men in any other way than in the complete concreteness, outwardness, bodiliness of history. Despising bodiliness shows that one does not take seriously the true historicity of God's revelation. "You find no word or commandment of God in the entire Scripture in which something material and outward is not contained and presented." The entire biblical history bears witness to this.[65] "The Spirit cannot be with us except in material and physical things such as the word, water, in Christ's body, and in these things on earth."[66] "Spirit" is not a transcendental sphere beyond all earthly history but precisely this history comprehended in God's word. And in this sense it is really important to remain on earth. For we remain most completely on earth precisely when we seek that which is above. Luther's interest in the bodily presence of Christ is part of his concern for the truly essential context of this theology of history. He had good reason to say that his opponents "wanted to have mere spirit" and for classifying them with the enthusiasts in this respect. The objections of the opponents have their source in a total view of spirit and history which Luther quite rightly felt was unbiblical and came from "another spirit than we have."[67]

Luther could also express this complete opposition in the differing concepts of the glory of God on both sides. The opponents felt that it was not worthy of God to be really present in bread and wine on the altar. "It is not proper" and "it doesn't fit" are expressions which Luther uses to express their thoughts.[68] Luther saw this as a "worldly and fleshly" concept of the glory of God which views it as being constituted by his transcendence. The

---

[65] *WA* 23, 261; *LW* 37, 135 f.

[66] *WA* 23, 193; *LW* 37, 95.

[67] "To Abraham he gave the word including with it his son Isaac [I Sam. 15:2 f.]. To Noah he gave the word including with it the rainbow [Gen. 9:8 ff.]. And so on. You find no word of God in the entire Scripture in which something material and outward is not contained and presented. . . . So too, here in the Supper, together with Christ's body crucified for us we have been given the word that is present in order to be eaten physically." *WA* 23, 261; *LW* 37, 135 f. *WA*, Br, 5, 340; cf. Sasse, *op. cit.*, p. 265.

[68] *WA* 19, 486; *LW* 36, 338.

truth is, however, that God's glory consists in his condescendence, in his entering into the world and into its trouble and shame. "The glory of our God is precisely that for our sakes he comes down to the very depths, into human flesh, into the bread, into our mouth, our heart, our body; moreover, for our sakes he allows himself to be treated ingloriously both on the cross and on the altar."[68]

Luther, however, was concerned not only with the question of whether the real presence is necessary, worthy of God, and meaningful, but also with the other question as to whether or not it is possible and not something absurd. Are Christ's flesh and blood really in the bread and wine on the altar? Did Christ not ascend to heaven? There he is present with God according to his humanity. He is in heaven and not on the altar.[70] Luther could only answer these questions by placing the real presence in the larger context of his christology. The conflict about the real presence gave his christology its final form and has dominated Lutheran theology since then.[71] Christology and the doctrine of the Lord's Supper have mutually conditioned each other.

Luther's basic christological thought must be stated at the beginning of our discussion. "There is no God apart from Christ." God is present for us only in Christ's humanity. "Wherever Christ is present there the deity is fully and completely present." The opposite is also true.[72] God, however, is omnipresent and works in all things. Wherever he is, Christ also is. If Christ is sitting at the right hand of God—then the right hand of God must be his presence which both transcends and is immanent in everything rather than a particular place in heaven. And Christ must be omnipresent also according to his humanity. As such, however, Christ's humanity is something which we cannot grasp and cannot under-

---

[68] *WA* 23, 155, 157; *LW* 37, 71 f.
[70] *WA* 23, 116, 119; *LW* 37, 46 f., 49.
[71] P. W. Gennrich says: "Luther's christology is not a product of the controversy about the Lord's Supper. On the contrary, Luther's position in the controversy about the Lord's Supper is the necessary result of his basic christological position. The controversy about the Lord's Supper however certainly stimulated Luther to expand and specially emphasize certain powers in his christology; what he here develops, however, is already contained within the context of his entire understanding of Christ as the basis of his theology." *Die Christologie Luthers im Abendmahlsstreit* (1929), p. 129.
[72] *WA* 23, 131 ff.; *LW* 37, 55 ff. *WA* 30ᴵᴵᴵ, 132 f.; Sasse, *op. cit.*, pp. 250 f.

stand." For it is one thing to ask whether God is present and something quite different to ask whether he is present for me. God's right hand is everywhere; but I cannot get hold of it everywhere. Rather, God must "limit himself for your benefit and meet you at some definite place. God's right hand does this when it enters into the humanity of Christ and dwells there. There you surely find it." The same is true also of the omnipresent humanity of Christ. When it is "present in and above everything, as is the nature of God's right hand," we cannot comprehend it. But Christ limits himself with his word, "This is my body," to the bread and commands us to grasp him there. Just as the incomprehensible and omnipresent God draws near to a man in the humanity of Jesus Christ, so the incomprehensible and omnipresent humanity of Christ again draws near to and can be grasped by men in the Lord's Supper. It is God's love that makes him reveal himself in such a concrete form. And he remains free to choose the form in which he will be concretely present. God's revelation is in its concreteness always contingent and underivable, and it can be received only by faith which accepts it as an absolute gift."

THE REAL PRESENCE AND THE GIFT OF THE LORD'S SUPPER

The real presence, that is, the bodily presence of the true body and blood of Christ in the bread and wine, occurs in the community celebration of the Lord's Supper in that the pastor who acts as "the mouth of all of us" performs and speaks (or sings) the ordinance instituted by Christ." Within this "ordinance of Christ" the decisive element is the words: "This is my body," and "This is my blood." Then, as now, they bring about that which they express when the pastor speaks them in the community. Christ's body and blood are present through the power of these words of Christ."

 WA 23, 151; *LW* 37, 68 f.

 WA 23, 267; *LW* 37, 140.

 WA 38, 247.

 "We must turn our eyes and hearts simply to the institution of Christ and this alone, and set nothing before us but the very word of Christ by which he instituted the sacrament, made it perfect, and committed it to us. For in that word, and in that word alone, reside the power, the nature, and the whole

What does the bodily presence of Christ in bread and wine effect? All receive it, not just those who believe,[77] and it brings
about the same gift for all. However, it works salvation only for
those who receive it in faith in Christ's words.[78] For the others
who do not believe and therefore are unworthy, and who receive
it only physically and not spiritually, that is, not in faith, it works
as a poison and brings about death under judgment.[79] Luther thus
teaches that the unworthy also receive Christ's body and blood
orally; he bases his position on Paul's statements in I Corinthians
11. The reality of the real presence and of its reception is determined by Christ's words and therefore, is independent of the inner
attitude of the recipient and of whether he believes or does not
believe.[80] We cannot understand this statement either as a relapse
irreconcilable with Luther's basic position or as a leftover of a ma-
terialistic sacramentalism. For Luther attributes this same double
effect, which he (and Paul) ascribes to the sacrament, also to the
word, and emphasizes the correlation between word and sacrament
at this point.[81] In both instances the presence of grace places man
in a situation of decision, either for life or for death.

What is the saving effect of the real presence? How is it related
to the essential gift of the gospel, the forgiveness of sins? By putting the question in this way, we once again take up the problem
which concerned us in our consideration of the first phases of Luther's doctrine of the Lord's Supper.

Even when Luther most strongly emphasizes the real presence,
the real and genuine gift of the sacrament remains the forgiveness
of sins. The forgiveness of sins depends on the fact that the New
Testament is present in the sacrament, which in turn depends on
the presence of Christ's body and blood. This is how Luther sees
the connection. "These words form [*fassen*] the bread and the

---

substance of the mass." *WA* 6, 512; *LW* 36, 36. "You have here Christ's
body and blood by virtue of these words which are coupled with the bread
and wine." *WA* 30^I, 224; *BC*, 448. For a more exact presentation of Luther's
understanding of the real presence, cf. Hans Grass, *op. cit.*
   [77] *WA* 26, 490 f.; *LW* 37, 352 f.
   [78] *WA* 26, 353; *LW* 37, 238.
   [79] *WA* 23, 179 ff.; *LW* 37, 85 f.
   [80] *WA* 30^I, 224; *BC*, 448.
   [81] At Marburg he explicitly drew the parallel to II Cor. 2:16. *WA* 30^{III},
119; cf. Sasse, *op. cit.*, p. 239.

cup into a sacrament. The body and blood contain [*fassen*] the New Testament; the New Testament conveys [*fassen*] the forgiveness of sins; the forgiveness of sins brings [*fassen*] eternal life and salvation."⁸² By the power of the word of Christ, body and blood are the "treasure through and in which we receive the forgiveness of sins." "Christ bids me eat and drink in order that the sacrament may be mine and may be a source of blessing to me as a sure pledge and sign, indeed, as the very gift he has provided for me against my sins, death, and all evils."⁸³ Body and blood thus guarantee that we receive the forgiveness of sins. They are a guarantee, however, which from the very beginning stands in an interrelationship to the forgiveness of sins. What is involved is precisely the same human life of Jesus which he risked for us on the cross. We can see that Luther, when he speaks of the Lord's glorified body, never forgets that it is the body which has been given into death. The glorified body remains the crucified body.

The effect of the Lord's Supper, like that of the sacraments generally, is that faith or its equivalent, the new life, is strengthened and increased constantly.⁸⁴ Faith needs this "re-creation" and "strengthening" because in this life it is constantly attacked and endangered by the devil and the world. Thus, the Lord's Supper is of help particularly when temptation attacks.

But the answer to the question about the effect of the real presence cannot stop at this point. Does not the word give the same thing, for example, in confession and absolution? The unique significance of the real presence of the body of Christ filled with the Spirit was too great to permit an answer to this question simply in terms that the body and the blood are the guarantee, and especially, the vehicle of forgiveness. For this reason, Luther attempts to demonstrate that there is a particular saving effect of such bodily eating of the body of Christ. "So, when we eat Christ's flesh physically and spiritually, the food is so powerful that it

⁸² *WA* 20, 478. Cf. *WA* 30ᴵᴵᴵ, 133; cf. Sasse, *op. cit.*, p. 253.

⁸³ *WA* 30ᴵ, 225; BC, 449.

⁸⁴ "Therefore, it is appropriately called the food of the soul since it nourishes and strengthens the new man. The Lord's Supper is given as a daily food and sustenance so that our faith may refresh and strengthen itself and not weaken in the struggle but grow continually stronger. For the new life should be one that continually develops and progresses." *WA* 30ᴵ, 225; BC, 449.

402   *The Theology of Martin Luther*

transforms us into itself and out of fleshly, sinful, mortal men, makes spiritual, holy, living men. This we are already, although in a hidden manner in faith and hope; the fact is not yet manifest, but we shall experience it on the Last Day."[85] But Luther had very frequently attributed this same transformation of the flesh into spirit to the spoken word of preaching which brings Christ into us. For this reason, Luther first describes a unique saving effect to the sacrament by taking up the thought of Irenaeus and the other Greek fathers that the body and blood of Christ are a food which makes the body immortal. Christ gives us his own body as a food "so that with such a pledge he may assure and promise us that our body too shall live forever; for here on earth it partakes of an everlasting and living food." If these words seem to say that the bodily eating of Christ's body was a guarantee to the soul that the body would be raised, other passages leave no doubt at all that Luther thought of a physical effect resulting in resurrection and not only an assurance of it. "The soul sees and clearly understands that the body will live eternally because it has partaken of an eternal food which will not leave it to decay in the grave and turn to dust."[86]

With this, the real presence received a peculiar effect corresponding to its peculiar significance. Since this is given only to faith, one cannot characterize the thought as magical. However, it clearly leads beyond Luther's basic principle of the relationship between word and sacrament. The sacrament now has two high points. It is, however, characteristic that Luther seldom mentions this idea of the physical effect of the sacrament outside of his polemical writings. The fact that it is completely missing in the catechisms is of particular importance. The *Small Catechism* summarizes the "benefits" of the sacraments in three terms: forgiveness of sins, life, and salvation. These three terms are basically only one: forgiveness. "For where there is forgiveness of sins, there

---

[85] *WA* 23, 205; *LW* 37, 101.
[86] *WA* 23, 155, 191, 205, 253 ff.; *LW* 37, 71, 93 f., 100, 130 f. On Irenaeus, see *WA* 22, 233; *LW* 37, 115-120. *WA* 30ᴵᴵᴵ, 126; cf. *Sasse, op. cit.,* p. 248. Luther makes the same statement in discussing baptism. *WA* 30ᴵ, 217; *BC*, 442.

are also life and salvation."[87] Luther's ideas about the physical effects of the Lord's Supper do, however, meet the demand of a doctrine of the sacrament that the validity and independent significance of the sacrament is established together with the preached word. Usually, however, Luther defines the uniqueness of the sacrament in other terms, as we have already seen (cf. p. 347).

---

[87] "He who believes these words has what they say and declare: the forgiveness of sins." No mention is made of anything else. *WA* 30$^\mathrm{I}$, 391; *BC*, 352.

28

ESCHATOLOGY

FOR FAITH, salvation is a present reality. Luther strongly emphasizes this fact. "Where there is forgiveness of sins there are also life and salvation," now, in this present moment. Salvation is no longer only a future event. In this life, however, the Christian has it only in faith and not yet in experience, not in complete, unbroken, uninterrupted, constant, and uncontradictable experience. Faith is continually attacked by the temptations arising from the contradiction between the reality it sees and the salvation that is present but hidden from sight. "We do not wait for forgiveness and all graces as though we would not receive them until the life to come; rather, they are now present for us in faith, even though they are hidden and will be revealed only in the life to come."[1] Christians therefore wait for the final revelation. We have repeatedly discussed this eschatological dimension of various topics of Luther's theology, for example, in the doctrines of Christ's work and of righteousness through faith. To be a Christian is both to have and at the same time not to have, to be and at the same time not yet to be. We are in the process of becoming Christians. Therefore those things which faith has already received point it forward to the eschaton. This is true not only of the life of the individual Christian but equally of the situation of the church in the world and of the lordship of Christ in history. The church must yet endure the bitter suffering brought upon it by the pressure and resistance of the world and of Satan. Theology is and remains theology of the cross; therefore it necessarily becomes eschatology. Faith eagerly waits and hopes for the future when Christ's lordship will be revealed. Luther's theology is thoroughly eschatological in the strict sense of expecting the end of the world. His thoughts about the eschaton are not a conventional appendix but a section of his theology which is rooted in, indispensable to, and

---
[1] *WA* 17^{II}, 229.

a decisive part of the substance of his theology. Luther did not merely repeat the old traditional answers to the central questions of eschatology. In this doctrine too, he is the Reformer.

DYING VIEWED IN THE LIGHT OF LAW AND GOSPEL

Luther's theology of death is expressed particularly clearly in his powerful interpretation of Psalm 90.[2] Just as natural man, by his own powers, is not able to understand the true nature of God's law and yet imagines that he can fulfill the law's demands, so he also fails to recognize the seriousness and the burden of death. People usually understand death as a "natural" event, as a particular example of the transitoriness of all creatures; they therefore recommend that we should not take it too seriously—Luther was thinking of ancient classical authors as well as of his contemporaries.[3] Holy Scripture, however, opens our eyes to what really happens when we die. Dying is more than a biological phenomenon. It is a human reality; and this distinguishes it from the ending of plant and animal life. Plants and animals do not come to an end because of God's wrath, but according to a "natural order" established by God. "The death of a man is, however, an infinite and eternal misery and wrath." For man is a creature created in the image of God, to live eternally and immortally in relationship to God and not to die. His death is not the result of a natural process created by God. Rather death is "laid upon him and executed on him through God's wrath."[4] This is why men draw back in terror in the face of death and experience horror such as no other living being experiences.[5] We must understand our mortal fate theologically within the relationship between God and man; for this relationship is the decisive and all-embracing destiny of man.

---

[2] *WA* 40ᴵᴵᴵ, 485 ff.; *LW* 13, 75-141. Luther delivered these lectures between October, 1534 and May, 1535. Due to illness, as well as for other reasons, the lectures were interrupted for long periods of time. Rörer took notes and reconstructed them; Veit Dietrich edited them and published them. We still have Rörer's notes of these lectures as well as the printed text.

[3] *WA* 40ᴵᴵᴵ, 485; cf. *LW* 13, 76.

[4] *WA* 39ᴵᴵ, 366 f. *WA* 40ᴵᴵᴵ, 513; *LW* 13, 94.

[5] *WA* 39ᴵᴵ, 367.

The Theology of Martin Luther

In this discussion, Luther never thinks merely of physical death
or of the decline of life as such, but he centers our attention on
personal center and depth of life.[6] Death in and by itself is no
game for children. In death we stand on the edge of the abyss
and we must "spring from the certain and secure edge of this life
into the abyss." We must do this even though we see and feel no
bottom and ground on which we can gain a foothold; we take the
chance on God alone.[7] No one therefore confronts death without
fear and trembling, even though he is like the heathen and the
saints and does not feel God's wrath.[8] But if that is all that were
involved in death, it could still be borne.[9] There is, however, much
more, for "Death always appears in the company of sin and law."[10]
This means: In the collapse of our earthly life, we sinners experience the "no" God speaks to us in his wrath.[11] The experience of
God's wrath in death is eternal death. God punishes us in death
because of our guilt. "Where death, however, is deserved and
earned because of sin, the wrath of God comes and makes death
unbearable so that we can neither find nor feel anything else than
death."[12]

> In the midst of death behold
> Hell's jaws gaping at us![13]

Only Christians and God-fearing men are completely aware of
this depth of death. Luther could say: "Our death is a more terrible thing than all death not only of other living beings, but
also than the troubles and death of other men. What of it when
Epicurus dies? He not only does not know that there is a God,
but even fails to understand his own misery and recognize the
disaster which he is experiencing. Christians, however, and God-
fearing men know that their death, together with all the other
miseries of this life, is to be equated with God's wrath. Therefore
they find themselves compelled to struggle and fight with the

---

[6] *WA* 40ᴵᴵᴵ, 487; *LW* 13, 78.
[7] *WA* 19, 217.
[8] *WA* 19, 218.
[9] *WA* 19, 217.
[10] *WA* 31ᴵ, 146; *LW* 14, 83.
[11] *WA* 19, 217. *WA* 40ᴵᴵᴵ, 487; *LW* 13, 78.
[12] *WA* 19, 217.
[13] *WA* 35, 454; *LW* 53, 276.

wrathful God in order to preserve their salvation."[14] Only the Christian is completely awakened by God's word to an awareness of his situation before God and thus to a full comprehension of his humanity. Only the Christian therefore is completely awakened to the fate of death as well as to God's wrath and the law in general.

All this is true of dying when it is viewed in the light of the law. The Christian, however, not only stands under God's law, but he hears the gospel at the same time. This gospel completely transforms all his experience of God's wrath, including death. The man who is proud and rebels against God encounters God's "no" to him in the destructive experience of death. When he, however, humbles himself under this experience and flees to the mercy God offers him in the gospel, then he, under the "no," also receives God's great "yes" to him in Christ. Then the condemning "no" of God's rejection is converted into the fatherly "no" of God's gracious visitation which removes his old sinful nature from him through death and gives him a new nature through Christ. Death becomes "a father's rod used to punish his child."[15]

Death then fulfills God's promise to Christians in their baptism, that is, their sin is put to death.[16] This begins in earthly life through the tasks and the sufferings which God lays upon a man, but it is completed only in physical death and then "instantly."[17] Thus everything depends on the fact that the Christian acknowledges the gracious meaning of dying by dying willingly. "The best that can happen in death is that our will accepts it."[18] No man

---

[14] *WA* 40ᴵᴵᴵ, 554; *LW* 13, 112.

[15] *WA* 31ᴵ, 160; *LW* 14, 90.

[16] Cf. *The Holy and Blessed Sacrament of Baptism* (1519), *WA* 2, 727-737; *LW* 35, 29-43. For Luther's understanding of baptism, cf. chapter 26 above.

[17] "Meanwhile, since holiness has begun and is growing daily, we await the time when our flesh will be put to death, will be buried with all its uncleanness, and will come forth gloriously and arise to complete the perfect holiness in a new, eternal life. . . . All this, then, is the function and work of the Holy Spirit, to begin and daily to increase holiness on earth . . . when we pass from this life, He will instantly perfect our holiness and will eternally preserve us in it." *WA* 30ᴵ, 190; *BC*, 418. By using "instantly," Luther refers to Paul's description of what will happen to those Christians who are alive on the Last Day [I Cor. 15:52]. In both cases, the change takes place "instantly." "When we have been reduced to dust, then at last sins will be entirely extinguished." *WA* 39ᴵ, 95; *LW* 34, 164.

[18] *WA* 10ᴵᴵᴵ, 76. See the entire sermon which is very rich in meaning. *WA* 10ᴵᴵᴵ, 75 ff.

can do this by himself. He can do it only by the power of the
death Christ endured in complete obedience. Since God uses a
man's death to set him free from himself and from death, the Christian desires death. Luther prays, "Help us not to fear but to desire
death."[19] And he confesses, "We should be happy to be dead and
desire to die."[20] He understands Christian perfection specifically in
terms of the desire for death. The final result of sanctification in the
Christian's life "is that he becomes perfect and gladly gives his
life into death; with Paul [Phil. 1:23], he desires to depart so
that all sin will cease and that God's will may be fully accomplished in him."[21] Thus the law of death also becomes a form of
the gospel for the Christian. "Death, then, which previously was
a punishment of sin is now a remedy for sin. Thus it is now
blessed."[22]

Death, freed of the wrath of God in this way, is now really
a sleep. "Death is become my slumber" is the way in which Luther puts it in his hymn paraphrase of Simeon's song [Luke 2:29-
32].[23] Or to illustrate with another picture which Luther used in
his *Treatise on Preparing to Die* (*Sermon von der Bereitung zum
Sterben*) (1519); death is only "the narrow gate and the small
way to life," corresponding to the narrow exit through which a
child is born into this world from the body of his mother. Thus,
when a man dies, he passes through the narrows and straits of
anxieties to be born into the world to come. "Thus a dying man
must courageously enter into anxiety with the knowledge that there
will be great space and much joy afterwards."[24] This is dying as
faith sees it in the light of the gospel. The voice of the law says,
"In the midst of life, we are in death." The voice of the gospel
says, "In the midst of death, we are in life."[25]

The Christian, however, hears the voice of the gospel only as a
man who still stands under the law as a sinner and also hears the
voice of the law. If this is true of faith generally, it is particularly

[19] *WA* 6, 14.
[20] *WA* 12, 410. *WA* 39ᴵ, 512.
[21] *WA* 17ᴵᴵ, 13.
[22] *WA* 10ᴵᴵᴵ, 76.
[23] *WA* 35, 439; *LW* 53, 248.
[24] *WA* 2, 685.
[25] *WA* 40ᴵᴵᴵ, 496; *LW* 13, 83. Cf. *WA* 35, 453 f.; *LW* 53, 275 f.

true in the face of death. It means that here too, faith must constantly and repeatedly overcome the temptation which comes from the reality of dying under the law.[26] The Christian does not succeed in viewing death in the light of the gospel once for all; rather, as a sinner he constantly comes from standing under the law and therefore views dying in the light of the law. In this trouble he must constantly reappropriate the gospel and the meaning which it gives to death. Here too, faith is moving, fleeing, struggling, and breaking through. Whoever does not keep this character of faith in mind must find an unbearable contradiction between the various things which Luther says about the death of a Christian. As we have seen, Luther can say that Christians experience death as a terrible thing in a way that all other men do not. For only Christians know of God's wrath and consciously confront it in death. In distinction from all other men they are completely alert to God's law. In other places, however, Luther seems to say the exact opposite. "A Christian neither tastes nor sees death. That is, he does not feel it and is not terrified by it, but goes into it calmly and peacefully as though he were going to sleep and were not really dying. A godless man, however, feels death and is eternally terrified by it. The word of God makes this difference. The Christian has this word and holds fast to it in death."[27] Luther says both the one and the other. This means that faith constantly comes from the first position and always ends at the second position. As long as a Christian is on earth he as a sinner comes out of this conflict with God and therefore also from under God's wrath and law. He neither can nor may bypass it but he may and should constantly allow himself to be called and carried away to the gospel of Christ, through the promise of God's forgiving and redeeming mercy. Thus faith constantly stands in conflict with the immediate experience and feeling of bitter death. The Christian feels death, but he does not want to feel it. He rises above this feeling.[28]

---

[26] If we really believed we would not fear any more, and we would not rebel against death. *WA* 39[II], 276.

[27] *WA* 17[II], 234.

[28] "He feels death, and yet he refuses to feel it or call it death but clings to the gracious right hand of God." *WA* 31[I], 160; *LW* 14, 90.

Therefore the Christian continues to sing songs such as, "In the Midst of Life We Are," that express the anxious questions and prayers arising from the "pains of bitter death."[29] Even the melancholy first lines of every verse of the hymn, "In the Midst of Life We Are" are not pre-Christian but Christian. Luther did not wish to replace "In the Midst of Life We Are" with "In Peace and Joy I Now Depart,"[30] but composed both for Christians and wants them to sing both.

> Whither shall we flee away
> Where a rest is waiting?
> To thee, Lord Christ, thee only.

This is where faith flees from the anxiety it feels when it confronts God in death. And it is this movement which then enables it to sing:

> In peace and joy I now depart,
> As God wants me.
> Content and still in mind and heart,
> He doth save me.
> As my God hath promised me,
> Death is now become my slumber.

THE SLEEP OF DEATH AND THE RESURRECTION

Luther thinks of the future for which the Christian hopes primarily in terms of what happens to the individual man in death and beyond death. Luther's certainty that there will be a new life arising out of death is based on the totality of God's redeeming work in Christ. We have therefore constantly referred to this point in our preceding discussions. The heart and center of this whole position is the resurrection of Christ Jesus and the victory over death which he won in it. This is the only true comfort for all of us who must die. Luther bears powerful witness to this through his references to Paul's statements in I Corinthians 15, in his sermons on this chapter, and elsewhere.[31] Christ is risen as the "first fruit." His resurrection promises the bodily resurrection of

---

[29] *WA* 35, 453; *LW* 53, 275 f.
[30] *WA* 35, 438; *LW* 53, 248.
[31] *WA* 36, 478-696.

all who are his own through baptism and faith." Through the resurrection of Christ the Head, the greatest part of the general resurrection has actually already taken place."

Luther always bases his expectation of a life beyond death on the resurrection of Christ—even though he frequently does not explicitly refer to it. In such cases, he begins with the First Commandment or with the introduction to it, "I am the Lord your God" or a similar word of God addressed to man." He interprets such passages as Jesus' answer to the Sadducees in Matthew 22: "God is not the God of the dead but the living." (This does not mean that Christ was of no importance for Luther in this particular approach to the resurrection. For Luther, the introduction to the First Commandment and the other statements of God which he quotes are nothing else than a summary of the gospel of Jesus Christ. What is essentially said is, "I am the Lord your God." "My God," the God who wants to save me, is never any other than the "God in Christ." Luther therefore considers it to be self-understood that Christ is implicitly included in such words of God.) Luther applies this syllogism when he says: If God introduces himself to you as your God, then you are alive to God even when you die." If God speaks to you, then you are involved in an immortal relationship; for God speaks only to those who are alive. It must follow that God raises the dead. This makes them "immortal." Anyone with whom God speaks, whether he speaks in wrath or in grace, is thus certainly immortal. The person of the God who speaks and his word demonstrate that we are such creatures, the kind of creatures with whom God wishes to speak in eternity and in an immortal way."" Thus every statement in which God makes himself known as our God and every word which God speaks to

" Cf., e.g., "Even if I die, so what? I will still sing, for Christ is risen and he is the first fruits. I have him, I believe in him, and I am baptized in him—and he has promised that he will take me to himself." *WA* 36, 543. Cf. *WA* 37, 67 ff. See also the explanation of the second article in the *Small Catechism* where Luther says: "Even as he is risen from the dead," *WA* 30¹, 297; *BC*, 345.

" *WA* 36, 547. *WA* 37, 68.

" *WA* 43, 479, 481. Cf. *WA* 31¹, 154; *LW* 14, 87.

" "Therefore they may live forever; otherwise he would not be their God." *WA* 31¹, 155; *LW* 14, 87.

" *WA* 43, 481.

us already bear witness to the resurrection of the dead."[17] According to Luther, this holds true for every man—even though God
does not speak with him in grace but "in wrath." There is no
basis for a man to escape from, or to run away from, his relationship to God through bodily death. The fact that God has spoken
to him remains his inescapable fate. For the believer, however,
God's word to him which preserves him through death is identical with Christ's word. The Christian holds fast to the word when
he dies, and it gives him the certainty that he will be awakened
out of death.

All certainty about the situation beyond death thus depends on
the word of God and of Christ.[38] For this reason Luther can answer the question about where we shall be in death only by referring to the word of God or of Christ. Christians rest in "the bosom
of Christ."[39] This, however, is nothing else than Christ's word, for
example, "Whoever believes in me will never die" [John 10:26]
or some similar statement. This is what a man must hold to when
he dies. In this he finds a place to rest in peace; for he is then "held
and preserved in the bosom of Christ to the Last Day."[40] This deep
insight demonstrates the significance of Luther's reformation for
eschatology. The traditional doctrines said much about the various
places where the souls of the dead were. Topographical maps of
the intermediate state [*Zwischenzustand*] were available.[41] Luther
criticizes them very sharply and proceeds from topographical to
theological discussions in the certainty that all who die in faith
have their "place" in God's word and Christ's promise.[42] They

---

[17] *WA* 43, 479.

[38] "My word is eternal and in this word you are eternal." *WA* 31¹, 456;
LW 14, 134 f.

[39] *WA* 43, 361; *LW* 4, 313.

[40] "Man's soul or spirit has no resting place where it can remain except for
the word of God, until it comes to the full vision of God on the Last Day. . . .
When we die we must take courage and commit ourselves with strong faith to
the word of Christ which says, 'Whoever believes in me will never die,' [John
11:26] or some word like this, and die and go to sleep upon it and thus be
held in the arms of Christ preserved to the Last Day." *WA* 10ᴵᴵᴵ, 191. Cf.
WA 43, 361; *LW* 4, 314.

[41] *WA* 43, 361; *LW* 4, 314 f.

[42] The fathers of the Old Testament rest in Abraham's bosom; that is the
word of promise given to Abraham. "So all of the fathers who lived before
the birth of Christ have gone to Abraham's bosom, that is, they died firmly
believing this word of God [Gen. 22:18] and they have all fallen asleep, are
preserved and protected in this word, and sleep in it until the Last Day as
though this word were a bosom." *WA* 10ᴵᴵᴵ, 191.

"rest" and "sleep" in the bosom of Christ. This is Luther's definitive statement about the condition of the departed. In order to understand its significance completely, we must view it against the background of the development of eschatology since the time of the New Testament.

The hope of the early church centered on the resurrection on the Last Day. It is this which first calls the dead into eternal life (I Cor. 15; Phil. 3:20 f.). This resurrection happens to the total man and not only to the body. Paul speaks of the resurrection not of "the body" but of "the dead." This understanding of the resurrection implicitly understands death as also affecting the total man. Together with this hope for the resurrection on the Last Day, we find still another thought in Paul. Dying leads immediately to full participation with Christ and life with him (II Cor. 5:6 ff.; Phil. 1:23). The apostle apparently felt that there was no contradiction between these two thoughts. In this letter to the Philippians, he first says that he expects to be immediately united with Christ, and later says that Christians expect to receive a new bodily existence, and therewith life out of death, from the Lord when he comes again. Paul makes no attempt to reconcile the two thoughts. In any case, it is Christ who waits for us in death and at the end of the world. Compared with this certainty, other questions are of no importance.

The church's doctrine of eschatology, however, attempted to put these two expectations of hope into a temporal relationship to each other.* This is done through the concept of an "intermediate state" between the death of the individual and the Last Day when he will receive a new bodily existence. Body and soul must be thought of dualistically. In death, souls separate themselves from bodies and continue to live without bodies either at some place set aside for those who are saved and for those who are lost or in some sort of a halfway house (as was commonly taught by theologians up to and including Augustine). Others maintained that those who did not go to purgatory entered into either heaven or hell immediately after death. This would mean

---

* Cf. my *Die Letzten Dinge* (4th ed.; Gütersloh: Bertelsmann, 1933), pp. 144 ff.

that the souls of the blessed are already with Christ, are already blessed with the vision and enjoyment of God, and participate in his eternal life. The Last Day will only intensify their condition through the resurrection of their bodies. Souls will receive their bodies back again in a glorified condition; and this makes their salvation complete. No emphasis is, however, placed on this second factor but only on the first, that is, that souls are truly alive and blessed already before the resurrection. Thus the original biblical concepts have been replaced by ideas from Hellenistic gnostic dualism. The New Testament idea of the resurrection which affects the total man has had to give way to the immortality of the soul. The Last Day also loses its significance, for souls have received all that is decisively important long before this. Eschatological tension is no longer strongly directed to the day of Jesus' coming. The difference between this and the hope of the New Testament is very great.

Against this background, we can measure the significance of Luther's Reformation for eschatology. Luther admittedly shares the dualistic definition of death as separation of soul and body; accordingly, he also teaches that the souls enjoy a bodiless existence until the Last Day." For this reason it is all the more significant that the decisive New Testament insights reappear in Luther and once again become the dominating elements in his thinking. Luther generally understands the condition between death and the resurrection as a deep and dreamless sleep without consciousness and feeling. When the dead are awakened on the Last Day, they will—like a man who wakes up in the morning—know neither where they were nor how long they have rested. "For just as a man who falls asleep and sleeps soundly until morning does not know what has happened to him when he wakes up, so we shall suddenly rise on the Last Day; and we shall know neither what death has been like or how we have come through it."" Luther

---

" "Only a part of man dies." *WA* 36, 241, cf. *LW* 51, 234. "Thus the spirit comes from the same seed as the body does and yet it can be separated from the body, but afterwards they shall again be reunited." *WA* 39ɪɪ, 386. Cf. *WA* 39ɪɪ, 354. Cf. my *Unsterblichkeit und ewiges Sterben bei Luther* (Gütersloh: Bertelsmann, 1930), pp. 36 f.

⁴⁵ *WA* 17ɪɪ, 235.

therefore says nothing about souls without their bodies enjoying true life and blessedness before the resurrection. They sleep in "the peace of Christ."[46]

Some Bible passages do compel Luther to make certain exceptions to the rule that the dead sleep. God can also awaken them for a time—just as he allows those of us here upon earth to alternate between waking and sleeping. And the fact that they are asleep does not hinder souls from experiencing visions and from hearing God and the angels speak.[47] And yet, all of this changes nothing in the decisive factor that the full significance of the biblical concept of resurrection appears in Luther's thought. The Last Day has decisive significance also for the individual. Christ awakens a man—not only his body—from the sleep of death and only then gives him blessedness. The Christian is already well taken care of in the sleep of death, since he sleeps "sweetly" with Christ and in His bosom. The blessedness of life with Christ is, however, something quite different than a sweet sleep; it is bound to that condition of being awake which comes only with the resurrection on the Last Day. "We are to sleep until he comes and knocks on the grave and says, 'Dr. Martin, get up.' Then I will arise in a moment and will be eternally happy with him."[48]

At the same time Luther can, as the Apostle Paul does, stress the fact that Christ and eternal life await us immediately beyond death. Speaking of Urbanus Rhegius (the reformer of Lüneburg) Luther says, "We are to know that he is blessed and that he has eternal life and eternal joy and participation with Christ in the heavenly church. For now he has learned, seen with his own eyes, and heard those things which he here in the church on earth explained according to God's word."[49]

---

[46] "Then it must cease and let us sleep in the peace of Christ until he comes and awakens us with joy." *WA*, Br 5, 240. "There can be no doubt: he must be sweetly and softly sleeping in eternal peace of Christ." *WA*, Br 5, 213.

[47] *WA* 43, 360; *LW* 4, 313. *WA* 43, 480 f. *WA* 10^{III}, 194. Cf. Julius Köstlin, *Theology of Luther*, trans. Charles E. Hay (Philadelphia: Lutheran Publication Society, 1897), II, 577.

[48] *WA* 37, 151.

[49] *WA* 53, 400. Speaking of another man who died, Luther says: "Sickness carried him off to heaven to our Lord Jesus Christ." *WA*, Br 6, 301; *LCC* 18, 64.

Holding these two views beside each other creates no difficulty for Luther. For he knows that our earthly concepts and measurements of time are no longer valid beyond death. For this reason, lapses of time such as we experience here are set aside. "Here you must put time out of your mind and know that in that world there is neither time nor a measurement of time, but everything is one eternal moment."⁵⁰ Thus the "intermediate state" is compressed together into a very short period of time. For those who have died, the Last Day comes very soon after their death—even "immediately" when they die. "Each of us has his own Last Day when he dies."⁵¹ Therefore we arrive at the end of the world and the Last Day at the moment of our death. And yet it comes no sooner to the departed than to us and to all generations after us until the temporal end of the world.⁵² Because our periods of time are no longer valid in God's eternity, the Last Day surrounds our life as an ocean surrounds an island. Wherever we reach the boundaries of this life—whether in dying yesterday or today or at some other time or whether at the end of the world—everywhere the Last Day dawns in the great contemporaneity of eternity. This understanding of the Last Day as something which is always near and even present when we die is the unity in which those two lines of expectation, which we found previously in Paul, flow together without excluding each other.

---

⁵⁰ *WA* 10ᴵᴵᴵ, 194. "Since there is no measuring of time in God's sight, a thousand years before him must be as though it were only a day; for this reason the first man Adam is just as close to him as the last man who will be born before the Last Day, for God does not view time on its horizontal but rather in its vertical dimension." *WA* 14, 70.

⁵¹ *WA* 14, 71.

⁵² "In that life a thousand years before God will not even be one day. And when we are resurrected, it will seem to Adam and the patriarchs just as though they were living a half an hour ago. There is no time there. . . . In God's view, everything takes place at once. There is no "before" and "after." And the patriarchs will not reach the Last Day before we do." *WA* 12, 496. "Just as soon as your eyes are closed, you will be awakened. A thousand years will seem as though you have slept a half an hour. As we do not know how long we are sleeping if we do not hear the clock striking during the night, so in death a thousand years will pass away still more rapidly. Before we shall be able to look around, we shall be beautiful angels." *WA* 36, 349. "This entire time which exists since the beginning of man's creation will seem to Adam, when he arises from the dead, as though he had slept only one hour." *WA* 40ᴵᴵᴵ, 525; *LW* 13, 101. Note that Luther thinks of time as being set aside not only subjectively for those who sleep but also objectively in God's eternity.

Later Lutheran Church theology did not follow Luther on this point.[63] Rather, it once again adopted the medieval tradition and continued it. Before the resurrection, souls live in a blessed condition with Christ even though they are without bodies. But how can they then really look forward to the resurrection and to the Last Day? "It would take a foolish soul to desire its body when it was already in heaven!" is the way Luther once put it.[64] The resurrection once again lost the total meaning which it had in the early church. The dualistic understanding of the soul conquered once again. Seventeenth century Lutherans moved away from Luther's idea that souls sleep in death. It made them uncomfortable and they sought to reduce its significance by reinterpreting it in terms of their own doctrine.[65] Only the body sleeps, the soul remains awake. There is no condition of death for the soul. Thus the significance of death on the one hand and of the resurrection on the other is greatly weakened. All the life beyond death that Luther expected comes fully and completely from God's awakening of men. Later piety and theology is no longer completely dependent on the hope that God is able and wills to call us out of death. Rather, it has available a metaphysical doctrine of the soul which was proved on the basis of Bible passages. God's resurrection no longer has total, but only partial, significance for life after death.[66]

With the New Testament, Luther teaches the resurrection of all the dead and not only of the believers.[67] All enter into judgment. The believers enter into eternal life with Christ; evil men enter into eternal death with the devil and his angels. Luther expressly rejects the idea that the devil will finally also be saved.[68]

---

[63] On the eschatology of Lutheran orthodoxy, see Hans Emil Weber, *Reformation, Orthodoxie, und Rationalismus* (Gütersloh: Bertelsmann, 1940) I², 241 ff.

[64] *WA*, TR 5, 5534.

[65] For a more explicit description, cf. *Die letzten Dinge*, p. 150.

[66] For a description of the way in which this change is reflected in the Lutheran hymns of the seventeenth century, see my essay, "Luthers Gedanken über die letzten Dinge," *Luther-Jahrbuch*, XXIII (1941), 18 ff.

[67] Cf. the explanation of the Third Article in the *Small Catechism*: "He will raise me and all the dead and grant eternal life to me and to all who believe in Christ." *WA* 30¹, 250; *BC*, 345. Cf. *WA* 26, 509; *LW* 37, 372.

[68] *WA* 26, 509; *LW* 37, 372.

THE GOAL OF HISTORY AND OF CREATION

The Christian expectation of the Last Day is concerned not only
with the fact that the individual man has a limited future, but also
with the fact that history and the world are coming to an end.
Luther maintains both emphases. Just as he sees Christians as
people who are moving toward death and resurrection and en-
courages them to desire it, so he also reminds them of the end of
the present form of this world and the coming of the day of
Jesus Christ and teaches them to desire it. This is nothing new
in relationship to the New Testament. However, compared with
the eschatological tradition of the medieval church, it is something
new.[58] Since the church's victory in the fourth century, its expectation of the coming of the kingdom of God became less and less
intense. And since Tychonius and Augustine, the millennium (the
thousand year kingdom) of Revelation 20 is no longer understood
in terms of the end of history but in terms of the history of the
church. Christ has conquered and now through his church exercises the lordship of which the Apocalypse speaks.[59] The traditional
pictures of the future were always preserved in dogmatics. But
they lost the emphasis which was once placed upon them. In comparison to the early Christian church and the church in the time
before Constantine, the consciousness of history has been basically
changed. Eschatological interest is now almost entirely concerned
with the future of the individual man. This is the only point at
which the theological doctrine of eschatology undergoes further development. But it had no effect upon the question about the end
and goal of history.

The intense expectation of the coming of the kingdom, however, was preserved among those outside the mainstream of the
church. Beginning with Joachim of Flora, the repressed stream of
chiliasm once again breaks into the open. It now appears in combination with a new and radical criticism of the church which had
conformed to this world. One can no longer attribute the true lord-

---

[58] Cf. the more extensive description in my *Die Letzten Dinge*, pp. 299 ff.
"The end of the world [*Eschaton*] . . . has been domesticated, and subsumed
within the church."

[59] T. F. Torrance, "Die Eschatologie der Reformation," *Evangelische Theologie*, XIV (1954), 60.

ship of Christ to such a church. One must therefore await the coming of his lordship in a new age. This view of the history of the church affected all of the critics of the church and the radicals during the later Middle Ages. And through them it influenced the Hussites and the Anabaptists. The traditional expectation of the coming of the antichrist was related to reality in a sinister fashion. The hierarchy is the realm of the antichrist and the world church is the Babylon of which the apocalypse speaks.

Now Luther agrees with the catholic church in its rejection of chiliasm.[61] He too does not interpret Revelation 20 in terms of the end of history but as a description of the church. The millennium lies in the past and was brought to an end through the coming of the Turks or with the papacy becoming the antichrist.[62] Luther's theology, in distinction from that of the official teaching of the church, however, once again revives the eager expectation of the coming of Jesus common to the early Christian church. Luther, in opposition to the Roman glorification of the church, most definitely emphasizes the hiddenness of the church of God, the form of a servant in which Christ's lordship appears, and the power of Satan on earth and particularly in the church. Therefore he most eagerly awaits the Last Day when Christ will finally overcome Satan.

The medieval church also spoke of the Last Day. It placed the emphasis, however, completely on its significance for the individual as the day of judgment. One need think only of the hymn, "O Day of Wrath, O Day of Mourning" (*Dies irae, dies illa*).[63] Certainly the New Testament teaching that Christ would return to destroy the antichrist was preserved. And the concept of the antichrist was a very meaningful one in the popular consciousness of the Middle Ages.[64] The church of the Middle Ages, however,

---

[61] *WA* 41¹, 121; *LW* 13, 263 f. [Cruciger's reconstruction of sermon notes].

[62] *WA*, DB 7, 409; *LW* 35, 405. Cf. *WA*, DB 7, 469 [the marginal note to Revelation 20]. *WA* 53, 152, 154. Cf. Emanuel Hirsch, *Hilfsbuch zum Studium der Dogmatik* (1937), p. 264.

[63] The translation by William J. Irons may be found in *The Lutheran Hymnal* (St. Louis: Concordia, 1951), No. 607.

[64] On the following, cf. Hans Preuss, *Die Vorstellungen vom Antichrist* (Leipzig: Hinrichs, 1906) and P. Steigleder, "Das Spiel vom Antichrist" (Dissertation, University of Bonn, 1938.)

with the exception of its radical critics, expected the antichrist to
be an individual person who will come at some future time and
incorporate within himself all the enmity to Christ which has been
present in history and raise it to its highest power. The imagery
of the legends describes his life and his abuses in individual detail. People were worried that he might come in the near future;
and they therefore attempted to compute the time of his coming.
But in spite of all this, the concept had little relationship to reality. Luther, however, finds the antichrist in the papacy. For the
papacy places itself above God's word and thereby above God and
Christ by abandoning the comfort of the gospel and placing the
human doctrines of work righteousness in the place of the gospel.
And, according to Daniel 11:36 and Paul's prophecy in II Thessalonians 2:4, these are the decisive characteristics of the antichrist."

Thus the early church's thought is again loaded and ready for use.
The fantastic legends were destroyed with a single stroke and replaced with the bitter reality which was visible to everyone in the
papal curia. Luther was indeed not the only one who characterized
the papacy as the antichrist; other reformers and revolutionaries,
one thinks primarily of the Bohemians, had also done this. And
yet, Luther does not simply repeat the Hussite thesis. His basis
was completely new. The Bohemians called the papacy anti-Christian because of its unchristian life. "Luther, however, was not so
much concerned with the life as with the doctrine, not with the
works but with the faith, because this is the root from which the
branch and the fruits grow . . . thus Luther's antichrist differs from
the antichrist of medieval opponents of the papacy exactly as the
theology of the Reformation differs from pre-Reformation theology."" For Luther, eschatological events are taking place in the
midst of the present. Because the antichrist is already present, Luther expects and hopes that the end will come in the near future
and desires it. The Middle Ages feared the Day of Wrath but Luther desires the coming of Jesus, because he will bring an end to
the antichrist and bring about redemption. Luther can call it "the

---

" *WA* 39ᴵᴵ, 381. *WA* 51, 509. *WA* 7, 741 f. Cf. Preuss, *op. cit.*, pp.
149 ff., 156, 177; further references will be found there.
" Preuss, *op. cit.*, pp. 153, 177.

most happy Last Day."[67] Therewith the early Christian attitude toward the Last Day was renewed and brought back to life.

Luther finally concludes that the antichrist is to be found only in the papacy, that is, in a power within the church itself—although his opinion on this question varies somewhat from time to time. Basically he does not see the antichrist in the external oppressors of Christendom—which in his time were primarily the Turks. In the *Smalcald Articles* he says: "The pope is the real antichrist who has raised himself over and set himself against Christ, for the pope will not permit Christians to be saved except by his own power, which amounts to nothing since it is neither established nor demanded by God. This is actually what St. Paul calls exalting oneself over and against God. Neither the Turks nor the Tartars, great as is their enmity against Christians, do this. . . ."[68] At another place Luther declares: "I do not think Mohammed is the antichrist. He does things too obviously; that black devil is so easily recognized that neither faith nor reason can be deceived. He is like a pagan who persecutes the church from outside it, as the Romans and other pagans have done. But the pope of our time is the true antichrist. He has a very crafty, beautiful, and glorious devil who sits inside the church."[69] Certainly the church of Christ must recognize and prepare for the fact that political powers will be opposed to the Christian community. Luther repeatedly emphasizes that the persecution of the church through the world in this sense cannot be avoided and is even the normal situation.[70] The New Testament bears witness to the terrible battle of political religion in the form of the emperor cult against Christianity (Rev. 13).[71] The most serious danger remains, however: that power

---

[67] *WA* 53, 401. *WA*, Br 2, 567; *S-J* 2, 130; *WA*, Br 9, 175 [a letter to his wife in 1540]. A sampling of references in letters written in 1543 and 1544: *WA*, Br 10, 275, 277, 284, 287, 398.

[68] *WA* 50, 217; *BC*, 300.

[69] *WA* 53, 394. *WA* 26, 507; *LW* 37, 367.

[70] *WA* 51, 217; *LW* 13, 167 f.

[71] In an interpretation of Rev. 13, Luther interprets the first beast as referring to the Roman Empire and the second as referring to the empire of the pope. He sees the first only in the past. Luther did not know of any political world power of his time to which he could apply Revelation 13: 6 f. The ancient empire had fallen, but the pope had re-established it. "For the pope has restored the fallen Roman Empire and conveyed it from the Greeks to the Germans, though it is an image of the Roman Empire rather than the body of

within the church which distorts Christ, which underlies the mis-
leading power of false Christs (Mark 13:6, 21), that falsification
of the kingdom of Christ which makes it a power of this world
and the falsification of the gospel which makes it a law (the Grand
Inquisitor!), and the glorious theocratic church which forgets the
cross. The words "antichrist" and "anti-Christian" are so loosely
used in our own time that they need to be restored. They dare not
become an expression for every power which fights against and op-
presses the church and Christianity. For the original biblical sense
of the terms describes opposition to Christ by imposters who seem
to resemble and pretend to represent Christ. The antichrist appears
within the church itself; as such it is the most dangerous form
which Satan can assume.

Luther's view of the Last Day and his eager desire for the coming of the kingdom are preserved among his pupils and friends.
We find it in the hymn written by Erasmus Alber:

> Your dear children are waiting all:
> For the world apart to fall,
> The devil's power to pass away,
> And he be damned to hell alway."

Nikolaus Herman puts it the same way:

> For your coming, Lord, we're waiting all,
> And listening for the trumpet's call.
> Lord Jesus, come—do not delay
> And help your church—we are afraid."

Christians at the time of the Reformation were aware of their

---

the Empire as it once was." It is "the imperial papacy," that is, the papacy "has
also become a worldly kingdom." Thus Luther can simply summarize the content of Revelation 13 as "the abomination of the papacy in worldly life." The
prophecies in this chapter seem to him real only as a picture of the papacy.
WA, DB 7, 413 ff.; *LW* 35, 405 ff. Cf. *WA*. DB 7, 451 ff.

" *Dein lieben Kinder warten all,*
wann doch einmal die Welt zerfall
und wann des Teufels Reich vergeh
und er in ewigen Schanden steh.
Reprinted in P. Wackernagel, *Das deutsche Kirchenlied von den ältesten
Zeiten bis zu Anfang des 17. Jahrhunderts,* 3 (1870), 879.

" *Dein Zukunft. Herr, wir warten all,*
Horchen auf der Posauen Schall,
Komm, lieber Herr Christ, machs nicht lang,
Hilf deiner Kirch, denn ihr ist bang.
Reprinted in Wackernagel, *op. cit.,* p. 1217.

position and knew where they stood in the midst of the history of the world and eagerly desired the coming of the day of Christ.

In the seventeenth century, however, this emphasis recedes into the background. To a large extent piety becomes a private matter. Christians are concerned with their personal and individual salvation. The first result of this was that few hymns are written about the church except by Johann Hermann. There are also fewer and fewer hymns that express hope in Christ's final victory and in the coming of his kingdom. The basic form of eschatological hymns is the hymn for the dying with its prayer for a blessed end and the certainty of eternal life with Christ. People desire heaven and heavenly salvation, which is indeed thought of as being experienced within the community of Jesus, but not in terms of Christ's coming on the Last Day. We can observe it also in the hymns of Paul Gerhardt whose work otherwise covers almost the entire content of the Christian faith. His Advent hymn, "O Lord, How Shall I Meet Thee?" does indeed contain one verse which could be understood in terms of the Last Day:

> What though the foes be raging,
> Heed not their craft and spite;
> Your Lord, the battle waging,
> Will scatter all their might.
> He comes a King most glorious
> And all his earthly foes
> In vain His course victorious
> Endeavor to oppose.[74]

But he only occasionally emphasizes this. His hymn, "About the Last Day [*Vom Jüngsten Tage*]":

> The time is coming near,
> Lord Jesus thou art here.[75]

describes only the blessedness which the individual experiences in seeing Jesus and tasting eternal joy with him. There is not a word about the battle and the victory of God and the Christian community, nothing about looking forward to the breakthrough of God's kingdom in glory. Pietism changes this situation, particularly the pietism of Württemberg with its theology of the history

---

[74] *The Lutheran Hymnal,* No. 58 (vs. 8).
[75] *Die Zeit ist nunmehr nah,*
Herr Jesu, du bist da.

of the kingdom of God. Phillipp Friedrich Hiller should be named first but Christoph Gottlieb Blumhardt and Johann Christoph Blumhardt should not be forgotten. In spite of their chiliasm, they stand closer to Luther than seventeenth century Lutheran orthodoxy does. They once again make us aware of an indispensable part of the hope of the New Testament which Luther had restored to the church.

Luther, as does the New Testament, expects not only that the individual will continue to exist in the future beyond death and that history will come to an end and be completed in the ultimate kingdom of God, but he also expects the future renewal of the entire world and its perfection as God's creation. Christ's resurrection guarantees not only the bodily resurrection of Christians but also the redemption and the perfection "of all creation with us" according to Romans 8:21.[76]

God's eschatological dealing with man and with all creation correspond to each other in the fact that both man and all creation are, through God's creative act, to be transformed out of their present form into their future and final form. Just as man, as he lives on this earth, is "simple material" which God intends to reshape into the form he wills for man's life in the future, so all of creation has been subjected to vanity and is material which God will use in creating its future glorious form.[77] God thus does not abandon his creatures and his creation but transforms, renews, and glorifies them. It is his good creation and he rejoices in it. God is thus leading men and all creation to an eternal goal. Luther's eschatology is not a worldless eschatology, as the eschatology of seventeenth century orthodoxy was, but includes all creation.[78]

The correspondence goes even beyond this. As all men must pass through the judgment of death and through the corruption of their bodies and can only enter into the glory of eternal life in this way, so the present form of this world must be destroyed through fire before a new and final world can be created.[79] Luther bases all

[76] *WA* 37, 68.
[77] *WA* 39[I], 177; *LW* 34, 139.
[78] Cf. *Die letzten Dinge*, pp. 351 ff.
[79] *WA* 39[I], 95; *LW* 34, 164. Cf. *WA* 10[I,2], 116 f. *WA* 41, 307 ff. *WA* 45, 229 ff.; *LW* 12, 118-121. *WA* 49, 503 ff. *WA* 14, 72.

this on Bible passages such as Romans 8:20 ff.; II Peter 3:10, 13; Isaiah 65:17, and others. The emotion and the realism with which he could express his hope for the glorious form of the creature as distinguished from its present condition is well known. Yet every attempt to picture eternal life and the new creation in detail is placed under the condition: "We know no more about eternal life than children in the womb of their mother know about the world they are about to enter."[80]

---

[80] *WA*, TR 3, No. 3339

APPENDIXES

APPENDIX ONE

"AND THOUGH I HAD ALL FAITH"

LUTHER'S INTERPRETATION OF I CORINTHIANS 13:2

Werner Elert begins the paragraphs dealing with "love of the neighbor, of the enemy, and of the brethren" in *The Christian Ethos*[1] by referring to the problem which Paul's statement in I Corinthians 13:2 appears to create for the evangelical doctrine of justification and renewal through faith alone. He therewith takes up a problem which Luther repeatedly discussed. Roman Catholic polemicists had often quoted this passage against Luther and the Lutherans in general in order to prove that "faith alone" is contrary to Scripture.[2]

At first glance, Paul's statement seems to create several difficulties for Luther. (1) The Reformer had repeatedly emphasized the entirely natural necessity which causes love to be born out of faith. Faith and love belong inseparably together. There is no true faith which does not immediately become "active through love"; and there is no true love which does not spring from faith. Faith makes us righteous and pure. How can faith then exist without love? "Wherever there is true faith, the Holy Spirit is also present. And where the Holy Spirit is present, love and everything else must be there. How can he then speak as though someone might have faith without love?"[3] It is then "surprising" that Paul here speaks of a faith which is able to move mountains, and yet is without love. (2) If faith can exist without love and if the apostle explicitly states that anyone who has no love is "nothing," then it is obvious that faith does not justify itself alone. And it was in this sense that Roman Catholic theology asserted I Corinthians 13 as an argument against Luther's doctrine of justification. "Here the Papists say that faith alone does not justify but that

---

[1] Werner Elert, *The Christian Ethos*, trans. Carl Schindler (Philadelphia: Muhlenberg Press, 1957), p. 269.

[2] Cf. Calvin's interpretation of this passage in *Commentary on the Epistle of Paul the Apostle to the Corinthians*, trans. John Pringle (Grand Rapids: Eerdman, 1948), I, 419 f. and *Institutes of the Christian Religion*, ed. John T. McNeill and trans. Ford L. Battles (Philadelphia: Westminster, 1960), I, 553 f. Also the *Apology of the Augsburg Confession*, BC, 127, 218.

[3] *WA* 17ᴵᴵ, 164.

love is also needed." And it appears to be true that I Corinthians 13 "speaks very forcefully against those of us who teach that we are justified by faith alone."[4]

Luther was thus required to deal exegetically with this passage on several occasions—even apart from the fact that it is the Epistle for Estomihi [Quinquagesima Sunday; the Sunday before Ash Wednesday], and therefore had to be repeatedly interpreted in his sermons. Luther follows the hermeneutical principle that this passage must be interpreted in view of the totality of Paul's doctrine and particularly of I Corinthians. "This one passage must not conflict with, nor overthrow, all the other statements which Paul makes about faith; these assert that faith alone gives justification."[5] To conclude on the basis of I Corinthians 13 that love "justifies" would be contrary to Paul's proclamation and intention expressed elsewhere throughout this whole letter.[6]

At first, Luther was not completely certain about the interpretation of this passage, and it was sometime in the 1530's before he worked out the interpretation which he then maintained throughout the rest of his life. It is worth the trouble to trace the development of his interpretation. For the decade between 1525 and 1535, our sources are two sermons and Luther's manuscripts. After that our material is drawn from the disputations.

In the collection of Lenten sermons of 1525, Luther's sermon on the Epistle for Estomihi Sunday presents three possible solutions of the problem which the text presents.[7] (1) We can understand vs. 2 of I Corinthians 13 to mean that Paul was speaking not of Christian faith which brings love with it by its own power but "of a common faith in God and his power." Understood in this sense, the faith of I Corinthians 13:2 is one gift among and similar to the others that Paul discusses in these chapters, that is, such as speaking with tongues, prophecy, knowledge, "and the like." This faith can work miracles even though it is not "Christian faith." Luther declares that even Judas, the betrayer, performed miraculous signs.[8] "Christian faith" makes us righteous and pure and therefore brings love with it. But the miracle-working faith of I Corinthians 13:2 is a completely different kind of faith. It does not transform the heart but is simply a

[4] *WA* 49, 351.

[5] *WA* 17^{II}, 164.

[6] *WA* 39^{II}, 193; *LW* 34, 309.

[7] *WA* 17^{II}, 164 f.

[8] Calvin treats the passage in the same way [cf. n. 2]. The basis for this interpretation is obviously Mark 6:13.

"gift" which has as little effect upon the personal life as the other gifts; Luther names reason, health, eloquence, and riches. All these remain outside of the person and leave it untouched and untransformed.

(2) We can, however, interpret the passage to mean that Paul is speaking not of a common faith in God but of genuine Christian faith. He would then be speaking of men who do miracles through the power of this Christian faith. But then it is precisely faith's power to work miracles which makes a man proud so that he succumbs to the temptation of pride. Therewith he falls both from love and from faith. Thus Luther attempts to solve the problem not by understanding this verse in terms of some other kind of faith than Christian faith but by distinguishing two stages of Christian faith. At first, this faith which has love with it is the true faith. Then, however, it loses the nature of true faith because of its pride.

(3) The third possible interpretation is that Paul uses an impossible example in order to demonstrate as strongly as possible the absolute necessity of love. In fact, it is not possible that that faith which moves mountains could be without love. Paul, however, assumes this impossible situation in order to strengthen his assertion that even such a gloriously strong faith would be "nothing" without love. Luther feels that Paul here speaks of an unreal possibility, just as he does in vs. 1: ("If I speak with the tongues of men and of angels . . ."); in both cases he speaks of something which is "not possible." It is simply impossible for a man to speak with tongues of angels. Verse 2 is thus to be understood in analogy to vs. 1. Verse 2a also describes an impossible situation ("If I understood all mysteries") for in fact it is impossible for anyone to understand all mysteries, that is, the entire Holy Scripture "for it is an abyss which no one can plumb in all eternity."

Luther considers that this third interpretation is the best—although he does not reject the first two. John Gerhard follows him in this.[*] Luther himself, however, never again returned to the interpretation of the passage which he preferred in 1525. He probably felt that it did not do justice to Paul's text. The reference to the analogy of vss. 1 and 2a, which are also supposed to describe impossible situations, is not convincing. For that analogy could only assert that it is equally impossible to speak with the tongues of angels and to understand all mysteries as to have a faith which can move mountains. That is not, however, what Luther wishes to demonstrate. He wishes to show the impossibility of a faith which is without love. The "impossible example" in vs. 2b lies in the condition "and had not love"; in vss. 1 and 2a, how-

---

[*] *Loci Theologici,* ed. Preuss (Berlin: Gust. Schlawitz, 1865), III, 472a.

ever, this impossible example is stated in the hypothetical conditions. This, however, destroys the analogy between vss. 1, 2a and 2b.

It is certain that the apostle speaks hyperbolically in the first verses of Chapter 13. He describes the highest and ultimate possibilities given to the Christian. Paul would have known Jesus' statement in Mark 11:23; he would therefore have thought of them as possibilities and not impossibilities, and would not have thought it impossible to find a faith in the Christian community that could move mountains. Perhaps Paul thought of speaking in the tongues of angels and understanding all mysteries as only an eschatological possibility,[10] but even then it is still a possibility. But even if speaking in the tongues of angels and understanding all mysteries before the Last Day exceeded the possibilities of any historical man, even of the Christian, Mark 11:23 still asserts a man could have that faith which can move mountains. Paul indeed uses an illustration, just as Jesus did, in order to describe the ultimate power of faith. But he then considers the possibility that such a powerful faith would not have love. This is, however, by no means intended to describe an impossibility, such as Luther would like to find at this place. In Corinth Paul was facing a gnosis which was lacking in love. Corresponding to this, he also considers the possibility of a strong faith which is loveless. To deny that would rob this passage of its depth and its stimulation for all who believe. Elsewhere Paul is also aware of the combination of faith and lovelessness. In Romans 11:17 ff. he was dealing with Gentile Christians who "believed" but at the same time stood in danger of having a loveless pride and of arrogantly despising unbelieving Israel. Therewith they stood in danger of falling away from faith into security. This, however, demonstrates that the third interpretation of I Corinthians 13:2 which Luther considered and preferred in 1525 is not Pauline. And Luther did not maintain it. Five years later we find him teaching the first two possibilities which he had considered in 1525.

We find the earliest proof for this in the marginal notes which Luther made in his New Testament in 1530.[11] At first Luther declares that Paul in I Corinthians 12:9 ("to another faith by the same Spirit") does not speak of a justifying faith but of that faith which makes itself outwardly known through its confession. In the context, Paul is discussing those gifts of the Holy Spirit which are manifest in the Christian community. And even Balaam and the heretics and the godless have had such a faith; the faith of the godless is demonstrated by

---

[10] A. Schlatter, *Paulus, der Bote Jesu* (Stuttgart: Calwer, 1934), p. 354.

[11] *WA,* DB 4, 479 f. For a discussion of the genuineness of the material, cf. *WA,* DB 4, 439 ff.

Matthew 7:22. The godless also have all the charismatic gifts mentioned in I Corinthians 12 and thus also the miracle-working "mountain-moving" faith of I Corinthians 13:2. (This means that Luther understands faith in I Corinthians 12:9 and I Corinthians 13:2 in the same sense). There can be no question that Balaam worked miracles through his prophesying and blessing just as Paul did. These miracles are the common property of the believers and the nonbelievers. Therefore the question which concerned Luther in 1525 as to whether Paul in I Corinthians 13 understood the hypothetical conditions in the sense of unreality or of possibility has lost its significance. In any case it cannot be finally decided. Everything considered, the passage in I Corinthians 13:2 is concerned with a working of miracles which is granted not only to Christians but also to those outside of Christianity.

Luther, however, did not let the matter rest with this interpretation. This is indicated by a manuscript of the same year (1530) which, together with many others, probably constituted a draft for the treatise on justification which Luther planned but never wrote out. Veit Dietrich has transmitted it.[12] One difficulty had remained in the interpretation indicated in Luther's marginal notes. Can that miracle-working faith of which the Lord spoke so highly simply be put into the same category with the undeniable miracles of the "godless"? According to I Corinthians 12:9, it is a gift of the Holy Spirit and it is apparently true faith. Furthermore, how can we say that a man who has such faith that it demonstrates its genuineness by his great deeds and miracles still should be called a "nothing," as Paul puts it? He by no means lacks that "fruit" by which true faith can be recognized. The Lord himself says in Mark 9:39, "No one can do a mighty deed in my name and soon after speak evil of me." Here again we see how Luther's theology was limited by Scripture. And Scripture contains not only Matthew 7:22 but also Mark 9:39. The fact that both passages are found indicates a great tension and even an apparent contradiction. In the one case miracles done in the name of the Lord indicate that one stands in a living relationship to him and thus belongs to him. In the other case, even such deeds done in his name do not prevent Jesus from rejecting their doers. "I have never known you." How is this tension and this contradiction to be resolved? Luther finds a way out by converting the theologically unbearable contemporaneity of miracle-working faith and lovelessness into a temporal succession, as he did in the second solution considered in 1525. He declares that the faith that works miracles is indeed true faith; but if the man who has this faith does not produce love then he also falls away from faith,

---

[12] *WA* 30ᴵᴵ, 674. Cf. *WA*, DB 4, 480, n. 1 and *WA*, TR 1, No. 1063. For the history of the text, cf. *WA* 30ᴵᴵ, 652 ff.

and this faith in fact becomes "nothing."[12] The faith which does not achieve love is then no longer itself, but it has become brashness and presumption and despises both the word and the brethren. Luther repeatedly saw this happening in his own time. At first men fervently received the gospel, then they did not endure in faith. Dependence on the word was replaced by religious presumption on the basis of faith; and such a perversion of faith—even though it pretends to be faith—naturally does not lead to love. Luther explains that Paul confronted this situation in the community in Corinth. He directs this against those who pretend to be believers, who made a good beginning in faith but now are very proud of their faith, even though it is no longer really faith. Thus faith without love is not genuine faith but a faith distorted into presumption and arrogance. Luther cites Balaam, Saul, Ananias, Sapphira, and Müntzer as examples of this disintegration of faith and the perversion of genuine faith into presumption. All of these people once truly believed and what they did in that faith was good; this is also true of the people of whom the Lord speaks in Matthew 7:22. They, however, then become different people.

The basic elements of these thoughts reappear in the sermon on I Corinthians which Luther preached on Estomihi Sunday, February 19, 1531.[14] He begins by pointing out that a man cannot at the same time have a faith which moves mountains and yet be without love or be evil. "Our Lord God does not use rascals to perform his miracles."[15] It is impossible that faith and lovelessness could occur at the same time; rather, they must follow each other. Luther says someone at first had faith and then lost it. He still boasts about it but does not have it any more. Now, however, the sermon of 1531 introduces a new thought which goes beyond Luther's previous interpretation; in any case Luther did not express it in his discussions of the second possible interpretation in 1525 and 1530—even though he may very well have thought it: Even though a man loses faith, he still might retain the gift of performing miracles granted to such faith. Faith and the gift of faith are thus distinguished. Balaam is again used as an example; but now Luther says that he was a prophet and had faith but fell away from faith—and yet the gift of prophecy remained.

---

[13] This makes it clear that Luther's understanding of the essential necessity by which true faith leads to love is—in spite of the illustrations from nature—not to be understood as an automatic psychological process. The believer must and can be summoned to realize the full nature of faith only because it is possible that he believes and yet at the same time lacks the love which the essential nature of faith demands. Cf. my *The Divine Command*, trans. Franklin Sherman ("Facet Books—Social Ethics Series," 9; Philadelphia: Fortress Press, 1966), pp. 38 ff.

[14] *WA* 34¹, 162 ff.

[15] *WA* 34¹, 167.

This can also happen to a baptized Christian who falls away from faith. In spite of it, he retains the gift of baptism, the forgiveness of sins.[16] Accordingly Luther can make the following statement about a miracle-working faith that remains without love: "Whoever has had faith at some time but now has no love, no longer has that faith, rather he has lost the faith even though he has performed miracles through faith. Such a faith is then either not a true and genuine faith or it was never present."[17] All that is left is the "appearance" or "echo" of an imagined faith.[18]

Luther maintains this solution of the problem in his Estomihi sermon of February 8, 1540.[19] "What is missing? Love. And where that is missing, it is impossible for true faith to be present even though it may have been earlier. For it can happen that what was once truly present can be removed afterwards through pride." Here, too, then, Luther expresses the thought that the people whom Paul is thinking of in I Corinthians 13:2 probably had true faith but have lost it without losing their power to perform miracles.

Luther did not only deal with this passage from Paul in his sermons. It was only natural that he should repeatedly concern himself with the theological significance of this passage in his controversies with the Roman theologians about justification by faith alone. The preliminary studies made in preparation for a treatise on justification (which we have discussed on pp. 433, 434) indicate this. So do the disputations conducted under Luther's direction. In these he had to think about I Corinthians 13:2; this resulted in the discovery and expression of theological insights which we quite understandably do not find expressed in the sermons to the Christian community.

I Corinthians 13:2 is frequently discussed in Luther's disputations between 1535 and 1544.[20] It is usually introduced because the participants in the disputation quote it against justification by faith alone and Luther replies. Sometimes, however, Luther takes the initiative and discusses this passage in the theses which he composed and then expands his thoughts in the course of the disputation. The extent to

---

[16] *WA* 34¹, 167.
[17] *WA* 34¹, 168.
[18] *WA* 34¹, 168. The text is difficult: On the one hand, that ability to work miracles which remains after faith has been lost appears to be God's gift. At the same time, however, Rörer's notes indicate that Luther said: "If a false faith can work miracles, it does so because it is moved by the devil or permitted by God." Does Luther distinguish between the God-given possession of the ability to work miracles and the application of this gift which is motivated by the devil?
[19] *WA* 49, 27.
[20] *WA* 39¹, 74, 77, 279. *WA* 39¹, 114; *LW* 34, 183. *WA* 39¹¹, 190, 193, 198; *LW* 34, 307 ff., 316. *WA* 39¹¹, 235 f., 241 f., 247 f., 310.

which Luther was concerned about the significance of this passage
for the purity of the doctrine of justification is apparent from the fact
that in 1535 he planned to conduct a special disputation about this
passage and even wrote down a short draft of theses.[21] The most significant of all of his statements on the subject are the last theses of
the disputation of July 7, 1542[22] and particularly the theses for the
disputation of April 24, 1543[23] as well as some of his explanations in
both these disputations. These last theses are exclusively devoted to
the problem which I Corinthians 13:2 created. They are Luther's last
extensive statement on the subject; after this we have only a very brief
opinion in his disputation of December 12, 1544.[24] At the same time
they are the most definite, the most fruitful, and theologically most
important. Here the thoughts which Luther had already expressed
during the 1530's are summarized and discussed in all their aspects.
We have gathered together the thoughts presented in these disputations and classified them according to their primary content.

(1) Luther emphasizes as he has done earlier, for example, in his
marginal notes to the New Testament (cf. p. 432), that I Corinthians
13:2 cannot possibly be cited as an argument against "faith alone."
For here Paul is not even considering that justifying and genuine
faith in Christ but the "faith of godless men who still do good works."[25]
True faith cannot possibly be meant because that results in love. The
people whom Paul wishes to correct are, however, characterized by
the fact that they sin against love.[26] Luther thus understands the description of the essence of love in I Corinthians 13:4-6 as the opposite of what Paul finds within the Corinthian community. Luther
bases this conclusion on the entire letter and probably specifically on
the largely negative formulation of these verses. Of the fifteen brief
sentences which the apostle uses to describe love, no less than eight
are in the form of negations. This means that the statement in I Corinthians 13:2 is to be understood as aimed at people who called themselves Christians and who did great things with their faith but had no
love—and this proved that their faith was false and meaningless.[27]
Luther establishes the basic principle[28] that all corresponding passages
in Paul, James, and John which summon men from a mere faith to
love are to be understood as spoken to people who were proud of

[21] *WA* 39^I, 76 f.
[22] *WA* 39^{II}, 190; *LW* 34, 306 f.
[23] *WA* 39^{II}, 235 f.
[24] *WA* 39^{II}, 310.
[25] *WA* 39^I, 74.
[26] *WA* 39^{II}, 233.
[27] *WA* 39^I, 279 f.
[28] *WA* 39^I, 279

their faith and their charismatic gifts but at the same time were self-seeking, loveless, arrogant, bestial, and brutal men.[29]

(2) As I Corinthians 13:2 shows, such men have a "faith" and are able to work miracles with it. Luther usually calls this faith a false, empty, imagined, hypocritical, and dead faith. It is "dead" because it does not depend on Christ and is not active in love. It is the faith of the godless. At the same time, however, the context of I Corinthians 13:2 leads Luther to understand this faith as a gift of the Holy Spirit[30] And in the disputation of October 16, 1535 Luther considers not only the possibility of interpreting "faith" in I Corinthians 13:2 as referring to that faith of the godless which has nothing to do with Christ, but also that Paul could here be speaking of those who have begun in true faith but have not persevered in it.[31] Therewith Luther once again takes up the second possibility which he considered in 1525, as well as in his manuscript of 1530, and in his sermon in 1531. One can see that even in 1535 he is not yet completely certain about which faith Paul was thinking of. In his later discussions, however, he no longer mentions the second possibility. At the same time Luther's awareness of the Lord's word in Matthew 7:22 ("Did we not do miracles in thy name?") always must have reminded him of the possibility that I Corinthians 13 might describe the fall from faith of those who once had true faith. However that may be, Luther, in accordance with his basic understanding of I Corinthians 13:2, concludes that even a distorted, false, imagined, or dead faith can do great works and miracles and even "move mountains." But how can a dead faith do such very living works as moving mountains and healing the sick? Such a faith is not dead, but thoroughly active. And in the disputation of July 7, 1542 Bugenhagen presents the argument that the cause must correspond to the effect, specifically that the cause must be as alive as the effect is.[32] Luther replies with the thought which he had already expressed in the disputation of October 16, 1535,[33] in the theses of July 7, 1542, and in the disputation itself even before Bugenhagen raised this objection.[34] "Whatever lively works dead faith does, however, are done by the public performance of [the office or] the ministry," that God has given.[35] This is true of those who hold political offices, as well as of those who hold ecclesiastical offices. Godless authorities do good works and work wonders because of the

---

[29] *WA* 39^I, 280.
[30] *WA* 39^I, 77. *WA* 39^{II}, 236.
[31] *WA* 39^I, 74.
[32] *WA* 39^{II}, 198; *LW* 34, 315.
[33] *WA* 39^I, 74.
[34] *WA* 39^{II}, 190, 193; *LW* 34, 306, 309.
[35] *WA* 39^{II}, 198; *LW* 34, 315.

public office in which they stand.[36] "We cannot deny that miracles can be done by godless men with dead faith, particularly when they are in office or in the Christian community."[37] "For dead faith is efficacious by reason of both the community and the ministry of the divine word."[38] God has done "many good things through Balaam and the impious prophets and tyrants and still does them, because whatever the ministry has, is not of itself, but of God. For that reason it is effective through the power of the Holy Spirit although in ungodly persons."[39] Other examples cited by Luther in the above named passages are Caiaphas, Alexander the Great, Judas, the pope, and naturally, the false teachers in Corinth against whom Paul writes.

All this means that God gives authority to perform great works and miracles (and accordingly also the necessary "miracle-working faith"[40]) to those to whom he commits a public office, whether in government or in the church, because of, and for the benefit of, their office. Church officials do miracles and greater deeds than "private believers" as long as they are in office or the Christian congregation.[41] The authority to carry out these deeds is not given to them because of their person but because of their office. This office is not something which is at their disposal, but is a tool which God uses to carry out his works just as he uses these as officials. God works through them. But this work completely bypasses them as persons. The office and the person must be strictly distinguished. The person may be godless and yet God works through him because of his office. The tension seems to be almost unbearable; the teachers in Corinth were "servants of the devil" (Luther probably thought of II Corinthians 11:15), and yet they work miracles with their false faith! The Roman pope is a tool of the devil, and yet one must admit that he can do miracles by the power of his office.[42] The work done by godless officials by the power of their office can be of great historical significance. And yet the faith by which such great deeds are done is dead and accordingly the works too are dead—even though men may think they are "very much alive" as Bugenhagen said,[43] in the theological sense they are dead."[44] For the

[36] *WA* 39[I], 74.

[37] *WA* 39[II], 190; *LW* 34, 306.

[38] *WA* 39[II], 193; *LW* 34, 309.

[39] *WA* 39[II], 198; *LW* 34, 315 f.

[40] Luther says these Corinthian teachers *credebant magna miracula. WA* 39[II], 193; *LW* 34, 309 f. He says the same of the pope: "Thus we also concede that the Roman Pontiff . . . is entirely able to rely on miracles [*miracula credere*] by virtue of his ministry." *WA* 39[I], 193; *LW* 34, 309. The phrase implies both the confidence that we can do miracles and the miraculous power that flows out of this trust.

[41] *WA* 39[II], 236.

[42] *WA* 39[II], 193; *LW* 34, 309.

[43] *WA* 39[II], 198; *LW* 34, 315.

[44] *WA* 39[I], 74.

person has not been made alive by that true faith which leads to love. God's wonders are done through godless men. Luther refers to the fact that godless men also rule in the church. And the word and sacraments which they administer are greater than all miracles, for they convey eternal life; and even this could be given through Judas![45] Godless men can teach true doctrine, administer the sacraments, and rule the holy church.[46] Luther here applies the doctrine which Augustine developed in opposition to the Donatists in terms of the Lutheran understanding of the means of grace.

Luther particularly emphasizes the distinction between the person and the office in his sermons on the Sermon on the Mount in 1532.[47] "On this basis you may judge everyone who occupies an office in Christendom. Not all those who occupy an office and who preach are Christians, or godly people. God does not ask about that. The person may be anything he pleases; but the office is right and good nevertheless, since it does not belong to man but to God himself."[48] Then Luther declares the same to be true of official persons in the world. In full agreement with what he has said about miracles in his disputations he here states, "It is true as I have said, that God does not let any signs take place through wicked men unless they are in public office, since God does not grant signs for the sake of their person but of their office."[49]

(3) Luther distinguishes between saving faith in Christ and miracle-working faith. A man who has the latter and can rely on his power to do great miracles (*credere magna miracula*), may be an unbeliever according to the standard of faith in Christ and be lost in spite of all his great works. Luther cites Judas as an example.[50] Faith in one sense of the word can be unfaith is another sense, as works which are "living" because of their human dynamic and their historical effectiveness may also be "dead" works when viewed theologically (See no. 2).

(4) Luther declares that great deeds of the unbelievers are also done by the power of the Holy Spirit.[51] His concept of the "Holy Spirit and his work is thus a very broad one,[52] as is the Old Testament's concept. The Spirit's working is not limited to the granting of faith in Jesus Christ but also includes the authority to carry out great historical

---

[45] *WA* 39^II^, 190; *LW* 34, 306.
[46] *WA* 39^II^, 236.
[47] *WA* 32, 528; *LW* 21, 276-280.
[48] *WA* 32, 529; *LW* 21, 277.
[49] *WA* 32, 531; *LW* 21, 279.
[50] "They relied on great miracles. Meanwhile, however, they remained unbelievers." *WA* 39^II^, 193; *LW* 34, 310.
[51] *WA* 39^II^, 198; *LW* 34, 316.
[52] See *WA* 39^II^, 239.

works apart from such faith. The Spirit works not only in the history
of salvation [*Heilsgeschichte*] but also in the political history of the
world; he works not only in the realm of the church but in the pro-
fane and godless world. "The Holy Spirit or his gifts"—Luther is
thinking of I Corinthians 12—"may be granted and be present even
without faith in Christ and love,"[53] that is, also to godless men who
are Christians only in name. They are not limited to the community
of believers.

(5) Faith in Christ and the gift of miracle working faith have a
completely different significance in the church than they have in the
world. The works of a "mountain-moving" faith are valid both before
God and men.[54] As Paul says in I Corinthians 12:7, they are given
and intended for "the common welfare." Luther translates *"gemeinen
Nutzen"* as for the "benefit of the church."[55] This is true of all the
categories of gifts, offices, and works named in I Corinthians 12:4 ff.[56]
God uses them for the benefit of the church and of the nations. But
as someone may occupy an office without having personal faith, and
without having faith in Christ and without having love, for the sake
of his office be granted miracle-working faith as well as the other
charismatic gifts named in I Corinthians 12,[57] so the man who bears
the office and possesses the charismatic gifts and deeds granted together with it has no personal benefit from all of this,[58] but is damaged
by it. Thus those who possess this kind of gift do not profit from their
office and their mountain-moving faith and their great deeds in terms
of their own personal salvation, but are injured in their souls and are
lost because of it, since their great gifts and works make them proud.

Faith in Christ is completely different. In distinction from that miracle-working faith which is granted because of the office, faith in
Christ has no public significance and effect at all. In the primary
analysis, it is a private affair between God and the believer. It has
saving significance only for the man who himself believes and is thereby justified, whereas offices in the church are given for the salvation

---

[53] *WA* 39[II], 236.
[54] The text of *WA* [and *LW*] reads: "Even if such people receive no benefit
for themselves by these acts, but harm themselves, nevertheless what they do
before God and men is valid." I feel that a comma should follow *faciunt* in
the Latin text and this thesis would then read ". . . nevertheless what they do
is valid before God and men." *WA* 39[II], 190; *LW* 34, 307.
[55] *WA* 39[II], 236.
[56] *WA* 39[II], 237.
[57] *WA* 39[II], 236.
[58] "Even if such people receive no benefit for themselves by these acts . . ."
WA 39[II], 190; *LW* 34, 307. "The ministry is of no advantage to its possessor."
WA 39[II], 236. Luther here echoes Paul's "I gain nothing" in I Corinthians
13:3.

of others and the official himself may be lost.⁵⁹ Faith first becomes active after a man is justified in his faith. That kind of faith which is a charismatic gift granted to an office is thus active in a primary sense, whereas saving faith in Christ is active only in a secondary sense. But the miracles which are done by this faith active through love are not inferior to the "moving of mountains" and similar deeds. On the contrary, faith in Jesus Christ which is active through love is able to do things which even that faith spoken of in I Corinthians 13:4 ff. cannot do. Faith in Christ overcomes the sins of lovelessness which Paul lists in I Corinthians 13:4 ff. and "triumphs over them in obedience to righteousness." It thus conquers sin, the world, and the devil—and this is something far greater than moving mountains. To love God and the neighbor willingly and constantly, without seeking a reward, may very properly be called "raising the dead."⁶⁰ Luther expresses the thinking of the apostle when he asserts that the value and effect of extraordinary charismatic gifts are far inferior to what faith does when it is active in love. (Paul makes the comparison with that which *love* does; Luther compares the two kinds of *faith;* in substance they are both thinking about the same thing.) Luther, as does Paul, instructs Christians not to put too high a value on gifts of the sort named in I Corinthians 12 even though the Spirit gives them. They are far less significant than the great miracles which a simple, and in no way extraordinary, faith in Christ does in love.

(6) The extent of Luther's distinction between miracle-working faith and saving faith in Christ is apparent from his theses of April 24, 1543, which compare miracle-working faith to the inner dynamic of the great and heroic men of world history. He finds these two "similar." "Heroic men" must be motivated by an extraordinary trust if they are to do anything great or memorable. Strength and power alone are not enough. There are many who lack neither of these but yet lack that inner dynamic and confidence and therefore achieve nothing. This dynamic comes from God. According to Jeremiah 51:11 He stirred up the spirit of the kings of the Medes against Babylon. For the welfare of Syria, he awakened Naaman who was still an idol worshiper and was gracious to him [II Kings]. We can see that God has always distributed glorious and marvelous gifts among unthankful pagan people. He is able to give great things to his people and do great things for them, both through believing as well as through godless men.⁶¹

---

⁵⁹ "Faith in Christ results in the justification only of the one possessing such faith." *WA* 39ᴵᴵ, 236.
⁶⁰ *WA* 39ᴵᴵ, 236.
⁶¹ *WA* 39ᴵᴵ, 237.

In the brief form of disputation theses Luther here takes up the idea of the "miracle men" or "healthy heroes" which is part of his understanding of the theology of history and which he had presented more extensively in his interpretation of the Psalm 101 in 1534/35. He clearly distinguishes the history of the world from God's dealing with his people and his church. But Luther's God also rules over the history of the nations—as the Old Testament prophets recognized and proclaimed. God "awakens" the heroes, the great princes, and states-men; he "teaches" them and "puts ideas into their hearts"; he "stirs up their thinking and their courage" and he "gives things into their hands."[63] The pagans "know from experience that there has never been a man of great deeds or any extraordinary man who has not been specially inspired by [*sine afflatu*] God."[63] Luther cites Cicero at this point. And in the theses of 1535 he uses the same expression *afflatus* which undoubtedly is also to be understood in the sense of inspiration by God. As we have previously mentioned, Luther does not even avoid saying that God's Holy Spirit works in the history of the world and in heroic men. Certainly this is a different work than his moving the heart to believe in Jesus Christ. The Spirit, however, gives diverse gifts not only in the church—as described in I Corinthians 12—but also in the world. And if Luther finds that the deeds of these miracle men have their source in God's working,[64] there can be no doubt that he does the same with the unusual confidence and faith of the heroes of history—even though it has nothing to do with faith in Christ.[65]

In the close of our presentation we must still ask whether Luther's last interpretation of I Corinthians 13:2 fully expresses the thinking of the apostles.

There can be no doubt that Luther expresses Paul's intention when

---

[63] *WA* 51, 207; *LW* 13, 154 f.
[63] *WA* 51, 222; *LW* 13, 174.
[64] Cf. *WA* 39ᴵᴵ, 198; *LW* 34, 316. "If a prince rules well then it is not because he has been born with the talent nor because he has learned it from books, but because he has been taught by the inspiration of the Holy Spirit." *WA* 40ᴵᴵᴵ, 209.
[65] I can thus no longer support the position which I took in my essay, "Luther und die politische Welt," *Schriftenreihe der Luthergesellschaft* (1937), No. 9, p. 11. I there asserted that Luther never speaks of the Holy Spirit when he speaks of "miracle men." At that time I attempted to differentiate between the concepts "inspiration" and "being given the gift of the Holy Spirit"; also I distinguished between "the inspiration of political leaders" and the fact that the "Holy Spirit is present only in God's people," (*ibid.*, p. 4). This dis-tinction is, however, not valid for Luther. This also means that I must retract the statements which I made in opposition to Siegfried Leffler in my essay, "Politisches Christentum," *Theologia militans* (Leipzig: Deichert, 1935), No. 5, p. 11. Luther speaks of the working of God's Spirit in a much broader sense than contemporary theologians do. It appears that he does this under the in-fluence of the Old Testament.

he does not equate the "faith" referred to in our passage with that faith which is common to all Christians and through which a man is justified. He is correct in understanding it as a special charismatic gift not granted to all Christians comparable to those gifts mentioned in I Corinthians 12:9.[66] (One could also think of a particularly strong faith; Paul elsewhere obviously distinguishes various levels of faith, Romans 12:6).[67]

We must still ask, however, whether Luther rightly interprets Paul when he characterizes miracle-working faith simply as false, as imagined faith, as autocratic, as "heroic" faith produced by a man himself, and as imagined faith because it is without love. Luther feels that such a faith says, "I will believe; if it is true, let it be true."[68] Such a faith would make a man a Christian only in name, not in reality; actually he would remain an unbeliever. Did Paul actually think about the faith which works miracles in this way? Paul definitely knows that the "man of sin," the "blasphemer" will do mighty deeds, great signs, and miracles at the time of his appearance (II Thessalonians 2:9). There is therefore a demonic and devilish analogy to the miracles of Christ, of the apostles, and of Christians. There is nothing specifically messianic, apostolic, or Christian about the miraculousness of such works in themselves. This, however, does not in any way change the fact that Paul understands the miracles performed by the apostles and by the other charismatic figures in the Christian community as having been done by the power of Christ (Rom. 15:18). This means that Paul also recognized the faith in which they were done. Paul numbers it among the manifestations of the Holy Spirit. For Paul, however, there is no Spirit except the Spirit of Christ. The three statements in I Corinthians 12:4-6 show that this is the context of I Corinthians 12:14. The charismatic gifts, including the charisma of miracle-working faith, are given by the one Spirit, the one Lord, the one God. The correspondence or, much more correctly, the unity of the

---

[66] Hans Lietzmann, . . . *An die Korinther* I, II, *Handbuch zum Neuen Testament* 8 (4th ed.; Tübingen: Mohr, 1941), p. 57. Calvin, *Corinthians* I, 401 f. and *Institutes* III, 2, 9; *LCC* 1, 553 f. Calvin refers to the fact that the word "faith" has many meanings. In each usage one must ask about its special meaning. The Roman theologians failed to do this and thus improperly use this passage in arguing against the significance of faith for salvation. In this particular passage, faith is one of the particular charismata of I Corinthians 12, that is, partial faith. Calvin characterizes it as partial faith "because it does not grasp the entire Christ but only the power of working miracles." For this reason it can for a time be the possession of a man who does not possess the spirit of holiness, that is, a man who is wicked, and it can be misused by him. "No wonder if it is separated from love."
[67] Cf. H. D. Wendland, *Die Briefe an die Korinther, Das Neue Testament Deutsch* (6th ed.; Göttingen: Vandenhoeck & Ruprecht, 1954), p. 94.
[68] *WA* 39ᴵᴵ, 247.

Lord and of the Spirit exclude the possibility of Paul saying as Luther does that "the Spirit, or the gifts which he grants, can be present
even without faith in Christ . . ."[69] Luther must assert this because his
understanding of faith eliminates the possibility of a faith in Christ
which would be without love. God can certainly work such a faith but
it cannot possibly be the same as saving faith in Christ. Luther must
therefore make a sharp distinction between the faith of I Corinthians
13:2 and saving faith in Christ. He minimizes the significance of the
former by calling it "hypocritical," "put-on," and "false."[70] In Luther's
thinking, men who have such a wonder-working faith (without love)
are unbelievers when judged by the standard of faith in Christ.[71] The
question is whether or not Paul would have agreed with this. Is Luther's alternative between true faith which is active through love and
"false," "hypocritical," or "put-on" faith, adequate in view of the faith
of which Paul speaks in I Corinthians 13:2? Paul depreciates that
faith only comparatively in its relationship to love (I Cor. 13:13) but
not in and of itself. Luther declares that faith which does not result
in love is no faith at all.[72] Paul declares that the man who has only
this faith without love is "nothing." He does not say such faith is no
faith at all. Paul and Luther do not basically disagree on the fact that
true faith by its very nature must necessarily lead to love. For Paul
love belongs to "the essence of faith"—to use Albert Schweitzer's
phrase.[73] Things which essentially belong together can still be separated from each other psychologically and empirically. We already
referred to Romans 11:17 ff. where Paul is confronted with the saving faith of a man who believes only for himself but not for others
and therefore violates love in his attitude toward them: he assumes an
arrogant attitude toward them because he has been given grace to believe. The possibility then exists—as Paul most seriously emphasizes—
that such a faith is in deadly danger of being changed from faith to
pride (Rom. 11:20). Luther also views the situation in this way. If
a man falls out of love, he cannot escape also falling out of faith.[74]

Luther is closest to Paul in the second of the interpretations which he
considered in 1525 and which he then held in 1530/31. But Paul
speaks to the Corinthian community in precisely this critical situation
in which genuine faith worked by Christ but lacking in love is pres-

[69] *WA* 39ᴵᴵ, 236.

[70] It is hard to understand how Luther could think of this faith at the same
time as being worked by the Holy Spirit. *WA* 39ᴵᴵ, 236.

[71] *WA* 39ᴵᴵ, 193; *LW* 34, 310.

[72] *WA* 39ᴵᴵ, 236.

[73] *The Mysticism of Paul the Apostle*, trans. William Montgomery (New
York: Holt, 1931), p. 307.

[74] *WA* 17ᴵᴵ, 165. *WA* 34ᴵ, 168.

ent. He is confronted with a faith which really trusts in Christ's power and in this confidence is able to work miracles and "to move mountains." "But the possibility exists that a man can put himself above God and remain selfish even in his preaching, knowledge, believing, and sacrificing."[75] And yet faith according to its nature lives from the all-inclusive love of Christ and is oriented to it. If a man becomes narrow and hinders the dynamic of love which proceeds from Christ by countering it with the selfishness which still lives in everyone, then faith denies its basis and therewith loses its essential nature. It is faith, even strong faith, certainty of salvation, power to undertake great things and to work miracles, but it is a selfishly limited faith; therefore it is on the way to pride and thus to a deceptive certainty of salvation and to the loss of salvation. The apostle in I Corinthians 13 tries to stop its movement down this deadly incline.

---

[75] A. Schlatter, *op. cit.*, p. 356.

APPENDIX TWO

"LOVE AND THE CERTAINTY OF SALVATION"

LUTHER'S INTERPRETATION OF I JOHN 4:17a

Luther's theology revolves around the assertion that we receive justification and therewith salvation through faith alone. God's promise applies to us apart from every condition on our side. We have only to trust ourselves to God's promise; this is what Luther calls faith. All this is true not only of the beginning of the Christian life but also of its continuation until the Last Day and thus also of the final judgment. Now it cannot be denied that in the New Testament the certainty of salvation is often connected not only to faith as pure receiving but also to love. The apostles know of a faith which fails to rescue a man from destruction because it lacks love (I Cor. 13:2; James 2). Such statements of the New Testament present a problem for the central theses of Luther's theology. And Luther constantly made new attempts to arrive at a true understanding of these passages which would bring them into harmony with his basic insight. It is significant that his interpretation of these passages changed in the course of his life. This reveals that he had difficulties with these passages. It is true, for example of I Corinthians 13:2 ("And if I have all faith . . . but have not love, I am nothing").[1] The same is true also of I John 4:17a. It is worth the trouble to consider Luther's interpretation of this Johannine passage in more detail.

The passage reads: "In this is love perfected in [bei] us, that we may have confidence for the day of judgment."[2] The context, particularly vss. 16 and 18, must be considered in the interpretation. The meaning appears to be that the complete reality of love manifests itself in the Christian's joyful expectation of the day of judgment. Exegetes have repeatedly asked whether such love is God's love to men as Christians experience it or whether it might at least also include the love of Christians.

---

[1] See Appendix One.

[2] The Greek text is: Ἐν τούτῳ τετελείωται ἡ ἀγάπη μεθ᾽ ἡμῶν, ἵνα παρρησίαν ἔχωμεν ἐν τῇ ἡμέρᾳ τῆς κρίσεως. The Vulgate reads: in hoc perfecta est charitas Dei nobiscum (since the revision of 1529: in nobis), ut fiduciam habeamus in die judicii.

In his lectures on I John in 1527, Luther understands this love primarily as God's love toward us.[3] Certainty that God loves us gives us certainty and confidence on the day of judgment. Calvin understands the passage in this way. The statement "that we may have confidence" describes "the fruit of divine love toward us." "Love is perfect in us" means that God's love is given to us in full measure. Believers are not terrified when they hear about the last judgment; rather, they come before God's judgment seat with certainty and good courage because they are absolutely convinced of his fatherly love. Thus the progress of Christians in faith can be measured by the good courage with which they await the day of judgment.[4]

This interpretation fits into the theology of the Reformers without difficulty. However, it cannot be maintained. In interpreting I John 4:17, we dare not separate God's love from that human love which it kindles. We can do this as little in considering vs. 17 as in vs. 16 ("whoever remains in love"). "Verse 18 undeniably reveals a reference to the love of men—we have a right to be confident in our attitude toward divine love only insofar as and because we love."[5]

Luther did not continue to interpret "perfect love" in vs. 17 as referring to God's love for us; rather he understood vs. 17 in terms of the Christian's love which shows itself in good works and fulfilling the Ten Commandments. The question is thus raised of how Luther's theology of "faith alone" can come to terms with a text which so obviously relates certainty of salvation and confidence in view of the last judgment to the perfectness of love. This obviously calls the Reformer's doctrine of justification into question. If the Christian's own love has any significance at all for his certainty of salvation, then it would seem that the Christian must consider his relationship to God in terms of what he is and has achieved. However, Luther had already sharply rejected this when he opposed scholastic theology and its concept of faith formed by love [*fides caritate formata*].[6] He felt that it asserted that faith justifies because it is "formed" (or validated) by love. That, however, was contrary to Paul and the gospel. Faith does

---

[3] For this love of God is so great that we can be confident on the day of judgment, when the whole world trembles. . . . Therefore we have such knowledge and faith through love that we can stand in judgment [according to the notes of Jakob Propst]. In Rörer's notes we read, ". . . [insofar as we know] God's love *and we love him,* we shall also be able to have confidence in him in the day of judgment. . . ." According to Rörer, Luther connected our love for God with our certainty of God's love. *WA* 20, 757.

[4] Calvin, *Catholic Epistles,* trans. John Owen (Grand Rapids: Eerdmans, 1948), p. 244.

[5] F. Büchsel, *Die Johannesbriefe. Theologischer Handkommentar zum Neuen Testament* (Leipzig: Deichert, 1933), XVIX, 37 f.

[6] Cf., e.g., *WA* 39ᴵ, 318. *WA* 39ᴵᴵ, 207, 213, 214.

not first become righteousness through love; "Faith by itself is already
a perfect righteousness; it is love that is imperfect. We, however, need
a perfect righteousness. How can we have it if our love is imperfect?
The answer is: Through Christ whose righteousness is absolutely perfect; we appropriate this righteousness for ourselves through faith."[7]
Faith, however, is nothing else than an attitude of pure dependency
and receptivity which appropriates Christ's righteousness for itself.[8]
As such, faith works our righteousness, that is, the righteousness of
Christ imputed to us. Faith by itself does not make us righteous as a
human quality but as the only possible attitude in which we can receive Christ's "alien" righteousness. There can therefore be no mention of the faith formed by love in the discussion of justification. Love
follows out of faith and is its fruit; but it does not give a quality to
faith before God. We are not at all concerned with faith as a human
quality, but only as an attitude of pure receptivity.

In spite of all this, love is a significant factor in the context of Luther's doctrine of justification. Most certainly, everything depends on
faith and on faith alone. But is everything which claims to be faith
and appears to be faith really faith? False, empty, dead faith also appears to be faith. Luther saw it with his own eyes. Therefore he necessarily had to ask the question about the marks of genuine faith. And
here the connection between faith and love, between faith and ethos
as the fruit of faith becomes significant. In his *Preface to Romans*
Luther defines faith as "a divine work in us which changes us and
makes us to be born anew of God, John 1 [12, 13]. It kills the old
Adam and makes us altogether different men in heart, spirit, mind,
and powers; and it brings with it the Holy Spirit. Oh, it is a living,
busy, active, mighty thing, this faith. It is impossible for it not to be
doing good works incessantly. . . . Whoever does not do such works,
however, is an unbeliever."[9]

Luther here follows the lead of Paul's statement about "faith active
through love" (Gal. 5:6) and of the "catholic" epistles, particularly
I John. In a sermon on I John 4:16 ff. preached in 1545,[10] Luther asks
his hearers: "Where is the fruit that shows you really believe?"[11] This
means that fruit in life shows whether faith is genuine. For this reason
the preacher admonishes his congregation: "Christ has not died so that
you could remain such a sinner; rather he died so that sin might be put
to death and destroyed and that you might now begin to love God and

---

[7] *WA* 39^{II}, 214.
[8] *WA* 39^{I}, 45; *LW* 34, 110.
[9] *WA*, DB 7, 11; *LW* 35, 370.
[10] *WA* 49, 780 ff.
[11] *WA* 49, 783.

your neighbor. Faith takes sins away and puts them to death so that you should live not in them but in righteousness. Therefore demonstrate by your works and by your fruits that you have faith. If you are a usurer. disobedient, and not industrious in your vocation then see whether or not you believe. For faith is the victor and the conqueror that overcomes the world. ... [Whoever believes] will say it with his deeds—or forget about having the reputation of being a believer.... Love follows true faith.... One should do everything that is good so that faith does not become an empty husk but may be true and genuine."[12] Love and its manifestation are thus the criterion for genuine faith.

II Peter 1:10 constantly reminded Luther of the necessary relationship between faith and ethos and of the significance of works for the certainty of salvation. "Brethren, be the more zealous to confirm your call and election (through your good works)." The second part of the fifth petition of the Lord's Prayer (Matt. 6:14 ff.) did the same.[13] This passage relates my certainty of God's forgiveness to my forgiving my own neighbor. In a disputation conducted in 1543, Luther refers to I Peter 1:10 together with I John 4:17. Love is the testimony of faith. It makes us confident and certain of God's mercy. So we are commanded to make our calling more certain through good works. Thus the fact that we have faith appears when works follow. If no work is present, then faith has been completely lost for the fruit bears testimony about the tree.[14]

In this sense Luther interprets I John 3:18 f. in his lectures on I John. ("Little children, let us not love in word or speech but in deed and truth. By this we shall know that we are of the truth and reassure our hearts before him ...")[15] Here, as in Peter, brotherly love appears to be the outward testimony of our calling, that is, we establish ourselves as what we in truth really are, for we sincerely and truly love the brother and anyone who is weak. ... Through this certainty we are able to assure our hearts that we have the faith. This is a great consolation.

Together with the thought that love makes faith certain of its genuineness and truth, Luther also points out that faith requires exercise in order to become strong. Faith exercises itself in its works and fruits. Faith is always struggling with a bad conscience and with consciousness of being guilty before God. It overcomes this more eas-

---

[12] *WA* 49, 783.

[13] Cf. the passages quoted in my *CW*, pp. 644 ff. See particularly *WA* 32, 423; *LW* 21, 149 f. Even though the sermons on Matthew 5-7 have probably been edited by someone else (*WA* 32, LXXVI), the genuineness of their content is confirmed by other Luther passages which are unquestionably authentic.

[14] *WA* 39ɪɪ, 248.

[15] *WA* 20, 715 ff.

ily when it serves the brother in love.[16] Thus, according to I John 3:
18, the heart is comforted and strengthened before God and becomes
confident in its relationship to God. The Reformer's typical reservation remains very clear: works do not bring about righteousness! Nor
are they a barrier to faith; on the contrary, they promote faith.[17] We
note that neither works nor love are to be considered in our justification before God. They are, however, of importance for that faith
which justifies, insofar as they make us certain that we have a powerful faith. According to Luther, we cannot bring our love before God
simply because that love remains imperfect and we need a perfect
righteousness before God. We neither can nor should bring anything
at all to God as though we were or had achieved something. We are
right with God only when we assume a purely receptive attitude. The
relationship of love to faith does not infuse an ethical quality into
faith above and beyond its mere receptivity. Faith is, and remains
nothing else than the readiness to receive God's promise and work.
The question is, however, whether faith really receives, as it thinks it
does, or whether it only imagines that it does and thus deceives itself
and others. Our receiving of God's love must of necessity manifest
itself in our now living in love; as Luther says, our deed now proclaims
that we believe and have received salvation. Luther thus places faith
and love in disjunction whenever he asks what makes a man righteous
before God. He joins them together, however, when he asks whether
the faith with which a man wants to receive justification is genuine
faith in his specific case, that is, whether it really receives God's love.

In 1532, five years later, Luther again interprets I John 4:17 in a
series of sermons on I John 4:16 ff.[18] This later interpretation is quite
different from that of 1527. It also differs from his interpretation of
the corresponding passage, I John 3:19 f. He now recognizes that perfect love includes the love which Christians have. This corresponds
to his exegesis of I John 3:19 f. in the lectures. However, the confidence or joy which love gives is no longer understood in terms of
man's relationship to God. Luther rather distinguishes a twofold joy
(or "courage" or "boast")[19] and correspondingly a twofold fear[20] which
is overcome by the Christian's joyfulness. This victory results in a
corresponding increase in joy. On the one hand, the Christian on the
day of judgment stands before God the Lord as his judge and must
fear his wrath. This is the "fear which falls down from above."[21]

---

[16] *WA* 20, 716. Cf. *WA* 36, 467.
[17] *WA* 20, 716.
[18] *WA* 36, 416 ff.
[19] *WA* 36, 454.
[20] *WA* 36, 464.
[21] *WA* 36, 462.

Before God, every man is lost because he is guilty when judged by the high standards of God's commandments. "I am a sinner in your sight."[23] On the other hand, however, when death and the day of judgment come—yes, even before this, in life itself—Satan, death, the world, and the neighbor against whom I have become guilty, so very guilty, rise up to accuse me.[24] They accuse me of lacking good works and transgressing God's commandments. And this, too, I must fear. This is the fear which comes from below, that is, from the world.[24]

The first fear, the "basic fear before God,"[25] cannot be overcome in any other way; and my joyfulness and my confidence before God cannot be established in any other way than with Christ and with God's work of salvation in him, that is, by faith in Christ. The fear which we feel toward God because of our sins "is conquered only through faith." Faith works the "most important joyfulness,"[26] and our "chief glory."[27] The fear which "falls down from above" cannot be overcome "except through baptism and the gospel. This gives great courage that we cannot find in ourselves but only in Christ."[28]

But the fear which I feel because Satan, death, the world, and my neighbor accuse me, must be overcome in another way. And my joyfulness in the face of it must have another foundation. This is given by good works and love. Before God we always have a bad conscience. But in relationship to demonic powers and to men we should, like Paul (I Cor. 4:4; II Cor. 1:12; II Tim. 4:7), have a good conscience[29] because of the manifest love for our neighbor toward whom we in our calling have fulfilled the Ten Commandments.[30] This love is definitely not perfect before God.[31] And the Apostle John does not intend to say that when he says that love is perfect. Love is perfect when it has content and is not a mere empty husk, not false, and not "only a rattling of our teeth" with "nothing behind it."[32] In view of Paul's statement, Luther asserts that it is possible for a Christian to have love that is perfect in this sense, that is, it is possible that the Chris-

---

[23] *WA* 36, 462.
[23] *WA* 36, 445, 466, 474.
[24] *WA* 36, 472.
[25] *WA* 36, 463.
[26] *WA* 36, 448.
[27] *WA* 36, 455.
[28] *WA* 36, 472.
[29] *WA* 36, 455, 449.
[30] "You should therefore not have the kind of love which exists only in your mouth, for that is meaningless love; rather you should have that full love which makes your heart joyful so that even when death and judgment come, you will be able to say: 'In spite of this I have done this and this for my neighbor.'" *WA* 36, 444.
[31] *WA* 36, 445.
[32] *WA* 36, 444 f.

tian has fulfilled his obligation to his neighbor. Thus "through firmly grasping right works" love silences the accusations of the others and no longer needs to fear.[33] I can fully and faithfully fulfill my calling in an orderly fashion; and in every case that is a service of love. Luther personally asserts that he has fulfilled the office of the ministry in this way.[34] For this reason the glorying and courage of a good conscience does have a place.[35]

Under no circumstances, however, does it mean adequacy before God. The Christian standing before God and under God's observation may, in opposition to accusations made by demonic powers and men, well boast that he has faithfully fulfilled his calling in love, but he may never do this in order to establish his relationship to God.[36] For no man can stand under the commandments as God himself interprets them.[37] Luther thus sharply distinguishes a twofold oughtness in God's commandments: on the one hand, that which God expects of me and, on the other hand, that which my neighbor and the world can expect of me. God the Lord demands more than my neighbor and the world can demand. There is all the difference in the world between having to answer to God and to my neighbors and the men and the powers who acccuse me. "I will not come to terms with God in any other way than through Christ."[38] "I must speak differently with God," that is, than with men and powers.[39] I can only speak to God in such a way that I point to Christ and hold fast to him.[40]

Thus I can insist that I have acted in love only when I speak with men and demonic powers but never when I speak with God. I neither can nor may think that I have been saved by acting in love or have created my own salvation. Luther never tires of emphasizing this. Two completely different dimensions are involved. And Luther says that his opponents are constantly confusing the two.[41] That fear which produced Psalm 6 ("Rebuke me not in thy anger, nor chasten me in thy wrath") is cast out not by our love but only by Christ and by faith in him.[42]

On the other side, however, living and working in love and the joy which it gives on the day of judgment is of great significance for the Christian when he confronts his accusers—even though it does not

---

[33] *WA* 36, 455, 466.
[34] *WA* 36, 470, 474.
[35] *WA* 36, 451.
[36] *WA* 36, 466, 455, 463.
[37] *WA* 36, 451.
[38] *WA* 36, 453.
[39] *WA* 36, 470.
[40] *WA* 36, 448, 450, 455, 463.
[41] *WA* 36, 466.
[42] *WA* 36, 477.

establish his salvation. To have to appear on that day without works of love would mean to be afraid and, according to I John 4:18, fear has to do with punishment. For the accusations of men and of other authorities do strike our conscience. "Whoever is terrified feels great agony for the conscience is the greatest cross on earth."[43] If we have no works, our heart becomes fearful and trembles under the accusations of Satan and of men. "It pains a man to have to admit: 'I have not done right. I have despised authority and have not honored my teacher and my spouse.'"[44] "That hurts" is Luther's translation of John's "fear has to do with punishment" (RSV).[45] And this is in addition to the fear of God's wrath which every man must have. How can a man get rid of this double burden? "If you want to take the sting out of what your neighbor and the devil say and out of God's wrath you have a doubly difficult task. Yes, dear fellow, it is more than you can do."[46] Luther can say, "I must also bring that glory [which comes from works of love] with me or God will not treat me in a friendly way."[47] He can also say that it "damages" faith to have no work. It must be exercised "and kept moving."[48] It is difficult for a Christian to believe in the hour of death if he has no experience or signs of faith. "It is difficult to hang only on the mere grace of God."[49] This is how far Luther goes in urging that faith be exercised in love and its works. Faith is in trouble when it has not been tested in life and when it lacks the "signs" which such testing produces.

This may be also put positively. Entering into judgment with works of love does not bring anyone salvation. Salvation comes only from God's forgiving grace. These works of love are, however, the "crown" of which the Apostle Paul speaks in II Timothy 4:8, "Henceforth, there is laid up for me the crown of righteousness which the Lord, the righteous judge, will award to me on that Day." Although the Christian is and remains a sinner before God, God will give the crown to him because he has tirelessly continued to serve the world in spite of its unthankfulness.[50] Luther thus distinguishes between blessedness

---

[43] *WA* 36, 477.

[44] *WA* 36, 471. Cf. "If this [awareness of good works] is not present when death comes, the heart begins to melt away in the body just as salt dissolves in water." *WA* 36, 466.

[45] *WA* 36, 475, 477.

[46] *WA* 36, 471.

[47] *WA* 36, 446.

[48] *WA* 36, 467.

[49] *WA* 36, 446.

[50] *WA* 36, 462. Cf. the printed edition prepared by Cruciger. Luther also distinguishes between the blessedness which is the same for all and the honor and the glory which is given in varying degrees according to the amount of suffering endured for Christ's sake. Assuming that the following text accurately reflects what Luther said, Luther could even speak of Christians receiving

and salvation on the one hand and the crown or the praise, the honor, the glory on the other.

This glorying in view of one's works of love is admittedly a very minor sort of glory when it is compared with faith's glorying for the sake of Christ. The confidence which it brings is of a lower grade and yet we must have it so that the world cannot accuse us before God.[51]

On the other hand that is not yet the final word. Luther's pastoral theology must also speak a word to those who, because of their lack of works, are so terrified by the accusations of men and of the authorities that they completely collapse in despair. God does not want that to happen. The fear which arises from a lack of love in our lives admittedly causes agony. But Luther constantly emphasizes that the Christian still should not collapse in despair. For God has commanded us to believe and to be joyful in him. "Faith and not fear should be in control"; even though, as we have already heard, faith is "weakened" when it is not tested in love and through sins against the commandments. But Luther's reference does not imply that a man will be damned because of such weakness.[52] Whoever does not have works should really not despair; he too can be saved through faith in God's grace. Luther in his lectures on I John 3:19 f. in 1527 had said that we should certainly be concerned to have the good conscience that comes from living in love. But even if we have no works or if our works against love accuse us, that is, if we cannot achieve that living love described in vs. 19 which "reassures our heart before God," we are still not left without comfort. Rather, we should remind ourselves that God not only advises but expressly commands us to hope in him. Therefore whatever may happen we should not despair. For the highest commandment, the sum total of the gospel, is that we should in faith grasp the grace which is offered to us; and this makes us worthy before God.[53]

Thus the dialectic of the relationship between faith and love is adequately treated on all sides. We are saved only through faith in that

---

"merit and reward" from God. "In this sense we concede that Christians have merit and reward with God, but not in order to make them children of God and heirs of eternal life. Rather, it is intended to console believers who already have this, to let them know that he will not leave unrewarded what they suffer here for Christ's sake, but that if they suffer much and labor much, he will adorn them specially on the Last Day, more and more gloriously than the others, as special stars that are greater than others. So St. Paul will be more brilliant, more bright and clear than others. This does not refer to the forgiveness of sins nor to meriting heaven, but to a recompense of greater glory for greater suffering." *WA* 32, 543; *LW* 21, 292 f. Cf. *WA* 36, 635.

[51] *WA* 36, 456 ff., 477.

[52] *WA* 36, 470 f.

[53] *WA* 20, 716. Propst's *"non desperabis"* is the proper reading. Rörer's *"non sperabis"* is an error.

grace offered to us in the gospel and through nothing else. True faith, however, demonstrates itself in love. If it is missing, then it is difficult for faith to be faith and to overcome the accusation of a bad conscience with the joyful certainty of salvation. Yet we cannot tell anyone in such a situation to do anything else than to believe. If you have no works, then do not be without faith.[54]

Is Luther's interpretation textual? Does it correspond to the theology of I John?

Luther refers to the fact that I John at one place binds salvation to faith in Jesus Christ and at another place to love. In I John 4:15 we read, "Whoever confesses that Jesus is the Son of God, God abides in him, and he in God." Verse 16, on the other hand, reads ". . . he who abides in love abides in God, and God abides in him." Luther says, "Both are true . . . both are written."[55] We must, however, distinguish between the two in this way. Faith helps us to have "the most important joyfulness" in relationship to God; love makes us joyful in relationship to the Christian community and to the world. "Through faith I glory in the fact that I belong to God; through my works and love I glory in the fact that no one has anything against me."[56] It is, however, hard to find this distinction in the text. There can be no doubt that John, in vs. 17, uses "confidence" or "joyfulness in the day of judgment" to indicate confidence in relationship to God and not only in relationship to men and other accusers. The meaning of the text is that salvation, "remaining in God," is connected with faith and love in the same way without any distinction in the judicial court before which each is effective. I John understands faith and love as an inseparable unity. Therefore, salvation can be connected with the one as well as with the other.

The differentiation which Luther attempts is foreign to the text. In both cases it is God's judgment and God's court that are involved. No mention is made of the men and the demonic powers who are against us and accuse us.[57] And in this respect, Luther was closer to understanding I John 3:19 in his lectures of 1527 than at this time; for then he probably recognized that John connects our certainty of our salvation before God to love. In another respect, however, Luther deviated from John even then. For John thinks of the life of love as quieting the accusing heart. The additional reference to the fact that "God is greater than our heart" and knows all things, leads neither

---

[54] *WA* 20, 716.

[55] *WA* 36, 447.

[56] *WA* 36, 454.

[57] Walter von Löwenich, *Luther und das johanneische Christentum* (1935), pp. 28 f.

beyond nor away from this fact, for precisely this certainty is bound to the Christian's living in love.[58] Luther, however, does not assert— as the text does—only that we who live in love are able to quiet our hearts but also considers the additional possibility that such love which can calm the heart is absent. In this case, Luther refers us to God's commandment not to despair but to believe and apparently under-stands the statement in vs. 20 that God is greater than our heart in this sense. "The conscience is a single drop whereas God reconciled with us is a sea of comfort."[59] According to Luther, then, vs. 20 refers to the possibility that we lack love. The text provides no basis for the change of relationship; on the contrary, the accusation of the heart is confronted with the certainty that God, who sees through us com-pletely, sees that love in us which is present as his gift in spite of everything which must otherwise condemn us.[60] For John the fact that God "knows everything" (vs. 20) means that he knows the depth of our hearts better than we and knows that we are motivated by his love. Luther, however, understands this as meaning that the confusion and shame of my heart so condemns me that "I do not know what I should say to myself"; God however knows "where I should come out," and "even if I do not know the outcome, he himself knows" that my sin is taken from me in forgiveness.[61] For John, love is the decisive factor in this entire section; both in vs. 20 and in vs. 19 it is love that makes us confident and which dares and makes possible the faith mentioned in vs. 20. (Büchsel puts it that "we must really practice love to be able really to believe in love.") Luther, however, sees vs. 20 as show-ing a shift from love to faith.[62]

Luther's distinction of a double fear and a double joyfulness, be-tween a good conscience in relationship to men and authorities and an evil conscience in relationship to God thus has no basis in the text of I John. Luther can, however, point to Paul in support of his po-sition and he repeatedly quotes him in his interpretation of I John 4:17.[63] He bases his position on the fact that Paul who witnesses to that grace which declares the godless to be righteous, at the same time desires "the glory" which no one can take from him, seeking after and even announcing that he has achieved it—a good conscience

---

[58] Cf. F. Büchsel's interpretation of I John 3:19 f., *op. cit.*

[59] *WA* 20, 716.

[60] Büchsel says: "God does not because of our sins forget the love which remains in us." *Op. cit.*, p. 58.

[61] *WA* 36, 717 f. Luther is, however, aware of the difficulty of the passage and apparently also of his own interpretation. *WA* 36, 716 f. Luther asks why it is that John does not say "can do everything" rather than "knows everything."

[62] *WA* 36, 717.

[63] In *WA* 36, 449 f., 455, 465, 471, Luther refers to I Cor. 4:4 or to II Cor. 1:12.

before men, the church, and the world." God's judgment of him and man's judgment of him are two different things. Confronted by the criticism and the accusations of men, even of Christians, Paul confesses that he has a good conscience (I Cor. 4:4; II Cor. 1:12). He rejects their criticism. But God's judgment is quite a different matter. Even his good conscience before men does not justify him before God (I Cor. 4:4b). In the face of God's eschatological wrath he will, like all Christians, be saved not by his good conscience before men but rather only through the crucified Christ (Rom. 5:9). This is the pattern of the double dimension in which Luther thinks. Paul also knows the double courtroom.

We could also refer to I Corinthians 3:12 ff.: here Paul considers the possibility that the works of a Christian—he was thinking primarily of the messengers of the gospel—may be revealed as nothing and burned in the fire of judgment. Thereby he suffers damage—our interpretation may be based on other statements of Paul. He then has no glory as a servant of Christ who has worked faithfully. He will however, be saved through grace in spite of it "and yet as one who passes through fire." This describes the trouble that a man will be in if he appears for judgment without "fireproof" lifework and, at the same time, the grace that will rescue him in spite of it. This is the scriptural basis for Luther's distinction between the glory which the works of love give to us and the glory which is ours in faith in the reconciling Christ. The Apostle Paul distinguishes between the blessedness which is given to all who believe in Christ and the glory which is given by our lifework. Obviously, this glory counts not only before men and powers but also before God, for he who works in the service of Christ will receive a reward, each one according to his work (I Cor. 3:8). God gives this reward and it is something else than rescue and salvation. The apostle makes the same distinction that Luther does between that blessedness which is one and the same for all and the honor or glory which comes in degrees.

Luther, as we have seen, also understood II Timothy 4:7 f. in terms of this distinction. Here faith does not glory before God because of Christ its Lord, but love glories in the work which it has done." According to Luther, the crown of righteousness which the apostle expects is not to be understood as blessedness but as the glory and honor which will be granted to the true worker and warrior according to the measure of his faithfulness and his exertion in working and suffering." Luther interprets this passage according to the analogy of the totality

---

" *WA* 36, 453.
" *WA* 36, 453.
" *WA* 36, 462.

of Pauline theology, but the post-Pauline author who speaks in II Timothy 4 certainly understood it otherwise: for him, the crown is salvation.

As we have seen, Luther's interpretation of I John 4:17 was not constant but changed. How did he understand this passage at the end of his life? If I understand the situation correctly, he did not again repeat the distinction between two kinds of confidence which he made in his sermons in 1532. He constantly emphasized that love is a hallmark of genuine faith, not only for other people but also for the believer himself. This means nothing else than the certainty that one's own faith is genuine cannot be achieved without love. Thus, however, the same must be true about the certainty of salvation and the certainty of God's mercy. The confidence which love gives is valid not only in opposition to the accusers but also in relationship to God himself. The man who has this confidence is certain that God is merciful because he is certain that his own faith in the gospel is genuine. This is how Luther's last interpretations of I John 4:17 are to be understood. This is true particularly of that passage from the disputation of 1543 to which we have already referred (see p. 449): "Love is the evidence of faith and makes us confident and certain of God's mercy."[97] Then Luther repeats I John 4:17 and interprets it differently than he did in 1532.

Luther's last sermon on our text preached on June 7, 1545 from which we have already quoted certain sections on p. 448 is not to be understood as meaning anything else than this. After the preacher has summoned us powerfully to prove our faith by our life and has expressed his own confidence in this regard, he continues: "If I did not have this certainty before God in the last judgment and before you . . . [Rörer's notes are interrupted at this point and continue after the lacuna with] I know then that my faith is not vain."[98] The meaning is clear: If I were not certain that my faith was genuine—because I had proved it with my deeds—and were not confident in my relationship to God and you, my neighbors, then I would be lost. Here too, as in 1532, God and the neighbor stand alongside each other, but not as though the confidence which flows from faith being proved by love were of significance only in relationship to the neighbor. No, confidence in relationship to God also depends on love. The distinction made in 1532 does not reappear later. Luther's final interpretation gives the genuine meaning of the text.

---

[97] *WA* 39ɪɪ, 248.
[98] *WA* 49, 784.

INDEXES

INDEX OF NAMES

INDEX OF SUBJECTS

Type, 11 on 13 and 10 on 13 Garamond
Display, Weiss
Paper, Spring Grove E.F. with Titanium

Printed in the United States
83104LV00001B/1-60/A